C. R. ASHBEE

C. R. ASHBEE

ARCHITECT, DESIGNER & ROMANTIC SOCIALIST

ALAN CRAWFORD

YALE UNIVERSITY PRESS

NEW HAVEN AND LONDON · 1985

For Felicity

Designed by Gillian Malpass
Colour illustrations originated by
Hongkong Graphic Arts Ltd, Hong Kong
and printed by Jolly and Barber Ltd, Rugby, Warwickshire.

Filmset in Monophoto Bembo and printed in Great Britain by
BAS Printers Limited, Over Wallop, Hampshire.

Library of Congress Cataloging in Publication Data
Crawford, Alan.
   C. R. Ashbee.

   Includes index.
   1. Ashbee, C. R. (Charles Robert), 1863–1942.
2. Artists—England—Biography. 3. Arts and crafts
movement—England. 4. Guild of Handicraft (London,
England) I. Title.
N6797.A76C7 1985   745′.092′4 [B]   85-40459
ISBN 0-300-03467-9

Frontispiece. C. R. Ashbee photographed by Frank Lloyd Wright, December 1900.

PREFACE

The first eight chapters of this book are a biography of Charles Robert Ashbee; the next six chapters deal with his work as an architect and designer; and the last two serve to draw together the themes of the book as a whole. This arrangement in three parts is not ideal, and I am afraid that it is more ponderous than its subject deserves. But at least it is clear; and I do not know of any other arrangement that would do justice to the variety of Ashbee's activities, and yet would not be shapeless. The relationship between the first two parts of the book is almost the same as that implied in the phrase 'life and work'; but I have been careful not to use those words because there is much in Part One that is work of the most important kind.

When quoting, I have not corrected or altered the spelling or grammar of the original texts, except that obvious typing errors have been corrected, and '+' has been altered to 'and'.

'Idealism' and 'Idealist' with a capital letter have been used to refer to the philosophical tradition which derived from Germany and which had an important influence on Ashbee's ideas; while 'idealism' and 'idealist' refer to a hopeful and visionary cast of mind which, as it happens, was equally important in Ashbee's life. 'Romantic' and 'romantic' have been used in a way that reflects a similar distinction between ideas and personal temperament.

I have used the phrase 'Arts and Crafts Exhibition' with a capital 'E' to refer specifically to the exhibitions organized by the Arts and Crafts Exhibition Society.

I am grateful to Felicity Ashbee for permission to quote from the writings of her father and mother and to reproduce her father's drawings and designs; and I would like to thank other copyright holders: Jonathan Cutbill (the unpublished writings of Edward Carpenter), the Provost and Scholars of King's College, Cambridge 1985 (the unpublished writings of G. L. Dickinson), Jane Wilgress (the unpublished writings of Alec Miller), Mrs Pamela Diamand (Plate 5), Sir John Rothenstein and Michael Rothenstein (Plate 38), and Mary Lutyens (Plate 91).

My thanks go to various other members of the Ashbee family, Francis, Richard and Olivia Ames Lewis, Helen Cristofanetti Ashbee, Dulcie Langham and Jean Langham, Conrad and Judy Marshall-Purves; and particularly to Mary Ames Lewis, Ashbee's eldest daughter, and her husband Ted.

I would like to thank the University of Leicester which gave me a research fellowship at the Victorian Studies Centre to write this book, an embarrassingly long time ago.

For help of various kinds I am indebted to W. P. Anelay, Victor Arwas, Paul and Stefan Asenbaum, Henry Baker, John Beer, Jim Benjamin whose knowledge of Ashbee in the United States is greater than mine, Jim Berrow, the late Sir Basil Blackwell, John Brandon-Jones, S. E. H. Broadwood, Professor Allen Brooks, Michael Brown, Ann Burnett, John Burrows, the Signori Calabró, Anthea Callen, Robin Carver, John Catleugh, Donald Chesworth, Jerry Cinamon, Peter Cormack, Anne Sophie Cox, A. R. W. Cox, David Cox, the late John and Lavinia Cox, the Dowager Countess of Cranbrook, Patrick Crawford, Susan Crawford, Count A. Czernin, Laurence Davis, Joyce Donald, the late Professor H. J. Dyos, Robert L. Edwards, Gyula Ernyey, Marian Wenzel Evans, Stuart Evans, Colin Franklin, Christopher Fyfe, Andor Gomme, Roderick Gradidge, Hilary Grainger, Arthur Grogan, the Hart family of Chipping Campden, Graeme Hindmarsh, Lady Hobart, Dr Stefan Holčík, Gordon House, Peter Howell who first stirred my interest in many of the things this book is about, John Jesse and Irina Laski, Klio Kemeny, Anthony D. King, Mary Lago, Ray Leigh, Roger Lipsey, Coy L. Ludwig, Dr and Mrs K. Lumsden, the late Philip Mairet, George Malcolm, Phyllis Marsh, Michael Mason, Christina Melk, Peter Miall, Mervyn Miller, Ben Milstein, Hofrat Professor Dr Wilhelm Mrazek, Stefan Muthesius, Meg Nason, Edward Newton, the late Henry T. Osborn, David Ottewill, Mr and Mrs J. F. Owen, the late Sir Nikolaus Pevsner who, with characteristic generosity, helped this book along in its earliest days, John Phillips, Dr Colin Phipps, the late Harold Pyment, Margaret Richardson, Godfrey Rubens, the late Sir Gordon Russell, Elizabeth Rycroft, Shahar Shapiro, the late Misses Mary and Dorothy Shaw-Hellier, Douglas Shepherd, S. Durai Raja Singam, Margaret Smallwood, Cameron O. Smith, Jane Spring, Seamus Stewart, the Revd Anthony Symondson, Paul Thompson who supervised my first research on Ashbee, Lynne Walker, Elizabeth Watson, Douglas Webster, Robert Welch, Michael Whiteway, Glennys Wild, Richard Wildblood, and Professor Robert Winter.

I would particularly like to thank the staff of the reference departments of Birmingham City Libraries for their courtesy and helpfulness; and also the staff of King's College Library, Cambridge, who have care of the Ashbee Journals, especially the late Tim Munby, Librarian, and Dr Michael Halls, the Modern Archivist.

Among the staff of museums, galleries and auction houses I am particularly grateful to Dr Sigrid Barten of the Kunstgewerbemuseum, Zurich; George Breeze, Annette Carruthers and Mary Greensted at Cheltenham Art Gallery and Museums; Robert Coats at the Museum of Modern Art, New York; John Culme, Philippe Garner and Philip Gibson at Sotheby's, London; Sharon Darling of the Chicago Historical Society; Rowland Elzea of the Delaware Art Museum; Wendy Evans at the Museum of London; Dr Irmela Franzke of the Badisches Landesmuseum, Karlsruhe; Susan Hare of the Worshipful Company of Goldsmiths, London; Dr Carl Benno Heller of the Hessisches Landesmuseum, Darmstadt; Dr Karel Holešovský of the Moravská Galerie, Brno; R. A. Kennedy of the Scolton Manor Museum, Haverfordwest; Juliet Kinchin, Brian Blench and Rosemary Watt of Glasgow Museums and Art Galleries; Professor Edelbert Kob of the Vienna Secession; Milo Naeve and Lynn Springer Roberts of the Art Institute of Chicago; Paul Needham of the Pierpont Morgan Library, New York; Jan-L. Opstad of the Nordenfjeldske Kunstindustrimuseum, Trondheim; Cavan O'Brien of Fischer Fine Art Ltd, London; Bruce Brooks Pfeiffer of the Frank Lloyd Wright Foundation, Taliesin West; Barley Roscoe of the Crafts Study Centre, Bath; Dr Elizabeth Schmuttermeier of the Österreichisches Museum für angewandte Kunst, Vienna; Martin Segger of the Maltwood Memorial Museum, Victoria, British Columbia; Dr Heinz Spielmann of the Museum für Kunst und Gewerbe, Hamburg; Peyton Skipworth of the Fine Art Society, London; Julian Treuherz of Manchester City Art Gallery; Timothy Wilson at the British Museum; and finally at the Victoria and Albert Museum, Shirley Bury who has brought together the finest collection of Ashbee's silver and jewellery anywhere in the world during her many years' service in the Department of Metalwork, Martin Chapman, Simon Jervis, Julian Litten, Eric Turner and David Wright.

Friends more knowledgeable than I am in aspects of Ashbee's work have read individual chapters of this book for me; and I am grateful for their comments to Margot Coatts, Craig Fees, Seth Koven, Gerald and Celia Larner, Andrea Schlieker, Gavin Stamp, Peter Stansky, Robert Thorne, Clive Wainwright and Christian Witt-Dörring.

David Cripps did most of the new colour photography for this book and I would like to thank him for some enjoyable sessions and fine photographs; and I thank Sutton Webster for his meticulous draughtsmanship in plates 84–5 and 116. At Yale University Press I am indebted to John Nicoll for his confidence in this book, to Susan Haskins for copy-editing, and to Gillian Malpass for the very great care and sensitivity with which she has handled its design and production.

My last thanks go to my wife Jane for help too subtle and various to be set down here; to Fiona MacCarthy from whose portrait of Ashbee in *The Simple Life* I have learnt more than I can say; to Andrew Saint for much encouragement, the pleasures of argument, and the meatier footnotes in Chapter Ten; and to Felicity Ashbee for her patience, help and friendship: this book is dedicated to her.

Alan Crawford
Birmingham
April 1985

CONTENTS

PART ONE

CHAPTER ONE
CITIES OF YOUTH AND THOUGHT
1863–1886

HAMBURG

As he grew old, Charles Robert Ashbee liked to recall a pleasant garden in a stately old city at the mouth of the Elbe; it was not part of Germany in those days, it was *Freie Hansestadt Hamburg*; and there were small children who 'sat about a great table and drank their milk from silver mugs, just as they do in *Grimm's Fairy Books* to this day, and ate crusty white rolls with slices of black rye bread and ginger cake. And out of the tall panelled room you look through the pleasant garden across a great lake, and on it were swans . . .'[1] It seemed as if the happiest times of his childhood had been spent in this still, old-fashioned world; and at its centre was the vivid, patriarchal figure of his grandfather, Charles Lavy, in a canary-coloured dressing-gown, who had stayed up to greet a family of Ashbees, weary and sea-sick after their three-day crossing from England.[2]

Charles Lavy was 'a merchant of the old school' who conducted his business according to a strict code of personal honour, and was respected throughout the small and traditional mercantile community of Hamburg. He made money carefully and consistently, and enjoyed a modest and cultured domestic life in which the display of wealth was avoided equally consistently.[3] Another of Ashbee's memories was of the day he went with his grandfather to see an old street in the harbour of Hamburg, the *Holländischer Brook*:

some fifty gabled houses in a row, a medley of red tiles with green copper spires beyond, in front the footway, at back the canal. The houses had great attics to their steep-pitched roofs, there were cranes attached to them to haul in the merchandise . . . I recall a pleasant smell of bales and spices, something faintly aromatic in among cordage and canvas . . . He pointed out one of the houses to me. 'That is where I learned business!' And then he shrugged his shoulders. 'It's a pity, isn't it, that the whole street, in Bismarck's great scheme for the reconstruction of the harbour, is doomed!'[4]

For most of Ashbee's career these childhood images of Hamburg lay at the back of his mind, gathering a romantic glamour to themselves. Occasionally, when he visited Hamburg as an adult, and saw how his grandfather's values had been ousted by the brash materialism of his cousins, they would come vividly alive; but their influence on his own ideas was quiet and steady, rooting his ideals of personal values, and smallness of scale in work and industry, in the immediate past, in old-fashioned capitalism; and so giving a curious twist to his Romantic socialism.

The Lavys had no sympathy with Bismarck, Prussian nationalism or the vision of a unified or more efficient Germany; they were Jewish, but not orthodox, and

1. Hamburg in the 1870s.

3. Henry Spencer Ashbee: one of his book-plates, designed by Paul Avril.

2. Mrs H. S. Ashbee and her son in about 1863.

they were Anglophile, trusting in England as the guardian of free trade and old-fashioned liberalism.[5] Charles Lavy had married an English wife, three of his daughters married Englishmen, and one of them, Ashbee's mother, went to live in England. Elizabeth Josephine Jenny Lavy was a beautiful young woman of twenty-one when she married, small in figure and with an uprightness and firmness of view which seemed to go with her size (Plate 2). She worshipped her successful and masterful husband, and ran the Ashbee household with efficiency, an impossibly high sense of the duties of servants, and an equally high but quite realistic sense of her duties as a wife. Her friends were few, but very close; and to most of her acquaintances she must have seemed charming and accomplished (she was said to play the piano excellently), but somehow more resolute than ordinary mortals. A gentler, weaker side was revealed most often to her only son, on whom she doted; and is now recalled in his memoir of her, 'Grannie', the simplest and least dogmatic of his books. The chapter called 'A Bundle of Letters' shows a woman of intense, fussy affection, sometimes funny, sometimes helpless before family troubles.

The letters are almost all written on Sundays, you feel in them the very atmosphere, and on the whole it is the wet Sundays when the happiest letters are written . . . 'Do not practise upon your constitution—porridges, my darling, are very nutritious, but a good cut of

2

not too underdone beef is better . . . Take care of yourself, my darling—it is very cold. Do you want any more oil, powders, biscuits, mittens, gloves, mufflers, money &c?'[6]

A relationship which began as the spoiling of a favourite child by an otherwise strict parent grew into a mutual dependence and affection of unusual strength and proportions. As an adult, Ashbee used to call her 'the Little Mother', and that bantering and impersonal name helped him to express, and to hide, his affection for her, perhaps the deepest and sometimes the most difficult love of his life.

The man she married in 1862, Henry Spencer Ashbee (Plate 3), was a merchant like her father. Born in 1834, he had worked for much of his life for a firm of textile warehousemen in London, listed in 1862 as Copestake, Moore, Crampton and Company, at 5 Bow Churchyard, 50 Cheapside and 58–63 Broad Street, City.[7] Part of his job was travelling on behalf of the firm, and though his family were not poor, he seems to have had to work his way in life without much help. The diaries he kept in his twenties reveal a bookish, rather earnest young man, suffering the loneliness of commercial travelling and the grinding imperatives of a self-help philosophy, without recognizing the nature of either deprivation.[8] Occasionally, he travelled abroad for the firm, and it was, presumably, on such a journey that he met Elizabeth Lavy. The marriage brought H. S. Ashbee the reward of his endeavours. With a view to his daughter's future position, Charles Lavy financed the setting up of a London trading house, Charles Lavy and Company, independent of the parent firm, and with H. S. Ashbee as the senior partner; the business of the house was exporting machinery, Sheffield goods and textiles to Europe. Ashbee was thus established as a merchant in his own right; and when he brought his bride back from Germany they settled in a newish and substantial villa in Spring Grove, Isleworth, on the western outskirts of London, where their first child and only son, Charles Robert, was born on 17 May 1863.[9]

BLOOMSBURY

About two years later, however, the Ashbees moved to 46 Upper Bedford Place in Bloomsbury, and it was in this dull- and respectable-looking house that Charley, as he was known to his parents, grew up. It was a curious move, since Bloomsbury had for some years been losing its status as a fashionable quarter and the aristocrats, professional men and merchants had been giving up its bleak brick terraces to professional offices, lodging houses and artists. Perhaps the explanation for the move was that H. S. Ashbee wanted to be near the British Museum and to cultivate the acquaintance of scholars and bibliophiles. He seems to have inherited an interest in books and literary scholarship from his father, and his ambition, which grew as the success of Charles Lavy and Company gave him opportunity, was to establish himself as a scholar, bibliophile and man of taste. Besides his library, which included such items as a set of Nichols's *Literary Anecdotes* 'extended from nine to forty-two volumes by the addition of 5,000 extra plates', he also built up a collection of paintings, indulging a safe taste for modern English water-colours and genre.[10] On his death, *River Scene with Ruins*, then attributed to Richard Wilson, went to the National Gallery, W. P. Frith's *Uncle Toby and the Widow Wadman* to the Tate Gallery, and some two hundred works by Turner, Bonington, Prout, Cattermole, de Wint, Cozens, David Cox, William Hunt and John Varley to the South Kensington Museum.[11]

Such things were not much in evidence, one imagines, when the Ashbees first moved into 46 Upper Bedford Place. In 1866, about a year after the move, a baby girl called Frances was born, and two more sisters followed, Agnes when Charley was six, and Elsa when he was ten. The children were much in the company of their mother and their German governess, and the atmosphere seems to have been one of calmness and solicitude among 'the golden console tables, the Victorian glass tube lustres, the grey and purple Axminster carpet, and the great Dresden clock and ornaments beneath their domes of glass'.[12] The chief excitement of the children's life might be a Christmas party with the children of Nicholas Trübner, the publisher, or an attack of the measles, a holiday in Blankenberghe or a visit to Ashbee relations in Kent.[13] And when spring came,

my father would don a smart top hat, stick a cigar in his mouth, mount the box of his landau and drive us to Bushey Park. The ritual was of Spring and carefully observed; the hamper with the picnic under the chestnut trees, the state apartments in Hampton Court Palace, the Maze, the swans, the deer, and the drive back in the evening. He always drove himself. He affected a somewhat rakish bucolic manner on those occasions, the Kentish sap rising.[14]

This was the ordinary life of the Victorian middle class, well-regulated and genial, and there was little to disturb its even tenor. Once, it is true, young Charley was standing by the window and heard the unemployed march chanting through central London; and another time, aged eight or nine, he spent all his pocket money to buy a suit of clothes for a boy who swept a crossing in the Tottenham Court Road, and was told by his father that he had done a very silly thing. Much later on, when he looked back on these incidents, they seemed to shine with meaning; but to the growing boy they were probably just another puzzle.[15]

On Tuesday evenings the Ashbees entertained, and the children would be aware of this, afraid perhaps that they might be brought down to be shown off to the guests. There were scholars and literary people, like H. F. Turle, the editor of *Notes and Queries*, to which H. S. Ashbee became a frequent contributor, G. W. Reid, Keeper of the Print Room at the British Museum, and, as a young man, Laurence Gomme, folklorist, antiquary, and local government officer. There were merchants and foreign visitors who had to be entertained for the sake of the firm; and architects like Alexander Graham, Secretary of the Royal Institute of British Architects, and W. H. Crossland, who built Royal Holloway College.[16] And there were bibliophiles like Richard Cordy Jefferson, Robert Samuel Turner, who threw himself down a lift shaft in Brighton rather than break up his library to pay his debts, and, particularly frightening to children, Richard Burton 'looking like an Arab sheikh with his long beard and the cruel scar across his face'.[17]

Meanwhile, Charles Lavy and Company was prospering; branches were opened in Manchester, Sheffield, and Bradford, and in 1868 the first European branch in Paris. Ashbee travelled to Paris fairly often after 1868 and it may be that it was in France that he developed an interest in that aspect of book collecting for which he is best known, erotica. In his diaries of visits to France, the name of bibliophiles with this interest occur very frequently; Henry Cohen, Eugène Paillet, and Alfred

4

Bégis in Paris in 1873, Frederick Hankey and Gustave Brunet in Bordeaux in 1875, and Jules Gay, author of *Bibliographie des principaux ouvrages relatifs à l'amour* in Brussels in the same year.[18] He bothered to record only a few business meetings, and there is no mention of respectable scholars of the sort who made up his London circle. One can well imagine how his interest in this kind of book-collecting might grow up in the social isolation of Paris.

At all events, the collecting of rare and exquisite items of erotica became one of his chief preoccupations, and he laid the foundations for the supremacy of his collection in 1877 when he bought most of the library of an expert but penurious collector, James Campbell Reddie, for £300.[19] As well as collecting books, he set about listing them, and produced three bibliographies of erotica whose descriptions range beyond his own collections and are still today the nearest the subject has come to standard works. The first, privately printed between 1875 and 1877, was called *Index Librorum Prohibitorum*, the second *Centuria Librorum Absconditorum* (1879), and the third, *Catena Librorum Tacendorum* (1885). The set of three has the common vernacular title *Notes on Curious and Uncommon Books* and the author appears under the pseudonym Pisanus Fraxi, that is, Ash and Bee Latinized and anagrammatized into a suitably scatological form.

It is hard to know what to make of this side of H. S. Ashbee's life. It is tempting to picture him as a raffish figure, a rebel against Victorian prudery; there is a tradition in the Ashbee family that he had a second family in Paris, and it has even been suggested that he was 'Walter', the author of the erotic autobiography *My Secret Life*, a marathon account of mid-Victorian sexual experiences; these are speculations.[20] His diaries, with their monotonous, stiff and impersonal entries, suggest rather a dullish man of ordinary views, accepting the orthodoxies of his time and class, liberal economics, the sanctity of the family, the dominance of the male, someone whose chief peculiarity was a kind of literary acquisitiveness, an endless sniffing after notes and queries. Yet the foremost collector and bibliographer of erotica in Victorian Britain can scarcely have been completely conventional, nor would a rugged Bohemian like Burton have dined with him often if he had been completely dull; perhaps the truth is that he was not a revealing diary writer. His son, who actually had good reason to dislike him and thought the erotic books should be destroyed, recalled nevertheless his sensitivity, the range of his knowledge, and a certain tough and useful sophistication.[21]

There are occasional references to erotica in his diaries, sandwiched between family affairs and those of his literary circle. They do not ruffle their dull and formal surface at all. On 21 June 1875 he noted receipt of the first proofs of *Index Librorum Prohibitorum* from the printer. Six days later he wrote, 'My wedding day, 13 years married, do not think it possible for any man to have a better wife, or nicer children, am perfectly happy. Drove my dear wife and children to Bushy Park where we picnicked. Glorious weather. Spent a most pleasant and enjoyable day, were quite alone.'[22] And he did not conceal his interests from his family, though he must have hoped that the children would not distinguish them from all the other mysterious goings-on of grown-ups. When travelling with them on the Continent, he visited collectors of erotica; and he spent the winter evenings of 1875 at Upper Bedford Place, correcting the blundering passage of his printer, J. H. Gaball, through the jungle of languages ancient and modern, and the battery of typefaces, which represented for Ashbee the taxonomy of the infant science of erotic bibliography.[23]

Collectors of erotica, like Ralph Thomas, Richard Burton and Richard Monckton-Milnes, were welcome at his dinner-table. But they probably met more often at 4 Gray's Inn Square, where Ashbee had rooms and where he probably kept his collection of erotic literature.[24] Gray's Inn was an exclusive male preserve, full of lawyer's offices and the private chambers of gentlemen. It was the perfect setting for the bookish sexual fantasies of a small group of men who, were it not for their age and the *de luxe* bindings, would have resembled a group of boys at a boarding school poring over girlie magazines. It was a normal part of mid-Victorian respectability that Ashbee should have had rooms and habits of life that were separate from, and not to be questioned by, his household and family; there need be no tension in his life, so long as Gray's Inn and Upper Bedford Place were kept apart. Interestingly, it was the assumption of male dominance in family life that C. R. Ashbee found most unattractive in his father.[25]

And no doubt part of the allure of erotica for Ashbee was the special challenge that it offers to the book collector, with its pseudonymous authors and faked bibliographical details; he had a passion for listing and tabulating. During the 1870s and early 1880s he was in keen pursuit of such items; in the mid-1880s his attention shifted to *Don Quixote* and he set about assembling the largest collection of Cervantic literature outside Spain.[26] In 1895 he published *An Iconography of Don Quixote 1605–1895*, in which he recorded every known illustration of this work; and at his death in July 1900 he was planning, according to one source, 'an elaborate bibliography of every piece of printed matter in French by Englishmen' and, according to another, 'a dictionary of all books in which Don Quixote is mentioned'.[27] Such lunatic dreams of completeness are as characteristic of H. S. Ashbee as his interest in erotica, perhaps more so.

His strange pursuits did not, as we have seen, disturb the orderly life of 46 Upper Bedford Place in the 1870s. The children were educated at home at first, and then the girls were sent to the North London Collegiate School whose headmistress, Frances Mary Buss, was a friend of the family. Mrs Ashbee had firm and progressive views about women's education, and

'did her duty by' and was inordinately proud of her three daughters in whom she saw beauties unperceived by the world. They were educated, drilled and disciplined in the most perfect way and on the most modern principles. In the teeth of the conventions of her decade she sent them, all dressed in jerseys and with hair plaited in a neat and sanitary manner to the neighbouring high school, then just on the rise of the wave. Women's education was in the air, and the girls were given 'every advantage'.[28]

But her progressive views did not, or were not allowed to, extend to her beloved son, who was given the conventional education of a wealthy merchant's son. At the age of about ten, a dreamy and puny child, he was sent to a preparatory school, and then, in 1877, to Wellington College, one of the newest and most expensive of the Victorian public schools.

At the very end of his life, Ashbee wrote an autobiographical novel about his schooldays called 'Trivialities of Tom', to amuse his grandchildren.[29] It presents a striking picture of a delicate and sensitive boy, quite out of place in the coarse and regimented life of a mid-Victorian public school. He is ill-equipped to take part in the regulation games, though a good swimmer, and is bullied for reasons he does not understand. He finds security in becoming an intellectual rebel. With two friends he forms a tiny clan called 'The Independents', who question official Christianity, cut games to read Dickens and Thackeray in the rhododendrons, and organize elaborate tricks to discomfort the headmaster, such as setting light to an endless trail of matches along the floor of the college chapel, during the reading from Genesis, 'Let there be Light'. This was more than a schoolboy joke; there were public figures present, and the point of the exercise was that Ashbee, who organized it, should not own up, and thus make a cruel and public spectacle of the ineffective headmaster, the Reverend E. C. Wickham. Donnish and aloof, Wickham was a most unpopular head, quite lacking in the forceful personality of his predecessor, E. F. Benson, who had built up the college since its foundation in 1859.[30] His appointment in 1873 was followed by a breakdown of discipline in the college, reaching a peak in the summer of 1880. 'Trivialities of Tom' breathes a spirit of hatred for Wickham which is quite unusual with Ashbee, though perhaps it was common enough in the college at that time.

But the 'Tom' of Ashbee's novel is a romantic simplification. In the luxury of reminiscence, Ashbee has recast his school-days in the light of his later, anti-Establishment attitudes, and has forgotten his more orthodox career, as revealed in the college records. He has forgotten the tentative youth who won a school prize for his essay 'On the Microscope' and only then began to feel himself gaining in position and influence; he has forgotten the prizes he won for free-hand drawing, and the compliments the Prince of Wales paid to his acting on Speech Day, 1882. He ended his career as editor of the college magazine, head of his house, and a school prefect. Perhaps he was a rebel; but he has forgotten that public schools are large and appallingly subtle institutions and are well able to find room for, even promote, a few young rebel intellectuals.[31]

He left Wellington in 1882, and it was his father's plan that he should join the firm of Charles Lavy and Company but the boy refused. Not that he had anything else in mind; it was just that he did not want to be a merchant. It is in this slightly mysterious episode—it comes to us only through family tradition—that we first get a sense of Ashbee as someone resolute and distinct, more than just the object of his mother's affections or a colourless name in his father's diaries. As might be expected, his mother took her son's part and, in an effort to find a career acceptable to son and husband, went the round of London publishers some time in the autumn of 1882. One of the last offices they visited was that of Nicholas Trübner, and there they met Charles Kegan Paul. Instead of offering the young man a position, Kegan Paul suggested he should go to university; within a few months Ashbee had secured a place at King's College, Cambridge.[32] His father, who perhaps hoped that Charley would decide to join the firm after all when he came down from Cambridge, agreed to indulge his son's uncertain preferences; but at the same time, as if to encourage him to manage his own affairs, he presented him with £1,000 and told him to fend for himself for the next three years. Such a sum, after the basic expenses of college life had been paid, would call for care and self-restraint if it were to last out the time. Perhaps H. S. Ashbee recalled his own stern and industrious youth, before the cultured leisure of his middle age.[33]

C. R. Ashbee owed a great deal to Kegan Paul for his suggestion. Early Victorian Cambridge had been a sleepy and irresponsible place where a man of lively mind might spend, as Macaulay spent, three profitable and leisurely years, and have no one to thank but himself at the end of it. But in the 1860s reforming dons like Henry Sidgwick, F. D. Maurice and J. R. Seeley set about changing the tone of Cambridge life, bringing it intellectually and educationally alive. They drew the university into the current of contemporary debate, accepted the challenge of Comte and Darwin, argued the claims of science, religious belief and history, and searched for an account of men and society larger, more subtle and more individual than the orthodoxies of utilitarianism. They believed that it was the duty of dons to train young men for public and professional life, and they worked to extend their teaching beyond the limits of formal lectures, into the common and informal life which the college system made possible: the intellectual, moral and personal development of each undergraduate was their first concern, the proper object of their scholarship and intellectual enquiry.

Their views gathered weight in the university in the 1860s and 1870s, and reform was most evident at Trinity and King's. A small college with a strong intellectual tradition, King's already enjoyed a fuller common life than other colleges because both dons and undergraduates had been drawn, until 1865, exclusively from Eton. These traditions were maintained, though not always easily, when entry to the college became more open, by dons of reforming sympathies, notably Henry Bradshaw, the University Librarian, and the portly figure of Oscar Browning. Browning gathered round himself a large and admiring circle of undergraduates, and founded a Dante society, which gave an excuse for taking undergraduates to Italy, a Mozart society whose repertory seems to have consisted of German student songs, and a Political Society whose meetings he chaired, his face covered with an enormous red pocket handkerchief. Dons of lesser showmanship might have been forgiven for thinking that these societies were formed less for the cultivation of art and thought than for the cultivation of 'O.B.'; but for all his egotism, Browning was a real teacher, 'Falstaffian', one of his pupils called him, 'shameless, affectionate, egoistic, generous, snobbish, democratic, witty, lazy, dull, worldly, academic', and an intellectual midwife, above all, in the Socratic tradition.[34]

After the heavy connoisseurship of 46 Upper Bedford Place, where the things of the mind were reduced to antiquarianism and acquisitiveness, and after the meagre and tedious conformity of Wellington, it was an extraordinary experience for Ashbee to come upon the communal intellectual life of King's in the 1880s. Here were men who were interested in ideas, and, what was even more wonderful, in his ideas. It made him very happy, and only the best and simplest metaphors are appropriate to this stage of his life, an awakening, a flowering. It is from this time that the earliest of his Journals survive; their long and irregular entries, sometimes sententious, more often vivid and telling in their impressions of people and ideas, are about as different as could be from the neat, matter-of-fact entries of his father's diaries; in the Cambridge years they document the unfolding of a young man's spirit (Plate 4).

The whole experience of Cambridge was so important for Ashbee that it is worth

4. C. R. Ashbee in about 1883.

5. Goldsworthy Lowes Dickinson. A drawing by Roger Fry, 1893.

dwelling on these years, and particularly on his intellectual life. He was not an original, and not always a very coherent, thinker; but his attitude to life, to his work, his surroundings, and even his relations with other people, was persistently, even irritatingly, intellectual; and there were a few fundamental beliefs to which he came in these Cambridge years and from which he seems not to have moved for the rest of his life. Not that he stopped thinking after Cambridge, but that his attention moved into another sphere. Those 'isms' with which he was so taken up at Cambridge, Ruskinism, transcendentalism, socialism, became the starting point for practical experiments; they were first principles, and they stood, almost unchanged, throughout his career.

Unfortunately, his Journals tell us little about his first year at Cambridge because he destroyed all Journal entries before 17 February 1885, half-way through his second year, leaving only a handful of letters before that date. These give only glimpses: he organized some kind of school for working-class children in Cambridge, an early expression of what was arguably his greatest talent; and he edited the *May Bee*, an ephemeral snippet of undergraduate journalism whose seven numbers appeared daily in May Week 1884.[35] He wrote an article on 'The Workman as an Artist' which was published in the *Building News*, and he is said to have started 'a society for discussion which was to spread throughout the world and which, in fact, collapsed after his first term'.[36]

One can be fairly sure who the first members of that society would have been, for during his first year Ashbee was drawn into a small circle of slightly older, high-minded and clannish undergraduates whose greatest pleasure was to sit up all night discussing the nature of the world and the cure for all its evils; the friendships he found among them, no less loving for being intensely intellectual, were the greatest discovery of Ashbee's years at Cambridge. There was Arthur Laurie 'the most speculative and bold of that little sect, a chemist, a Henry Georgite, a perpetual talker . . .'; Arthur Stevenson, whose Tyneside family have been described by Mark Girouard as a textbook example of the flowering of late Victorian wealth in liberal and cultured reformism; Arthur Berry, a serious-minded Unitarian and a brilliant mathematician who taught in an adult Sunday school throughout his undergraduate career; Arthur Grant who became professor of history at Leeds University; and James Headlam, later a distinguished diplomat and historian.[37]

But above all, and closest to Ashbee, there was Goldsworthy Lowes Dickinson (Plate 5), bony and affectionate, no longer the callow and conventional youth who had come to Cambridge from Charterhouse two years before, but a natural King's man, earnest and acute, the best type of new undergraduate. 'It is twelve o'clock,' Ashbee wrote in February 1885. 'G.L.D. has just left me after our usual nightly converse,—thought tellings, soul searchings, heart sighings, poetry overbabblings and suchlike, that to our other friends would seem either affectation or inanity, but which to us are the spirit of life.'[38] It was an odd friendship, considering how different they were in intellectual temperament. Dickinson was a careful thinker, with an English philosopher's sense of how little one can know; while Ashbee, as Dickinson himself recalled him at this time, was 'a long youth, enthusiastic, opinionated, Schwärmerisch'.[39] But Dickinson admired Ashbee's capacity for practical, philanthropic work, his 'saner and more concrete views'; while Ashbee found in his older friend an intellectual guide.[40] He had discovered Shelley at Wellington, but Dickinson had gone before into the visionary and inexhaustible world of Plato.

Ashbee's Journals allow us to eavesdrop on the meeting of this little sect, though generally all one can catch is certain recurring names and phrases—Plato, the Soul, socialism, Henry George and land nationalization, Emerson, Carlyle, transcendentalism, and others spoken more faintly, Schopenhauer, Swedenborg, even Madame Blavatsky.[41] The strain of Philosophical Idealism in their talk, though more to be expected in Oxford than in empirical Cambridge, and particularly at the Balliol of T. H. Green and Arnold Toynbee, was typical of the philosophical mood of late-nineteenth-century England. The rational and empirical orthodoxies of the mid-century—laissez-faire economics, utilitarian philosophy, the development of natural science and its apparent challenge to religious belief—seemed to have stripped the world and man of any spiritual resonance; it seemed that Plato, Hegel and Coleridge, and the transcendentalism of Carlyle and Emerson might give a point of view that would make sense of spiritual realities and personal morality.

Now Ashbee was no philosopher, and he took away from these discussions no great skill in philosophical argument, far less a systematic grasp of the nature of things, but rather an image of the world that was basically dualist. The homely didacticism of Emerson appealed to him most and he perhaps read Plato in that light; and came to look on all material things and the manifold details of experience as the revelations of a deeper spiritual reality. The work he did, the objects he designed, the movements he espoused, were all the workings out of what, if the notion were not so woolly in his mind, one could call a single coherent spirit. He often described himself as a 'Practical Idealist', and the title was a handy one, partly because professional descriptions, such as architect or designer, never quite exhausted the range of his activities; and partly because it underlined the moral idealism of his work. But it also had a quite specific philosophical meaning: he saw himself as realizing spiritual meanings and potential in the ordinary practical world.

Ruskin was another name heard faintly in these discussions, though he was perhaps not so much of a hero to others of the little sect as to Ashbee, whose interest in art and architecture was developing at this time. The most fruitful and, as it turned out, unshakeable convictions of his life seem to have been found in reading Ruskin; one would not guess it from his Journals of this date which are fuller of Plato, but it showed as soon as he left Cambridge and began to teach and lecture. From Ruskin he learned to see art, architecture and the decorative arts as the reflection of the social conditions in which they are made, and to bring them within the scope of morality. Ruskin could read the history and health of a whole society in its buildings and works of art; the stones of Venice spoke to him; and he would discriminate with extraordinary fineness and persistence between the truthfulness and honourableness of one work and another. It would be hard to exaggerate the influence on Ashbee of this way of thinking; by temperament, talent and conviction he was both artist and social reformer, and this yoking of themes (it did not seem like yoking to him) informed all that he did and wrote. Like Ruskin, he started from the assumption that the roots of art lie in the soil of society, and that the first question to be asked in any sane order of things was, what *ought* to be made.

He learned from Ruskin to see the carved detail of mediaeval buildings as full of life, individual, changeful, flawed and imperfect, and above all free; the mediaeval craftsman was a rude and vital figure, standing upon the scaffold at Beauvais or Rouen, beside whom the modern workman seemed fettered and lifeless. It was not the particular beauty of the mediaeval work which mattered so much as the general lesson it implied: that men could be happy in their work, and that when they were, that work was art. And he learned to question the economic system and industrial achievements of nineteenth-century Britain; to see *laissez-faire* economics as abstract and unfeeling, greed and materialism in rational dress. Asked in one of his Cambridge examinations to define 'value' and 'riches', Ashbee did what Ruskin had done in *Unto This Last*, rewrote current economic theory in the more humane terms of social affections and the aspirations of the spirit. 'Value', he said, signified 'the strength or availing of anything towards the sustaining of life . . .'; and his papers were torn up.[42] Of how things were made, and what it was like to work in industry, he knew as little as any other young middle-class Londoner of his time; and that is partly why he was so ready to accept Ruskin's occasional onslaughts on the industrial system, on the division of labour as a murderous dissection of experience; on the use of machinery as the inhuman and convulsive emblem of a society gone mechanical in heart and head.

Men may be beaten, chained, tormented, yoked like cattle, slaughtered like summer flies, and yet remain in one sense, and the best sense, free. But to smother their souls with them, to blight and hew into rotting pollards the suckling skin which, after the worm's work on it, is to see God, into leathern thongs to yoke machinery with,—this is to be slave-masters indeed . . .[43]

Denunciation was not a part of Ashbee's temper, but the effect on him of such scalding rhetoric was profound. His legacy from Ruskin was a long, patient, and professedly practical questioning of the value of modern industry.

It is not clear from Ashbee's Journals how much he knew of William Morris at this date. He may have read pamphlets, or the collection of Morris's early lectures published in 1882 as *Hopes and Fears for Art*; and he would certainly have known of Morris as a poet, decorative artist and a recent convert to socialism. In those early lectures, Morris, like Ruskin, idealized the mediaeval craftsman. The decorative arts were held in honour then, he thought; it was the Renaissance which introduced the cruel divide between the fine and decorative arts, raising painting and sculpture, as the works of genius, out of the reach of the people, and degrading the other arts as merely useful and unexpressive. The decorative arts survived this élitism unevenly, in some parts of Europe longer than in others, and were eventually destroyed by the Industrial Revolution. The urgent need, he wrote, was for those arts to recover their dignity; the craftsman must come up with the artist. This was to be the principal platform of the Arts and Crafts Movement.

Morris added to what Ruskin had written a sense of tradition and of Englishness; it was not the stonecarver of Rouen he idealized so much as the English yeoman at his cottage door, a humbler, domestic creation, and there was a sense in his writings of a vernacular tradition surviving, in the corners of the English countryside, perhaps until the eighteenth century. Ashbee thought of Morris as a man who could revive that tradition by force of genius, and remake the golden chain which linked the present with the past.[44] Morris also carried out a more sustained and clear-eyed critique of mechanized industry than Ruskin's glancing invective. What, he asked, painting a picture of shoddy products and vulgar luxuriance, could one expect of men whose work was little more than minding machines or acting like them? The health of the decorative arts depended not on taste or principles of design, not on education or the public, but on the healthy and happy experience of the men who produced it. 'If I could only persuade you of this,' he told an audience in Birmingham in 1879, 'that the chief duty of the civilized world to-day is to set about making labour happy for all, to do its utmost to minimize the amount of unhappy labour . . . I should have made a good night's work of it.'[45] There were thus two strands in Ashbee's self-education at Cambridge, one Idealist, the other broadly speaking Romantic. They were not strangers to each other. Coleridge and Carlyle belonged to both, and the writings of Emerson could furnish texts for sermons on the simple domestic arts. But there was a different emphasis in each. Plato and Emerson were restful and contemplative; they had their eye on eternity. Ruskin and Morris were the children of history, holding up the present to the judgement of a Romantic past: they were specific, drastic, and welcome to Ashbee, who wanted to make the world a better place.

But when it came to making the world a better place, Ruskin and Morris were not the clearest of guides. Their ideas were radical and, at an intellectual level, that was part of their attraction; but just what was one to *do* in the service of such ideas? One could start with the arts themselves, architecture and the decorative arts in the nineteenth century. But if what Ruskin said was true, if the arts were an index of the state of society, how much further would one have to go? What had begun as Ruskin's commentary on building details in late mediaeval Venice, neutral and specific, could cast a shadow over the present day, and then not only on its art, but work as well, and what beyond? It might not seem much to ask that men should be happy in their work, but that might also be to strike at the roots of industrial society, at established power and wealth and social relations. Ruskin must always have seen this, and praised those Venetian capitals perhaps just because they implied the ruin of the industrial world he knew; but in the history of his practical efforts, and of the Guild of St George in particular, there was always a large and saddening gap between aspiration and achievement.

Morris began, in his early lectures, by considering the fate of the decorative arts, and their immediate relationship to methods of production. But he was a dogged thinker, and honest with himself, and found he could not stop there. In 1883 he became a socialist, and during the next few years his convictions deepened and grew clearer: there could be no healthy art while men were not free, while industry and economic life were based on the exploitation of one class by another. His socialism grew out of his Romanticism and his attachment to the decorative arts—their full, creative life implied a standard—and it was a committed socialism, not the indulgence of a distinguished figure playing at politics. These were just the years when Ashbee was at Cambridge, drinking the strong wine of Ruskin's prose.

It was a stark challenge which Ruskin and Morris issued; but it was softened for Ashbee and thousands of others by a quirk of British culture, by the fact that the country where the Industrial Revolution began was still half in love with other and older ways of life. The tastes and attitudes of the upper and middle classes were permeated by a mild and nostalgic anti-industrialism which, while it did not disturb the fabric of industry or the sources of wealth, fostered social values and cultural ideals of a quite different kind. It was remarkable how little the nineteenth-century aristocracy and landed interest were displaced by the urban middle class, in comparison with Germany for instance; and how the aspirations of the middle class were shaped by gentry values. Industrial wealth was used to turn the sons of its possessors into 'gentlemen' who, by definition, stood at a distance from trade and industry. The public schools trained for the Church, the Army, the professions, public service, but not for industry. Geography strengthened the split, with industry concentrated in the north, power and influence in the south. The village and 'the countryside', things old and untouched by the despoiling hand of industry, were powerful themes in literature and art and, most pervasively, in landscape taste: those leafy middle-class suburbs thick with gardens, those 'cottages' old in appearance, new in planning, comfort and technology, dotted among the Surrey hills, accessible by train. Britain might have her great cities, but it was the Romantic image of villages and fields and yeomen stock which excited national pride.[46] The same tastes and attitudes could be found in other countries, but none was so uneasy about its industrial achievements as Britain. They were the ground from which Ruskin and Morris's invective grew; they blurred the challenge and offered blander forms of discipleship. When, after Cambridge, Ashbee was asking what he was to do in the service of these ideas, he did not have to choose between Morris's socialism and inaction. All sorts of genteel Ruskinism were available, and Morris could be reduced to sighing among flowered chintzes, taste masquerading as social conscience. The Arts and Crafts Movement itself was as much a product of this cosy, popular anti-industrialism as of Ruskin's searing insights and Morris's courageous logic.

13

In his second year at Cambridge we find Ashbee applying himself, rather uncertainly, to the history tripos. There are jocular letters to Oscar Browning about essays on 'The Law of Nature' and 'Ancient and Modern Wills'—he took readily to the mocking, slightly theatrical style of the Browning circle—and later in the year he is assured by Dickinson 'that this burying of oneself in "treaties" and "international law", and "mediaeval periods" and "seven years wars" etc is necessary intellectual training . . .'.[47] The history tripos was only twelve years old in 1885 and had been given its early shape by J. R. Seeley, the Regius Professor of Modern History. He taught history in 'broad sweeps', marshalling his well-researched material into characterizations of periods whose significance for the present was unmistakable; there was also a good deal of political theory in the tripos and it was meant to be, as Seeley's supporter Oscar Browning put it, historico-political, a training for public life. In the 1880s this view was successfully challenged by those who believed that the tripos should encourage a more scholarly and supposedly scientific approach, including the study of original documents.[48] But Ashbee did not sympathize with the scholarly view, though he found much to admire in the teaching of one of its most influential advocates, Mandell Creighton. He said of scientific history, as Mrs Gamp said of Mrs Harris, 'I don't believe there is no sich thing.'[49]

Seeley's picture of history with its broad sweeps and its bearing on the present was much more congenial and seemed to lend itself to his Idealist speculations. For if history moves from one coherent period to another, what is that coherence but the expression, at each stage, of the Idealist prime mover, the 'Spirit of the Age'? Once brought within the Idealist vision, Ashbee's historical studies came alive and influenced the whole of his later career. The sense of the past, and particularly of the English past, which informs so much of his work, is a sense of successive periods, each having its own character; the sense he had of his own time and of his own work, was the feeling of an age seeking its form, the 'Spirit of the Age' seeking expression through its different manifestations. The only difference was that the politicians, diplomats and lawyers of his Cambridge studies were pushed summarily from the centre of the stage, and their place taken by poets, artists, thinkers, whose right to that place lay not in superficial power or privilege, but in the deeper privilege of the spirit; and in the drama of the present day, whose title was as yet undecided, Ashbee himself hoped to have a part.

Most of the little sect were older than Ashbee and took their triposes sooner—Dickinson, Laurie and Grant in 1884, Stevenson in 1885. As was usual for good 'reading men' in those days, they did not leave the university immediately, but in Ashbee's second year there was a slight loosening of the group. Arthur Laurie was up in the north of England, doing University Extension lectures; and in the early summer of 1885 Dickinson went off to stay with Harold Cox at Craig Farm, near Farnham, to prepare Extension lectures for the coming year.[50] Cox, an ex-King's man, a socialist, and a devotee of the simple life, was trying to make a success of this small, new farm on rather unprofitable ground, and Dickinson, eager to share in common and practical work, helped on the farm in between writing lectures and reading Plotinus. As a farmhand he was not an immediate success: 'It may look simple,' he wrote, 'but I assure you there is an art in manipulating the teat of a domestic cow not easily fathomable. It will ever be a sorrow to me: but the

6. Edward Carpenter at Millthorpe, near Sheffield.

fact remains; I can't milk a cow!'[51] The aim of the lectures which Laurie and Dickinson were preparing on behalf of the University Extension movement was to make the benefits of university education more widely available, no longer a matter of class privilege, and to a degree to lessen class divisions and resentment; the movement answered very well to the mood of the little sect, in whose discussions socialism figured as largely as Idealism, the demands of social action challenging the claims of intellectual and moral perfection. Austen Leigh, the Provost of King's, recognized 'socialistic enthusiam' as 'the main current of new feeling among thoughtful young men' in the College in the 1880s.[52] This socialism was not intellectually sophisticated, nor did it involve any specific political allegiance. It was essentially a response to class divisions, which seemed to be growing in late nineteenth-century Britain; a mixture of angry youthful idealism and of upper-class notions of duty tinged with panic: the important thing was to get in touch with the working class, and to get at the common humanity below the differences of class. There was a good deal of Matthew Arnold and Ruskin in this, and nothing of Marx, and their socialist activities were characteristically miscellaneous: canvassing in school board elections, supporting a Fellow of King's who was running as a radical MP for North-West Suffolk, inviting the anarchist Stepniak to lecture at Cambridge.[53]

For Ashbee at least, these vague socialist ideas, which could have subsided simply into a restless dissatisfaction, were given shape and direction by his meeting with Edward Carpenter (Plate 6). Carpenter had been a missionary for the University Extension movement in the 1870s in Sheffield.[54] In 1883 he bought a small farm at Millthorpe, near Sheffield, and divided his time between market gardening, writing and political campaigning with Sheffield socialists. Ashbee was attracted, not by the politics alone, but also by the way of life at Millthorpe, one of the most persuasive embodiments of the simple life, with overtones of Emerson at Concord; by Carpenter's personality, gentle, thoughtful but with a cast of mind which seemed to rank him with the 'prophets' of Victorian thought; and by the nature of his

15

socialism, as expounded in a long and, it now seems, unreadable poem in the style of Whitman, *Towards Democracy*. Carpenter set the innocent muscularity of those who make and do against the artificiality of modern society, the unreality of gentlemen and moneymakers. His socialism was an ideal of comradeship among simple honest ordinary lives, a remaking of social relations at their personal roots.

After the foundation of the Independent Labour Party in 1893 British socialism was drawn more and more into the paths of conventional politics, and Romantic socialism such as Carpenter's began to seem exotic and peripheral. But that was not a point of view of the 1880s, and one cannot understand Carpenter or Ashbee except in the context of a much less exclusively political socialism than has been normal in Britain, at least until the 1970s. In the 1880s organizations like the Progressive Association, the Fellowship of the New Life, the Fabians and the Social Democratic Federation were a focus for discontented middle-class intellectuals with a wide range of ideals; Jim Joynes and Henry Salt, both schoolmasters at Eton, came to socialism via Henry George and land nationalization, Shelley and vegetarianism, William Morris by way of Ruskin and the decorative arts. They wanted to change the social and industrial structure of society and at the same time to find a new way of life, simpler, more honest and feeling in its personal relations, more creative.

Ashbee first met Carpenter on 14 May 1885, and his response was tentative: 'Met tonight Edward Carpenter . . . we had an hour's talk together, on land nationalization &c—but did not go deep—he was not of a disclosive nature.'[55] It was not until the winter of that year that he got to know him better. At that time Dickinson was in Mansfield, desperately learning his Extension lectures on Carlyle, Emerson, Browning and Tennyson by heart and delivering them right over the heads of his audience in radical clubs and mission halls. He was not far from Millthorpe, and in early December Ashbee came up to stay with him.

It is these few minutes of soul-outpouring between friends that are the only things worth having in life—a kindling of the imagination. We don't want anything else than that—all should be subservient to it. Goldie and I sat over the fire in the 'Commercial Room' of the George Inn in Stamford from 9 to 1 this evening and talked and talked in the very Elysium of mental understanding. It was just like Cambridge over again—he coming to my room, and Plato, and the burden of the soul, or feelings fraught with Emersonian illumination and noble Carlylian pessimism.[56]

One wonders what the other occupants of the Commercial Room at the George Inn made of the numinous couple by the fire.

Two days later Ashbee wrote: 'I dwell tonight under the roof of a poet. Edward Carpenter seems to me to come nearer to one's ideal of *The Man* than anyone I have ever met.'[57] The house was simple, with a kitchen and living-room serving all purposes, and bedrooms above. Carpenter introduced him to Albert Fearnehough and his wife and daughter, with whom he lived, and showed him his treasured letters and portraits of Walt Whitman, giving him a reproduction of one portrait as a keepsake. The next morning Ashbee, Dickinson and Carpenter went for a walk in the woods round Millthorpe. Ashbee had the feeling that 'The morning was bright and buoyant, harmonizing with our spirits as we measured them afterwards—Goldie and I. We agreed that it was the being near Carpenter that had elated us, and drawn us out of ourselves into another world, another cycle of feelings.'⁵⁸ Two days after that found Ashbee and Dickinson at Lincoln, where they 'read the *Phaedo* together and communed with eternity' until one o'clock in the morning in the parlour of the White Hart Inn.⁵⁹ Back in London for a family Christmas, Ashbee found it 'gloomier than ever, but *I* much refreshed from inhaling of the fresh clear atmosphere of *Millthorpe* the ideal, the poetic . . . a glimpse into the real and the true which we are apt to forget in a world of smoke and folly etc.'⁶⁰ After Christmas Carpenter was in London and asked Ashbee and Dickinson to hear him lecture on 'Private Property' to the Hammersmith Branch of the Socialist League in the converted stables of William Morris's Kelmscott House. They were asked to supper afterwards and

Goldy . . . succeeded in drawing the old man out on the first principles of Socialism, and a splendid conversation followed across the table, we all listening intently and now and then putting in a word. Old Morris was delightful, firing up with the warmth of his subject, all the enthusiasm of youth thrilling through veins and muscles; not a moment was he still, but ever sought to vent some of his immense energy. At length banging his hand upon the table: 'No' said he 'the thing is this, if we had our Revolution tomorrow, what should we Socialists do the day after?' 'Yes, what?' we all cried. And that the old man could not answer: 'We should all be hanged because we are promising the people more than we can give them!'⁶¹

After supper they walked back as far as Bloomsbury with George Bernard Shaw; he agreed with Morris—'the first persons to be killed in the Revolution when it does come will be we Socialist leaders'—and he left them on the corner of Goodge Street, wondering.

Back in Cambridge, the approach of the history tripos was made more bearable for Ashbee by his growing friendship with Roger Fry, then in his first year at King's reading science.⁶² Fry was another of those for whom coming to Cambridge was like being born again. He came from a family in which long traditions of Quaker austerity were compounded by an intense intellectualism: his father was a distinguished judge of severely logical mind, with a keen interest in science. A slightly eccentric preparatory school and the high-minded atmosphere of Clifton College had done little for him, and he arrived at King's docile, strict with himself, and unprepared for intellectual freedom. In photographs of this date (Plate 7) his expression is ungainly and quizzical, and there seems to be none of that marvellous openness and mobility which shines from the face of the mature Fry. He probably got to know Ashbee through their common interest in art, something that Fry's rigorously intellectual upbringing had not attended to; though Ashbee was acute enough to recognize that 'he has the aesthetic quality much further developed than I'.⁶³ By the end of the term, they were close friends and spent part of the vacation together at the Frys' country home, Failand House, near Bristol, sketching the churches of Somerset.

But before Failand there had to come Millthorpe, for Ashbee. Carpenter met him off the train and took him to see some of the Sheffield factories and workshops.

Coming fresh from one's political economy books, especially those who with Fawcett sing of the golden age that has dawned, one little realises what the life of these factory hands, men, women and children, really is. Grimy, grinding, deadly monotony . . . Beal

7. Roger Fry in about 1886.

and Son is a thriving Sheffield manufacturer who makes thousands and thousands of uncanny knives—some stamped out of Bessimer steel and all scamped, bad, piece-paid work, and exports them to savages in the Pacific Islands. On every blade there is stamped 'Superior'. To think there should be a lie stamped on every blade![64]

And on the following day he visited a steel foundry:

'Twas very wonderful. Vast engines plying armour plates. Great brawny men wheeling hither and thither molten ingots of steel. The blast furnace shooting its white blaze of light and sparks into the sky, while the great sun itself was trembling in sickly violet rays beside it. There is something mighty and beautiful in all this. I insist again that it is to *this*, our art must turn. It is folly for us to seek the beautiful outside life. We must seek it in the actual conditions of things and when once we begin to seek we shall be able to separate the ugly from the beautiful. A whole epic is in one of these factories a world of sorrow of beauty of ugliness of power of pathos of heroism. And as for mere external loveliness and wonder! Why we sat for 20 minutes, watching in astonishment![65]

The difference in his response to these two workshops, the Ruskinian condemnation of the manufacture of domestic goods, and the romanticising of heavy industry in the manner of Walt Whitman, is typical of Ashbee's as yet untried aesthetics. In the previous September, describing the scenery as he travelled through Carlisle he noticed a 'sylph-like, cloud-soaring Homeric factory chimney in the distance', actually the tallest in England at that date.[66] Eleven days later, his mind clearly running on themes of art and work, he wrote:

From Henrici in Aachen I once learnt the beauty and loveableness of the domestic in architecture . . . From old Mrs Laurie in Edinburgh I caught the suggestion that our vast capital

18

in young artists who fly high with weak wings,—talents who follow after genius, might better devote themselves to domestic and decorative art, (instead of painting pictures that nobody wants to buy) . . . Would not this be a good basis for the art of our Democracy? The young artist becoming the working man—the clever working man an artist—talent the only leveller. It would look well if in the internal decoration of some town hall we frescoed and panelled the walls with paintings of factory chimneys fuming into cloud and the ruby glow of the furnace piercing the impenetrable gloom of grey;—the predominant grey, as I have seen it often in splendid cloud effects,—passing through the 'Black Country' or in the London streets. And there *is* beauty in all this—a gigantic beauty in the harmonies of colour—in the gloom and sorrow of the thought conveyed.[67]

There is a healthy variety of intellectual influence in this passage. Those ideas which place Ashbee so centrally in the Arts and Crafts Movement he formed not just from reading Ruskin but also from talking to Arthur Laurie's mother, and to Karl Friedrich Wilhelm Henrici, Professor of Architecture at the Technische Hochschule in Aachen, with whom he stayed in 1884.[68]

There is also, in this passage and in Ashbee's contrasting judgements on Sheffield workshops, an interesting mixture of ideas; on the one hand, the sense of the artist turned craftsman, the dignity of the decorative arts, and on the other, a sense of beauty hidden in the world of industry. This was a beauty which Ruskin would have found sad and incomprehensible, and perhaps rightly so, for it is hard to see that there was beyond mere 'external loveliness and wonder'. But it was important to Ashbee because his socialism, tinged with Whitman, taught him that an art which was not rooted in this 'real' industrial world was mere middle-class studio artifice. Both convictions remained with him during his career, the idea of craftsmanship providing an all-absorbing vehicle for his Romanticism, at once practical and theoretical, immediate and specific, while the beauty of industry remained pale and elusive, a theoretical preoccupation in his writings.

From Sheffield they went up to the farm at Millthorpe.

Hoeing today and digging, much manipulation of the spade and the gavelock. Digging up and replanting of raspberries with Carpenter and chatting to him the while on Socialism, on Sir Henry Maine and Democracy on Wagner and all the most delightful subjects imaginable. Character and Humanity seem to unfold to me here. I know several of the labourers—Carpenter's friends—now and I seem to be getting nearer to them—finding out that they are human beings with souls inside them. If one could only shake off this devilish gentility! Why is one reared according to so purely artificial a standard?[69]

With the end of his Cambridge years in sight, Ashbee was making practical plans during the spring. His parents had moved into a grander house in Bloomsbury two years before, at 53 Bedford Square. But after the comradeship of Cambridge and the simplicity of Millthorpe he did not want to live there, and must have told his mother so in the spring of this year, 1886.[70] Besides, he had been sure for some time that he wanted to be an architect; and if his father still hoped that he would join Charles Lavy and Company, this decision must have widened the gap between them. In June and July he was up in London, going to see architects—Somers Clarke the Younger and G. F. Bodley—and staying at Toynbee Hall, the university settlement in the East End. All the idealism of his university days led there, a permanent centre of university influence among the working population of London.

I arrived here last night, my object to explore. I hope perhaps to live here later for a while, but rather as a sop to my own conscience, having now for three years talked philanthropy I'm desirous of doing something. Yet I mistrust myself and this place also; myself for insincerity, Toynbee Hall for what seems at first sight a top hatty philanthropy.[71]

Then, on 8 July, he went back to Cambridge for the last time as an undergraduate, for what reads almost like an orchestrated finale of those glorious years. 'Notwithstanding the childlike ruses and stratagems of my good mother to keep me on in London, the gloomy and grimy, for a few hours more, I have escaped for the last time into this fairy city of youth and thought'.[72] Fry was there, and Dickinson, his closest friends, and best of all, Carpenter.

Edward Carpenter came up this evening to stay with me. After supper we had a delightful walk through the green cornfields in the afterglow. He unfolded to me a wonderful idea of his of a new free-masonry, a comradeship in the life of men which might be based on our little Cambridge circle of friendships. Are we to be the nucleus out of which the new Society is to be organised?[73]

The Journals say no more, at this stage, about the heady vision of the 'new free-masonry'. Carpenter probably talked to Ashbee about homosexuality that evening. He was himself homosexual, and much of his later work was an attempt to bring about an understanding of sexual variety. He was relaxed, loving, and honest with himself, and when, a few years after this, his lover George Merrill came to live with him openly at Millthorpe, theirs was a simple, gregarious domestic life, as thoughtful and challenging as his writings. He believed, in a way that is characteristic of the Romantic phase of socialism in the 1880s, that homosexuality could be a vital part of the new ideal for which they were working. He wanted not only to free it from the stigma of perversion, and to have people make a simple acceptance of different kinds of sexual affection and relationship; he also hoped that homosexuality could become a positive spiritual and social force, breaking down the barriers of class and convention, and binding men together in comradeship. Comradeship, that current of affection which he had recognized with a leap of joy when he first read the poems of Walt Whitman, was the essence of the new freemasonry.

Ashbee was also homosexual, and the intense friendships of his Cambridge days seem to be shot through with such affections. But it is doubtful whether he was able to recognize that it was natural for him to love other men until these final days in Cambridge with Carpenter. Nothing in his background or upbringing would have prepared him for this difficult discovery; and as an undergraduate he seemed puzzled and detached about sex.[74] He must have had a sense of these affinities in the company of Oscar Browning and in the pages of Plato's *Phaedrus*; but recognition comes in stages. Dickinson, whose affections lay the same way, recalled with perfect clarity that he did not realize that he was homosexual until 1886, when he fell in love with Roger Fry.[75] Ashbee's friendship with Carpenter, which developed so strongly in his later Cambridge days, must have helped him to understand the nature of his affections, and the idealized vision of comradeship must have made it easier for him, for he was always puritanical by temperament and uneasy in personal relations unless he could throw over them some gloss of social or intellectual significance.

It was important that things should be made easier for him, because the social pressures against homosexuality in late Victorian Britain were unusually fierce. The law, which for centuries had applied only to buggery, was widened in 1885, when the Criminal Law Amendment Act made all male homosexual acts illegal. The new scope of the law seems to have reflected a hardening of public attitudes and the success of the reformers who saw homosexuality as a threat to the family and social purity, on a par with prostitution. At the same time, and partly in response to the Act, homosexuals took on a more distinct identity; groups were formed which gave some organization to its shifting, twilight world; the word itself, only recently coined, began to have currency in England in the 1890s; and it found spokesmen prepared to bring it as an issue into print, John Addington Symonds, Havelock Ellis and Edward Carpenter.[76] On that walk through the cornfields Carpenter had introduced Ashbee not only to his own sexuality, but also to the social world of homosexuality; this was not just a personal matter. He spoke of 'a new free-masonry, a comradeship in the life of men', language which suggested a clandestine society on the one hand, and an open expansive socialism inspired by homosexual affections on the other. Both meanings were apt, for the weight of society's disapproval made both secrecy and sublimation typical patterns for homosexual behaviour. It was to be a question in Ashbee's career, how he would respond to the illegality of his own emotions.

After a week or so, Carpenter went back to Millthorpe. From there he wrote a tough letter of thanks, which can stand at the close of Ashbee's education. Carpenter may have forgotten about it, but Ashbee did not, and much of the rest of his life was a working out of its hints and exhortations.

Millthorpe
29 July 1886

Dear Charlie

I have got back to my lair—and have a very pleasant recollection of Cambridge. *How to reconcile that freedom and culture of life with self-supporting labour*—that is the question that vexes me. Here in the agricultural parts (and in Sheffield) we have practicality—deadly dull, worn out and grimy—at Camb you have lawn tennis and literature—and *4* men to support each of you.

What is to be done?—it is really horrible to see the despair and gloom in wh. the mass of the people live. Will the wealthy come and give *everything they have* and live right in the midst of these toiling suffering hordes. Nothing can be done any other way, and can—will—that be done? It is all dark and dreadful.

And you are depressed. Going to put on the chains so nicely—and do work about which you don't care a damn! Well perhaps you had better do it—3 years is not much—*you* have plenty of time before you. As Dickinson says, it does not much matter what you do as long as you keep true to the ideal. But I conjure you—get to know the people—you will never understand yourself or your work till you do—don't be baffled till you know them thoroughly—that is the only thing that will save you from the deadly torpor of a profession. 'The corn whitens to the harvest and the workers are few.'[77]

CHAPTER TWO
EAST LONDON
1886–1891

TOYNBEE HALL

Carpenter's letter ended with an invitation for Ashbee and Dickinson to come to Millthorpe at the end of August; and so they did. Initiated into the mystery of comradeship, Ashbee now felt himself one of the elect, passionate and high-minded. 'Edward's idea is still burning within me,' he wrote from Yorkshire. 'I feel so proud that he should have chosen me as a vessel in which to place it.'[1] Much of the rest of life, the 'world' which he was about to enter, seemed dull and unredeemed, and he wrote to Fry of the need to stand up against convention outside the magic Cambridge circle. 'We must work together and help each other through.'[2]

Then he went off to the north of France, sketching as he had learnt with Fry earlier in the year, catching vivid impressions, looking in a building not for design but for atmosphere and romance; even the restored Gothic of Viollet-le-Duc at Pierrefonds set him dreaming: 'It is all so beautiful and perfect that one does not think oneself in a real world at all but sits in the court there and expects every minute to see the Sieur D'Orleans himself emerge from his chamber and descend the grand staircase.'[3] After France, there were relations in Germany to be visited, and there he did some more sketching, but the dream was broken. 'N. German Gothic doesn't do after France!'[4]

This was all in preparation for an architectural career, and on 19 October 1886 Ashbee started work in the office of Bodley and Garner at 7 Gray's Inn Square. Immediately, Carpenter's fears of the deadly torpor of a profession fell away, and he wrote to Fry: 'I don't regret going to Bodley, he is a splendid man and is always helping and teaching his pupils. I like too the spirit of the office, art is studied in about as sacred a way as it can be and there is no commercialism admitted.'[5] George Frederick Bodley was, by this date, rising sixty, the most distinguished church architect of his day. There was an atmosphere of religious dedication in his, as in some other Gothic Revival offices, and he would sit, muttering as he designed, 'I wonder what Ruskin would make of that?'; when, that is, he wasn't taking half-crowns off his pupils at whist. Ashbee always looked back on his days with Bodley with affection.[6]

The other members of the office he knew well enough after a few months to characterize with relish. There was Walter Tapper, whose efficiency made up for Bodley's appallingly unbusinesslike habits, 'a dapper little gentleman with a baldish pate': William Bucknall 'an ex-Swedenborgian, now Church of England . . . too oppressed with the weight of a few dominant ideas'; and Francis Inigo Thomas, 'the aristocrat . . . A man of much power but wasting himself in frivolity and the "old chappie" style of humour.'[7] High Church connections were strong in the office, and Ashbee, who had been taken, on childhood Sundays, the round of all known denominations, must have been an oddity there. His loose and un-Anglican beliefs certainly jarred on the 'gentle and pious' John Ninian Comper:

I like him very much and truly wish I could get him to like me, beyond a mere toleration of something leperously unorthodox. I know I am intolerant myself about 'parsonifications'—I try not to be but Comper is so good and so very ecclesiastical. His only interest is saints, and a couple of clergymen, his speciality drawing angels . . .[8]

But Ashbee had such enthusiasm and such an appetite for people and ideas that he could easily take in what he called 'a few church people of the narrow type'; and if he had any worries about 7 Gray's Inn Square, they were not about his colleagues, but about the fact that his father's chambers were only three doors away.[9]

After a day's work, Ashbee would not walk the half mile or so to 53 Bedford Square; instead he would turn east and take a bus to Whitechapel. The tide of social concern in the 1880s flowed the same way, and London's East End was the focus of the most sustained social crisis of late Victorian Britain. Middle-class London had been frightened by working-class riots in the West End in 1866; but fears subsided in the 1870s when it was believed that poverty and unemployment could be dealt with by a combination of carefully monitored charity and workhouse discipline. In mid-October 1883 this complacency was shattered by the Reverend Andrew Mearns with a twenty-page pamphlet called *The Bitter Cry of Outcast London*; suddenly the crowded dwellings and sweated industries, the disease and prostitution of East and South London became a major public issue. The exposé of slum conditions came with a sense of shock on a middle-class London which had grown more and more distant from the East End; and with peculiar force, for the root of the problem was no longer seen to lie in the fecklessness of a small part of the population, but in the condition of a dangerously large number, trapped in poverty by their circumstances and environment.

For trapped they were, in a period of severe depression, with major London industries in structural decline. The winter of 1885–6 was particularly severe, and on the afternoon of 8 February a public meeting of the unemployed in Trafalgar Square was followed by rioting in Hyde Park and St James's. For two days afterwards, middle-class London, deep in fog, was filled with rumours of working-class insurrection. William Morris thought these days 'the first skirmish of the revolution'.[10]

These events, and press accounts of the London slums as a dark jungle, full of hints of anarchy, inspired an epidemic of 'slumming'. Arthur Laurie who, like Ashbee, had come to live and work in the East End, recalled that 'After a good dinner a crowd of men and women in evening dress would be personally conducted through the worst slums known, prying into people's homes and behaving in an intolerable manner.'[11] Such sensationalism was particularly resented by the members of the University Settlement movement which was, by contrast, a sustained attempt to get to know the slums and their problems. In the early 1880s Samuel Augustus Barnett, a man of wide social sympathies, and the energetic vicar of St Jude's, Whitechapel, was in touch with a group of undergraduates at Oxford anxious to help him with his work. These were young men who were drawn towards social reform by the teaching of the Balliol philosopher T. H. Green.

In his lectures Green brought Philosophical Idealism powerfully and earnestly, if none too clearly, to bear on public life. Rejecting old-fashioned individualism on the one hand, collectivism on the other, he presented voluntary associations as the most hopeful form of social action: the merits of free, personal action, of self-help, could be combined with those of co-operation in voluntary bodies such as trade unions, co-operative societies and building societies. His vision of the social reformer as a type higher even than the saint must have appealed to undergraduate imaginations, and it is arguable that Green provided the philosophical inspiration whereby mid-Victorian liberalism came abreast of the social questions which were at the centre of domestic politics in Britain at the end of the century.[12] The public concern which followed the publication of *The Bitter Cry* focused the aspirations of Green's pupils and associates, and in November 1883 Barnett addressed a meeting in Oxford. It was decided to establish a university settlement in the East End, and Barnett was later chosen as the first warden. Funds were gathered in, premises were taken near St Jude's, and the first university settlement was opened in 1884; it was called Toynbee Hall after Arnold Toynbee, the most earnest and brilliant of that undergraduate circle, who had died in the previous year.[13]

The idea of the settlement was simply to bring the young men, fresh from university, into contact with the people of Whitechapel. As Barnett wrote:

little can be done *for*, which is not done with the people. It is the poverty of their own life which makes the poor content to inhabit 'uninhabitable houses'.

Such poverty of life can best be removed by contact with those who possess the means of higher life . . . It is distance which makes friendship between classes almost impossible, and therefore residence among the poor is suggested as a simple way in which Oxford men may serve their generation.[14]

The 'higher life' was a phrase often on Barnett's lips, and it came as near as anything to expressing the ideal of his Broad-Churchmanship, his sense of the spiritual influences passing through secular life and especially through secular culture. He believed 'that the Gospel of the higher life is not to be conveyed in any set phrase or by any one means. It now reaches men through the thousand influences of literature, art, society, which have been touched by the spirit of Christ.'[15] He held annual exhibitions of the work of old and modern masters to edify the poor of Whitechapel. 'Pictures, if they are of any value, are preachers, and their message is to the world . . .', he wrote, and added didactic catalogue notes to his exhibits, to make this clear.[16] His choice among contemporary painters fell naturally on Holman Hunt, Watts, Burne-Jones, artists whose work lent itself to this kind of explanation; his church was decorated by William Morris, and hung with drawings by Henry Holiday and pictures by G. F. Watts.

Philanthropic money to support the settlement was quick to come in, and Toynbee Hall soon had its own buildings, appropriately Tudor collegiate in style. Whitechapel was then one of the most crowded and deprived areas of the East End, the reception quarter for Jewish immigrants, its close-packed courts over-looked by a few barrack-like 'model dwellings', it streets crowded with buying and selling, 'the poor living on the poor'.[17] Toynbee Hall, described by Barnett approvingly as a manorial residence in Whitechapel, must have struck an odd note architecturally, and perhaps in other ways as well.

It was towards this building that Ashbee's steps were turned after a day's work. He had visited it in the summer of 1886, testing the ground, wary of what he thought might be 'top-hatty philanthropy'.[18] But all the idealism of his undergraduate days led to Toynbee Hall, and again his fears were unfounded. In a letter to Fry he sketched the model dwelling and a massive smoking chimney which filled the view from his room (Plate 9), and told him, 'Once and for all Toynbee is out of the charmed circle of grim and despicable detail and here is all the enthusiasm of the University collected and concentrated. There are some splendid men here and a deal of silent unostentatious heroism.'[19] Which was just as well, because his heart was still in Cambridge. His two soulmates were there together, Fry in his second year, Dickinson satisfying his urge to do some good by studying medicine. (After a year he decided that he did more good by wondering what Good is, and settled into a Fellowship at King's.)[20] Ashbee was up there twice before Christmas, and each time his Journal was ecstatic.[21] Then, after a weekend of comradeship, he would come back to the challenge of Toynbee; he made no passionate attachments there, but its idealism provided a wholesome, if sterner, diet.

The residents of Toynbee Hall were expected to spend some of their time in social or educational work, and it was through its wide range of evening classes, clubs and Extension lectures that the influence of the place was spread abroad. So from his earliest days as a resident, Ashbee offered a class on the writings of Ruskin; in the annual report for 1886–7 it is listed in 'Group A & B, Language Literature and Morals' alongside classes on English history, economics, German and Mazzini.[22] To spread the 'gospel' of Ruskin more widely, and to recruit members to his class, he also lectured on 'The Work and Teaching of John Ruskin' at working men's clubs. At Deptford Liberal Club on Sunday, 21 November, he gave his first lecture; he faced an audience quite different from the clever debating clubs of the university, and, to make the tyro still more nervous, the great John Burns was due to speak the following week. But the lecture was a success, and Ashbee felt that he was 'getting nearer to these men, and beginning to understand the Whitmanic position. Ruskin is little known but immensely appreciated, and they enjoy the fiery humour of Fors . . . the B.W.M. is no more a terror for me.'[23] He wrote to Dickinson about his conquest of the 'British Working Man', in great excitement, and got an amused, tart reply.

I hadn't somehow imagined you a successful sans-culotte, but then you're always developing some unexpected faculty. And it must be very pleasant to discover that one can drink whisky and fraternise with the BWM when necessary. It is still more astonishing that the B.W.M. should be keen on Ruskin; but I expect you gave them all the sweet and none of the bitter; i.e. all the Socialism and none of the hero-worship.[24]

He was probably right.[25] Deptford was followed by the West Ham Radical Alliance on the following Sunday, and by the Beckton Co-operative Society in the new year. Here the industrial landscape did not seem heroic any more (Plate 10), and the lives of the gasworkers horrified Ashbee. He saw 'Weary grey sallow lifeless faces grimed with dirt and utterly depraved . . . I had a small audience—some 30—

26

9. (above). Ashbee's sketch of the view from Toynbee Hall, October 1886.

Beckton Jan 18. 87 [illegible]
Progress to the Gas Hell.

10. *Progress to the Gas Hell.* A drawing by Ashbee inspired by a visit to Beckton in Essex.

they were very primitive but very appreciative—nothing tells but social questions and the putting of the awful question Why is all this so?'[26]

The Ruskin class started with only three members, but by the spring of 1897 it was probably about thirty strong.[27] They began by reading *Time and Tide* and parts of *Fors Clavigera*, then they went on to *Unto This Last, The Crown of Wild Olive, Munera Pulveris,* and *A Joy for Ever*; by 1889 they were deep in *Sesame and Lilies.* Similar groups of Ruskin enthusiasts were being formed in other parts of the country at this time, taking advantage of the new cheap editions of his works, reading set texts and meeting regularly to discuss them.[28] Most of them probably continued as placid study groups; but just as on occasions Ruskin would leave his books and throw himself into some practical experiment, so it was with Ashbee's class. After reading about the dignity of manual work, they wanted to do some; and it was decided that they should decorate the dining-room in the new Toynbee Hall buildings.

A decorative scheme was designed, to be painted in free-hand on the wall, and punctuated by modelled bosses or medallions; the coats-of-arms of Oxford and Cambridge colleges, modelled in clay, cast in plaster, painted and gilded, were to run in a frieze round the top of the wall.[29] Today, it is impossible to reconstruct what it looked like; the painted decoration has long since disappeared, though the heraldic frieze remains, and the medallions, dotted across the wall; each of them is modelled with a crudely stylized tree, the 'T' of Toynbee Hall putting forth leaves and branches. Recent investigations of the layers of paint on the wall showed hints of the original scheme, leaves and branches surrounding the medallions, it seems, but no more.[30] But for six weeks in the summer of 1887 Ashbee's class worked away, like Rossetti and his friends in the Debating Hall of the Oxford Union thirty years earlier, enthusiasm triumphing over inexperience, and Ashbee

27

rejoicing in the generosity and comradeship which the project had called up—'the men and boys of my class gave over 2000 hours of their spare time', he reported proudly.[31]

That summer he could feel something real growing in his hands, a new and practical East End scheme to which he could commit himself; while in the West End, at 53 Bedford Square, there was crisis and pain. There is nothing to show what the crisis was; only oblique and anguished notes from the participants. On 21 June, having fled to Cambridge to escape the celebrations for the Queen's Jubilee, Ashbee wrote, 'Plighted a troth to my well-beloved the promise of which may I never be called upon to fulfill . . . I will stand the test if it comes and with his helpful love destroy the family ghost.'[32] His affections circled round Fry, his closest comrade now, as he looked for security among the difficulties of Bedford Square. On 7 July his mother wrote to him simply, 'My dear Boy, I am reading the life of Christ. It does me good'.[33] And three days later his father wrote in his diary, 'My Silver Wedding, one of the most unhappy days I ever spent, let me forget it.'[34] Perhaps it was the old hurt, now so much sharper, that caused the crisis, the fact that Charley would not go into the family firm; perhaps that was poisoning relations between his parents. In this year H. S. Ashbee made his assistant Arthur Petersen a partner in Charles Lavy and Company; if things had turned out differently, he could have given that position to his son.[35]

The dining-room was formally opened on 8 September, though the frieze was not finished until the following year. 'A delightful speech from Kegan Paul—a good evening cheered by the love of my men and boys. *The inauguration of an idea.*'[36] In August Ashbee had gone to lunch with Burne-Jones to talk about the idea of an art school: 'He sitting stately at the head of his table in blue and silver,—grey beard peaked, Velazquez-like,—with blue shirt Morris-like, and silver studs and amethyst set in silver . . .'.[37] In October he discussed a 'guild' with Edward Carpenter.[38] And then, in December, he went to see William Morris. Here, above all, he looked for support, for was not Morris the best-known figure in the world of the decorative arts, and a socialist to boot? But he was disappointed. Morris was by this time convinced that the salvation of the arts lay, not in the arts themselves, but in the remaking of society, indeed in a revolution so catastrophic that it would sweep away much of the present fabric. And it was less than three weeks since Bloody Sunday, when he had stood at the approaches to Trafalgar Square in a crowd of demonstrators and watched the mounted policemen advance; three demonstrators were killed. He could see no point in art schools or guilds.

William Morris and a great deal of cold water. Spent last evening with him—by appointment—à propos of Art Schools.

He says it is useless and I am about to do a thing with no basis to do it on. I anticipated all he said to me. If I could draw him it would be thus [Plate 11], a great soul rushing through space with a halo of glory round him, but this consuming, tormenting and goading him on.

I could not exchange a single argument with him till I granted his whole position as a Socialist and then said 'Look, I am going to forge a weapon for you; and thus I too work with you in the overthrow of Society.' To which he replied, 'The weapon is too small to be of any value.'[39]

Ashbee was disappointed, but not deterred. As an Idealist he believed in the power

11. *Soul of William Morris*. A drawing by Ashbee made after he had been to see Morris, December 1887.

of voluntary associations and small, personal groups; the 'Spirit of the Age', the Emersonian 'Oversoul', would manifest itself in such small centres of the new life sooner than on the large theatre of politics, and social change would come imperceptibly as one Idealist group answered to another. So he wrote a 'Proposal for the Establishment of a Technical and Art School for East London' and circulated it in the winter of 1887–8 among those public figures—and they were not a few—who were concerned with the East End and with the future of art and education.[40] The essence of the proposal was to set up a workshop and a school together. The men in the workshop would teach in the school, thus 'reproducing one of the best features of the mediaeval workshops of Italy'; while the pupils in the school would be gradually drafted into the workshop. £300 was asked for to cover rent, tools and salaries for the first two years, and a start would be made with 'Simple but high class work in wood and metal (repoussé) . . .'.

The resources of Toynbee Hall were enlisted. Holman Hunt was asked to advertise it when he opened the annual Whitechapel Picture Exhibition in March, Walter Crane, Edmund Gosse and Alma-Tadema were invited to speak to public meetings at Toynbee, and on each occasion the press was supplied with copies of the proposal.[41] Restless and eager, Ashbee spent the spring gathering in money, support and contacts. W. B. Richmond wrote, 'Tell me a Sunday evening when I may come . . . and I will speak to your people from the bottom of my heart'; and then sent four pounds in a postscript.[42] By June a little more than the £300 asked for had been given; the top floor of a warehouse at 34 Commercial Street, almost next door to Toynbee Hall, was rented as a workshop; and the 'Idea' could be realized. On 23 June 1888 the School and Guild of Handicraft was formally opened at Toynbee Hall by the Rt Hon. Sir William Hart Dyke, Vice-President of the Council of Education, under the presidency of the Marquis of Ripon. After the ceremony there was a visit to the workshops and *The Times* reported that the brick walls and the ceiling rafters had been painted 'in various tints'; that prints, plaques and work by members of the Guild hung on the walls; and that the beams were inscribed with suitable texts, including Ruskin, sternly pointing the workman in the way of salvation: 'Life without industry is guilt, and industry without art is brutality'.[43]

In bringing the School and Guild into existence, Ashbee drew largely on the enthusiasm and movements of the day. The sense of crisis over the East End, and the cult of slumming gave him a ready audience; and in circulating his proposal he made use of the well-established philanthropic network of Toynbee Hall. Some important contacts were his own, like Charles Kegan Paul; others were almost certainly enlisted through Barnett: Walter Crane, for instance, and Mrs Russell Barrington, protectress of G. F. Watts and *grande dame* of the Holland Park artistic set. And of the subscribers to the School and Guild of Handicraft during its first three years between a quarter and a half were already supporters of Toynbee Hall and its other enterprises.[44] What is more, Barnett was in a position to provide guidance as well as support; he had, after all, been preaching the gospel of social reform through art for some years in Whitechapel, and encouraging craft teaching in his Church school against strong opposition.[45] In the weekly half-hour talks which every Toynbee Hall resident had to have with the warden, Ashbee may have learnt much, though he would never have admitted it later.

The idea of a school connected to a workshop also seemed to be in tune with the times. The Department of Science and Art, established at South Kensington in the 1850s to promote training in the applied sciences and applied arts, had only succeeded in encouraging theoretical teaching in the schools under its aegis; its attempts to improve the standards of technology and design in British manufactures had no real bearing on workshop practice, because of the rationalist theories of its promoters and its horror of intruding on the free market. By the 1870s alternatives to the department's system were being explored. In 1873 Henry Solly set up the Trade Guild of Learning, later the Artisan's Institute, a working-class organization intended to fill the gap left by the decay of the traditional apprenticeship system in London; in 1878 the establishment of the City and Guilds of London Institute allowed the funds of City companies to be used to support trade classes, and by the 1880s the technical education movement was well under way, with the foundation of Regent Street and other polytechnics, and of the National Association for the Promotion of Technical Education in 1887, Canon Barnett being among its founding members. In art schools—Ashbee's proposal seemed to bear on technical and art teaching—the movement towards a more practical approach was led by J. C. L. Sparkes at Lambeth School of Art in the 1860s and 1870s, and by Edward R. Taylor at Birmingham Municipal School of Art in the 1880s; both introduced what amounted to craft teaching as an alternative to the 'South Kensington' system with its emphasis on precisely defined drawing skills and designing purely on paper.[46] Ashbee's idea of a craft school in the East End, with a workshop at its centre, simply took these ideas one stage further; and in this climate of ideas it was sure to be supported; only time would reveal its radical and awkward aspects.

Finally, the Guild of Handicraft was of a piece with the decorative art movements of the 1880s. In his proposal, Ashbee had said: 'Our endeavour will be to make work of such quality as shall satisfy the demand of the professional public rather than of the Trade. As an architect myself . . . I can testify to the need for such work.'[47] He presented the Guild as decorators catering to advanced architectural tastes, and placed it in a line of descent which starts with Morris and Company, established in 1861, making stained glass, furniture, fabrics and wallpaper. Watts and Company was set up in the early 1870s by Bodley and Garner with G. G. Scott, Jun., to cater for a slightly more refined ecclesiastical taste; while in 1882 A. H. Mackmurdo and others founded the Century Guild, a loose assocation of architects, designers and craftsmen producing fabrics, furniture, metalwork and ceramics. The Guild's aim was 'to render all branches the sphere no longer of the tradesman, but of the artist', language echoed in Ashbee's proposal.[48]

The Guild of Handicraft were to be 'artistic' decorators; but they would also be philanthropists. The leading idea of the Guild and School was to provide worthwhile work, the products came second; and in that respect they were closer to the Home Arts and Industries Association, set up in 1884. The 'Home Arts' organized craft classes throughout the country, not for the sake of cultivating skills—and much of their work was distinctly amateurish—so much as for the sake of providing 'improving' activities for the working class, a counter-attraction to the pub in towns, a palliative to seasonal and female unemployment in the country. Ashbee may have been acknowledging a debt to the 'Home Arts' when he said that the idea of his School and Guild was 'adapted from the practice of Mediaeval Italy and Modern America', for part of the inspiration behind the 'Home Arts' came from C. G. Leland, who ran craft classes for poor children in Philadelphia.[49]

The 1880s were an important decade for the Arts and Crafts; the Movement became aware of itself then. The Art Workers' Guild was formed in 1884, and it became the focus of the revival of craftsmanship in London, a club for like-minded architects, artists and designers, an élite which gave a sense of belonging to a movement. It was by nature a rather withdrawn organization, and the Arts and Crafts Exhibition Society, set up in 1888, gave the Movement a more public face—and its name, for it was at a preliminary meeting of the Society on 25 May 1887, that T. J. Cobden-Sanderson coined the phrase 'Arts and Crafts'.[50] The writings of Ruskin, the standards set by architects like Philip Webb, Street and Bodley, the lectures and example of William Morris, had created a climate in which 'Arts and Crafts' became a watchword, a name which stuck; and it was in that climate that the Guild of Handicraft began.

None of which is to deny the peculiar quality of the School and Guild. In the context of social experiments in East London in the 1880s, it was more down-to-earth than the activities of Toynbee Hall, the evening classes and the boys' clubs, with their constant hint of condescension; and though it was much less far-reaching than the work of social statisticians like Hubert Llewellyn Smith and Sidney and Beatrice Webb, it implied a richer sense of the socialist ideal. In the context of the Arts and Crafts Movement, it was the most radical workshop, addressing itself to the problem posed by Ruskin—how to find satisfying work in industrial conditions. All other Arts and Crafts workshops were dilettante by comparison, concerned with narrower issues of design and workmanship, or they were concerned with humanizing leisure, not work, like the Home Arts and Industries Association.

The Guild was, in short, original. It was shaped by a young man of twenty-five, working without any professional or much family support, trying to give a practical shape to four or five years of speculation. In the midst of organizing lectures and appealing for money, he was reading Blake and trying to make sense of East London in the light of his Cambridge speculations. 'I must create a system or be enslaved by another man's', he quoted, and designed a letterhead for the School and Guild on the Blakean theme of Los, Poet and Craftsman (Plate 95). And the City of Golgonooza, he wrote, following Swinburne, 'inspired art by which salvation must come'.[51] In Blake Ashbee saw the Romantic image of the artist and prophet striving with society, and gathered hope for what he planned to do; in these emblems of social struggle, these brave, cloudy images, we come as close as we can to his hopes for the infant Guild.

THE GUILD OF HANDICRAFT 1888–1890

The Guild of Handicraft started life with four members, besides Ashbee, and a capital of only £50, the £300 and more raised by subscription being reserved for the School.[52] Some, perhaps all, of the Guildsmen were drawn from Ashbee's class at Toynbee Hall, and it was a matter of luck that they had the right combination of talents. There was Fred Hubbard, a gentle, slightly prim idealist, who used to work as a clerk in a city office nursing unsatisfied artistic desires; he was responsible with Ashbee for decorative painting and general administration.[53] John Pearson, the senior metalworker, was already a skilled craftsman and designer, specializing in decorative repoussé work, and his wares were useful in bringing the Guild favourable notices at exhibitions; the art loving public began to take note of the School and Guild at Toynbee Hall.[54] In the workshop, on the other hand, Pearson was less of an asset for the collaborative spirit of the Guild seems to have been lost on him. It seems that he rarely executed other people's designs; he probably did not teach in the School, and in 1890 he was almost expelled for running his own workshop outside the Guild. It was probably his thorny, unco-operative individuality that Ashbee was referring to when he wrote about 'our quaint genius . . . our strongest and weakest point'.[55]

John Williams, the other metalworker, was much more the stuff of which the Guild was to be made, relatively unskilled, but with talent and idealism lying hidden to all but Ashbee's eye. In July 1888 Ashbee sent him to Cambridge and wrote to Fry:

make him very comfortable, initiate him a little into the mysteries of Cambridge—show him the best things in the way of decorative work that might be of use to him to design from for his metalwork . . .

You will find J.W. very silent—so draw him out a little and put some animal magnetism into him. He is one of those strong silent receptive natures that love you for what small kindness you can give them.[56]

One wonders what William's silence concealed, whether it was shyness, or placidity, or pain and puzzlement at the difference between his circumstances and those of his new, educated friends. Ashbee continued to draw him out, and he certainly responded to this process, for he became one of the most active and committed members of the Guild, and a designer of some skill.[57]

The fourth founding member, C. V. Adams, cabinet-maker, was also the most important. It was he who turned Ashbee's schemes into real workshop organization. He was an active trade unionist and fiercely democratic, but rather reserved in temperament, so that Ashbee found him difficult to get to know; but together they worked out the rules of the Guild as a co-operative workshop; and in its day-to-day running Adams, as shop steward and later as manager, gave continuity, while his weight, added to the opinion of the men, stopped Ashbee in his enthusiasm from dictating too much. He was, in effect, co-architect with Ashbee of the Guild as a workshop experiment, and when he finally left in 1897 Ashbee described him as 'the man who has done more than anyone towards making the place what it is, and a man with a wonderful tact and strength of character and absolute power over the men'.[58]

The nine months or so that Ashbee had spent advertising the Guild brought in some work to keep these four, and a chubby-cheeked apprentice called Charley Atkinson, busy. There is a letter from Fred Hubbard of August 1888 discussing, with tantalizing obliqueness, various early commissions.[59] And T. C. Horsfall, who ran an art museum in Ancoats, a slum area of Manchester, had asked in May for 'a beautifully framed copy of some edifying picture'. The Guild framed for him a reproduction of Holman Hunt's *Triumph of the Innocents*, which had been voted one of the three most popular pictures by visitors to Canon Barnett's Whitechapel Picture Exhibition in that year. The frame, made by Adams, incorporated a quotation from Ruskin, lettered and illuminated on vellum by Ashbee and Hubbard; the pictures at Ancoats were normally 'explained' in this way.[60] And meanwhile Pearson and Williams were producing repoussé work which was seen by the public when the Arts and Crafts Exhibition Society held its first show in the autumn of 1888 (Plates 12, 157); it must have been a nervous time, a 'first' for the organizers as well as for Ashbee and other exhibitors; but it was a success and Walter Crane

12. Typical early repoussé work by the Guild of Handicraft.

wrote to Ashbee congratulating him on the Guild's repoussé work.[61] Then, some-time round Christmas, came a commission for furniture and metalwork from Herbert J. Torr of Riseholme Hall, near Lincoln; it was not a large commission at first—the Guild could scarcely have handled it if it had been—but designs for Riseholme were produced at intervals over the next three years; and the Guild had found a sympathetic client.[62]

In January 1889 the Guild formed itself into a committee—not, one would have thought, needed in so small a workshop; but Canon Barnett had formed a committee for the School of Handicraft, and a counterweight was necessary. The Guild committee started by setting out the rules for the conduct of the workshops, something Ashbee rather enjoyed. His own position, with the title of 'Hon. Director', was left undefined for the time being; but the sharing of profits was carefully regulated. At the end of each year, the profits were to be shared among the Guildsmen, those who had earned most in wages receiving the largest share. However, the first twenty pounds of each Guildsman's profits were to be allotted in the form of capital investment in the Guild, so that each should have a stake in it; and the Guild's capital was to be built up in this way as well as by loans. Provision was made for Guildsmen to find work away from the Guild when times were slack and return later, providing that they left their capital untouched.[63] As for the management of the Guild, it seems to have been assumed that the final authority lay with the Guild itself meeting in committee, though the relations of the committee with Ashbee and other managerial figures were constantly adjusted. The minutes for 1892 record an example of Guild democracy. Ashbee offered to take over the finances of the Craftsman Club which were a burden to the Guild, and to run it as a private concern; but Adams and Williams objected that this would introduce an element of autocracy into the Guild, and a compromise arrangement had to be adopted.[64]

These rules are of interest as the principles of a co-operative workshop. In the Co-operative Movement as a whole, Ashbee's scheme can only have been of peripheral importance, for the real advance in co-operation in the East End at this date was made in distributive societies; on co-operative workshops Charles Booth simply commented that 'their career has been neither long nor brilliant'.[65] And there is no evidence among the papers of the Guild of any connection with other co-operatives. Ashbee's sense of the value of co-operation was in tune with the reforming liberalism of T. H. Green: not that it gave control of the workshop to the men, or that it gave them profits at the end of the year (for various reasons, it did not often do that), but that it educated them and gave them a sense of involvement in the workshop. In the earliest days, with only a few members, an elaborate system of co-operation was superfluous; it probably worked best in the middle years of the Guild, when there were about thirty workmen; and there were profits in those years. Later, as the Guild grew and profits shrank, its virtues came to seem more and more theoretical.[66]

During the rest of 1889 the Guild made steady progress, adding a few new craftsmen and apprentices to its number, making new contacts, finding new commissions. In the spring Holman Hunt asked them to make the repoussé copper frame he had designed for the large version of *May Morning on Magdalen Tower, Oxford*, a prestigious job. Not having designed so large a frame in copper before, Hunt

34

was nervous, but Williams and the other craftsmen met his expectations perfectly, and he wrote to Hubbard of his friends' 'outburst of admiration at the appearance of the frame . . . I wish Ruskin could see the work . . .'.[67] And in the summer the Guild even opened a so-called 'country branch' in the 'New School' at Abbotsholme, Derbyshire. One of the new cabinet-makers, H. Phillips, went to live at the school when it opened in September, and taught carpentry classes; an arrangement that lasted, not without difficulties, for at least two years.[68]

It had been in October 1888, on a longed-for weekend at Millthorpe, that Ashbee had met the redoubtable Dr Cecil Reddie, and then, or soon after, heard of his scheme for an 'Educational Laboratory', a public school purified of Establishment values and brought into line with the latest ideas. At Abbotsholme, living languages were taught instead of dead ones, sports were supplemented by farm work and craft classes, and Anglican orthodoxy was replaced by humanist Christianity of the broadest and most uplifting kind. Setting aside the bizarre Germano-scientific language which Reddie used to describe his experiment, this must have been seductive to Ashbee, especially when he remembered his own arid schooling; besides, Edward Carpenter and Charles Kegan Paul were supporting the scheme; and there was a broad sympathy between the 'New School' movement and the Arts and Crafts: the same belief in 'Nature' and in the balance of head- and hand-work.[69]

As the Guild became better known, Ashbee was asked to speak in public about his work; and in October he lectured on 'Decorative Art from a Workshop Point of View' to the Edinburgh Congress of the National Association for the Advancement of Art and Its Application to Industry. It was a racy, aggressive piece which, without adopting a political stance, left no doubt about where he stood.

The key to the study of most things nowadays is the social question . . . The studio is a happily situated nest, somewhere in the region of villas and top hats . . . It is ornamented with all the conventional gusto of the prevalent Queen in-Anne-ity . . . The workshop is almost as light as the studio, though less pleasantly situated, and near the racket of some big thoroughfare . . . The place is in a condition in which no housewife would enter it, and the glue pot is simmering on the stove pipe.

The militant spirit of trade unionism, he told his audience, would provide the spirit of collaboration needed to produce great decorative art, would be

our substitute for the monastic ideal, or the creative enthusiasm of the Guilds . . . The destinies of British art and industry must eventually be decided by the British working classes; even as they are at present slowly and surely solving our social and economic questions, and in the end it may yet be told how from the obscene bulb of the plutocracy sprang the tulip of the new civilisation.[70]

A few weeks later, in the more relaxed atmosphere of the first smoking concert of the Guild's Craftsman Club, he spoke in public again, but in a lighter vein, and entertained the Guild with a recitation of 'Ellen McJones Aberdeen'.[71]

By this time, the Guild was seven strong, about as many as the workshop in Commercial Street could hold, with three or four apprentices (Plate 13). Three new cabinet-makers had joined, including Walter Curtis, an unobtrusive figure who was to remain with the Guild for almost twenty years.[72] And later, in 1890, two important recruits were made on the metalworking side, Bill Hardiman and W. A. White. Ashbee liked to talk about how he had 'found' these two, Hardiman

13. The workshop of the Guild of Handicraft at 34 Commercial Street. (From C. R. Ashbee (ed.), *Transactions of the Guild & School of Handicraft. Vol. I.* (1890), p. [18].)

earning fifteen shillings a week trundling a cat's meat barrow in Whitechapel, White working in a 'cutting city bookshop', both rather well-paid jobs by East End standards, in fact.[73] What excited Ashbee was their inexperience as craftsmen: untainted by contact with the metalworking trades, they were the material out of which the Guild traditions of skill and style should be built up, and in 1889–90, when his training with Bodley was drawing to a close and he could find more time, Ashbee settled down to work out the rudiments of the Guild style in metalwork. He had some skill and experience himself in modelling, and Hardiman's talent lay that way, and so they began to teach themselves the technique of modelling and casting, working in silver for the first time (Plates 174–5). They were learning from materials, from the examples of the past, and from each other; an Arts and Crafts workshop was coming into being.[74]

THE SCHOOL OF HANDICRAFT 1888–1890

Many of the early letter-heads and prospectuses refer to 'The School and Guild of Handicraft' in that order; and there is a sense in which the School had priority. It was natural that fund raising and philanthropy should be directed to an educational rather than a workshop scheme; and equally natural that the School should show more immediate results than the little quartet of workmen. In its first year the School had about eighty students, and some classes were over-subscribed.[75] The classes were on weekday evenings, generally at eight; Williams taught metalwork, clay modelling, wood carving and plaster casting; Adams and Hubbard taught carpentry; Ashbee took the men's decoration class, and the boys' was taken by Hubert Llewellyn Smith, of whom much more later, helped by Roger Fry.[76]

As for the kind of pupils it attracted, one can only guess. Arthur Laurie, who was living at Toynbee Hall in 1888 and teaching at the People's Palace down the Mile End Road, said that the boys in his classes 'came from the small shopkeepers, foremen and the aristocracy of the working class', and that may be a guide, as many of his pupils also went to the School of Handicraft.[77] A survey of pupils carried out in 1891–2 showed that there was an overwhelming majority of school teachers, for whom special classes were held from January 1889; the rest were, on average, a little over twenty years old and thinly spread among the craft trades, jewellers, engravers, sign-writers, decorative painters and so on, plus a sizeable bunch of embroidery students of 'No Occupation'.[78] In the teaching there was, one imagines, no special educational system or philosophy as there is so often in progressive schools, simply the assumption that with patience the Guildsmen could impart their own experience and skills to the pupils, as the craftsmen in the Guilds of old were thought to have taught their apprentices. It was naïve of Ashbee to believe that experience could so immediately provoke learning, but it was at the core of the Guild idea.

In the early months the School was very much under the wing of Toynbee Hall, Canon Barnett being one of those philanthropists who was more interested in the School than in the Guild. He chaired the School committee, and there were two other Toynbee Hall representatives on it; but the arrangement did not last long. In December 1888 we find Ashbee writing of Barnett:

He is primarily a eunuch in spirit and heart—that is the reason for his cold-blooded saintliness. He plays fast and loose with the moral enthusiasm of young men and has not the strength either to lead or be led by them . . . In his method of working he is Jesuitical and crooked . . .

Ashbee determined to be a little calculating himself:

My line of action . . . shall be this. To work with Barnett trusting him as far as I can . . . but biding my time, keeping the sacred lamp of the New Socialism always before me . . . making the bulwarks of real human love so strong in the hearts of our men and boys that no castrated affection shall dare face it.[79]

The language is strong for Ashbee, the sexual imagery unusual; he felt betrayed. Barnett's strength lay, as Beatrice Webb saw, in his 'fathomless sympathy'; he was so quick in the uptake. But through some disagreement or clash of temperament Ashbee could only see the dark side of this protean character; Barnett seemed a philanthropic middleman, with no clear convictions of his own.[80] Arthur Laurie felt equally disillusioned: 'Nothing will keep me at Toynbee,' he wrote to Ashbee. 'We must prepare for the inevitable.'[81]

Ashbee, Laurie and others on the School committee were now not only disappointed in Barnett, but tired of Toynbee Hall. As residents, they were supposed by the interested middle class to be noble young men doing good for the poor, especially after Mrs Humphry Ward's novel of the Settlement movement, *Robert Elsmere*, was published in 1888; but they did not feel noble. The limelight thrown by the press on one small area, the troops of idiotic West Enders on their slumming sprees, all made Whitechapel seem unreal, and the six barbaric murders committed by Jack the Ripper between August and November 1888 in the streets round

I (above). The School of Handicraft Boys' Club on holiday. A drawing by Ashbee, 28 July 1889.

II. Cyril Kelsey. A drawing by Maxwell Balfour, 12 November 1899.

14. The Craft of the Guild sails away from Toynbee Hall. (From C. R. Ashbee (ed.), *Transactions of the Guild & School of Handicraft. Vol. I.* (1890), p. 25.)

Toynbee Hall brought all the sensationalism of the press to bear. Ashbee and his friends simply wanted to get to know the ordinary people of East London in an ordinary way, and especially the Labour leaders; that was how their socialism would grow.[82] And so, like others at Toynbee in these years, they decided to move 'further east' (Plate 14). They found a house at 49 Beaumont Square, just south of the Mile End Road, and on 25 March 1889, Ashbee wrote in his Journal:

Everything is done now. And the world's great age begins anew again ... For myself I feel like Sinbad, I have shaken the old man of the sea off my back and the fresh breeze of the infinite ocean fills me. Barnett is compassed ... We sign the Beaumont Square lease tomorrow.[83]

After Easter Ashbee moved into 49 Beaumont Square, and with him Arthur Laurie, Hubert Llewellyn Smith who, as an undergraduate at Oxford moved in the Toynbee Idealist circles and was now helping Charles Booth with his survey of the *Life and Labour of the People in London*; Arthur G. L. Rogers, who was active on a local vestry, and Hugh Fairfax-Cholmeley, whose family were Yorkshire land-owners and almost disowned him for his socialism; in the East End he was known as 'the Chump'.[84] In May Ashbee gave an address at the opening of the Guild's Craftsman Club, and announced that they had moved to 'that portion of London which is essentially the workmen's quarter'; the language of colonial exploration which had become so familiar in East London came easily to him; here, he said, 'these five have planted the flag of a new colony round which the Guild and School may rally later'.[85]

As it turned out, the Guild and School never got to Beaumont Square; they remained for the time being in Commercial Street, but control of the School passed from Toynbee Hall to the Beaumont Square contingent, plus Ernest Debenham, who had been a friend of Ashbee's at King's and at Toynbee, though he never moved into Beaumont Square.[86] Number 49 often swarmed with the meetings of the School Boys' Club, and in the summer of 1889 they took them on holiday in the country, staying in an oast house in Kent belonging to one of Ashbee's rela-tions, who read Ruskin and Plato and Swedenborg, to Ashbee's delight.[87] They slept in hammocks, until some joker let them down with a crash in the early morn-ing; they splashed in the sea at Seasalter, paid reverence to Gothic in Canterbury and had tea in the deanery garden, and dinner in a hotel; and all the while the grown-ups—Ashbee, Llewellyn Smith, Laurie and Williams—sketched, while the

15. The Guild and School of Handicraft in crisis. (From C. R. Ashbee (ed.), *Transactions of the Guild & School of Handicraft. Vol. I.* (1890), p. 26.)

boys planned a rebellion against the adults who made them do the washing-up (Plate I); it was, according to a diary kept by one of the boys, slavery, but at the end of the holiday 'both parties agreed to have slavery abolished and from that time to have free labour as there was so much work to be done packing up'.[88]

All this is what Ashbee had been working for, the five idealists in their little house deep in the East End, holidays in Kent with the Boys' Club, the stuff of comradeship. And yet nothing remains of Beaumont Square in his personal papers, not even a pen-portrait of the inevitable dypsomaniac landlady. It may be that he did not wish to recall an episode which was soon clouded in painful disagreement. During the first year of rule from Beaumont Square, there were worries over fees; the School was not paying its way.[89] Then in June 1890 some members of the School committee put to its second annual meeting a draft constitution. It gave 'sole and absolute control over the management, direction and finance of the School' to the committee.[90] That struck at the root of Ashbee's idea, that the School should be, as it were, the teaching wing of the Guild.

At the same time Ashbee proposed to appoint a boy as his secretary in the School, perhaps from among the students; that was where his strength lay, in his hold over the young; but the move was opposed by most of the committee.[91] There was a flurry of meetings in August and September, recorded in two different sets of equally elliptical minutes (Plate 15). Ashbee himself added to the confusion by his inventive and, to all appearances, unconstitutional manoeuvrings.[92] The outcome was that all the members of the School committee except Ashbee and C. V. Adams, the newly appointed Guild representative, resigned. On 30 October 1890, and with due ceremony, Ashbee and Adams handed over their powers as a committee to the Guild.[93]

The débâcle was perhaps inevitable, for despite the idealism and the comradeship, there were two quite different ideas about craft schools at Beaumont Square. On the one hand there was Ashbee, for whom it was essential that the School of Handicraft should be 'dependent not on South Kensington grants, or even permanently on private subscription, but on the success of the Guild; a body of self-supporting independent craftsmen'; if need be, the Guild would subsidise the School to keep fees down.[94] On the other, there was the rest of the Beaumont Square group, perhaps led by Llewellyn Smith, who wanted the School to have its own freedom, to set its own fees and control its own educational work. Smith, in particular, must have seen the School in the context of technical education as a whole, for he had been assistant secretary of the National Association for the Promotion of Technical Education since February 1888; he was campaigning for better trade and craft training in London and throughout the country because he saw an educational and social need for it; to tie the School to the fancies and fortunes of a small craft workshop must have seemed only quirky and frustrating.[95] The whole of the later history of the School was to revolve around this point.

ESSEX HOUSE 1891

Ashbee and the Guild now stood alone. It must have been strange to look back on those first years at Toynbee Hall, after he came down from Cambridge brimming with idealism; all his energies had been devoted to gathering people in, making friends where he could for his particular East London experiment, publicizing the scheme which took shape on 23 June 1888. And ever since then, almost without knowing it, he had been shaking people off, gradually losing his middle-class allies and helpers, as he found that their aims were not quite the same as his own, as if he was possessed by a hatred of colleagues and collaboration, restless until he was king in his own castle. First there was Barnett, who seemed a mere Christian in socialist clothing; and now, more painfully, the Beaumont Square contingent. In January 1891 Llewellyn Smith opened the Whitechapel Craft School in Little Alie Street, near Toynbee Hall. It was just like the School of Handicraft, except that the Guild element was missing. And on its committee there were Charles Kegan Paul, Hugh Fairfax-Cholmeley, Arthur Rogers and, bitterest of all because he had been one of his dearest friends, Arthur Laurie.[96] All the comradeship and idealism of Beaumont Square seemed to have been lost.

But there had been gain as well. Ashbee's large hopes of making the world a better place, stirred by his Cambridge reading, had been brought down to practical proportions. He had a sense of direction now. Living in an atmosphere of Balliol Idealism, he had found a role for himself as the social reformer T. H. Green so much revered. He would not live for himself alone, as an architect and designer, nor would he take to organized politics; his would be a middle way, and he would join the ranks of those so sharply and dismissively evoked in the Communist Manifesto as 'economists, philanthropists, humanitarians, improvers of the condition of the working class, organisers of charity, members of societies for the prevention of cruelty to animals, temperance fanatics, hole-and-corner reformers.'[97] It was fortunate that the Arts and Crafts Movement provided just the setting in which his particular brand of reforming activity could flourish, for it reached the stage of organized action, of coming before the public, just as Ashbee started his Guild. In a workshop devoted to the revival of crafts his talents as a designer and his beliefs as a reformer, which might have followed different paths, could work together; and he was strengthened by the knowledge that his Guild was part of a larger movement, even if it was a movement whose name was heard more often in Holborn and Hammersmith than in the Mile End Road.

After the dispute over the School Ashbee must have moved out of Beaumont Square; but it is unlikely that he went to live in his father's house in Bloomsbury; and for some months we simply do not know where he lived. Lanky and intense,

41

16. C. R. Ashbee surrounded by the emblems of the Guild and School of Handicraft. A plaster roundel of 1891, possibly modelled by Ashbee himself. (Private collection).

17. *Craft of the Guild*. A plaster roundel probably designed by Ashbee and executed by Ashbee and Bill Hardiman.

with big searching eyes, he must have seemed an isolated and rather difficult figure. Meeting him at Holman Hunt's a couple of years before, Stopford Brooke had described him as 'more *petit maître* than ever'; and though it seems strange that someone so devoted to improving work in the East End should seem a fop, that was how he struck people. He did not have an easy, conversational way about him, he could not chat; he had always to be discussing things, with intensity. Lacking in social graces, having to make his own way because he had decided that no one else's would do for him, he fell easily into the habit of adopting mannered and exaggerated attitudes.[98]

The Guild was now his own little kingdom. Comradeship was as strong as ever, though possibly not expressed in the intense and intellectual manner of his Cambridge days. There were Guildsmen, no doubt, who would have found any expression of such affection disturbing and offensive; but for some of the younger men, and those who had most to learn perhaps, like Williams, Hardiman and the young apprentice cabinet-maker, Charley Atkinson, Ashbee had a special affection; and in a sense it was the Guild itself, an idealized group of comrades banded together against the forces of commercialism, which was the normal object of his intellectualized and puritanical emotions (Plate 16).[99] On an ordinary day in the workshops, on Boys' Club outings or at smoking concerts, he could still feel 'Edward's idea' burning within him.

And the fame of the Guild was spreading. In September 1890 Ashbee spoke at a meeting to promote the recently established Birmingham Guild of Handicraft, whose name acknowledged part of its inspiration; this new workshop had grown, like the Guild, out of craft classes for working men and boys, and it was supported by many members of the city's earnest, wealthy and cultured nonconformist élite. Under Ashbee's friend Arthur Dixon its simple metalwork and its social ideals were to make it one of the most interesting and ambitious workshops in the Arts and

Crafts.[100] Later in the year, as if to affirm the strength and continuing life of the Guild, Ashbee published *Transactions of the Guild & School of Handicraft. Vol. I*, a history of his little enterprise and a record of some of the lectures given to the School by artists such as W. B. Richmond and Henry Holiday (Plate 185).[101] There were no recriminations in Ashbee's history, though he saw how important the separations had been, from Toynbee Hall and then from Beaumont Square; instead, he hit on the delicate and telling device of recording these events in pen drawings at the top and bottom of the page, the personalities suppressed, the turning points in the history of the Guild underlined. And the story ended on a note of hope, for now the Guild was to have a new home.

In the summer of 1890 Ashbee had brought news to the Guild of Essex House, 401 Mile End Road, on the borders of Mile End and Bow (Plate 18). It was a large, plain brick house of *c.* 1700, presumably built by some merchant when it stood on the rural outskirts of London. Now it looked down on the broad and busy Mile End Road with its shops and public houses, and the narrow streets of artisan houses spreading to either side. In its dignity and isolation it seemed to symbolize what the Guild stood for, older values than those of nineteenth-century industrialism. There was even a faint memory of the country under the industrial grime, 'a couple of good box trees, three or four pears and crabs, some cherry trees, laburnum and ash, and a number of vines'.[102]

Right opposite the house was a narrow alley called Brantridge Street, a slum of the most horrific kind, and there were pockets of similar poverty in Stepney and Bow Common; but the area as a whole was, in Charles Booth's terms, 'fairly comfortable', an area of artisans and skilled workmen in permanent employment, particularly in the streets next to Essex House, round Tredegar Square. That was one of the attractions for Ashbee. The move further east from Toynbee, of which this was the second stage, was not, as one might think, a move deeper into deprivation, but away from it, away from the sensationalism of slumming and an immigrant population in Whitechapel who were relatively inaccessible to the social philosophies of Ashbee and his friends; those philosophies could only take root in the outer suburbs of the East End, with their 'solid English industrial population endowed with noticeable vigour and independence of character'.[103] It was from such a population that the Guild would draw its strength.

Inside, the house was well proportioned, with a fine staircase and panelled rooms. It was easy to see how it could be used for Guild offices and meeting rooms; the lighter metalwork could be done in the house, and Ashbee could have a bachelor flat there. The cabinet-makers and the newly established smithy would have to go elsewhere, but there was permission to build new workshops in the garden. On 17 January 1891 Ashbee signed a twelve-year lease on behalf of the Guild, and they moved in in the spring.[104] A large plaster medallion, showing the 'Craft of the Guild' was hung on the stairs (Plate 17), and one of the metalworkers was set to fashioning a suitable bellpush with 'Guild of Handicraft' in fat, arty letters. Soon the dirty earth of the garden appeared to be broken by a mass of small shoots: white pinks were growing there in unlikely profusion. They were a hint of what the Guild might do in its new home, and this flower, with so full a history in the decorative arts, so rich in associations, became the favourite emblem of the Guild.[105]

CHAPTER THREE
THE NINETIES
1891–1897

Ashbee's energy was extraordinary. He worked and worked, took his play very seriously and then, just occasionally, he would drop everything and get away. One of those moments came after he had signed the lease for Essex House, and in February 1891 he left for Italy with John Williams.[1] They spent six weeks there, and he came back to England refreshed. He was a single man, rising thirty, with few ties, little need of creature comforts, and an enormous appetite for work. His energy had been concentrated on establishing the Guild, and on his work as an architectural pupil; now, in the early 1890s, he took up new kinds of work. For some years he lived at Essex House, and the Guild remained the centre of his life; but he also had an architectural office, at first in Lincoln's Inn and then in Chelsea; he started teaching for the University Extension movement; he started an ambitious survey of London's historic buildings; he lectured, he wrote and he travelled. His life in the 1890s was so many-sided that a single narrative cannot do justice to it; and consequently the different sections of this chapter do not all follow each other in chronological order but run, in some cases, side by side.

THE GUILD AND SCHOOL

Once they were established at Essex House, Ashbee planned to expand the Guild. It was, he thought, passing from childhood to adolescence, 'a young concern which has begun to feel growing pains . . .'.[2] And he issued one thousand £1 promissory notes with the intention of registering under the Industrial Societies Act, and issuing ordinary shares, in 1892.[3] As so often, he was running a little ahead of practical realities.

The cabinet-makers were almost without work, and in July 1891 one of them was temporarily laid off. October showed that the Guild as a whole had made a loss over the half year; and by February 1892 things had not improved: first John Williams, then Williams and Adams, and then Ashbee had to make loans to the Guild during the spring, because of the lack of capital.[4] The Guild might have foundered completely at this stage, but for a large order which came in in the summer: panelling, decorative painting, leatherwork, metalwork and furniture for Bryngwyn, a country house in Herefordshire, all to Ashbee's design. It was worth about £350 and by the end of 1892 the Guild showed a reasonable profit; the Bryngwyn order was followed by another in 1893 which threw all the Guild's

18. Essex House, 401 Mile End Road.

19. The Guild of Handicraft in about 1892. From left to right, back row: John Pearson, C. V. Adams and W. J. Osborn; seated: W. A. White, George Kirtland, Reinhart Read and Walter Curtis; front row: Charley Atkinson, H. T. Dennis, Arthur Cameron and A. G. Rose.

earlier work into the shade, the furnishing of a town house in Chelsea which Ashbee was building for his mother, in circumstances which will appear later.[5]

No sooner was the Guild on the way to financial security than it was beset by other difficulties; its carefully devised democracy was under strain. In the early days, when there were only five or six members, the workshops could be run by the whole Guild in committee. But by 1892 it was about a dozen strong; the earliest surviving photograph of the Guild shows most of the Guildsmen and three apprentices, at about this time (Plate 19). They were a cumbersome committee, and as the Guild grew, more management was needed. So it was proposed to elect a small executive committee consisting of Ashbee and a representative from each workshop; the full Guild would only meet every six months. It was a reasonable proposal, but it threw the Guild into violent and unexplained convulsions. Just before the election John Williams resigned, saying that he 'had no longer any confidence in the members of the Guild and . . . some of the members had not any confidence in him, . . .'; the Guildsmen, astonished, put off the election. Three days later, John Pearson, the other principal metalworker, offered his resignation; and four days after that Ashbee issued a fierce and urgent letter saying that '*much, much* more government is wanted . . .'. He proposed that the executive committee should consist only of himself as 'Hon. Director', and an elected manager, as the representative of the Guildsmen. His nominee for manager was C. V. Adams, 'the man whom we all trust and respect'.[6]

And so it was. The resignations remain a mystery, and Williams's was also a real loss to Ashbee, though he continued to act on the School committee. On 8 September 1892 Adams was elected manager, and from that time onwards the Guild met only twice a year, with no fuss and little exceptional business.[7] Under the joint direction of Ashbee and Adams the Guild entered a long phase of steady and uneventful growth. Year by year new Guildsmen were recruited; new skills were taken up, such as leather work and enamelling, while silverwork and jewellery became the Guild's strongest lines; and there was an all but steady rise in annual profits.[8] The minutes of the Guild during these years are formal and terse, a sign perhaps that the Guild had reached maturity.

Not so the minutes of the School. Ashbee brought the School to Essex House full of hope, like the Guild. As if to show that it could flourish without Llewellyn Smith and the others, he started two new courses, in life drawing and embroidery; even more ambitious courses were planned, brazing and metalwork, gold- and silversmithing, a Guild and School printing press.[9] But, as in the Guild, hopes outstripped performance. The School fees were still not enough to cover costs. The classes for teachers were running at a loss, and in May 1891 the Guild agreed to provide teaching free, as it had promised the year before.[10] But that could not go on for ever.

At the time, it looked as if it would not have to. The Technical Instruction Act of 1889 had placed the responsibility for technical education with the newly established county councils; and it allowed them to raise a penny rate for the purpose. In the following year, a hitch in the parliamentary progress of a quite unrelated act—Local Taxation, Customs and Excise—diverted considerable revenues from a tax on spirits from their original object to those of the Technical Instruction Act.[11] After 1890 everybody in the technical education movement, rich until then only in committees and good intentions, was talking about 'whiskey money'.

The Guild and School were soon involved. In 1891 they were asked by Essex County Council to advise on the development of craft education. Ashbee took the hint and circularized all county councils, offering to send them schemes of training, teachers and inspectors from the Guild.[12] In 1892 the Guild published *The Manual of the Guild and School of Handicraft* for the guidance of county council teachers, an unpretentious little book with introductory chapters by Ashbee and practical essays by Adams and Williams. By July 1892 Ashbee could claim—he was inclined to give himself the benefit of any doubts when compiling statistics—that instructors had been sent out to some forty centres.[13]

But none of that solved the problems of the School at Essex House. Its debts to the Guild increased in 1891–2 from £135 to £233.[14] A grant from the London County Council, on the other hand, would have solved their problems. To an urgent philanthropic entrepreneur like Ashbee, always impatient of bureaucracy, it seemed an easy matter to claim a small share of the whiskey money. But unfortunately it was not. For months in the life of the School, and then years, whiskey money remained simply a tantalizing hope. In January 1891 Ashbee applied for a grant to cover the cost of setting up the School at Essex House and was told that the county council was not yet ready to consider the matter.[15] A year passed; in the spring of 1892 the LCC appointed a Special Committee on Technical Education, with Sidney Webb as chairman and Llewellyn Smith as secretary. Smith was asked to report on the existing provision for technical education in London, and did so with exemplary speed. The Guild applied a second time in September, and were again deferred, pending the establishment of a Technical Education Board to administer the whiskey money, as Smith recommended.[16] While the debts of the School of Handicraft mounted up, the machinery of the County Council ground slowly forward. The Technical Education Board met for the first time in April 1893 and a circular was issued. Llewellyn Smith, appointed to the Board of Trade, could not be secretary, and his place was taken by Dr William Garnett. Two members of the School of Handicraft went to see Garnett and were told, 'if you conform to the requirements of the circular you will not fail to receive assistance'.[17] The whiskey money was within reach.

Ashbee made the School conform to the circular, a tedious business, foreign to its traditions and idealism. The informal system of 'workshop evenings', when any student could turn up and get on with his work, had to be adapted to the rigid 'class system' of the circular; registers had to be kept and the minute statistics of educational bureaucracy recorded.[18] In October 1893 the School applied for £700 to £900, partly for running costs and partly for development.[19] Nothing more was heard of the application, and no grant was made. In the winter, they took over ironwork classes from University House, in Bethnal Green, part of the Oxford House Settlement, and set up a special forge; the County Council said that they would probably help once the classes were established. An application was made; and it was refused.[20] The School's debt had by now reached £400. An inspector from the Technical Education Board was promised in the summer of 1894 and duly came; but no grant followed.[21] All the golden vistas opened up by whiskey money seemed to be closed, blocked, at least in Ashbee's eyes, by the unhelpful figure of Dr Garnett.

All classes except those on Friday evenings and Saturday mornings were closed down in September 1894; a claim for £72 was made to the Board, and refused. On 30 January 1895, the School closed down completely. The committee met only once more, in November, to ratify the last annual report, a long, bitter, and no doubt thoroughly one-sided account by Ashbee of *A Nine Years' Experiment in Technical Education*, and of the unhelpful part played in that experiment by the LCC's Technical Education Board.[22]

The minutes of the Technical Education Board, though orderly and specific, are not full, and they do not show why the School's applications were refused. (In fact, only one application seems to have got as far as the Board. Were the others not in the form which could be submitted? Or was Garnett blocking them?) Ashbee thought, probably rightly, that a private enterprise like the Guild and School was distasteful to municipal socialists, who preferred to put their money into the large, new polytechnics—arid educational machines in Ashbee's eyes. That was speculation; but the Guild of Handicraft was almost certainly at the root of the problem. The Technical Instruction Act was carefully framed so that public money was not granted to institutions connected with manufacturing or trade, with the world of private enterprise; and in his report of 1892 Llewellyn Smith had identified two London art schools as being connected with manufacturing and commercial concerns. One was the Royal Female School of Art in Queen Square, Bloomsbury, run in conjunction with the commercial Chromolithographic Art Studio for Women; the other was the School of Handicraft. He was not sure whether the manufacturing connections of these schools placed them outside the scope of the Act, and so made them ineligible for whiskey money. Each case, he thought, would have to be settled by legal experts. Ashbee had always insisted that the School was quite independent of the Guild in its management and finances, and Llewellyn Smith took note of this; but it may be that the Technical Education Board was not convinced.[23] If so, the failure of the School must have been all the more painful, for the connection with the Guild was essential to it, and arguably its most interesting feature even to this day, for it was an attempt to break down the walls which education builds up around itself. Ashbee could have been forgiven if he had felt that there was more in this than just falling foul of the terms of a particular act.

The episode showed how far his own efforts were at odds with the growing specialization of life, with the tendency of education to become a world apart.

This was Ashbee's first major disappointment. All through his career he was attracted to progressive institutions, organizations and movements whose ideals were cousins to his own. He thought of them as facets of a single creative movement, the working out of the 'Spirit of the Age'. Weaving alliances with them, he often found individuals who shared his idealism; but never institutions or organizations as a whole. They were weapons taken up in hope, but they always turned against him. There were to be many more disappointments.

UNIVERSITY EXTENSION

Back in September 1891, when his hopes for the School of Handicraft were at their highest, Ashbee organized a conference at Essex House on 'University Extension'. R. D. Roberts, the Secretary of the London Society for the Extension of University Teaching, was present, and the conference resolved that an Extension centre should be set up at Essex House under the aegis of the London Society. Some time later, Ashbee issued a leaflet advertising the centre; their object, he said, was 'to give a higher and more definite aim to that movement for technical education' and 'to apply to handicraft ... that wider and more liberal training which the Universities can provide'.[24] The first course at the centre was to be twelve weekly lectures by Ashbee on 'The History of English Handicraft'.

University Extension was a development of the nineteenth-century tradition of extending the benefits of knowledge. The idea of diffusing knowledge for its own sake was combined with that of tempering some of the inequalities of the age. There were dons within the universities who wanted to teach a wider spectrum of society; there was a demand for such teaching from northern co-operative societies; and there was an obvious gap to be filled in the higher education of women. It was in Cambridge in the early 1870s that the University Extension movement took shape and the London Society for the Extension of University Teaching was started in 1876. Oxford University adopted Extension in principle in 1878, but did not achieve much until they appointed the buoyant twenty-four-year-old Michael Sadler as secretary; that was in 1885 and he was to become one of the most influential policy-makers in modern English education. The system worked through local centres set up by supporters of the movement; each centre ran courses of lectures chosen from the range offered by the University's team of part-time and very itinerant lecturers. History and literature were the favourites, and arts subjects were generally more popular than science. Though the movement hoped to reach artisans and working men, most of its students were middle class, and most of the middle-class students were women.[25]

Ashbee was familiar with Extension from Cambridge, where Lowes Dickinson and Arthur Laurie had both been lecturers; Arthur Berry became the secretary of the Cambridge Delegacy; and R. D. Roberts, the secretary in London, had been on the fringe of their Cambridge circle.[26] Over the years, Ashbee had arrived at a rather special point of view on the movement. Most Extension lecturers taught academic courses characteristic of the universities; their topics and teaching methods may have been modern in emphasis, but they assumed that the pursuit of knowledge for its own sake had its proper rewards, personal and social. Ashbee took a different view of liberal culture, as the references to handicrafts and technical education in his original manifesto suggest; it did not seem to him complete and valuable in itself. Unless it touched the ordinary lives and practical skills of working men, University Extension would be mere dilettantism, 'a hackneyed boiling down of the latest academic ideas for the consumption of the middle class'.[27] Liberal culture as Ashbee saw it was simply the fine flower and full understanding of the practical culture of the workshop. He liked to talk of 'grafting the humanistic on to the industrial', university education on to the local trades.[28] When he embarked on Extension lecturing, he was not taking a new path; he was simply opening another wing in the temple of his idealism.

As things turned out, the idea of a centre at Essex House never came to anything. The Joint Board of the London Society approved of the centre, but found the syllabus of Ashbee's course on 'The History of English Handicraft' too vague and would not sanction it; hearing that he had already advertised it with placards in the East End, they were considerably put out, and the whole idea of a centre seems to have fallen into abeyance.[29] But Ashbee had by this time been accepted as a lecturer by the Oxford University Extension, where Michael Sadler was setting up new classes and introducing innovations like summer schools and travelling libraries. In January 1892 Ashbee began a course of six lectures in the furniture-making centre of High Wycombe; where possible, he would tailor his courses to the local industry, and here his title was 'Design in Its Application to Furniture'.

On the evening of Monday, 11 January 1892 about fifty students assembled and were given special interleaved syllabuses; they were to use the blank sheets for copies of the lecturer's blackboard sketches. The first lecture, on 'The Meaning of Design', was comfortably general; remember, they were told, Pugin's aphorism, 'Ornament your construction, do not construct your ornament'.[30] After that, the lectures alternated between the general and the particular. First there was a whirlwind tour of European history, each age seen through its characteristic furniture: 'in the abbey of the fourteenth century monk, in the hall of the sixteenth-century noble, in the boudoir of the eighteenth-century lady, in the model dwelling house of the nineteenth century workman'.[31] Then there was an exercise 'On Good and Bad Furniture', with the students bringing examples to class; they returned to the history of English furniture in the fourth lecture, before the nettle of local industry was grasped in the fifth lecture, 'On Chairs in general and High Wycombe Chairs in particular'. The syllabus reads like a music hall version of Ruskin:

The chair and its various moral attributes. The propriety of a chair, the dignity of a chair, the nobility of a chair. Of chairs that are immodest, unmannerly, and vulgar. Of chairs that hurt you. Of how chairs fit to their possessors, and why their possessors grow fond of them. Of the old German family chair. Of grandfather's chair. Of the machine in the modern chair industry, the chair of the million, and the chair that has lost its individuality.[32]

Any students who had come expecting to hear about inlays, or the merits of Sheraton as a model for modern work, were by now disabused, and not surprised to find that the last lecture was about the Arts and Crafts Exhibition Society, the trade unions and 'the dependence of the craft on social and economic questions'.[33]

D. S. MacColl, who marked the exam papers written at the end of the course, found the students breathless and overstretched. 'A more limited subject seems to be desirable. The history of chairs for instance . . .'[34] It was a normal practice for lecturers to make a report to the Delegates in Oxford, and Ashbee's was written in his best crusading style. The course as a whole has been satisfactory, but 'more should be done by the University for the artisan. Our methods of teaching are too academical, we want some ways of linking the life of the workshops in a little self-absorbed industrial centre like High Wycombe with our educational curriculum.'[35] This was not an admission of failure; Ashbee did not think *his* teaching 'too academical'. He was using the report to preach about the Extension movement in general; and he returned to the point in an article on 'University Extension and Working-Men' in the *Oxford University Extension Gazette* that autumn: the Extension movement must recognize the constructive spirit of trade unionism and must look for support, not to the masters of industry, but to trade unions as a whole; that was the only way that the movement would be brought home to the working man.[36]

The course at High Wycombe must have whetted Ashbee's appetite, for he immediately took on four more, and during the next eighteen months he taught eleven courses in all, in places as far apart as Newcastle-under-Lyme in Staffordshire and Barnstaple in Devon. At the height of his enthusiasm he was spending two days a week on Extension work, much of it in trains; he even sacrificed his precious Wednesday evening suppers at the Guild. In the autumn of 1892 he started a second course at High Wycombe on 'The History of English Handicraft'; all that talk earlier in the year about trade unions and the deadly effect of commercialism had not gone down well, it seems, for he got only ten students at a time when the average in extension lecturing was nearer a hundred. But he treated them as a faithful few, and taught the course through to the end; one of them, a 'dreamy polisher . . . all akindle with social questions' even joined the Guild of Handicraft.[37] That course was taught on Mondays; on Tuesday evenings he was in Birmingham, centre of the art metalwork industry, with 'Design in its application to Metalwork'; the course was organized by the Birmingham Guild of Handicraft and, as might be expected, it went well.[38]

On the following afternoon, forty miles or so to the north, it was 'Architecture as the Language of the English People' in Newcastle-under-Lyme, *a tour de force* of Idealist history. 'All art is the expression or index of a nation's social system, . . .'[39] And so we find the high water-mark of English Gothic in the fourteenth century answering to the 'fulness of chivalry' and seventeenth-century styles heavy and pedantic, echoing the temper of Puritanism. The story converged naturally on the present day and its architectural problems; and so did the examination Ashbee set at the end: 'Give a short sketch of architecture under Queen Victoria and state what probability you see of the formation of a common style, giving a forecast of its characteristics.'[40] It was all challenging stuff, but delivered, really, at the wrong time of day; the middle-class ladies of Newcastle-under-Lyme regarded it, to Ashbee's disappointment, as 'a pleasant afternoon's relaxation'.[41] 'The History of English Handicraft' delivered in the evening to an audience of artisans from the local pottery industry was much more rewarding.

He kept up the same pace in the early months of 1893, with four lectures each week in the West Country; 'Architecture' on Thursday afternoons to the boys of Bath College, and then to a general audience in the evening; 'Architecture' again to the ladies of Clevedon on Friday afternoon—'a little shaking up will do them no harm and their ideas about Trades Unions are rather antiquated'—and 'English Handicraft' in the evening.[42] But his enthusiasm was beginning to wane; his reports were more matter-of-fact, there was less of the crusading spirit of the previous year at High Wycombe. Part of the trouble was that the Extension atmosphere was so polite, his audience so often made up of middle-class ladies on whom, for all their culture and intelligence, his message could take no hold. Two courses in the autumn of 1893 only confirmed his sense of the problem. 'Architecture' at Newbury provoked the comment, 'the audience drive up in their carriages, the footmen wait without while the young ladies receive culture within'.[43] A twelve-week course on 'Design as applied to Furniture' at Barnstaple was equally depressing, though in a different way; the course was probably directed at Shapland and Petter, a large local cabinet-making firm; but Ashbee found that the employers were 'Plymouth brethren *v. godly* and *v. mean*—and they will not do anything at all for education but look at it merely from the point of view of the market. On the whole the educational outlook for Barnstaple is about as bad as it can be ...'[44] After Barnstaple, Ashbee taught no more courses for almost two years. It was not that he had lost faith in the work, for he remained on Oxford's register of lecturers; but he was busy with a new enthusiasm, the Watch Committee, and he was perhaps tired. It was a struggle just to get people to recognize his special point of view; and he had made no lasting progress in the 'grafting' he felt to be so important.

He started teaching again in 1896, two of his old six-week syllabuses, one at Fleet in Hampshire and the other at Gloucester. In the autumn of 1897 he put 'Architecture' and 'English Handicraft' end to end to last twelve weeks in Tamworth; but somehow it was not satisfactory. His reports were short, and bland, as if his heart was not in it. And to make matters worse, the sympathetic Michael Sadler was replaced as secretary at Oxford by J. A. R. Marriott, who wrote chilly letters when Ashbee complained about the travelling library.[45] In the winter of 1898–9, Ashbee agreed to teach twelve weeks at Darlington, but refused to take on a course at Harrogate on the same journey. This was a breach of normal Extension practise, and from then on relations with Oxford began to crumble. The Darlington course was cut from twelve to six lectures, and in a mood of injured pride Ashbee wrote to the Delegates saying he would resign unless he were promoted to the full-time staff, a proposal which could not possibly fit in with their arrangements or his other commitments. On 2 December 1898 the Delegates called his preposterous bluff and he must have resigned soon after.[46]

Here was another failure, a disappointment almost as great as the closure of the School of Handicraft. He had wanted to bring the Extension movement into touch with what he saw as the real interests of working men, but its audiences remained largely middle class and its teaching entirely academic. And these hopes were not as pious, the failure not as inevitable, as one might think. Ashbee's recipe for organizing the movement through labour organizations, had, in fact, a lot to be said for it. There was a strong working-class demand for adult education, witness the success of the Workers' Educational Association after 1903, and those Extension centres which attracted the largest working-class audiences were precisely those run by co-operative societies, at Hebden Bridge from 1886 and at Oldham in the 1890s. Ashbee's belief that the Extension movement had to be taken to the working class was not unrealistic, and was shared by many leading members, including Michael Sadler and Oxford's most popular lecturer, the Reverend Hudson Shaw. The difficulty was to involve the co-operative societies and trade unions as such, rather than just particular branches; and despite negotiations and conferences throughout the 1890s, this was never achieved.[47]

As for his educational philosophy, 'grafting and humanistic on to the industrial', that does seem to have been a difficult idea and one not paralleled elsewhere in the Extension movement, except possibly in the work of Patrick Geddes. In a sense, it echoed the simple and attractive idea put about by Ruskin and Morris, that making and thinking go together, and that head-work and hand-work have an equal dignity; and it is an idea which has a wide, if often problematic, currency today as 'liberal studies' in technical and art education. But two things were difficult about Ashbee's version. One was that he hoped to make this grafting a normal activity of University Extension, when the movement itself obviously reflected the separation, so deep-rooted in British education, between vocational training and liberal culture. Most Extension lecturers were sure that liberal culture alone was their proper field, and lectured on 'English History from the Reformation to the Revolution', 'The Romantic Poets', or 'The Earth's Crust'.[48] The other difficulty was that Ashbee's idea seemed to depend on a specifically Idealist, dualist point of view. As material objects have a spiritual dimension, so the workshop is incomplete without its own spiritual history, and that is liberal culture. In his lectures he would move easily between everyday objects, chairs, jewels, buildings on the one hand, and the academic history he had learnt at Cambridge, the rise of feudalism, constitutional monarchy on the other. This was grafting in practice. One wonders whether the students who watched him leap so nimbly about the field of western culture could see what he was driving at, or were simply bemused.

Probably their strongest impression was of his commitment, of a zeal more common in the preacher than the teacher. All his courses converged, whatever their topic, on the present day and on some of his cardinal beliefs, workshop reconstruction, hopes and fears for architecture, the future of the Arts and Crafts. There was little play of mind here, little pleasure in knowledge for its own sake, and perhaps too ready an assumption about the needs of his students. If they reacted like the rest of his acquaintance, then most of them would have been puzzled, and a few, a saving few, drawn close and set alight by his enthusiasm.

A FEW CHAPTERS

In September 1894 Ashbee published *A Few Chapters in Workshop Re-Construction and Citizenship*, his first substantial book.[49] The slightly puzzling title—I have seen it shelved in one library with books on the repair of industrial buildings—referred to its double theme: 'Workshop Re-Construction' meant the refashioning of the industrial system; 'Citizenship' was an educational ideal, a sense of beauty and a reverence for tradition which would be part of a common culture, national not personal attributes. 'To train a child as Pantagruel was trained,' was Ashbee's ideal,

53

'or in the manner in which Vittorino da Feltre sought to bring up the young Gonzage in well balanced grasp of ethics, music, art, languages, history and athletics ...'[50] 'Citizenship' was a word much used by T. H. Green to refer to the duties and values which individuals share with the community; Ashbee added the sense of a common culture as exemplified by the finest periods of European civilization, and particularly by the Renaissance.[51] In its scope, the book was a new departure for Ashbee. It was not an apologia for the Guild and School, which were hardly mentioned, but a working out of his ideas over the whole field of education, architecture and the industries concerned with the decorative arts.[52] It showed what he had learnt in Whitechapel and Mile End, in talking to workmen and employers, Board school teachers and ragamuffin children; and it is the only piece of Arts and Crafts literature written from the point of view of the East End.

His argument was simple. 'The Art problem must be worked out through the social problem.'[53] Picture exhibitions and polytechnic classes in design served little purpose; the only real art was in the workshop, where it was grounded in ordinary life, and in the workshop the solid, unmistakable force was trade unionism. There was no point in working against the men; they would have to be given a larger share in the running of the workshop, and in their incoherent strength lay the hope for art.

I do not say that the artisan has any appreciation of the sense of Beauty, far from it, but I affirm that if we could look for its development anywhere, it is with that portion of the community who are seeking to break its commercial traditions and to construct a newer social order, in which, let us hope, the sense of Beauty may find more room for growth.[54]

In saying this, in looking away from art to its roots in society, Ashbee was thinking like Morris. But his expectations were quite unlike Morris's: no revolution, but small-scale, gradual change, the life of the workshop evolving from within.

The dignity of labour, the standard of life, the necessity of leisure, the need for the curtailment of unnecessary and unproductive labour, and of national waste, the province of the machine, its position as the basis of social re-construction, these are all primarily workshop problems, and will, in due course, be settled from within, not without, in fact, are now being settled.[55]

This mild progressivism was Ashbee's alternative to the radical socialism of Morris, and it was a doctrine as characteristic of the 1890s as Morris's was of the 1880s.

It was a lively book, written in a bold and individual spirit; Ashbee did not feel the need to be serious all the time, and laid about his enemies with bantering satire. Much of the argument was carried on through a series of personae, types of the different parties involved in workshop re-construction. There was the Reverend Simeon Flux, an East End Churchman whose expansive gospel of culture brought the fashionable ladies of Bayswater flocking to his sermons, but somehow did not touch the people of his own parish—a wicked thrust at Canon Barnett. There was Archibald Pushington, a Liberal MP and a large manufacturer in the decorative arts, a kindly, cynical spokesman for the employers, who subscribed to Ashbee's schemes, bought paintings of the most progressive kind, and was utterly immovable on the rights of private property; and his timid designer, John Penny-

III (above). Design by Ashbee for part of the procession of the Fair Cities at the Art Workers' Guild masque, June 1899. The part of Venice, on the right, was played by Janet Ashbee.

IV. Design by Ashbee for the Citadel gardens, Jerusalem, about 1919–20.

worth, who had read his Ruskin and was a bit of a radical in his way, but had to think of his wife and children; then Thomas Trudge (the working-class names were sadly coy), a down-to-earth, conservative trade unionist for whom wages came first; and Timothy Thumbs, Cockney headmaster of an East End Board school, a born teacher, who brought beauty and history to his pupils in the teeth of the educational system.[56] Ashbee moved between them like an interpreter, drinking port with Mr Pushington in Kensington and smoking a pipe with Thomas Trudge in the Mile End Road, and seeing all their points of view; for though they were his puppets, this was a kindly device and he did not score points off anyone except Flux; they all had a part to play in workshop re-construction.

In the closing pages of the book, he rehearsed its theme in a more exalted style; and as part of this peroration, he wrote a long passage on comradeship, the least rhetorical part of which reads as follows:

It is not new in itself; this, the feeling that drew Jesus to John, or Shakespeare to the youth of the sonnets, or that inspired the friendships of Greece, has been with us before, and in the new citizenship we shall need it again. The Whitmanic love of comrades is its modern expression. Democracy—as socially, not politically, conceived—its basis. The thought as to how much of the solidarity of labour and the modern Trade Union movement may be due to an unconscious faith in this principle of comradeship, is no idle one. The freer, more direct, and more genuine, relationship between men, which is implied by it, must be the ultimate basis of the re-constructed Workshop.[57]

This was more than he had said before in print, and some years later it was quoted by Edward Carpenter as evidence of the place and power of homosexual affections in work and industry.[58] It is clear that Ashbee was prepared to speak out about homosexuality in the wake of Carpenter; and he also belonged to one or two groups which provided support and understanding for homosexuals. He may have been a member of the Order of Chaeronea, a secret society and pressure group for homosexual reform started in the mid-1890s, whose principal figure was the odd, cricket-loving and obsessively mysterious criminologist George Ives, a friend of Ashbee's.[59] Much later, he joined the British Society for the Study of Sex Psychology, founded in 1913, in which homosexuals were strongly represented. It was on behalf of this society that he approached the Trustees of the British Museum with an (unsuccessful) request for access to the catalogue of the Private Case in the Library of the Museum, in which as it happens his father's collection of erotica was also kept; an episode whose complexities would, if more were known about it, tax the skill of the most sensitive biographer.[60]

In the art world to which Ashbee belonged there were homosexual enclaves. Charles Kains Jackson published occasional poems on boy-love in the *Artist and Journal of Home Culture* of which he was editor, and there was a homosexual circle in Christchurch, Hampshire, in the 1880s, around the house of J. W. Gleeson White, who later became the first editor of the *Studio*.[61] Ashbee's work was published in the *Artist*, and he must have known Gleeson White; but there does not appear to be any evidence of homosexual links. Equally, Ashbee did not know Oscar Wilde, though he once had the chance of meeting him, when Wilde read *A Few Chapters* and sent the following message to Ashbee through George Ives: 'Tell him that I have read his book and disagree with everything he has said and the way

56

20. 4 and 6 St Leonard's Street, known as The Old Palace, Bromley-by-Bow, East London. (From Ernest Godman, *The Old Palace of Bromley-by-Bow* (1902), plate 2.)

in which he has said it.'[62] Ashbee chose not to follow up this challenge, 'I fancy because I was afraid of his mind . . .'; later, he regretted the decision.[63]

THE WATCH COMMITTEE

After it passes Essex House going east, the Mile End Road becomes Bow Road, and just as it skirts the church of St Mary Stratford-le-Bow, it passes above what was once the mediaeval village of Bromley-by-Bow. Little sense of a village survived the nineteenth century, and now there is none, just blocks of flats and new, massive, droning roads. But when Ashbee came to Essex House there was still a mediaeval church in St Leonard's Street, and nearby there stood a large old brick house with sash windows and odd wings at the corners (Plate 20); part of it was used as a colour works, and the rest was let off as a lodging house. In the late autumn of 1893, the London School Board bought it, planning to build a school on the site. Their land surveyor was rather surprised when the housebreaker put a high value on the materials, but they went ahead with their plans nevertheless.

Ashbee was only just in time to save the best of the seventeenth-century ceilings from the workman's pickaxe. For the School Board had bought a manor house of about 1600, one of the finest surviving in London; it had been altered in the eighteenth century and its corner towers lowered; but inside there was still an original panelled 'state room', its chimneypiece carved in an outlandish classicism and antique heroes modelled in plaster on its ceiling; and there were two more fine ceilings and an original staircase besides. Postmen and land surveyors knew it as 4 and 6 St Leonard's Street; others as The Old Palace, Bromley-by-Bow, because of its traditional association with King James I. Things had gone too far to save the building, but somehow Ashbee arranged for the panelling and ceiling of the state room to be given to the Victoria and Albert Museum where they are displayed. The fire-place had already gone to a dealer in the Brompton Road, but the School Board were persuaded to buy it back and present it to the Museum.[64]

It was the waste which infuriated Ashbee.

We now have on the site of King James' Palace a well-built Board School, and by well built I mean of course built in accordance with all the ordinary regulations, sanitary, solid, grey, grim and commonplace. What we might have had with a little thought, and with no extra expense to the rates, would have been an ideal Board School with a record of every period of English history from the time of Henry VIII as a daily object lesson for the little citizens of Bromley, . . .[65]

Afterwards, he took every opportunity to castigate the School Board for want of imagination.[66] But the School Board was not to blame. They simply did not know what they had bought. If the blame lay anywhere, it was with the British system—or lack of it—for protecting historic buildings, and with the want of something less exalted than imagination but just as necessary, information.

In 1893 Government protection of historic buildings in Britain consisted of the Ancient Monuments Protection Act of 1882, which allowed the Board of Public Works to acquire and maintain any of sixty-eight specified monuments, provided that the owner agreed; almost all of them were prehistoric, earthworks, burial mounds and stone circles. The provisions of the Act were extended in 1900 to include some mediaeval structures, but it was still narrow in scope: all Church property and all inhabited buildings were excluded. The scheduling of ancient monuments in private hands had to wait until 1913; buildings other than monuments were not protected until 1932; and, incredibly, no government list of buildings other than monuments was provided for until the Town and Country Planning Acts of 1944 and 1947.[67] Compared with most European countries, Britain's statutory protection for historic buildings was niggardly and unsystematic; France, though its system was over-centralized *and* chaotic, could boast seventy years of active government conservation, since the establishment of the Commission des Monuments Historiques in 1830.[68]

It was a feature of British conservation that responsibility was thrown much more on to voluntary associations, and particularly on to the Society for the Protection of Ancient Buildings, founded by William Morris in 1877. ('Ancient Buildings' meant, most often, mediaeval churches, but secular buildings and those of the sixteenth, seventeenth and eighteenth centuries also came within the Society's scope.) The SPAB was essentially a pressure group, and since few historic buildings were protected by law, its only weapon was persuasion: writing to the owners of threatened buildings, writing to the press, raising the support of local antiquarians or kindred societies. It was a more consistently successful lobby than one might expect, partly because the Society's four hundred or so members included some influential figures. But it too was unsystematic. A small voluntary society, busy with current cases, could not find the time to identify and list all the historic buildings in the country, and even if there were a list, without statutory protection there was no way of knowing when a building might be threatened, as the case of the Old Palace showed. To say that many buildings slipped through the Society's net would be to imply that it had a net at all.

In all this London presented something of a special case. In the heart of the capital the problem of identifying was not so great, for the buildings of 'Old London' were much admired: topographical artists sketched them, antiquarians wrote books about them, the Society for Photographing Relics of Old London recorded them from 1876 to 1888. The problem was to save them from demolition, for they were peculiarly vulnerable. Many were clustered along the Strand and Fleet Street, in Holborn and the Inns of Court, and in parts of the City of London. But the Strand was to be widened; the great Kingsway scheme would cut through a maze of seventeenth-century streets in Holborn; and in the City, increasingly empty at night, banks and offices exchanged their old-fashioned domestic dress for the grandeur of classicism six storeys high. There was no battle royal, as their might be today, between conservationists and developers. The SPAB fought valiantly, but the two sides were not evenly matched. The mood of the antiquarians was elegiac; they wrote books with regretful titles like *London Vanished and Vanishing* and *London City Churches Destroyed*, and got on with the recording. In the suburbs, the problems of redevelopment were almost as great; but there was also the problem of identifying buildings. The old houses of Fleet Street were well known, but what of those in Bromley-by-Bow? Antiquarians were probably as ignorant of the East End as philanthropists had been ten years before, when the slumming began. The Old Palace made Ashbee realize that the first step was to make the buildings known, to draw up a list.

And so, in March 1894, he found himself sitting down to write a circular, as he had done so often for the Guild and School, putting forward the idea of a watch committee for Greater London, to compile 'a register in which all work of an artistic and historic interest shall be catalogued'.[69] On 16 March he went to the Architectural Association to hear Francis Masey talk on 'Old Architecture in East London' and stood up afterwards to tell people about the Watch Committee; that brought in recruits from the newly founded Architectural Association Camera Club.[70] And money came in from William Morris, Walter Crane and George Frampton among others.[71] On 25 June the Watch Committee met for the first time at Essex House, eleven strong; they elected Ernest Godman secretary, which was important; and they endorsed Ashbee's idea that they should make a start in East London, which was even more important. He had drawn a line north from Aldgate for twenty miles, and then let it describe an arc eastwards, down to the Thames, taking in parts of Middlesex and Essex. That would do for their first year's work.[72]

They were a mixed bunch, the early members of the Watch Committee. There were young men from the Architectural Association; a couple of East End Board school teachers, one of whom, Harry Lowerison, also worked for the *Clarion* newspaper—its tone of self-conscious socialist jollity spilled over into his letters; there was, as there always is, a local historian, Alfred P. Wire, who had been working for many years along the lines of the Watch Committee; and there was, as if for the sake of the inconsequence, a music publisher, Spedding Curwen. Some were amateurs in the recording of historic buildings, and after a few weeks Lowerison wrote, 'I have been over my "beat". Can you recommend any little manual of domestic architecture? We shall need such.'[73] So, a good deal depended on the secretary, curly-headed, old-maidish, methodical Ernest Godman, who was also Ashbee's architectural pupil (Plate 21). He and Ashbee made an odd pair, the one all fire and go, the other plodding along; but Godman was thorough, and he had a real interest in the detail of old buildings. It was lucky that the day-to-day business of the Watch Committee was in his hands.

A week later the Committee met again, and divided up their segment of London

21. Ernest Godman, drawn by F. W. Sargant in the life class at Essex House, 26 January 1894.

22. (facing page left). A shop on the corner of Bow Lane, Poplar, East London. An early photograph taken for the Watch Committee.

23. (facing page right). The doorway of a house in Old Ford Road, Bow, East London. An early measured drawing for the Watch Committee.

into twenty-six survey districts. They were to scour the streets for anything that looked old or architecturally interesting. Once a building was identified as noteworthy, details were filled in on a standard form, photographs were taken, measured drawings were made (Plates 22–3). Churches were omitted, perhaps because they were already well documented, and the large, well-known houses were visited on Saturday afternoons by the whole Committee. Ashbee was after the overlooked, the chance survival among the acres of suburbia, so there was no substitute for foot-slogging, and they attacked some out-of-the-way places. Various Guildsmen took Mile End, and Francis Masey, a connoisseur of East End architecture, opted for London Dock, Shadwell and Wapping; but there were also the northern suburbs, flanking the dismal River Lea; villages once, dotted with early Victorian merchants' houses, and then covered with artisan streets when the cheap workmen's fares came in; they were just what Ashbee had in mind. Godman took Walthamstow, and the breezy Lowerison was not deterred by Upper Edmonton and Tottenham Hale: 'I have explored my "district" thoroughly I think, pressing Parson, Postman and Policeman into service and now await further orders.'[74] Most popular with the surveyors, understandably, were the fringes of Epping Forest, Chingford, Chigwell, Loughton and Waltham Abbey, not villages any more, but not yet part of London. The search seemed less desperate where there was still a sense of the past.

Ashbee thought it would take a year to survey all the districts and publish their findings. Then they could tackle other suburbs, 'the Chelsea, Battersea or Highgate districts, which also often need a little thoughtful and tactful care in the matter of the preservation of their historic monuments'.[75] But he was too optimistic. In October F. W. Sargant, a Chelsea artist friend, wrote saying that he was leaving town, and would his work on Waltham Abbey and High Beech do in the spring? In March 1895 the architects Smith and Brewer, who had taken on Whitechapel, reported that they had an architectural job that would keep them busy for weeks;

and in April, with only two months to go, the Committee found that only a few districts had been finished, and those were by Ashbee and Godman.[76] As always in such things, the enthusiasm of the organizers outstripped that of the other helpers.

And Ashbee himself was subject to distractions. On 21 September 1895 the *East London Observer* reported a proposal to demolish Trinity Hospital in the Mile End Road (Plate 24). Built in 1695, the Hospital provided almshouses, according to an inscription, for 'twenty-eight decayed Masters & Comanders of Ships or ye widows of such'; there were cottages in two long wings of brick, enriched with the emblems and attributes of seamanship, flanking a garden of easy formality, the view closed by a pedimented chapel; and the wings, being of unequal length, were joined by a graceful curving screen. Once, you could have watched from its windows as the ships moved slowly down the Thames; now it was an island of old-fashioned quiet in the Mile End Road, a little masterpiece of the age of Wren.[77] The Trinity

24. Trinity Hospital, Mile End Road, London E1. (From C. R. Ashbee, *The Trinity Hospital in Mile End* (1896) plate 2.)

Corporation, who administered the Hospital, argued that retired seamen now looked to them for pensions rather than accommodation in the Mile End Road; and they proposed to realize the value of the site. That called up all Ashbee's anger and energy.

He got in touch with the SPAB and the Metropolitan Public Gardens Association and organized a campaign in the national press. And since the Charity Commissioners were to hold a public inquiry into the proposal, the conservationists asked to be represented. The Charity Commissioners took the view that matters of architectural and historic interest were not relevant; but, in the event, on 27 November counsel did appear for the conservationists who now included the Commons Preservation Society, the Kyrle Society and the newly founded National Trust; the Charity Commissioners were represented by Mr G. S. D. Murray, a 'shrivelled up little nincompoop' in Ashbee's opinion.[78] Things did not go well for the conservationists. The relevance of architectural and historic interest was still in doubt, and the arguments put in favour of pensions were impressive. Worst of all, the closest precedent seemed to be that of Emmanuel Hospital, Westminster, when Mr Justice Chitty, only a year before, had ruled out arguments of architectural and historic interest and allowed the demolition of the Hospital.[79]

After the inquiry, Ashbee sat down and wrote *The Trinity Hospital in Mile End: An Object Lesson in National History*, an extended version of the case he had prepared. Perhaps he felt that now, more than ever, a record was needed.[80] It was a surprising book. Though it was a monograph on a particular building, much of it was devoted to the corporate life of the Mariners' Guilds in the Middle Ages and the creation of the British Navy in Stuart times, before Trinity Hospital was even built. There was only a short description of the building itself, and a speculative attempt to connect its design with John Evelyn and Christopher Wren; there was no assessment of its architectural quality, and no acount of its life and associations over two hundred years. This was entirely in keeping with the way Ashbee looked at old buildings, not as architectural compositions, but as the outcome and expression of changes, broad, slow-moving changes, in society; and it was also in keeping with his reasons for saving them, which were social as well as aesthetic. To Ashbee the Trinity Hospital, for all its late seventeenth-century date, was an expression of the charity and fellowship of the Middle Ages, and of the honour and glory of the British Navy; these were traditions which lived on, even in the Mile End Road in 1895; traditions compared with which the pensions proposed by the Trinity Corporation were a nineteenth-century parody of charity, a 'money-dole', social affections commuted into cash.[81] The illustrations of ancient sea captains playing draughts and chess in the Hospital, or scanning the naval intelligence at their leisure, were no doubt intended to underline this point (Plate 25).

The book must have been finished by the middle of March 1896, when Ashbee went to the United States. He came back on 11 May, and on 27 May *The Times* reported that the Hospital would not be demolished because there were sufficient funds for its upkeep and no want of beneficiaries. The conservationists had won. Ashbee was scornful of the technical reasoning, for he could never understand why public bodies acted on the limited grounds of their charters and not of a larger idealism; but he was pleased with the result. 'It will not unreasonably be asked,' he wrote as the book went to press, satisfaction giving wing to his verbosity, 'would

25. Inmates of Trinity Hospital playing draughts. (From C. R. Ashbee, *The Trinity Hospital in Mile End* (1896), plate 12.)

the Commissioners' decision have been the same had there not been so great a public outcry against the destruction of the Hospital.'[82] He knew that the answer was probably not, and that the result was due more to him than to anyone else. It was a personal victory.

Survey work, meanwhile, progressed unevenly, despite the tireless Lowerison who wrote, 'Apportion me another district. I've got a bike now, and can fly, look you, can fly.'[83] But once again the LCC seemed to hold out some hope. In 1896 the Council agreed in principle that it might act in the case of threatened historic buildings; and they accepted the Watch Committee as pioneering a list of such buildings, and in July 1897 agreed to pay for the printing of the first volume of

26. A house in Old Ford Road, Bow, East London. A drawing for the Watch Committee, probably by F. C. Varley.

the survey results.[84] Excited by these possibilities, Ashbee concentrated on getting the survey results published. They had amassed drawings and photographs (Plate 26); Godman was urged to get all the details in order; and a number of topographical drawings were made by the Chelsea artist F. C. Varley, perhaps to supplement the photographs.[85]

Then there were delays in the production of the first volume which neither the Committee's archives nor the minutes of the LCC really explain. The months slipped by and no volume appeared. At this rate, Ashbee fretted, it would take eighty years to deal with the whole of London 'by which time the London of 1899 would be—where the commonsense people are rapidly trying to place it—used up for concrete'.[86] History has not proved him wrong. While the matter was out of his hands, he may have thought that he had slipped into yet another institutional *mésalliance*, like the School of Handicraft or University Extension. Once again there was the sympathetic individual, like Llewellyn Smith or Sadler, and this time it was the Council's statistical officer, Laurence Gomme. Gomme was no mere administrator. He had a breadth of view that complemented Ashbee's, drawing on his studies of folklore and primitive government; he saw how the government of London, even in its newest form, had deep popular and historical roots; and he knew that a city's historic buildings were a part of its identity. He also knew how to handle committees, and while Ashbee complained of the LCC that 'like the

64

mills of God they grind exceeding slow', Gomme oiled the wheels; and as a result the first volume of the *Survey* was published in the autumn of 1900.[87]

Ashbee wrote a long introduction to the first volume which explained why the Watch Committee chose those apparently unprofitable suburbs. They wanted to redeem them. In their searches they had come across some twenty former estates levelled by the grim eastward sprawl. Why could not the big houses be given new uses so that they would stand as a link with the past; why could not new roads follow existing avenues and respect the trees, the gardens be kept for common enjoyment? No reason, Ashbee said, but sordid utilitarianism.[88] The introduction ended with a burst of Ashbee rhetoric:

In fine, we plead that the object of the work we have before us, is to make nobler and more humanly enjoyable the life of the great city whose existing record we seek to mark down; to preserve of it for her children and those yet to come whatever is best in her past or fairest in her present . . .[89]

It was typical of Ashbee that he should place the grounds for conservation in the life of the people at large, and it set him a little apart from the conservation movement of the time. Conservationists easily adopted narrow, professional criteria, and when reporting on particular cases the SPAB would naturally assume that the grounds for conservation were self-evident, arguing only that this ceiling was 'a beautiful example of Jacobean plasterwork' or that inn 'a picturesque feature in the architecture of the High Street'.[90] Buildings were judged by the standards of the professions then most friendly to the cause; they spoke, like architects, of the beauty of a building, or, like scholars, of its historic interest. All this was natural and important; scholarship and discrimination were needed, because beauty and history were the stuff of the movement; but it was the language of a refined and sober élite, safe and hermetic. Ashbee was important in a different way, because he kept his eye on why buildings should be saved, whom they were saved for—'the life of the great city'; and because his reasons for saving them, as in the case of Trinity Hospital, were not only aesthetic and historical, but also social. He showed that conservation was not just for the professionals.

By the time the first volume was published, the Watch Committee had shifted its attention from the East End to Chelsea, and added an MP, two peers and a High Court judge to its numbers; it was now called, rather cumbersomely, the Committee for the Survey of the Memorials of Greater London.[91] During the next few years Ashbee was a campaigning chairman, but less concerned with survey work; the death of Ernest Godman in 1906 and the pressure of Guild affairs at that time loosened his ties with the Committee; in 1907 he handed over its direction to Philip Norman, one of London's best-known antiquarians; and when the second *Survey* volume, *The Parish of Chelsea (Part I)*, appeared in 1909, its scholarship, more substantial than that of the first, was due to Walter Godfrey, with whom the Committee was to be associated for more than fifty years.[92] The partnership with the LCC was strengthened in 1910, when the Council undertook to research and write alternate volumes of the *Survey*, and this arrangement lasted until 1954 when the Council took over the whole project. The Committee was wound up in 1965, shortly after Walter Godfrey's death.[93]

Nowadays the conservation of historic buildings is an elaborate affair, with its pressure groups and its legislation, its listed buildings and its conservation areas. *The Survey of London,* as it is now known, is carried on by a team of scholars who are paid by the Greater London Council. Their scholarship is meticulous, and the stately blue-bound volumes are published at the slow but steady rate of about one every three years. It is strange to think of Ashbee as the founder of this great series, for he was no scholar; strange too that he should have taken up such a project at the busiest point of his career. But then in 1894 conservation was in its infancy, and an enthusiast had to turn his hand to all sides of the work. His contribution in those pioneering days was considerable. It is not just that the Trinity Hospital still stands; or that the Survey has since grown into an impressive undertaking. It is also that, in the 1890s, Ashbee was a very modern conservationist. The Watch Committee was, it seems, the first society to record buildings by combining photographs, measured drawings and historical research; its scheduling of buildings anticipated the government system by exactly fifty years; and, above all, Ashbee's peculiarly broad approach to conservation, his sense of its social values, his awareness of its context in development and planning, and of the need for new uses, seem more and more a necessary part of conservation policy today.

AMERICAN INTERLUDE

One of the odd things about Ashbee's life in the 1890s is that there are very few entries in his Journals in the mid-1890s, none at all in 1893, 1894 and 1897. But in the middle of this busy silence there are six weeks of long, frequent, irregular entries, from March to May 1896. They are in his regular Journal manner; he keeps close to the events of the day, savouring their mood and excitement, analysing character; and he also stands back, in the pose of the Practical Idealist who reflects on art and society, sifting the living energies of the time from the dead wood of materialism and convention.

He spent those six weeks lecturing in the United States. On arrival in New York, he wrote,

I have set myself during the six weeks before me in the States to study as far as I can American character—actual contact after some years of theoretical study. It must be premised that I start with a favourable bias, with a trust in the future if not the present of Democracy.[94]

This was a voyage of investigation, carefully prepared and intellectual. He had an ideal picture of America, built up around the idea of 'democracy', and he was going to see how true it was. 'Democracy' meant, not a system of government, but the mass of people, tousle-haired and ordinary. After kings and princes, aristocrats and bourgeois oligarchs, this was the time of democracy, a chance for each individual to find dignified work and a satisfying life. Like Walt Whitman, Ashbee could see the mass of the people and at the same time look into one man's eyes; and it was probably Whitman's writings which shaped his expectations during those 'years of theoretical study'. To Ashbee America was the special home of this democracy, a young society unstratified by class; it lacked traditions of culture and citizenship which he valued, but he expected the greatness of opportunity, the generous sense of the here and now, to make up for that.

Much reading of Whitman was not necessarily a good introduction to the United States in the 1890s; though to Ashbee it seemed to be. Whitman's sense of the many different kinds of people and walks of life, the catalogues of trades and occupations which march across his pages like multi-coloured puppets, all seemed to present a picture of a rough, workaday America, real enough to Ashbee,

Where the cheesecloth hangs in the kitchen, where the andirons straddle the hearth-slab,
   where cobwebs fall in festoons from the rafters;
Where trip-hammers crash, where the press is whirling its cylinders,
Wherever the human heart beats with terrible throes under its ribs . . .[95]

But *Leaves of Grass* had been published in 1855, and things had changed since then. There had been the traumatic experience of the Civil War; and America in the 1890s was less rural, and less innocent, than it had been in 1855.

The lecture tour was organized by Henry Winchester Rolfe, an East Coast academic who was working in University Extension. Ashbee probably met him in Oxford in 1892, at one of Michael Sadler's Summer Schools; Ashbee had been lecturing on 'The Renaissance as expressed in the Design of the XVth and XVIth Centuries', Rolfe on Hawthorne, Thoreau and Emerson.[96] He was a very unworldly intellectual, too much in love with teaching and ideas for his own academic good, as it later turned out, and Ashbee liked people like that. Rolfe met him off the boat, and with time only for a stock impression of New York— 'good but godless'—they travelled down to a reception in Philadelphia given by Ashbee's hosts, the American Society for the Extension of University Teaching. He was to give a series of six weekly lectures on 'The Historical Conception of English Character and Citizenship' in Reading, Pennsylvania, about forty-five miles away. On 23 March Ashbee stood up in the Reading YMCA, wearing the gown of a Cambridge graduate, with a snow-storm howling outside, and began with 'The Workman of the Middle Ages'. He told his audience that mediaeval guilds were trade unions devoted to standards of work and life; and that mediaeval society made for discipline and aesthetic sensitivity; the ideological drive was there, cushioned in history. In the following weeks he spoke on 'The Gentleman of the Renaissance', 'The Puritan' and 'The Citizen of Greater England'; and ended with a rousing call to cultural unity, presenting the traditions of citizenship which he had described as an inheritance common to English-speaking people.[97]

His audience was enthusiastic, and rather more cultured than Extension audiences were supposed to be. In England Ashbee would have detected a drawing-room atmosphere and reacted angrily, but in the States he approved:

There is a great deal in this American enthusiasm for culture. Strip it of its European significance and apply it to the huge democratic average—a Democracy which is all middle class—and its significance is immense . . . it will not be long before men will say to themselves—why go on acquiring? It does not go to the filling and enriching of life! Then will begin our aesthetic reaction and we shall have our Donatellos and Giottos of Democracy. That is a far cry perhaps but they have the sense of communal life which makes such an art possible and they have it much more strongly developed than we.[98]

He was still thinking in the terms he had brought from England.

But foreign countries are unpredictable. In between lectures the different feel of ordinary American life began to catch hold of him and kept him puzzled. Some things were very like England, like the Drexel Institute in Philadelphia—'about as model a polytechnic as it could be, better even than ours—but just about as stuffed full of emptiness as ours'.[99] Others were not; he visited a farming family in Holicong:

At table waited the negro boy he was black as night and hideous as a demon in one of Dierick Bouts' pictures. There came over me a creepy repellent feeling as he touched and brushed past me, I realized how deep-seated and intense the racial emotion must be for I somehow experienced the direct opposite to the sensation of pleasure and kinship and the desire for sympathy that I feel towards any youth of my own species.[100]

He felt safer in the decorous atmosphere of the Ivy League universities. At Cornell he found technical training combined with a command of just that leisure he thought America needed so badly: 'I see here one of the great centres of future America.'[101] At Princeton he lectured on 'Cambridge University', ranging wide as usual, so that afterwards one of the professors came up to him and said, 'Yes, that is the thing to make for—the re-union of the English-speaking peoples—a federation of England with her colonies and America.'[102]

Later in April he spent some days in Boston, but that most English of American cities did not excite him. He was introduced to Charles Eliot Norton, Harvard professor and man of letters; Ruskin had said he was 'a *gentleman* of the world, whom the highest born and best bred of every nation, from the Red Indian to the White Austrian, would recognize in a moment, as of their caste'; but Ashbee found him simply 'elegant and pessimistic'.[103] He admired the murals by John Singer Sargent on the top floor of the Public Library—he had seen them being painted at Morgan Hall in the Cotswolds a few years before.[104] And he was taken round Prospect Union, an educational settlement, by Robert E. Ely, but could not enthuse. 'I am so sick of "Toynbee Halls".'[105] At least it was better than the rather distant hospitality of most Bostonians he met.

I have seen a good many people now and there's a certain air of the draper's store about their cordiality that makes you want to touch it with finger tips for fear you should soil it, . . . Dear little Mr Eley's three over-poached eggs and the cup of cocoa, to which he insisted on treating Rolfe and myself at the Crimson Cafe for lunch at Harvard yesterday meant much more than the many effusions of more 'eminent Bostonians' . . .[106]

In New York he was taken to see the best of America's art industry, but there was little that satisfied his rather special criteria. At the showrooms of the Gorham Manufacturing Company, one of America's leading silversmiths, he was

wearied with many hours of commercialism and shown endless symbols of waste and luxury—nothing that revealed to me any joy or character in the producer. That is and remains to me the only test, not of every concrete case but in the abstract, of a work of industrial art.[107]

But the glass works of Louis C. Tiffany and Associated Artists were more heartening:

These works are the right sort—bar the 'paying' element of which there is a good deal;—

68

but there is distinct artistic genius, or as Josiah Wedgwood might have called it 'taste' behind them. I was much interested in watching the women at work, the peculiar interest being that the method required the leaving of much discrimination in colour and form to them.[108]

The last few days of his trip were spent at Concord, Massachusetts, with Rolfe and one of the daughters of Ralph Waldo Emerson. The farmhouse peacefulness, the old-fashioned Puritanism, the sense of an American tradition, seemed to throw the events of the past weeks into perspective. It was not just 'the chance of genius, the Emerson, Hawthorne, Thoreau tradition that hangs about the place', Ashbee thought, it was a whole way of life that set the lie to 'the great new commercial cities of enterprise and drive . . . they are mutually destructive these two . . . if one of them is right the other must be wrong . . . no community can finally prosper without a preponderance of the former'.[109] The 'great city', he concluded, was a lie, a phase of modern life that had to be worked through, to find a more balanced condition of things.

He sailed from New York at the beginning of May. On the 11th the ship docked in Liverpool and the train cut down through Cheshire, Warwickshire, Northamptonshire, to London:

I never realized before until I had been to the States how surpassingly beautiful England was. The green fields and hedgerows set all my blood tingling. Is there anything like England in the world anywhere. Any spot where is so much life, so much history, and so much beauty all in such a tiny compass together . . . Would I swap my tiny work of Art for that great Continent yonder with its endless noughts? not I![110]

In terms of his original, rather intellectual expectations, the trip had been something of a failure. He had gone expecting a new industrial democracy, raw and untutored but open to idealism, and he had found too much materialism and misdirected energy. His Journal entries were guarded and impersonal, as if he had wandered, Whitman-like, identifying with everything and everyone, and yet finding no one; there was no sense of discovery, and no romance even, until he met a young Chicagoan on the ship coming home 'as fresh and wild and untamed as any Boeotian'.[111] And yet something in the United States must have attracted him, something that didn't surface in the Journals, for he returned a few years later, and many times after that. And as he got to know the country more, it came to have a special place in his ideas and affections.

CHELSEA

There were legal papers waiting for him in London, for he was in the process of buying a couple of artisan houses at the western, seedy end of Cheyne Walk in Chelsea. In the end he never built on the site, but at one point he actually planned to move the workshop of the Guild of Handicraft from the Mile End Road to Cheyne Walk; so important had Chelsea become to him. It was in the mid-1890s that Ashbee established himself as a Londoner of two worlds, Mile End in the east, and Chelsea in the west.[112]

Chelsea in the 1890s was still much as Carlyle had described it in the 1830s;

its population had doubled, but it was still 'very dirty and confused in some places, quite beautiful in others, abounding in antiquities and the traces of great men . . .'.[113] There were mean streets which reminded Charles Booth of Mile End or Bethnal Green; and there were the early Georgian houses at the start of Cheyne Walk, with their tall and sumptuous wrought iron gates, Chelsea Old Church, Wren's Hospital, and the river itself, though its picturesque and muddy edge had been replaced by the dull efficiency of the Embankment in the 1870s.[114] With the Embankment came other changes. Large middle-class houses in the latest architectural style were built on the estates of Earl Cadogan and the Metropolitan Board of Works; wealth and fashion were drawn a little westwards from Belgravia, and Chelsea began to count MPs, connoisseurs and aristocrats among its residents. And at the same time members of the literary and artistic *avant-garde*, following Carlyle himself, Leigh Hunt, Rossetti and George Eliot, adopted Chelsea as their *quartier*, making its ordinariness somehow special, exclusive. 'A dinner party in its august cliques', said one London guide book, 'is not to be lightly undertaken; you feel as you enter that this is indeed a holy place.[115]

Exclusive Chelsea was epitomized by the dandified figure of James McNeill Whistler, with his contempt for the Philistine. He was not much in the public eye in the 1890s, but the most talented artists of Chelsea felt themselves more or less his disciples: P. W. Steer, so very English, everyone said, yet as close as England comes to comparison with Monet; the blond, patrician Walter Sickert, exercising his genius for discovering 'the dreariest house and most forbidding rooms in which to work' at that same seedy end of Cheyne Walk.[116] When the young William Rothenstein was leaving the studios of Paris in 1892, Whistler had said, 'Of course you will settle in Chelsea', and it was the obvious place: 'The name itself, soft and creamy, suggested the eighteenth century Whistler's early etchings, Cremorne, old courts and rag shops.'[117] His first studio was in Tite Street, the heart of the artists' quarter. Whistler had built his famous White House there in the 1870s, and Oscar Wilde lived for a time at Number 16.

It was an English Bohemia, with a dash of bourgeois reserve in it. There were easy morals and sometimes an electric air of homosexuality about the place; but there were also respectable, domesticated painters, like the Glaswegians who settled in Chelsea in the 1890s, James Guthrie, John Lavery and E. A. Walton. Chelsea artists commonly met at the Chelsea Arts Club, 181 King's Road, though Whistler and his cronies had liked to drink at the Six Bells a little further down; and they exhibited with the New English Art Club, founded in 1886. The public thought of the NEAC as impressionist, which was scarcely true; but its members looked to France for inspiration and painted for tone, colour and light, not narrative, and that in itself was a great change in England. The club was certainly the liveliest exhibiting society in England in the 1890s, and a serious rival to the Royal Academy.

The Winter Exhibition of the New English Art Club in 1891 included two items by Ashbee, a 'Set of experiments in design in its application to leather' and a design for a suit of armour. (To a small scale: the armour was part of the props for G. F. Watts's painting, *The Court of Death*.[118]) With these bizarre exhibits, Ashbee first appeared on the Chelsea scene. How he came to be invited is not known; it may have been through Roger Fry who was studying painting under Francis Bate, the secretary of the NEAC; or it may have been through Fred Brown, the

27. C. R. Ashbee in about 1900.

principal organizer of the club: Ashbee himself attended Brown's classes at the Westminster School of Art, and when Brown became principal of the Slade School of Art in 1892 Ashbee followed him there, attending classes throughout 1893.[119] Both Schools would have introduced him to Chelsea artists. He never penetrated to the inner circle of the Chelsea art world, he was too little concerned with painting for that. But he counted some of its leading figures among his friends, D. S. Mac-Coll, George Clausen, William Rothenstein, E. A. Walton; he began to specialize in designing houses for artists on the river front—Edwin Abbey referred to him as 'the studio-building gent'; and he was elected to the Chelsea Arts Club in 1894.[120]

It is odd that Ashbee should have wanted to shine in Chelsea. Art for Art's sake was almost exactly the opposite of what he stood for; and he was probably never fully in sympathy with the NEAC; compared to the Pre-Raphaelites they were dilettante and short of ideas, he thought.[121] But then it was not an intellectual or a stylistic allegiance that attracted him to Chelsea. His appearance, in fact, gives rise to an intriguing explanation of his motives (Plate 27). There was something of the poseur about him, and he liked to time his entrances into a room for dramatic effect.[122] The soft hair parted in the middle of his forehead, the searching gaze, the full moustache and the slight, tufted imperial, the studied uncertainty about the tie, all these recalled a celebrated Chelsea personality, and when Ashbee wore an eyeglass, round 1900, the resemblance to Whistler was complete.[123] Was he setting himself up as the dandy of the decorative arts? Perhaps he was. At all events

71

Chelsea was much more to Ashbee than just a place to live. The geography of London echoed his preoccupations. It was as if, having laboured almost alone for seven years in the East End, in the stern world of work and social reform, he needed to refresh himself in the world of art, to replenish his resources.

The chance to establish himself in Chelsea came in 1893 out of the painful circumstances of his parents' marriage. How bleak the atmosphere was at 53 Bedford Square in the early 1890s, just what finally destroyed the affection between the acquisitive bibliophile and his resolute little wife, one can only guess. The legal deed which separated them as man and wife is dated 30 January 1903, so perhaps the crisis came some time during the year before. Ashbee's Journals make only the most passing allusion to these dark events, and when, many years later, he tried to tell his own children what happened, his account was as charming as a fairy story, and as unbelievable. 'And so it came that one day she just passed as moving sunlight out of the house, and all her children, believing her to be right, went with her.'[124] Where Mrs Ashbee went is not known, though she seems to have stayed briefly at Essex House, and then, some time in 1893, she bought a freehold building plot from the Cadogan Estate. It was Number 37 Cheyne Walk, Chelsea, and on it stood the charred remains of an old pub, the Magpie and Stump, burnt down seven years before. Here Ashbee would build a house for her, and they would build a new life together (Plates 105, 146–50).

There was Chelsea magic even in the burnt-out shell at Number 37; Rossetti and George Eliot had lived nearby, and there had been an inn on the spot since Elizabethan times, traces of which came to light during the excavation of the foundations. Ashbee built these memories into his new house; it declared itself as belonging to an artist and to Chelsea of the olden time. 'The Ancient Magpie and Stump' was inscribed on the porch, and a magpie was carved on a corbel at street level. The handles on the grey oak entrance doors were modelled in bronze as naked boys 'with every detail shown to perfection' as one of Ashbee's secretaries was later scandalized to discover.[125] Inside it was not just the early Renaissance painting in a pierced bronze frame or the blue and white Nanking china that struck the visitor, it was the ordinary things, the door furniture so obviously original, the entire absence of mantelshelves, of which Mrs Ashbee disapproved, the little beads of coral and enamel hanging from the lights. One was for ever, aesthetically, on one's toes.

To this strange house, part showroom for the Guild of Handicraft, part *salon* for its talented director, and part home, Mrs Ashbee came with her two younger daughters, perhaps in the spring of 1894. (The eldest, Frances, had married in 1890 and took no sides in the division of the family.) Agnes, at twenty-five was an artist and bookbinder, and a rather melancholy beauty.[126] John Brett, the painter, thought her a 'stunner' in the old Pre-Raphaelite way. Elsa, twenty-one, had taken a degree in maths at Girton, and was now reacting in favour of sports and frivolity.[127] They were well-educated women of confined experience; to neither did husbands present themselves as an easy way out; and the air at 37 Cheyne Walk was often brittle with their tensions. Their brother had his architectural office in the house, and a bedroom, and he moved across the restricted firmament of his womenfolk like a domestic shooting-star, busy with his many concerns. His mother loved it, especially when they entertained. In the drawing-room on the first floor, with its chimney-breast painted by Roger Fry and its views up and down the Thames (Plate 28); or sitting at the head of their long, narrow dining-table, with a bag of knitting slung over the back of her chair so that no moment should be idle (Plate 150); she was the hostess and he the principal attraction.

On Saturday, 22 June 1895, for instance, she invited her friends to 'A Modern Morality Play' written by her son. The invitation carried a little vignette of the Magpie and Stump as a many-gabled inn of the olden time. Ashbee had written a script which dressed up Chelsea's sacred cows as personifications, as in the old moralities: the 'New Woman', a 'Chorus of Chelsea Artists', the 'Great Lady dwelling upon Chelsea Embankment' who finds that what with appreciating Wagner, buying Mr Conder's fans and trips to Toynbee Hall, life is almost too wonderfully full. The first act was all clumsy knockabout satire, and probably quite enjoyable, but the *Zeitgeist*, originally introduced as a comic character, was transformed halfway through into a serene and beautiful heroine, who shifted the production onto a higher plane, all bland progressivism and sub-Shelleyan quatrains. Fashionable Chelsea, no doubt, began to shift restlessly in its seats.[128]

The part of one of the Chelsea artists was played, rather unwillingly, by the

28. The drawing-room, 37 Cheyne Walk.

seventeen-year-old Janet Forbes. She was the daughter of a prosperous stockbroker who had been a supporter of the Guild and School of Handicraft from its earliest days, and lived in sober comfort in a large, sharp-featured Gothic house overlooking the common at Godden Green, near Sevenoaks in Kent (Plate 89). F. A. Forbes was a sweet and speculative man, a good linguist and an accomplished musician, honest as a rock, Scottish nonconformity at its best. He married Jessie Carrick, who was Scots nonconformist too; she had grown up in faintly Bohemian surroundings in St Petersburg, and both her brothers, Janet's uncles, lived and worked in Russia. (One of them was a doctor and named the sanatorium which he ran in the Khirgiz steppes of Central Asia after his niece; it is called Janetovka to this day.[129]) There was more to the Godden Green household in this way than the usual image of the Home Counties stockbroker might suggest. Their only daughter was a solitary and serious child. She had a younger brother, Nevill, to whom she was deeply attached, a pale boy whose mandarin behaviour amused her, and she loved her father dearly; but she never had friends of her own age, and did not seem to need them. Towards her mother she somehow felt nothing, maternal pleas for affection filling her with dumbness and panic.

When she was fifteen she was sent to Berlin with her governess to broaden her education. She learnt to be an industrious pianist but, thankless child, showed not a trace of homesickness. In the following year, 1894–5, she stayed in Paris with a family of opera singers who were perhaps more exotic than her parents realized. She became a little worldly and wore her hair in *bandeaux* after the fashion of a famous dancer; and the easy goings-on and flirtations in the household fascinated and puzzled her. She wondered about sex, but no one ever told her anything, and she never asked. When she came back from Paris, at the time of the 'Modern Morality Play', she was almost beautiful (Plate 33). The *bandeaux* suited her thick brown hair, and she had lovely grey eyes. She looked at things simply and objectively, and but for the precious fact, which everyone who had to do with her seemed to ignore, that she was still, emotionally, a child, she was ready for life. What Sevenoaks had to offer in that way was yet to be seen.

She had never liked Mr Ashbee. As a girl she found him ridiculous. He contradicted her father, turned his toes out, lounged against the mantelpiece, and touched her hair in an aggravating way. And after Berlin and Paris it was just the same. He came down to Godden Green in February 1896 and she was continually reminded of Tennyson's line: 'So spake he, clouded with his own conceit.'[130] She felt suggestible in his presence and hated herself for it. Asked to choose gifts from among Ashbee's exhibits at the Arts and Crafts Exhibition Society that year, she wrote in her Journal:

I consider with horror how easily I am influenced by the opinion of others. . . . If he finds something is beautiful, then I too at once think it beautiful. It is ghastly and I am fighting hard against it, but so far without success. Can he really have a hypnotic power over me?[131]

While she saw him only occasionally, it didn't seem to matter. But in January 1897 her art teacher, Miss Halhed, decided to hold her Saturday morning lessons not in Sevenoaks but in a real Chelsea studio; she chose a studio that Ashbee had converted from an old skittle alley at the back of the Magpie and Stump. When the lesson was over, Janet went in to lunch with the Ashbees, marginally sensing the tension among the women. Ashbee came in late and ate 'in a rather august way he had', asking her questions about her reading.[132] Afterwards he took her into his office and let her rummage among old letters for autographs of the famous which she collected. He talked to her about Browning and Ruskin and Shelley, and made her little presents of books. Despite years of eager reading, these were unknown territories to her. On succeeding Saturdays he talked to her in the same way, like a schoolmaster with a bright pupil.

The Chelsea classes lasted for twelve weeks, and then Janet went away on holiday. Ashbee wrote her a short, business-like letter saying that a copy of *Sesame and Lilies* was coming under separate cover; the quotation from Emerson he had been searching for was thus and thus; her next subject was to be 'Conceptions of Womanhood'.[133] Janet no doubt did her best with that. In August, when she was back at Godden Green, he came down to stay and they went out riding together. (She despised his loose but actually quite competent seat.) After a little time, quite without preface, he proposed to her.

He was calm and matter-of-fact. The horses kept a steady pace. His way of putting things was entirely to her liking, but what should she make of his proposal? Did she love him? What could she compare this to? He talked on quietly and reasonably: she should not make up her mind there and then, it was unfair to expect her to; she should take her time to think about it, and talk to her parents. Janet was carried along by his good sense, and she felt drawn to him just because he did not force himself upon her. She felt inclined to accept his proposal. Her parents knew better than to stand against her independent will, and packed her off to Yorkshire to stay with friends and get used to the new situation.

When he learnt that she had accepted him, Ashbee wrote her a long letter; it was all about comradeship.

You at least shall claim the whole of my philosophy of life as far as I am able to formulate it.

Comradeship to me so far,—an intensely close and all absorbing personal attachment, 'love' if your prefer the word,—for my men and boy friends, has been the one guiding principle in life, and has inspired anything I may have been vouchsafed to accomplish in the nature of the influencing or the building up of character.

Some women would take this and perhaps rightly as a sign of coldness to their sex, and they would shrink from a man who revealed himself thus, and fear a division of affections. *That* depends upon the woman. I have no fear that you will misunderstand, and thus, not fearing feel that it were almost superfluous for me to tell you that you are the first and only woman to whom I have felt I could offer the same loyal reverence of affection that I have heretofore given to my men friends. Will not the inference be obvious to you? There may be many comerade friends, there can only be one comerade wife! ... Each new link forged in the chain, makes the chain stronger. It strengthens us, and it increases our power of giving—it brings us nearer to the universal sympathy which is the essence of that religion, whatever its various dogmas or creeds may be, in which you and I have been brought up.

But these things are so hard to write about.[134]

They *were* hard to write about. It took courage for him to be candid. And yet it was easy also, for his philosophy of life seemed cool and complete. It might have been harder if he had simply said 'I love you.'

75

CHAPTER FOUR
SUCCESS
1897–1902

TRULY A STRANGE WOOING

Janet liked the letter, with its vouchsafes and its heretofores. It was not an ordinary wooing, not the sort of thing you read about in books. But she did not want that. Demonstrations of affection, even when actually felt, bored her. Here was an older man, who cared for her; he was intellectually commanding, and moved in a world that seemed much more refined than hers; she liked the sound of his voice and felt a little bit spellbound in his company, proud to be chosen as the one comrade wife. His very sexlessness appealed to her placid and unready heart; he was safe. In the ballrooms of Sevenoaks, surrounded by clammy young men, she had simply felt confused and a little disgusted. They were all prospective husbands, and she had been educated to this stage—marriage was obviously the next step; but she could not choose any of them.[1] She wrote a letter in reply, using his elevated tone and turns of phrase, reaching out to her strange lover; she hoped, she said, to enter 'though at first in a small, yet in an ever-increasing measure' the circle of his comrades.[2]

And he, who had never been interested in women before, found himself taken by her charm. She was fresh and undemanding, and something of a tomboy; he reckoned, with a rather frightening realism, that she would make a very special addition to his circle. Besides, she offered an escape from the Magpie and Stump. That house had seemed so full of new opportunities four years before; but, now that he had rejoined his family, his sisters' jealousy of his place in his mother's affections made it unbearable. There was no warmth between him and Agnes now, and Elsa was inaccessible behind the angular fortifications of her feminism. He could not live with them any longer; but with Janet he could make a fresh start.[3] And perhaps there was more to it than that; perhaps she attracted him just because she did not belong to the clever and rather artificial world of Chelsea which he had created around himself; her unusual upbringing, with no school and much experience of Europe and people and music, had been the right one, and she had developed a tough and natural intelligence, perceptive, inquisitive, and downright; perhaps he wanted that, almost without knowing it.

After a fortnight, Janet came home. Their engagement was to be secret for a while, so that they could get to know each other better; but as it turned out she could only see him occasionally, squeezing herself into his hectic timetable between Extension lectures in Tamworth and interviews with titled ladies; many letters passed between them. The Guild, he wrote, was in a turmoil; the Grand Duke Ernst Ludwig of Hesse wanted the furniture for his palace at Darmstadt ready for

29. The summer of 1899: Ashbee and the young men of the Guild at Tintern Abbey, Monmouthshire.

a visit from the Tsar of Russia, and showered them with telegrams and visits from imperious German dignitaries.[4] He had to say goodbye to a dear comrade, a member of the Guild, leaving for South Africa; it was only later that he told Janet of their last night together, of their kisses and 'the white light of his love'.[5] On top of that, C. V. Adams, for so long the mainstay of the Guild, left in October in an atmosphere of tension and some acrimony for a better paid and more responsible job at Heal's.[6] Janet wrote to say how sorry she was about this, but her own thoughts were on happier things. Where would they live? In one of his houses? Ashbee replied that he had already earmarked a building site on Cheyne Walk for them, but would she not consider at least starting their married life at Essex House, by his side? That would be an education. And then there were the wedding presents: 'What shall we do to escape them? . . . Beg them to avoid *silver* unless it's bought at the Guild!'[7] He ended with arrangements for them both to go and see a performance of *The Tempest* by the Elizabethan Stage Society, in the Egyptian Hall of the Mansion House.

The theatre was always one of Ashbee's enthusiasms. When the Shakespearean season was on at the Lyceum Theatre in London, he would book a block of seats for the Guildsmen, and get them to read the play together before they went.[8] In the 1890s he would have sympathized with Bernard Shaw and the drama of ideas, which challenged the stagecraft and melodrama of the older, Victorian actors' theatre. But his particular enthusiasm was for the rediscovery of Elizabethan and Jacobean drama, of major talents besides Shakespeare, and of the formal qualities of spoken verse. This was a specialized and academic affair in the 1880s and 1890s, which stood apart not only from stragecraft and melodrama but also, more radically, from the realism of the proscenium arch and illusionistic scenery. At its centre was the doctrinaire figure of William Poel who insisted that Elizabethan and Jacobean plays should be acted according to their original conventions, a platform stage, the costume of the day, little or no scenery and few or no breaks in the performance. The Elizabethan Stage Society was founded in 1894 to foster productions of this kind, and Ashbee was a member from the beginning; he thought Poel 'one of the finest artists we have in modern London'.[9] So, in among reports to Janet about the Guild's exhibition at Keller and Reiner's in Berlin, and apologies about asking her to fair-copy his translation of Cellini's *Trattati dell' oreficeria e della scultura*—'. . . it is so abominably written—mostly "train and omnibus work"'—he was wondering how you could graft modern words and music, modern ideas onto the tradition of Elizabethan drama.[10] Or, for that matter, Greek drama; he thought it had the same formal principles, the same kinship with music and dance; after a performance of Aristophanes' *Wasps* at Cambridge in November he was delighted to hear the undergraduates shout their appreciation for a solid quarter of an hour.[11] His own *Modern Morality Play* of 1895 had been a light-hearted attempt at such a grafting. But now, in 1897, he began his own series of revivals of English drama, taking the Guild along with him. It was, after all, a revival of English dramatic traditions parallel to that on which they had been engaged for many years in the decorative arts. He started with a most unpromising piece, *The Masque of Narcissus*, an arcane university burlesque of 1602, recently edited from a manuscript in the Bodleian Library, and thick with Latin tags. It was first performed in July at the Magpie and Stump, and then again in November in front of the boys of Charterhouse School, the actors being drawn from the Guild of Handicraft (Plate 30). It must have creaked terribly in performance, but for Ashbee the value lay as much in the doing of it as in the quality of the performance. After Charterhouse he wrote to Janet, 'It does my boys no end of good, this sort of thing, and cannot but make better artists and workmen of them.[12]

They had planned to be together at Christmas; but Janet had to go to St Petersburg to stay with her cousins, 'great bearded fellows ... with great wolf eyes and long tawny hair ...', and Ashbee spent Christmas in Paris with Philip Dalmas, a clever, moody composer friend of Edward Carpenter's, and Leonard Borwick, a pianist with whom Janet had, curiously enough, been half in love earlier in the year.[13] They were trying to shape a new kind of play, based on Greek drama with modern music and lyrics by Ashbee in a strange 'diamond-shaped metre', full of Maeterlinckian mysticism; 'a whole creative week', he wrote, 'which has been about as full of real life as it can be'.[14] Janet thought it sounded chaotic. Halfway through he lunched with the dilettante Comtesse de Béarn, for whom he designed some exquisite enamelled clocks, waited on by footmen of overpowering discreetness, with truffles wallowing in aspic, and 'infinite suggestions of other footmen through half opened Louis Quinze panelled doors ... You will appreciate the transition from all this to Phillip's humble flat up the ricketty staircase 'au cinquiéme' ...' where they lived on nuts, using the shells to feed the fire, and wrestled with the 'Drama'.[15]

Janet was wrestling with humbler but more painful problems. Ever since she had decided to marry him she had been wondering whether it was the right decision. The whole thing was so definitely *not* overwhelming. She became quite ill with worry. Ashbee was well aware of this, and while she was still in St Petersburg,

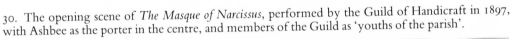

30. The opening scene of *The Masque of Narcissus*, performed by the Guild of Handicraft in 1897, with Ashbee as the porter in the centre, and members of the Guild as 'youths of the parish'.

31. The men of the Essex House Press. Thomas Binning is the bearded figure on the right.

he wrote her a long better of reassurance, cast in the form of a fable about a suave and green-eyed 'Demon Doubt'.[16] The Demon, he related, had come and sat at the end of his bed and told him that he was a fool to marry; his new wife would claim more and more of his affections, the Demon said; his comrades would fall away one by one; he was not the man for it. But he had dismissed the Demon by pledging his faith in Janet. So the letter ran. The only trouble was, his dismissal did not read nearly as convincingly as the Demon's vivid and magnificent rhetoric. The letter only served to show that his feelings too were divided. If the engagement had been broken off early in 1898, it would not have been surprising. As it was, Ashbee's sisters gossiped, the engagement had to be made public in March, and the Demon was banished, officially.

They watched their new house that Ashbee had designed going up on Cheyne Walk; and he at least escaped his doubts by keeping busy; Walter Crane asked him to dress up as Mrs Grundy in a satirical lament on the demise of Art at the Art Workers' Guild, the clubby refuge of Arts and Crafts men; he was urging Godman on with the Survey, rescuing St Mary's, Stratford-le-Bow from over-restoration by Sir Arthur Blomfield, and despatching pages of his translation to Janet.[17] The Cellini was to have been printed in Whitechapel, but March brought exciting developments. The Kelmscott Press had just printed its last book and was closing down. In Wolverhampton there was a vigorous, wealthy young brewer who was more interested in books and paintings than in brewing beer, called Laurence Hodson. He owned manuscripts by Morris, paintings by Rossetti and Burne-Jones, etchings by Whistler, sculpture by Rodin and books printed by the Kelmscott and other private presses; Morris's last pattern design was made for his house, Compton Hall.[18] Hodson had known Ashbee for some years and seems to have come to him early in 1898 suggesting that the Guild should take over the staff and equipment from the Kelmscott Press, and continue the tradition.[19] At the end of March Ashbee wrote jubilantly to Janet:

The great event of the week has been the purchase of the Morris press by the Guild of Handicraft ... next Monday there will be vans of presses and gages and chairs and tables and paper and machinery—lock, stock and barrel—moving East from Hammersmith. We are thinking of a musical procession![20]

Three printers came with the presses (Plate 31), including Thomas Binning, a trade unionist of long standing who claimed to have been the one to convince William Morris of the value of political action; 'a quiet refined old gentleman' he seemed to one of the Guildsmen's sons, 'very well read'.[21] Within a month the first sixteen pages of the Cellini were in proof. Ashbee could reflect with pride on this last addition to the workshops of the Guild; the workshop hallowed by the 'master-craftsman' would now be called the Essex House Press.

In May, he escorted his future mother-in-law, in a feather hat and parasol, up ladders and across planks to the precipitous top of their new house, and, planning his autumn engagements, decided that they should get married before he started Extension lecturing at the end of September.[22] Looking further ahead, he pondered on married life and the future of the Guild. In 1896 he had taken a little weather-boarded cottage called Poynett's, near South Benfleet in Essex, partly for the Guild boys to get out into the country, and partly to escape from his sisters. Now he was thinking of building workshops there, moving everyone out to Essex for good. 'To train up little children or fine craftsmen in London', he told Janet, 'is a cruelty unmentionable.'[23]

The Guild in 1898 was buoyant and, barring the occasional crisis, efficient; the half-year ending 31 December 1897 had been their best so far, with more than £100 in bonuses for the Guildsmen.[24] This was an important stage for the Guild. It had always been interesting socially and artistically; now it seemed to be successful financially. Ashbee revived the idea of registering as a limited company. While they were still a private concern, all the Guildsmen were answerable in the event of heavy debts, and the thriftier among them were anxious to limit their liability. At the same time an issue of shares would provide capital for expansion.[25] They had considered registration in 1891, without result, and again in 1896 when Ernest T. Marriott, a London architect who had been a pupil of Ashbee's, offered to invest £1,000 if Ashbee could find an equivalent sum. He could not; but in the winter of 1897 the idea came to the surface again with an offer of practical help from Rob Martin Holland, a young director at Martin's Bank. On 8 July 1898, the Guild was registered at 'The Guild of Handicraft Limited'.[26]

The articles of association, handsomely printed by the Essex House Press, record a brave attempt to preserve the special character of the Guild. Its self-government was now challenged by the authority of a board of directors, responsible to share-holders. So the Guildsmen were given the right to elect their own representative on the board, the labour director. And their financial stake in the Guild was now represented by five pounds invested by each Guildsman on election and two and a half per cent deducted weekly from wages to build up his holding.[27] Though they were only a small proportion of the total investment, the Guild holdings were impressive. Of the 3,864 shares taken up, the twenty full Guildsmen apart from Ashbee held 632; Ashbee held 688 and his mother 840. The remaining 1,704 shares were held by eighteen private shareholders, of whom the largest were Willie Gibbins, a Birmingham manufacturer friend of Ashbee's and a King's man, with 500; Laurence Hodson with 350 specifically for the Press, Rob Martin Holland with 236 and, curiously, the Reverend Hastings Rashdall, historian of the mediaeval universities, with 200.[28]

It is difficult not to see registration as a high point in the history of the Guild, ten years of earnest effort crowned with success. They were now a substantial workshop attracting prestigious commissions, exhibiting throughout Britain and in Europe, and consistently well reviewed in the art press.[29] Ashbee himself seemed to enjoy this phase; he was less embattled and intense, readier to relish life and its varieties. And yet he looked on success with a questioning eye. Here was the Guild taking on men, and with every one it became less personal, less 'human' as he would have said; and as for the new outside finance, it might be needed, but it only put back the day when the Guildsmen would, as he hoped, become sole owners of the business.[30] Actually, business success only mattered to Ashbee because it allowed him to continue with something quite different, the personal experiment of the Guild, the attempt to enlarge that elusive creative freedom of the craftsman of which Ruskin had written. In a small workshop like the Guild, so much set against the way of the world, business success would always be, at best, ambiguous.

On 8 September 1898, an uncomfortably hot day, Janet and Ashbee were married, and the Guildsmen at the wedding struck an interesting note among the ices, white satin and Sevenoaks notables. They left the reception at Godden Green in an open dog-cart, instead of a brougham, a concession to Janet's growing unorthodoxy, and travelled by train to Cannon Street, talking of this and that. A cab took them through Whitechapel to Mile End. It had been Janet's idea that they should spend their first night there, though her parents would not think of them living in the East End. Essex House was empty except for the housekeeper, and they ate a simple supper, the pervasive smell of fried fish drifting in from outside, keyed up to a sickening intensity by the heat. A group of Guild boys dropped in on their way home and the newly married couple stood at the top of the stairs, unseen, listening to the boys discuss the wedding; then they went to bed. There were two small beds, and Janet lay there, frightened as a hare, turning and turning in her mind impossible ideas about the 'marriage night', while Ashbee undressed next door. In his flannel night clothes he looked unfamiliar somehow. He got into his own bed, smiled at her reassuringly, and blew out the light.[31]

MARRIED LIFE

They spent their honeymoon at The Clergy House, Alfriston, on the South Downs, a fourteenth-century timber-framed house which had the distinction of being the first building to be acquired by the National Trust. The good weather held, and there was a lovely late summer fulness about the place; they ranged red apples along the beams of The Clergy House and swam in the Cuckmere River nearby.

Janet took off her stays by the river's edge, and never wore them again. It was, in a way, a sacrament of her new life, like the service in church a few days before. Ashbee, though, who did not stand like her on the threshold of adult life, was anxious to preserve the continuities. He wrote to his mother as soon as they arrived, urging her to get closer to the sisters now that he was gone; the letter ended, 'I shall always love you more than anyone else in the whole world'.[32]

His Extension lectures were in Darlington, due to start on 29 September, so after a fortnight they went north, staying at Holmesfield, just outside Sheffield. Ashbee must have talked to Janet a good deal about Edward Carpenter, and now he took her over to Millthorpe to meet the prince of comrades, sage and father figure; Philip Dalmas was staying nearby as well. They kept a fairly regular Journal together now, and Janet's entry shows that she was impressed. But she wrote blandly, as if she felt she had to rise to the occasion: Carpenter and Dalmas were 'two personalities of the greatest human interest and vitality'.[33] She could do better than that. In her husband's world she was bound to be something of an acolyte at first, echoing his opinions, even picking up a little of his flowery, cloudy way of writing. Luckily Dalmas played the piano a lot, including a sonata he had dedicated to Ashbee, and Janet felt on safer ground there, sure of her own taste. On the way south again they stayed near Wolverhampton with Colonel Shaw-Hellier, an aristocratic old soldier who pottered around his estate, half out of touch with the world, but in love with music and architecture; Ashbee thought he was homosexual. They inspected the ancient Wodehouse at Wombourne, where he lived, looked over the chapel Ashbee had built for him (Plate 104), and admired his furniture and bric-à-brac; 'refinement and luxury', Janet noted, but 'softened by the custom of centuries'.[34]

All these introductions were preliminary. Married life really began for Janet when they got back to London and she found herself the mistress of two servants, an account book and a house with a view over the river. 74 Cheyne Walk was an artist's house, of the sort Ashbee designed elsewhere on the Embankment; it had a big studio which they called the Music Room and used for entertaining (Plates 106, 108). It was bare and unlived in, of course, the more so because the architect had exercised his refinement in leaving many things like mouldings out, concentrating attention on a few decorative features, emblems of his presence: the copper front door embossed with pinks (Plate 32), the stained glass roundels by Christopher Whall in the ante-room to the studio, depicting Music, Architecture, Handicraft and—the particular note was struck here—Labour Organization.[35] Janet took readily to running the household, diverting Minnie the housemaid from her perpetual quest for a husband, and instructing Bertha the Polish cook. There were not many disastrous meals, and besides Ashbee never gave food the attention it deserved. After supper, if they were not dining out, he would work at his drawing-board, and she would read to him. In this way they covered much interesting ground, and in the enjoyment of Meredith and Leigh Hunt, Dickens and Sterne, they grew closer together.[36]

And the day was all hers, to go where she wished and do as she pleased, in which her husband rather encouraged her. She took up social work, visiting the poor in the grotesquely misnamed Sun Court, a desperate slum tucked close, very close, behind 74 Cheyne Walk, wondering with a keen sense of duty whether she should

32. The front door of 74 Cheyne Walk. (From *Neubauten in London* (Berlin, 1900), plate 11.)

33. (facing page). Janet Ashbee in the late 1890s.

learn to do the work more scientifically with the Charity Organisation Society; she went to lectures at the new polytechnic in Manresa Road, and plunged rapturously in the local swimming bath. She cultivated her husband's friends and clients, and could be seen threading her way fearlessly through the traffic on her bicycle, dressed in the uniform of her liberation, braced skirt, and a jacket of green Ruskin serge with a cap to match; no lace, no frills. (Little Mary Newbery, daughter of the headmaster of Glasgow School of Art, when staying with E. A. Walton and his wife at Number 73, saw her walking on the Embankment in a more outlandish, more Arts and Crafts kind of rational dress, with 'rather flowing white robes . . . the first grown up I had ever seen wearing bare feet and sandals [Plate 33]. Mrs. Walton disapproved . . .'[37]) It was all rather different from the proprieties of Sevenoaks—'interesting' was Janet's word for it; she seemed to have limitless energy, and was, at the same time, numbed by the newness of it all, endlessly open to new people and experienced, unaware of herself.[38]

Ashbee had always said that she should share in the life of the Guild, and so on Wednesday afternoons they would bicycle across London to Essex House; he throve on the pressures and artificiality of the West End, but liked to escape from them too, and his Wednesday evening suppers with the Guild were sacred. For Janet it was a new and absorbing world, and she spent hours in the workshops learning about the processes and getting to know the men. She was so open and straightforward that she was quickly accepted. To the apprentices and the Guildsmen of her own age she became an ideal figure, confidante, holiday companion, mother, sister, near and far, not challenging their relationship with her husband, but somehow making it less intense, less one-sided.

The Guild was very different now from the handful of men who had first set up shop in Essex House in 1891. There were about thirty workmen, if the apprentices were included, and all but five had joined since 1891. Among the cabinet-makers

34. Sid Cotton in the early 1900s.

35. (facing page top). The cabinet-makers of the Guild of Handicraft in about 1901. The bearded figure in the centre is Tom Jelliffe.

36. (facing page bottom). The metalworkers of the Guild of Handicraft in about 1901.

(Plate 35) the old guard consisted of W. J. Osborn, now manager of the Guild as a whole, who lived in an exalted atmosphere of his own, surrounded by price tags and visitors' books; Reinhart Read—Old Dick Read as he was known—a stern old radical who had gone to prison for his trade union beliefs in the 1870s; Tom Jelliffe, a sturdy, bearded sixty-year-old craftsman of uncompromising skill— 'There were no refinements of lap or mitre dovetailing which he did not know and use . . .'; Walter Curtis, 'very staid and upright', who was scarcely mentioned once in Ashbee's Journals; and the portly A. G. Rose who was because Ashbee was tickled by his pretentiousness: 'He knows that Thursday is my day for bringing cultured and intellectual visitors round the shops; and Carlyle's *French Revolution* lying negligently at the corner of his cabinetmaker's bench . . . creates an impression.'[39] The brightest new face in the woodshop was that of Sid Cotton (Plate 34), who had come to work at the Guild in 1896, when he was thirteen. He was a summer's day kind of boy, a 'hysterical cabinetmaker' Janet called him.[40] Happy, boisterous, brainless and endlessly forgivable, he could also be truculent and bad tempered, and indulge in biting sulks for days on end. Ashbee loved him through all this, and liked to think of times when Sid showed that he had learned something; floating together in a punt on the Thames, Sid dipping for lily-leaves and arrow-heads, and saying 'how fine they'd be for inlay'.[41] The geometry of the leaves, Ashbee thought, appealed to the budding soul of the cabinet-maker. Or was it just that Sid Cotton had the mother-wit to know what Ashbee expected him to say?

The cabinet-makers had the reputation of being stolid, inartistic and able to look after themselves; if there were crises and commotions in the Guild they usually came from the jewellers and silversmiths (Plate 36).[42] Part of the trouble was the repressive character of W. A. White, the foreman, sensitive in his craftsmanship, heavy-handed and tactless in his dealings with the men. He lacked the element of comradeship, Ashbee thought. His large flat feet and unbending boots seemed

to bespeak the man, and in the shops they called him 'the Whale' or 'the Old Man'.[43] Bill Hardiman, the other pioneer of Guild silverwork, was kindly, and an excellent modeller, but simple-minded and unstable: persecution mania was beginning to take hold of him.[44] Among the younger men, Arthur Cameron's rather coarse handling of bird, beast and flower forms seemed full of life and possibilities, and Ashbee said, 'if I could afford to break up my copy of the Stones of Venice I would tear out and frame a certain famous picture of "Noble and Ignoble Grotesque" and give it to Arthur'.[45] But Arthur was a conceited, sharp-tongued young man who had once been expelled from the Guild for using bad language; he gave the others nicknames, but resented his own, 'Chooka Chooka the music hall ape', though it was given in admiration for his rendering of the music hall song of that title.[46]

Cyril Kelsey (Plate II), silversmith, was not like the other Guild boys, 'this long lath of a lad with his hungry intellectual face the beaky aztec nose and the goggling eyes'.[47] He had had some education, and lived in a flat in Battersea with his neurotic mother, who earned a meagre living lecturing on hygiene for the LCC. He was a sad, scraggy demanding boy, clever but raw, and to find some protection in his bleak world of shabby gentility, he clothed himself in exaggerated intellectual attitudes; he paraded unrelated scraps of academic learning, and was nicknamed 'the Professor' by the Guild in revenge; he built up great edifices of dogmatic free thought from which he could shake his fist at God and the world, neither of whom were especially kind to Cyril Kelsey. And perhaps what he wanted all the time— what he needed—was a more robust affection than he got from his mother, who idolized her only son and troubled him with 'hygienic clothing and hysteria'.[48]

When they sat down to supper on Wednesday evenings it was mostly the apprentices and the younger Guildsmen who came. And it is they whose antics fill the pages of the Ashbee Journals, Cyril, and Sid, and Arthur, and Alf Pilkington, 'the Wild Man of Poplar', and Lewis Hughes, the gentle Welsh blacksmith nicknamed 'Jacko' from his great big eyes and crestfallen air of an organ-grinder's monkey.[49] This was the part of the Guild most dear to Ashbee. He recruited these boys not so much because he saw signs of fine craftsmanship in them as because they had some kind of human 'stuff' about them, a challenge to his educational idealism. Ned West was a meagre, surly boy, seared by an oppressive Puritan upbringing,

But I liked the boy's face and in the study of human nature if one is prepared to back one's own judgement there is a certain instantaneous look of the eyes which is worth everything else in the world ... I doubt very much whether I shall ever make a craftsman of Ned West ...[50]

Ashbee would interview these boys, asking them questions about anything but their skill or trade, about swimming or their family or what they read; and all the time he would be sketching, noting the colour of their eyes or the line of their lips.[51] And then the choice would be made, with a long gaze and a handshake, not because the boy would be good at the craft, but because the craft would be good for him. For Ashbee to educate, to shape character, was an unavoidable instinct.

At supper it was his habit to direct the conversation towards the topics of the day, keeping up the tone while the boys appreciated his generous slices of mutton.

And Janet would support him loyally until her sense of humour got the better of her and she would say something that turned the conversation into less educational channels. Afterwards they would gather round and sing songs, in the garden if it was summer, round the fire in winter; if White came he was put at the back because his voice was appalling. The boys were taught folk songs and traditional rounds and catches, and Janet could help a lot there. The popular music of the day had little place in their sing-songs; this was not vernacular song in the obvious sense, but a vernacular revived (like the Arts and Crafts as a whole) from a healthier-seeming and more Romantic past. To the Ashbees it seemed unlikely that real popular song, untainted by commercialism, could have survived the industrial age.[52] At other times, they would read plays, the Elizabethans of course. When the evening went well—and that did not mean that pitch or diction were perfect, but that the men and boys got into the spirit of it—then something important had happened, something close to what the Guild was about.[53]

Late in 1898 Cellini's *Treatises* appeared, a sober and practical volume, dedicated to the metalworkers of the Guild of Handicraft; its only real readers, Ashbee thought, would be found in Arts and Crafts workshops run 'with the enthusiasm of the artist rather than the itching fingers of the tradesman'.[54] He was busy with a report on the restoration of the church at Horndon-on-the-Hill in Essex, and busier still with preparations for the masque.[55] This curious extravaganza had started in a small way, at a meeting of the Art Workers' Guild on 'Masques and Pageants' in April 1897; but it grew, slowly at first, and then uncontrollably. The architects, painters, sculptors and craftsmen of the guild versified, argued, rehearsed and argued again; lavished disproportionate care on the stage and its furniture; drove their womenfolk to extraordinary lengths of patient needlework; and produced a gorgeous and ephemeral spectacle, *the* event of the Arts and Crafts Movement, a demonstration of its varied talents and of its blessed irrelevance. Somehow the moment was ripe. It was to be formal, like the old masques, design, pageantry, allegory, but not an antiquarian revival, for there was a symbolic and processional strain in the Arts and Crafts which found a welcome expression in the masque: it was as if their allegorical figures had stepped out of the picture frames, down from the sculpted friezes, and now enjoyed the extra freedom of verse, music and dance.[56] And, being the Arts and Crafts, it was didactic, an allegory of London and the artists' hope for their city, touching and specific. The title was to be *Beauty's Awakening: A Masque of Winter and of Spring*.

Ashbee was an enthusiastic masquer, if difficult to work with. In one scene a troop of grotesque capering demons with names like Bogus and Bumblebeadalus and Slumdum were denounced as the scourges of London. For this Ashbee wrote some boisterous doggerel in the manner of Thomas Hood, a favourite author; it was full of local colour, meaty rhymes and clumsy satirical swipes at the Establishment:

> Room for this picturesque waxworks of Daedalus
> Room for the London of old Bumblebeadalus!
> The London of vestries, of jobs and of lies,
> Of puffs and of posters, of signs in the skies,
> Of crawling busses and crowded trains
> Of river monopolies, unflushed drains, . . .[57]

That would not do. It upset the Faerie Queene mood of the rest of the libretto (today Ashbee's verses alone are readable); and it would also upset the Mayor and Corporation of the City of London, for the masque was to be performed at the Guildhall. Selwyn Image and J. D. Batten objected; Ashbee revised his verses, but not enough; Henry Wilson objected, and Christopher Whall tried to make peace.[58] From a corner of the Music Room at 74 Cheyne Walk, Janet watched them:

the comfortable Selwyn Image, like a glorified Pickwick ... the gentle Walter Crane, vaguely passing from group to group, the worst chairman of a meeting imaginable ... Louis Davis wandered round the room in his absent triangular way ... and Wilson, who looks like a seedy bank clerk, and is perhaps the greatest artist of the lot, sat and moped and cavilled ...[59]

In the end, the masque was performed on 27 June and the three following nights, and Ashbee's speeches were left out, for lack of time so they said. The front of the stage was covered with a massive Byzantinesque arcade by Wilson, rich in imperceptible symbolism. At the back lay Fayremonde, the Spirit of Beauty, sleeping. Little girls in ragged leafy dresses danced beautifully in the wind, echoing the passage of time. Enter the prim book illustrator Paul Woodroffe as Trueheart the Knight, clad in armour; enter Lionel Crane as the Dragon Aschemon, waddling in his cage of *papier-mâché*. They fight; the Dragon is slain. The (now wordless) Demons dance a caper, and then appears the gorgeous and solemn procession of the Fair Cities, threading its way through Wilson's forest of columns, the high point of the masque (Plate III). It is, though, always in danger of collapsing into giggles: Athens wears only a little *crêpe-de-chine* dress because 'the more Art, you know, the more Nood'; two Greek youths in her train (Guildsmen of Ashbee's) think everyone is looking at their bare knees; Florence (Agnes Ashbee) is in agony because Elsa has bound her hair up so tight; and Nuremberg (Walter Crane) has Cyril Kelsey *and* Sid Cotton in his train. By way of *dénouement*, Trueheart wakes Fayremonde with a kiss, and the distraught figure of London is given a place, triumphantly, among the Fair Cities, wearing an enormous copper crown. It has to be buttoned under her chin. The masque was quaint and disjointed, and no doubt its allegorical meaning was lost on the Mayor and Corporation, but it was undoubtedly beautiful to watch. Howard Walker, an American architect who was staying with Ashbee, thought that it was remarkable that so many talented men should be so under-employed.[60]

After the masque in June and July, the next excitement for the apprentices of the Guild of Handicraft was the river trip in August. There had been river trips since about 1891, but 1899 was memorable, a week of sunshine rowing down the wooded valley of the Wye, remote, green and spectacular (Plate 37).[61] The boys stripped off and turned a beautiful golden colour, there were songs and recitations round the camp fire with Lewis Hughes always asking for more. Janet revelled in the primitiveness of it all and devoted herself to drawing out the difficult characters. Sid Cotton, as it happens, was in a mood for three days, 'cross and snarly as a bear', but Cyril, the prickly egotist, was gentle and affectionate: 'It is now no rare thing to win a smile from him, and occasionally I even find his long cold fingers twisted into mine and (by the camp fire, be it understood) feel the roughness of his tangly hair against my face.'[62] The last camp was in the meadow below

37. The Guild river trip of 1899.

Tintern Abbey. Art and Nature, Wordsworth and the glories of English Gothic conspired, and Ashbee took the boys, in the Essex House Sports Club blazers, to admire the noble ruin (Plate 29), bringing home to them, no doubt, in the brilliant Monmouthshire sunshine, the lesson of Gothic craftsmanship, to be carried back to Mile End.

That autumn there was one of the big Arts and Crafts Exhibitions, perhaps the most impressive ever; the Arts and Crafts movement was at its height, still producing new developments, still satisfying the critics. The Guild exhibited two striking writing cabinets, with spots of colour showing through the open-work of their metal fittings (Plate 140), and a wealth of fine metalwork and jewellery.[63] There was an assurance in the bold curves of the tableware, an easy fertility in the variations on flower and insect forms for jewellery. It was partly that Ashbee in the midst of all his other activities, had discovered a facility for designing with wirework, and partly that there was a growing maturity among the metalworkers and jewellers themselves. Excitable they might be, but they were the Guildsmen whom Ashbee found he could coax towards designing. As for the art press they seemed to take the quality of the Guild's work for granted. The *Studio*, instead of commenting on their designs, printed a long disquisition on the unique collaboration among its metalworkers; while the *Artist* simply noticed the Guild's 'first-class craftsmanship' and commented 'we have ceased to expect anything else as possible from there'.[64]

The Guild put on another play in December, Beaumont and Fletcher's *The Knight of the Burning Pestle* and on this occasion William Poel helped to train the actors.[65] It was an obvious choice, this tale of Cockney apprentices larking about as Knight

91

(Arthur Cameron), Squire (Alf Pilkington) and Dwarf (Sid Cotton) in the manner of Don Quixote; the train-bands at Mile End recalled the Boer War volunteers; and the sturdy burlesque called for no particular refinements of acting; W. A. White was magnificent as the grocer constantly interrupting from the audience, and, in the lunatic excursion to Moldavia in Act IV, Cyril Kelsey as the gorgeous Princess Pompiona, 'his girlish face under the green veil and black tresses' was, unbelievably, 'the prettiest thing in the play'.[66] The Guild's rickety performance was, no doubt, a long way from the original: a sophisticated upper-class parody of the *passé* romanticism of the shopkeeper class, performed before a select audience. But then Ashbee had a very simplified view of Elizabethan drama as 'popular' and unprofessional, and he believed that they were performing the play 'much as it might have been rendered in the time of James I by any group of half-fledged 'prentice lads, who . . . formed such a scratch company as might have acted at Grocer's Hall, or elsewhere, on a festival night'.[67] It was common in other vernacular revivals of that time for the relatively 'polite' works of the sixteenth and seventeenth centuries to be mistaken for the humblest of their time.

After Christmas the Ashbees went to stay with friends of Janet's just outside Paris. Listening to Wagner at the opera, Ashbee sensed the passing of one of his youthful heroes: 'my whole conception of the province or *purpose* of Art has so completely changed. English Dec. Art, the discovery of old music, the elizabethan drama and the greek play have done it. The realism of Wagner makes my flesh creep.'[68] They were, one imagines, an amusing couple to entertain, Ashbee always ready with an opinion on the topics of the day, Janet tempering his dogmatism. He was in any case mellowing; his socialism in particular, was less tangible now; artists and politicians, he would say, had drifted apart since the heady days of the 1880s and he thought John Burns and Sidney and Beatrice Webb were as materialist and mechanical in their thought as anyone.[69] They dined a good deal along Cheyne Walk; with Leonard Courtney, distinguished Liberal MP, now in the political wilderness because of his opposition to the South African War; with Wickham Flower, no longer in the Swan House which Shaw had built for him, his flat crowded with art treasures; with some South Africans in Rossetti's old house where they met Aubrey Beardsley's model, 'such a mass of all the decadent affectations that I feared every minute she would drop like a broken necklace into her soup plate'.[70]

If the sophistication of Chelsea sometimes seemed a little tainted, there were friends of Janet's like Hugh Spottiswoode of Eyre and Spottiswoode, the Queen's printers, and his beautiful wife, Sylvia.[71] Hugh was a businessman of the right (Ashbee would have added, rare) sort, sensitive, humorous, idealistic, and Ashbee enjoyed his company over cigars after dinner, or in flannels at his idyllic Cornish seaside house, Porthgwidden, when they could argue about 'human values' in business. Then, among new friends, Laurence Housman was to count for much (Plate 38). The Ashbees got to know him in about 1900 when he was known as a slightly precious Romantic writer and a brilliantly decorative illustrator of books, one of those the publisher John Lane called his nest of singing birds; what is more he was on the way to becoming a playwright, a champion of feminism, and a rebellious and iconoclastic social critic. He was gossipy and self-possessed, greeting with equally humorous satisfaction the success and failure of his work; though a

38. Laurence Housman. A drawing by William Rothenstein, 1898.

homosexual, he tended to treat Ashbee, the busy idealist, with comic reserve, finding Janet's less university and up-to-the-minute intelligence immediately attractive. He and Janet soon became regular correspondents and the letter-writing went on for fifty years.

Another new friend was the beautiful and cat-like Gwendolen Bishop whom Janet met at a gathering of one of those societies devoted to rational, healthy and artistic dress.[72] Gwendolen wore the loose, flowing clothes of reform with a natural, sleepy grace, not as a gesture of principle. She gave Janet courage. They went often to the swimming bath together, and though they only talked about clothes, more seemed to be said. Gwendolen was supremely 'interesting'; she was a talented amateur actress; she lived in a flat surrounded by cats, the walls stencilled with blue lotuses. And, in an unlikely sort of way, she had a husband. 'Ground between office millstones' at Marion's, a photographic company, Gerald Bishop (Plate 57) was sober, idealistic, an advocate of Ebenezer Howard's idea of a Garden City, planted out in the country beyond London.[73] Before Letchworth was started, no one could tell that this was anything more than the vision of a crank. When the Ashbees came to dinner, Gwendolen wore a spare white frock and sandals, her feet 'long and slim like the feet of a mediaeval French saint'; Gerald sat quietly at the end of the narrow black table in a rather unconvincing brown velvet coat.[74] Neither the food nor the conversation were memorable, but the Bishops seemed to stand for something; or for several things.

The Guild was doing well; they had opened a shop in the spring of 1899, Number 16A Brook Street, just off Bond Street, and were making good profits.[75] Up till then they had relied rather on commissioned work; anything made for stock could only be sold at exhibitions, or to such visitors as came to Essex House, but now they could reach a larger public, and the balance of their work would change accordingly; the silversmiths and jewellers, in particular, would have to keep the shop supplied. 'Essex House is roaring along', Ashbee wrote to Janet in March 1900, enclosing a blurred snapshot of various apprentices fooling in the yard: they had, for some reason best known to themselves, painted the words 'Joe Chamberlain' on the garden roller.[76] At Easter they were at Alfriston, in The Clergy House again, with Charley Downer, Alf, Sid, Jacko, Ned West and Cyril. Leonard Borwick, the pianist, was there too, wondering if he should take up the 'simple life'. They had a sing-song for his benefit, and Janet was proud to report that all the Guild's airs and catches were 'carolled forth' with good spirit.[77]

On 29 July 1900 Henry Spencer Ashbee died, at Fowlers Park, a large house at Hawkhurst in Kent, where he had been living for some years. So far as is known, he had not written or spoken to his son since the separation eight years or so before. The principal beneficiaries of his will were Arthur Petersen, his business partner, and Louisa Maud Ashbee, a cousin. He bequeathed his pictures to the English nation and his library to the British Museum. His son was only mentioned once in the will: each of his three daughters might claim forty shillings each week, provided that they were in indigent circumstances and 'not living with my son Charles Robert Ashbee'.[78] There is no entry in the Ashbee Journals, no letter, nothing at all, to show what if anything he felt. It was not until much later, when the Guild was in serious financial difficulties, that he was ready to admit how different things would have been if he had had some money of his own.[79] (Some months later, the Trustees of the British Museum invited him to choose books from those they were not interested in keeping; enjoying the irony of it, Ashbee made a selection for the library of the Guild.[80])

That summer, things were rather flat. There was a river trip, up the Thames from Oxford to Lechlade and back, mooring the boats at Kelmscott for a visit of piety to Morris's quiet, grey manor house. But it was the wettest expedition for years.[81] Ashbee made a journey to the Belgian coast, for he was one of a number of architects invited to develop the *plage* at Westende with colourful and expressive buildings, but nothing came of that.[82] And Alf Pilkington went to join the Army in South Africa. Ashbee had tried to persuade him not to, but in the end he accepted with grace because Alf was so much of a soldier, and 'after all one must pay a little penalty for one's Imperialism and one's admiration for Kipling'.[83] All excitement was reserved for the autumn, when long-standing plans at last matured, and Ashbee made a second visit to the United States. This time it was to be for three months, lecturing for the National Trust.

AMERICAN SHEAVES AND ENGLISH SEED CORN

The National Trust was set up in 1895 to acquire and hold land and buildings for the nation. Much of its character and appeal lay, and lies, in that double loyalty, the sense of an inseparable Englishness in old buildings and fine scenery. Both seemed to be threatened in 1895 by the urban and industrial changes of the last hundred years; and were to be preserved, as much as anything, for the benefit of the new urban population. Ashbee was, of course, in sympathy and became a member of the Trust's council in July 1896.[84] Its earliest acquisitions were not the great country houses for which it is famous now, but scattered areas of natural scenery and small buildings like The Clergy House at Alfriston. There were only 245 members in 1900, yielding a subscription income of £277. 3s. 6d.[85]

The immediate purpose of the tour was, no doubt, to raise funds, and a broadsheet had been prepared listing the sums needed.[86] There were Anglo-American connections to be exploited here, for one of the first American state organizations, the Trustees of Public Reservations in Massachusetts, had been inspired by English experience and advice in 1891, and four years later the National Trust itself based its constitution on that of the Massachusetts Society. But there was a good deal of sensitivity about asking for American money for English purposes, and Ashbee spent some time encouraging his audiences to look at his mission in a different light. He would stress the need for a sister organization in the United States:

Button up your pockets if you will against the ruined abbeys and falling palaces of England, let the records of her poets, her statesmen, her kings be neglected; allow that they are too large and too remote a subject for you to deal with; but at least mind what lies at your innermost heart at home. Regard the history that you have and the beauty that surrounds you as your own Trust at least.[87]

Or, more ambitiously, he would urge them to see it as a question, not of England or America, but of the common inheritance of the English-speaking peoples; the history of England was the history of the race.[88] This was not special pleading on Ashbee's part; he had spoken in this way on his last visit to America, and it was the essence of his particular, cultural version of the then so prevalent imperialism.

Janet went with him, and he also took his mother who had been seriously ill during the year; he thought a complete break might do her good. They crossed in the middle of October. Rolfe was the transatlantic organizer as before, and from Quebec they travelled down to Concord to meet him and pick up old threads. The first lecture was a success. Ashbee talked about England's architectural inheritance, its mediaeval abbeys, and Elizabethan country houses, and the Trust's work to safeguard it for the future. He played, no doubt, on the topical ambiguity of the word 'Trust', honoured in England, but compromised in the United States by the activities of the 'Robber Barons' of the business world. And, as always, he took a wide brief, preaching about what life might be like in these industrial times, the inspiration of great thinkers such as Thoreau and Emerson, the reality of the hustling Yankee, whose education had scarcely begun.[89] There seemed to be a lot more to discover on this tour. It was partly that the Arts and Crafts Movement in America had developed enormously in the intervening years, and Janet was particularly eager to explore. In Boston, which had drawn such a dry and dismissive response from her husband in 1896, she went to see the printer Daniel Berkeley Updike at his Merrymount Press, 'discoursed learnedly on uncials and Jensons and presswork and heavy inks . . .', and admired the type pages of Bertram Grosvenor Goodhue.[90] That evening, they dined with Charles Eliot Norton, who was the first president of the Society of Arts and Crafts in Boston; there was 'quite a little knot of typographists' there, Updike and Goodhue, and also Bruce Rogers of the Riverside Press.[91] For seven or eight years now, the sturdy black types and dense scrolling borders of Morris's Kelmscott Press had set the fashion in this quarter; but tastes were changing. Norton, perhaps aware that the Essex House Press continued much of this tradition, 'flung down the gauntlet by declaring that he disliked all Morris's typographical work, type, paper, drawing and style all *ugly* . . .'.[92] It was the austere, more purely typographical work of the Doves Press that was to set the standard in Boston from now on.

The tour progressed from Harvard to Philadelphia, where Ashbee found a congenial atmosphere, like that of the Art Workers' Guild, among the architects of
the T Square Club; then on to Bryn Mawr College and to Pittsburgh, 'the only
city I have visited in America that seems to be without any sort of public spirit
or any sense of citizenship'.[93] Janet meanwhile had gone to Washington, partly
to prepare the ground for Ashbee's visit there, partly to be on her own. It had
been a mistake to bring 'the Little Mother', a very great mistake. Somehow Janet
had not seen it before; in London a busy life kept them separate enough, but now
that they were thrown together it was obvious. He was as much married to his
mother as he was to her. He stood almost exactly between them in age, and his
love for his mother was very strong. Janet saw with alarm how his feelings for
her were changed by the presence of his mother. He was usually genial and cheerful
with her, if a little distant, but when they were all three together he became tense,
a shutter went down over his eyes, and he showed signs of being ill. The worst
of it was that he seemed unaware of these tensions himself, as if numbed by the
cross-currents of his affections. Janet could see that there was no relief for her
jealousy as long as the tour lasted, so it was a pleasure to busy herself about the
British Embassy with arrangements for a lecture there; other chances of escape
would come.[94]

They were together again in Chicago, the most memorable part of the tour.
Ashbee had not been so far west before, and the city came upon him with peculiar
and welcome force. He felt at home, intellectually, in Chicago's progressive architectural circles, round the disciples of Adler and Sullivan, where German Idealism
reigned; and it was as if all his hopes and fears for the new industrial democracy
were concentrated in the city's frantic streets; hopes in the idealism of Jane Addams
and the Hull House Settlement, modelled on Toynbee Hall and one of the thriving
centres of the Arts and Crafts Movement in Chicago; fears in the brash, unregulated
development of the business centre, the cavernous streets and the raucous presence
of the elevated railway. In the middle of all this he could see the special quality
of the new steel-framed buildings: 'Chicago is the only American city I have seen
where something absolutely distinctive in the aesthetic handling of material has
been evolved out of the industrial system.'[95] Not that he appreciated the contributions of individual architectural firms, such as Burnham and Root or Holabird and
Roche; typically, he attributed the distinctiveness of these buildings to the spirit
of the place, to 'the storm and stress of this terrible and wonderful city'.[96] This
was, he felt, the most American place, the city where the world's industrial problems
were at their most acute, and their most hopeful.

Characterizing a whole city can be a dangerous business, especially when you
have been there only a few days, as Ashbee found when he lectured to the Chicago
Architectural Club at the Art Institute. Chicago, he told them, was one of the
great 'bear cubs' of modern democracy, a city without any history and with only
a dawning appreciation of the arts. He went on to talk of a 'Nameless City' on
two rivers 'covered with the slime of factory refuse. Soft coal is burned and chimneys tall and unsightly belch forth a pall of filth.'[97] His audience thought he meant
Chicago, and when he had finished showing his National Trust lantern slides the
hall was almost empty. The Chairman remarked crisply that he had not expected
to be asked to preserve 'old ruins in England dear to British hearts', and the next
day the *Chicago Tribune* published the headline:

39. Cartoon of Ashbee in a Chicago newspaper entitled 'To Enlighten a Foreign Critic'. The Chicago citizen is saying 'Sir, we have the ruins all right, but we are tired of preserving them. They won't keep.'

CHICAGO'S ART UNDER THE LASH
C. R. Ashbee of London Tells Architectural Club
This City Has No Appreciation of Beautiful in History
HIS AUDIENCE AGHAST
Many of His Hearers Refuse to Countenance His Remarks by Remaining
and Leave the Hall
WANTS TO SAVE CASTLES[98]

He had, in fact, been talking about Pittsburgh, but his abrasiveness had turned away what should have been a favourable audience, for the Architectural Club was receptive to people of the Arts and Crafts persuasion.[99] The local press had a field day (Plate 39); but in the end the *Chicago Tribune* came round and wrote a leader supporting him.[100] In a later lecture he explained the misunderstanding, but gave no quarter—it was the Chicagoans who had thought he meant them. And then he ended with an extraordinary tribute: only once before, he said, had he felt as he did in Chicago, and that was long ago in Cambridge when he had leaned over the bridge at King's, wondering at the beauty and history of the place in the moonlight; he had felt then what great hope and opportunity there was for idealism in the modern industrial world; and he had felt it again in Chicago.[101] Ashbee was not one to pay empty compliments; he meant what he said.

The last day in Chicago was the most enjoyable, partly because it was spent in the more congenial atmosphere of the suburbs, and partly because Ashbee's guide was Frank Lloyd Wright; they had met, it seems, over the supper-table at Hull House.[102] Wright took him over his recently completed house for Joseph W. Husser in Buena Avenue, a house poised on the verge of the maturity of the 'Prairie Houses'. Ashbee found it 'one of the most beautiful and the most individual creations I have seen in America' and Wright 'far and away the ablest man in our line of work that I have come across in Chicago, perhaps in America'.[103] It was a perceptive judgement, for Wright was scarcely known outside Chicago, but it was compounded of all sorts of things: admiration for Wright's flamboyant personal style and debonair good looks, a common taste for Whitman and rhetoric,

97

the 'originality' of the houses themselves, which Ashbee thought proper to the place. Every city, he had told the Architectural Club, has its own personality. 'You notice the frigid social atmosphere of Boston, the apathy of St Louis . . .'[104] Who could express the storm and stress of Chicago? Ashbee had met Louis Sullivan 'in whom the Chicago spirit finds such curious and restless expression', but he guessed that Wright would show himself greater than his master.[105]

Wright's head was full of the ideas which appeared two months later in his lecture at Hull House on 'The Art and Craft of the Machine'; Ashbee was a convenient sounding board.

He threw down the glove to me in characteristic Chicagoan manner in the matter of Arts and Crafts and the creations of the machine. 'My God,' said he, 'is machinery and the art of the future will be the expression of the individual artist through the thousand powers of the machine, the machine, doing all that the individual workman cannot do, and the creative artist is the man that controls all this and understands it.[106]

Ashbee loved arguing about 'the Machine'; and Wright could be scathing in his criticism of English Arts and Crafts as sentimental; there was the making of a good argument here. But somehow it did not happen, perhaps because Ashbee's position was not quite what Wright supposed. He was no simple machine-hater; the machine was as important to him in his way as it was to Wright; he saw it as the starting-point for reconstruction; he saw its glories and its crimes almost as Wright did; and its future lay for him too in 'control'.[107] 'He was surprised to find', Ashbee wrote, 'how much I concurred with him, but I added the rider, that the individuality of the average had to be considered . . .'[108] There, in that pallid abstraction, 'the individuality of the average', there was something to argue about if they had cared to pursue it. For Ashbee never saw the machine as Wright did at Hull House, as a pervasive and pulsating force in which the modern architect could and should glory. What Ashbee cared about was the creative life of the average workman, something for which there seemed to be no room in Wright's technological opera, between the heroic figures of the Artist and the Machine.

At Hull House, Ashbee had been given an invitation to stay in another settlement in New York, so after two days in St Louis and a lecture at the British Embassy in Washington, they found themselves in the slums of the Bowery. Ashbee no doubt thought that to sip champagne with ambassadors one week and make friends with street urchins the next was the way to see America; but it was hard. The 'Little Mother' had to give up after a few days, and by the end of the week both Ashbee and Janet wanted a bath.[109] They were well into December now, and the tour was drawing to an end. After Christmas Janet escaped again, to see a friend in Syracuse, and then on to East Aurora, near Buffalo, where Elbert Hubbard had his Roycroft workshops. A showy charismatic ex-soap salesman who marketed a cheerful and pre-digested gospel of Culture and the Sayings of Great Men, Hubbard had been inspired to start printing by meeting William Morris in 1894; this led to bookbinding, metalwork and, just beginning in 1900, furniture-making. On a snowy day in late December, Janet found 'a home-like Carpenterian breath about the place', and sat down to supper at a table loaded with 'crackers and cookies and cranberry jelly, apples and a vessel containing that terrible thing known here as tea'.[110] Afterwards she gave a short talk about the National Trust and, feeling the sympathy of the place, went on to talk about the work of the Guild. In the morning she was shown round the stone-built workshops: 'Great bits of purple and brown and grey, put crudely together by the Roycrofters who keep their builders living near as the medieval folks did, and in the intervals of book-making lend a hand to spread mortar or to adjust a corner stone.'[111] The workers were mostly local and there was a cheerful, community atmosphere. This was before the days of Karl Kipp and Dard Hunter, and Janet could see that much of the Roycrofters' work was crude and ill-designed; the simple furniture was better than the books. But she could not help liking Hubbard. Behind the affectations and the name-dropping—he claimed to know Ashbee quite well until he found out who she was—she saw a natural, humorous man, laughing at himself and making her smile. She was something of a scalp-hunter as far as character was concerned, and Hubbard was a prize.[112]

They were to end the tour at Concord, to reckon up with Rolfe, and touch the magic Emersonian ground, ideal America. On the way they stopped at Boston, where Updike remarked that you had only to look at Roycroft books to see that they had been printed in the intervals of building walls, and Ashbee visited the silver workshops of the Gorham Manufacturing Company at Providence, Rhode Island (he had seen their New York showrooms in 1896). Frank Lloyd Wright's arguments were in his mind.

Two things emerge for me as convictions from this visit—first that the application of machinery has been carried to a pitch of excellence and precise skill in its use for the making of silverware that no firm in England can come anywhere near, and second that we are as equally far ahead of them in the production of really individual work . . . I have a sort of conviction—this place has brought it more home to me than any, that the whole fabric of mechanical production will be slowly and surely undermined—that indeed is what is going on in England at the present moment, even more than American Competition.[113]

That sense of undermining, of the Arts and Crafts building up new values in industry, was what he had meant, six years before in *A Few Chapters*, by the reconstruction of the workshop, its gradual transformation from within.

From the point of view of the National Trust, his tour had not been an unqualified success. He had raised more than £100, but he left the money in Washington for American purposes. He had modified the idea of setting up a society in America on the lines of the National Trust, as he realized how strong the local loyalties of American states and cities were; and he left a working committee in Washington to set up a council which would simply act as a federal body with representatives from existing historical and amenity societies throughout the country, a quite different model. News of the council's progress reached him occasionally in England during the next months, but it does not seem to have had a long history.[114] As for the unity of the English-speaking peoples, he believed in that as much as ever, but somehow it had not taken hold, and he wrote in irritation, in his *Report* to the National Trust, about American schools where everything before 1776 was treated as foreign history.[115]

During the crossing to England, he and Janet found opportunities to be alone together and they talked about England, and the countryside and the Guild; it was a dream they shared. The idea of moving the Guild out of London had been

99

lying to one side of their lives for some years; it had not gone away, but had gathered strength. They would have to do something. They reached London on 22 January, the day on which Queen Victoria died. It was raw, miserable and foggy. Ashbee felt how complicated things were. There was a sense of loss, of loyalty to something old and intangible, the Queen and, beyond her, his country. And there were the bright, unchallengeable spots in his American tour, Concord, Wright, the Bowery, the pride of ordinary men in a society of levellers. There was a title for a book there, he thought, 'Democracy and the Feudal Idea'.[116] It was never written.

BACK TO THE LAND

All Ashbee's early work, the foundation of the Guild in Whitechapel, the move to Mile End, was urban in inspiration. It grew out of the Settlement movement and the concentration of philanthropy on East London; indeed, it could scarcely have happened anywhere else, and Ashbee loved the place; the intensity of his idealism lit up its gloomy, squalid streets. In one of his favourite lines from *The Knight of the Burning Pestle*, a Cockney apprentice says to his mother, 'is not all the world Mile-end, Mother', to which she replies, 'No, Michael, not al the world, boy, but I can assure thee Michael, Mile-end is a goodly matter . . .'[117] In the late 1890s that line came to have a melancholy ring for Ashbee. Perhaps it was the success of the Guild that was responsible. The sulphurous smoke that blackened the garden at Essex House, the jarring bustle of the Mile End Road, these things could be overlooked in the heat of the battle, indeed they seemed a necessary part of it. But now the Guild was established, fêted even, they were obvious and appalling. His idealism was not of a kind to stand still. He would crown success by giving his workmen the surroundings that their work deserved. The Guild would go out into the country.

There were several strands of thought in Ashbee's growing enthusiasm for the country. There was a Romantic view of the country as pure and natural, a little bit of Eden, everything that the city is not. This was, since he had lived in London almost all his life, a city-bred Romanticism of the sort that adds a solemn tone to green fields seen from trains; but it was important nevertheless; it enriched the idea of moving out into the country, making it seem like a passage from one way of life to another. And it had been with him for a long time; much of the critique of the modern industrial world which had shaped his ideas since Cambridge was grounded in the concept of Nature. When Emerson walked in the woods at Concord, he saw the sun setting behind the trees; but he also saw Nature, the grand, organizing principle of the universe. There lay, he wrote, 'the advantage which the country-life possesses, for a powerful mind, over the artificial and curtailed life of cities'.[118] Ruskin and Morris told the same story; and it is surprising, in a sense, that Ashbee had resisted the lure of Nature for so long.

Country themes also ran through the Romantic socialism which he had espoused in the 1880s, and Robert Blatchford's *Clarion* newspaper fostered cycling clubs and field clubs 'to bring the town dweller more frequently into contact with the beauty of nature; to help forward the ideal of the simpler life, plain living and high thinking'.[119] The supreme example, of course, was Edward Carpenter, who had started market gardening at Millthorpe in 1883. To do without the clutter of objects, servants and formalities that made up so-called civilized (and that meant city) life, to walk freely and naturally in sandals and homespun clothes, to concentrate on those things which make life worth living, health, affection, work, the things of the spirit; this was the 'simple life'. It had always appealed to Ashbee without ever quite making its mark on his appearance or habits of life; one of the attractions of going out into the country was that you could take up the 'simple life' in earnest.

Then there was a tougher strand of thinking about city life. Some social reformers in the 1880s and 1890s argued that urban problems such as ill-health and unemployment could be solved by repopulation of the countryside: the crowding of population into cities should be reversed. General Booth of the Salvation Army proposed this in his famous book *In Darkest England and the Way Out* (1890), and the Garden City idea so dear to Gerald Bishop was another example of this current of opinion. In his plans for the Guild in the country, Ashbee included the idea of smallholdings, so that the Guildsmen could produce most of their food, and work rather shorter hours.[120] He was quite speculatively grafting on to the Guild the ideas of Jesse Collings, MP, and the 'Back to the Land' movement, which aimed to establish independent peasant owners on smallholdings throughout the country, and so to recreate the 'yeomanry' that was once the 'backbone' of England.[121]

Such ideas, in Ashbee's case as in others', were given special force round 1900 by the Boer War. Here was a great nation held to ransom, apparently, by a handful of herdsmen and farmers; during the recruiting campaigns in the big cities an alarming number of men had to be turned away as unfit to fight, and the figures in the East End were among the worst; it seemed obvious that city life was sapping the health of the nation. In 1901 Seebohm Rowntree published *Poverty: A Study of Town Life*, which put the statistical side of the argument; the influential collection of essays *The Heart of the Empire*, published in the same year, put the social side.[122] Ashbee was always most aware of social issues when they were most topical, and it is no accident that his own *Endeavour towards the teaching of John Ruskin and William Morris*, which came out just before these two titles, included a chapter on 'The Centre at Essex House and the Possibility of Shifting it into the Country'.

There was, finally, the feeling that the craftsmanship of the Guild had a special sympathy with the countryside. Ashbee talked of the Guildsmen 'going home' to the land, as if they had somehow always belonged there.[123] It was a strange idea, which flew in the face of the facts, for the Guildsmen were almost all Cockneys, and the sophisticated trades they practised were entirely urban in their history and character. But it was in keeping with the Romanticism of the Arts and Crafts Movement, which found its spiritual home in the countryside. Spiritual, note; not actual. The Movement had its country workshops round 1900, but most of them were philanthropic, set up to provide local employment. The leading architects and designers, with their workshops, were to be found in London and other large cities, and on the whole they stayed there. Ernest Gimson and the Barnsley brothers, who settled deep in the south Cotswolds in 1892, were the exception at this stage, and theirs was a fairly unambitious move. Only the three architect-craftsmen were involved, and they waited to build up their workshops until they had settled into the country life. It was Ashbee, typically, who put the Romantic ideals of the Arts and Crafts Movement most daringly and literally to the test, who took one of

40. Members of the Guild river trip of 1901 their blazers embroidered with emblematic pinks. From left to right they are, standing: Maitland Radford, Fred Pontin, Gwendolen Bishop, Will Fenn the office boy, George Hart, Sid Cotton, Ashbee and Simeon Samuels; sitting: Charley Downer, Janet Ashbee, Lewis Hughes, Cyril Kelsey and George Colverd.

its largest and most rootedly London workshops out into the country to find its spiritual home.

The lease on Essex House was due to expire in September 1902, so the Guild had to find a new home soon.[124] On his return from America, Ashbee took up the idea of building new workshops at the western end of Cheyne Walk, at 115–16 Cheyne Walk and 3–4 Little Davis Place, the property he had bought about five years before; clearly he did not feel that the country move had to be immediate.[125] But the scheme fell through, and it may have been this failure that persuaded Ashbee to look outside London straightaway. He inspected a water-mill at Sundridge, just the other side of Sevenoaks from Godden Green, but it was not suitable; and he looked at a site at Letchworth in Hertfordshire.[126] It was one of the saddest twists of fate in his career that he did not settle there, for two years later it was chosen as the site of the first Garden City. A little town of roughcast houses, such as would have delighted Ashbee, with red tiled roofs and green painted windows, grew slowly there; its earliest inhabitants included many middle-class idealists who believed in Romantic socialism, the 'simple life', free thought and the Arts and Crafts; they would have made perfect clients for the Guild. But no one was to know that in 1901, and the search continued.

The summer passed according to the happy pattern of those years. Weekends were spent at The Court House, Long Crendon in Buckinghamshire, a timber-framed building of about 1500, also just acquired by the National Trust. (The Guild had abandoned Poynetts a year or so earlier, giving way before the tide of suburban development.) Ashbee, who was cavalier about dates, urged Frank Lloyd Wright to come and stay in this 'romantic little fourteenth century place built before iron was known and Chicago was still a swamp ...'.[127] In July he was fighting on behalf of the Watch Committee to save the buildings of Christ's Hospital. The school was moving out of London, and the site was to be cleared and sold to pay for new buildings at Horsham. Fragments of the fourteenth-century Greyfriars convent, buildings by Wren, archaeological remains, and an open space in a crowded and historic area were at risk. At the end of the month Ashbee was called with other conservationists to give evidence and spent 'Most of the day at the House of Commons fighting the Philistines—and Lord! there were a host of them'.[128] There was, of course, no protection for the buildings in law and the issue turned on the needs and responsibilities of the school governors. 'It makes one gnash one's teeth that one should always have to plead for English history and for what is noble and dignified in life, on side issues.'[129] The case was lost, as Ashbee feared it would be; Philip Norman described it as 'perhaps the heaviest blow which has been dealt to lovers of old London for many years'; and Ashbee had to content himself with a long and splenetic letter to *The Times*.[130]

The river expedition in August, down the Severn from Shrewsbury, was welcome as ever (Plate 40). The sun shone, Janet swam with Gwendolen Bishop, naked and ecstatic, Cyril was angelic, and they read *Huckleberry Finn* out loud. Ashbee felt as if he had been let out of prison, realizing 'what it means to be free from squalor and ugliness, to be for ten days in sun and fresh air, to see birds and beasts and flowers, running water and glowing colour, to hear silence . . .'.[131] It seemed that there was just a chance that they might get the Guild out into the country soon. Rob Martin Holland, whose family owned Overbury Court, by the edge of the Cotswolds, told Ashbee of a little town in north Gloucestershire that might meet their needs, Chipping Campden (Plate 41). They went to have a look on their way back to London.[132] There was an early eighteenth-century silk mill, long out of use, with three long floors of workshop space. There would be difficulties, of course, in finding houses for all the Guildsmen, but such problems must have seemed trivial as Ashbee walked along the High Street, its gentle curve lined with handsome stone houses, scarcely any later than the eighteenth century, most of them of the seventeenth. It was as if time had stood still and the Industrial Revolution itself had never happened. The beauty of the masonry, the colour of the stone, weathered to greys and browns from its original creams and fawns, darker

41. The High Street, Chipping Campden, in about 1900.

still on the roofs, the sense of a distant prosperity waiting to be revived, the tower of the fifteenth-century parish church looking down over the High Street, these things must have told Ashbee that this was to be the future home of the Guild. There is no sign that he hesitated for a moment.[133]

During the autumn he was busy designing a new house on Cheyne Walk, writing letters to *The Times* about labour problems and trade unionism, and working on his most ambitious printing project yet, *The Prayer Book of King Edward VII*, a 'sumptuous and magnificent' folio edition of *The Book of Common Prayer*, in memory of the king's accession.[134] At the end of November he and Janet were in Cambridge seeking expert advice on the theology of his illustrations from F. Crawford Burkitt, an Anglican scholar who took an interest in the Guild. Burkitt did his best, making St Augustine sit down when he met the seven English bishops, instead of standing up as Ashbee had him. But his scholarship could make little impression on the latitudinarian Ashbee, for whom the Church of England and its *Prayer Book* were the expression, not of particular beliefs, but of the evolving religious consciousness of the English people.[135]

Investigations into Chipping Campden had been going on meanwhile, and in mid-November Ashbee took the foremen of all the Guild workshops down there to see for themselves. There were, apparently, cottages to let in the town, so accommodation would not be a problem, and in the end sixteen houses were found to be standing empty.[136]

We went over the silk mill again, measured it up, peered through the green and bottle glass panes, studied the girth of the plum tree growing round the stonework, tipped the old mad woman with the ringlets, climbed up and down the empty 17th cent. houses, explored the town hall and the reading room, asked endless questions and finally in the words of the exceedingly stolid Bill Thornton, the foreman of the smithy, professed ourselves as 'very agreeably surprised'. There now, the country has charms after all, and it seems as if the Great Move were at last coming off.[137]

The Guild as a whole was then consulted. It was discussed on 6 December, and the debate turned—'gyrated like an autumn leaf' was Ashbee's phrase—not round the question of the move so much as round the question of wages, for the directors had suggested a possible reduction in wages in view of the lower cost of living in the country. In the end they adjourned the meeting with the decision that each Guildsman should make up his own mind and hand in his vote accordingly. They would meet again in a fortnight's time to hear the result of the ballot.[138] By then Ashbee was down at Waterside, Drayton St Leonard, a cottage in Oxfordshire which had had to replace the lovely Court House after disagreements with the National Trust. In the ballot, twenty-two Guildsmen were in favour of the move, eleven against, and one unrecorded. The cabinet-makers, 'the stolid Trade Union shop' as Ashbee saw them, and the blacksmiths were in favour of the move; the silversmiths and jewellers and the printers were divided. Lewis Hughes, the organ-grinder's monkey, took the train to Oxfordshire and walked eight miles through the snow to bring the news. 'I am glad', Ashbee wrote in the Journal on Christmas Day, 'to think that the men themselves have decided that on the whole it is better to leave Babylon and go home to the land.'[139]

The Guild play that year (they had missed one the year before, the Ashbees being

42. Ben Jonson's *The New Inn*, performed by the Guild of Handicraft and friends at 74 Cheyne Walk in January 1902. Ashbee, in the part of Lovel, is at the extreme left with Sir Glorious Tipto (Arthur Cameron) next to him; the bearded figure in the centre is W. A. White as Goodstock, and Gwendolen Bishop, playing the part of Lady Frances Frampul, is on the right.

away in America) was Ben Jonson's comedy *The New Inn* (Plate 42). December found them 'studying its every nook and corner, hammering away at the old Titan's meanings, and fitting all its infinite universal things onto modern life and character'.[140] Casting was easy, as its burlesque fitted the characters of the Guild like a glove, and Arthur Cameron presented Sir Glorious Tipto as if to the manner born; though they all had difficulty, little wonder, in getting their tongues round Jonson's marvellously close-packed figurative diction. For Ashbee the great attraction of the play lay in its philosophy, its climax in the alehouse symposia of Acts III and IV, where Jonson defined Love and Valour 'as no other poet, not even Shakespere has done it'.[141] (At least not so Platonically, Janet might have thought: 'Love is a spiritual coupling of two souls, / So much more excellent as it least relates / Unto the body.') Two performances were given in January at 74 Cheyne Walk, before hundreds of invited guests, the ante-room and gallery to the Music Room making a kind of inner stage. The play gave scope for music, and they sang rounds and catches to seventeenth-century tunes as they marched in procession round the room, giving the play that dignity of form which Ashbee missed so much in modern theatre. After the last performance, he made his usual Thursday morning tour of the workshops and felt a sense of satisfaction among the men, a sense of 'something well and happily done'.[142]

It was a fitting way to say goodbye to 74 Cheyne Walk. Ashbee was keeping his office on at the Magpie and Stump, but they would have to let the house, just as they were growing fond of it. One day early in March, when the details of the move were almost settled and they had found themselves a wonderful late fourteenth-century house in Chipping Campden, Janet was walking along the Embankment and saw Minnie the housemaid talking to a stranger at the copper door. Reaching the house she ushered in an old gentleman in a cocoa-coloured overcoat and a craped silk hat 'of that exactly cylindrical form affected by Parisians'.[143] Memories of a drawing by Nicholson flitted through her mind, and she realized whom she was talking to. It was Whistler, old and very ill, curled and corseted, come to see if he could rent the house. It was not just 74 Cheyne Walk they were saying goodbye to, it was Chelsea, and an epoch in their lives.

CHAPTER FIVE
THE COTSWOLDS
1902–1908

The Cotswolds are a country of differing moods. There are the wolds proper, bare and bracing hills netted over with dry-stone walls, good mainly for grazing; there is no intimacy under their vast skies. And then there are the stone-built towns and villages in the valleys, not cosy exactly, but close-packed and out of the wind. Chipping Campden is one such, lying in a fold near the northern edge of the wolds, and to Ashbee it seemed like Utopia. In the peaceful atmosphere of this secluded and dignified little town, he thought he could give a new romantic fulness to the achievement of the Guild, a reward, in a way, for years of struggle in East London. Visiting journalists rhapsodized over this Cotswold idyll, a workshop set down among orchards, a quaint, neglected town brought back to life. In the story of the Guild, the Campden years have a rich romantic bloom upon them.[1] And yet they were also years of pain and tension; there were times when the warm, grey-brown stone of Campden must have seemed cloying and remote, times when relief could only be found out on the naked wolds, walking in the wind.

The story of Campden was long, easy to read on the face of its buildings, and hard to end, in 1902, any way but sadly. The noble and intricate parish church of St James stood for the town's prosperity in the Middle Ages, when the Cotswolds were covered with sheep and their wool was brought to Campden to be sold and dispatched all over Europe. The substantial seventeenth-century houses in the High Street belonged to the time when Campden was a quiet country town, the wool trade having passed to Stroud, but prosperous enough, its special glories being the long row of many-gabled almshouses below the church, and the arcaded Market Hall (Plate 50) built by Sir Baptist Hicks with money earned, not from the land, but from banking and selling silk in London. In the eighteenth century silk weaving flourished in the town, supplying the ribbon trade at Coventry, and country classicism was added to the handsome miscellany of the High Street. Ashbee relished the beauty of all this for its own sake, a delicious and improbable dream after Mile End, and also as a text, a demonstration of the dignity and fruitfulness of everyday work in the pre-industrial era. It bore out so well all that he had learnt from Ruskin and Morris that he consistently mis-dated it, calling it 'mediaeval'.

Building continued in the nineteenth century, with even a note of modernity: the fifteenth-century Grammar School was rebuilt in the High Street, and the Oxford, Worcester and Wolverhampton Railway arrived in 1853. The station was built more than a mile outside the town, and Campden was left at peace, its contacts with the changing world of the nineteenth century tangential, occasional. The

43. Chipping Campden in about 1900: St James's church and the farm which stood in the grounds of the ruined Campden House.

people of Campden spoke with a rich Gloucestershire dialect, sprinkled with thees and thous; at Whitsun each year, on Dover's Hill above the town, they had traditionally held the famous Dover's Games, two days of wrestling, shin-kicking, gambling and dancing, a festivity started in the early seventeenth century in a polite mediaevalizing spirit. Unfortunately, they had degenerated by the 1840s into rioting and crime, spoilt by gangs of ruffians from Birmingham and the industrial towns, and they had to be stopped.[2] At the mid-century too the silk trade died away and farming became the principal source of livelihood in the town. English farming had never been as efficient and productive as it was in the late nineteenth century; but it was in competition with the vast and partly mechanized farmlands of America and there was, in an era of free trade, no protection against foreign imports. Efficient and productive as it may have been, English farming became less and less profitable.

As the agricultural depression of the late nineteenth century deepened, Campden became poorer and its population declined. Strangers were corrected if they called it a village, but, truth be told, it was no longer a town, and the mayor's robes hung in a cupboard at the grocer's, from which they could be borrowed for amateur theatricals.[3] The farm workers lived like strangers in the merchants' houses of more prosperous times; a handful of farmers held sway on the Rural District Council; and at the apex of this little hierarchy stood the Earl of Gainsborough, a small, gentle man, a descendent of Sir Baptist Hicks; though not provincial in his views, he was too much afraid of controversy for Ashbee's taste.[4] Taking visitors round Campden, Ashbee would note the houses standing empty or divided up, with doorways botched and casements hanging loose; he would talk of the large modern farms employing only a few men, or of the waste of sporting estates; men were being driven off the land and into the great cities.[5] It was a popular explanation, especially with 'Back to the Land' reformers; and it encouraged Ashbee to think that he was reversing the trend. But it was also simplistic, gilded with romanticism. Rural poverty was due, not so much to landed greed or a flight from the land, as to economic depression, to an industry that could not pay a living wage.

And then, in the 1880s and 1890s, the first tourists began to arrive in this quiet, conservative place. The cult of the Cotswolds had begun. At first the leaders of the cult were artists and architects: Morris and Rossetti in their little grey manor house at Kelmscott; the American illustrators who, in the mid-1880s, settled at Broadway a few miles from Campden, delighted with the quaintness of the place, Edwin Abbey, Frank Millet and, for a time, J. S. Sargent; and then Guy Dawber, whose lectures and drawings in the 1890s brought the simple dignity of Cotswold buildings to the attention of architects. In 1895, Mary Anderson, heroine of the London stage, settled in Broadway and gave the village its fashionable *cachet*; bankers, novelists, connoisseurs and aristocrats summered there from now on.[6] Campden, being more out of the way, took longer to discover. Charles Rennie Mackintosh was there in 1894, sketching; postcards were produced and the tourists began to come from Cheltenham and even Birmingham. In 1902 *Country Life* printed an article on the town by a Birmingham publisher in a sighing, old-world style, and Laurence Housman, hearing that the Ashbees fancied they had discovered the place, protested that it was one of his old haunts.[7] If, as Ashbee argued, the great cities were drawing life out of the countryside, they were also, in their way,

44. Part of the frontage of Woolstaplers' Hall, High Street, Chipping Campden. The entrance was introduced by Ashbee in 1909, replacing a window of, apparently, nineteenth-century date.

sending it back. Campden was on the verge of a twentieth-century revival. With the modern age of tourism and mobility it entered possibly the most prosperous stage of its history, certainly the most ironic; for the more people came to Campden in search of its peaceful charm, the more certainly that charm retreated before them. The arrival of the Guild of Handicraft marked the beginning of this stage.

Ashbee did not surrender himself immediately to the joys of country life. There was always business to attend to at the Magpie and Stump and, using the excellent railway service, he could leave Campden at half-past seven in the morning, change at Oxford, and be in Paddington by half-past ten. (Such toing and froing, though it did not make for the 'simple life', had a way of keeping his rosy ideal of country life fresh and young.) It was only in about 1904–5 that he began to concentrate more of his work in Campden and brought his secretary, Hilda Pook, down; and even then he could often be seen, dictating away to her busily, in the trap on the way to the station.[8] The fact was that his sense of the country was more a matter of intellectual appreciation than of feeling; and the longer he spent in Campden, the more he had to come to terms with some unwelcome facts about country life, its intellectual blankness and *longueurs*, a pace of life so slow that it sometimes seemed to have stopped.

Janet took to it all much more readily. In a tunic and sandals, her hair kept short to save trouble, she was in her element. She had, after all, grown up in the country at Godden Green. They had taken a house in the High Street of Campden, paid for by her father; much altered during the past hundred years or so, it nevertheless dated in part from the fourteenth century and was said to have been used by the wool merchants of the Campden staple (Plate 44). Ashbee dropped its trite surburban name, The Hollies or some such, in favour of the more original Woolstaplers'

Hall, and set about exploring the fabric. He revealed, behind false ceilings and partitions, a fine upper room of the fourteenth century which they called the library, and used for reading and writing, quiet talks and Guild sing-songs, all the things they loved best.[9] Their furniture was workaday and slightly nomadic, though not all cheap; with Morris hangings and stray bits of peasant pottery it gave a pleasant, unstudied atmosphere, that let the old house breathe and be itself. 'A room', Janet wrote in a trenchant attack on 'artistic' interiors in the *Dress Review* at about this time, 'is a place to work in, to rest in, or to entertain in, not a museum of things or a palette of colours.'[10] The garden at Woolstaplers' Hall was disappointingly small, but Janet chose a sunny spot in the churchyard, and could be found there in the early summer of 1902, entertaining her friends, reading Dostoyevsky and laughing with the Campden children who took to her smiling natural ways. Packing to go to London in early June she realized how quickly the weeks had passed: for the first time she felt that Campden was home.[11]

The workshops came down from London by stages. The old silk mill in Sheep Street was put in order and renamed Essex House (Plate 45); electric light was installed, the first in Campden, so that they could do a full day's work in winter (the Guild's working day started at seven and ended at five thirty), and a shed was built in the yard to house the timber they now had to stock, and the woodworking machinery (Plate 94).[12] On 2 May the young men of the Guild piled their bicycles into the train at Paddington and Ashbee, anxious that they above all should be properly introduced to their new home, came with them. They got out at Moreton-in-Marsh and rode across the hills, approaching Campden from the south. Almost sixty years later one of them could still recall the marvellous sight of the tower of the parish church standing up against a thundercloud, golden in the sunlight.[13] Last to arrive, in August, were the printers, who installed themselves on the ground floor of the mill, with the Guild offices; the jewellers, silversmiths and enamellers were on the floor above, and the cabinet-makers and woodcarvers at the top. Ashbee's office was in the house next door, swathed in the branches of the ancient plum tree, and the blacksmiths, in the nature of their trade, were housed separately in the yard.[14] The workshop windows looked out on to orchards and the surrounding hills; once the garden was laid out and in bloom, the workshop paradise would be complete.

Some of the men moved into empty houses in the town straightaway, while Charley Downer and Fred Brown, unable to make up their minds, hesitated in rooms at the Rose and Crown. To make things easier, the Guild had leased a row of six recently built cottages in Sheep Street as a temporary expedient. It was not altogether a success.[15] Herbert Osborn, for instance, was an ivory turner, brother of the manager, W. J. Osborn. He left a decent flat in Bethnal Green, with privacy and internal plumbing, to come to Campden, expecting fresh air and a pleasant garden. No. 6 Sheep Street had no garden, just a narrow yard at the back common to all six cottages, with six outside lavatories in the middle. The hearth was far too small to cook on, and there was hardly any choice in the shops. Mrs Osborn sat down and wept. Some of the other families in the row went back to London as soon as they could; the Osborns stayed, and got a better house after a year, but Mrs Osborn never took to Campden, hardly ever went out, and made no friends.[16] This was one of Ashbee's blind spots. The young and unmarried

Guildsmen were his chosen company; he gave time to the married Guildsmen too, but their wives scarcely entered into his reckonings. And it was for the young men that he set up a hostel at Braithwaite House in the High Street, with guest rooms for Guild visitors. They would practice, Ashbee said, flying rather high, 'that healthier and simpler hosting which so often appeals to the Englishman at the Guest Houses of American colleges'.[17]

The great move worked many changes in the Guild. Some of the older men could not bring themselves to leave London, and there were obvious gaps among the younger ones. Cyril, the hungry and pretentious Professor, had gone to join the Army in South Africa, as he had always threatened to do; good riddance, Ashbee told himself, and yet he half hoped Cyril would come back: 'there was something curiously lovable in this boy though he was as cold and unresponsive as a fish'.[18] Lewis Hughes quarrelled with the manager and went off to join a trade blacksmiths', leaving Ashbee mortified, the boy seemed to have so much soul; after that it was poverty, a Welsh coalmine, a milk round in London and trouble with the police; jarring echoes of 'Jacko's' life reaching Ashbee in Campden from time to time.[19] The less than promising Ned West came down to Campden and made two appearances in the High Street, the first as a seedy urbanite, 'a presbyterian cut about his black coat, an entirely superfluous cane in one hand and in the other Darwin's

45. The old silk mill, Sheep Street, Chipping Campden. Light and power were provided by a 12 horse-power oil engine housed in the small single-storey building on the left.

'Origin of Species' . . .', the second, 'white as wax . . . clad in a scarlet bathing suit . . .', leading the local boys out on a country run.[20] So there *was* good in the boy, but no time to find it out, for in June he collapsed with enlargement of the heart and was taken back to London. Of the colourful crowd who had wrung so much affection out of Ashbee and Janet, only Sid Cotton and Charley Downer remained.

There were many newcomers too, for by the end of 1902 the Guild was employing as many as seventy-one men.[21] Most of them are just a name; a few stand out because they drew Ashbee's admiration and interest, like Will Hart (Plate 46), a carver and gilder who was known as 'The Skipper' because he had been in the navy, and took charge of things with quiet, unflappable confidence. He was everything that Ashbee was not, steady, unimaginative, careful of detail, and Ashbee idolized him. But this could only be admiration from afar. All the aspirations that made Ashbee's life so strenuous and complicated and worthwhile, even comradeship, slipped off the sides of Will Hart's massive commonsense.[22] Will Hart's shopmate, a small, likeable Scotsman called Alec Miller (Plate 47), was also new. Only twenty-three, he had ten years of carving in a Glasgow workshop behind him, and had read and admired that literary production of Ashbee's London years, *A Few Chapters in Workshop Re-Construction and Citizenship*. He came to Campden unprepared for the glorious aptness of the Guild's new home, unable to read 'the history embodied in those stone-built houses, so rich, so substantial, and of such beautiful stone. I simply walked on and on, in an ecstasy of pleasure, with no thought but just wonder.'[23] Alec Miller was modest and reserved, and his special qualities only revealed themselves to Ashbee slowly, his delicate skill, his creative power, above all his reading and thinking and his love for beauty. Here at last was Ashbee's ideal craftsman, the fine flower of the practical culture of the workshop, the humanistic grafted, as he had never so convincingly seen it, on to the

46. (facing page left). Will Hart in about 1905.

47. (facing page right). Alec Miller in about 1907.

48. Fred Partridge. A drawing by Willie Strang, 1903.

industrial.[24] Soaked in nineteenth-century Romantic writers, self-taught with a steady, speculative cast of mind, all daylight and no dogma, Alec Miller could argue with Ashbee about Meredith and Plato, and understand the larger ideas behind the Guild. Ashbee was charmed, and at times chastened, by his tough and unpretentious clarity.

These new recruits altered the character of the Guild rather; they tended to be older and already skilled, like the silversmith Sidney Reeve, who had been an art master in Bewdley, Worcestershire; there was no more fishing of likely strays off the streets of East London.[25] Fred Partridge (Plate 48), the son of a dispensing chemist from Devonshire, was an accomplished jeweller, trained at Birmingham Municipal School of Art; in the summer of 1901 he attended a class in Barnstaple run by Jack Baily, a silversmith from the Guild, and in 1902 Partridge came to Campden.[26] With his shaggy hair, flannel shirt and sandals ('Jolly Art Dress', the men called it), he could have walked out of a novel. He was skilled (perhaps the best jeweller the Guild ever had), something of a lady's man, and fiercely, intellectually, at odds with the world. Janet exercised her finest discriminations on his charm which she thought Celtic at bottom, and on his physiognomy: that mouth, it was too curved and unstable to be quite safe; in a way he reminded her of Cyril.[27] Perhaps these new men were not so different, so mature, after all. The Guild's most fascinating human problem having gone to the war, Fred Partridge stepped into his shoes.

By September the Guild had brought about a hundred and fifty men, women and children, mostly Cockneys, into this sleepy, agricultural town, whose own population was then only fifteen hundred, most of whom had never travelled further than the nine miles to Evesham. The effect was predictable. 'Who bist thee?' shouted the local boys in the school, and the Cockney newcomers shouted back, mocking the rich country dialect; then the fighting started.[28] Their elders were no better, quickly forming two camps, 'Campden' and 'Guild'. It has to be said that the people of Campden had a real grievance, for the Earl of Gainsborough had evicted some of his local tenants in order to get a higher rent from the Cockney newcomers. Hence some of the houses standing so invitingly empty. (Ashbee knew nothing of this.[29]) Hence also, in retribution, the two prices in Campden shops, one if you were local, another if you were Guild. And then, the Ashbees must have been puzzling to the gentry: Mrs Ashbee wore such odd clothes, and refused to ride side-saddle.[30]

The church in Campden never got over the Sunday in June 1902 when the Guild honoured the Lord's Day with a bicycle ride to Warwick and were observed, as they swept back into Campden, healthy and happy, by the vicar's wife and daughter (Plate 49).[31] Quite soon, relations were such that the Ashbees would not worship in Campden, which was inconvenient, for living in the country made them want to go to church at the weekend. But soon they discovered the little church at Saintbury, on the other side of Dover's Hill, where the vicar, with the improbable name of Muriel Nason, administered a seemly ritual and was no part of the rural establishment. Ashbee was asked to read the lessons, and they would often stay to lunch afterwards, when Janet felt the difference between this household, penniless, chaotic and full of children, and her own.[32]

In October 1902 the Guild held an exhibition at the Woodbury Gallery in London. Now that they were nearly a hundred miles from most of their clients, it was more than ever important to keep in the public eye. Some of the Guild's finest work was put on show in the gallery in New Bond Street, accompanied by a pamphlet with illustrations of Campden sleeping in the summer sun (Plate 50).[33] 'We begin to think,' it declared,

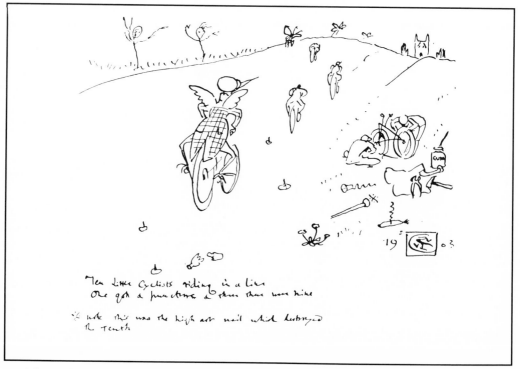

49. The craftsmen of the Guild of Handicraft bicycle into Chipping Campden and the church holds up its hands in horror. A cartoon by Walter Crane of 1903. (From C. R. Ashbee, *Caricature* (1928), plate 82.)

50. Four views of Chipping Campden, drawn by E. H. New and first published in C. R. Ashbee, *A Description of the Work of the Guild of Handicraft* (1902): (a) the parish church and almshouses; (b) Grevel House; (c) the High Street and Market Hall; (d) the High Street looking towards Middle Row.

it is not necessary to look any longer to the great towns, least of all to London, as centres of life, inspiration, or education; and that a little Cotswold village will probably be found to possess many things that make for the building up of character and that good craftsmanship which is its expression. We at least intend to try, and we look into the future with hope and confidence.[34]

For someone who despised advertising, Ashbee was a remarkable publicist. The poverty of the Guild's East End home had lent it a kind of glamour in the 1890s; now he offered the public the mellow and more seductive image of the happy craftsman in the Cotswolds. This was not deliberate image-making. For Ashbee, Campden really was Utopia, and he gave the town a title, taken from the seventeenth-century Utopian writer Tommaso Campanella, which he had reserved up till now for the sacred Cambridge of his youth; he called it, with sublime disregard for the English weather, his 'City of the Sun'.

COCKNEYS IN ARCADIA

It was always the intellectual side of things that interested Ashbee. In November he had a good after-dinner argument with Hugh Spottiswoode about machinery. 'Give me your work of handicraft', said the King's Printer, 'and I will reproduce it by machinery a thousand times and at a fraction of the cost. Is it any the less beautiful?' 'Maybe not,' said Ashbee, 'but ultimately it is the pleasure of the producer that sets the standard.'[35] Arguing round this point, the kernel of the Guild, helped him to hammer out some general principles:

1 Machinery is necessary in modern production, so also is human Individuality.
2 The recognition of ethical principles in economics postulates a good and a bad in the production of machinery.
3 Machinery in so far as it destroys human Individuality is bad, in so far as it develops it is good.[36]

A fortnight later, Laurence Hodson wrote, wondering if Ashbee was the right person to design a church he was planning in the High Anglican spirit; the 'hopelessly uncatholic' character of the *Prayer Book* Ashbee was printing gave him pause. Ashbee wired, 'Send me your definition of Catholic and I will answer your letter', and letters then flew between Campden and Wolverhampton over Christmas. Hodson was vigorous and historical. 'Catholic' for him meant the rule of life of thirteenth-century Christendom, Christian civilization at its peak; Ashbee was prim and uncommitted; he meant by 'Catholic' what the dictionary meant, 'all-embracing'; the Church must come abreast of modern life, it must accept historical and scientific criticism, and the secular idealism of the times, if it was to give a lead. Hodson may not have found these demands for relevance intellectually convincing, but he seems to have felt their force, for Ashbee got the job.[37]

Christmas was good at Campden, with big fires and bracing talk, and time to pause. Gerald and Gwendolen Bishop came down; and Gordon Craig's production of *Bethlehem* in London was a talking point, for Laurence Housman wrote the play, Gwendolen Bishop played the Virgin Mary and the music was written by Joseph Moorat, who lived in Campden. They sang carols in black gowns with white hoods, shepherding a flock of red-bonneted children with coloured lanterns, a sight to see in Campden High Street, and the Guild performed *The New Inn* again, in the Town Hall. Tickets were sold to raise money, for Ashbee was planning to build a bathing lake—the boys and girls of Campden had no right to look so unhealthy he thought. Willie Strang, blunt-headed etcher and painter and a good friend, came down for that, and drew portraits of Ashbee, Janet and the new elect among the Guildsmen, Miller, Partridge and Will Hart.[38] And there was a young writer staying, a starveling young man with a shock of straight hair, whom Hodson had found to organize a memorable exhibition of fine and decorative art at Wolverhampton. He could tell stories of sea-faring and vagrant life in America which neither his years nor his friendship with W. B. Yeats would have led you to expect. His name was Masefield, and the Guild's performance of *The New Inn* was a revelation to him. 'The play was first rate,' he wrote to his sister, 'on a stage without any beastly tawdry scenery, and all the actors trying to speak verse poetically, not to gain applause by rolling their eyes and striking attitudes . . . it was the finest thing I'd ever seen on stage.'[39] Tucked in among these expansive literary and artistic people was May Hart, an enameller from Birmingham, 'formal, well trained', wrote Ashbee with slightly menacing approval.[40] She was unofficially engaged to Fred Partridge, the charmer; but how reliable was he? At the time of the great move, the Guild had started a bookbinding shop in the High Street, run by a young woman who had studied under Douglas Cockerell. Janet had already done much to dilute the male ethos of the Guild, but in the summer of 1902, they found themselves adjusting to the Amazon figure and long mannish strides of Annie (usually known as Statia) Power.[41] 'I say, isn't she FINE?' Partridge had said, after she first came to tea at Braithwaite House; he showed her how to make a ring, they went on walks together, and took up illuminated lettering.[42] 'And so', wrote Janet, who enjoyed the clear lines and strong colours of this romance, 'the little girl in Birmingham was forgotten and the two young people led a life of thoughtless and delicious intimacy.'[43] Things came to a head in the new year, and Ashbee, who thought he stood *in loco parentis*, was brisk and censorious. He told Partridge that if he wanted to remain faithful to May Hart he must give up Statia Power *and* leave the Guild; his job was at stake.[44] And Partridge did just that, writing a few days later: 'I think you are a peculiar man and I don't like you.'[45] Even Janet did not see how dictatorial her husband had been, and she reflected mildly that 'It does seem hard that he should lose a good berth, and we should lose one of our best jewellers because of the "way of a man with a maid". It's one thing to introduce female labour at the Guild and another to solve the problems that arise from this step.'[46]

After the dust of the Partridge affair had settled, Ashbee and Janet got ready to go to South Africa, a voyage they had been planning at least since peace was declared, in May of the previous year.[47] They sailed on 30 May, and two days later Campden held a grand Whit Monday fête: decorative floats processed through the town, representing local trades (Wixey, the grocer, got up as an Indian tea merchant), and the old and new industries of Campden—wool, silk and now the Guild of Handicraft; all Ashbee's hopes were there. Then came *The Bride's Ransom*, an open air melodrama with Guildsmen as sinister brigands and much letting off of blank cartridges, followed by a (surely unnecessary) burlesque of the same play, and a nigger entertainment, both organized by the Guild enamellers, Cameron

51. Four Guildsmen in Campden, left to right: John Cameron, metalworker; William Mark, enameller; Arthur Penny, chaser and silversmith; and Arthur Cameron, metalworker and enameller.

52. Arthur Cameron with his wife, his brother John, and his eldest son Arthur on his knee.

and Varley. The whole thing was a joint effort; it entertained some three thousand spectators in blazing sunshine and showed, besides, that the people of Campden had come to accept the Guildsmen, 'who', a local paper remarked, 'may by this time be looked upon as townspeople rather than strangers'.[48] The friction of the first few months of the Guild's arrival had almost disappeared; and the Guildsmen who felt so out of place at first were beginning to feel at home (Plate 51); under a photograph of Arthur Cameron and his family outside a trim little cottage, Janet wrote with affectionate irony, 'Picture of reformed Cockneys in Arcadia'. (Plate 52).[49]

The South African visit was a voyage of exploration as much as anything; Ashbee was fascinated by imperialism. It was probably suggested by Lionel Curtis, whose friendship with Ashbee reveals some of the subtler connections in turn-of-the-century reforming ideals. Curtis was a budding administrator, not a mandarin but a prophet whose burning zeal put his colleagues in mind of Isaiah. In the 1890s he had lived in a block of workmen's model dwellings in Stepney, and dressed as a tramp at night to beg for bread, trying, like Ashbee and others, to get beyond the unrealities of the Settlement movement; he shared his flat with Owen Fleming, chief architect to the LCC's Housing of the Working Classes branch, and Fleming had done some repair work on the old Clergy House at Alfriston; when it was acquired by the National Trust, Curtis seems to have been one of the earliest tenants.[50] In the late 1890s he was private secretary to Leonard Courtney and then to the chairman of the LCC, and in 1898 Ashbee restored a pair of urban cottages at the end of Cheyne Walk, in one of which J. M. W. Turner died, for Curtis and his artist friend Maxwell Balfour to live in.[51] Curtis enlisted as a bicycle messenger in the South African War, and joined Lord Milner's staff in the work of reconstruction when it had ended. He was one, perhaps the leader, of the group of former Oxford undergraduates (Balliol and New College) who came out to South Africa and were derisively known, from their youth and inexperience, as 'Milner's kindergarten'.[52] A subtle thread of idealism seemed to run from East London through Chelsea and Alfriston on the Sussex Downs to the Cape, and

Ashbee was following it out; following too a number of his Guildsmen whom patriotism or ill-health had taken to South Africa; Huey Baines, one of the first and certainly the most dearly loved of the Guild apprentices, was living now in Kimberley.[53]

It is not strange that Ashbee, though something of a socialist, should also have been an imperialist; or that he should have set Kipling's *Recessional* to music for the Guildsmen to sing. A commitment to social reform at home was often married, at the turn of the century, with imperialism in foreign affairs; Joseph Chamberlain, the Colonial Secretary, was the classic example, and his imperialism was partly inspired by Ashbee's teacher, Seeley in *The Expansion of England* (1883); the politics of one wing of the dominant Progressive Party in the LCC were of this kind. As usual in such matters, Ashbee's position was neither exclusively political nor easy to define. He was, so to speak, a cultural imperialist, accepting as a force for good the growing sense of national identities throughout Europe, wishing to keep the culture and traditions of his own race distinct, and then seeking to foster the varieties of British life across the world; that, in a muddled way, was the point of the union of English-speaking peoples about which he lectured in America. In all this he took for granted the military and economic exploitation which are the groundwork of imperialism; Africa, then the focus of European ambitions, he seemed to accept as a blank map, void of Africans.[54]

They had six weeks to spend, and progressed slowly along the coast. In Cape Town Ashbee admired Groote Schuur, the fantastically Cape Dutch house designed for Cecil Rhodes by Herbert Baker; he was shown round by Baker's partner, Francis Masey, who had been one of the founder members of the Watch Committee.[55] East London, six hundred miles up the coast, cosmopolitan, slightly American in flavour and yet English at heart, fitted his idea of imperialism: 'England surely is not, cannot any longer be looked on as a country . . . England has become a principle . . .'[56] In Durban he met the educationalist E. B. Sargant, whom he had not seen since Toynbee Hall; Sargant was planning a school of architecture and applied arts, and threw out the idea of a guild of handicraft linked to the school. Already the tour was bearing fruit.[57] But questions of race made Ashbee uneasy. Curtis had said that South Africa could not take just any kind of immigrants, the rejects and failures from the industrial system; if a Guild were set up, the work could only be done by skilled craftsmen; and Ashbee agreed that it seemed the only practical system in South Africa, though 'it gives one an uncomfortable doubt as to the issue . . .'; as for the Africans, he did not know what to think, was puzzled chiefly that he could not bring his socialist principles to bear; talking to Curtis and a crowd of ex-Toynbee Hall men in Pretoria, he noted 'how completely the English Socialist changes when brought into immediate touch with the native question. His universalism goes at once.'[58]

It was here, in the Transvaal, that Ashbee's interest was greatest, for Milner was concentrating his work on unification in this former Afrikaaner colony and in the flimsy, upstart town of Johannesburg whose mining wealth was so much the object of British imperialism. Curtis was the town clerk of Johannesburg until 1903, when he was moved to Pretoria, with responsibility for all towns and cities in the Transvaal. And Herbert Baker had been brought from the Cape to introduce 'a better and more permanent order of architecture'.[59] On a rocky plateau in Parktown, the mining magnates' suburb north of Johannesburg, Baker built himself a house; mingling the Mediterranean and the English countryside, sturdy walling and airy loggias, the Stonehouse looked out across the veldt to the distant Magaliesburg Mountains, veiled in blue. Though ostensibly Baker's own house, it was in effect the home of the kindergarten at this time; they were all bachelors, and Ashbee found its ambience irresistible, this group of young idealistic upper-class Englishmen living together, a house 'full of clean white boys' Kipling had called it.[60] And as for the architecture, Ashbee was entranced:

Baker's own house . . . springing like a jewel castle from out of the rock, its arcades and stoeps, its red cedar shingled roof, the open court, the white columns the pergola with the circular garden below and the wonderful veiled view into the sunset light is one of the most exquisite pieces of architecture I have seen.[61]

There was no puzzlement here; architectually at least, in Herbert Baker's hands, South Africa made sense.

Ashbee took orders for Guild work in South Africa, the furnishing of a new house for Curtis, and furniture for Rust en Vrede at the Cape, a house originally designed for Cecil Rhodes, but hardly started at his death; Baker was now completing it for the Witwatersrand mining magnate and Progressive politician, Abe Bailey, who saw himself as Rhodes's successor. Ashbee was to design bedroom furniture for the house, including rush-seated ladder-back chairs and a bronze bed with 'little lions in the manner of Alfred Stevens'.[62] On these commissions, and on his conversations with Curtis, Baker, Sargant and others, Ashbee based a scheme for 'the Establishment of Arts and Crafts in South Africa'.[63] First there was to be an exhibition of English Arts and Crafts work at Bevern's showrooms in Johannesburg; if that went well, workshops would be started, and Ashbee would send men to set up a South African branch of the Guild; finally there would be a school of architecture, its teaching modelled on that of the Central School of Arts and Crafts in London. The scheme was ambitious, but not impossible in the context of British reconstruction in South Africa. Baker had felt the lack of skilled craftsmen in his Johannesburg work, and Curtis would have voiced Milner's eagerness to welcome skilled British immigrants of the right kind. In the end, though, nothing came of it. Ashbee came back from the South African trip with a couple of commissions and his sense of imperialism enriched and slightly troubled.[64]

Back in Campden, things had gone on quietly. The water had been let into the new bathing lake, but the puddling had cracked in a very dry June, so that was going to cost more; Jack Baily had got married.[65] In Chelsea, Whistler had died at 74 Cheyne Walk, his decline brought on, so his friends said, by the noise of building work Ashbee was doing next door. He had never liked the house anyway, and described it as a 'successful example of the disastrous effect of art upon the middle classes'; a typical Whistler jibe that, carefully sharpened, and wide of the mark.[66] The rest of the summer seemed to be filled with gossip and visiting friends. Ashbee went to London in somewhat rustic dress, it being August, and saw Laurence Housman, who told Janet he could scarcely take his eyes off her husband's cuffs, 'there was a sort of 'il n'y a pas de quoi' air about them—like a "Swiss Roll" coming undone'.[67] Gwendolen Bishop came back from Italy, a little hardened, Janet thought; she was much taken up with a theatrical crowd now, who called themselves 'The Dancers' and professed Nietszchean irresponsibility.[68] Janet herself went to London to shop, and called on her friend, the beautiful, intellectual and untidy Helen Wrightson, whose life seemed increasingly and casually strewn with babies. Ashbee had just built a cottage for the Wrightsons in Buckinghamshire (Plate 129): 'and Helen loves her new cottage all but the chimney; and her friends and her lovers stand afar off and shoot out their lips and say Tush, so we would not have it, but in her heart [she] does not mind'.[69]

Campden itself could provide a peculiar kind of social life. For two summers, Sidney and Beatrice Webb had taken a house near Campden, working away on their massive history of local government, Beatrice experimenting the while on a dim, orderly, near-vegetarian diet, macaroni, cereal pudding—'grape nut is my favourite'—and so on; she wanted to make herself more efficient, and was curious to see how healthy she could keep on 'so cheap and easy a fare'.[70] Ashbee was delighted to find this opportunity for intellectual cut-and-thrust, unexpected in the country; there was nothing he liked more than arguing with LCC Progressives. One afternoon that September they were getting ready to go to tea with the Webbs (two of the Mitford girls, Lord Redesdale's daughters from nearby Batsford, would be there, and Joseph Chamberlain's daughter, Beatrice). To her surprise, Janet found herself swept into her own drawing-room by 'two wonderful ladies'. One was Lady Elcho, whose country house at Stanway nearby was one of the spiritual homes of 'The Souls', that clever and powerful coterie of refugees from the beefy brainlessness of British aristocratic life; the other was the famous actress, Mrs Patrick Campbell. Mrs Campbell bombarded Janet with bright and foolish questions. 'Tell me what it feels like to be as strong as that!' she said, and (pointing to the arcaded Market Hall), 'I suppose you've had a lot of monks and that here, haven't you?' She swept round the Guild workshops, and then accompanied them to tea at the Webbs's, where she scattered her charming inanities freely over the tea things and the piles of Blue Books. Sidney Webb, in Janet's well-chosen words, sat on the edge of his chair and tried to let himself down to the level of Mrs Campbell's conversation.[71]

By the autumn of 1903 the great *Prayer Book* was ready and it was published in October (Plates 193–5); that was none too soon, for there was a good deal of capital tied up in it. For a few days a special vellum copy was displayed in London, before it was presented to the King. The Guild's new showroom was used for this, Dering Yard, 67A New Bond Street, just round the corner from their shop. It had been opened earlier in the year because the shop was too small for exhibitions and for selling furniture.[72] In December another important publication appeared, the first part of *The Essex House Song Book*, the repertoire of Guild songs, sung after Wednesday suppers in Mile End, or round the camp fire on river trips, now edited in a substantial and lasting form by Janet (Plate 197).

It was a typical Ashbee production, racy, eclectic, a little self-conscious, practical—if the songs were not sung it lost its point—and traditional in a special sense; the history of English song quarried, not with scholarly detachment, but with an eager sense of its modern value, its idealism. It owed a good deal, both in the selection of songs and in its spirit, to the folk song revival of the time; and in the preface Janet acknowledged *English Country Songs* (1893) by Lucy E. Broadwood and J. A. Fuller Maitland as the source of twenty-nine songs, while *Songs and Ballads of the West* (1891–2) and *A Garland of Country Songs* (1895), both by Sabine Baring Gould and H. Fleetwood Sheppard, were acknowledged as the source of twenty-six more.[73] 'Folk song' was a fairly new term at this date, and it reflected the view of authors such as these, that such songs were not a quaint by-way of literature, but a surviving and essentially rural tradition of popular music; for them the only proper way to tap this tradition was to record both tune and text from performances by country singers; though they were not above 'improving' what they heard, making it more polite and literary, before they published it.

Fuller Maitland, Broadwood, Baring Gould and others belonged to the first phase of the folk song revival, publishing in the late 1880s and early 1890s; there was then a lull until about 1903, when Cecil Sharp, Percy Grainger and Vaughan Williams began to introduce more thorough and accurate standards of recording. Sharp, in particular, has come to be revered as the great archivist of English folk song in the twentieth century; though he too would edit out modern and urban elements from the songs he heard, in order to preserve his Romantic image of folk song as the expression of a primitive, rural culture. For the revival was not simply a matter of musical tastes; nor simply of musical patriotism, recovering English traditions after decades of dominance from Germany; it had hopes of finding a larger 'Englishness' in the rural past, and it had wider associations, unease with modern, urban life, a sense of primitive, redeeming vigour in the working man. 'The English labourer is now an important factor in politics,' wrote Baring Gould in 1895; 'that he has been a factor in English music has not been recognised as it ought . . .'; and the revival was, according to another enthusiast 'part of a great national revival, a going back from the town to the country, a reaction against all that is demoralising in city life'.[74]

Ashbee would have been drawn to the revival even if he had not learnt to dislike Wagner in the 1890s, it echoed so exactly his own Romantic, anti-modern socialism. If anything he was closer to its second phase. He thought Baring Gould 'an awful old bowdlerizer'; and the *Essex House Song Book* is a much tougher and less sentimental selection than Baring Gould's comparable *English Minstrelsie: a National Monument of English Song* (1895).[75] The Ashbees could have made good use of Sharp's more thorough researches, and it is a pity that their interest developed when it did; for it was in September 1903 that Sharp heard John England, the vicarage gardner at Hambridge in Somerset, singing *Seeds of Love* as he mowed the lawn, and took up his lifelong work of recording songs; and by that time parts of the *Essex House Song Book* were ready for the press. Later, in 1910, Sharp came down to lecture in Campden, and the Ashbees did some recording of their own, noting the songs sung by Old Shepherd Hedges in the Campden almshouses.[76]

The *Song Book*, however, was more than a collection of folk songs in the rural sense of the revival. Many of the entries were traditional popular songs preserved not in oral tradition but in literary and indeed urban sources, particularly the broadside ballads which were sold in the streets in the eighteenth and nineteenth centuries. Antiquarian interest in such things was strong in the mid-Victorian period: the Ballad Society was founded in 1868, and in her editing Janet seems to have drawn on the work of one of its leading members, the music publisher William Chappell.[77] Chappell's *Popular Music of the Olden Time* was published in 1855–9, and a second edition, heavily revised by H. E. Wooldridge, appeared in 1893 as *Old English Popular*

HONEST DOVER'S FANCY.

Words by John Masefield. 1904.
Air: "Greenwich Park." 1608.

Campden town
Is quiet after London riot;
Campden street
Is kindly to the feet;
Campden wold,
So bonny to behold,
Is merry with the blowing wind & glad with growing wheat.

Campden fields
Are covered up with buttercup,
And bluebells slight
That tremble with delight;
Cuckoos come
When blossom's on the plum
And blossom's on the apple trees in petals red and white.

Campden woods
Are ringing with the blackbirds singing
Thrill! thrill! thrill!
O merry orange bill!
Sweet! sweet! sweet!
Says the chaffinch in the wheat;
All the pretty birds that are do delicately trill!

Dover's Hill
Has bramble bushes full of thrushes;
Tall green trees
That set a heart at ease;
Soft green grass
Where little rabbits pass
To nibble yellow buttercups amid the honey bees.   V.—41

53. A page from *The
Essex House Song Book.*

Music. Janet seems to have used both editions, moving from one to the other in order to find the earliest date, the most traditional-sounding version.[78] And interestingly, Ashbee seems to have hoped that their own collection would have something of the romance of street literature, for he published it in parts, a few sheets at a time, 'much in the manner', he said, of James Catnach, the famous early nineteenth-century printer of broadsides and ballads, though Catnach's cheap and garish sheets were very different from the exquisite productions of the Essex House Press.[79]

In introducing the *Song Book* Ashbee said that it would include 'Sullivan and Chevalier, and what is best in modern music hall and melody'.[80] But in fact there were few popular songs of the day in the collection, and most of the modern songs which were included had been written by the Ashbees or their friends. Moorat and Janet wrote some of the music; Masefield celebrated Campden's quiet, out-of-town beauty in *Honest Dover's Fancy* (Plate 53), and Laurence Housman wrote a maypole song with a chorus:

There Broadway lies keeping her flocks under hill,
There's Willersey sleeping, and sleeps with a will;
But Campden, Chipping Campden, Broad Campden, I say,
Is waking to life on this first morn of May![81]

Ashbee himself had written several songs over the years on Guild themes: a lament for the destruction of the Old Palace, Bromley-by-Bow 'by the notorious School Board of that year', for instance; or *The Master Craftsman's Song*, written in memory of William Morris and dedicated to Sid Cotton.[82] His ideals for the Guild ran through it all, perhaps were most subtly reflected here, and so was his patriotism; it was meant, he said, to be 'English in the greater sense of the word'.[83] It never sold very well: the original edition of three hundred was reduced to two hundred, and some of that had to be remaindered. Perhaps it was the publishing in parts that put people off, perhaps it was just too special to the Guild, though Ashbee loved it all the more for that. It would need a public educated to his rather special way of enjoying music before the *Song Book* could reach a wide audience, educated not just to 'appreciation', but to singing together and learning from the past, a sense of music as both social and traditional.

The Guild went on working steadily, larger now than it had ever been. At the beginning of 1903 Ashbee had stood at the crowded private view of the Arts and Crafts Exhibition, noting philosophically how much excellent work people had sent in, and wondering what it all meant, in the larger development of civilization.[84] He would have done better to have seen it in the hard light of competition. For about three years Liberty's had been selling silver and jewellery under the name of 'Cymric' sufficiently like the Guild's work to challenge it in the market. Working out in the country, the Guild could ill afford to lose any sales, and in the face of this competition it seems to have been agreed that the jewellers and silversmiths should work on designs that would be sure to sell, cheap and trifling though they may be. It drove Janet wild with vexation. 'Here is Liberty', she wrote in the spring of 1903, 'putting £10,000 into the Cymric Silver Co., and we struggling to get our hundreds, and having to potboil with vile brooches etc. to make ends meet.'[85] Janet had, it seems, got her figures wrong, but by the end of 1903, when the annual report was prepared, it was clear that the Guild was not as buoyant as it had been. Sales were higher than in the year before, but so was expenditure; the new showroom at Dering Yard was presumably responsible for both rises. With the Guild stretched in this way and a net profit of only £410.0s.3½d., the directors were unable to advise the payment of a dividend, for the first time since registration.[86]

While the unwelcome details of these finances were being audited in Clifford's Inn in London, Janet was deep in conference with Gerald Bishop in his rooms in the Adelphi, devising *A May Day Interlude* to be performed at the Whit Monday festivities in Campden; the country move had such various consequences, hard economic facts, rich possibilities for the imagination. It was a piece of neo-pagan myth-making, celebrating seasonal rebirth, innocent, and compelling to its authors. Five hundred copies were printed at the Essex House Press and distributed throughout the town. 'Winter' and his drab attendants took their stand in the Market Hall; boys and girls dressed in white and carrying flowers and green branches entered as the 'Procession of Summer'. A wax doll, 'the Spirit of Earth, the symbol of the sap of things that rises each year in man and beast and plant . . .' hung from

54. Billy Payne as Jack-in-the-Green.

the May Garland.[87] Billy Payne as 'Jack-in-the-Green', his costume stitched all over with ivy (Plate 54), welcomed 'Summer' with the refrain 'High, low! High, low! All the earth is gaily!' and then the children danced round the Maypole 'as wildly and unrestrainedly as possible'.[88] After that, the people of Campden went on with their usual Whit Monday procession, followed by the fête in the afternoon, with teas, coconut shies and other rituals unknown to the author of *The Golden Bough*.[89]

The summer seemed to be full of tensions. Ashbee was amused and annoyed when Archie Ramage, the young blue-eyed socialist compositor who had started the Campden Labour Union, had his honesty questioned at a public meeting by Lord Harrowby, a local peer; Ramage was a favourite of his, a thinker like his fellow Scot Alec Miller, and an asset to the Guild.[90] Janet crossed swords with Lady Gainsborough over Campden schoolgirls not being taught to swim: 'One has only to look at the anaemic and sickly women (I could cite a score) and girls here to grasp how their physical development has been neglected.'[91] Ashbee was nursing a scheme to print the Bible, but the finances would not come right; Essex House books cannot have been selling well, for the Press was put on short time in about July.[92] In August he went off to France with his favourite young Guildsmen, Alec Miller, Will Hart, and George Chettle, a new architectural pupil, 'a long thin rather charming brown-eyed creature with lots of stuff in him'.[93] That at least was delightful; they read, sat in the sun, sketched the cathedrals and argued about the philosophy of religion; and gradually (the serious purpose of the holiday) Ashbee's moustache, shaved off at Christmas so that he could play the part of Sir Peter Teazle in *The School for Scandal*, recovered its former luxuriance, his imperial its tentative tufts.[94] Janet meanwhile was enjoying a bachelor existence in rented rooms in Oxford, attending occasional lectures on biblical studies and entertaining her friends.[95] She was left even more to her own devices in these years, with Ashbee so much away, for it was that kind of marriage—large freedoms and companionship. They were together again at the end of the month, staying with the Hodsons in the wet Welsh mountains, working out the difficult *Bible* finances; Ashbee wrote to the philosophical Alec Miller of his admiration for Hodson's mind: 'quite unmetaphysical . . . but as for aesthetic criticism it goes as a bee to its cell, plumb in sunlight'.[96]

One of Ashbee's Campden schemes, however, was progressing. Though the closure of the School of Handicraft in 1895 had put an end to most of his educational work, he had set up the rather grandly named Trustees of the Gallery and Library of the Guild and School of Handicraft in 1901, chiefly to take responsibility at Essex House for the loan exhibits he organized from the South Kensington Museum.[97] Once the Guild was settled in Campden, these exhibits were displayed in the Grammar School; classes were held in carpentry, life-drawing and suchlike, and lectures were given, including Willie Strang on Holbein, Granville Barker on producing Shakespeare, and Ashbee on 'Old Time Campden: Its Life and Sports'. The structure of State-aided education in Britain meanwhile was transformed by the Education Act of 1902, which transferred responsibility from school boards to the county councils under the Board of Education, and made the first substantial provision for secondary and higher education. For Ashbee this meant that the work of the School of Handicraft, abandoned for lack of subsidy, could be revived; there were grants to be had from the Board of Education and Gloucestershire County Council, and 'higher education' under the Act seemed to offer more scope to Ashbee's kind of teaching than the terms of the Technical Instruction Act, to which he had had to conform in the 1890s.[98] Quite soon his ambitions outgrew rooms in the Grammar School; facing the corner of Sheep Street and the High Street stood Elm Tree House, three storeys of seventeenth-century ashlar with a large disused malt house at the back; in the spring of 1904, Ashbee started to repair and adapt it as a school. Two libraries and a caretaker were to occupy Elm Tree House, classrooms for cookery, woodwork, metalwork and enamelling went on the ground floor of the malt house, and over them a long room was turned into a gallery and lecture room, its beams painted with improving texts from Emerson, Blake and others, just like the workshop in Commercial Street all those years ago (Plate 55); one of the inscriptions (author happily unknown), exhorted the audience to 'give to harrows, trays and pans/Grace and glimmer of romance'.[99]

It was sometimes said in Campden that the School of Arts and Crafts was exclusive, the preserve of the Guild; a charge that Ashbee was quick to refute. In 1905–6, he reported, there were 22 Guildsmen out of a total of 330 students.[100] He meant the School to provide higher education under the 1902 Act for the town and district as a whole; he meant it particularly for the young men who spent their evenings loitering on the corner of Sheep Street, that 'evil corner' as he called it.[101] Like many of the classes of the Home Arts and Industries Association, it was an attempt to bring some leavening, some 'higher life', into the occupations of the countryside. In the new School buildings he planned to teach much more than craft classes: vocal and instrumental music were taught by Mr J. B. Matthews, organizer of the Cheltenham Music Festival, and needlework, cookery and hygiene by, apparently, the ladies of the Gloucester School of Domestic Education. There was land at the back of Elm Tree House where gardening classes could be held, young men and boys growing beans, parsnips, onions, peas each on his own little plot. And the weekly lectures would complement these homely skills with cultivation of the mind; in 1904–5, Janet gave a series of lectures on 'The Growth and Influence of Music', during which George Chettle, Ashbee and Janet herself sang songs, and her father played a violin sonata by Attilio Ariosti; at other times Walter Crane spoke on 'Design in relation to the Crafts', Thomas Adams, Secretary of the Garden City Association, on 'The Garden City Movement, or the City of the Future' and Edward Carpenter on 'Small Holdings and Life on the Land'.[102] It was typical of Ashbee that he could bring distinguished lecturers down to Campden to talk to a mixed and country audience, and all without a hint of condescension; for he simply assumed that others shared his enthusiasms.

In September 1904 Ashbee and Janet went to Hamburg for a cousin's wedding, and on the way stopped for supper in Chelsea with the De Morgans. The great potter was just closing down his works, and did not expect to reopen them, a fact which afforded him odd but entirely characteristic amusement. 'My potting days are over', he said ruefully, waving his head over a soup plate and wondering whether Ashbee might take on any of his men; but, said Ashbee, 'we have as much sail as we can carry, and times are bad'.[103] The wedding was awful, a bourgeois saturnalia, relentless and uninspired. Ashbee thought of his dead grandfather, and of his simplicity of life.[104] Back home in Campden, he prepared astutely for the formal opening of the School buildings by asking Lord Gainsborough, originally an opponent of the scheme, to take the chair, and Lord Redesdale, much the most cultured of the local aristocrats, to give an address.[105] On 20 October, the platform was crowded with local grandees and educational administrators. Mingling with

55. The lecture room and gallery at the Campden School of Arts and Crafts.

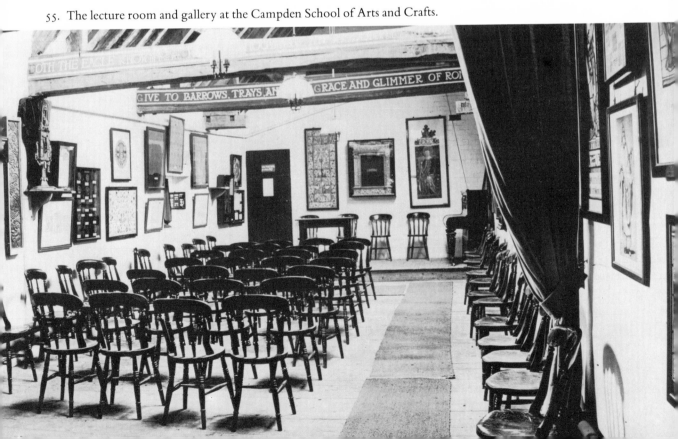

and managing these notables, Ashbee 'felt like a sort of aesthetic punch and judy man', aware that it was he and not they who really counted.[106] He was actually entering on an institutional alliance much like those which punctuated his earlier career, but in his enthusiasm he could afford to overlook their outcome.

A prospectus for the Essex House Press *Bible* was issued in November; it was to have about sixty 'bold decorative woodblocks' by Willie Strang and subscribers were invited for an edition of three hundred copies.[107] But Christmas was bleak. Ashbee was in Droitwich, a parvenu little spa which can have held few charms for him, hoping to cure the lumbago which afflicted him.[108] Meanwhile at the Guild's shop and gallery in the West End, its pendants and brooches, muffin dishes and decanters should have been selling well with the approach of Christmas; but in fact sales were down below the usual level; it seemed to be the same all along Bond Street. The Guild's yearly profit had been low in 1903; in 1904 it was even lower, £94.10s.4d. With so much of the Christmas stock unsold, the workshops in Campden were put on short time in the new year, and some of the men were laid off.[109] The state of trade had given rise to rumours during the year, and, to keep the shops better informed, it was agreed that a quarterly bulletin on the state of trade should be posted up. Morale was low, and the directors heard, after the annual general meeting in February 1905, of a 'want of confidence between the men and the Board'.[110]

TENSIONS

Ashbee had plenty to think about in Droitwich. It was almost three years since the Guild had arrived in Campden, buoyed up by several years of healthy trading and good profits. Gradually, the profits and the buoyancy had disappeared. But while the economics of the Guild faltered, the rest of its life, what Ashbee called the 'human' side of the Campden experiment, flourished. Campden and the Guild had come to enjoy each other's company; indeed, the townspeople so much enjoyed the Craftsman Club which the Guild had set up in the High Street, with its billiard room, its bar and its large, new gramophone—can the Ashbees have approved of such a new-fangled musical machine?—that they all but took it over early in 1905.[111] Ashbee's literary friends relished the town in their different way. Housman, Masefield, Ashbee himself, Janet, Gerald Bishop were all writing songs and poems about Campden, and planning to collect them all together and attach them by a common title to the memory of *Giles Cockbill*, a mid-Victorian farm labourer and a famous local character; Ashbee had a photograph of him as an old man in corduroys and a stove pipe hat.[112] Sitting waist-deep in a brine bath in Droitwich, Ashbee must have pondered on the perversity of things. Without the profits that now seemed to be slipping from their grasp, none of the rest of their romantic Campden existence was possible.

Yet there were times when Campden seemed, quite simply, full of resonance to his literary and historical imagination. In January of that year, 1905, they played *As You Like It*; and just as Beaumont and Fletcher had written about Mile End, so, Ashbee thought, Shakespeare had almost written about Campden:

56. Charley Downer as Touchstone.

'As you Like it' is essentially a local play. The Forest of Arden is not far away, Corin and Silvius were as likely as not Cotswold shepherds, Audrey must have come from the Wolds; and Shakespeare might have seen, probably did see, Charles the Wrestler challenge the lads of Campden, Weston, Aston and Willersey at the games on Dover's Hill.[113]

Some of the casting was literal, as Ashbee liked it; Silvius was played by Ron Haydon, a real shepherd carrying the crook with which he had been handling ewes in the market place that day, and Audrey by Kate Haines, 'a right-down country wench . . . a foil to Charley Downer's delicious Cockney Touchstone' (Plate 56).[114] To Campden audiences these homely ambiguities between on and off stage were probably just as much fun as Shakespeare's game of mistaken identities. Indeed twentieth-century Campden and the Forest of Arden became so inextricably confused that Hilda Pook, Ashbee's capable and personable secretary, was known as Phoebe from then on, and a few years later she married none other than Silvius, her 'young swain'.

The older shepherd, Corin, was played by Fred Griggs, one of several artists who settled in Campden more or less in the wake of the Guild. George Loosely was the first, a Chelsea artist who used to rent the skittle alley studio behind the Magpie and Stump; he came soon after the Guild arrived and Ashbee converted a barn into a studio for him; from which, Janet credibly relates, he attempted to woo the Amazon Miss Power by telepathy; and succeeded.[115] Griggs arrived in the summer of 1904 on a noisy and unreliable Rex motortricycle, to do the drawings for the Cotswold volume in Macmillan's *Highways and Byways* series. He was then just a shy and meditative architectural illustrator, not yet the author of the great etchings of mediaeval architecture real and imagined, which are the most intense vision of Gothic England in modern times. He was so taken with Campden that he decided to settle there, and lived at first in Braithwaite House, where he got on well with the aspiring young men like Miller and Chettle. With Ashbee, however, he did not much sympathize. They shared the same enthusiasm, for Campden, for the Arts and Crafts. But Griggs's faith in these things was dark and mystical (he became a mediaevalizing Roman Catholic); he would not, like Ashbee, enlist them in the service of a secular Utopia.[116] Also Catholic was Paul Woodroffe, the book illustrator, whom Ashbee had already employed once or twice for the Essex House Press; by this date he was also working in stained glass. He arrived in 1904, buying a cottage next door to his brother-in-law, Joseph Moorat, in Westington, which Ashbee enlarged for him (Plates 122–3). Under its deep thatched eaves he lived a life of strict devotion, a beaky, austere man to look at, though kindly; he longed to inspire in his own assistants the mood of easy camaraderie that prevailed between Ashbee and the Guild, but he never could. Janet tried to like him, but he was terribly innocuous, hard to like or dislike very much; in her correspondence with Laurence Housman Woodroffe figured as 'Bête Grise'.[117] None of these artists actually joined the Guild; indeed they were rather studiously independent; but their presence in the town was sympathetic; they gave an extra momentum to the Campden experiment.

Ashbee crammed his days as full of various activities as ever. He had started Extension lecturing again, and drew up an ambitious 'Three Years' Scheme of Study . . . Adapted to the Needs of Workmen' with the help of the Extension Board of London University; of this he taught a first course on 'The Workman and Crafts-manship' at the South-Western Polytechnic in Chelsea in the early weeks of 1905.[118] He liked the class, practical workmen for the most part, and they seemed to catch his drift; discussing the influence of machinery on craftsmanship, they agreed that it was necessary to treat the question as an ethical one:

the men voted that 60% of the machinery was good, and 40% was bad. They then asked themselves why this 40% was bad, and they concluded (a) that it disorganised the workshop (b) that it destroyed man's proper training, (c) that it destroyed his individuality.[119]

Janet meanwhile was fighting the Campden Rural District Council elections, not, she said, on politics, but on issues that needed a woman's touch, health, sani-tation and relief of the poor; she was the first woman in the district to stand for election. But since such elections turn on rates, and Janet recommended the adoption of the Housing of the Working Classes Act and the strict enforcement of the Health Acts, it was clear that her policies would be expensive. In the event she was defeated, despite campaign leaflets finely printed at the Essex House Press; and George Haines and Ulric Stanley, farmers both, kept their seats.[120]

Perhaps Ashbee hoped, by keeping busy, to keep the difficulties of the Guild at bay. But it did not work. As the summer approached, Janet could see that he needed help she could not give; astute, and perhaps a little desperate, she asked Alec Miller to take him away in June, out of the Guild atmosphere; and they went up to Scotland, to Oban. They took Meredith's *One of Our Conquerors* and Shelley's translation of Plato's *Symposium*, but their heads were stuffed with literature any-way; and for a few wonderful Highland days they read and bathed and talked. He was never, Alec recalled, in a more simple and affectionate mood. One day they were on the island of Kerrera, and Ashbee told him for the first time about his father and the disinheritance. If he had been a rich man, Ashbee reflected, he could have helped the Guild.[121] And then, because life is absurd, their holiday was cut short. Alec had suddenly to go to Glasgow and have all his teeth out. Ashbee went back to Campden, and the rush and pressure resumed. Within a week or so he was off to Budapest to design a house.[122]

His clients in Budapest were Zsombor and Elsa de Szász; he was a member of the Hungarian Parliament, a nationalist and a landed gentleman who read his Ruskin, which meant for Ashbee that he was as good as a socialist; she was expansive, sharp-witted and Anglophile.[123] The house was to be in the Stefania district of Budapest, a fine site on a broad street lined with acacias (Plate 133); it was altogether an attractive job, and the de Szász were just the kind of cultured and idealistic clients Ashbee liked. Their tables were piled with copies of the *Studio*—'The ghosts of one's transgressions', Ashbee remarked coyly, 'arise and rebuke one . . .'—and there was the chance of fat commissions for the Guild.[124]

This was not, in fact, Ashbee's first contact with Hungary. In 1899 a Hungarian economist with Ruskinite sympathies called Gyula Mandello had come to Essex House in the course of his researches, looking at the same time for wedding furniture. Ashbee produced many designs for him, ranging from an interior in Budapest, through furniture, silverwork and jewellery down to a book-plate; so far as the records go Mandello seems to have been Ashbee's largest single client.[125] Then, in 1900, Mandello sent a young, highly strung and intensely idealistic aristocrat, Ervin Batthyány to see Ashbee; he wanted to study Edward Carpenter and had read, Ashbee thought, more Tolstoy than was good for him; they spent a weekend in Cambridge together.[126] Batthyány later had an important role to play as an anarchist in Hungarian revolutionary politics. In 1904, Zsombor de Szász visited the Guild's showroom at Dering Yard, and that presumably led to the present commission; while Mandello was now talking of Ashbee designing a house for him at Bratislava.[127]

With such contacts, Ashbee could hardly have chosen a more interesting time to come to Hungary. For almost thirty years, under a Liberal government, Hungary had been subject to the economic and political hegemony of Austria under the Hapsburg emperors; they had been years of modernization, of industrial development promoted by foreign investment and the urban bourgeoisie; Budapest had equipped herself with the attributes of a modern capital, boulevards with fashionable cafés, museums, an opera house, a university. In 1903 the Liberals were ousted by a coalition of socialists seeking democratic reform and the National Party, a largely landed interest opposed to the Austrian alliance. De Szász came from the intellectual gentry, an important element in the National Party, and Ashbee sympathized with his host's aspirations: they tallied with his own beliefs in racial distinctness, and he was impressed by the evidence of a surviving rural culture, 'a fine, stalwart, self-dependent peasantry'.[128] The political skill of the Emperor Franz Joseph was enough to make this socialist–nationalist coalition ineffective, but the fluid situation in Hungary acted as a forum of release for the tensions created by Liberal rule. There were strikes in that summer of 1905; dissident intellectuals took the part, more or less, of the urban workers; and socialism, if not revolution, was in the air.[129]

Budapest was beautiful in Ashbee's eyes, not the architecture, but the feel of the place, the stuff of history and race, physical types and life in the streets, out of which he could fashion his sense of the Hungarian. He had an idea for a statuary group to go in the hall of de Szász's house, something gessoed and richly coloured, to be done by Alec Miller; a young boy, *The Spirit of Modern Hungary* would be poised between a female saint, the Church, and a crowned king; there would be a doubtful movement in the group, the boy half held, half escaping from them (Plate 64).

Will the little winged creature fly away from Church and State? from the beauty of the tradition of a thousand years? will it make its own way? will it be held back, take the halo and the crown again?[130]

The image, like the movement of the youth, was deliberately ambiguous. In a published commentary Ashbee identified the crowned figure as the Austrian Empire, which made the group a tentative image of de Szász's nationalism; but when he wrote to Alec Miller about it, the figure was King Matthias of Hungary; since a winged youth for Ashbee suggested the hopes of an industrial democracy, the group then seemed to suggest the radical and socialist aspirations abroad in Budapest that summer: 'when they come into Mr. De Szasz's Hall', Ashbee told Alec, 'these ultramontanes, and conservative nobles, the radical nationalists and Socialists, they will all just read the symbolism and read it right their own way.'[131]

The sun shone, and he sat for hours by the Danube, watching the swimming, the clear water sparkling on the young men's backs; lumbago seemed a thing of the past. Sometimes it was so hot he could not bring himself to work, or even write to England; he just lay there feeling deliciously pagan. In the evening he would talk politics with the de Szász. 'They are really charming people', he wrote to Janet. They had a little daughter of three and a half, 'brown-skinned, bright-eyed, close-cropped' Irmelin; and she, Ashbee said, was even more interesting than politics.[132]

Janet must have screamed. How could he write to her about children in this way? Did he not know the strain she was under? Or was he trying to tell her, guardedly, that he too cared about little children? She loved him; he was kind, subtle and intelligent; and she knew that their relationship was large and reasonable, her daily life more interesting than that of many wives. But she wanted him to make love to her. 'Anything but this temperate gentle touch', she wrote in a private diary.[133] When they first got married it had been an adventure, still part of growing up for her; but that was seven years ago. Slowly she had come to think that they would never make love, that he was, simply and altogether, homosexual. By the time they came to Campden, she had resigned herself to an unwanted celibacy.[134] Her resolution was strong, but the strain was always there, becoming acute when she saw her friends marry and have children. Intellectual comradeship was much. But she wanted a warmer, more physical relationship, a more domestic life.

Earlier that year, in March 1905, Janet had been godmother to one of the Nason children, and that had been a turning point. She was, in the superficial phrase, 'good with children'. At the christening the baby seemed to belong to her in a kind of dream life, and also to Gerald Bishop; it was she who had suggested that Gerald should be godfather. He was like her father in a way, gloriously conventional, not likely to be noticed in a crowded room, but very real (Plate 57). To her friends Janet always seemed so very capable, and Ashbee thought her so; but Gerald treated her as if she were vulnerable; he called her 'Little One' and refused

57. Gerald Bishop.

to take her seriously; it was an enormous relief. The christening seemed to seal an affection which had been growing between them for some years, lost years for him in many ways, for Gwendolen, searching with her theatrical friends for a more exotic range of experience than came with being married to the manager of a photographic firm, had left him. Ashbee saw their affection growing; he was not jealous; in fact he was almost pleased, for he could see that Janet found in Gerald something that he could not give her. And she, little lion, hoped in her happiness that she could love them both.

While he was in Budapest, Janet sent him a love poem she had written for Gerald, saying she had 'found it in a ballad book, an old Welsh song', and did he think it early eighteenth century or what?[135] She seemed to be warning him of the seriousness of her affections, but sadly he missed the point; he thought it really was old. (Masefield was not so deceived; he thought Janet had written 'a most lovely thing' and so did Yeats.[136]) When he came back, Janet and Gerald went off on holiday together to Norfolk, bicycling along the long flat roads, staying at little inns and visiting country churches. The countryside was glittering in the August heat, and they seemed to move through a magic and isolated atmosphere, church after church. She would not let him make love to her, then or later; that was taboo. But she was full of happiness, refreshed after the strain of many years. If it kept its place, she thought, this happiness could last.[137]

She came back to Woolstaplers' Hall to find her husband busy as usual, playing waterpolo for Campden, writing to *The Times* on 'The Hungarian Question', and lecturing at the University Extension summer school in Oxford.[138] The Guild was still in trouble, with sales down by twenty-five per cent in the first half of the year; but since the spring the manager, W. J. Osborn, had been drumming up work for the Guild among architects, and the effects were beginning to be felt. Gradually the shops returned to full time during the summer, except for the Press, which was now sustained only by a trickle of orders given, it seems, to keep them in work.[139] Among these was a book of poems by Ashbee, *Echoes from the City*

58. The gardening class at the Campden School of Arts and Crafts.

of the Sun, published in the autumn of 1905. He wrote in a lush and self-conscious style, like an undergraduate, which makes them difficult to read now, but some of them are intriguing as biographical fragments, such as the tribute to Cambridge with the refrain, 'Oh I belong, oh I belong!' There is also a suite of love poems addressed to a 'Comrade'; but it is impossible to tell now who the comrade might be; perhaps it always was. The book did not sell well, and joined several earlier titles from the Press piled on the stock-room shelves. That Christmas Janet took down a copy of the Press's edition of Baldassare Castiglione's *The Courtyer*, the famous symposium on the qualities of a Renaissance gentleman; and she wrote in it, 'To one of the "good courtyers" Gerald Michael Bishop from his "especial and hartye friend" Janet Ashbee.'[140]

The Campden School of Arts and Crafts flourished that year, its fortunes rising as the Guild's declined. Teachers were sent out into the surrounding villages, Ebrington, Mickleton, Aston Subedge, Saintbury and Shipston, where Hilda Pook taught shorthand. The gardening plots at the back of Elm Tree House yielded their first fruits (Plate 58); and the Campden curriculum was broadened. A laundry class was started because it struck Ashbee as absurd that in Campden, his haven of self-sufficiency and the simple life, shirts had to be sent to Evesham to be starched. (In the event it did not catch on, the women of Campden resisting the idea that laundry could be *taught*.) The young men and boys were invited to attend physical drill classes under the watchful eye of a former Army drill sergeant (Plate 59); and the art of lead glazing was taught by Paul Woodroffe's foreman. The lectures

134

this year were on a single theme, 'Great Englishmen': Ashbee on Henry V, Mase-field on Nelson, Abbot Gasquet on Thomas More. But something of the old 'mixed assortment' remained: additional lectures included Captain R. Montagu Glossop on his experiences of fighting in the China seas, followed by demonstrations of Japanese wrestling.[141]

In January 1906 the Guild played *The Knight of the Burning Pestle* once more. It made Janet think of all that had happened since 1899, when the Guild had been so new to her.

Nearly 4 years in this little grey city—it seems more like 40! The weather-worn dove-coloured stone has a way of catching and fixing one's affections; and even the opposition, the Vicar, the pig-headed farmers, the stupid politicians .. are all part of it–and seem as necessary as the mist and the rain and the rheumatism and the muddy roads . . .[142]

She reflected on how the cast had changed; Arthur Cameron had grown too portly to play the Knight/Apprentice Ralph; Charley Downer, a beardless Mistress Merrythought in 1899, now had an exquisite moustache. Cyril Kelsey, the startling Princess Pompiona, was now a broker's clerk in London, 'the proud possessor of a bowler hat, and a dress suit, *and* a young lady . . .'.[143] Ernest Godman, aged thirty, was dying of consumption, and Sid Cotton, the last of the hilarious and troublesome apprentices, turned out to be consumptive too. He had left the Guild in 1905, and was now with Alf Pilkington in Canada, building railway carriages. Janet imagined him, 'trapping skunks and inlaying parlour cars'.[144] She was in a melancholy mood: 'The gaps yawn so many and so wide–I think we are growing old.'[145]

The shareholders of the Guild of Handicraft Limited faced a bleak prospect; the balance sheet for 1905 showed a substantial loss of £958.[146] It was now a ques-tion of how the Guild could survive, if it was not to close down straightaway. Ashbee went to see Martin Muir, who ran the London showrooms of the Birming-ham Guild of Handicraft, and got from him the advice that they should do more work 'for the trade', concentrating more on standard lines to be sold to retailers and architects, less on individual work sold to the public directly.[147] The advice was to be expected for the Birmingham Guild was itself becoming more like a professional firm of architects' craftsmen; Ashbee had watched with dismay as 'idealism' had given way to 'business sense' in its counsels; he blamed it on the Chairman of the Board, William Kenrick, a local Liberal worthy and brother-in-law of Joseph Chamberlain.[148] It was a bitter pill, to have to ask the Birmingham Guild for advice.

A good deal of responsibility, not all of it welcome, now fell on Rob Martin Holland, the kindly, cultivated banker who had been a director with Ashbee since 1898. He was the obvious source for business advice, and by now the largest single investor in the Guild, with over a thousand shares. Five days before the annual general meeting he wrote to Ashbee, agreeing with Muir's advice and adding some of his own:

You sometimes tell me that you wish you could suffer fools gladly, as you say I do, well I wish it too, for then instead of having so many enemies in Campden and the neighbour-hood, you would have friendly sympathy with the Guild and its objects and a great deal of local work which goes elsewhere.[149]

135

59. (following pages). The young men of Chipping Campden performing exercise number thirteen, 'Double knee bending with arms bending and stretching'.

Two days before the meeting he returned to the charge: 'we have perhaps paid more attention to what we like and consider good art, than to what our customers want. This is a wrong attitude. Our first essential is to find out what our customers want, and give them that at as low a price as possible.'[150] This too must have been hard to accept; they had been making 'vile brooches' for some years, against their will, and here was one of the directors arguing that they must go even further down that road. The crisis probed the very nature of the Guild. Could it be run according to such principles and still retain its idealism? Would it not be better for the Guild to give up now, rather than prolong its existence by compromising with business sense?

The shareholders did not think so. Idealism apart, the Guild's finances were in such a poor state, its stocks and assets so difficult to dispose of, that they had little to lose by carrying on. A committee of inspection was formed, consisting of the directors plus Hugh Seebohm, Gerald Bishop and E. Peter Jones, a manufacturer of corrugated iron and one of a circle of excellent clients Ashbee had in Wolverhampton. Reforms were begun. The gallery at Dering Yard was given up, a clearance sale was held in April and May, and the men were put on short time.[151] Most important of all, changes were made in the management of the Guild. In April, Gerald Bishop wrote saying that 'efficient continuous management' was what the Guild needed, and what it was not getting from Ashbee; an educated man with business skills and experience was wanted, who would take over the management, leaving Ashbee to look after the designing and the 'human' side of the Guild. 'One of the great factors of success in an undertaking', wrote Gerald, stretching the goodwill of his friend to its utmost, 'is the recognition of one's own limitations.'[152] However unwelcome this truth may have been to Ashbee, it was accepted by the committee of inspection, and at the beginning of the summer Mr J. T. Webster was appointed full-time manager of the Guild (Plate 60).[153]

COLLAPSE

The most painful part of the reorganization was the closing down of the Essex House Press. They had pinned their hopes on printing the *Bible*, a long, serious job. But only forty subscribers could be found, and more were needed to make it pay. They had a Guild sing-song in the library at Woolstaplers' Hall that June, the first for a long time, rounds and catches, Purcell and Schumann, but it was spoilt for Ashbee by the thought of the Press, and of losing Archie Ramage.[154] The presses and equipment stayed with the Guild, in case they should be able to start work again, and in August Ashbee helped to list them all with Thomas Binning, whose livelihood they had been for fifteen years. It was, he wrote, rather like taking the inventory of a man's life.[155]

At another of the sing-songs that summer, in August, the German architect and designer H. E. von Berlepsch-Valendas sat in a corner and admired the high cultural tone of the Guildsmen; in fact he admired everything. Reporting on his visit in a German magazine, he recalled how he had stepped down from the train outside Campden and found

around me wonderful meadows, fields shining like gold in the midday summer sun . . .

60. The Guild of Handicraft, probably in the winter of 1906–7. Ashbee is not present, but the new manager of the Guild is seated in the middle, in a dark suit and particularly crisp collar. From left to right, in the back row, are: Arthur Cameron, metalworker; Tom Hewson, silversmith; George Hart, silversmith; unknown; George Vickery, secretary; Walter Curtis, cabinet-maker; Will Hart, carver; Tom Jelliffe, cabinet-maker; Wally Curtis, cabinet-maker; Alf Smith, gardener; William Wall, cabinet-maker; Edward Williams, secretary; Alf Keyte; Herbert Osborn, ivory turner; Jack Baily, silversmith; Fleetwood C. Varley, enameller; William Mark, enameller; Charley Plunkett, French polisher, and Jim Pyment, cabinet-maker. Middle row: Bill Thornton, blacksmith; Dick Eatley, pressman; Bill Scurr, jeweller; — Webster; J. T. Webster, manager; Arthur Naylor, secretary; unknown; Bill Wride, cabinet-maker, and Charlie Daniels, jeweller. Front row: Walter Edwards, silversmith; Alec Miller, carver and modeller; Bert Humphries, silversmith; Micky Moran, jeweller; Arthur Bunten, cabinet-maker; John Cameron, metalworker; Mark Merriman, enameller; Stanley Keeley, metalworker, and Wilfred Merriman, office boy.

above me the blue sky, great white sailing clouds; I was surrounded by the hot dry chirping of crickets, the buzzing of mosquitoes and—after the train had disappeared behind the next hill—only the brooding August mood . . .

He met Janet:

Nor was it a nervous lady in a machine-embroidered modern sack-like reform costume 'sicklied o'er with the pale cast of thought' who offered me her hand with a friendly smile . . . Her hand, it was not white, not lined with strongly protruding blue veins—no it was brown, sunburnt, a working hand, not the hand of a drawing room lady—this hand belonged to a female apparition whose radiant health-exuding beauty gave her a victorious air.

He was shown round the workshops:

out of the window there were lovely views into gardens, a glimpse of distant hills, of hazy blue undulating terrain.

He met Ashbee:

A tall, slim but muscular looking man with a springy walk stretched out his hand to me. With certain people one has only to look into their eyes to know who one is dealing with. This calm but certain eye, the entire likeable expression of the face, it harmonised with everything else. 'Would you like to come for a walk with me? I have to supervise the rebuilding of a partly ruined small mediaeval monastery near here. It is being changed into a country house.'

And finally, after the sing-song:

139

61. Ethel Coomaraswamy weaving at the Norman Chapel, in about 1909–10. As Ethel Mairet, she became one of the leaders in the twentieth-century revival of English hand-weaving.

62. Ananda Coomaraswamy.

I stood in the moonlit quiet road with its old steep-roofed houses and thought and thought: was I dreaming or was all I had seen and experienced in the course of a few hours reality? No, no, it was reality, happy reality.[156]

Such was the rosy light in which outsiders saw the Guild. Ashbee, having to deal with a different kind of reality, felt the pressure of worry mounting again, and in August escaped for a holiday in Cushendun, County Antrim, where Masefield had rented an abandoned coast guard station. It had thirteen windows looking out to sea, none of which saw the sun; the coastline of Northern Ireland was bleak and unkempt, Masefield had toothache, and it rained all the time.[157] Ashbee's gloom was simply transposed into another key.

The 'partly ruined small mediaeval monastery' was just about as romantic as it sounded: the nave of a Norman chapel with a late mediaeval priest's house added to it, in the sadly derelict hamlet of Broad Campden, about a mile away (Plates 70, 124–7). Tumbledown and overgrown, its simple stones had a primitive appeal for Ashbee: Campden before its mediaeval glory even. He wanted to live there himself, but money was the problem, and he ended up repairing it for somebody else.[158] The amorous jeweller Fred Partridge had a sister, Ethel Mary (Plate 61), who had married a tall, meditative young man called Ananda K. Coomaraswamy (Plate 62); he was Anglo-Sinhalese, olive-skinned, learned, and slow in his movements. Although he grew up in England, Coomaraswamy had been appointed to direct a mineralogical survey in Ceylon from 1903 to 1906; after that they would return to England, and had decided to settle in Campden. The erosion of native life and manners in Ceylon by industrial civilization preoccupied them both, and Coomaraswamy's interest was shifting from mineralogy to the traditional art and craftsmanship of India and Ceylon; he was surely drawn to Campden by the presence of the Guild.[159] Campden's artistic circles promised to be that much more interesting when the Norman Chapel was ready to receive them. In the meanwhile they kept the cabinet-makers in work with orders for furniture.

Some of this work can be seen in photographs of the Guild which were taken in the late autumn or winter of 1906–7 (Plates 63–4), one of several efforts to publicize its work and claw back customers.[160] Guild clients were invited to replace the 'rubbishy, tawdry and commercial silverwork' which they might have received as wedding presents, with new Guild silverwork engraved with the names of the givers, thus retaining 'the sentiment of the gift, while getting rid of its inutility or ugliness'.[161] And Guild advertisements began to appear in the *Architectural Review*.[162] All this must have jarred on Ashbee; he disliked advertising and, to make things worse, most of their material was now printed, in the absence of the Essex House Press, in a catchpenny style he would have found tasteless.[163] Just before Christmas Rob Martin Holland and Gerald Bishop came down, no doubt to jaw about the future of the Guild; Janet was in hospital for a minor operation, and Ashbee sat up in the small hours, trying to write her an amusing letter, but it was no good: 'the interminable black rain of the Cotswold nights is going drip drip with that incessant thirsty gurgle down the drainpipe, and my brain is like a racing clock. Add to that there's simply no news, not even the tiniest morsel of scandal!'[164]

And then two weeks passed, and in January 1907 they were in Sicily, perched, as the guidebooks say, on a craggy mountainside among the spurge and prickly pear, high above the sea at Taormina. It was like England in April, with the almond blossom out and heavy showers passing to leave the air clear, the ancient sea sparkling and still. Taormina was a town with a sophisticated lotos-eating immigrant population, a resort for artists, a resting place for tubercular Englishmen, and a gathering ground for homosexuals. Italy censured such affections less than England, and Ancient Greece had seemed to show their highest, most ideal development; in Sicily, Greece and Italy met. The local photographer in Taormina, Baron Wilhelm von Gloeden, was famous for his soft, quasi-classical studies of Taorminese *ragazzi*, naked and artistically posed.[165] It was Colonel Shaw-Hellier, the old soldier from Wolverhampton, who had invited the Ashbees. After a brief and disastrous excursion into marriage, he had given up the Wodehouse at Wombourne, and come to live, as Janet put it, 'in this Old Man's Paradise'.[66] He had bought a site with a spectacular view down the Straits of Messina, and Ashbee was to build him a £2,000 house among the olive trees and orange groves. At the back of the site was the church of San Pancrazio, built on the ruins of a Greek temple dedicated to Isis—massive stonework at the base of the walls, plastered baroque above (Plate 65). Ashbee liked that; he liked to think that things were pagan underneath.

They had six weeks to spend, took picnics out to the neighbouring villages, sat in on the colonel's peculiar, high-pitched cosmopolitan parties, ate the excellent marmalade he made, and did the rounds of Sicilian architecture by train and mule.[167] Sicily was a revelation to Ashbee. He had never been so far south in Europe

63. The Guild blacksmiths, Bill Thornton at the back of the workshop on the left, and Charley Downer at the front. The decorative hinge hanging over the bench was destined for a grand piano made for Ananda Coomaraswamy.

64. The Guild carvers, Alec Miller at the back of the shop, Will Hart at the front. Behind Alec Miller are the model and roughed-out carving of *The Spirit of Modern Hungary*, the statuary group designed for Zsombor de Szász's house in Budapest.

65. The site chosen for Colonel Shaw-Hellier's house at Taormina, looking towards the church of San Pancrazio. A drawing by Ashbee, probably of January 1907.

before, and Greece had always been for him a country of the mind. Now, in the sunlight, his vision of Ancient Greece, country of good-natured simplicity and boy love, came alive. Janet read to him from the *Idylls* of Theocritus while he sunbathed, and he could instantly see the spirit of it all in 'the little wild untamed singing boys that run along the roadside for a smile from you . . .'.[168] He could see it among the Doric temples and the almond blossom at Agrigento, a subtle and local spirit, not to be captured in the damp and earnest north, with its 'black lumps of stone with rotten Greek mouldings—banks, exchanges, mansion houses . . .'.[169] He saw Sicily crowded with races in a long and colourful history, and the spirit of Greece persisting in the 'Byzantine paganism' of the mosaics at Monreale, a warrior Christ in strength and splendour, and carried up even into the eighteenth-century Palladian time. ('Oh but the faces of the priests! . . . There are troops of them about here in long black petticoats and black beaver hats. I feel as if I wanted to strip them, whip them, and then wash them in the water of paganism again . . .'[170]) The classic spirit was dead now of course, and no one understood, let alone would pay for, that love of form in building, 'unless it be some dear old-fashioned, lovable belated English country gentleman'.[171] Somehow, all this was to be built into the colonel's house.

On his return, Ashbee had to sit down with his fellow directors in front of the balance sheet for 1906; it showed a staggering loss of £1,994. Their overdraft at the bank was now creating an intolerable burden of interest, and though they felt that they had brought the management into good order, something urgently needed doing. At the annual general meeting, deferred to 18 May, the shareholders approved the issue of £1,000 in preference shares paying six per cent, the money to be used to pay off the overdraft.[172] It was not a hopeful measure, they were simply trying to buy time. Ashbee wrote a letter to the shareholders, urging them to take up the shares: there was so much more than investment at stake, there was the work of the Guild, the life of its members, the revival of a decaying Gloucestershire village.[173] Some did, admitting that it made no business sense, others did not; one heard with regret that the Guild might be wound up and wrote to Ashbee, 'I think it is a matter of great regret that this litle oasis of human life should be submerged in the unintelligent ocean of competitive industry.'[174] Ashbee might not have mixed his metaphors, but he could not have put it better.

Everything seemed to have a gloomy reflection that summer. He went to a meeting of the Art Workers' Guild in June when Willie Strang was in the chair, but it was dull. William De Morgan had closed down his works again, and this time it really was for good; the meeting, happening to be about pots and potting, soon became a general lament on the effects of commercialism. Afterwards Ashbee, Selwyn Image, and Cecil Brewer went to console themselves with a glass of old port at Henekey's in High Holborn, a favourite haunt of Arts and Crafts men. Among the seventeenth-century columns and the giant casks of wine, they drank a toast to the glory of the Lord who looks after patient artists in evil days, and Image, 'who has that air of immaculate benevolence which appears to come of close communion with a somewhat Anglican Almighty', developed some elaborate theory about how all economic activity was converging towards giant trusts, vast concerns of which artists would in the future be mere trivial appendages.[175] It was all very depressing. 'Everything is decaying', he intoned gravely from under his large silk top hat, 'even taste in wines.'[176]

Ashbee thought his shareholders 'the most charming and enlightened in England', but they could only find £600 of the £1,000 he needed.[177] In the autumn it was decided that the Guild of Handicraft Limited should go into liquidation. Late in October the Guildsmen met to see if anything could be done for those who did not want to leave Campden. Ashbee said bravely that the limited company was only an episode, that the Guild could not be so easily destroyed; and in a sense that turned out to be true.[178] But there was no denying that they had reached the point they had been struggling for several years to avoid. The Guild had not ceased to exist perhaps; but it had 'gone under'—there were many phrases in which its failure could be expressed. Letters of commiseration began to arrive. Laurence Hodson wrote briefly; he might have been able to help but he had financial difficulties of his own and had had to sell his best Pre-Raphaelites at Christie's the year before.[179] Nevill, Janet's brother, recalled some charcoal cartoons of Capital and Labour which hung on the stairs at Essex House; it seemed so wrong that Capital should triumph.[180] Cecil Brewer wrote: 'I only want to shake you by the hand and tell you how I (in common with, I am sure, many others who may sometimes have been critics) have admired your pluck in sticking to your ideals.'[181]

There were, of course, post-mortems on the Guild, and many reasons were given for its failure. Some said it had grown too large and was overburdened with office clerks and administration; the Guildsmen who set up their own small workshops in Campden after liquidation rather took this view, and their own modest success bore them out.[182] In a way, Ashbee agreed with them; it had always irked him to have to keep perfect accounts for the limited company; but he also looked outside the Guild for explanations.[183] He pointed to a period of acute commercial depression in the Campden years, and its effect on the luxury trades such as the Guild served, first felt in about 1904.[184] He pointed to the competition from retailers like Liberty's, with their cheaper versions of Arts and Crafts wares; and to competition from amateurs who put little or nothing for their labour into the price and so could undercut the Guild; they were middle-class ladies for the most part, and the Guildsmen referred to them, with biting condescension, as 'Dear Emily'.[185] Finally, he pointed to the difficulties of running a skilled craft workshop in the country; not just the obvious problems of transport and communication, lack of contact with clients and so on, but the basic difficulty of employment. In London things had been flexible; when orders were low, Guildsmen could go and find work in a trade shop; a postcard would bring them back when things picked up; the Guild rules provided for this. In Campden it was not easy to lay men off when times were bad; there was nowhere for them to go; they had to be kept on, making stock for which (times being bad) there was no demand. By 1907 the Guild had accumulated so much stock that light fittings costing £5 in labour and materials had to be sold off for 12s. 6d.[186]

There is much to be said for Ashbee's diagnosis. The competition from Liberty's and amateurs was real enough; the point about the inflexibility of employment in Campden was well made; and the Guild had gone through difficult times. But the diagnosis put too much responsibility on to outside circumstances. The 'three successive years of commercial depression' to which Ashbee referred in 1907 are not easy to identify in the world at large.[187] General consumer expenditure on the sort of goods the Guild produced rose steadily between 1900 and 1908; there were no significant dips in 1904, 1905 and 1906, the years which Ashbee said were difficult.[188] And even in the little, luxury world of the Arts and Crafts, it is hard to parallel Ashbee's experience. He wrote, 'All the other workers in the Arts and Crafts tell the same story, and it is noticeable that many of them in the last year have gone under, or have closed their workshops.'[189] But the only other casualties among the principal Arts and Crafts workshops during the years 1904–7 were William De Morgan and Harold Rathbone's Della Robbia Pottery. At the same time several new workshops were started up; Elmdon and Co., a London furniture workshop, Reginald Wells's Coldrum Pottery in Kent, and Robert Paterson's The Crafts in Glasgow.[190] The setting up of firms like these does not suggest an Arts and Crafts Movement staggering under the effects of economic depression.

Equally, Ashbee's argument about the difficulties of working in the country is not exactly borne out by the experience of other country workshops. Some of those which were fostered by the Home Arts and Industries Association survived into the 1920s.[191] The Arts and Crafts colony at Haslemere in Surrey actually grew in these years, with the addition of several workshops.[192] Ernest Gimson and Ernest Barnsley only started continuous furniture production when they opened their Daneway workshops in 1902, just as the Guild arrived in Campden; but they carried on until after the First World War. Their work fell, for the most part, into the luxury class, but they suffered no loss of trade like the Guild; their difficulty was rather in completing the orders they received, since they never employed more than fifteen men.[193] All these workshops differed from the Guild in the way they grew up in the country: they developed more or less gradually, they employed local as well as imported workmen, and they did not become very large: these differences may have been crucial.

The Guild of Handicraft failed because it was out of place in the country, too big, too sophisticated. It was naïve of Ashbee to think that a workshop employing as many as seventy men could be set down in the country all at once and survive; its skills belonged to the city, and so did its patterns of employment; when bad times came in the country, it could not respond. The 'great move' was probably the fatal step in the history of the Guild not, as Ashbee argued, because it was impossible to carry on a flourishing workshop in the country, but because of the way he went about it. With typical enthusiasm he tried to take the country by storm, forgetting how much a product of East London the Guild of Handicraft was. The boldest and most imaginative act of his career was also the most disastrous, and the irony was worthy of him.

Round Christmas, with liquidation certain, the Guildsmen began to leave. Mr Webster went, loaded down with expressions of regret and approbation, to pursue a successful career with a well-known manufacturer of sanitary ware in the Potteries.[194] Fleetwood Varley returned to London, where Liberty's were glad to buy his enamelled landscape plaques for the top of their cigarette boxes.[195] A number of metalworkers gravitated naturally to Birmingham. Tom Hewson, silversmith, drifted into unemployment and drink; Walter Edwards worked as a silversmith at first, and then got a job at Cadbury's, supervising the making of the moulds in which chocolates are made. Mrs Ashbee was to look out, he wrote, for chocolates with 'a touch of Ashbeeism' about them.[196] Edwards was one of those who looked back on his time in the Guild with affection; he lived in a 'cottage' in Acacia Road in Bournville, the Cadbury's model estate, and called it 'Campden'; the pierced metal sign still hangs above the door.[197]

Not all the Guildsmen left Campden; some decided to stay on, running their own workshops under the general title of the Guild of Handicraft. Jim Pyment, the sturdy foreman of the woodshop, started a building and joinery business; Bill Thornton and Charley Downer carried on the forge, truculent but inseparable; George Hart, Will's brother, and Jack Baily ran a silversmiths' workshop on the first floor, while the Australian Bill Mark worked by himself as an engraver and enameller, and Ted Horwood as a jeweller. Alec Miller and Will Hart, Ashbee's favourite craftsmen, set up as carvers and architectural modellers on the top floor, and what with various helpers, notably Charley Plunkett, the Cockney French polisher and old-fashioned free-thinking radical, there were still some dozen Guildsmen living in Campden.[198] In Pyment, Downer, Miller and Hart, they had some of the most active and loyal members, and Ashbee could fairly talk of the reconstruction of the Guild. The workshops, if less crowded, had the same atmosphere; the Guild met regularly with Ashbee in the chair, and the minutes were duly taken. The most obvious difference, now that the Guild was no longer a business in itself, was that Ashbee's position was much less clear. He could scarcely call himself the director, there was so little for him to direct; and he had to content himself with a vague personal authority.

Life went on, and Campden could still please and surprise. In January 1908 Janet found herself at the Norman Chapel for one of the tea parties that had become a fixture since Ethel and Ananda Coomaraswamy arrived in the previous spring. Sister Nivedita, author of *The Web of Indian Life*, was speaking on 'Women's Ideals in India', but Janet found herself less taken by this cause than by the crowd of faces in the shadowy mediaeval library—gentry, farmers and the Guild were represented—and she wondered at the happy fate which had brought these two people to the Cotswolds; the impenetrable Anglo-Sinhalese scholar with his passion for argument and intellectual subtleties (she skirted him rather in her mind, thinking of race), and Ethel (Plate 61), who was older than him, tender and motherly, and just as fascinating as her brother Fred. To Janet she appeared as 'a strange little thin undeveloped figure—by day dressed in the gaunt sack-frocks of the Jaeger-and-

Godfrey-Blount School—but at night coming out like a brilliant moth in Eastern plum cherry and orange colours, with strange Singhalese jewels'.[199] She would make a good friend, Janet thought. 'Both of them live in their enchanted chapel, which glows rose-colour with linen and Morris hangings and oriental crimsons—like two elves, creatures that you cannot gossip with and that yet have something more human about them than the most ordinary of us.'[200] There had been magic of an architectural kind in the Norman Chapel when Ashbee had finished restoring it; the Coomaraswamys added another kind of magic of their own.[201]

Ashbee was not, as far as one can tell, cast down by the failure of the Guild. Within six months he had written a substantial book, *Craftsmanship in Competitive Industry*, with the defiant epigraph from Cecil Rhodes, 'If you have an Idea, and it is a good Idea, and you will only stick to it, you will come out all right in the end.' The recent history of the Guild, Ashbee said, was an object-lesson in the callous destructiveness of modern industry; it had been squeezed out of existence by the ordinary, unregulated operation of commerce and industry. The experience did not give him pause; it simply strengthened his conviction that craftsmen had to be protected against unfair competition from the factory system. In heavy industry, he argued, machinery might have free play. But in the manufacture of domestic products, in the industries which challenged the Arts and Crafts, there would have to be some limitation on machinery.

Something of this sort, a disillusionment with machinery, he thought, was already in the air, the Arts and Crafts showed that; but it needed to be strengthened. The craftsmen should unite into a single trade union, bringing pressure to bear from below; and there should be government legislation from above. Ashbee was rather coy about spelling this last point out, but it seems that he thought machine products should be taxed, to give the craftsman a chance.[202] This was very different from his hopeful individualism of the 1890s, when he had said that workshop problems would be solved from within, not from without; he had turned to legislation. This fundamental change of tactics was probably partly due to the unhappy experience of the Guild, and partly to Ashbee's habitual sensitivity to the current political climate. His idea of taxes in favour of craftsmanship was borrowed directly from the campaign for tariff reform which Joseph Chamberlain made a focus of British politics from 1903 onwards. Chamberlain proposed duties to protect British industry and colonial trade against foreign imports. Quite apart from his imperialism, Ashbee was glad to see the principle of free trade questioned. If that could happen in international trade, why not in home markets too? Why not tariffs to protect quality, a preferential system in favour of the Arts and Crafts? And it was probably no accident, that Ashbee turned to legislation just at the time when so much welfare legislation was coming on to the Statute Book, following the massive Liberal victory in the elections of 1906.

While he was writing this book, Ashbee was also working on a scheme to give the faithful remnant of the Guild some economic security. In the heady days of 1901, he had talked ambitiously about the Guildsmen taking up agriculture, on small holdings; in the event a few Guildsmen worked some garden plots, and Ted Horwood kept bees and chickens, but nothing was done on a large scale.[203] Now, he revived the idea; he got in touch with Joseph Fels, an idealistic American millionaire, who spent a large part of the profits of his Philadelphia coal tar soap business in taking the British urban unemployed 'back to the land' and campaigning across the world for a single tax and land nationalization.[204] Ashbee showed him the proof sheets of *Craftsmanship in Competitive Industry* in which a scheme for Guild land was sketched out, and he was impressed. He came down to Campden in April 1908 and warmed to the Guildsmen; Janet found him a 'small, grizzled close-knit bright-eyed Jewey little man'.[205] A seventy-acre farm just north of Broad Campden was on offer; negotiations continued throughout the summer and a 'Guild of Handi-craft Trust' was formed to hold the land along with the Sheep Street workshops. On 3 October Charley Plunkett, Ted Horwood, Jack Baily and Jim Pyment made definite offers to work part of the farm each, and five days later Fels bought it on behalf of the Trust for £3,500.[206] In nine months Ashbee and his hustling, imaginative millionaire had, it seemed, transformed the fortunes of the Guild; they were now, in a sense, closer to his original ideal, closer to the basic, elemental things of the countryside, than they had ever been. On 17 October 1908, Ashbee sailed from Southampton for his third lecture tour of America.[207]

ENVOI

Janet had been seriously ill at the beginning of the year with diphtheria; it meant complete isolation for a while, and a long period of convalescence at the time when Ashbee was working on the land scheme.[208] She was still in love with them both, her kind, preoccupied husband, and Gerald, squarish and greying at the temples, whose attentiveness moved her so. It seemed a challenge to her to sustain two kinds of love, both good; and in a way she was proud of herself; but the strain perhaps told on her in her illness. In May Ashbee was in Italy, seeing to the colonel's villa among other things, and Janet went to stay with Madge and Peter Jones, who now lived at Greenbank, a large, white, late Georgian house outside Chester, Peter Jones having moved his corrugated iron works from Wolverhampton to Ellesmere Port. Janet, whose sense of the qualities of things was much more acute than her husband's, caught for him the slightly pedestrian modishness of the house:

The furniture would amuse you—exceedingly good and well chosen but savouring of a hotel, 'no expense having been spared and every detail showing refinement and taste' as the ads say. Some very good old pieces of furniture—and *exquisite* oriental carpets, fine brocade—beautiful engravings of Romney and Reynolds—and generally an 18th century flavour. It is mostly too new, and wants knocking about and a bloom of wholesome shabbi-ness putting on it—but there is nothing to offend and hardly anything that savours of MONEY aggressively.[209]

Perhaps that was another reason by the Guild had failed; Ashbee could not quite manage the new eighteenth-century taste. A few pieces of the Arts and Crafts furniture he had designed for the Joneses in about 1900 could still be found at Greenbank, tucked away in the spare rooms.

By July Janet was still not fully recovered, and it was decided that she should, in her turn, have a holiday of escape, not to dreary County Antrim or to Oban, but further north still, to Plockton in the western Highlands, opposite Skye (Plate 66).[210] She stayed in a little ugly crofter's cottage belonging to a crazy, slatternly

66. The lochs of the western Highlands: a photograph taken on Janet Ashbee's holiday at Plockton.

philosophical friend of Alec Miller's. After a few weeks she was brown and bleached and salty from much swimming; in her long blue fisherman's jersey and loose skirt she seemed a picture of health to Gerald when he came to spend the last two weeks with her. They milked the cow at breakfast time, Janet made the coffee, and they pondered over what kind of nothing they should do all day. This was the 'simple life'. On the train, travelling home, Janet was acutely aware of crowds, and of the noise and squalor of Birmingham, where they parted.

Almost immediately afterwards, as if their happiness had been too complete, and indeed it had, Janet broke down. She could not sleep at night, and went to Godden Green to be taken care of, but to no effect. She was then put into a London nursing home under the care of the neurologist, Henry Head, to whom she told her love story with peculiar and characteristic objectivity, considering how her brave philosophy of human intercourse had been overturned. The American lecture tour was only a week or so away. Head simply forbade any communication between Janet and Gerald for six weeks, and she obeyed.[211] She was taken down to Southampton and went on board ship. Ashbee was late, as usual. She saw him approach, smiling, in a long, grey ulster coat and a soft hat. In a most unwonted way, he started to take care of her. They sat on the deck, wrapped in rugs, watching the grey Atlantic; he writing his lectures and occasionally stopping to ask for her comments, she sitting there, thinking over it all, finding herself again.

149

CHAPTER SIX
WHERE THE GREAT CITY
STANDS
1908–1918

America, as so often, gave back an echo to Ashbee's thoughts. In Philadelphia he met the Arts and Crafts architect William L. Price, who had started a community of artists and craftsmen at Rose Valley, thirteen miles outside the city in 1901; their furniture workshops were built in the ruins of an abandoned textile mill, an allegory of industrial change that Ashbee would have enjoyed. Joseph Fels was one of the backers of the Rose Valley community, and it was much like the Guild at Campden in spirit—and in its fortunes, for it more or less collapsed at about the same time. When they went out on a picnic together the men sat and talked socialism and single tax, while the women cooked porridge and eggs; this was the mood of the Arts and Crafts, and Ashbee enjoyed it.[1] But he was also aware of other forces in American life, an awareness that reflects a shift in his idealism. He sensed a power of organization and corporate life that seemed positive, and a sign of the times. He saw it in the early skyscraper architecture of New York: materialistic it might be, but at least it had character and style; and he saw it in the discipline of the footballers and the singing, chanting crowd at the Yale versus Harvard match. 'The country is moving as one,' he wrote, 'the football game is its microcosm ....'[2] That fitted in with his ideas about the Arts and Crafts, and their need to replace a temperamental individualism with large-scale organization. In the years that followed the liquidation of the Guild of Handicraft he did not believe any less strongly in the Arts and Crafts and in the idea that people need the satisfying work of craftsmanship; but he did come to feel that the Arts and Crafts Movement had got into something of a backwater; from now on, he thought more about the world to which the Arts and Crafts addressed itself, about ways of fostering it through larger organizations and the temper of society.[3]

In Chicago, that great 'bear cub of Democracy' with which he had wrestled so enjoyably eight years before, he found things curiously muted. He sat in Louis Sullivan's office, almost empty for want of work, while the old man read from the manuscript of his chaotic prose epic 'Democracy—A Man Search'. A commercial traveller came in to sell concrete and then went out again. The Whitmanic periods rolled on. At Hull House, Jane Addams had great dark rings round her eyes. 'We are in a period of reaction,' she said, 'and I think it's a bad time for ideas of all sorts.'[4] And Frank Lloyd Wright, with whom they stayed in Oak Park, seemed bitter and drawn in upon himself. They enjoyed the Wrights' big and boisterous family in the days just before Christmas, but Janet who was vulnerable herself, could feel the tension in their marriage, the loneliness of Catherine Lloyd

67. New York skyscrapers in 1913, with the Woolworth Building under construction on the left, and the almost completed tower of the Municipal Building in the distance.

Wright—'people do not kiss one in that way unless they are lonely in the midst of plenty'.[5] Ashbee, whose attention was focused as usual on less personal matters, concluded that Chicago had finally found its driving materialism too much; 'The soul of the city is sick . . .'.[6]

From Chicago they travelled west, spent Christmas in the wilds of North Dakota, and so came for the first time to the Pacific coast. Ashbee was captivated immediately, and characteristically attributed its fascination to the influence of oriental culture and 'the spirit of California . . . coming out of commercialism' rather than to the common attractions of climate and coastline.[7] They stayed with H. W. Rolfe and his family in a crazy bungalow on Sharon Heights about thirty miles outside San Francisco 'where every wind of Heaven beats upon it'.[8] The rain got in, soaked Rolfe's books, and drowned the children's guinea-pigs in the stable. Janet, who liked her Bohemianism to be efficient, found it all rather irritating.

Rolfe, now an associate professor of classics at Stanford University, had arranged for Ashbee to lecture to the whole university on 'The Arts and Crafts and the Spirit of Socialism'. Socialism was not a scare-word at Stanford then, but the lecture had gained advanced notoriety; unknown to Ashbee, Rolfe was locked in a long and unequal struggle with the autocratic President of Stanford, David Starr Jordan, a struggle to make the university more democratic and less hidebound academically. The lecture was to be a stage in that struggle. Ashbee rose to the occasion, the lecture took hold, the *Daily Palo Alto* reported pithily, 'Noted Architect Explains Craftsmanship Movement as Socialistic Rebellion Against Machinery', and Rolfe whispered to a sympathizer, 'We've won, we've won hand over fist.'[9] After the lecture Ashbee could leave San Francisco feeling that he had helped towards a more humane discipline at Stanford, but for Rolfe, the dreamy idealist, the victory was short-lived; a year later Jordan, using his power of dismissal, fired him as a misfit.

After San Francisco, Los Angeles was a disappointment, its Latin inheritance stamped out by commercialism.[10] But in nearby Pasadena Ashbee found an architect who made everything fall into place. It was only in 1904, after being in practice for a decade, that Charles Sumner Greene and his brother Henry began designing the low, open-structured wooden houses with deliciously soft obtrusive jointing, on which their reputation rests. Ashbee had come at the right time. 'I think C. Sumner Greene's work beautiful; among the best there is in this country.'[11] Greene seemed to epitomize the spirit that Ashbee had discovered on the West Coast: 'Like Lloyd Wright the spell of Japan is upon him, like Lloyd Wright he feels the beauty and makes magic out of the horizontal line, but there is in his work more tenderness, more subtlety, more self-effacement . . . perhaps it is California that speaks rather than Illinois . . .'[12] They drove round in Greene's new car looking at his buildings and visiting the workshops where his furniture was being made, probably for the Gamble and Blacker houses. Ashbee saw 'beautiful cabinets and chairs of walnut and lignum vitae, exquisite dowelling and pegging, and in all a supreme feeling for the material, quite up to our best English craftsmanship . . . I have not felt so at home in any workshop on this side of the Atlantic . . .'[13] In a way, it was chastening. Here is Greene, thought Ashbee, working quietly away at the heart of the Arts and Crafts Movement; and here am I, merely preaching about it. They ended the day up at Greene's house on the Arroyo, having tea with Mrs Garfield, widow of the murdered president. It was another typically Arts and Crafts moment, tempting him to deviate from his normal Journal style into that of a travelogue: 'We looked out on the mountains and discussed single tax in the intervals of tea and fingering the surfaces of Greene's scholarly panelling. As the afternoon wore on, a glorious sunset lit the snow of the mountains to rose red.'[14]

They made the return journey across America quickly, stopping for a visit to the Van Briggle Pottery in Colorado, and ending up as usual with the Emersons at Concord.[15] It had been Ashbee's longest American tour, and probably the most rewarding. He had brought back a big carving job for Alec Miller on the library at Bryn Mawr College, Pennsylvania; his takings had been good, for he had given forty lectures, mainly on the Arts and Crafts, at ten pounds each; and the West Coast had been a revelation, enlarging his sense of modern life; he even planned to follow it up with a trip to Japan.[16] As for Janet, who had been allowed no letters to or from her friends at home, on Dr Head's instructions, she was much better; the symptoms of her breakdown had disappeared. During the past five months she had been thrown together with her husband, alone with him in a sense; and if her affair with Gerald was partly a plea for a more loving marriage, perhaps that plea was answered now. Right at the end of the tour, in March, Ashbee's mother wrote to them about their plans for going to Japan, and she said, 'if there are any children by then, well you will not be able to go and you will both have your hands full with another sort of education'.[17] It seems that Janet had, in the isolation of the tour, been able to draw her husband closer to her.

CASTLES IN THE AIR

Ashbee came back to Campden on a new footing. To some extent he could pick up the threads of his old life; he chaired the meetings of the Guild, steering them with relish through the formal tangles of a dispute over the goodwill of the old company.[18] But there was no disguising the fact that his position in the Guild had changed. They had got on quite well while he was in America; he was not indispensable. For twenty years the Guild had claimed the best of his time and his idealism, and other things—architecture, conservation, lecturing—had come second. Now there was a change in his career. His extraordinary energies, instead of being focused on the Guild and Chipping Campden, were dispersed among many different schemes and projects, which he hoped would earn him a living and at the same time satisfy his idealism.

In the summer of 1910 he stood as a candidate for the Slade Professorship of Fine Arts at Oxford; it offered the hope of a small but steady income in return for a lecturing commitment that could be fitted in with his other activities. Typically, he planned to divert the academic traditions of the post towards his own idealism, telling the electors that he would direct the teaching of the Slade Professorship 'upon History, Sociology and Economics', which he took to be the roots of art.[19] If they were alarmed, he could claim the precedent of the first and most distinguished Slade Professor, John Ruskin. In the event they chose Selwyn Image, a safe, not to say benign, candidate and Janet spent the autumn sticking pins into the new professor from a distance.[20] But it was probably just as well; the confined and ornamental character of the post would have irked Ashbee.

At the same time he was working on an ambitious scheme to build a gallery for the Arts and Crafts, where craftsmen could show and sell their work, free from the competition of commercial retailers like Liberty. He showed elaborate designs to the Art Workers' Guild, exhorted the London County Council to provide a free site on Kingsway, walked up and down the terrace at Stanway explaining the scheme to Mr Balfour, the ex-Premier, and told Alec Miller there was a year's carving work in it for him.[21] But nothing came of it at that stage. Three years later, it was taken up by Lady Walburga Paget, one of Ashbee's 'permanent collection of titled hags' as Janet called them, 'a tall gaunt old Walkyrie of a thing . . .'[22] She introduced Ashbee to her son-in-law, the Earl of Plymouth, an influential figure in architectural circles, but he was then (1913) more interested in saving the Crystal Palace from demolition. Lady Walburga, with mad Teutonic logic, seized upon the notion that the Crystal Palace should become a gallery for the Arts and Crafts, and there was little Ashbee could do with the idea after that.[23]

That summer too Ashbee was acting as confidant to a troubled Frank Lloyd Wright. In the autumn of 1909 Wright had come to Europe with Mamah Borthwick Cheney, the wife of one of his clients, with whom he had been having an affair for some years, amidst considerable press interest and public controversy in Chicago. He had walked past the Magpie and Stump, unable to bring himself to knock and explain the breakdown of his marriage. Now he was living in the Italian sun at Fiesole while he supervized the lavish portfolio on his work being published by Wasmuth in Berlin. He wrote little, except to his mother and to Ashbee, saying he had sacrificed his family and the cause of architecture, but could not square things otherwise. 'I would give much to feel you my brother still, that would help.'[24] Ashbee, who knew something of the isolation which sexual unorthodoxy brings, replied that men like Wright 'when they have reached a certain stage of mental development, carry their God, their own Heaven and Hell, inside them . . .', which is just the sort of thing Wright would have said; but now, in uncharacteristically broken mood, he found it a demanding philosophy.[25] He came to Campden in September, visited the Guild and argued with Ashbee about architecture and Japan and mechanization, two arch-individualists each on his own hobby-horse. Ashbee used to say that they were at one on fundamentals, but perhaps it was just that their hobby-horses had the same names.[26]

It was on this occasion that Wright asked Ashbee to write the introduction to a short monograph on his work that Wasmuth was also publishing—a collection of photographs and plans of executed work to date usually known as *Frank Lloyd Wright: Ausgeführte Bauten*.[27] He chose Ashbee, he said, as 'a pure bit of sentiment on my part—because I liked you and I turned to you at the critical moment . . .'; but also perhaps because he was tired of the superficial praise of American critics; he found it galling to be continually type-cast as the moving spirit of the Prairie School.[28] The buildings illustrated were for the most part those subtly-interlocking, low-roofed, suburban houses which were his contribution to the Prairie style, plus two particularly challenging public buildings, the Unity Temple in Oak Park, Chicago and the Larkin Company Administration Building in Buffalo. This was, Ashbee argued in the introduction, a truly honest architecture, indigenous to the Middle West; and since it was free from the influence of European culture, unlike the architecture of the Eastern seaboard, it presented a special opportunity; here America

154

could find herself architecturally. He also admired Wright's stance in relation to 'the Machine', 'his determination, amounting sometimes to heroism, to master the machine and use it at all costs . . .'.[29]

It was typical of Ashbee that he should pay more attention to the ideas which he believed lay behind Wright's work than to the work itself. It was only towards the end of the introduction that he commented at all fully on the buildings and, as if taking care to qualify his admiration, took issue with the bareness of some of Wright's work. 'I have seen buildings of Frank Lloyd Wright's that I would like to touch with the enchanted wand,' he wrote; 'not to alter their structure in plan or form or carcass, but to clothe them with a more living and tender detail.'[30] It was just such a comment as an English Arts and Crafts architect would make, for American detail often seemed dead and hard to English eyes at this time, just as English drawings and details appeared imprecise to the Americans. Students of Wright's work have felt, perhaps because of this difference in sensibility, that Ashbee did not really understand what Wright was doing.[31] That may be so; but at the same time Ashbee's characteristic emphasis on ideas may have been important historically. The monograph, together with the larger portfolio of drawings which Wasmuth published, were influential in introducing Wright to Europe; their influence can be seen in the work of Peter Behrens, Gropius and Mies van der Rohe.[32] And while those architects no doubt learnt most from the photographs and plans, the emphasis in Ashbee's introduction may also have intrigued them, for it presented Wright's work as the expression of the ideals of honest modernity, freedom from historical styles, and machine architecture, which played such an important part in the early history of the Modern Movement.[33]

After Wright had gone, Ashbee set to work on a town planning scheme; London was full of embryo town planners that autumn. In 1909 Parliament had passed the Housing, Town Planning, Etc., Act, and though the powers it conferred on local authorities were in practice confined to housing developments on the outskirts of towns, it had the effect of alerting the professions on whose skills it called. 'Town planning'—the term itself was less than ten years old—became an issue. Ashbee, responsive as ever to progressive legislation, took up the cause, joining the *Architectural Review*'s Advisory Committee on Town Planning and Housing.[34] His scheme was a competition entry for the planning of residential development on the 6,000-acre Ruislip Manor Estate, on London's north-western fringe. This was the largest planning project since the Act and attracted more than sixty competitors, mostly architects.[35] Only a bird's-eye view of the centre of Ashbee's scheme (Plate 68) is known to survive, showing public buildings grouped around a large circular plot of grass, and the principal roads radiating outwards; the houses were not dotted with formless suburban individualism, but gathered together into strong, rather inward-looking groups. Such formal treatments were typical of the centres of other competition designs, but the Utopian echoes in Ashbee's design were particularly strong; echoes of the ideal cities of the Italian Renaissance, of Filarete and Francesco di Giorgio, in the circular and radial plan; echoes of Morris's vision of 'what a city might be; the centre with its big public buildings, theatres, squares and gardens: the zone round the centre with its lesser gildhalls grouping together the houses of the citizens'; and echoes, in the central park, public buildings, radial and ring roads and railway sidings, of the diagrams of 'Garden-City' in Ebenezer Howard's

RUISLIP GARDEN CITY
On this plan Public open spaces and permanent gardens only are coloured green.

Tomorrow: A Peaceful Path to Real Reform (1898), as if Ashbee had simply transferred them to the northern slopes of Middlesex.[36] In the absence of his plans for the whole site, it is not possible to judge how effective the scheme may have been; as it stands this highly finished bird's-eye view of a perfect world only serves to show that for Ashbee town planning was more concerned with the achievements of social ideals than with the management of physical change and growth. He was disappointed at Christmas when he found that the competition had been won by 'an entirely unknown man in a suburb, . . .' but his interest was by now well established.[37] Indeed, it was this interest in cities, what they stood for and the hopes they offered, which was the most obviously new element in his idealism during the post-liquidation years.

The early town planning movement in Britain was a miscellaneous, plural affair; the sense of a separate profession and of distinct skills was slow to emerge, and the first town planners were actually architects or surveyors, housing reformers, engineers or landscape architects. They did not all share the same view of what town planning was about. There were those in the nineteenth-century tradition of housing reform who saw town planning as a solution to the problems of over-crowding in cities: a matter of controlling densities and providing open spaces in suburban housing developments. One of the leaders of this group, the radical MP John Burns, was the principal author of the Housing, Town Planning, Etc., Act, and their interest is reflected in its title.

And then there were those who talked of 'garden cities' and 'garden suburbs'; which meant two quite different things. Garden cities meant building completely new small towns out in the country to check the sprawling growth of the big cities, a radical idea; garden suburbs on the other hand meant accepting the sprawl, and trying to plan the fringes of the great cities, as at Ruislip, on improved lines.

156

68. (facing page). The central part of Ashbee's town planning scheme for Ruislip, drawn by Philippe Mairet.

69. Patrick Geddes in about 1912.

As built, in the streets of Letchworth Garden City or the pathways of Hampstead Garden Suburb, they looked much the same, cottage housing at low densities, firmly and picturesquely grouped, the winding roads thick with greenery.

Another point of view was held by the staff of the newly established Department of Town Planning and Civic Design in the School of Architecture at Liverpool University. They believed in order: the different functions of a city should be clearly zoned, its roads and spaces laid out on axial lines. They admired nineteenth-century Paris and some modern American cities, and thought that the hotchpotch of nineteenth-century British cities needed 'pulling down, Haussmanising, and re-erecting on intelligent lines'.[38] They were urban in their tastes, and preoccupied with things architectural and monumental; they liked designing civic centres best.

And then there was Patrick Geddes, a lonely and distinct voice (Plate 69). Officially Professor of Botany at University College, Dundee, Geddes was the most extra-mural of academics. Round his Outlook Tower in the old town of Edinburgh he set up halls of residence to bring university students into touch with the life of the town; there was a craft school and a strong flavour of Toynbee Hall; he began an elaborate survey of every side of Edinburgh's life and history and cleared out slum courts to make communal gardens: he wrote on *The Evolution of Sex* and started a museum of all human knowledge; he was both gardener and polymath. Moving easily, perhaps too easily, across the field of human knowledge, he seemed to Janet, when he lectured at Campden in 1907, yeasty, suggestive, incoherent and irritating, a regular stage professor with his shaggy hair falling over his eyes.[39] Geddes believed that society, like nature, is subject to the laws of evolution; and he worked out that idea over a typically wide range before bringing it to bear on town planning in the early years of the twentieth century. As there is an art of town planning, he argued, so there is a corresponding science of civics, which seeks to understand the process of evolution in each city; intelligent planning could only be conducted within the context of civics, and planning projects should be preceded by a survey of all sides of a city's life, social, historical, economic, industrial, cultural. Other town planning enthusiasts advocated particular techniques of planning, of handling the physical environment; for Geddes, these things came later; the first thing was to understand the process of city life, the collective soul of the city.[40]

Ashbee sympathized with all these points of view. He knew about overcrowding from his East End days; his tastes inclined him to the garden city and garden suburb point of view; and he even admired the monumental, axial approach of the Liverpool School, seeing in it the expression of a corporate spirit. But he sympathized most with Patrick Geddes, calling him 'the finest educational revolutionary . . . now living and teaching in England'.[41] He had known him since the 1890s, but probably saw more of him after 1906 when Geddes became warden of a London University hall of residence on Cheyne Walk. On a spot which had once been Sir Thomas More's garden and was only a few yards from Ashbee's old home at Number 74, Geddes talked civics and sociology, and organized the re-erection of Crosby Hall, the great late mediaeval merchant's house from the City of London, which had been dismantled in 1908. Much of Ashbee's life had been about just these things, Chelsea, Utopia, old buildings, university idealism; and indeed, there was no one in Ashbee's career more like him than Geddes, though they never became close friends.

They started, it is true, from different intellectual premises, for Geddes was a Positivist, believing that understanding is derived by induction from scientific fact; and he knew, quite simply, a great deal more than Ashbee. But they both had the same intellectual temper, the same disdain for professional and academic boundaries; and as reformers their ideas converged. Geddes drew from Ruskin and Morris as well as from Huxley and Comte; and his sense of the evolution of industrial society corresponded closely with Ashbee's. He developed a distinction between two stages of industrial society: a first or palaeotechnic stage, characterized by coal, waste, materialism and individualism (the bad old nineteenth century); and a second, neotechnic stage, dawning in the twentieth century, characterized by clean hydroelectric power, conservation of resources and the natural growth of social ideals.[42] Ashbee would not have emphasized, as Geddes did, sources of power; but the distinction answers to Ashbee's sense, which we have seen at Providence, Rhode Island in 1901, and in *Craftsmanship in Competitive Industry*, that industry was developing in his time into a new and more humane phase. We shall see this hopefulness about the twentieth century growing in the next few years.

There were changes meanwhile in the domestic life of Campden. The Coomaraswamys were in India where Ananda was collecting work for an art exhibition at Allahabad; in September 1910 Ethel wrote to Ashbee saying that she was coming home, though Ananda would stay, and she would give up the Norman Chapel. He had fallen in love with another woman, though she could not bring herself to say so at the time, and their marriage was breaking up.[43] Life in Campden would be the poorer without them; but the Ashbees had always wanted to live in the Norman Chapel and now, when Ethel had cleared away the vibrant oriental furnishings, they were able to rent it, letting Woolstaplers' Hall in their turn. It

158

70. The Norman Chapel, Broad Campden, Gloucestershire.

was in their last months at Woolstaplers', on 25 March 1911, that Janet gave birth
to a baby girl, Mary Elizabeth. As soon as she knew that she was pregnant she
had written to all her friends, full of happiness that this should have happened after
so long. In the summer they moved into the Norman Chapel, and its massive walls
became Janet's fortress, a temple of domesticity, and sometimes a prison (Plate 70).
In this little hamlet, so much more remote even than Campden, she lived her latter-
day country life, a lady of the manor without the social hierarchy, mercifully.

Motherhood became her, as she had known it would, and now she had somewhere to stand, in her own right. Ashbee had wanted a boy and he was, just a little, put out; but he was happy for her, and he loved his little Mary more and more as she grew up.

All during these years he was working away at a big ambitious book called variously *Culture and Machinery* or *The Man and the Machine*.[44] He was so preoccupied with 'the Machine' at this time, and his conversation drifted so uncontrollably towards it, that Janet christened the subject 'King Charles's Head'.[45] When a departmental committee of the Board of Education was set up in 1911 to enquire into the working of the Royal College of Art, Ashbee took the occasion to publish the parts of this book dealing with art education under the title *Should We Stop Teaching Art*. It was prefaced by six axioms boldly printed in capital letters, like Otto Wagner's *Moderne Architektur* of 1895 and Ruskin's *Seven Lamps*. The first set out the belief which lay behind much of Ashbee's work, that there was no point in talking about, or working in, the arts if one ignored the context of industry.

AXIOM I.—MODERN CIVILIZATION RESTS ON MACHINERY, AND NO SYSTEM FOR THE ENDOWMENT, OR THE ENCOURAGEMENT, OR THE TEACHING OF ART CAN BE SOUND THAT DOES NOT RECOGNIZE THIS.[46]

Art teachers, Ashbee explained, had never got beyond the débâcle of the arts at the time of the Industrial Revolution; they had not adjusted to the new conditions. 'The first consistent attempt to give expression to the Arts under the condition of Machinery has been what is known as the Arts and Crafts movement.'[47] The last axiom set out what Ashbee saw as the achievement of the Arts and Crafts Movement:

AXIOM VI.—THE EXPERIENCE OF THE LAST TWENTY-FIVE YEARS HAS SHOWN THAT IN MANY TRADES AND CRAFTS THE DISTINCTION BETWEEN WHAT SHOULD AND WHAT SHOULD NOT BE PRODUCED BY MACHINERY HAS ALREADY BEEN MADE.[48]

They had come to see, he wrote, that 'it is now just as immoral to produce certain types of metalwork, or furniture, or clothing, under mechanical conditions as it is to produce lead-glaze ware unsafeguarded, or matches with the adjunct of phossy jaw'.[49]

The argument of *Should We Stop Teaching Art*, as one might expect, only touches lightly on the Royal College of Art; it took a wider view, arguing that Britain's art schools produced too many fine artists who only ended up as art teachers; that skill and imagination were stimulated artificially in schools and then checked unnaturally in life; and that the schools should be converted into State-subsidized craft workshops, which would endow the craftsmen the country really needed and at the same time provide more practical teaching. The heart of this argument went back to the old School of Handicraft in Whitechapel, but with this difference, that by 1911 Ashbee's tactics had changed and he was looking not to a quixotic band of idealists, but to larger institutions, the nation's art schools, and state subsidy.

1912 was much occupied with architectural schemes. There was a long slip of land at 40–45 Cheyne Walk, next to houses he had already built, and he was intrigued by its history: the mulberry tree said to have been planted by John Evelyn, the fragments, apparently, of old Shrewsbury House, giving connections with one of his Elizabethan heroines, Bess of Hardwick. He had designed several schemes for it over the years, and in 1907, when Patrick Geddes was campaigning to turn Chelsea into a university quarter, a 'Collegiate City', Ashbee turned one of his schemes for flats into a university hall of residence.[50] Nothing came of that, but in 1912, he recast the hall of residence as the 'London Fraternity House', a scheme with a distinctly overseas flavour; it was to be a group of hostels which would rescue American and colonial students from the squalid lodging-houses of Bloomsbury, and create 'the first great residential college within the London area' (Plate 114).[51] He lobbied the Senate of London University in support of the scheme, but without success; it was not built.[52] Then there was an equally fruitless scheme for rebuilding Morley College in South London; the only result of that was a protracted squabble over the payment of his fees.[53]

The gap between Ashbee's aspirations and what could be achieved seemed to widen all the time. Janet, on the other hand, now that babies were her business, seemed to grow stronger, more trenchant. That summer, with another baby on the way and her husband away in Suffolk, hob-nobbing with the aristocracy, she lost patience with his mannered letter-writing: 'Your letters are always interesting, but they generally make me angry, mostly I think because they show you at your very worst. You seem to slip out of my grasp and become again the self-conscious precieux you were when I found you—the man who reads over his letters and writes one word over another—as if his wife was a printer . . .'[54] It was not easy for Ashbee, just when his career seemed to be coming adrift, to live with someone who had so definitely got his measure.

Just before Christmas he was up in London for the King's College dinner, something he always looked forward to; it did not, though he was rising fifty, make him feel old. He came out of the Hotel Cecil and a young guardsman caught his attention in the Strand. His first instinct was to walk on and catch a bus, but he looked round and the guardsman looked round too. It was a straightforward homosexual encounter. The young man, Chris Robson, was stationed at Chelsea Barracks. Ashbee was going to Cheyne Walk, and they walked on together. Chris Robson told his life story, how he had worked on a farm in Yorkshire, and in an ironworks in Middlesbrough, and then joined the Coldstream Guards; they had some supper at the Magpie and Stump and then Robson had to go back to barracks. Ashbee felt 'stimulated and sappy, tingling in every vein of me . . .'.[55] They met again in January and Ashbee decided that they should read Kipling together, for Robson was rather wordless. Life is complicated. In February 1913 Janet had a baby, Jane Felicity, not a boy, not 'David' as Ashbee hoped. As the atmosphere of domesticity at the Norman Chapel deepened he felt, perhaps, on the edge of things. In May he went to France on holiday with Chris Robson, sending Janet a long, rather literal description of his companion. 'I need this other side to life still,' he wrote, 'I can't quite do without it—yet.'[56] Janet wrote back. 'I confess I had a few tears this morning over your description of your lover. But I never can repay your understanding and generosity of 5 years ago save 'in kind' . . . So bless you both.'[57]

The rest of Ashbee's letter was about Joseph Fels and rates of interest on the Guild estate. (That was one of the irritating things about his letters, they passed from personal to business matters without inflexion.) In his own theoretical way, and without any inclination to lift a spade himself, he had become deeply involved in the estate at Broad Campden. It had started as a way of supporting the Guild, with part of the seventy acres being farmed in the ordinary way by the silversmith George Hart, Will's brother, and the rest divided up as small holdings and allotments for the Guildsmen and others.[58] But now local people outnumbered Guildsmen among the tenants, and he looked on it as a venture in its own right. It was perhaps to represent the interests of the tenants that he served on the parish council at this time, though the most obvious (and predictable) result of his term of service was constant friction with the local farming establishment.[59] He would talk of the dignity of the country labourer who works his own land instead of someone else's; and of self-subsistence: a man should grow his food to eat, not to sell.[60] His hero on the estate was Charley Plunkett, the Cockney French polisher: 'His cabbages and potatoes are the best cabbages and potatoes and he bakes his own bread. His pig is a wonderful pig and he has eggs that are luxuries. He is a wise man and grows to eat, not to sell.'[61] In a way, agriculture was now twinned in Ashbee's mind with the Arts and Crafts. It was one of the 'great and beautiful things in life', things that a market economy could not comprehend.[62]

Here again his enthusiasm reflected recent legislation. The Small Holdings and Allotments Act which came into force in January 1908 was part of the Liberal programme of social legislation and a great deal more drastic than its predecessor of 1892, for it gave county councils the power of compulsory purchase against landowners. (Ashbee would have welcomed it for that alone.) It was effective in promoting smallholdings, especially in areas devoted to stock-rearing and market gardening, and this generated government and voluntary activity.[63] Ashbee entered into the spirit of the movement. In February 1912 he invited officials from the Board of Agriculture down to Campden to explain about credit banks and how to set up a co-operative. The thirty-five smallholders and allotment holders were probably rather bemused.[64] A little later he was working on a housing scheme for the estate, so that smallholders could be near their plots. The Agricultural Organisation Society, founded in 1901 to encourage co-operation among farmers, was drawn in to support the scheme, but Fels would not co-operate when his approval and financial help were sought. (He had just given £10,000 to the Single Tax campaign in China, and was paying his bankers five per cent on the sum.) The scheme was still stalling when Fels died in February 1914, and his executors decided to call in his mortgage on the Guild estate.[65] The whole venture might have crumbled in the summer of 1914, if a greater crisis had not intervened.

WAR

Ashbee's reaction to the war was odd. There was the first, obvious response: 'Aug. 5. 1914. I woke up this morning sobbing . . . All we have worked for, all we have hoped for the last 25 years . . . is to go by the board.'[66] But quite quickly he seemed to digest the war, accommodating it to his own ideas; his Journals grew fat with the record of long and intense discussions: '. . . the german war machine for me is only another and extreme example of the misuse of mechanism . . .', he wrote to Laurence Hodson in September, and in the same letter he spoke of the war as a protest against mechanism, men fighting because their life was ugly and colourless and drab.[67] He could see the loss and destruction—'The Arts and Crafts', he wrote,

162

'is practically defunct . . .' and yet that was also a clearing of the ground, an opportunity for reconstruction.[68] What the Journals do not tell in any detail is the humdrum story of a fifty-one-year-old architect and unattached idealist trying to find useful work. He went to the Home Office, the Foreign Office and the War Office, but they had no job to offer. By the late autumn it was looking as if a lecture tour in the United States would be the only way of earning some money. And then events took a curious turn.[69]

Lowes Dickinson was a thinker on whom the disaster of the war bore down with an almost personal force. He was permanently depressed and preoccupied by it. Staying at Hereford during the first week of the war, he jotted down two possible schemes for a peace-keeping body to settle international disputes; he was looking ahead to peace-time when such a body might be set up to prevent another disaster on this scale. This was the intellectual germ of the League of Nations. From Hereford he went on to Campden to stay with the Ashbees, and discussed his schemes with them.[70] Shortly afterwards he set up a study group to pursue these ideas, under the chairmanship of Lord Bryce, the former British ambassador to the United States; it was not a propaganda body and fought shy of publishing any statement for some years lest it should be ignorantly branded as pacifist. Ashbee was certainly not an important member of the Bryce Group, if he belonged to it at all; but it was important to the Group to keep in touch with American opinion, and it appears that around Christmas he was asked to maintain a liaison for them in the United States.[71] He was pleased to be associated with such thoughtful and progressive people, and to do something useful. In February he went to Whitehall for an interview with the Foreign Secretary, during which he found himself wondering whether Sir Edward Grey would be any different if he were not surrounded by Sir George Gilbert Scott's 'banal stencil decorations' in gold on sage green.[72] In March he sailed for America. 'For me,' he wrote, 'belief in America for all her filthy ways and her abominable manners comes to have more and more something of the nature of a religious faith.'[73]

As it turned out, this was only the first of three wartime lecture tours. During the next sixteen months he was in the United States for more than half the time, lecturing on his favourite topics, the Arts and Crafts, civics, the 'Man and the Machine'; and at the same time he was seeking out influential men, especially on the first tour, probing American support for the Bryce Group's ideas. In June 1915, with American opinion sharply altered by the sinking of the *Lusitania*, he attended a meeting in Independence Hall in Philadelphia when, on an afternoon so hot that delegates were dropping asleep from exhaustion, ex-President William H. Taft welded a distinguished collection of politicians, journalists and academics into the American branch of the League to Enforce Peace, on principles close to those of the Bryce Group.[74] After that he went to Theodore Roosevelt's home at Oyster Bay on Long Island because someone had said he knew better than anyone what Americans were thinking. Roosevelt told him that the peace ideas were premature, 'all tomfoolery, all slush', and that he did not agree with what Americans were thinking, 'I am red blood . . . I know a few sound red-blooded Americans here and there . . . but now the people think differently.'[75] Ashbee loved the drama of the man. He also enjoyed his own role as investigator. Finding out what Americans were thinking was an old pastime of his, and now he could give it a sense of urgency and importance. But when he got back to England, he found that all his probing did not count for very much. Everything was governed by the war and when Ashbee went to see Lord Robert Cecil, Under-Secretary of State for Foreign Affairs, he said he had not even heard of the League to Enforce Peace.[76] On later tours, Ashbee gave rather less time to his liaison work, more to his usual lecturing and exploring.

The lectures were a success. 'I feel that I am wanted, and that here I have something to say worth saying,' he wrote in November 1915 from Pittsburgh.[77] And when he was not lecturing he was exploring backwoods America: the women of Marie Garland's Home Colony Union weaving in the woods above Buzzards Bay, Massachusetts; the sadly deserted workshops of Ralph Radcliffe Whitehead's Arts and Crafts colony Byrdcliffe at Woodstock in the Catskills.[78] Best of all was the Thatcher's School in Ventura County, California, where the gilded offspring of American plutocracy was being educated in the open air: the boys riding naked and barebacked to their bathing pool put him in mind of the Parthenon frieze.[79] He looked at cities too, with a more expert eye, thinking that 'In America lies the real possibility of city life . . .'.[80] Any feature that was more than utilitarian excited him: in Kansas City it was the park system, in St Louis the siting and design of Washington University, in Portland, Oregon, the Library where the staff were so much more than custodians of books.[81]

In the spring of 1916 he stayed at Taliesin, Spring Green, Wisconsin, Frank Lloyd Wright's rural retreat in the land of his fathers. 'The house perches eyrie-like on the cliff—it might be an immense aeroplane at the moment before flight.'[82] Wright met him 'dressed in a sort of buff leather suit—like the puritan fathers—with a long black silk tie, and his long hair under a seal skin cap'; he was riding a wild brown horse called Kaiser and was defiantly pro-German; it was two years since a servant had gone berserk at Taliesin, killed seven people including Mrs Cheney, and burnt part of the house to the ground; Wright's hair had gone completely grey.[83] Ashbee stayed for five days, went over the drawings for the Imperial Hotel in Tokyo, and saw a good deal of Mrs Miriam Noel, with whom Wright was now living. he took a rather prurient delight in the irregular ménage, and wrote letters home full of knowing gossip. Janet, who disliked Wright anyway—'all his talk and gas and parade of it all'—took the same view as the American public, that promiscuity is not excused by artistic genius, and dismissed the whole thing as just another 'whoring episode' on Wright's part.[84]

That was the view from the nursery at the Norman Chapel, a judgement issued with all the force of motherhood and common-sense authority which Janet learned in these difficult and confining years. Isolated in Broad Campden, cut off from many of her friends by the war, she lived in the little circle of nanny and housemaids and children (Plate 71). Campden looked askance at her because her husband was half German and spent most of his time in America lecturing about peace.[85] But she was not dismayed. Now that she was a mother herself, she started, with typical forthrightness, a school for mothers; children were brought to her to be weighed, and a campaign was waged in favour of breastfeeding, striking fear into the hearts of those Campden mothers who preferred the bottle.[86] She was, in her own less theoretical way, as much a reformer as her husband. Of her own children, Mary was five when her father came back from America for the last time in May 1916,

71. Janet Ashbee and child.

a still and sensible child. The three-year-old Felicity, on the other hand, was quite wild, and given to waking up at midnight and talking with 'a sort of moonlight irrelevance and insouciance'.[87] There was another baby now, born on Christmas Eve 1915. Ashbee's letters from America that autumn had ended with the prayer, 'Let it be David, oh please let it be David', but it was a girl again, a restless little thing called Helen, who looked, however, very elegant at her christening in a Guild necklace.[88] The new clergyman, Janet was pleased to report, had a 'beautiful *non-*clerical voice and speech . . . and a very nice, comfortable, un-martyred, rather city businessman's (fish-in-bag) kind of face'.[89]

Ashbee had enjoyed himself in America, travelling unattached, with no responsibilities except to his lecture schedule; a very intellectual existence. Back in England he moped rather, restless for want of work. The war and his absence had done much to destroy what shape the Guild still had in its post-liquidation phase: Will Hart was fighting at the front and rose to the rank of major (that at least confirmed Ashbee's faith in him); Thornton and Downer were both hammering away in munitions factories; Ted Horwood, always one for tinkering with machines, had been taught to fly and was serving in Egypt, the Sudan and Salonika.[90] At home the School of Arts and Crafts was closed down in January 1916 by the Gloucestershire County Council on grounds of economy: 'in a mood of panic-stricken wrecking', Ashbee wrote, 'the work of 15 years is to be undone'.[91] And occasionally there was news of friends and former Guildsmen killed: in the summer of 1915 it was his beloved scapegrace Sid Cotton; Ashbee had last seen him in 1914, posing stylishly in Charley Downer's smithy in a loud canary-coloured check and bright yellow boots, the colonial gent visiting the old country.[92] Then, in the summer of 1916 it was Chris Robson, hit by a stray shell at Ypres. It happened in July and Ashbee somehow sensed it. He could write nothing in the Journals until he heard for certain in October.[93] He had still found, by this date, no useful war work to do. Then at the end of 1916 he saw an advertisement in the *Times Educational Supplement*; the Egyptian Ministry of Public Instruction was seeking lecturers in English to replace conscripted staff at the Sultania Training Collge in Cairo.[94] Ashbee applied and was appointed.

CIVICS

Cairo was a revelation to him, and all the more welcome because it fitted so closely to his own ideas about craftsmanship and pre-industrial traditions. He had guides show him the weavers and metalworkers in their booths by the side of the street; he saw musicians making beautifully fretted and inlaid instruments like lutes, and thought of the English craftsman Arnold Dolmetsch. 'I asked one if he would play. He ceremoniously shut the door of his little shop. Four of us sat down together and with a peacock's feather . . . he played delightfully.'[95] 'It is wonderful to see', Ashbee reflected, 'what one has so long been preaching—the cultural force of these hand processes.'[96] Later he could be seen, exploring the alleyways of Cairo, dressed in a white silk suit and a fez, armed with a fly-whisk, marvelling at the human cornucopia of the streets, a fellow in pink or blue leading an orang-outang, green clover, oranges, robes of lemon silk, drenched in the sun.[97] That was the secret: 'constant sun and open air is a preservative against mechanism and the factory system; a sort of quinine or tonic . . .'[98] His letters and Journal entries were lyrical; but somehow unobserved, as if he was seeing only what he wanted to see.

Janet's letters were not in the least lyrical.

Broad Campden. 22 March . . . Well, here we have 3 inches of snow, 15 degrees of frost, and a hurricane from the N.E.—and as a bonne bouche the exhaust pipe of the *furnace* has burst with the frost so *all* the hot water is pouring onto the Fern Patch and the *cold water* patiently climbing up into all the radiators—I really could have cried when I found out . . . There is nothing so soul destroying as an imperfect and badly contrived elaborate luxury.[99]

They kept arriving, these letters, sometimes months after they were written, interrupting Ashbee's sunlit idyll.

The Sultania Training College, he quickly found, was not an ideal institution. (All his life he believed that such an institution could be found, or created; that was perhaps the essential weakness of his idealism.) It was little more than an overgrown board school of the worst sort, run by administrators—dry, unimaginative Scotsmen, he tauntingly reported to Alec Miller—with an inflexible syllabus and meaningless discipline: the students flew to attention whenever they were spoken to, banging their squeaky desk seats. Here was the machine in Egypt after all, in the form of an uninspired colonial administration. He settled into the role of the rebel against the system, the real teacher who understands his students. He decided that they should read *Gulliver's Travels*. That was countermanded by the administration because it was a secondary school book and should have been read already. (Most of Ashbee's students had never heard of it.) But they read it all the same, unexpurgated. At a higher level, in the headquarters of the Ministry, he must have been appreciated, because there was talk of his being offered the vice-principalship of the College though nothing came of this. The whole place would have to be reformed of course, but he was flattered by the idea and wrote to Janet, guardedly, asking what she thought about starting 'a new creative life's work out here'.[100]

The answer came ringing back, late but passionate. The gap between his endless speculations and schemes and her own real and difficult life of babies' kisses and loneliness was finally too much for her.

do you want me to consider *me myself*, apart from THE WORK, I mean the human me, I, with my aspirations (for I too have them, and have them even *for myself*, tho' you have never asked what they are)—and I have them too for the children, and, separately, for you . . . What is 'Your love to us all'—sometimes I feel I want a little tenderness so dreadfully I feel I want to hurt you and *make* you feel something, if only pain—I don't suppose you know a bit what I mean . . . is one real flesh and blood—or merely a pen behind a brain with an intellect.[101]

She felt like Richard II with his warrant. 'Mine eyes are full of tears, I cannot see.' 'Goodnight,' she wrote, 'I suppose one ought to conceal all this under a terrible composure.'[102]

During the summer of 1917 Ashbee was back in England for about two months, and he saw his latest book, *Where the Great City Stands*, through the press. Like *Should We Stop Teaching Art* it began with a series of axioms, the first six much as before, and then four new ones. The theme of the book was stated in Axiom VII:

The new relationship of man to life which machine industry has brought with it, finds its fullest expression in the new life of our city. This implies that through the city and its proper adjustment to mechanical conditions will man realize again those finer values which the arts bring into life. Through the city we focus civilization.[103]

That last sentence caught the quality of Ashbee's idealism during these years and the way his ideas had changed since the time when the Guild had been the focus of his life.

Lecturing in Chicago in 1900 he had said

in the great cities of modern civilization we are creating a state of life that has become intolerable. Intolerable for its vulgarity, its sordidness, its squalor, its ugliness, its unreality, and above all for its waste, whether in London or in Chicago, whether in Pittsburg or in Manchester, in Cincinnati or in Sheffield, the great cities have either to be destroyed, or their whole conception of citizenship saved from the sordid materialism upon which it at present rests.[104]

Such trenchant anti-urbanism was to be expected when he was thinking of moving the Guild out into the country. Eight years later, in *Craftsmanship in Competitive Industry*, he analysed the failure of the Guild in Campden and gave full weight to the difficulties of working in the country; now, one would think, was a time for reconsideration, for looking on the great city in a kinder light. But in fact, Ashbee never thought of 'going back'.

when I put myself the question in the light of the last six years' experience in the country—was the thing worth permanently doing in the town, and would you for the sake of economic success have continued it or start it again, I answer, No . . . It would be comparatively easy with the experience of 20 years behind us to go back to London and start it all again—a new Guild of Handicraft in East London or elsewhere, many of its old members would return to it even there, but many would not, because they have seen how things can be better done; and some of us feel with Socrates that having once seen the Sun and learned the meaning of the shadows on the wall, we have no desire to go back into the den.'[105]

His faith in the country was not shaken; and his new enthusiasm for the city as the focus of civilization was not a reaction to the failure of the Guild in Campden. It was a response to new ideas, to the town planning movement in Britain, Germany and America, and particularly to the suggestive thinking of Patrick Geddes. Ashbee was moving on.

The subtitle of the book was *A Study in the New Civics*, which aligned it with Geddes, and in the first twelve chapters he traced the idealism of the book through many different channels of the nineteenth and early twentieth centuries, the Pre-Raphaelites and the Arts and Crafts, the Impressionists, the conservation movement, garden cities, the influence of Japan; this was Geddes' synoptic survey technique applied to the history of culture. The rest of the book expounded the new view of city life at which Ashbee had arrived, in a series of short chapters rich in example and allusion, loose in argument. He enthused about the civilizing value of small cities, about the regulation of building heights, and zoning for separate uses. He showed his admiration for the City Beautiful movement which had spread through America at the turn of the century: its civic pride and acknowledgement of the expert, its cleaner streets and generous park systems, its ambitious civic centres planned, and occasionally built, in the classical style, in all these he saw a dynamic reforming spirit.[106] And there were other topics less closely related to the theme of planning: drink, museums, neo-Georgian architecture. In a sense, *Where the Great City Stands* was a summary of Ashbee's work and ideas in the ten years since the liquidation of the Guild: the Fraternity House on Cheyne Walk, the Campden School of Arts and Crafts, even the League to Enforce Peace, all make an appearance. It was a mixture liable to puzzle reviewers, but a biographer understands. In Ashbee's case it is usually his life which throws light on his writings, not the other way around.

At the heart of the book was a sense of the city as a progressive social force, expressing the aspirations of the democracy towards a finer life. This was the new element in Ashbee's ideas, more a focus of hope than a specific model or programme for reform. From one point of view it seemed to have displaced the old idea of the Guild, for it was a larger and perhaps more realistic concept, and one which met his demand for more organization in the arts. But from another point of view, it was simply a sense of context, an intellectual vessel in which his earlier ideas would be carried, not greatly changed in themselves, but with greater force and a broader application. His favourite themes, education, the Arts and Crafts, the limitation of machinery, recurred throughout the book. And near the end he told the story of how he had been asked to advise on the setting up of an art institute 'in one of the great American cities of the Middle West'.[107] His advice was drastic: set on one side all thought of conventional art galleries or art schools, bring together a group of practising craftsmen, give them a setting in which to practise all the

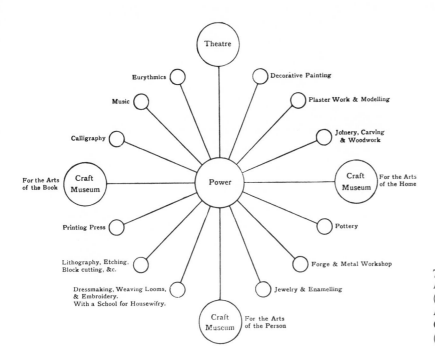

72. Diagram of an
Art Institute.
(From C. R.
Ashbee, *Where the
Great City Stands*
(1917), plate 98.)

arts, and endow them to teach and exhibit, but above all to perform and produce.
Each city should create such a cultural powerhouse in its midst (Plate 72).[108] The
idea was tangible, if Utopian, specifically civic, and had not been met with before
in Ashbee's writings in just this form.[109] But it had a pedigree, it was a harking
back. It revived the arguments from *Should We Stop Teaching Art*, and probably
also the scheme for an Arts and Crafts gallery on Kingsway—Ashbee's diagrams
were perhaps adapted from that. And then, at the heart of the art institute, there
was the Guild of Handicraft, the idea which had inspired Ashbee all his life. Housed
as it might have been in the sparkling stone of a civic centre in the Middle West,
the art institute would still have had its Charley Downer in the forge, its Bill Hardiman in the modelling shop.

The interest of *Where the Great City Stands* lies in Ashbee's peculiarly vital and
social sense of the city, qualities which the city borrowed, so as to speak, from
the Guild. It probably did not make any timely contribution to the developing
technical literature of town planning or urban government, but then it was not
addressed to a purely professional audience.[110] It is worth reading for Ashbee's
sense of the complexity of cities, of how they are made up of people and not just
streets, a social more than a physical fabric.[111] He knew what cities could express,
and that there might be an element of idealism in that. The title of the book, taken
from a favourite passage of Whitman, was its best summary:

Where women walk in public processions in the streets the same as
    the men,
Where they enter the public assembly and take places the same as
    the men;
Where the city of the faithfulest friends stands,
Where the city of the cleanliness of the sexes stands,
Where the city of the healthiest fathers stands,
Where the city of the best-bodied mothers stands,
There the great city stands.[112]

73. Ashbee's students at the Sultania Training College in Cairo, performing *As You Like It*.

74. Ashbee and friends on an island in the Nile.

Where the Great City Stands was published in December 1917, by which time Ashbee was back in Cairo. With his teaching contract due to end in the summer, he decided that his students should put all their energies into a performance of *As You Like It*, played 'as Shakespeare and William Poel would have rendered it', in local costume (Plate 73).[113] It was an experiment very much in the tradition of the Guild theatricals, and a good example of Ashbee's cultural imperialism: just as, in the United States or South Africa, he spoke of England as 'a principle', so now he spoke of Shakespeare as 'universal'. When a friend suggested that some of the literary traditions of the Elizabethans might be foreign to his students, he replied, 'those "brown boys" may even understand Shakespeare better than we'.[114] It was not, he argued, the gap between the cultures of England and Egypt which posed problems, so much as the gap between pre-industrial culture, whether Elizabethan or Egyptian, with its sense of beauty and idealism, and the materialistic culture of the modern Englishman. When the play was performed in April he felt vindicated: the Forest of Arden shepherds seemed to him quite at home as Fellaheen, and, as he wrote to Janet, 'Nothing can give *any* idea of the beauty of the colour . . .'.[115] After the play was over, he invited the whole cast to spend three days with him on an island in the Nile, where he could play at being the banished Duke (Plate 74). The students were to bring a blanket and towel, enough food and water, and possibly a book of verses. 'I will also', Ashbee announced, 'ask Whaba to bring the football.'[116] It was an oddly successful conclusion to his short and controversial career as a professional teacher.

The question of what he was to do when his contract ended was urgent, and he debated it with Janet through the slow and unreliable post. He still thought of Campden as his home and hoped to revive some sort of Guild activity there; but Janet had had enough of the Cotswolds: 'as we are on WILL NOTS—I *will not* stay here another winter alone with the children if you are away . . . Nothing will induce me to go through another winter like the 2 last have been, and National Causes leave me absolutely cold.'[117] In the end the problem was solved in a quite unexpected way. Ronald Storrs, the new Military Governor of Jerusalem, invited Ashbee to come to Jerusalem during the summer and advise on town planning.[118]

The uncertainties of war had taught even Ashbee not to put too much hope in such invitations; but it sounded interesting and he went.

His task in Jerusalem was to report on how local crafts and industries could be revived within the context of the repair and general planning of the Holy City, captured in December 1917 from the Turks; the military government were interpreting their responsibilities in a broad and imaginative way. It was a brief well suited to the author of *Where the Great City Stands*, and in fact it was partly because of the book that he was invited: the new city engineer had read and admired it. He threw himself into the work of gathering material, and during July and August he could be seen inspecting a Zionist knitting factory, or riding out into the villages to engage masons, or drinking coffee diplomatically with the Grand Mufti.[119] His report was complete by September, and he wrote to Janet telling her of all the things he hoped to do:

There's an immense deal one could carry through—given the power. The Mosques, and the Churches, and the Citadel that has not been touched since the time of Soleyman the Magnificent,—there are all the workshops and the Arts and Crafts to start again, paralized by the war, there are the bazaars or Súks to repair and reopen, the Guild organizations to start again, schools to establish, building permits to attend to and thousands of women to set off again at the most beautiful embroidery you ever saw . . . [120]

The report was a thorough document, illustrated with excellent photographs of surviving crafts, and it applied Geddes's survey technique so far as the limits of Ashbee's brief allowed.[121] It was well received by the authorities, but there was a question whether money could be found to implement it, and particularly whether a salary could be found for Ashbee to take charge.[122] September passed without a decision, while he waited to go back to England; and it was not until late October that the military authorities in Palestine decided that there could be no money for the work or for his salary. But Ronald Storrs, who had originally commissioned the report, was determined that Ashbee should be appointed, and promised to find a salary from other sources.[123] After all the difficulties and disappointments of the past ten years, Ashbee must have rejoiced to feel that his abilities were appreciated.

He sailed for England late in November. Back in Campden he gathered together the few remaining Guildsmen, for the new work which he had in prospect in Jerusalem meant that there had to be endings too. On 25 January 1919 seven Guildsmen gathered round the stove in Alec Miller's workshop for the last meeting of the Guild of Handicraft. They talked about what should happen to the Guild estate; Ashbee said something about the essence of the Guild being in the idea that inspired it, not in the tools and the workshops; and Alec Miller made a short speech on behalf of the Guildsmen, paying tribute to Ashbee.[124] The atmosphere of the meeting must have been a little unreal, for in fact the Guild had faded away in the years since liquidation without anyone quite being able to say when it had gone; and the craftsmen still working in the mill, Jim Pyment, George Hart, Alec Miller and others, had long been well established in their own right. But during the war years Ashbee had cherished hopes of reviving the Guild, of some recasting of his ideal. Now, with a new chapter opening in his own career, he finally gave up those hopes, and at that meeting, with the Cotswold hills outside covered in snow, the Guild of Handicraft formally ceased to exist.

CHAPTER SEVEN
JERUSALEM
1919–1922

THE HOLY CITY

Topographical artists in the nineteenth century would often take their stand on the Mount of Olives to the east of Jerusalem, or higher up on Mount Scopus, so that the Holy City lay before them, entire and self-contained; from that point of view it was an image of great power and antiquity. 'Walk about Sion and go round about the towers thereof. Mark well her bulwarks, set up her houses that ye may tell them that come after.'[1] In the distance, a few monuments stood out, the turquoise splendour of the Dome of the Rock, some minarets and the bulk of the Church of the Holy Sepulchre. For the rest the roofs of Jerusalem's houses, some roughly domed, spread like a web between the walls, the houses so interlocked and overlapping that they seemed like one continuous habitat; the walls themselves ragged and eroded by centuries of pilfering and decay, for Jerusalem was a cannibal city in its architecture, built out of its own ruins. What the artist saw was only the upper layer of an archaeology stained with blood: the kingdom of the Jews displaced by Roman rule; then Christian Byzantium, Islam with the building of the Dome of the Rock, the crusaders from the West in 1099 and the Mamluks of Egypt in the Middle Ages; the Ottoman Turks took power in 1517 and their rule lasted exactly four hundred years until General Allenby took Jerusalem from them. When the Western Allies dismembered the decaying Ottoman Empire at the end of the First World War they talked not of 'Empire' but of 'Spheres of Influence'; but they were the last in a succession of imperial conquerors for all that.

The sense of Jerusalem as a 'Holy City' could perhaps be preserved from a distance. But visitors received a very different impression when they passed through the gates and into the Old City itself. David Street and Christian Street ran along the lines of a Roman encampment to the principal points of the compass, dividing the city up into quarters, one each for Moslems, Christians, Armenians and Jews. For the rest it was a warren of alleys, not so much streets as narrow spaces behind and between the close-packed introverted courtyard houses; sometimes they would be built over the debris of earlier buildings, sometimes under the structure of later ones; in places they were filthy and deep in dung. This was not what the insular Victorian visitor expected of the Holy City. 'If the traveller have the courage to inhale the infected air of its close alleys,' reads a guidebook of 1843, 'he will soon hasten out of them, with the deepest impression of the misery and social degradation of their unhappy inhabitants.'[12] Occasionally, the alleys would open out to reveal some ancient and fragmentary relic, the Gothic façade of the Holy Sepulchre, or the pool of Hezekiah; but the only serene space in the whole city was the Haram

75. Jerusalem seen from the Mount of Olives.

es Sharif, the great stone-paved plateau at the south-east corner, a Moslem precinct crowned with the potent presence of the Dome of the Rock, and the Al Aqsa Mosque. This was also, in Jewish tradition, the site of the Temple of Solomon, and long rows of pious Jews would stand outside its enclosure along the Wailing Wall, praying for the rebuilding of the Temple. Of Spanish, Oriental, East European or Russian origin, they lived in the poverty-stricken Jewish quarter nearby, barely sustained by foreign alms, and devoting themselves to the pious fulfilment of the prescriptions of the Torah. This was the Holy City to which Ashbee came, its poverty and squalor only deepened by the violence of war.

It was not, of course, all that there was to modern Jerusalem. Outside the walls to the east lay the barren ravine of the Kidron Valley and the Mount of Olives, open land but for a scattering of Jewish tombs and the Christian sites of pilgrimage; but then to the north and west there were the modern suburbs—Arabs to the north, Jews to the west—whose huddled roofs of tile and corrugated iron touched the city walls at one or two points. It was in the west that growth was greatest, as the number of Jewish immigrants in the late nineteenth century increased; the pogroms in tsarist Russia in the 1880s brought many refugees; Zionism, the belief in a 'Jewish National Home', brought many more to the City of David and Solomon. As a movement, Zionism had its roots in the Jewish communities of Eastern and Central Europe. The Viennese politician Theodor Herzl was its founding father, but when he died in 1904 leadership passed to a Russian-born scientist working at the University of Manchester, Chaim Weizmann, a persuasive and, as things turned out, influential figure. The Jewish population of Jerusalem in 1896 was 28,000 compared with 16,000 Arabs; in 1912 the comparable figures were 45,000 and 25,000.[3] By the time of the First World War the main street of Jerusalem lay quite outside the Old City along the Jaffa Road, which ran through the western suburbs between foreign consulates, shops and hotels.

With its Jewish majority, Jerusalem was not typical of Palestine. At the first reliable census in 1922, there were 83,000 Jews in Palestine, out of a total population of 752,000, most of whom were Arabs. And yet Jewish, and particularly Zionist, interests were strong after the First World War, because they had the support of the British Government. In December 1916 Lloyd George and Balfour had succeeded Asquith and Grey as prime minister and foreign secretary; both supported Zionism from personal conviction, and from a sense of political advantage. They hoped to establish the Jews as a client people in Palestine and so buttress the British presence around the Suez Canal; they also hoped that Zionists in the United States and in Russia, whom they believed to be men of great wealth and influence, could help to bring their governments in behind the Allies, then at their weakest. Both these political considerations turned out to be irrelevant; but not before the British War Cabinet in November 1917 had issued the Balfour Declaration, which stated the British Government's support for the establishment of a 'Jewish National Home' in Palestine. The civil and religious rights of the existing 'non-Jewish' inhabitants of Palestine would, it was said, be respected.[4] Much of the troubled history of modern Palestine descends from the Balfour Declaration and its appallingly ambiguous wording. That the 'Jewish National Home' would be a stage on the road towards statehood, a prelude to the establishment of a Jewish state in Palestine, was the expectation of many Zionists and the fear, increasingly justified, of the

Arab population.[5] The British Government, on the other hand, persuaded by political pressure at home and an Evangelical Protestant conscience, presented itself simply as settling a much persecuted people in the land of their fathers; committing itself thereby to a new and latter-day colonialism on behalf of the Jewish people.

Half Jewish though he was, Ashbee brought to Palestine much the same attitudes and stereotypes as other British officials, and a rather greater sympathy for the Arabs than for the Jews. 'Through all the many types here,' he wrote in 1918, 'the Jew is distinguishable, lean, mean, griping, hard-featured, inquisitive, brainy, and every now and then, especially in the faces of the young men, with that look of curious dreamy intelligence discerning God, singly, far away through everything.'[6] The usual Anglo-Saxon prejudices are here: the faint sense of physical revulsion, the assumption of financial greed; but there is also a sense of Jewish intellect and idealism. Ashbee hated the Haluca Jews of the Old City as he hated the idle, sallow, over-dressed, leech-like votaries of any faith; but in the Zionism of the younger immigrants, with its strains of Tolstoy, socialism and a love of the land coming out of Russia, there were echoes of his own idealism; if only they had not been so arrogantly self-absorbed.[7]

For the Arabs he had great, if occasionally patronizing, respect. He had the kind of intellectual sympathy which falls easily in love with another way of life, and in Egypt he had fallen in love with that of the Arabs. To Dickinson he described them as 'dreamy, fatalist, aristocratic', the Zionists as 'tearing, strenuous, intellectual, nervy'; and to Janet he wrote that the Arab is 'not so clever but in many ways he's so much nicer than the Jew: not such a Modernist or Democrat but so much more of a gentleman'.[8] Interestingly, these antithetical stereotypes of Arab and Jew echo the values which shaped his own career. All his life he had been fighting against narrow, thrusting men who measured success in economic terms; at their worst the Zionists took this part; at their best they recalled his own frenetic idealism of the London years. The Arabs, on the other hand, with their ancient culture, seemed to stand for some of the things he valued most, particularly in the Campden years: they were like the land to him, large and passive, the cradle of craftsmanship. And yet, he never really saw them clearly as he did the Jews, perhaps because their language and their culture were learnt, for him; Arabs in his Journals are not so much individuals as types, representatives of a culture.

Ashbee sailed back to Jerusalem in February 1919, full of enthusiasm, running ahead of himself as usual, planning a great school of archaeology before he had even cleaned the muck from the streets.[9] He was going where his tastes would not normally have led him, as they would to northern France, or Sicily, or the Cotswolds; Jerusalem stood rather outside his sense of history. But the opportunity it offered was so great that he could easily embrace its foreignness; the revival of crafts, technical education, historic buildings and town planning were all to be part of his new post, all his old enthusiasms. On board the S.S. *Aronda*, sailing from Malta, he perhaps looked back to the time of the Guild, an episode which had been so satisfying and so all-consuming, which had given his life a shape and a direction. The ten years that had elapsed since liquidation had been an unsatisfactory decade: so many schemes that led to nothing, his domestic life disrupted by the arrival of children, and all the disorientations of the war. Now, with Jerusalem, it was as if he was being given a second career, another chance to reach Utopia.

76. Janet Ashbee with Mary, Felicity, Helen and Prue.

He did not underestimate the difficulties, recognized the contrast, as he wrote in *The Times*, 'between the Jerusalem of man's imagination ... and the actual Jerusalem left us by the Turk ... a picturesque but filthy medieval town ...'.[10] But he saw this contrast as a challenge: his job would be to clear away the detritus of the recent past and reveal 'the idea behind', to reveal what had made Jerusalem a 'holy city' for Jews, Christians and Moslems and so, in his judgement, a city of the mind. That the history of this Holy City was spattered with blood; that the more sacred it was to the different religious groups the more murderous they became towards each other, did not give him pause. Like others in the British administration, his attitude was secular and ecumenical: the Holy City was to be preserved as part of the history of the human spirit; this monument to centuries of religious belief, bloodshed and fanaticism was to be blandly cradled in the relativism of British imperial rule. So strong in Ashbee was this anti-sectarian ideal that he could even bring himself to say of the Dome of the Rock that it was not Jewish, not Christian, 'not even Moslem', but a building holy for all by its beauty.[11]

Janet followed him in the late spring, bringing the children with her. There were four of them now, a neatly descending sequence of girls (Plate 76), ranging from the capable Mary, now eight and old enough to help with the others, to the eighteen-month-old Prudence, who had come into the world while her father was in Egypt. Ashbee had busied himself arranging a house for them, and now that he had challenging work, respect, and an interesting post he felt, domestically, a little more in the ascendant. He had hired a plump and friendly cook called Haani, whose glass eye mesmerized the children, and a male servant called Hassan. He showed his family over the house and the girls settled who would sleep where; then he turned to Janet and explained that he would have one bedroom and she another. It was done, like his proposal of marriage, more than twenty years before, quite without preamble.[12]

This was only a temporary home, and there were further moves before they settled in a pleasant house in the Wadi el Joz below Mount Scopus, a quarter which would be called a suburb in relation to the city but seemed like country to the girls, surrounded by cornfields and olive trees. The only furniture they could get was makeshift, but it suited their tastes, and a few tiles let into the sideboard, some hammered copper Armenian dishes, and a serving girl from Bethlehem, her dress embroidered with fourteenth-century cross-stitching, all lent an air of distinction to their entertaining.[13] The older girls went off to school at the American Colony, a commune of gentle people waiting for the Second Coming, who gave a good, eccentric start to their education; and Janet, with all those frozen winters in the Norman Chapel behind her, seemed to mellow: her letters were now less hectic, and less amusing. Providing her husband's colleagues were intelligent, she would quite relish being a government wife.

The government on whose fringe Ashbee now found himself was a military one, the Occupied Enemy Territory Administration, under the overall command of General Allenby. Its standing derived from the fact of conquest, its task was to maintain the *status quo* in Palestine. The soldiers, though not particularly well equipped for colonial administration, were suited to the appalling problems left by the war, poverty, refugees, the collapse of government; less happy as the instruments of the Balfour Declaration. Most of them sympathized with the Arabs, and some had been involved in the Arab revolt in the Hejaz in 1916; they saw the Declaration as a betrayal of earlier British support for Arab nationalism, an injustice in Palestine and a political impossibility. By the time Ashbee arrived in the spring of 1919, the Administration was some fifteen months old and had reached a fairly settled position of opposition to the Zionist-influenced policy of the government in London.[14]

The administration presented itself to Ashbee chiefly in the person of Ronald Storrs, Military Governor of Jerusalem. A child of the privileged clerisy—his father had been a clergyman in Belgravia—Storrs had spent the first twenty years or so of his career as an administrator in Egypt, mitigating any narrowness of outlook in the British community in Cairo—the Turf Club point of view—by his growing acquaintance with and sympathy for what Europeans called 'oriental subtlety'; he had, he claimed, an *anima naturaliter Levantina*, and enjoyed nothing better than haggling with Moslem dealers in colloquial Arabic; he often got the best of them. He was an extraordinarily, and not quite exclusively, clever man, with an engaging way of reducing almost everything to the level of good manners. He wrote prose which combined the stateliness of Gibbon with the wordy subtlety of Henry James, and still managed to say something; and yet one wondered, in his subtlety and taste for the surface relations of diplomacy, whether anything mattered except words. No Zionist, he cultivated them, and was met by their mistrust.[15]

He was also a man of taste, who took more pleasure in the conservation of Arab monuments than in anything else in Egyptian politics and administration, and built up a fine collection of ikons, marbles and oriental carpets; one of his first and characteristic acts in Jerusalem was to issue an edict forbidding the use of stucco and corrugated iron in the Old City.[16] Beside the intellectual elegance of Storrs, eighteen years his junior, Ashbee's enthusiasms may have seemed unsophisticated; and yet he was delighted by 'our cheering brilliant governor', finding him 'full of fire, full of vigour . . . mercurial, brainy . . .'.[17]

Apart from Storrs, Ashbee's closest colleague was Ernest Richmond, son of the painter W. B. Richmond who had been a supporter of the Guild in its early days. Richmond was an architect, had worked in Egypt before the war for the Comité pour la Conservation des Monuments de l'Art Arabe, and had shared a flat in Cairo with Storrs. (It was he, in fact, who showed Storrs that the way to get to know Arabic and the Egyptians was to say the first thing that came into your head, sense

77. Ashbee as Civic Adviser in Jerusalem.

or nonsense.[18]) Like Ashbee, he had been called to Jerusalem in the early summer of 1918, to report on the structural condition of the Moslem shrines in the Haram es Sharif, particularly the Dome of the Rock, whose wind-racked north-west façade had suffered terribly in the winter of 1917–18. His responsibilities bordered on Ashbee's, they shared an office while Ashbee was preparing his report, and they got on well together. 'I count it one of the lucky chances of life', Ashbee told Janet, 'to have fallen in with one so sympathetic and of my own *"Weltanschauung"*'.[19] Ashbee's world view would not normally have comprehended someone like Richmond, who was given to brooding on life and its meaninglessness in a way not far removed from the fatalism of the Arabs, among whom he had many good friends; but his belief was of such a subtle, inward and melancholy kind that Ashbee could tease him and not feel challenged by it.[20] Sadly, Richmond's work on the Haram was complete in about a year, so only a few months after Ashbee had got back to Jerusalem, his most symapathetic colleague was taken from him.

Ashbee's title in Jerusalem was 'Civic Adviser', borrowed, he said, from the American habit of appointing an outside expert to report on a city's problems (Plate 77).[21] It was not a government post, since the military administration had not felt able to pay for the work Ashbee had recommended in his report; he was attached to the Pro-Jerusalem Society, a voluntary association set up by Storrs in September 1918 to preserve the amenities and antiquities of Jerusalem and foster its cultural life, aims as dear to him as any in the Holy City but not proper to a military administration. The Society paid Ashbee's salary, and he became its secretary and principal officer. During its eight years of life, and in a steadily worsening political situation, the Pro-Jerusalem Society remained Storrs's most cherished venture; not least because it was only round its council table that he could gather, besides scholars and architects, *all* the leaders of the city's political and religious groups: the Mayor and the Mufti, the Franciscan Custodian of the Holy Land, the Greek and Armenian

Patriarchs, the Chief Rabbi, the Chairman of the Zionist Commission and the Right Reverend the Anglican Bishop in Jerusalem.[22] Its meetings were conducted in French (with occasional asides in Arabic, Turkish, Hebrew and Armenian) and its members, however violently they might disagree on other issues, were united in their love of the Holy City; that in itself, for liberal administrators like Ashbee and Storrs, was commendation enough.[23]

Ashbee had an office in the governorate and was accepted by the soldiers as a colleague; they called him 'Civics'. One member of the administration who first met him in 1919 recalled 'a distinguished looking, loosely grown man in his middle fifties ... He walked about Jerusalem with the lope of a Bedu ... maddeningly vague and unbelievably clever.'[24] If they did not always understand what he was driving at, much could be forgiven in post-war Jerusalem, where the work of reconstruction was so unfamiliar and so full of hope. 'A bit of a Jewish showman, actor-Manager, he was maddening to work with. He was often laughing up his sleeve, or talking in a language far ahead of the era in which he was living.'[25] It was an arrangement which suited Ashbee, leaving him uncluttered by bureaucracy, at least for a time.

WORK UNDER THE MILITARY ADMINISTRATION, 1919–1920

However ecumenical its membership might be, the Pro-Jerusalem Society was limited in effect by existing interests; it was, after all, seeking to insert yet another, and a distinctly modern, point of view into a city already richly overlaid with values. The great religions took a jealous care of their sacred buildings and the Society did not intervene apart from helping with replacement tiles for the Dome of the Rock. The set pieces of guidebook Jerusalem, the Haram es Sharif, the Holy Sepulchre, the Wailing Wall, were outside its scope, so that its work could seem marginal; but Ashbee did not see it in that way. His view of Jerusalem was coloured by a romantic sense of the vernacular, and for him the essence of the Holy City lay in its secular and traditional fabric, its domed and interlocking houses, the pattern of its streets and markets (Plate 78), the definition it enjoyed as a walled city; it was built, he wrote, 'like an ant heap or a pack of cards'.[26] That was what he aimed to protect and enhance, and was able to do so because another of Storrs's early edicts had forbidden all building and demolition work without permission; Ashbee was given the job of vetting the applications and he dealt with five hundred in the first eighteen months, taking tradition as his guide in the Old City: red tiles were forbidden and low domed roofs insisted upon.[27]

Of special projects which the Society undertook, the first was the repair of the sûqs or bazaars, long covered streets lined with booths and lit with pencil-like shafts of light from covered openings in their vaulted roofs. The finest was the fourteenth-century Sûq el Qattanin, the old cotton market, which opened at its eastern end on to the Haram under a magnificent semi-domed portal (Plate 79). It was full of dung and rubbish, the doors of the booths had been used for firewood by the Turks, and part of the building was being gradually shaken to pieces by the twenty-horsepower engine of a flour mill. The Society spent £1,000 repairing it and bringing it back into use, and only just in time, for in mid-February 1920 Jerusalem

78. The streets of Jerusalem. 79. The Sûq el Qattanin.

was hit by a freak snowstorm which ravaged its more dilapidated buildings. In some of the booths, when cleared, Ashbee installed looms for the weaving industry he aimed to revive.[28]

The revival of traditional crafts had always been part of his plan, less for economic than for social reasons. He did not expect them to transform the economy of Jerusalem, recognizing that the Holy City would continue to depend on foreign alms; but he thought they would mitigate the idleness and parasitism which he believed that dependence encouraged. They were part of the traditional atmosphere of the city and would help to keep people busy. He thought that 'Work with the hands, the creative work, the work of the imagination applied to a man's personal labour, keeps men from empty political speculation. For every craftsman we create, we create also a potential citizen; for every craftsman we waste, we fashion a discontented effendi.'[29] Looms had been set up in Jerusalem immediately after the war by the American Red Cross in a similar spirit, to provide work for refugees, chiefly Armenian; Ashbee saw their potential in peacetime. A manager was appointed to run the workshops under the faintly Arts and Crafts style of the 'Jerusalem Looms' and by the end of the first year they were employing about seventy people producing cloth of a traditional pattern (Plate 80). It was, Ashbee wrote, 'financially a success far beyond our expectations. All *that* is Armenian and Muslim . . .'[30]

180

80. The apprentices of the Jerusalem Looms. (From C. R. Ashbee (ed.), *Jerusalem 1918–1920* (1921), plate 62.)

The Jerusalem Looms was later joined by the Dome of the Rock Potteries. Richmond's research, written up in June 1919, showed that about 26,000 tiles on the Dome of the Rock needed to be replaced, principally on the north and west sides; he also showed that furnaces of the eighteenth or early nineteenth century survived in the Haram.[31] Here was a chance to make replica tiles and revive a useful craft, if only the original methods could be rediscovered. Storrs recalled a Turkish bath tiled all over in delicate blues by an Armenian potter, David Ohanessian, at Sledmere in the East Riding of Yorkshire, home of the diplomat Mark Sykes, a romantic figure in Near Eastern affairs; Ashbee recalled how William De Morgan had passed on to him recipes and materials in 1909, urging him to start a pottery in Campden. Ohanessian was summoned from Damascus and the De Morgan materials were brought from England; tile-makers from Kutahia in Turkey, where the art had been revived before the war, were also brought in, and Ohanessian was astonished to find that De Morgan's plans exactly echoed the mediaeval pattern of furnace construction which had been abandoned in Kutahia in favour of a sixteenth-century type. After a few months of experiment, he was ready to start. The Mufti appealed to the Moslem faithful for funds; the Pro-Jerusalem Society, acting as an honest broker in all this, guaranteed Ohanessian's financial stability; and the Dome of the Rock Potteries was established, producing plates, jugs and bowls as well as tiles. Many of the tiles which grace the Dome of the Rock today are of their making, and the potteries still exist.[32]

The fantastic route by which authentic tiles for the Dome of the Rock were arrived at showed the extent to which Ashbee drew on the resources and attitudes of the Arts and Crafts Movement in his Jerusalem work. He spoke of the 're-establishment of workshop traditions', but re-establishment was a phrase more appropriate to some cases than to others.[33] Tile-making such as they now undertook had never, at least in Richmond's judgement, been native to the area; weaving had, but the Jerusalem Looms were started *de novo* and in slightly artificial circumstances; only in the case of the glass-blowers of the Hebron district, a handful of dour and farouche old men who greeted Ashbee's plans to revive their fortunes (of which more later) with their habitual fatalism, was he able to rekindle activity in surviving workshops.[34] In Ashbee's craft revivals the native traditions of Jerusalem were mingled with the skills and techniques of the western Arts and Crafts Movement, and particularly with that sense of the social value of craftsmanship that was so marked in him; Jerusalem was in a line of descent from Whitechapel, Mile End and Chipping Campden.

In rather the same way Ashbee grafted modern western ideas on to the fabric of Jerusalem in his ideas for the city walls. Built of great square blocks of stone by the Turks in about 1540, and so not as old, or as reverenced, as some other parts of the city, the walls were to Ashbee the key to its townscape. In 1919 they were badly in need of protection from the other buildings and the inhabitants of Jerusalem which they had originally been built to defend, from pilfering of the topmost stones, mounds of rubbish, encroachments by neighbouring buildings and (to western eyes) bizarre uses such as the man who used the upper part of St Stephen's Gate for baking dung cakes; prickly pear was growing everywhere.[35] Ashbee employed gangs of labourers to clear all this away and create a rampart walk along the top of the wall right round the city (Plate 81). Where the Turkish sentinels had walked in the sixteenth century to guard the city, the general public should walk now. The two-and-a-half mile circuit would take about an hour and would give a sense, Ashbee thought, of 'the largest, and perhaps the most perfect, mediaeval enceinte in existence. Carcassonne, Chester, Nuremberg, are parallel cases, but none of them comes up to Jerusalem in romantic beauty and grandeur.'[36] It was a good idea. The fact that the route fitted so closely over the historical path of former sentinels redeemed it from the vagueness that so often attaches to the nineteenth-century idea of a public open space; and though it was never completed so as to run right round the city, it is still an effective feature of the Old City today. At the same time, that sharp sense of the difference between public and private space which allowed Ashbee to sweep away encroachments so ruthlessly was not a part of Jerusalem's urban traditions; and in making Jerusalem more explicitly a historical city, Ashbee's rampart walk also made it more modern.

On the west side, south of the Jaffa Gate, the walls of Jerusalem build up to the mass of the Citadel. The Mamluks built it in the fourteenth century on the foundations of a crusader castle, and it incorporates massive stonework from the time of Herod at its north-east corner; it is a dramatic archaeological slice through the military history of Jerusalem, and the crowning image of the great walled city. Here Ashbee concentrated his efforts. It was full of refugees at the end of the war. 'There was much sickness, the misery and squalor were pitiful . . .', he wrote.[37] Some cleaning out was done inside the Citadel, though they made little impression on the debris of a demolished Turkish fortress; outside the fosse or broad surrounding ditch was full of dead carcasses and decomposing matter; this Ashbee managed to clear out completely on the east and south sides and laid the cleared ground out as the Citadel gardens (Plate IV). As the great rough walls advanced and receded the narrow slip of garden followed them round, terraced and stepped with small, rectangular beds. Low trees were planted, the accent always being on 'the solemn masses of the ancient stonework'.[38] Ashbee lavished great care on this garden and probably counted it one of his chief successes in Jerusalem, always thinking of it as a setting for the Citadel more than a garden in its own right.[39]

The Citadel gardens were only a beginning. He planned a whole sequence of parks, gardens and open spaces which would thread their way almost continuously round the Old City on either side of the walls; and among his Jerusalem papers are many small sketches for improving other derelict spaces and stretches of ragged

81. A drawing by Ashbee showing part of his plans for the Rampart Walk.

82. A street in Jerusalem, by the Karaim synagogue.

83. Ashbee's design for the same spot, tidied up and planted.

and decaying building work in the Old City (Plates 82–3).[40] He would tidy them up, repair the masonry, and plant them with herbaceous borders, rows of cypresses, clumps of olive trees and so on. There was more in this than mere prettification, even though trimness is the strongest accent in Ashbee's designs; such planting was necessary in the climate of Jerusalem, Ashbee argued, to reduce its scorched condition.[41] Beyond the walls of the Old City he planned a system of larger parks (Plate 84). At this point his work touched upon general plans for Jerusalem, of which two existed, one drawn up in 1918 by the city engineer, W. H. McLean, the other in 1919 by Patrick Geddes who turned up, uncannily, in Jerusalem to advise the

183

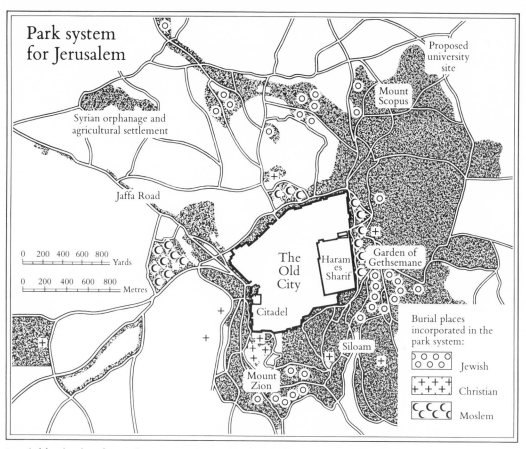

Park system
for Jerusalem

Proposed
university
site

Mount
Scopus

Syrian orphanage and
agricultural settlement

Jaffa Road

0   200 400 600 800
└──┴──┴──┴──┴──┤ Yards

0   200 400 600 800
└──┴──┴──┴──┴──┤ Metres

The
Old
City

Haram
es
Sharif

Garden of
Gethsemane

Citadel

Siloam

Mount
Zion

Burial places
incorporated in the
park system:

Jewish

Christian

Moslem

84. Ashbee's plan for parks in Jerusalem. (Adapted from C. R. Ashbee (ed.), *Jerusalem 1918–1920* (1921), plate 25.)

Zionists on their proposed university. Both plans dealt fairly narrowly with physical development, anticipating the spread of the new city towards the north and west, leaving the land immediately to the south and east of the Old City more or less undeveloped.[42] Ashbee's park system accepted this general approach, and from Mount Zion in the south-west, through the village of Siloam and the Garden of Gethsemane to the slopes of Mount Scopus in the north-east, a swathe of more or less open land between a mile and half a mile deep, was designated. To the north and west, where the new city approached the walls of the old, the ring of parks became a narrow strip; and small tongues and islands of the system were to be formed round burial grounds elsewhere.[43] He was applying here the lessons he had learnt from American planning, from Kansas City for instance; but at the same time the landscaping he planned for Jerusalem did justice to his acute sense of place. The trim and tidy aspect was confined to the gardens by the rampart walk; further out, he did not plan special or ornamental plantation. 'The bulk of the land will, it is hoped, remain under fellahin tillage or even in its present wildness.'[44] The controlling idea of the whole scheme was monumental, historical and symbolic: to preserve a clear space round the Old City and the burial grounds. Ashbee could fairly have written of his park system as he did of McLean's town plan: 'it isolates the Holy City; sets it, so to speak, in the centre of a park, thus recognising the appeal it makes to the world—the city of an idea . . .'.[45]

184

He was pretty continuously keyed up by his work at this time, and wrote to Lowes Dickinson, who was correspondingly depressed by the vengefulness of the Treaty of Versailles:

I am very happy because I'm so busy creating. We have really great things under way. I have started two new industries, restored some old streets, am laying out parks and gardens, saving the walls of El Khuds [it seemed natural to use the Arabic name for Jerusalem], have rebuilt Nebi Samuel, started an apprenticeship system among the weavers, am planning new roads, parks and markets, and making the designs for half-a-dozen important buildings. (In fact I've done more creative work during the last 18 months than I was permitted to do in England during the last 18 years.)[46]

But the military administration worried him. Bureaucratic impediments were beginning to multiply around him, and the soldiers could be maddeningly unco-operative, as when the Chief of Staff, Waters Taylor, destroyed all his plans for a municipal survey by refusing to pay the staff enough.[47]

The general political situation worried him too. Half in and half outside the administration, Ashbee watched political relationships worsen. By the end of 1919 the Zionists had effectively broken off contact with the administration; in February 1920 Arabs attacked Zionist settlements in northern Palestine. In March Herbert Samuel, the most influential Zionist politician in Britain, toured the settlements, ostensibly to advise the administration on finance, actually to decide for himself whether he wanted to head a new civil administration in Palestine. Ashbee and Janet, perhaps because they were not completely identified with the administration, were invited to accompany him.[48] At the beginning of April, during the Moslem festival of Nebi Musa, there were four days of rioting and bloodshed in Jerusalem, most of the victims being Jews of the Old City.[49] Ashbee, who had come to Jerusalem prepared at least to see good in Zionism, now began to see the ambiguities of the 'Jewish National Home' in a harsher light, as a claim to statehood and a direct challenge to the Arabs. During the rioting he wrote to Samuel: 'Until the Zionists frankly and openly disclaim all ideas of a Jewish state they will not win Palestine. But it has got to be an *absolute renunciation*.'[50] The Nebi Musa riots discredited the military administration and hastened the transition to civil government. Ashbee clearly thought that was the way forward, for when Samuel was appointed high commissioner of a civil administration at the end of April, he wrote to congratulate him: 'I can't tell you how many of us here not only long for but see the acute need for a Civil Administration and that soon.'[51] In July, with Samuel arrived in Jerusalem and the civil administration established, Ashbee recorded a second peak of hope in his Jerusalem endeavours: 'All here now is high hope. We shall at last really get constructive things done. The lines are all laid. We have only to go ahead.'[52]

WORK UNDER THE CIVIL ADMINISTRATION, 1920–1922

Given the Zionist sympathies of the British Government, Samuel was an obvious choice. He was a distinguished Liberal politician with seven years' experience in the Cabinet, the first non-baptized Jew to hold such a position; his Englishness was not in doubt, and though he was known for his Zionism, he was famous for his impartiality. Trim and compact in appearance, orderly and forceful in argument, he was a very cerebral politician. Ashbee watched him adopt his 'best bronze mask' in committee and wondered whether he was really a Zionist; or indeed really a Liberal.[53] In consultation with the Foreign Office and with Zionists in Britain, notably Weizmann, Samuel put together an administration that was broadly, though far from exclusively, favourable to Zionism. Storrs was asked to continue as governor of Jerusalem; Wyndham Deedes, a Gentile and a friend of Weizmann's, who believed in Zionism as the fulfilment of Old Testament prophecy, was appointed to the important post of civil secretary; Norman Bentwich, the lawyer son of a distinguished Zionist, was attorney-general. But as assistant civil secretary with special responsibility for Arab affairs, a man of fiercely anti-Zionist views was appointed, on Storrs's suggestion, none other than Ernest Richmond. Ashbee was glad to have him back. It was an appointment which could be seen by outsiders as balancing the others; Richmond was later to see it in another light.[54]

The coming of the civil administration lifted Ashbee's sense of frustration and during the honeymoon period of Samuel's régime (which ended with the Jaffa riots of May Day 1921) he felt able to work hard and confidently. More work was done on some of the original schemes: the rampart walk was all but completed; all the seven towers of the Citadel were repaired and exhibition rooms opened in the David and Hippicus Towers; the Citadel gardens were extended and improved, not without apt comment from Samuel himself:

I hope such a garden will not detract from the dignity of the wall. It ought to look rather grim and farouche. Flowers round its base may make it a little pretty and sentimental with an association of ivy carefully grown over the old cannon and trim gravel paths (with notice boards!) round the Norman castle walls.[55]

New work was also undertaken: exhibitions of local Arts and Crafts were organized, and, at Samuel's suggestion, a diplomatically trilingual system of street-names was hammered out in committee and, in some cases, executed by Ohanessian's Dome of the Rock Potteries in the form of ceramic plaques.[56] But there was, in a sense, less work to be done. Before, the Pro-Jerusalem Society had done the work thought not proper for a military administration; now there were government departments which could properly lay claim to that work, notably the Department of Antiquities and the Jerusalem Town Planning Commission; Pro-Jerusalem's role now seemed more confined.[57]

These changes did not trouble Ashbee at first. He was made secretary of the Jerusalem Town Planning Commission when it was set up in 1921, and this allowed him to deal with building permits in the city as he had done before. To provide a framework of control for these permits, the commission called for a further town plan which Ashbee drew up. McLean's plan of 1918 had aimed to control where new building went and what it looked like. By preserving a narrow strip of land around the Old City free of building, he made it the visual focus of his plan; he then laid out two great arcs around it, one covering the more sacred and precipitous south and east, where 'Buildings may be erected only with the special approval and under special conditions rendering them in harmony with the general scheme.'[58] In the other arc, covering the populous north and west, development

186

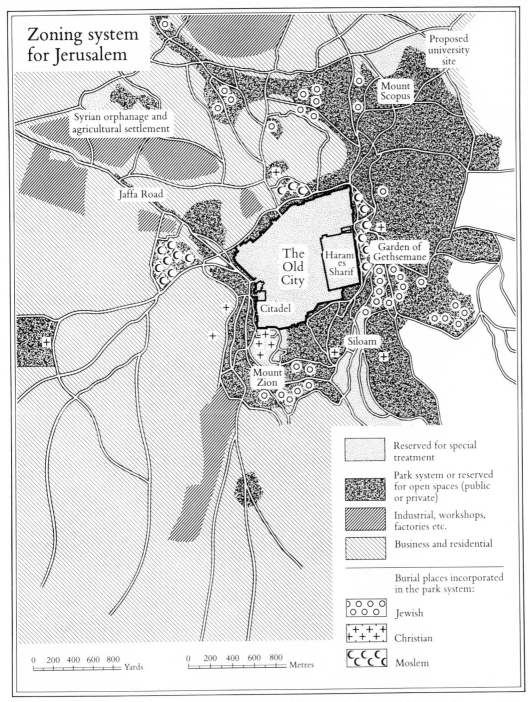

Zoning system for Jerusalem

Proposed university site

Mount Scopus

Syrian orphanage and agricultural settlement

Jaffa Road

The Old City

Haram es Sharif

Garden of Gethsemane

Citadel

Siloam

Mount Zion

	Reserved for special treatment
	Park system or reserved for open spaces (public or private)
	Industrial, workshops, factories etc.
	Business and residential

Burial places incorporated in the park system:

	Jewish
	Christian
	Moslem

0 200 400 600 800 Yards

0 200 400 600 800 Metres

85. Ashbee's plan for the zoning of Jerusalem. (Adapted from C. R. Ashbee (ed.), *Jerusalem 1920–1922* (1924), plate 35.)

was concentrated. Geddes's plan of 1919 was like McLean's except that it looked for a much larger area of parkland to the south and east, specified a business centre and town hall outside the walls, and provided a road system more sensitive to the contours of the site.

Ashbee's plan (Plate 85) was a development from both these, and from his own

Park System of 1920. It isolated the Old City in the same way, kept the south and east open, and anticipated development to the north and west; but the whole exercise was much more comprehensive. It took a larger planning area, including outlying villages, and it incorporated more elements of control: new bye-laws for the city, plans for local planning districts, and an elementary stage of zoning, with industry located on six sites.[59] It was unsophisticated by contemporary western or later Jerusalem standards, but then early modern planning in Jerusalem was necessarily experimental, a layering process by which one plan was superimposed on another, each providing new elements of information and control. In this sense, the Ashbee plan was a considerable advance and, in some respects, it worked; though Ashbee himself was doubtful whether the inhabitants of Jerusalem were ready for the discipline of zoning, his siting of industry was in fact effective.[60]

Back in October 1919, when his Jerusalem endeavours were only beginning, Ashbee's mother died, and he so far away. The Journals record nothing of his feelings, which were perhaps too wide and helpless to be written down. Agnes, who had looked after her mother to the end, scattered her ashes in the garden and closed up the house.[61] It was not until May 1921 that he could get back to England, and he arrived, late and lonely, on a Sunday night, his first experience of post-war London. Bed and breakfast and half a bottle of Bass at the Grosvenor Hotel cost him £1. 10s. Next morning, walking down Oakley Street to the Magpie and Stump, he panicked, fearing to see the bare bones and shell of it all; but Chelsea Embankment in the warm May sunshine charmed him out of that mood. It was 'quite lovely with its decorous houses and its red brick and its white paint and the old church and the irises'.[62] The house, for all his fears, seemed homely and welcoming; everything had been well kept, his mother's piano was in good condition and he had a sense of her presence about the place; so much of his life was there, and he felt content: 'the good and the beauty so utterly outweighs the evil'.[63]

Then he went to see friends, testing the mood of the country. All the time he was looking before and after, into the past and future, in this odd, isolated moment of his life. His Jerusalem appointment had a fixed term to it; would there be new work for him to come back to in England afterwards, could he pick up the threads; or would it be 'retirement'? He lectured to the Art Workers' Guild on his work in Jerusalem, and that went well.[64] On the same day, the librarian at Chelsea Public Library and the head of the Prints Department at the Victoria and Albert Museum asked him for specimens of Essex House Press work. 'Isn't it amusing,' he wrote to Janet, 'now that it's all over, and one is never likely to produce again to come back to England, a sort of Rip Van Winkle, and find oneself regarded as a classic!'[65] But life in the arts, the things that counted, did not seem to him to have survived the war.

The old curiosity shops have increased by a hundredfold—a sure sign that the crafts are dead . . . Strang is dead, Gimson is dead. Roger Fry's Omega Workshops are closed down. The private presses have stopped work. Rothenstein has given up his Gloucestershire home. The Daneway colony like our Guild is no more; except in each case, for a few stragglers.[66]

He wondered whether there would be anything to come home to, where the points of continuity were. If they lived in London, he thought, after Jerusalem, it could only be at the Magpie and Stump.[67]

Janet, however, had other plans for the future; as always, she resisted the atmosphere of that house, and now with so much more strength:

You know my ideal for the children's teens years—not a stereotyped hockey-playing £300 a year girls' school—but a year in Italy, a year in France and a year in Germany; where you and I all have knowledge and can put into them or draw out of them 3 times as much 'stoff' as any school can give with its unnatural class and non-family atmosphere—and air of hurry and competition. This we must *do before we get too old*, so that we don't have to say 'Oh no I am too tired to walk up to Fiesole.'[68]

Ashbee, who thought that formal schooling for girls could go too far, as in his sisters Agnes and Elsa, would have agreed with the educational point.

He returned to find the political atmosphere in Jerusalem had deteriorated once again following the Jaffa riots; Samuel now followed a policy of restricting Jewish immigration to appease the Arabs, and the early concord of his administration had disappeared. But during the summer and autumn, Ashbee was busy with a congenial and creative task which kept his mind off the larger situation. Samuel was proving a good friend to the Pro-Jerusalem Society, and he understood what Ashbee was trying to do, sympathized with his tastes; had he not, back in 1899, paid seven guineas for a piece of Ashbee silver at the Arts and Crafts Exhibition, a salt cup in the form of a little winged figure?[69] In 1921 he asked Ashbee to redecorate Government House on the edge of Mount Scopus, using local craftsmen as far as possible. Ashbee brought in masons, plasterers, blacksmiths, weavers, cabinet-makers and potters, relishing the polyglot confusion; his foremen spoke Greek, French, Arabic, Armenian, German and Turkish. The goodwill that creative work seemed to inspire was so different from politics, he thought. The carpets were bought elsewhere and some silk hangings were woven in Cairo, but the rest of the work was local and Lady Samuel's boudoir, the drawing-room, dining-room and library became airy white spaces touched with the colour of fabrics from the Jerusalem Looms and tiles from Ohanessian's potteries, and dotted with movable furniture to Ashbee's designs (Plate 86).[70]

The dining-room was lit by electroliers, clustered cones of bell-like mosque-lamps and glass beads, the work of the old glass-blowers whom Ashbee had discovered in Hebron, some twenty miles south of Jerusalem, their craft threatened with extinction by western imports and the war (Plate 87). With the Government House commission in mind, Ashbee built them a furnace by Ohanessian's kilns in the via Dolorosa, so that they could start work in Jerusalem. As soon as he had done this, one of the three old men went to Egypt; and the other two decided to harvest their tomatoes. If His Excellency wanted their glass he would have to wait. Ashbee, who had so often preached about the sympathy between agriculture and the crafts, now felt its awkward side. He tried to buy up the existing stocks of the little mosque lamps, but they had been smashed by the blacksmith's guinea-pigs; he tried via the police, to bully the two old men into starting work, but that didn't work: they insisted on being arrested (a bureaucratic impossibility) so that they could ride to Jerusalem in a car. In the end, with the tomatoes harvested, they started work a little late, and produced cascades of beautiful blue-green glass. Ashbee, watching over them, the architect and craft-revivalist in a hurry, reflected that perhaps they knew best.[71]

86. The dining-room, Government House, Jerusalem, as furnished and decorated under Ashbee's care.

87. A Hebron glassworker in his shop in Jerusalem.

In November 1921 Ashbee and Richmond set off on a tour of northern Palestine, looking for the remnants of local craft traditions, extending the work already begun in Jerusalem. As they travelled they read Rabelais and talked of what was poisoning the atmosphere in Jerusalem: 'politics and mistrust—or as Richmond with his burning pro-Arabism would say—the Jew'.[72] Richmond saw clearly that the British Government was Zionist in spirit as far as Palestine was concerned, governing the country with a show of fairness until such time as the Jews, by immigration, should be a majority.[73] Ashbee did not face the situation so squarely, but one can see his sympathies shifting towards the Arabs. When he first came to Jerusalem he had thought very highly of Bezalel, a Zionist school of Arts and Crafts established by Boris Schatz in 1906.[74] His admiration for its Arts and Crafts ideals remained undiminished, but he came to think it 'quasi-sectarian' and he was increasingly appalled by 'The slovenliness, the ugliness, the want of grace, the essential absence of any style which characterize the Palestinian Jew ...'—they were so unvisual, and at the same time so arrogantly ignorant of any other Arts and Crafts work: 'The young men of Bezaleel, and I have conversed with many, think that they are the only instance of such achievement, and their ignorance is pathetic.'[75] With every narrow-minded fanatic who came into his office, Ashbee's sympathies for Zionism diminished; and even in the best of them he could not stomach the old-fashioned idea of a national God—'there is no longer any chosen people ...'.[76] 'All this nationalistic religion', he wrote, after hearing a lecture by Norman Bentwich, '... is reactionary ...'.[77]

He was also now disillusioned with the civil administration, within which his own work had to be carried on and, what is most striking and dismaying in the shift of his attitudes, with Storrs, once the mainstay of his Jerusalem endeavours. In July 1921 he reported on 'a dreadful tea' with the Roman Catholics who wanted to build a basilica in the Garden of Gethsemane; Ashbee was opposed to any new building there but the governor failed to back him up. 'Storrs thought himself so brilliant and clever, but Monsignor Luigi Barlassina played him like a mouse ...'[78] It is not easy to see what lay at the root of this growing distrust, unless it was simply that Ashbee could not follow the Governor into the more sophisticated and pragmatic game of civil politics.

It was an odd event which finally destroyed his loyalty to the civil administration. During 1921, the administration had built a modern water-borne sewage system for the chiefly Jewish north-western suburbs round Me'a She'arim; the money had been provided by the Zionist Commission. In February 1922 the system broke down and deposited a pool of liquid sewage in the valley below the Arab suburb in which the Ashbees lived. The stench was awful. Ashbee asked the administration to find another house for his family, while the Arab householders petitioned for some kind of redress, with little effect. 'Had the situation been reversed', Ashbee reflected, 'and the drains of a Moslem slum voided into the best Jewish quarter, there would have been such an outcry in Israel as would have moved Wall Street and Park Lane.'[79] His request for another house was refused. He then offered his resignation as civic adviser.[80]

The drainage fiasco was only the occasion of his resignation; there was a tangle of deeper causes and it is perhaps surprising, considering how difficult he had always found it to work with colleagues, that he should have lasted so long—four years or so—in Jerusalem. The diminishing role of the Pro-Jerusalem Society probably had something to do with his departure: there were no major new projects under the civil administration and money was short; his original initiatives were increasingly taken over by government departments and he was not sure whether they would survive bureaucracy; for all his restlessness under the soldiers, he looked back with regret to the freebooting days of the military administration when Storrs's word, so firm and so enlightened, was law.[81] And then there was his growing hostility to Zionism and British policy in Palestine. In July 1922 the League of Nations approved the Mandate which sanctioned British rule in Palestine, and the streets of Jerusalem were full of rioting. Ashbee was scornful of the conduct of his colleagues: 'Storrs is still in England playing up for his title ... Deedes is in control and Deedes is parti pris for the Jews ... You cannot, unless you do it by force, govern against the will of 75% of the population.'[82] He had arrived at a settled view, that British government under the Mandate amounted to the imposition of minority interests upon the people of Palestine by force.

Leaving Jerusalem in the autumn of 1922, the Ashbees settled in the little seaside town of Bandol in Provence. It was like waking up out of a dream; Ashbee's preoccupation with that dry, glittering, dirty city collapsed, like a house of cards.[83] But he had reached a point politically where he could not disengage himself from the issue of Zionism, and he spent the next few months making a book out of his Palestine Journals, with their long, dislocated reflections on racial types and hopes for progress in the melting pot of Palestine. The manuscript dealt broadly with the issue of Jew and Arab, though from a settled point of view, for this was a diary of disenchantment. He had started off thinking that Zionists were typically interested in ideas, as he was; and found that they were only interested in power. 'And that is, I suppose,' he wrote, 'why I disbelieve in the Jewish National Home ... I was quite ready to believe. It is my four and a half years' close observation of the rebuilding of the Holy City by other than bricks of the mind that has brought me to this want of faith.'[84] He dealt less broadly, more bitterly, with certain personalities. All evidence of his earlier admiration for Storrs was omitted, and trivial gossip at the governor's expense introduced. Richmond saw it in draft and said it was too personal; the argument could be put as well through personae or embodiments of different points of view; so Ashbee introduced pseudonyms and cut some (only some) of the unkinder passages, and *A Palestine Notebook* was published in December 1923 in England and America.[85] What must have seemed to the general public a volume of interestingly firsthand reflections on the Palestine situation, partisan and in places obscure, was read in Jerusalem as a personal polemic. Richmond reported on its reception:

The Palestine Weekly gave two columns of abuse. The High Commissioner with twinkling eye used the word 'malicious' in speaking of it but his eye still twinkled. Ronald Storrs cannot smile about it. He is quite furiously angry ... The fashion seems to be on the whole thoroughly to enjoy the book and to disapprove of it when speaking in mixed company.[86]

As for the work which Ashbee left behind—his contract was due to run until July

1923—that went on. Clifford Holliday, an architect, was appointed to succeed him and much work was done in conservation and in planning, though the Pro-Jerusalem Society had to be wound up when Storrs resigned in 1926.[87] Richmond resigned in 1924, believing that his continued presence on the administration only served to obscure from the Arabs its true Zionist nature. The Mandate seemed increasingly impossible to sustain. There were violent political disturbances in 1929 and 1936 and in 1939 the British Government renounced its commitment to a Jewish state in Palestine, having spent twenty years fostering just such a thing. The Mandate was abandoned after the Second World War, but its consequences remain.

It would be easy to see Ashbee's work in Jerusalem, which ended so abruptly and on such a sour note, as misconceived, just as the Mandate was misconceived. But politics and planning did not mirror each other so closely, even though Ashbee sometimes felt they did, and the principles for the care and development of Jerusalem worked out under the Mandate have a lasting value. That has become more clear since the building boom which Jerusalem experienced after it was reunified in 1967: intensive speculative development, the easy glamour of luxury hotels and high-rise blocks, a master plan which, if it had been adopted, would have subjected the hills and valleys to a network of large roads and interchanges; western cities knew all this in the 1960s, but the effect on Jerusalem was all the greater for its intensely traditional character and delicate relationship to the landscape. The orgy was short, though some projects, long in the pipeline, are still going up; public protest forced a return to a more conservative policy, and the ideas which McLean, Storrs, Ashbee, Geddes and others had originally roughed out, their respect for the character of the Old City, became a normal part of Jerusalem's planning once more. The gardens recently designed by Ulrik Plesner around the walls of the Old City seem to take up where Ashbee left off; Mayor Teddy Kollek is repairing the rampart walk, and his Jerusalem Foundation recalls the Pro-Jerusalem Society.[88] Jerusalem is inevitably subject to westernization in the twentieth century; better that it should be the conservative planning for which Ashbee stood, sensitive to the special qualities of the Holy City, than the nowhere architecture of international hotels.

CHAPTER EIGHT
IN A KENTISH GARDEN
1923–1942

LOOKING BACK

In January 1923 Ashbee sailed to the United States for another lecture tour. Normally he liked nothing better than the close society of an ocean liner, the brief intense encounters, the discursive talk. But now he felt old and tired and disinclined to reach out to his fellow passengers. 'I'm sort of creeping back into my cold English shell . . .', he wrote helplessly to Janet, 'Everyone I talk with brings home to me how old and of the old world I am become.'[1] He was in no mood for America, and though he lectured in many of the eastern cities and as far west as South Bend, Indiana, his old expansiveness and zest for exploration seemed to have deserted him. 'I keep pretty quiet in my hotel with a few friends here and there.'[2] It was not that he had suddenly grown old, for he was only sixty, but that he had momentarily lost his bearings. In Washington he stood in the shell of the great Episcopal cathedral, unfinished at that time, listening to the wind blowing through the clerestory windows, and felt a kind of sympathy for this giant relic of the English Gothic tradition; it had been designed by Henry Vaughan, one of the most senior of Bodley's pupils, in association with the master himself, and it carried Ashbee back to that office in Gray's Inn Square where he had learnt his architecture; it all seemed very long ago. After three months, he sailed home, thinking he would never come to America again.[3]

'Home' was now the big, spiky Gothic house at Godden Green in Kent where Janet had grown up (Plate 89), and where her mother still lived, bedridden after a stroke, looked after by nurses. It was the obvious, perhaps the only, place for them to go, though it was probably only a temporary solution at first. The Magpie and Stump had been sold in 1921, and Janet seems to have revised her plans for educating the girls peripatetically; they went to English girls' schools at first, though each had a spell in Europe later on.[4] Ashbee might have liked to settle somewhere less prosaic than Godden Green, but as it turned out it suited him perfectly; his requirements, practical and spiritual, were those of a commuter; to live in the country within easy reach of London. And the country it certainly was, for the house stood in a large garden surrounded by fields; and nearby, though screened by trees, was Knole, not the most spectacular of Tudor or Jacobean country houses, but one of the most elaborate and unaltered; such houses had always been, for Ashbee, one of the most perfect architectural expressions of English national life. He came to see himself in these years as a country gentleman *manqué*, and cared, with a new and very practical enthusiasm, for the large and (to the children) deliciously rambling Victorian garden which his father-in-law had laid out, tending

88. Ashbee in the garden at Godden Green.

89. The Forbes's house at Godden Green, Sevenoaks, Kent, as originally designed.

90. The house as remodelled by Ashbee in 1924–5.

this little bit of England in the evening of his life. In the same spirit he took to genealogy, for his own ancestors came from Kent, and he had childhood memories of visits to his great-aunt Keyte at Westwood Court, near Faversham, where she offered them custards 'cool, superlative and stiff in their little white china cups'.[5] Overleaping the unsatisfactory parental generation, he traced his family back through the centuries, emerging triumphantly in the fifteenth century with a certain Robert Ashbee who had taken part in Jack Cade's rebellion and had been pardoned; here was the English yeoman stock, a parentage to be proud of.[6] And so he struck historical roots for himself in Kent, and, in a curious way, was more at home in the genteel atmosphere of Godden Green than he had ever been in Chipping Campden, so much more romantic and problematic. He was growing, in any case, more philosophical; no less anxious to set the world to rights, but less impatient about it.

Within a matter of a few years, the whole pace of his life seemed to slow down. After a career of frenzied and many-sided activity, much of it self-generated, he seemed to subside at Godden Green into an early and uncharacteristic retirement, and passed almost twenty years, fully a third of his adult life, in this quiet way. He still read and wrote and argued and wondered about the state of the world; 'King Charles's Head' made its regular appearance in the conversation; but nothing emerged into which he could throw himself wholeheartedly as he had into the Guild or Jerusalem.[7] It was perhaps a matter of temperament: so much of his extraordinary vitality may have been due to sublimated sexual energies, now dying down; and perhaps also a matter of circumstances: after Campden, and the war, and Jerusalem, he was badly out of touch with London and with professional life.

After they had been at Godden Green for about a year, old Mrs Forbes died, and they decided to buy the house from her trustees. It cannot have been to Ashbee's taste, and it was unmanageably large, so he decided to remodel it, by taking off its top storey, substituting a parapet for gables and eaves, adjusting the plan, and generally substituting for its Gothic austerities an air of neo-Georgian comfort and practicality (Plates 89–90).[8] Janet rejoiced in the more convenient plan, Ashbee in the library and study which he made out of the morning-room. Its walls were lined with his nine thousand or so books, and the Journals were in a place where they could be readily consulted; their fascination for him grew stronger every year. It was in this room that he would read out loud to the girls, taking them, unbelievably, through the *whole* of Morris's *Earthly Paradise*. This was his spy-hole on the world; from here he could write pithy letters to *The Times*, long discursive letters to his friends, articles, and the occasional book. As he had an out-of-doors, a garden persona at Godden Green, the country gentleman, so he had an indoors one, the journalist and man of letters. There had been an element of that in him ever since Cambridge and it had tended, for instance, to set him apart from his colleagues in the Arts and Crafts. Now, in his study, he was no longer architect or designer to any great extent, no longer educator or organizer, but he was still a scribbler, questing, eagerly topical, genuine, wide in his reading and reference and actually, with the passing of the years, less narrow in his aim.

It was in this study, during the mid-twenties, that he wrote an excellent piece of popular art history, a book on caricature. He had started to collect cartoons in about 1915, believing that they revealed 'the ideas behind the war'; he gave a talk on 'Caricature' at the Art Workers' Guild in 1927, and then Chapman and Hall asked him to write an introduction to the subject. In the old days he would have used the history of caricature as a peg on which to hang his own criticisms of society; he had treated the history of architecture in just that way as an extension lecturer in the 1890s, and theatened to do so again in his application for the Slade Professorship in 1910. But now he wrote a relaxed and undogmatic account of Daumier and Gill, Hogarth and Beerbohm, Raemaekers and Rowlandson, full of sympathy for the particular qualities of each artist's work. It was only at the very end that his attention began to shift towards 'the ideas behind', those large truths of life and society which so often mesmerized him, blurring his insights.[9]

From the study too he carried on a campaign against the inadequacies of contemporary planning. His work in Jerusalem had taught him too little to allow him to become directly involved in inter-war planning schemes, too much to allow him to stand by without comment. He wanted strong planning, but always from a specifically conservationist point of view. In the inter-war years, the years of ribbon development in housing, and of the growth of a mass market in cars, he was almost necessarily cast in the role of an embattled armchair critic, for the linear spread of suburbia and the development of the road system threatened what he valued most, the conservation of the past and of the countryside; planning, instead of minimizing the destructive effects of current developments, seemed to encourage them.

He was active in and around Sevenoaks; with a few others he set up the Sevenoaks and District Housing and Town Planning Association in 1924; and he fought against plans to run a bypass road through Knole Park.[10] The fight was successful; but it seemed to Ashbee a sign of the times that anyone should think of destroying Knole Park, and perhaps forcing the house to be closed to the public, for a mere charabanc and joy road, as he called it.[11] On larger issues he could only comment from the sidelines. In 1929 he spoke on the radio, in the early days of the British Broadcasting Corporation, asking 'Can We Save the Countryside?'; and he wrote many trenchant letters to *The Times*:

a lovely countryside is being transformed into a vulgar and unintelligent suburbia (30 May 1927). What we apparently have is a Ministry of Motor Transport; what we need is a Ministry of Transport (29 August 1930). There are many who, as a protection to the public against the anarchy of the road and the destruction of real values, envisage now an intelligent revival of the locked gate, the turnpike and the pale (26 September 1933).

His fiercest denunciation was actually in a private letter, to Fred Griggs in Campden. He wrote simply, 'The enemy to all architecture is the car.'[12]

He would go up to London quite often for meetings, and 1929 was a busy year in that way, for he was made Master of the Art Workers' Guild, a welcome honour, if a little late in the day. While in town he liked to look in on Hodgson's, the antiquarian booksellers in Chancery Lane, or to pick up some choice work he had done at his binder's, Charles McLeish in Little Russell Street. (Such purchases had to be smuggled into the house out of Janet's way, for she found it hard to reconcile his indulgence in such things with his constant reluctance to pay the rates.[13]) On one memorable evening in London he met Lutyens at a dinner of the Armourers' and Brasiers' Company, and they discussed Benson Court, Magdalene College,

91. Ashbee caricatured by Sir Edwin Lutyens, 1929.

Cambridge, a design by Lutyens which would have swept away some old houses in Magdalene Street. The great architect was drunk and could not remember who Ashbee was. 'Yes,' he said, 'I had a letter from Ashbee. Can you tell me what his alternative proposal for the street is?'[14] Ashbee explained, trying to insinuate his own identity, while Lutyens stared at the floor, counting the stars on the carpet. In the end the embarrassing situation was defused, with the help of one of Lutyens's legendary caricatures, Ashbee as a ghostly, bearded figure complete with halo (Plate 91). Twenty years earlier, it would have been galling for Ashbee to look on Lutyens's success, and to feel himself so much the forgotten man; but now he was more philosophical, content to be dismissed as a relic of the 'nineties, a saint in the style of George Bernard Shaw, who should long ago have gone to his reward. Success of the Lutyens kind was simply out of reach.

There was a kind of tranquillity about his life at this time; it invited him to look back, not brooding on the past but reflecting on it, often charitably. Passages in his early life would become clear in his memory and he could revisit them with detachment. For his own children he wrote a short and rather private book about his mother, *'Grannie': A Victorian Cameo*, which took him back through the painful history of mid-Victorian London, the mysteries of business and bibliophiles, the pompously furnished house in Bloomsbury. He deified his mother, of course, and left many things unsaid, but on the other hand he found he could now speak more generously about his father, and he wrote more simply than he had ever done, perhaps because he was confronting the primitive facts of his childhood. Laurence Housman thought it probably the best thing he had written, 'no pose about it, or grinding of any axe, social political or artistic'.[15]

Peckover: The Abbotscourt Papers (1932) was another kind of revisiting, an uncovering of the layers of romantic meaning which Campden (Peckover) and the Norman Chapel (Abbotscourt) held for him. The book had a complicated literary structure, and though Ashbee posed as the 'editor' of these papers on the title-page, it was all fiction, and of his writing. It told an imaginary story of the Norman Chapel changing its architectural shape from age to age, from Norman times through the crusades and the age of Erasmus down to the eighteenth century, adapting itself to the different uses and values of the time, yet always the same, the embodiment of tradition. Interwoven with this was a modern tale of idealists in the Cotswolds, a recasting of parts of the Campden story. Ashbee appeared as 'Harry Vere, Fellow of King's College, Cambridge—capricious journalist and litterateur' (an apt characterization that, at once ambitious and self-deprecating); Alec Miller as the Quaker stonecarver Richard Gurney; and Ethel Coomaraswamy as the mysterious, doom-laden lovable Lady Cecilia, standing in the ruins of her childless marriage, a portrait of the Modern Woman searching for love and integrity outside that institution. And all the time the Norman Chapel gathers a spiritual power to itself through the centuries, so that by the time of Lady Cecilia it stands, like Howard's End, for something more than the human participants in the story; it seems to speak to her. And she, thinking of the house and of the future, says to Richard Gurney (what Ethel Coomaraswamy would never have said to Alec Miller), 'I would like to have a child by you.'[16] Ashbee's writings contain no more curious or imaginative an expression of the place of architecture and history in people's lives.

Campden still fascinated him, and he went back there, as to Cambridge, not for nostalgic reasons but to check that its magic still worked for him. It was a touchstone. He stayed there in 1924 while the Godden Green house was being remodelled, and the surviving Guildsmen were flourishing: Jim Pyment with his building business, Thornton and Downer still in the forge, Alec, as much a sculptor as a carver now, in his studio, and George Hart farming part of the Guild estate at Broad Campden. Quite a colony of craftsmen was growing up in the town and that summer there was a big Arts and Crafts exhibition, its catalogue paying tribute to his pioneering work.[17] Six years later he returned, and reported 'great, and very interesting changes', most of them to do with the work Fred Griggs was doing to protect the character of the town through the Campden Society and the Campden Trust—'mostly composed of "our" people', Ashbee said.[18] It was Griggs who had saved Dover's Hill from being built on in 1926, and seen it transferred as open land to the National Trust. Ashbee admired all this, felt that the work he had begun was bearing fruit after all, and was delighted, when he walked down the High Street, to find that they were remembered. 'I can't tell you', he wrote to Janet, 'how many old women came toddling up to me in the street . . . seized me by the hand and said "*Is* Mrs Ashbee with you—give her my love!" I can't tell you who they all were though I knew their faces. You'll have to come. Forget and forgive—if I can you can!'[19] But for Janet memories of Campden in the war years were too painful, and she would not go back, at least during his lifetime.

America was another touchstone, but on the last occasion, in 1923, the magic had not worked. That was perhaps why, eight years later, he decided to go back, advertised his lectures, and set sail in September 1931. It was a great success. He lectured in New York on Jerusalem—'Toppling Towers and the Holy City Eternal'.[20] At Yale he was due to speak on 'The Gothic and Georgian Revivals and their Meaning' and characteristically abandoned his subject in favour of a stinging critique of the university's Gothic buildings as luxurious, untruthful, gloomily ornate and unrelated to their surroundings.[21] And in New York again he went to St Mark's in-the-Bouwerie to see a dramatization of *Conradin*, a ballad he had written twenty years earlier, while working in Sicily.[22] Here was fame indeed; the twenty-year-old Mary, who accompanied her father, was charmed and astonished to see how he was lionized in the United States. From on board the S.S. *American Farmer*, sailing home, Ashbee wrote happily to H. W. Rolfe, who had first brought him to America in the nineties, 'We've had a lovely time and my feelings towards U.S.A. are once more as of old. "Good old Eagle" has come back to me again!'[23]

In August 1932 Lowes Dickinson died, and the effect on Ashbee, who had seen him only recently on a visit to Godden Green looking well and cheerful, was disabling. It was as if a part of his life had gone, as well as a dear friend. Their springtime undergraduate love had long since changed into an intellectual friendship of a particularly elastic kind. They thought differently and worked differently, and yet it always mattered to Ashbee to tell Dickinson what he was thinking, to hear his response, not necessarily to get his approval. It mattered simply that Dickinson was there, at King's. Janet was in Germany when he died, and saw his obituary in *The Times* by chance. 'No—there is *no* meaning in anything really,' she wrote, 'I am so *so* sorry I am not with you—perhaps to make a sort of bridge back to life without a Goldie in it, unthinkable for you, I expect, after 50 years.'[24] She was right. For Ashbee it was the beginning of the end.

NO LONG FACES

There were other losses almost as great in these years; Edward Carpenter died in 1929, Roger Fry in 1934, though neither left him feeling as absolutely lonely as Dickinson. Good friends and colleagues from the old days of the Arts and Crafts went too, Selwyn Image, Lethaby and Henry Wilson around 1930. Ashbee would scan the obituary columns of *The Times* for familiar names, cutting out the entries and pasting them into the Journals. Sometimes they were people he had hardly known, though their paths had crossed—Aston Webb, the Earl of Crawford and Balcarres—and their deaths reminded him what a late Victorian he was. In 1937 came news of a different kind of passing: a letter telling him that Essex House in the Mile End Road had been pulled down to make way for a cinema.[25] Everything seemed to be slipping away.

He would sit in the study thinking about the past and the future; there were obituaries to be cut out and the Journals had to be got in order. They sat there on the shelves, the residue of fifty years, erratic, personal, often vivid and sometimes sententious entries, interleaved with hundreds of letters; he gave time now to getting them in order, rewriting, or at least recopying, some passages in the clear, angular calligraphic hand of his old age. In the 1920s he had looked back happily on the past; that was the secret of *'Grannie'* and *Peckover*. Now he was worrying about posterity, anxious that the story of the Guild and the quality of its idealism should not be forgotten. He worked over the Journals, picking out the important bits and boiling them down into six fat typescript volumes which he called 'The

Ashbee Memoirs'. There was some thought of publishing, but they were too long for that, and in the end he had four sets typed up, planning to deposit copies in the London Library, King's College, Cambridge and the Library of Congress in Washington.[26] The typing was done by Phoebe Haydon, his old and faithful secretary, who felt her own memories of Cheyne Walk and Chipping Campden come flooding back as she typed, and threatened to charge an extra five pounds for emotional wear and tear.[27]

It was in 1935, while he was in this mood, and sensitive to his reputation, that he received the draft of a learned article on '*William Morris, C. R. Ashbee und das zwanzigste Jahrhundert*'. He was staying at the Hotel Bristol in Cairo at the time, *en route* for Jerusalem, and he wrote to Janet, rejoicing in 'that most interesting essay of the learned German telling me how famous I appear to be!'[28] The learned German was Nikolaus Pevsner, and the article was published in the following year in the *Deutsche Vierteljahrsschrift für Literaturwissenschaft und Geistesgeschichte*.[29] It was a meaty and telling piece in the history of ideas tradition, breathing a bold socialist hope that art would no longer be judged by aesthetic standards but by the good it did for the community. Morris was seen as the first truly modern artist because he dared to concern himself with useful, unaesthetic things, Ashbee as 'a really original and extensive thinker'.[30]

Using such sources as were available to him, chiefly such books as *A Few Chapters in Workshop Re-Construction and Citizenship* and *Craftsmanship in Competitive Industry*, Pevsner presented Ashbee as working out Morris's socialist aesthetic through a mixture of Guild experience and hopeful, wider schemes of reform; what Ashbee would have called 'practical Idealism'. It was just such a picture as Ashbee himself would have drawn, and they parted company only on the question of 'the Machine'; here Pevsner found Ashbee sadly blind to the direction of history, unaware, in the critical years 1900 to 1910, of the coming revelation of the machine aesthetic in Gropius's model factory at the Werkbund exhibition of 1914 and in the establishment of the Bauhaus.[31] Ashbee did not take issue with this; those years were too real, too much a matter of personal experience, for him to be impressed by such determinism. He was not one, like Voysey, to protest at being identified with Modernism. He was flattered by the essay as a whole and wrote to Pevsner, praising the clear and scholarly handling of the subject, and contenting himself, on the question of 'the machine' with the muted comment: 'It has great good in it, but it needs, certainly in England, more intelligent control and direction than it receives.'[32]

By this time, by the second half of the 1930s, the girls were grown up and beginning to leave home. Mary was living in London and sang, for a season, in the chorus at Glyndebourne; Felicity, after studying at the Byam Shaw School, was enjoying some success as a painter: she was still living at Godden Green, running a children's drama group with enormous zest; Helen married an American astronomer, which gave an excuse for a final visit to the United States at Christmas 1938; and Prue, the youngest and sadly never her father's favourite, went to Dresden to study dancing and there got engaged to a penniless young artist, Horst Nessler. Trouble dogged their marriage from the start: the Nazis did not look kindly on his work, and Ashbee, with a strange attack of old-fashioned fatherly convention, refused to give his blessing because there was no settlement on his daughter.[33] The whole affair added to the tensions of these years, as the Godden Green ménage shrank back, and the house came to seem once more unmanageably large. Janet made desperate efforts to get out: there was talk of building a house in the grounds, or of moving elsewhere, even, in 1938, to Bath, but then Ashbee narrowed the choice impossibly by specifying an old man's paradise: 'a *small* 18th C. house with a library and two spare bedrooms . . . a small garden with lots of sun . . . and no cars within sound or smell'.[34] Nothing came of these ideas, and in the end Janet gave up. He seemed to have taken root in the house. It was kinder to leave him there, looking out towards the calm and lovely line of his lawn and trees, playing the country gentleman to the end.[35] The outbreak of war settled the matter once and for all.

Early in 1940, he went into a nursing home for a prostate gland operation, and then it seemed to take him a long time to recover. Two months later he was still in bed at Godden Green, irritated by his slow progress. What he did not know was that he had cancer of the prostate gland, and that a second operation to remove the growth was not possible. Janet, who had assured him that she was not made sick by the sight of blood, pus, urine or any other by-product, but only 'mental unrest or anxiety', decided not to tell him, fearing to destroy his cheerfulness.[36] For two years she lived under this strain; he, though increasingly weak, was as active mentally as he had always been, and, from his bed or deck-chair, carried on a long argument with H. W. Rolfe in California, about the rival virtues of English and American democracy. 'Yet, my dear friend,' he chided Rolfe, 'how strangely, childishly, ignorant you are of English democracy and the way it works . . . Our society here is no more *privileged* than yours . . .'[37] One night two bombs dropped in the garden, scarring the lawn which he had tended for almost twenty years—German bombers lightening their load on the way home. There seemed less for him to live for after that.[38]

He began to be a little feverish again about the history of the Guild. The Memoirs now seemed too long, and he put to Alec Miller the idea of something more specific, 'a human and vividly written history of the G.o.H'.[39] It was like him to see it in that way, the Guild as the important thing, not his career. Miller, though feeling a bit inadequate, agreed to do it and, since he now lived in California too, the load of bulky letters, books and manuscripts despatched from the long-suffering post office at Godden Green redoubled. As the planes flew over Kent during the dark months of the blitz, Ashbee could enjoy the curious sensation of thinking that his life's work was being chronicled on the sunny shores of the Pacific. The first chapter came back in February 1941, and he was delighted with its sober prose, its evocation of Campden in the early days, its sense of the ideas behind the Guild; nobody else in the Guild could have done it: 'most moving and beautiful', he wrote.[40] The bombers droned on overhead. On 17 April they dropped a parachute mine on the Embankment in Chelsea, destroying Chelsea Old Church and the neighbouring properties. Some of Ashbee's most memorable houses, including 74 Cheyne Walk, were reduced to rubble. He was driven up to London to see the wreckage.[41]

By the end of the year he was so frail that he had to have a nurse to look after him; in the clever hands of Mary Murphy, friend of a friend and a 'pseudo-nurse' as Janet put it, he did not feel quite so much that he was dying.[42] He still pottered among his papers, wondering what his place in history would be, telling himself that there was perhaps 'one little justifiable nook . . . men who had an idea'.[43] At the end of April 1942 Alec's second chapter arrived. 'You have put everything so delicately, so directly and so modestly,' Ashbee told him. 'I hope you will go on with it and in your own way. When we meet I will give you the data of the 13 years in East London . . .'.[44]

He died three weeks later, on 23 May.

When she had dealt with the practical matters, written to his friends and emptied the house, which had been requisitioned by the Army, Janet wanted to be alone and she went for a few weeks to Goathland, on the bleak and beautiful moors of north Yorkshire.[45] She must have been reminded of the time, forty-five years before, when she had stayed not far from there, at Kirby Moorside, trying to get used to the idea of marrying him.

After the war, the house was sold and his property disposed of according to his will; the best of the Journal volumes went to the Library at King's College, Cambridge. Janet went to live at Hest Bank, a genteel and overgrown seaside village on Morecambe Bay in Lancashire, all white stucco houses and grey sea. She lived on there quietly, fighting against arthritis, rejoicing in her grandchildren, and writing daily to her friends, page upon page of the big, round, emphatic, endearing scrawl. Some childhood scruple about not wasting paper had stuck with her for life and she would curl and crowd her parting thoughts and all her love round the narrowest margins and oddest corners of the page, rather than start another sheet. She died on 8 May 1961 having, characteristically, taken the precaution of writing her own obituary; there were to be, she told the readers of the *Lancaster Guardian and Observer*, 'no long faces or mourning at her departure'.[46]

PART TWO

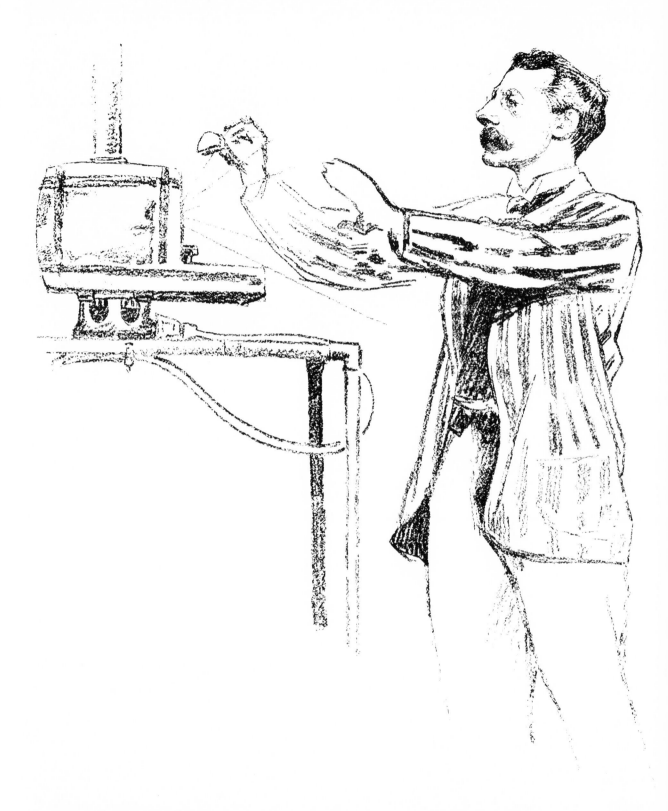

92. Ashbee confronts the enamelling furnace in the workshops of the Guild of Handicraft. There may be an element of pose in this picture, for other sources do not suggest that Ashbee was skilled in enamelling. (From a drawing by George Thomson published in the *Studio*, 1897–8, vol. 12, p. [31].)

CHAPTER NINE
THE ELEMENTS OF DESIGN

THE ARTS AND CRAFTS MOVEMENT

Ashbee's career was the story of many enthusiasms. He was always ready to take up a cause if he felt a progressive spirit in it; he would work at it for some years and then, if it proved intractable to his own ideas, or his circumstances changed, he would put it by. He was not dilettante in this; it was just that his enthusiasms went in phases. However, there was one movement in which he was happy to be involved from his earliest days in East London until the last years of his retirement; it was the frame and context for all his work as a designer; and, in a sense, it set him on his course. It is a good question whether, with his strong literary and intellectual interests, he would ever have turned to architecture and the decorative arts if it had not been for a movement of such intellectual character as the Arts and Crafts. He might have been, like his persona Harry Vere in *Peckover*, a capricious journalist and littérateur.

For the Arts and Crafts was an intensely thoughtful movement. Even though it idealized the humble productions of unlettered craftsmen, its ideals were ambitious in their range and sophisticated in their origins. Ask an Arts and Crafts man to give an account of his work and he would talk not only about techniques and materials, but also about the status of the decorative arts, the uses of wealth, the Industrial Revolution, work, nature, the home, honesty, simplicity and the Middle Ages. It was partly Ruskin who was responsible for this taste for generalities, for he fashioned from the carved detail of mediaeval Venice and the cathedrals of northern France persuasive social and personal myths, the dignity of the mediaeval craftsmen, and his satisfaction in the work; and William Morris too, who saw behind the vernacular buildings of the English countryside the figures of a sturdy but inventive yeomanry, shadowy but appealing. Members of the Arts and Crafts Movement naturally saw things in a double vision—the object never quite distinct from the maker—and when they started talking about art they could easily end up talking about society.

It was an essential, if paradoxical, part of their make-up that they should also be anti-intellectual; set against the idealized Middle Ages of Ruskin and Morris modern architecture and decorative arts seemed to them a dry, dull, theoretical affair, mere paperwork, a commercial pursuit. And so we find distinguished architects standing rapt in admiration before a simple cottage, skilled painters, an ancient treatise in one hand, stumbling through experiments in plaster or enamel, and sophisticated designers, back at the bench, trying to recapture the old uncertainties of the hand. They were not dogmatic about the processes they used, and they did not abandon the use of machinery; they simply kept it on the edge of things. But they did abandon the basic assumption that technology is progressive; they loved to revive discarded and archaic techniques, and looked more often to the past for better ways of making things than to the future. At the time people thought it odd that men of education and professional standing should humble themselves in this way, and that they should question the advances in technology on which the wealth of nineteenth-century Britain was founded. A hundred years later it is still difficult to know how seriously to take the Arts and Crafts; whether to see in it a crisis of confidence among artists, architects and designers, a deep dissatisfaction with the state of industrial society; or something more playful and mundane, not to be burdened by such large significance, romantic escapism, and eccentricity in the English tradition.

The Arts and Crafts was less concerned with what things look like, with style, than with how they were made and, taken as a whole, the objects which the Movement produced present a picture of splendid confusion. They might be plain or elaborately decorated, homely or exotic; they took their cue from Byzantium or Berkshire, the fifth or the fifteenth century. There was no single Arts and Crafts style. And yet there were, in this visual cornucopia, features which expressed the allegiance of their makers, elements of taste rather than of style, if the distinction will stand. There was a Puritan strain which liked things plain and homely and which, rather than decorate an object in the ordinary way, would make its methods of construction and its materials the focus of attention: buttressed walls and obvious riveting, the grain of wood and the texture of woven cloth. And at the same time there was a sensuous and entirely traditional delight in ornament. Many of the techniques which the Arts and Crafts loved to revive, like gesso or 'Limoges' enamelling, were essentially decorative; their natural ornament was slightly flattened and conventionalized but did not lose a sense of its fleshy origins; they controlled their ornament, bounding it with frames and mouldings, balancing it against plain surfaces; and they often gave it a quality of thoughtfulness, drawing on meanings and associations which lift it above mere decoration. Arts and Crafts ornament was, characteristically, serious and sensuous.

They worried a good deal about the dangers of copying the styles of the past, but in practice they drew fruitfully on the example of past work. The pre-industrial vernacular, such things as ladder-back chairs and peasant jewellery, provided them with exemplars for their designs, and a source of romantic associations. There was not generally any question of slavish dependence here, merely of using the past as a point of departure. They also worried about making their work 'too good', too smooth and finished, and preferred to fashion it according to the harsh contrasts of Ruskin's imagination, in which a smooth and perfect finish reveals the deadly influence of the machine, roughness and imperfection the touch of the living craftsman. It is this studied naïveté in Arts and Crafts objects which is most striking when they are seen alongside other work of the same date and standing. The Scottish architect Robert Lorimer, an Arts and Crafts man himself, found an apt phrase for it when he referred to the 'artificial crudeness' of some of the exhibits at the Arts and Crafts Exhibition Society in 1896.[1]

They were a small and self-conscious group, reacting against the mainstream of architecture and decorative arts in their time. As a historian, one wants to qualify their sense of singularity, to point out that their work and attitudes were a natural development from the revival of craftsmanship in the Gothic Revival, and that they were never entirely distinct from the world of commercial art production. But they rarely saw things in that way; they felt themselves to be antithetical, for they took as their mentors some of the fiercest critics of the age. What they saw in the shops they condemned as 'commercial' and went away and designed the opposite. Many of the qualities of Arts and Crafts objects can only be understood as a reaction against more general tastes; their deliberate ordinariness, for instance, is puzzling until it is set against what the Arts and Crafts saw as the showiness of much contemporary design. Of course, late Victorian architecture and decorative arts were much less benighted and much more various than the literature of the Arts and Crafts Movement would give one to believe; and it is only when the Movement is seen in the larger context of contemporary work that it can be properly understood and its stereotypes seen for what they are.

The most influential of these stereotypes arose from the emotive and ill-defined notion of 'the Machine'. According to the Arts and Crafts, the Industrial Revolution may have brought many benefits, but it also caused the degradation of the decorative arts as the old hand processes were displaced by the operations of 'the Machine'; the price of this substitution could be felt in the dull mechanical labour of Britain's factories and in the objects which came out of them, sometimes ill-made, often heavy with pretentious machine-made ornament, in dead and destructive imitation of the craftsmanship of the hand. Quite apart from the doubtful assumption that the appearance of an object will show that it was made either 'by hand' or 'by machine', this story does not fit the facts. It is true that there were great changes in the processes of production during the late eighteenth and nineteenth centuries; but it is far from true that steam power and mechanization replaced earlier processes across the board; and in the particular areas of architecture and the decorative arts their effect was only partial.[2] Factory production and large-scale mechanization were common only in the textile industry; in printing and in ceramics the production process was mechanized only in part. In decorative metalwork and jewellery, lathes, stamping presses and electro-plating were widely used, but finishing was generally done by hand, and small workshops were typical of the trade. In the building trade, the manufacture of parts and materials was increasingly mechanized, but building itself was still traditional hand-work; and furniture also could only be made up by hand. The Arts and Crafts thought of 'the Machine' as a generalized and relentless force; but in practice there were always checks, social, economic and technical, on the wider use of machinery; and there were very few decorative objects at the end of the nineteenth century which could be simply described as 'machine-made' rather than 'hand-made'.

And just as this negative and problematic stereotype of 'the Machine' was not drawn from any full, close or steady view of the circumstances of contemporary industry, so the large claims made for handwork by the Arts and Crafts were not brought to bear on those circumstances. They said that there was more dignity and satisfaction in hand-work than in machine-minding, an argument which, if taken at face value, ought to have turned their attention to those trades in which machine production was commonest. But in fact they confined themselves to architecture and the decorative arts, and often to those trades where machine production had made least inroads. Their anti-machine rhetoric cannot always be taken at face value; and on their lips 'the machine' was neither a descriptive term, nor a banner for reforming industry; it was a dismissive stereotype which served to set the industrial world on one side, and to justify workshops which, however large their claims and radical their craftsmanship, remained comfortably confined to the world of architecture and the decorative arts.

There were, perhaps, other and more familiar developments in that world which had a greater and more direct influence on their attitudes than mechanization. The simple increase in the quantity of production is not irrelevant: the growth in production and consumption as the population grew and levels of wealth rose. And middle-class shopping was important. In early and mid-Victorian shops, goods were not standardized and the customer depended on the shopkeeper for guidance on quality and price; in the late Victorian period larger shops began to appear which sold standardized goods at a fixed price: expertise and personal contact were replaced by a more anonymous commercial system; Heal's, Maple's, Liberty's, Howell and James, Mappin and Webb, were London shops of this kind specializing in the decorative arts; the large new department stores took the process one stage further by actually displaying prices. Buying in the decorative arts had become easier, more impersonal, and accessible to more people, with the choices swayed less by the shopkeeper's recommendation than by the larger force of fashion, fed by an illustrated press.

As for what was bought and the character of Victorian design, no earlier period can have enjoyed so varied and exact a sense of the styles of past civilizations, and while the mainstream of taste flowed in seventeenth- and eighteenth-century channels with a preference for Louis Seize, exotic forms from India, Japan and the Middle East were also common; no earlier period, likewise, had had so wide a range of technical skills available, especially in the field of ornament. There was a taste for density and rooms crowded with furniture, a romantic and sentimental taste which treated the common stock of natural ornament with a whimsical realism. If ornament was spared it was generally a matter of propriety rather than of taste, on objects of lesser dignity and value; for at this as at other times, the principal function of the decorative arts was to embellish domestic wares and so to provide a marker of wealth and social standing.

The people of the Arts and Crafts knew much more about these things which were close at hand and plain to see, then they did about machines in factories which they learnt about through the rhetoric of Ruskin and which, so far as one can tell, they rarely visited. It was arguably the growing involvement of the decorative arts with a modern market economy, and the unusual wealth of skills, styles and ornament, that shaped their reaction. When they saw street upon street of terraced houses, each with its decorated lintel; or row upon row of identical painted china vases, and condemned them as cheap and tawdry, pretentious and mass-produced, they were responding, with a touch of English upper-middle-class *hauteur*, to the sight of the decorative arts being brought into the market place, brightly lit and ticketed, and exercising that primitive form of aesthetic discrimination which assumes that the more often an object is reproduced the less its value becomes. When they set up the ideal of the craft workshop of pre-industrial times, were they not looking for a comforting alternative to the complex and impersonal commercial world, a work-place in which the craftsman would set the standards and not middlemen? And when they designed in their serious and sometimes austere way, so different from the mainstream of taste, were they not moved by the belief that the decorative arts have other purposes than simply underlining social status or promoting the fashionable market; that the architect and designer is an artist who must do what he thinks right?

IDEAS ON ART, ARCHITECTURE AND DESIGN

Ashbee was fond of theorizing and quasi-philosophical speculation—it was his way of taking things seriously—and he had very definite theories about architecture and design, though he never gave a separate account of them. It would be pretentious to speak of his 'aesthetics' for he was no philosopher; and it would be misleading to treat his ideas as a blueprint for his work as a whole for that was shaped as much by taste and fashion, the limitations of materials and techniques, and the expectations of clients as by more intellectual considerations. But with someone as intellectual as Ashbee one can no more overlook his theories of art than his theories of friendship, cities, education or the countryside.

The root and ground of his ideas was what he called, with some slight embarrassment, the 'Religion of Beauty'; the belief, as he once told Alec Miller, 'that the fact of Beauty is the crowning proof of the Immortality of the Soul ...'; they were discussing religion, not art, at the time.[3] No one except Plato, he wrote in the same letter, 'and a few of the neoplatonists and renaissance men have ever worked at a philosophy of aesthetics ... The Divine Beauty is too much for any of us, we can only get it dimly through the earthly revelation ...'[4] In *A Book of Cottages and Little Houses* he proposed a scale of values in architecture: first its practical aspects, then its human qualities, its expressiveness, and finally its aesthetic quality, 'the Soul of Architecture'.[5] Elsewhere, he roughly annexed the image of the cave in the Seventh Book of Plato's *Republic*, intended as a myth of human knowledge in general, and applied it to art: buildings, works of art and craftsmanship are, as material objects, merely shadows cast on the wall by the light outside; what give them their value is 'the light behind'.[6]

There was also a dynamic side to this idea for the Spirit, according to German Idealism, works in history. 'We artists ourselves', Ashbee once wrote, 'are too apt to think that we are the discoverers of forms that come new to us. It is not so. We ourselves are but the instruments through which breathes the Over-Soul, the Zeitgeist.'[7] The artist was at best an interpreter whose job it was to feel the spiritual pulse and movements of the time, and to express them in the language of his art. That, Ashbee thought, was what Frank Lloyd Wright had done so well in the Middle West: 'This land, pierced by the great trunk lines of the Middle West, the new cities of the miners, the cattle breeders, the canners and the grain exporters, the men of ideas and invention, make a new appeal ... It is the architect's business to express life, and to ennoble it in the expression. Frank Lloyd Wright has done this ...'[8] The idea of a spiritual dimension in art also helped Ashbee to make sense of his own work as a designer, of the Guild, and of the Arts and Crafts as a whole. Whether he was arguing with his kindly pragmatic banker friends, or standing in the Arts and Crafts Exhibition wondering what the point of it all was, it was to the idea of the spiritual in art that he turned.

We pull ourselves up oftentimes, and ask, why do we go on, what is it all for? This mere trifle of mine, of what use or beauty may it be, will it give any one delight? May be not, may be it is useless and unlovely, and will give no man pleasure, what then? Why just this, we are brought face to face with the ethics of production; the artist producer stands forth. This trifle of mine is a mere symbol, the thing itself is empty, vain, its goodness consists in the spirit put into it, and the doing it, its creation by us, reflects a greater doing, symbolizes a creation elsewhere, in which we are sublimely and unconsciously taking part. We talk of a piece of machine-made work as soulless, what a deal we mean when we say that! So let us continue to make our trifles, remembering always that they are symbols only. This, if you will, is the Idealists' Gospel of Work . . .[9]

The notion of symbolic trifles, airy though it may be, was to have its consequence for the objects Ashbee designed.

Among philosophies of art, Ashbee's belongs with those which see art, not in its own special terms, but as the expression of circumstances outside itself. 'The origin of style', he told the Architectural Association in 1892, 'lies not in the theories, not in the forms, of Art, but in the social relations of men to men . . .'[10] He was not proposing here a tool for the analysis of works of art, the results of which could only have been crude and forced, but rather a sense of where the roots of artistic problems lay; there could be no hope for a healthy art until the social and economic conditions which nurtured it were reformed.

William of Wykeham, Henry Harland, Henry Eveleigh, John Thorpe, Huntingdon Shaw, Viansen, Torrigiano, Thomas Chippendale, all men who left an indelible mark on English craftsmanship knew their trade, no men more so, but set them in the modern workshop, in Sheffield smithies, Shoreditch woodshops, Birmingham metal shops, and we should see the high technical skill doubtless remaining, but infinitesimally narrowed down, and all the energy of genius thrown into grasping the social and economic condition under which the whole complex web hung together. It is these social and economic conditions which we architects have first to understand and then to control, if we are to lift the great Art we profess once more upon the pedestal that should receive it. Art, Architecture, the Crafts, are for the moment, alas, by the way.[11]

For William Morris, the logic of this argument led to revolutionary socialism; for Ashbee, it led to the little world of the Guild of Handicraft, his own attempt to create art out of the social relations of men to men.

One of the common ideals of the Arts and Crafts Movement was that craftsmen should if possible become designers in their own right, and Ashbee subscribed to this idea in a general way. But he did not set great store by individual talent; he was much more interested in the human average, and what made the ethos of the Guild so fascinating socially (and its work so uneven artistically) was that it was made of stuff more various, more everyday, and much more challenging personally than artistic talent. When Ashbee chose men to work for him, trusting to his power of instinctive choice, he was looking for character: 'the best craftsmanship almost always postulates the best moral backbone. I really care very little whether I have the rarer aesthetic qualities in my people provided I can make sure of the homelier stronger and more trustworthy things.'[12] This is not to say that he set himself a social rather than an artistic goal; it was just that he could not see one apart from the other, believing that the things which made for good craftsmanship were in the end neither technical nor aesthetic, but moral and social.

To exalt the craftsman and his experience as Ashbee did was also to invert the usual order of things, in which the workshop exists to meet the demands and standards of the consumer. In Ashbee's economy it would be the other way round. The craftsman's pleasure in his work—its spiritual significance—was the keystone of his industrial philosophy and it was not to be sacrificed to merely commercial considerations.

We may ... in our reconstructive efforts, set aside the commercial traveller's plea that it is the market, the consumer, that must determine what shall be produced. In the future it will be the producer that will determine.[13]

He had, in fact, little interest in the consumer. The charge is often brought against the Arts and Crafts, and against William Morris in particular, that their products were so expensive that they could be bought only by the rich, that they failed to make 'good design' widely available. Such a gospel of good taste, such consumer-socialism, had no appeal for Ashbee. When Rob Martin Holland asked him what was the point of producing private press books for epicures, he simply said, 'I don't see it that way! The Morrisian point of view—to wit that in Art one must just go ahead and produce the best one can and not bother about the rest is good enough for me.'[14]

In September 1885, while he was still an undergraduate, Ashbee went to look at the building of the earliest stages of the new cathedral at Truro, a late work of the Gothic Revival, compelling in its completeness and correctness. He did not know what to think. 'It seems fine and yet out of place somehow ... It all resolves itself into this question which, if I become an architect I must solve, Will 19th Century Gothic do?'[15] Truro provoked the same doubt in other architects; it posed a question for the time: should one so closely reproduce the forms of thirteenth-century Gothic in the late nineteenth century? Could one do it with conviction? In Ashbee's case this mood of doubt was reinforced by the philosophical ideas which he was discovering at this time. Belief in the *Zeitgeist* seemed incompatible with Revivalism. If the forms of Pearson's Gothic at Truro were vital in the thirteenth century, shot through with the 'Spirit of the Age', what were they in the nine-teenth? 'We know', Ashbee wrote much later, 'that if we practise an Art that is no longer in and of our own time, that Art is of little consequence.'[16] And of the Philadelphia architect, 'Rose Valley' Price he wrote:

He has, like most of us who have studied the Arts and Crafts and felt the humanity underly-ing the movement, the conviction that if the movement is to find itself it must speak in a voice of its own and not in the language of back numbers, the beaux Arts, the 'old colonial'. His own beautiful handling of Reid's store in Walnut Street is a good expression of the man and he has no patience with the scholarly work of MacKim and White and others who stand for traditional culture.[17]

The building whose contemporary spirit Ashbee commended here, the premises of Jacob Reed and Sons, 1424–6 Chestnut Street, Philadelphia, was actually an adventurous, eclectic design in reinforced concrete with strong Byzantine elements.[18] Ashbee's modernism, though it rejected the scholarly revivalism of a Pearson or—he was sad to say—of a Bodley, was not like that of continental theorists in the 1920s and 1930s who sought to exclude all reference to the past from their buildings and designs. He naturally accepted that the past is a part of the present, an inheritance of examples, inspiration and constraints: 'we can no more escape the past than we can our own shadows', he wrote, 'and it is the glory of a great people to live in the present and yet not forget its past'.[19] The work of the past presented itself to him as tradition: 'Our canons of taste in building as in all art, are modelled upon the past.'[20] It presented itself as a language of association which could add meaning and dignity to modern work: examples in later chapters will demonstrate this idea. And it presented itself as an example: he thought a silversmith's workshop, for instance, should have a knowledge of what earlier silversmiths had done, 'English, German, Spanish, French, Italian, and above all Greek and Byzantine . . .'.[21]

Ashbee had a rather university-trained sense of the past, and it is worth looking more closely, for instance, at his accounts of the history of English architecture and decorative arts, because they give some of the intellectual flavour of the man. In lecture series for the University Extension such as 'The History of English Handicraft' and 'Architecture as the Language of the English People', he would start with the Middle Ages, and the flourishing of a great craft tradition. A popular culture expressing itself in stone and wood, glass and metal, was supported by the patronage of the monastic communities and by the craft guilds, which maintained standards of workmanship. The architecture of the Middle Ages developed in a stately curve from the sturdy but redundant work of the Normans to its apogee, the Decorated style in the time of the Edwards, an age which saw, by no accident, the flowering of chivalry, the verses of Chaucer and the preaching of Wyclif. (An old-fashioned preference this, when Perpendicular was increasingly popular among English architects.) The Renaissance saw the completion and decadence of the high traditions of craftsmanship developed in the Middle Ages. It was an age of learning and secular culture, foreign influences and intellectual excitement and discovery; it replaced the community of the mediaeval abbey with that of the great country house, elegant, aristocratic and, in Ashbee's eyes, no less admirable; he could not bring himself with Ruskin and Morris to disapprove of a time which produced humanists like Thomas More, Erasmus and Sir Philip Sidney.

He would pass quickly over the late seventeenth and eighteenth centuries, a time of pedantry in the arts, Puritanism in religion, and the growing influence of the middle classes; the period reached its proper conclusion in Sir John Soane's museum, 'A perfect specimen of the worst taste of the worst period'.[22] His picture of the nineteenth century was dark (the Industrial Revolution) and confused (the babble of styles), lit fitfully by the idealism of the Oxford Movement, Ruskin and the Pre-Raphaelites.

The outline of this account, the glories of the Middle Ages, the Soanean nadir, would have been widely echoed at the time, but Ashbee's was quite a particular point of view. Unlike some Arts and Crafts writers, he showed little romantic appreciation of vernacular and primitive building: the cottage and the yeoman's house made no appearance; Anglo-Saxon architecture had 'little architectural importance' for him; and he did not attempt like Morris to draw a popular history out of the fabric of anonymous buildings.[23] Equally, he stood apart from the scholarly traditions of architectural history as they had developed in the nineteenth century: there was no close observation of buildings, and little concern with the history of construction or the development and classification of styles. Instead he presented architecture and the decorative arts in parallel to the social and political history of England, a mirror held up, so to speak, to the kind of history he had learnt at Cambridge.[24] In this he was influenced by J. R. Green's enormously popular *A Short History of the English People* (1882), which introduced an element of social history into the narrowly political traditions of English history writing, and moved cultural achievement nearer to the centre of the stage:

If some of the conventional figures of military and political history occupy in my pages less than the space usually given them it is because I have had to find a place for figures little heeded in common history—the figures of the missionary, the poet, the printer, the merchant or the philosopher.[25]

Ashbee recommended *A Short History* to his students as the backbone of their course of reading.

His feeling for architecture and the decorative arts was thus shaped more by his sense of its cultural context than by the simple pleasure of seeing, and it is not surprising that his picture of history had only a tangential effect on his work as a designer. One can feel it, for instance, in the mood he created for his studio houses in Chelsea and in the Elizabethan authors he liked to print at the Essex House Press; but at other times his taste and his sense of history would be at odds, and the exemplars for his furniture and metalwork were often drawn from the seventeenth and eighteenth centuries, which his academic perspective condemned as decadent.

On the question of mechanization, we have already seen how the larger issues which this seemed to raise preoccupied Ashbee; the story of the Guild was an attempt to make a place for traditional craftsmanship and hand-work in an increasingly industrial world. On the more specific question of the place of machinery in architecture and the decorative arts, his position was simple. He believed that work in which machinery played a leading part could not be creative; it was soulless. He also believed that the craftsman set the standard, not the consumer. It followed that machines should only play a subordinate part in architecture and the decorative arts. He would use them, as the Greeks used slaves, for dull and heavy work, the preliminary sawing of wood, the rolling and milling of metals; he would even use them for more advanced processes:

I have no objection to using the dental fret for modelling in silver, or a steam drill, for boring and punching, still less do I mind the polishing lathe, or belting it to the engine, but if the doing of these accessories—for observe they are accessory, not vital, to my craft as a Silversmith,—disorganizes the economy and inventive power of my workshop, then as a Silversmith I am better without them.[26]

He would not allow them to dominate the workshop, to dictate its pattern of work. This argument was, like so many Arts and Crafts arguments about 'the Machine', insensitive to the number and variety of processes which could be brought under that heading; it was uncertain in its application. But at least its internal logic was clear. It did not challenge the use of machinery in heavy industry, it did not rule out the possibility that machine-made objects might be beautiful.[27] It simply set those matters on one side. The touchstone in the workshop, as in the rest of Ashbee's philosophy, was the creative experience of the craftsman.

It is noticeable how some of the most familiar Arts and Crafts ideas have not figured in this survey of Ashbee's beliefs: that architecture is the Mother Art to which all others are subordinate; that there should be no division between the fine and decorative arts; that designs should be based on materials and construction; that ornament applied for its own sake is worthless. Ashbee did in fact subscribe to these ideas.[28] But they do not bulk large in his writings. In practice his whole career was dedicated to working out Arts and Crafts convictions such as these, which were broadly speaking derived from the writings of Ruskin and the early lectures of William Morris. But when he came to writing books and articles, he was influenced by a slightly different intellectual tradition, that of Idealism. It was not a point of view foreign to the Arts and Crafts; Carlyle and Emerson were an inspiration only less strong than Ruskin and Morris; Voysey and Baillie Scott both saw their furniture, houses and so on in an Idealist light, as having a spiritual value. But it was a point of view which Ashbee arrived at before he became an architect or a designer, and it had its roots in German philosophy: it encouraged him to take a wider and intellectually more ambitious view of things than the Arts and Crafts' rather homespun version of Ruskin and Morris. It is no accident that some of the most ambitious (though not always the clearest or most persuasive) thinkers in the Arts and Crafts were influenced by Idealism, Mackmurdo, Cobden-Sanderson, Henry Wilson, and Ashbee himself.

WORKSHOP PRACTICES

For most of his career, Ashbee ran two offices, one for architecture, the other for decorative arts produced by the Guild of Handicraft. It was a slightly complicated arrangement, but he was not so scornful of professionalism as to think that he could run an architectural practice from the workshops of the Guild, at least when they were in the East End, and so he made himself accessible to clients. Indeed he took pride in the title of architect, describing himself on letter-heads and in print as 'C. R. Ashbee, M.A., Architect'. By contrast, he described himself as 'Designer' on only one occasion, so far as is known, when he was elected to the Art Workers' Guild in 1891.[29]

His first architectural office, opened in September 1890, was actually right next door to the abhorred Soane Museum, at 15 Lincoln's Inn Fields; but he did not have to endure this for long, for in 1894 he moved into the self-contained set of rooms he had designed for himself at the back of the Magpie and Stump. Here there was an outer office for a secretary and an inner sanctum where he worked and interviewed clients, 'a little chilly room hung with cold chaste blue linen . . .'.[30] There were assistants and pupils in a studio upstairs, but just how work was shared out, and whether they took any responsibility for design is not clear.[31] The first and most important of them was the meticulous and reverential Ernest Godman— he could not bring himself to call Ashbee 'C.R.A.', though everyone else did and Ashbee liked it. He joined Ashbee in the early 1890s, and though Ashbee would sometimes smile in a superior way at Godman's 'careful architectural soul', he could not have run the office without him. When Godman fell fatally ill with consumption in about 1904 the office was under considerable strain.[32]

After Godman came Austin Gomme, the son of Laurence Gomme of the LCC, in about 1896, a talkative, indolent, charming young man; then Charles Holden in 1897; Gabriel Stevenson, assistant from 1902 to 1907, who was remembered for the care he took of the office cat; George Chettle, who came as a pupil in 1904 and eventually became a partner in the practice in about 1912; and Philippe Mairet, a thoughtful young artist who was employed as a draughtsman from 1906 to 1908, and intermittently after that.[33] It was always a small office, with rarely more than two assistants and a pupil at the busiest times, and unsophisticated in its drawing techniques.[34] Ashbee's staff were not as consistently dim as Voysey's pupils, but it was not an office to which bright young men were attracted, as they were to Belcher or Lutyens. The only architect of special talent among them was Charles Holden, who arrived full of an enthusiasm for Whitman which must have been irresistible to Ashbee. He probably contributed a good deal to some of Ashbee's most original designs for houses in Chelsea, but after a year or so he left because he wanted to 'get among the philistines'.[35] Ashbee's office was hardly the place for him, having too much the atmosphere of an artist's studio, high-minded and faintly Bohemian.

It is more difficult to be sure of the way designing was carried on in the Guild, partly because it was meant to be a more collaborative affair, and partly because it is poorly documented. Ashbee had little to say about it in the Journals or in print; none of the Guild's office papers seem to have survived; and though some drawings do survive, they are only a small proportion of the total number that must have been produced.[36] It is reasonable to assume that Ashbee designed the great majority of Guild products; but this can only be an assumption for, with the exception of designs for the Essex House Press, the majority of Guild products cannot, at present, be firmly attributed.[37] In the chapters which follow it will often be said that 'Ashbee' designed this or was responsible for that, for it is difficult to gather work of this kind together, or to explain it, without assuming such attributions; in the chapters on furniture, metalwork and jewellery, the reader is asked to retain a sense of scruple.

When Guild products were not Ashbee's work, they were often designed by Guild craftsmen, as the ethos of the Arts and Crafts required. Some brought their skills with them to the Guild, like John Pearson and Fred Partridge; others, like John Williams, Bill Hardiman and the unsympathetic but gifted W. A. White, discovered their talent by working in the Guild. How far the Guild progressed in this direction can be judged from the catalogue of the Arts and Crafts Exhibition Society for 1903 which lists designs from eleven different Guildsmen besides Ashbee. A certain amount of Guild work was also done to the designs of outside architects, such as Baillie Scott, Charles Spooner and Charles Holden; but it is hard to say how much of the Guild's output was of this kind; though quite a number of architects used the Guild, none of them seem to have done so very regularly.[38]

Ashbee was actually less interested in making designers out of individual Guildsmen than in making design a collaborative affair between himself and the Guildsmen, and so developing a common Guild style.[39] He wanted to make room

93. The Gallery at Essex House where loan exhibits from the South Kensington Museum were displayed. The showcase contains local and traditional jewellery, and electro-types of metalwork.

for his Guildsmen to exercise their Ruskinian freedom, and there was always the practical consideration that his own skills as a craftsman were limited to modelling in plaster and wax; he would often need to take advice. Writers in contemporary periodicals sometimes noticed how sketchy Ashbee's instructions were and regarded this absence of dictation in design as a special feature of the Guild.[40] George Hart, one of the silversmiths from the Campden period, recalled how Ashbee would only make rough sketches at first and then, on one of his regular tours of the workshops a few days later, would take the design further in consultation with the craftsman.[41] This practice was, however, more successful with some Guildsmen than others. The metalworkers responded to it, and one can see how scarcely any guidance from Ashbee would be needed for designs that became traditional in their repertoire: the early repoussé work or the simple silver of *c.*1900.[42] The cabinet-makers, on the other hand, the 'stolid Trade Union shop', always wanted to be told what to do.[43]

Ashbee encouraged the Guildsmen to study old work, in the belief that their craftsmanship would benefit from the influence; and he naturally turned to the collections of the South Kensington Museum, which had been formed originally for just this purpose, the instruction of workers in the decorative arts. When he was living at Toynbee Hall and working in Bodley's office he would spend his Saturday mornings at the museum, sketching.[44] Later, he was able to arrange for loans from the collections to be made to the Guild: a room was set apart at Essex

House and a changing selection including metalwork, jewellery, wrought iron and pattern designs was put on show (Plate 93).[45] When the Guild moved to Campden the loan collection was housed at first in the Grammar School and then in the lecture room at the back of Elm Tree House (Plate 55). Ashbee's idea was not that it should be used as a quarry for designs, but that the spirit of old work should influence the workmanship of the Guild; and he was happy to report, after the first year of the scheme, that it did: 'I have noticed in the course of the year frequently how details of shape, metal, inlaying, carving, modelling or designing generally have been influenced to the good by some specimen of work exhibited in the Trustees' Gallery.'[46]

Just as the gallery reflected Ashbee's sense of the value of historical exemplars, so the use of machines in the Guild reflected, at least to some extent, the clear distinction in his mind between routine processes and creative work. The metal-workers used electrically-powered equipment for buffing and polishing, at least at Campden, but no other machinery it seems. In the woodshop there was a lathe for turned work, foot-powered presumably, and a morticing machine and a trimmer worked by leverage; the blacksmiths had a simple, heavy hand drill. The bulk of machinery in the Guild was used simply for cutting up wood, and at Campden that was concentrated in a large shed a little distance from the main building (Plate 94): off the overhead power shaft ran a band saw, a planer and, on the extreme

94. The Guild's woodworking machinery at Campden.

left, a circular saw. Ashbee included a photograph of the latter in one of his books over the schoolmasterly caption 'Circular Saw in the Guild's Power House, illustrating the right use of machinery'.[47] In any strict view, of course, the equipment of the Essex House Press should count as machinery, for printing has always been a mechanical process and enjoys few of the delicate and immediate operations of the hand so dear to the Arts and Crafts, no hammering or modelling, carving or painting. But Arts and Crafts enthusiasts felt that they could talk of 'hand-printing' because they worked slowly, producing short runs on presses of traditional design, and Ashbee, with the rest of them, overlooked the anomaly.

For the first ten years or so, most of the Guild's work was done for particular clients; there must always have been a certain amount of work done speculatively, and some of the many ornamental copper dishes probably fall into this category; but it seems to have been in a minority and the arrangements for selling Guild work to the general public were rudimentary.[48] When Ashbee took visitors round the Guild on Thursday mornings they could no doubt be persuaded to buy something, if only as a memento of a journey so deep into the East End; and sales could also be made at some exhibitions, particularly those organized by the Arts and Crafts Exhibition Society: in the 1890s the Guild's small metalwork and inexpensive jewellery sold well.[49] But such exhibitions did not happen very often. The later 1890s saw a shift of emphasis towards selling to the general public, perhaps encouraged by Rob Martin Holland, as a director of the new limited company. When the West End shop in Brook Street was opened in 1899, metalwork, jewellery and books could be sold where they were likely to be bought, and as a matter of fact other Arts and Crafts workshops had shops nearby, Morris and Company, W. A. S. Benson, and later the Artificers' Guild; the process was completed by the opening of the gallery at Dering Yard in 1903, big enough to hold furniture. We have already seen some of the consequences of this shift in the workshops of the Guild; others follow in the chapters on metalwork and jewellery.

Ashbee did not choose to make the Guild better known by advertising in the press, until he was forced to it by the circumstances of 1906, but then the admiring articles which were written about the Guild in the art press during the 1890s probably made it unnecessary; he did, however, issue discreet catalogues from 1895 or so onwards, which could be circulated to clients of long standing or future promise.[50] On the whole it must have been an uncertain business selling the Guild's wares, for though Rob Martin Holland argued that you should aim to give the customer what he wanted, Ashbee would argue that it was the producer, not the consumer, who set the standard. One could scarcely expect a strong policy from someone who was so out of sympathy with the commercial world, and who set his own artistic principles so much higher than the requirements of clients and customers.

As for the people who bought the Guild's wares, no full list of clients survives to give an accurate picture of them. They must have been drawn from the upper and middle classes and they must have been admirers of the Arts and Crafts, for the products of the Guild, though not all expensive, were generally slightly dearer than their commercial equivalents; it is perhaps not surprising that many of those who bought Guild wares at the Arts and Crafts Exhibitions, or visited the gallery at Dering Yard, came from Kensington and Chelsea.[51] But beyond this one can only get partial impressions. There was a sprinkling of aristocrats among them, like Viscount Halifax who bought at Arts and Crafts Exhibitions, and the Duchess of Leeds, for whose villa on the Italian Riviera Ashbee designed furniture, fittings and silver; there were businessmen like Hodson and Peter Jones in Wolverhampton; and there were collectors and connoisseurs like Pickford Waller, whom Janet visited in 1903 and did not take to: 'acres of EHP books all locked away so nice and tight and Mrs and Miss wearing GoH brooches, it was so overpowering ...'.[52] And it may be that clients often chose the Guild's designs from conviction as much as taste, sympathizing with its social ideals: T. C. Horsfall and Charles Rowley, both from Manchester and both men of ideas, perhaps belong here, and so does the Guild's largest client, Gyula Mandello from Hungary.[53]

Finally, a note on Ashbee's work as a designer for manufacturers; he was not so entrenched an enemy of industry as to refuse such work. In about 1897 the Falkirk Iron Company approached a number of designers connected with the Arts and Crafts asking for designs for fireplaces and other ironwork that would be sympathetic to cast iron; Voysey, George Jack, William Scott Morton and Ashbee were among them. Ashbee took a lot of trouble experimenting with patterns in mahogany and gesso made up at the Guild and produced half a dozen designs (Plate 152); but in the event they did not sell well and were discontinued.[54] Then in the early 1900s he designed some piano cases for John Broadwood and Sons, a firm long associated with progressive cabinet-making (Plates 142, V). These commissions do not amount to much, but Ashbee must have done other work outside the Guild, for in 1911 he wrote that he had also designed for manufacturers of bedsteads, wallpapers, clocks, pottery, metalwork, organs and books; so far little substantial information has come to light on any of these commissions.[55]

EMBLEMS AND SYMBOLS

Ornament is a part of Ashbee's design work as a whole and is best dealt with in the chapters which follow. But there is one aspect of it which calls for a preliminary explanation: about half a dozen images which Ashbee uses frequently seem to act as emblems or symbols: the pink, the ship, the tree, the sun, the circle or sphere, the winged youth and the peacock; the intellectual background to these images needs to be explained.

Ashbee's whole cast of mind encouraged him to give a spiritual meaning to decorative images. He believed, with Emerson, that 'It is not words only that are emblematic; it is things which are emblematic. Every natural fact is a symbol of some spiritual fact.'[56] We have seen how he thought of the whole activity of the Guild as symbolic; and the neo-Platonism which seemed to him to offer the fullest philosophy of art was also perhaps the richest source of symbolic imagery in western art apart from the Christian tradition. He was interested in the ideas of Emanuel Swedenborg, with his sense of correspondences between the natural and the spiritual worlds; among nineteenth-century painters his heroes were Burne-Jones and Watts, painters of the Idea; and he was aware of symbolism in late nineteenth-century French art, being an admirer of Puvis de Chavannes.[57] His preoccupation with symbolism was perhaps at its strongest in the early days of the Guild, and Roger

95. Design by Ashbee, apparently for a letter-head, 1888.

AND·THEY·BUILDED·GOLGON:·
·OOZA·TERRIBLE·ETERNAL·LABOUR·
STRIVING·WITH·SYSTEMS·TO·DELIVE
·INDIVIDUALS·FROM·THOSE·SYSTEMS·

Fry, when teaching at the School of Handicraft, found the students 'too much absorbed in the hidden meaning of things to trouble about correct drawing.'[58]

The traditions of ornament to which he turned for exemplars in designing for the Guild were full of motifs which were possibly symbolic in their origins and certainly lent themselves to emblematic treatment. The Guild's senior metalworker, John Pearson, introduced ships, fish, trees and peacocks in his repoussé work, motifs apparently inherited from his employment in William De Morgan's tile works.[59] We know that Ashbee studied the textile collections of the South Kensington Museum, and in English embroideries of the late sixteenth and seventeenth centuries in particular he would have found roses, pinks, peacocks and the characteristic decorative treatment of small sprigs of fruit and flowers known as 'slips' which recur, for instance, in his enamelled fireplace at 37 Cheyne Walk.[60] The choice of motifs in sixteenth- and seventeenth-century embroideries was influenced, it is said, by the Renaissance taste for emblem books and quaint and curious devices.

Ashbee's emblems have something of the character of the *imprese* or devices which were so popular in the Renaissance; they are badges of his personal endeavour and that of the Guild; and he may have seen particular scope for symbolism in the flowers, birds and animals that are dotted so freely across the surfaces of sixteenth- and seventeenth-century embroidery. But the meanings which he attached to his favourite motifs were much less complex and arcane than those of the Renaissance. They were simple, and moralizing in tone; and they reflected a nineteenth-century, not a sixteenth-century view of the world. One of his earliest emblems, taken from a quite different but potentially just as arcane source, will illustrate the point.

In Ashbee's Journal for January or February 1888 there are drawings copied from the title-page and other parts of William Blake's *Jerusalem*: facing them are quotations from the same poem in which Los stands in London building Golgonooza: 'I must create a system or be enslaved by another man's / I will not reason and compare: my business is to create.'[61] Ashbee was just now in the middle of his tense and hopeful struggle to bring his idea for a school and guild to fruition; and about ten pages later there are draft designs for a decorative panel, apparently a letter-head for 'The Art School and Guild, Toynbee Hall' (Plate 95).[62] A far-beaming sun shines on a mountainous landscape, and by the edge of a lake or sea stands a city like Blake's Golgonooza in *Milton* with 'mighty Spires and Domes'; elsewhere in *Milton* we read that 'Golgonooza is named Art and Manufacture by mortal men'.[63] In the foreground blacksmiths are hammering the sun on an anvil. This is the forge of Los, Poet and Craftsman, spiritual revolutionist, Blake's mightiest image of the

'Creative Imagination'. Los is associated with the sun, indeed he creates the material sun each day, and the hammering is a properly Blakean image of the Imagination as the creator of the world. As an inscription to the design Ashbee ran together several passages from *Jerusalem*: 'And they builded Golgonooza: terrible eternal labour Striving with systems to deliver individuals from those systems.'[64] The design owes little to Blake's drawing style and the whole conception is quite un-Blakean, for nothing in the Prophetic Books could be rendered in this static and two-dimensional way. The selection of images is Ashbee's own, and they are combined to express the aspirations of the Guild: the building up of an ideal community in the city, London/Golgonooza; and the correspondence between the little world of day-to-day craftsmanship and the 'Creation elsewhere', the Ideal world. In Blake Los and his furnaces are if anything 'in' Golgonooza, an image of intense, inward creation; Ashbee puts a reach of water between the forge and the city and so introduces an extended and moralistic image, with overtones of a life's journey or quest: in another version of this design, a small ship sets sail towards the city.[65]

Almost unknown at his death, Blake's work was for many years obscured by the difficulty of much of his poetry and his odd method of publishing it by illuminated printing; if he was known he was thought mad for all but the simplest of his poems. He became something of a cult, however, in the 1860s and 1870s among the Pre-Raphaelites, and in the 1880s the artists and writers connected with the Century Guild were equally enthusiastic: much has been made of his influence on the development of Art Nouveau in England.[66] Still rejected by the intellectual and literary establishment, it was as a cult figure for rebellious artists and aesthetic coteries that Blake was best known in 1888 and Ashbee's admiration was probably tinged with anti-Philistinism. Even within the cult, appreciation was generally confined to the shorter and simpler poems and there was no easily available text of the difficult Prophetic Books until E. J. Ellis and W. B. Yeats published their edition and commentary, *The Works of William Blake, Poetic, Symbolic and Critical* in 1893. That Ashbee should try to fashion a mythology for the Guild directly out of *Jerusalem* and *Milton* shows how much Blake meant to him; he probably had to go to the British Museum to do it.[67] But as a guide to the persons and places of Blake's imagination, Ashbee seems to have taken Swinburne's *William Blake: A Critical Essay* (1868), which interpreted those persons and places as the types of moral attributes, and presented Blake as a champion of individual liberty and a kindred spirit with Walt Whitman; an interpretation accessible and sympathetic to Ashbee and apparently reflected in his legend 'Striving with systems . . .'.[68] Ellis and Yeats presented a different Blake, the heir to a long and occasionally occult tradition of symbolism, a picture substantiated by much twentieth-century scholarship. Ashbee must have been aware of this sort of thing in Blake, of Swedenborg and neo-Platonism; but he was not, like Yeats, attracted by symbolic *systems*, preferring more or less isolated images and symbolic meanings. A parallel and simpler example is the title he gave to the Boys' Club of the School of Handicraft, 'The Rose and the Ring', an image which he glossed as follows: 'That Art . . . is only noble in service . . . the completed work . . . is noble in proportion to its communal, not its personal significance . . . has not our first study been when we meet on Wednesday evenings to draw the flower within the limits of the circle, the flower in service?'[69]

THE GVILD & SCHOOL OF
HANDICRAFT,
34, COMMERCIAL ST., E.

SEPT., 1890

DEAR

THE MEMBERS OF THE GVILD OF HANDICRAFT
HAVE THE PLEASVRE TO INFORM YOV, AND ALL
INTERESTED IN THE MOVEMENT, THAT ON SEPT-
EMBER THE THIRTIETH, 1890, THEY ARE OPENING
AN OFFICE IN THE WEST END, AT 15, LINCOLN'S
INN FIELDS, W.C.

ALL MATTERS OF ART, WITH THE EXCEPTION
OF SVCH WORK AS IS EXECVTED IN THE
WORKSHOP FROM THE DESIGNS OF OVTSIDE
ARTISTS & ARCHITECTS, WILL THERE, IF NEED
BE, RECEIVE THE IMMEDIATE SVPERVISION
OF MR. C. R. ASHBEE, ARCHT. & HON. DIRECTOR
OF THE GVILD, WHO WILL HAVE HIS OFFICE
ADJOINING.

ALL BVSINESS COMMVNICATIONS SHOVLD BE
MADE, AS HERETOFORE, TO THE SECRETARY, AT
THE WORKSHOP, 34, COMMERCIAL ST., E., WHICH
WILL BE OPEN, AS IN THE PAST, TO ALL CLIENTS
AND VISITORS VNTIL THE IMPENDING REMOVAL
OF THE GVILD INTO LARGER PREMISES.

THE GVILD.

TO

P.T.O.

96. A printed circular of
September 1890. Height
20.8 cms.

The explanation of symbolism commonly suffers from the obvious being overlooked in favour of the high-flown, so it is best to start with what seems to be
Ashbee's most straightforward motif, the white pink. This flower and the more
elaborate carnation were often represented in late fifteenth-century Flemish manuscripts, whose borders are filled with lifelike flowers, birds, animals and insects.
Half-menagerie, half-seedsman's catalogue, this decorative treatment was carried
over into the borders and ornamental letters of sixteenth-century printed books.
Late sixteenth-century English embroideries used similar motifs, drawn apparently
from such printed books and from herbals; and in these textiles pinks and carnations
were only less popular than roses, as they were, it seems, in English gardens of
the time.[70] Ashbee's earliest dated design is on a circular dated September 1890
(Plate 96); the petals seem to be intertwined with initials, perhaps 'CC' for the
Craftsman Club.[71] The circular speaks of the 'impending removal of the Guild
into larger premises', a reference to Essex House in the Mile End Road which Ashbee

97. The Craft of the
Guild rides at anchor:
from a Guild pamphlet
of September 1889.
Diameter of original:
9.9 cms.

had seen in the summer of 1890 if not earlier.[72] The *Transactions of the Guild &
School of Handicraft. Vol. I.*, which Ashbee produced at the end of the year, carried
the pink as an emblem (Plate 185), and clearly connected it with Essex House.[73]
Ashbee must have noticed, during the summer, that there were white pinks, with
their single, five-petalled ragged flowers, growing in the garden at Essex House
and, delighted that one of the favourite and most decorative flowers of the
Elizabethans should grow in this unlikely spot, decided that it should be the emblem
of the Guild.[74] From now on the pink was used, in various designs more or less
reflecting sixteenth-century decorative treatments, on letter-heads and ephemera
replacing the Golgonooza design, on a proportion (a fairly small proportion) of
Guild products, and on almost all the books that Ashbee wrote or printed.

On the panelled staircase at Essex House there hung a large modelled roundel
of a ship, with the inscription 'Craft of the Guild' (Plate 17); one can imagine
visitors smiling weakly at the too obvious pun.[75] In another design, a printed
roundel on an early Guild pamphlet, the craft of the Guild rides at anchor by a
cliff with a tree above; in Renaissance imagery such a scene would be emblematic
of life's uncertain journey (Plate 97); and in a third, equally traditional, printed
image, the craft is blown out into the open sea, the tree here clearly marked with
the 'T' of Toynbee Hall (Plate 14).[76] These images took the craft beyond punning:
they told the story of the Guild's separation from Toynbee Hall; and they also
caught the sense of the Guild as an experiment, a voyager through the uncharted
waters of the new industrialism.[77] Such stylized galleons were also used in much
the same way in English book-plates by Arts and Crafts artists, as an emblem of
intellectual discovery.

The tree motif was among the earliest of Ashbee's designs, for he used it on
the walls of the dining-room at Toynbee Hall; and it is at its richest emblematically

98. 'Guild Workshop Record Book
Sept. 89'. The original, in the Library
of the Victoria and Albert Museum,
is 44 cms high.

carved and painted on the cover of the Guild Workshop Record Book (Plate 98).
Its roots spread along the base of the design and its topmost branches embrace
the sun: it is associated with the Tree of Life or 'World Tree' which has its roots
in the underworld, passes through the world of men and spreads its branches in
the heavens. Carlyle had written of Igdrasil, the Scandinavian world tree, as binding
together past and present, and in the closing words of *The Laws of Fésole*, Ruskin
spoke of 'this fair Tree Igdrasil of Human Art' which 'can only flourish when its
dew is Affection; its air, Devotion; the rock of its roots, Patience; and its sunshine,
God'.[78] For Ashbee the roots of the tree perhaps lay less in moral or religious than
in social grounds, for he liked to think of art as rooted in the social world, imagination drawing support from the soil of every-day life.[79] The medallions which hang
in the tree like circular globes of fruit belong to a conventional treatment of the
Tree of Life in mediaeval manuscripts and the printed books of the sixteenth and
seventeenth centuries: in the literature of Christianity, alchemy and the Cabala,
the Jewish mystical tradition, it was used to represent the relationship of parts to
a larger whole, offshoots to a common source. On the Record Book, medallions
for Toynbee Hall, the Craftsman Club, the Rose and the Ring Boy's Club and
the Guild and School itself, hang in the branches of Ashbee's endeavour.[80]

And then there is the sun, beaming at the head of the tree; one of the most
important of Ashbee's images, for he used it often and it carries 'higher' meanings
perhaps than some of the other emblems. There was an approved Guild of Handicraft way of rendering the sun, with far-darting rays alternately wavy and straight,
which, though it could have come from many sources, perhaps derives from Blake;
the human face on the cover of the Record Book is not usual.[81] We have seen
the Blakean sense in which Ashbee first depicted the sun: as a symbol of the Imagination and of the relationship between the creative microcosm of the Guild and the

226

99. *Spirit Weft*, a design by Ashbee of 1888. Height of original: about 8.8 cms.

great world. The sun is also the central image in the rather static world of Platonism, 'the top' to quote an eighteenth-century writer 'of all the visible Creation, and the brightest material Image of the Divinity'.[82] Ashbee seems also to have thought of it as a distant sun, the image of an ideal state and human life as a journey towards it. What this adds up to is that in Ashbee's imagery the sun casts an Ideal light, both in a specific philosophical sense—the light outside the cave—and in a moralizing one. On many Guild designs it acts as a kind of blazonry, an inscription of the spiritual meaning of the work, for those who care to read.

Circles are a snare to the iconographer for they are liable to so many interpretations and can be spotted in so many places; but fortunately there is an explicit commentary on one aspect at least of Ashbee's circle motifs. Returning to the British Museum at the beginning of 1888 we find him writing in his Journal: 'This art school weighs upon my mind. Wish to goodness we could start. Everything waiting!'[83] Then he launched into a quasi-philosophical speculation under the heading

Spirit Weft. Oddments

The world exists by virtue of its Ideas. At the end of the last century a symbol fell—the symbol that contained the idea of *Permanence* On the electric surface of the world a new Idea was flashed, *change* and the possibility of *progressive change*. Evolution became the watch word of men. The Spiral Thought has engaged men since, and will till the Spirit woof which weaves round, and weaves out the world touches another electric flash upon its Surface.[84]

On the facing page he then drew an image of this idea, with its echoes of traditional spiral symbolism and of the looms of Enitharmon in Blake: a cocoon-like image surrounded by gyrating or spiralling lines (Plate 99). Several years later, talking to himself in the Journals about true and false philanthropy, he wrote, 'Each man

100. A design for a mantel-piece frieze on vellum by Ashbee, executed by Ashbee and H. Dancey, 1889. (From the *Studio* 1895, vol. 5, p. 128.)

must work and emit from his own centre, and his greatness depends on the centrifugal and centripetal forces of which he is the symbol.'[85] The idea expressed on a large historical stage by the 'Spirit Weft' is here transposed to the individual.

In traditional symbolism the spiral is important as confounding centre and circumference, and as a symbol of change within repetition, cyclic progression; in Blake it is spoken of as 'the vortex', an image of the spiritual journey, and Emerson wrote an essay on 'Circles' which applied a whole imagery of cyclical progression, infolding and outfolding, to human life; Ashbee's idea followed these. Spirals occur often in his designs, either as a contained circular movement as in the Spirit Weft, or in a linear way, as in the rolling movement of a frieze; in either case they may have the sense of the movement of the spirit. One rather curious and ambitious version is a design painted on vellum by Ashbee and a student of the School of Handicraft in 1889 or so (Plate 100). A muscly Blakean figure struggles through a wood towards the sun; on four circles are inscribed a passage from the Fifteenth Canto of Dante's *Inferno*: '*Si tu segui tua stella non puoi fallire a glorioso porto.*' These words were spoken to Dante and his guide by Ser Brunetto Latini, one of a company of sodomites among the shades, and might well have provoked special recognition among homosexuals. However, Ashbee altered the setting of this episode from the open plain to a wood, which allows the quotation to be read also in the simple, moralizing sense of a dark and difficult journey, a struggle to remain faithful to an idea—'if you follow your star . . .'. So far we have only an ambivalent image; but the meanings are further complicated by the fact that two of the circles gyrate. Ashbee's spiral imagery here transposes the isolated moral struggle into a larger and less personal process of spiritual evolution, and so gives the design a further dimension.[86]

There are spheres or globes that float in some of Ashbee's designs, in a way that recalls Burne-Jones, but the most obvious emblematic use is in conjunction with the figure of a winged youth.[87] This figure first appears in a niche fashioned out of the gable kneeler of 74 Cheyne Walk, a pert little figure standing on a sphere (Plate 110); this is in 1897, at a time when learned sources played a less important part in generating Ashbee's emblems. The most striking version is on a salt cup of 1899 (Plate 101) in which a winged figure supports a sphere, like the Renaissance motif of Atlas upholding the world; he also holds a sphere of amber and stands on a hemisphere. Learned reference is scarcely needed to explain the image: it is the winged spirit of imagination and idealism, the embodiment of Ashbee's ideals

101. A salt cup in silver and amber, designed by Ashbee, 1899. 17.1 cms. high. (Victoria and Albert Museum).

for the Guild; 'where machine reduplication enters', he wrote, 'the winged spirit flies away'.[88] Ashbee of course regarded every product of the Guild as a symbol; what the salt cup did was to make that explicit.

As a symbol, the peacock (Plates 178–9, XVI) has had surprisingly different meanings: in Christian iconography it is a symbol of the Resurrection; in modern times it has become a symbol of pride. One of Ashbee's earliest uses reflects the modern sense, a peacock embossed on a coal scuttle with the legend 'The Pride

229

of Life'; but there was more to his sense of the image than that.[89] In 1892 his friend D. S. MacColl designed a binding for Ashbee's catalogue of the first Arts and Crafts Exhibition; it was called 'Peacock and Fountain' but Ashbee thought the fountain looked more like fireworks and wrote a bantering letter to MacColl's sister Elizabeth, who actually made the binding.

Tell him from me that I hold the peacock a most fitting symbol of the Arts and Crafts, tell him that I most sorrowfully allow that it started with a splendid tail—all eyes and pride—and that the tail subsequently came off in fireworks—tell him however too that the peacock is also the symbol of the Resurrection . . .[90]

Ashbee said he would bring another volume for her to bind, and the peacock would be reunited with his tail. He was only playing with words, but the association of the peacock with the Arts and Crafts is interesting, as if Ashbee enjoyed that side of the Arts and Crafts that relished colour and ornament and jewellery and display, and was not Puritan. There was a provocative phrase of Ruskin's at the beginning of *The Stones of Venice*, 'Remember that the most beautiful things in the world are the most useless; peacocks and lilies for instance . . .'[91] It may be that Ashbee's peacocks have this sense, flaunting his pleasure in proud, redundant, unfunctional beauty.

The importance of symbols in Ashbee's work should not be exaggerated. The majority of Guild designs did not employ them, even when Ashbee's fascination with symbolism was at its height in the late 1880s. When they did, the symbols did not convey a distinct message, they simply added an intellectual resonance to the objects. Ashbee's images cannot be separated into those which are purely symbolic and those which are purely decorative. And of course all the images to which he attached special meanings were commonplace in late nineteenth-century decorative art; the trees, ships and suns which seemed so potent to him can be found on every frieze and fireguard, bedstead and bookend in the 1890s without much hint of arcane associations; and no one would have wondered at peacocks after Whistler, the Aesthetic Movement and 49 Prince's Gate. On the other hand, it would be a mistake to dismiss these symbols as peripheral. They went to the heart of what Ashbee was doing, and were an apt expression of his attitudes. The meanings of his symbols converge on his life's work and ideas: the Guild as a voyage of discovery, art growing out of the soil of social life, the immanence of the Spirit and its working in history, the aspiring imagination: these are the things he believed in.

He was not unusual in adopting this language for there was an element of symbolism in the work of many Arts and Crafts designers and it was often, like Ashbee's, self-conscious, expressing the aspirations of the Movement itself; much of the Arts and Crafts imagery of spring and rebirth, for instance, proclaims the renewal of art through the Movement. Lethaby's *Architecture, Mysticism and Myth* published in 1891, was influential, and encouraged some Arts and Crafts architects to see their work as a little creation, the building up of their own earth and their own sky; the language of this idea, Microcosm and Macrocosm, can seem slick and pretentious, and particular applications of Lethaby's ideas, such as the Cosmic Eggs which perch on the porch of Mary Ward House in Tavistock Place, Bloomsbury, can sound absurd when pointed out in isolation, but the idea itself, to look on building in this light, has an attractive seriousness about it. Ashbee's image of the sun has the same idea of the microcosm in it, but in general his symbols are closer to those of artists with more literary imaginations. Some of his favourite emblems can be found in the decorations which Walter Crane designed for his long and cloudy poem on the theme of evolution and social progress, *The Sirens Three*.[92] Some also are found in the work of Charles Ricketts and Charles Shannon, who were admirers—more scholarly admirers than Ashbee—of Blake and Renaissance imagery.[93] Ricketts and Shannon moved in literary circles and Yeats was among their friends; symbolism in the Arts and Crafts was not entirely separate from symbolism in literature in the 1890s, and there was perhaps some common spirit between Ashbee and his workmen beating out peacocks on coal scuttles in the East End and the young Irishman in Dublin, his room hung round with tapestry 'full of the blue and bronze of peacocks', studying the transmutation of the world through alchemy.[94]

CHAPTER TEN
ARCHITECTURE

THE NATURE OF GOTHIC

Ashbee's master in architecture, George Frederick Bodley, had an extraordinary visual memory and a liking for cigars. When he was looking at a church he would borrow a chair, light a good cigar, and sit in the churchyard quietly absorbing the fabric, moving occasionally from one viewpoint to the next. When the cigar had burned down to the butt, he would get up and go inside. He had no sketch-book and took no notes and yet he could remember everything he saw.[1]

By the time Ashbee joined the practice of Bodley and Garner they were the leading English church architects, and their churches reflected Bodley's feeling for English fourteenth-century Gothic, always alive and scholarly in their detail, often sumptuous in their furnishing and colour-work. Some of their pupils and assistants, such as W. H. Bidlake, F. C. Eden and especially John Ninian Comper, carried this kind of work into the twentieth century. Ashbee worked on some of the finest of Bodley and Garner's buildings, the churches at Hoar Cross in Staffordshire and Clumber in Nottinghamshire, monuments to aristocratic High Church piety, and Hewell Grange in Worcestershire, a great Elizabethan mansion for the Earl of Plymouth.[2] But his own architectural practice can hardly have been more different; he designed relatively few buildings; most of them were modest houses for middle-class clients; and all of them were designed in a quite different spirit from his master's reverent absorption in Gothic.

Two of Ashbee's early works will show how different his architectural temperament was. His design for an 'Oxford University Extension College', shown at the Royal Academy in 1892, is his first known architectural work (Plate 103). It was a model design for a possible centre for the University Extension work on which he had just embarked with such enthusiasm, and contained lecture rooms and a library. The treatment was a very broad late Gothic, except for the entrance, a Tudor-arched doorway framed by pilasters and an entablature in the Renaissance manner. This 'fusion between the late Gothic and the Renaissance' was, Ashbee explained, 'a reference to that earlier and greater extension of the Universities when Colet lectured at Oxford and Erasmus led the new learning of Europe from his little cell at Queen's.'[3] That is, a time round 1500. The point is clear enough: the architectural treatment symbolized the flowering of Renaissance learning on the stock of the mediaeval universities. But as architectural history it was nonsense. If Ashbee had attended, as Bodley did, to the fabric and history of English building, he would have taken account of the fact that both Oxford and Cambridge were remarkable throughout the sixteenth and well into the seventeenth century for their

102. Repairing Elm Tree House, High Street, Chipping Campden, in 1904.

103. Oxford University Extension College, of about 1892. (From the *Architect*, 1893, vol. 49, p. 83)

104. (facing page). The chapel and part of the entrance front, The Wodehouse at Wombourne.

architectural conservatism, clinging to late Gothic in the teeth of fashion, and quite out of step with the world of letters. But Ashbee was not interested in architectural history for its own sake, as we have seen; he was interested in architecture as history, as an expression of and parallel to the social, political and cultural context; in a way his sense of architecture was influenced more by three years of academic study at Cambridge than by four years in an architect's office.

In 1895–7 Ashbee carried out alterations and additions to a country house, The Wodehouse, at Wombourne near Wolverhampton for the eccentric old soldier, Colonel Shaw-Hellier (Plate 104). The house was said to be of fourteenth-century date and later, and Ashbee built a new chapel and a billiard room, restored part of the open timber roof, and added new chimney-stacks; he also simplified the roof line, replacing some pretty Georgian gables with a parapet in some places and with his own, rather similar, gables in others.[4] Bodley had worked on the house in the 1870s and Ashbee drew on his experience as a pupil, giving his gables a profile which recalled those at Hewell Grange, and beyond them Montacute, which Ashbee thought 'the most beautiful house in England and therefore in the world'.[5] If Bodley had added a chapel to the entrance front of The Wodehouse it would have been Gothic, and one can imagine how handsomely its broad expanses of stonework and delicate tracery would have contrasted with the rest of the house. But it was ten years since Ashbee had stood in front of Truro Cathedral and asked 'Will 19th Century Gothic do?' and he had pretty well decided that it would not. So here, to the Gothic detail of his chapel window, he added a tall sweeping concave gable that suggested seventeenth-century town houses in Holland and perhaps in London. It was obviously meant to continue the 'Dutch' theme of his other gables, but it was out of scale with them and out of character with the chapel. Colonel Shaw-Hellier was a High-Churchman, but Ashbee gave him something more like those nonconformist chapels of *c.* 1900 which aimed to be up to date and appealing by combining Gothic with the prevailing secular styles.

The mongrel character of the Wodehouse chapel is a symptom of Ashbee's uncertainty, at a time when he was trying to find a manner more congenial to him than that in which he had been trained. By the time work on The Wodehouse had finished he had found it, and his houses of the late 1890s show him working in a plainer and less scholarly style than he could have learnt from Bodley, the style in which much of his best work was done. It seems to have been the strength

and limitation of his architectural talent that he was happiest working with plain surfaces and simple details; when he felt it proper to draw on what historians of vernacular architecture call the 'polite tradition', as in his handful of unexecuted designs for public buildings, the details were generally awkward and ill-digested.[6] In this respect he was like many other Arts and Crafts architects; he valued the materials and treatments associated with humble buildings partly as a matter of taste, and partly as a matter of conviction, for the ambivalence of simple vernacular forms answered perfectly to his typically Arts and Crafts mixture of modernism and traditionalism: they seemed to have been freed from the academic catalogue of styles and yet, at the same time, they kept hold upon tradition.

The list of Ashbee's architectural works at the end of this book contains ninety-one entries, of which fifty-nine were actually built; they were mostly middle-class houses and they fall, broadly speaking, into three groups: houses in Chelsea, houses in Chipping Campden, and a number of cottages and smaller houses linked by their size and treatment rather than by where they are. It does not seem a large body of work when compared with the 360 buildings of a busy and professional architect like Ernest Newton, or the 308 of Baillie Scott who worked through the inter-war period; but it was broadly comparable with the work of Arts and Crafts architects who, by choice or circumstance, kept their practices small, such as E. S. Prior. Ashbee's many other commitments, and especially the Guild of Handicraft, would have prevented him from running a larger practice even if he had wanted to. And though he liked to present himself as an architect, most people probably thought of him first of all as that energetic, many-sided and in the end unplaceable figure, the director of the Guild of Handicraft. It is noticeable that some of his wealthy friends, like Hugh Seebohm and Rob Martin Holland, who were eager to support his work in the Guild, went to other architects when they had building work to be done.[7]

One of the oddest features of Ashbee's architectural work was that almost half of his executed designs were within walking distance of his own front door. One explanation of this is that thirteen of his designs were either for himself or for his family or for the Guild. Another is that he wanted to act as his own builder and employ workmen directly on his buildings, and that was only practical if the building work was close at hand. In *A Few Chapters in Workshop Re-Construction and Citizenship* Ashbee had preached the virtues of the 'direct labour' system, which was also used by other radical Arts and Crafts architects, such as W. R. Lethaby and E. S. Prior.[8] It would get rid of the contractor, whom Ashbee saw as merely an entrepreneur, someone who reduced building to cash transactions, fed on mistrust and got between the architect and the workman. It would be an education for the architect: 'The architect must take off his top hat, and discontinue poking at the workmen's clay model with his two foot rule when he makes his didactic visit to the contractor's shop. In this school he must set to work in an apron with the other workmen.'[9] If it had continuity, the builders would get to know their architect: 'let our plasterers get into the knack of knowing how I want my cornices to break round the window architraves, and my bricklayers, from experience of working with me, how I like my arches to rake, and my smiths to remember that I always swear when they file fine the edges of my scrolls . . .'.[10]

And it would not only be the architect who would benefit:

it is not from vanity of my own style that I want my plasterers, and bricklayers, smiths and joiners, to be in sympathy with me, but because, by this sympathy, and owing to the fact of our continuous co-operation, I shall become the vessel through which the tradition of our re-constructed workshop is to flow . . . our newer system of responsible co-operation will inevitably approximate to the mediaeval guild system, in which the workman was enabled to put his own individuality into his work.[11]

In this, as so often, Ashbee was in tune with progressive opinion, for there was a good deal of dissatisfaction with the contracting system at this date, and a number of experiments in 'direct labour', such as the LCC's Works Department.

The District Surveyor's returns for South Chelsea record work by Ashbee on Cheyne Walk six times between 1896 and 1898; on all six occasions he was listed as the builder.[12] He was trying out his idea: 'I engaged my own foreman and workmen, entered into direct relations with tradesmen and local authorities, paid my own wages, and took up contracts for the execution of works.'[13] The returns also list Ashbee as the owner in five cases, and his mother in the sixth. The experiment called for continuity, and Ashbee seems to have acquired leaseholds and freeholds on Cheyne Walk in order to promote development and so keep his building guild going. The irony of it was that he was acting just like a small speculating builder, but for the opposite reasons.[14] When he moved to Campden he revived the experiment. But by then he had realized that it could not succeed if left to the efforts of a single architect. It needed a whole combination of builders to give the labour market stability and so provide leisure and the opportunity for good work.[15] Only then would the modern building trade correspond to his ideal, the Guild system of the mediaeval builders; only then would modern life correspond to the conditions which had created 'the greatest Architecture of all time'.[16]

In his way, Ashbee was as great an admirer of Gothic as his master Bodley. But it was another kind of Gothic; not a vision of noble stonework in a country church-yard, veiled in cigar smoke; but a myth of work and art and happiness created out of the social conscience and historical imagination of John Ruskin.

HOUSES IN CHELSEA

Almost all Ashbee's Chelsea designs, and all his executed ones, were concentrated in one stretch of Cheyne Walk, west of Oakley Street and Albert Bridge, looking out over the grey, slow-moving Thames. It seemed, in the 1890s, a quiet and old-fashioned place, lined for the most part with unpretentious artisan houses of many dates; though it was now part of London there was still a faint sense round the Old Church that Chelsea had once been a village. The building of the Embankment from the Royal Hospital to Battersea Bridge in the 1870s had changed things rather, replacing the jumble of wharves and waterstairs which lined the river bank with a modern, decorous promenade.[17] And at the same time, the artisan housing of eastern Chelsea, nearer to Kensington and Belgravia, began to be displaced by large brick town houses; Richard Norman Shaw, E. W. Godwin and Bodley were among the architects. This change of scale, texture and social class had scarcely reached the stretch of Cheyne Walk where Ashbee worked by the 1890s, but there was a big, red, modern block of flats called Rossetti Mansions near the Old Church; and there was no reason to suppose that the tide of fashion and property develop-ment, flowing from east to west, would stop at Oakley Street.[18]

The new middle-class houses of Chelsea were commonly in the 'Queen Anne' style—indeed they made it famous—and Ashbee's houses belong, in a sense, to this tradition. They had few or none of the surface beauties which played such an important part in 'Queen Anne', exquisite cut and moulded brickwork, or fanci-ful window details. But they shared the underlying qualities which can be seen in such classic 'Queen Anne' town houses as those by Richard Norman Shaw on the Embankment: extreme individuality; bays, oriels and porches so massive as to replace the sense of a flat façade with features by one that is deeply modelled; and such exuberant proportions that, while each design groups happily with equally exuberant neighbours, it would be hopelessly unwieldy left to itself. There is a particularly close relationship, too, between Ashbee's houses and the 'Queen Anne' studio houses built by E. W. Godwin in Tite Street, Chelsea, for Whistler and others. They have the same rather gaunt quality, as if they were the fruit of more difficult thought than the work of Shaw and Ernest George; and the same note of austerity in the interiors. Since Ashbee's houses were more or less round the corner from Tite Street, and some of his clients, whether hoped for or achieved, lived in Tite Street, they can be thought of as an extension of the Tite Street community.[19]

His first house in Chelsea was 37 Cheyne Walk, 'The Ancient Magpie and Stump', of which we have already seen much, for no house played a bigger part in Ashbee's life (Plate 105). It was built in 1893–4; and in 1895 the *Studio* published an article about it.[20] The journalist described the outside as 'not, at first sight, notably different from many a good new house in re-erected Chelsea ... a good modern house of the very eclectic style so absurdly miscalled Queen Anne' and then hurried eagerly in to enjoy the decorative delights of the interior (Plates 146–50).[21] Most comment since has been of this kind, and has missed some of the peculiarities of the house. But the *Builder* in 1897 noticed the abnormally large size of the egg-and-dart ornament under the cornices and commented 'the incident is in keeping with the naïveté of style characteristic of the Georgian era and especially of Chelsea architecture, and the house keeps up the traditional local character ...'.[22] It was a perceptive comment for it picked up the local and antiquarian threads which Ashbee had woven into the design. The house was built on the site of a sixteenth-century inn, burnt down in 1886, which was perhaps just as well for the *Studio* referred to it darkly as 'notorious'. After the lapse of a few years, Ashbee was able to resurrect its quaint name, purged of grosser and more recent associations, to lend romance and continuity to his mother's house.

Another, and in its way no less explicit, reference to Old London was the massive three-storey oriel, which was based on the early seventeenth-century wooden front of Sir Paul Pindar's house in Bishopsgate. The broad idea of one bay superimposed on another with continuous glazing had inspired Shaw at New Zealand Chambers in the City of London, for instance; but Ashbee's version was so close in plan (though not in elevation or section) as to amount almost to a copy of the Paul Pindar front. That had been a *cause célèbre* in 1890 when the house had been demolished amidst the protest of conservationists to make way for an extension to Liverpool Street Station; and though Ashbee does not seem to have taken part in the protest, he must have known the front well, as it was only a few minutes' walk from the workshops of the Guild. It may be that, in designing a copy for the front of his mother's house, Ashbee was not only exploiting its virtuoso plan and antiquarian associations, but also trying to give it some kind of extended, substitute life.[23] If so, the irony is painful, for Sir Paul Pindar's house lasted almost three hundred years and the wooden front still has a kind of life in the Victoria and Albert Museum; Ashbee's lasted for only seventy-five.

The Magpie and Stump was Ashbee's first executed design, and it is not surprising that its street front should be a little uncertain. It probably worked well close to where one could enjoy the rippling brickwork of the oriel; but a large and more architectural view, such as that in Wasmuth's *Neubauten in London*, shows Ashbee hovering between two different treatments. The main façade, with its plain brickwork and heavy cornice seems to be a reaction towards a more sober mood after the fantastically elaborate Flemish façades of Ernest George's town houses of the 1880s. The oriel, on the other hand, is a deliberately picturesque feature, though with more of Shaw in it than George. When Shaw used such heavy off-centre oriels, he tied them into the rest of the wall with all sorts of busy ribs and courses of projecting brickwork; but that was just what Ashbee was trying to do without.

105. 'The Ancient Magpie and Stump', 37 Cheyne Walk. (From *Neubauten in London* (Berlin, 1900), plate 7.)

The elements of 37 Cheyne Walk seem, as a result, ready to fall apart; though it is possible that Ashbee actually intended this loose effect, suggesting a façade that had been added to.[24]

After the Magpie and Stump Ashbee did not design any new buildings on Cheyne Walk for three years, though he enjoyed repairing Carlyle's house at 24 Cheyne Row in 1895, as a monument to the Scottish sage.[25] When he started designing again it was on a quite different basis. He did not wait for clients to come to him; he went out and bought land, designed houses to go on it, and showed them to friends, colleagues and estate agents in the hope of attracting clients; and when he saw property on Cheyne Walk that seemed ready for development he would make designs, even though he did not own it, hoping to stimulate work. He was both architect and speculative builder, and at times, as he gathered mortgages together on some properties to pay for building on another, he seemed more like a businessman than he had ever done.[26] He built seven new houses in all on Cheyne Walk, but they were only a fraction of his full output of designs for the riverfront; there are drawings for no fewer than twenty-one sites, for some of which he designed five or six different schemes at different times.[27] And yet, because he did not like to think of himself as a businessman and did not preserve his business papers, we know almost nothing about the background to these activities: we do not know where the money came from; or what his purposes really were, whether to provide himself with an income from property, to stimulate architectural work for himself, or to give his experiment in direct labour continuity.[28] He worked in this way all through his career, and he confined himself almost entirely to Cheyne Walk, so fascinated was he by the riverine scene.

His first acquisitions seem to date from 1896. In May he bought a slice of property at the western and less fashionable end of Cheyne Walk, numbers 115–16 running back to 3 and 4 Little Davis Place.[29] He was thinking, it seems, of building workshops for the Guild there and carried out some works at the back of the site in 1898; then in 1901, as the search for the Guild's new home became more urgent, he bought an adjoining property, 27 Riley Street, possibly with Janet's father's help.[30] The Guild, of course, did not materialize on this site; it was perhaps too far west to take fashionable town houses; and it lay fallow for some years. Then in 1914 Ashbee and Chettle designed several schemes in an attempt to make something of it, culminating in an expensive house with a front in a late seventeenth-century manner, and views up the Thames. Nothing came of that either.[31] But in the summer of 1896 Ashbee had also entered into a legal agreement with R. C. H. Sloane Stanley who owned the Sloane Stanley estate in Chelsea.[32] It was a small estate by London standards, and lay mostly between Fulham Road and the King's Road west of Old Church Street, but there was a narrow tongue running south of the King's Road towards the river.[33] Ashbee was interested in its southernmost tip, the row of a dozen or so humble and heterogeneous houses lying between Old Church Street and Danvers Street which, until they were thrown open to the river by the Embankment, had formed the north side of Lombard Street. There seemed to be scope for new building here. Ashbee referred occasionally to 'my Sloane Stanley building estate' and 'the Sloane Stanley building agreement', but it is not clear just how large his property was or what the terms of the agreement were.[34] It may be that he acquired building leases in return for an undertaking to make designs and promote development on this short stretch of the river.[35] At all events, this property turned out to be much more productive for him than 115–16 Cheyne Walk, and he built four of his most interesting houses here.

Ashbee had now to find clients for the buildings he proposed, and he looked almost exclusively among artists. In 1896 the painter E. A. Walton was renting a studio at the Magpie and Stump; he became a client; and it may have been through him that Ashbee designed a bizarre studio house for James Guthrie in 1896, with two big circular windows on the front, like eyes.[36] Walton and Guthrie belonged to the group of Scottish painters known as 'the Glasgow Boys' whose reputations spread well beyond Glasgow in the early 1890s; they admired Whistler and it was almost inevitable that they should come to Chelsea, though in the event Ashbee's design for Guthrie was not used.[37] But his contacts with artists grew, and during the next twenty years he designed studios and studio-houses for almost every site on Cheyne Walk with which he had to do. His pursuit of artists was not merely canny, not just a recognition of the fact that Chelsea was becoming an artists' quarter and that an architect must specialize; mixed with that realism was a romantic sense of Chelsea's life and traditions, as we shall see, a myth of history typical of Ashbee in which painters played an important part.

His first executed design in this new phase was 72–3 Cheyne Walk, built it seems between December 1896 and the summer of 1897 (Plate 106).[38] It was built over two of the earlier, narrow plots on the Sloane Stanley estate, and was in fact two separate dwellings, though that fact was rather suppressed by the broad and puzzling frontage, a trick played in other 'double house' designs in London by E. W. Godwin and J. M. Maclaren.[39] Number 72 consisted of a single-storey sculptor's studio at the back of the site and bachelor accommodation on one floor immediately over the archway; this was built for John Wenlock Rollins, a minor figure among the distinguished tribe of sculptors trained at the South London Technical Art School, who had worked with Ashbee at Essex House in the early 1890s.[40] Number 73 was a studio house for E. A. Walton for whom Ashbee provided a dining-room on the ground floor, two small sitting-rooms stacked one above the other over the entrance hall, these being essentially annexes to the studio which occupied the whole of the rest of the first and second floors, and bedrooms in the roof.

Houses for artists with purpose-designed studios were essentially a late nineteenth-century phenomenon, some of the earliest being those designed by Shaw and others round Holland Park. In these houses, the studios were designed for entertaining clients and the public as well as for painting in, and the rest of the interior had a marked air of comfort and elegance, as if to vouch for the soundness of the artist's work. The studio houses in Tite Street by Godwin, however, had a rather different atmosphere: the studio was still the focus of the house, but there were scarcely any other reception rooms besides a dining-room, and the interior was more likely to reflect a fashionably Whistlerian austerity.[41] Ashbee's plan at 73 Cheyne Walk was of this kind. There was no comfortable drawing-room with quaint alcoves or sunny bays; if one came to see the Waltons, it was for art or nothing. The studio was the all-purpose room, combining the functions of work-room and gallery with the breadth and view of the *piano nobile* drawing-room

so appropriate in town houses overlooking the Thames; and perhaps it also had something of the primitive feel, so dear to the Arts and Crafts, of a 'houseplace', one big room in which almost everything is done.

The street front of Number 72–3 showed none of the uncertainty there had been three years before at the Magpie and Stump. The façade was still a flat wall with projections, but the different parts were no longer at odds. The wall was broad, with expanses of plain brickwork, and its surface flatness was emphasized by those windows whose frames were brought out almost flush with the brickwork. (This practice was forbidden by the bye-laws when the Magpie and Stump was designed; it was permitted by the London Building Act of 1894 and Arts and Crafts architects rejoiced in it.[42]) At the same time, the projections from the façade, all oriels, were so treated in plain or white painted wood with roughcast spandrels as to suggest the slightest structural continuity with it. It was as if the wall were a flat canvas on which the architect had placed, with painterly discrimination, certain features. Mark Girouard has suggested that some of Godwin's houses in Tite Street were designed as arrangements in line, form and colour, in the same spirit as Whistler's increasingly formalist painting of the 1870s; and it may be that something of the kind was happening here.[43]

It was a much cleverer façade than the Magpie and Stump, perhaps because it was plainer; and Ashbee's new resourcefulness can be measured by the different and quite independent characters it took on from different points of view. Looked at in elevation, it was the painterly elegance that was striking, the fastidious placing of elements; in perspective its bulky oriels and freely-placed features had a typically Arts and Crafts honesty about them; closer to, there was the old-fashioned look of the oriels, recalling London houses from before the Great Fire, the rustic quality of the roughcast, closer here to central London than Voysey had brought it, and the reticence of the brick- and woodwork.[44] This was the first house in which Ashbee had used such simple, country elements as roughcast and exposed eaves rafters, and its subtlety and expressiveness show how much happier he felt with them.

At roughly the same time as he was working on 72–3 Cheyne Walk he devised an ambitious scheme for a large and neighbouring site belonging to the London County Council, on the corner of Danvers Street and Cheyne Walk roughly where Crosby Hall now stands (Plate 107); it was part of a larger property between Danvers Street and Beaufort Street, left in the hands of the LCC by compulsory purchases connected with the rebuilding of Battersea Bridge in the 1880s; Ashbee's offer of £70 *per annum* ground rent was accepted by the Council in June 1897, subject to the approval of his building plans.[45] Ashbee called his building Danvers Tower, and the original plans were for a composite studio-house for Edwin Abbey, the American painter and illustrator, the sculptor John Tweed, who came from Glasgow, and Ernest Oppler, a painter; Walton seems to have helped to gather clients once again. Ashbee's handling of the site was simple and effective: he put bulky wings on Cheyne Walk and Danvers Street, butting up against a big pale tower at the corner, and he used colour distinctively: bands of red brick and pale roughcast, yellow stonework and green Westmorland slates. But his planning and construction must have been sketchy, for the LCC's architect, Thomas Blashill, found serious defects in the plans submitted for his approval; there were overloaded

106. 72–3 and 74 Cheyne Walk. (From *Neubauten in London* (Berlin, 1900), plate 16.)

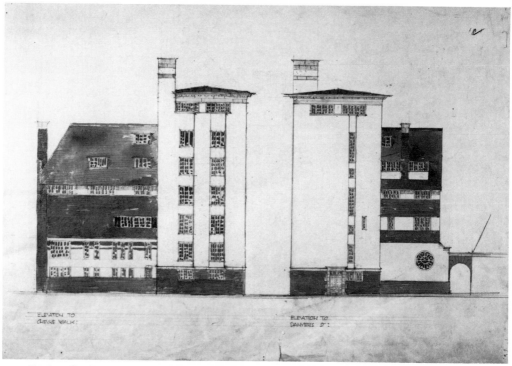

107. Design for Danvers Tower. This design belongs to the scheme for six or seven flats, some with studios, which probably dates from early 1898.

girders and walls weakened by too many flues, and as a whole the plans did not show 'the usual architectural skill and knowledge which is the case with other sets of drawings for buildings on the Council's land'.[46] Ashbee made amendments, but not enough, and then abandoned the studio-house idea in favour of a block of four or five studio-flats and two ordinary flats, designed, it seems, early in 1898. This change of plan was made without much alteration to the general shape of the wings and tower, for Ashbee did not always work out his elevations rigorously from within as Arts and Crafts architects are supposed to have done, and the distinctness of his tower, for instance, did not reflect equally distinct internal arrangements.[47] This scheme was still far from satisfying Blashill, or the requirements of public health and the Building Act, and in March 1898 the negotiations broke down in an atmosphere of bitterness; Ashbee said Blashill was 'a thundering old jackass'.[48]

Of Ashbee's unexecuted designs, Danvers Tower is the one whose failure should be regretted most. It would have been a landmark on Cheyne Walk, well loved by now, colourful and, provided the great blank roughcast sides of the tower were well maintained, arresting. It was a young man's design, self-consciously progressive and aware of what other people were doing. Godwin had piled up a stack of studios at 46 Tite Street in about 1884 and called it Tower House; and Voysey had published designs for two roughcast, tower-like houses for artists.[49] The wings, in their effort to keep a domestic and eventful character while being stretched to five or six storeys, recall, ironically, the work of the Housing of the Working Classes Branch of the LCC Architect's Department at the Boundary Street Estate in Bethnal Green. Owen Fleming, the chief architect of the Branch, and Blashill's subordinate, was a personal friend of Ashbee's; and though the blocks at Boundary Street most like Danvers

244

108. The studio or Music Room, 74 Cheyne Walk. (From *Moderne Bauformen* (Stuttgart), 1903, vol. 2, plate 75.)

Tower—Cookham, Clifton and Laleham—date from 1897–8, they may well have been on the drawing-board earlier.[50] But perhaps the most important influence on the design was the presence in Ashbee's office of the twenty-two-year-old Charles Holden, who was said to have been responsible for much of the invention of Danvers Tower.[51] One of the merits of the design is its handling of scale: the tower reads as a massive thing, yet it was only about six feet higher than 72–3 Cheyne Walk; such cleverness and sense of massing was commoner in Holden's work than in Ashbee's.[52]

When Danvers Tower was disappointingly rejected in March 1898, building work was well in hand on the house in which Ashbee and Janet would live when they got married, 74 Cheyne Walk, which seems to have been paid for by her father.[53] Ashbee designed it as an artist's house with a studio filling the whole site at basement, ground floor and mezzanine levels except for the staircase hall and a small galleried ante-room at the front (Plate 108).[54] Neither he nor Janet needed a studio; they called it the Music Room and furnished it in their casual and spartan way; but Ashbee may have felt that a studio-house was a good long-term investment on this site, or may just have liked entertaining in its austere and Bohemian

245

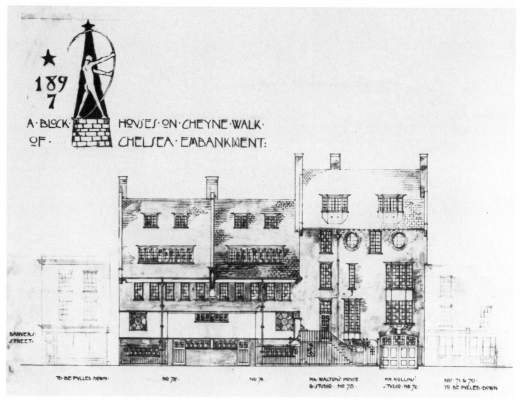

109. Designs for 72–5 Cheyne Walk.

atmosphere better than in a conventional drawing-room.[55] In the compact houses that Ashbee designed the studio dictated the planning as well as the atmosphere, and at 74 there was no room for a kitchen in the basement, or for back stairs. The kitchen was on the first floor with the study and dining-room, and the bedrooms above that in the roof. It was an unorthodox arrangement, but Ashbee and Janet had talked much of living the simple life when they got married, and if they could not do without servants altogether, they could at least show their common humanity with the cook and the housemaid by rubbing shoulders on the stairs.[56]

The street front of 74 Cheyne Walk was Ashbee's most puzzling elevation (Plate 106), for what with the lowness of the eaves and the stepping back of the ground floor and mezzanine, there was scarcely room for an elevation in the ordinary sense at all. The origins of the puzzle lay round the front door, in the large and unexpressive two-storey 'projection'—there is no more appropriate architectural term, for it was scarcely a porch or a bay. Part of its character was simple, since it looked like and was no doubt meant to be seen as the honest outcome of the plan; though it was not that, for the turning of the stair it contained could have been brought within the main wall. But it also looked like something so familiar and yet so unexpected that it can only tease the spectator until it is spelled out. Its size in relation to the main block, the large blank area of roughcast, the high rows of small windows, the door, so undemonstrative until you discovered the copper panels decorated with pinks in repoussé (Plate 32), harbingers of the art within, all these things suggested a service wing or extension built at the back of a town house. Philip Webb said that most backs of houses gave him pleasure, and perhaps Ashbee

246

was giving a clever twist to a familiar architectural saw when he gave 74 Cheyne Walk, instead of a Queen Anne front, a Mary Ann back.[57] If so, it was typical of the *faux-naif* strain in the Arts and Crafts, with its worship of the kitchen and all things plain and homely; and we shall see that this was not the only time that Ashbee treated the front door of one of his Chelsea houses as if it were a servants' entrance.

An elevation of 72–5 Cheyne Walk, done in 1897 (Plate 109), shows that Ashbee originally hoped to echo the design of Number 74 at Number 75, an arrangement which would have given more breadth and presence to the principal elevation and left the entrance projection more subdued. But as it turned out, his client for 75 Cheyne Walk, Mrs William Hunt, was not an artist and was so far unlike his other clients as to own a carriage (Plate 110).[58] Ashbee kept the same general arrangement

110. 75 Cheyne Walk.

111. The porch, 39 Cheyne Walk. 112. The entrance, 38 Cheyne Walk.

as at Number 74, except that, instead of giving the bottom of the house to a studio he gave it to the carriage, coachman and horses; and instead of repeating the projection as on Number 74 he ran it the full width of the façade and pierced it with a carriage entrance. It was an extraordinary arrangement, probably unique in London and presumably smelly; yet in Ashbee's rather special terms he had turned the situation to good account, for not only was Mrs Hunt's front door even less demonstrative than his own, her front even more obviously a back, but he was able to treat the now broader projections as a roof garden in front of the drawing-room and so encourage the life of the house to spill out into the public street in a pleasant, unbuttoned, riverside way.

75 Cheyne Walk was designed in 1901–2 and built as soon as the Ashbees had left Number 74 to live in Campden—it was the noise of this house being built which drove their tenant Whistler into such a frenzy—so it has taken us out of chronological sequence, for in 1898–9 Ashbee built 38 and 39 Cheyne Walk next door to the Magpie and Stump (Plate 113).[59] These are the only houses by Ashbee that survive today on Cheyne Walk. If they are approached with an innocent eye, Number 39 will be readily intelligible. The porch (Plate 111) and the neat row of windows suggest a town house, and though there is a hint of rusticity in the band of roughcast to the second floor and the low deep eaves, it is charming, petite, and quite explicit. But Number 38 is a puzzle. Indeed, one wonders if there is a Number 38. The semi-circular arch in the half-basement (Plate 112) looks more as if it were a servants' entrance than a proper front door. And the rest of the

248

113. 38 and 39 Cheyne Walk.

façade has no striking features of its own, apart from the asymmetrical gable, which serves to link the high parapet of Number 37 with the low eaves of Number 39. If this is a separate house, then it seems to be simply a useful, unemphatic piece of infill.

The degree of Ashbee's sophistication, the mastery he now had over his town house façades, can be judged from the fact that the circumstances of the design of these two houses were almost the exact opposite of what they suggest. They were designed and built as a single job. But Number 39, which seems so much to set the tone was a speculative development, probably by Ashbee himself, with no client to press his point of view; while Number 38, which seems so unassertive, was built as a studio-house for Miss C. L. Christian, an artist from Tite Street, who had very particular requirements.[60] Ashbee clearly delighted in making things seem other than they were, and in the bald appearance of supposedly forced-upon-one solutions. The gable looks as if it has been obliged to dive down picturesquely to pick up the eaves; the design seems just as clever when one knows that the eaves were probably pushed down to make room for this eccentric effect. As in much good Arts and Crafts architecture, invention is here the mother of necessity.

The detail of these houses is instructive. The two-inch, handmade Bracknell brick, set in thickish mortar joints, the creamy-grey roughcast which originally extended across the upper part of Number 38, give an old-fashioned, out-of-town character; while the decorative details introduce a more sophisticated but no less traditional note. The elements of the porch to Number 39 are those of an early eighteenth-century town house—cantilevered canopy of the scroll and bracket kind, fanlight, cornice and panelled door; but each element is restated in an Arts and Crafts idiom, free in design, broad and rough in execution. The canopy has an exaggeratedly shallow *cyma recta* profile, the fanlight is a peacock in wrought iron, the cornice looks like egg and dart from a distance, but it has been rendered in a primitive way, and Ashbee's favourite Elizabethan sprigs or 'slips' introduced; and a close look also shows that the panelling of the front door has been only roughly worked, as if to insist that it is honest craftsman's work and not the slick neo-Georgian of the commercial decorator. The asymmetrical gable on Number 38 echoes one slightly less dramatic at 45 Cheyne Walk, only a few yards away, which Ashbee may have thought was part of old Shrewsbury House.[61] Even the railings with their golden balls, once seen never forgotten, show modern versions of English smiths' work of *c.* 1700 in their scroll patterns and clustered columns, and even a simple overthrow. Most comment on these houses has emphasized the novelty of their design and called them 'Art Nouveau', or more aptly 'Free Style'.[62] The point is well made; and if these houses can be grouped with others of their date, it must be with the fresh and original Passmore Edwards Settlement in Tavistock Place of 1898, by Ashbee's friends Cecil Brewer and A. Dunbar Smith. But contemporaries noticed rather how old-fashioned these houses were, and the *Builder* commented on a drawing of Numbers 38 and 39 at the Academy: 'a house front in Old London style, brick below and plaster or roughcast above, with all the small-paned windows right up to the face of the wall; ... the whole thing has character, though rather of an archaeological kind'.[63] There were many such old house fronts in Wych Street and Holywell Street off the Strand, a warren of second-hand booksellers doomed, at this date, by the scheme for Kingsway.[64] It would have been typical of Ashbee to rebuild such houses in a modern way, as he had done with the Paul Pindar front.

After the Guild moved to Chipping Campden in 1902 Ashbee worked less continuously on designs for Cheyne Walk; but there were flurries of activity in 1907 and 1912. This was the time when English architects heard much, from Reginald Blomfield, Mervyn Macartney and others, of the virtues of 'English Renaissance', of the dignity and restraint that could be found and emulated in English buildings of the time of Wren.[65] The freedom that had seemed so attractive in the years before 1900, the asymmetry and the playing with individual features and little awkwardnesses, now began to seem self-indulgent. Ashbee was no less a creature of fashion than most architects, and though he disliked Blomfield and deplored neo-Georgian as an easy, mechanical, merely scholarly style too well suited to rich men's houses, he was clearly swayed by the popularity of English Renaissance.[66]

In 1907 and 1912 he designed schemes for a crescent of tall brick town houses on the corner of Cheyne Walk facing Chelsea Old Church in a simple version of this style.[67] And at those dates also he returned to the former site of Shrewsbury House, 40–45 Cheyne Walk which, as we have seen, fascinated him so.[68] Most of this site, which ran back almost four hundred feet from Cheyne Walk, was vacant and presumably ready for building round 1900; it belonged to the Artisans Labourers and General Dwellings Company.[69] Ashbee does not appear to have acquired leases on it, but he designed six different schemes for it, including two schemes for flats and an adaptation of these as a university hall of residence in 1907, all in a classical manner; these culminated in his 1912 proposal for a £45,000 'Fraternity House' for American and colonial students living in London.[70] Feeling that he should bring together old and new and give a visual sense of the union of the English-speaking peoples about which he had lectured in America and worried in South Africa, he designed a women's hostel and a married hostel at the rear of the site in a curious, many-windowed version of English Renaissance, and then set down in Cheyne Walk, next door to his own diminutive Number 39, a men's hostel eight storeys high whose massing and emphatic piers read unmistakably as a tower, and recalled, almost as unmistakably, the architecture of American universities (Plate 114). On all three blocks he formed the parapet out of a succession of tiny crow-stepped gables; 'it was not to have only the Oxford and Cambridge tradition', he wrote: 'it was to have some of the Scotch and some of the American quality, it was to be a creation essentially suitable to London'.[71] It may not have been the tallest building in London, but if it had been built its only rival for some years in sheer verticality would have been H. P. Berlage's 1914 office block at 32 Bury Street in the City of London.

The Fraternity House was not quite the pipe-dream that it seems, for London University seemed likely to concentrate itself in South Kensington at this time, not Bloomsbury; Ashbee must have been aware of this, as was Patrick Geddes, who had spoken of the need for an Outlook Tower in Chelsea such as he had established in Edinburgh, a hint perhaps taken up into Ashbee's design. But in the end it came to nothing, like Ashbee's other schemes in these years. It was now almost ten years since he had built anything on Cheyne Walk; but one last design remained to be executed. In 1897 he had acquired the freehold of 70 and 71 Cheyne Walk, a slip of land lying awkwardly within the Sloane Stanley estate but not

114. The men's hostel, part of Ashbee's design for a 'Fraternity House' at 40–5 Cheyne Walk. Etching by Stanley Mercer.

115. (facing page). Perspective drawing of 71 Cheyne Walk. The narrow windows in the side wall were probably not executed.

part of it.[72] There are almost a hundred drawings for this site in Chelsea Public Library, many of which precede the executed design; and they show how Ashbee experimented with designs for his properties, taking them up and putting them down, looking for ways to attract clients. Numbers 70 and 71 were two small terraced shops of identical plan, and at different times Ashbee proposed to keep them and put a studio behind (1907); to refurbish them and add a storey in the roof (possibly 1910); to rebuild to the existing plan, adding more storeys and English Renaissance façades; to rebuild Number 71 only, squeezing the plan and accommodation of 74 Cheyne Walk on to this narrow site behind another English Renaissance façade; and to cover the whole site with a town house for a family (two nurseries and no studio).

Then, in about July 1912, a client appeared in the form of a lady artist, Miss Daisy D. Ladenburg. For her Ashbee designed a tall, three-bay studio-house, to be known as 71 Cheyne Walk though it covered both plots. It was faced in an attractively provincial way, in silver-grey brick with scarlet rubbers, and it was crowned with a deep cornice; but the rest of the façade was completely flat apart from a light wrought iron balcony to the central first floor window. It was an all but symmetrical design and as formal as any house Ashbee had designed on Cheyne Walk.[73] The designs are dated July and August 1912, and building work had begun by late September.[74]

But then, at the last minute, the elevation was altered dramatically (Plate 115).[75] The plan and the facing materials remained much the same, but Ashbee changed

the street front from three to four bays, recessed the lower storeys in the way Norman Shaw had done at the Swan House on Chelsea Embankment in the 1870s and threw a bold gallery and false cornice across his façade. This made, of course, all the difference, and what had been his most formal design now became one of his most picturesque. He had fallen back on methods he had used so often and so well on Cheyne Walk, a broken, additive façade, bold elements, an awareness of the river: and he was drawing on one design in particular, the flat façade, deep cornice and massive feature of 37 Cheyne Walk. On one of the last drawings before the executed design there is an oriel window rather like that at 37 Cheyne Walk, and a porch exactly like.[76] 71 Cheyne Walk brings us full circle in Ashbee's riverside designs.

Looking back on the Cheyne Walk houses, it is the richness of meanings and allusions, the range of effects Ashbee achieved, which are so striking; the elegant formalism of Numbers 72–3, the rusticity and provincialism, the clever pretences, façades looking other than they are, the mock humility and the harking back to Old London and Old Chelsea. These were speaking designs which worked chiefly by the associations they created rather than by virtue of composition or visual form. Yet one cannot pretend that their meanings were obvious; they were unusual in town houses, and they have to be won from the fabric by explanation. Some of these houses were illustrated in contemporary publications devoted to London houses, notably *Neubauten in London*, a series of superb photographs and plans published by Wasmuth in Berlin in 1900; and the equally excellent series of drawings by Curtis Green which appeared in the *Builder* in 1896–9 under the title 'London Street Architecture'. In both publications the buildings by Norman Shaw, Ernest George, Mackmurdo, Fairfax Wade, Stokes or Balfour and Turner showed that there were conventions in the design of late nineteenth-century town houses which could be followed with fruitful results, a dignified and welcoming porch, regular distribution of the windows, the meeting of wall and roof boldly and elegantly detailed. Ashbee rejected these conventions in favour of low-key, reticent and difficult effects; and when he put the back of 74 Cheyne Walk at the front, or asked Miss Christian's visitors to come in through something very like a tradesman's entrance, he seemed to be flaunting town house proprieties deliberately, to be slumming. Paradoxically, it was in the most eloquent of his designs, Numbers 38 and 39 and 72–5 Cheyne Walk, that these ambitious effects of reticence and mock humility were strongest. The building papers of the time, unable to accept the rather special effects Ashbee was aiming at, usually described his houses as eccentric or affected.[77]

Another paradox in these houses was that though they looked pragmatic and informal, as if they had been designed from the inside out, and perhaps added to as occasion arose, almost the opposite was the case; the arrangement of the elevations and the requirements of the plan were often only loosely related while Ashbee was designing. We have seen how the outside of Danvers Tower stayed the same while the inside was changed (and the construction severely criticized), and how, in giving Numbers 38 and 39 such dramatically different profiles, Ashbee really took the façade as his starting point. He could be deceptive. Of the free disposition of elements on the façade of 72–3 Cheyne Walk, Raymond McGrath wrote in 1934:

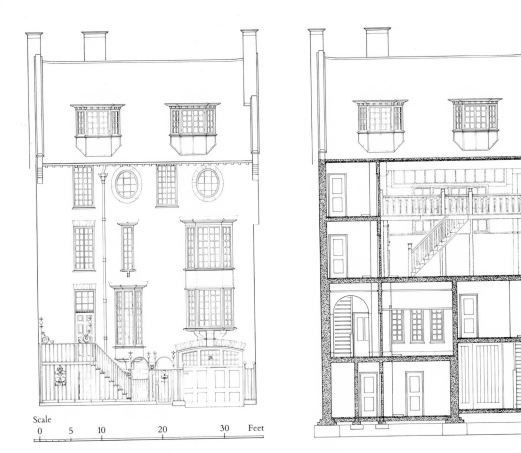

Scale
0   5   10   20   30   Feet

116. Elevation and cut-away drawing of 72–3 Cheyne Walk.

about 1900 ... Buildings were no longer looked on as pictures in stone or brick but as structures with a form which was the natural growth of the plan. The houses in Cheyne Walk are structures of this sort. The house front is a statement of a free plan. There is nothing of that false balance which is simply the balance of two more or less equal halves.[78]

McGrath had read the façade in one of the ways that Ashbee intended. But he had clearly not read the plan or been inside the house. If he had, he would have seen that Ashbee's elevation, so far from expressing his plan, rather belied it (Plate 116). The large oriel linked the sculptor's sitting-room with the lower right-hand corner of Walton's studio; the tiny flat oriel grouped that part of the studio with the various sitting-rooms; and the rhythm of the windows under the eaves was quite independent of the fact that one lit a sitting-room and the rest the studio gallery. There was freedom here, but it was precisely a freedom from functional constraints. It does not matter very much what kind of windows go in the south wall of a studio, and Ashbee took advantage of this to treat his façade as a free and engaging composition.

In looking at Ashbee's houses one by one we have not had, perhaps, the best point of view for looking at them, the wide, raking, changing view of someone walking along by the railings of the Embankment, who would see them as groups and as part of the streetscape of Cheyne Walk (Plate 117). 'When we design in the town', Ashbee wrote, 'we think, or we ought to think of the street ...', and

117. 71–5 Cheyne Walk and neighbouring houses in 1938.

in the hall of 39 Cheyne Walk he had Fleetwood Varley paint a frieze of all the
houses in Cheyne Walk from one end to the other with his own houses standing
up amongst them (Plate 151).[79] The deliberate variety of his designs, and some
of their odd and unbalanced features, such as the projections on Numbers 74 and
75, make particular sense when they are seen in this light, as incidents in the
streetscape: the roof lines shifted from parapet to gable to eaves, and from high
to low, the elevations from flat to modelled, regular to irregular, and the front
doors performed a strange, see-saw-like dance from street level up to raised ground
floor and down to half-basement; it was almost as if he wanted to hide the hand
of a single architect behind the appearance of some anonymous building process.
It was, of course, a picturesque and not a formal streetscape that Ashbee was creating
and contributing to: Cheyne Walk was not a Classical terrace to which purely
architectural criteria could be applied by extension; it was just a collection of houses,
a church, some trees and the river, a pleasant, miscellaneous place, full of history,
like a long thin village. What mattered here were scale, incident, variety and association, the criteria of streetscape, not the stricter language of architectural form.

256

There were echoes of Old London in Ashbee's houses, as we have seen, and perhaps memories of the Hamburg he had known as a child, with its narrow, picturesque waterfront façades; a writer in a Viennese magazine even saw a resemblance to old Scottish town houses.[80] One would particularly expect echoes of Old Chelsea here, for the place meant so much to Ashbee; but at this point the argument takes a curious turn. There were individual allusions, in the gable of 38 Cheyne Walk, for instance, and Ashbee's chimney details and his use of Westmorland slate perhaps owe a debt to Wren's Royal Hospital. But in the general character and grouping of his designs he did not take his cue from surviving buildings, from the surrounding streets. He ignored the large and handsome eighteenth-century houses on Cheyne Walk, east of Oakley Street and immediately west of Battersea Bridge, and the plain artisan terraces of later date offered little to his taste. He did not try to build in keeping. Instead he designed the kind of homely and unpretentious streetscape one might see in any English country town, houses only roughly aligned, all sorts of different materials, a roofscape of abrupt changes, and yet everything more or less in scale.[81] This was new building designed to catch the mood and history of the place as Ashbee understood it, a generalized, small-town picturesque which would serve as an image of Chelsea when it was still more or less a village, before it became part of London.

If there were allusions to Chelsea streetscape in Ashbee's designs—and the point is tentative—they were to buildings which no longer existed, to those which stood on the river's edge before the Embankment was built, and particularly to the jumble of houses, workshops, wharves and pubs which once formed the south side of Lombard Street, where some of his own houses were built (Plate 118). Here there were

118. Chelsea Old Church and the back of Lombard Street, seen from Battersea Bridge. (From Walter W. Burgess, *Bits of Old Chelsea* (1894), frontispiece.)

dramatic changes of roof line, humble backs and galleried projections not unlike Ashbee's. He would not have known these buildings himself, because they were demolished when he was a boy, but he would probably have known of the views in Walter Burgess's handsome book of etchings, *Bits of Old Chelsea*, published in 1894 with a text by Lionel Johnson and Richard le Gallienne.[82] It would have been characteristic of Ashbee that he should try to give his new, middle-class houses, built under the régime of the bye-laws, something of the relaxed character of their humbler predecessors. (Today an architect who shared Ashbee's vaguely socialist sympathies would have agonized over the process of gentrification in which he found himself involved, and would have hesitated to add to the injury of displacing Chelsea artisans the architectural insult of echoing the picturesque charms of their humble houses in the grander ones he designed. But Ashbee does not seem to have seen things in that light.)

In 1900 Ashbee gave a lecture in the United States called 'Chelsea or The Village of Palaces'. 'The whole Embankment', he said, 'is full of painters, poets, politicians, wits and worthies from one generation to another'—Whistler, Rossetti, Dyce, Maclise, George Eliot, Carlyle and Turner in the nineteenth century; in the eighteenth, Girtin, Gillray, Smollett, Horace Walpole and Steele; in Tudor times the queens whose houses gave him his title and above all Sir Thomas More, 'England's greatest Chancellor, the man who was her first historian, who fixed her language, who formed her oratory, who pointed to her Utopia'.[83] All this in a mere village 'hard by London, yet not of it' with no great political or academic institutions, yet 'a village dedicated to the most sacred, moral, intellectual and aesthetic traditions of English life'.[84] The reason for it all, he said, was simply tradition:

It is history that ties them, as it ties us, together, the painters go where the painters have been, the poets love each others society, the architects and builders take up the spirit of the life and give it concrete expression as each age gives them their bread, and all are moved by some historic sentiment that makes them love to be where greater than they have been before.[85]

Most of what Ashbee did on Cheyne Walk makes sense in the light of this lecture, the antiquarianism, the slumming and above all the jumbled streetscape were all designed to give a sense of Chelsea and its traditions, of an intellectual village with deep roots in the past. 'The Chelsea of today', he wrote in the same lecture, 'is primarily the home of artists.'[86] It is only when Ashbee's houses are seen in the light of his special sense of history, of literary, political and cultural traditions running in parallel with architecture and giving it meaning by association, that they can be seen as he saw them, as the setting and embodiment of a flourishing cultural tradition; in what had been a village of palaces, he was now helping to build an urban village for artists.

It is difficult to know what to compare Ashbee's houses with. Norman Shaw in Cadogan Square and Ernest George in Harrington Gardens had built houses next door to each other which could be seen as a picturesque group. But these were imposing town houses which asserted their individual identities, whereas Ashbee's houses merged their identities more or less in that of the street. E. S. Prior's waterside hotel and lodging houses at West Bay in Dorset, and Ernest Newton's shop, bank and inn in the High Street, Bromley, Kent, were both groups designed with as much attention to picturesque streetscape as to individual designs; but neither showed quite that prolonged and personal rapport with one place that Ashbee had with Cheyne Walk.[87] Probably the nearest comparison is with the work inspired by Patrick Geddes in the 1890s and carried out by S. Henbest Capper and other architects in restoring and rebuilding the tall and picturesque town houses of Edinburgh's Old Town.[88] Geddes's effort to create a sense of intellectual community in the Old Town, and his architects' loose and Romantic sense of Scottish town building, both have their parallels in Ashbee's work. But perhaps it is not surprising that there are few comparisons to be made. It has rightly been said that Arts and Crafts architects were not good at producing town houses, and Ashbee's must count among the few consistent examples; to express his sense of an urban village he designed houses that were not just countrified, demure and honest-looking, as Arts and Crafts houses typically are, but also clever, reserved, sophisticated and ambiguous. The kind of urban picturesque that he practised was actually rather rare.

For some years these houses worked as Ashbee intended them to do, for Chelsea was the artistic quarter of London in the early twentieth century and his houses caught or created, it is hard to tell which, the peculiar atmosphere of the place.[89] And then in May 1941 Sydney Castle, who did bomb damage reports for the *Illustrated Carpenter and Builder* found himself in front of a mass of rubble between Old Church Street and Danvers Street: 'Those fronts,' he wrote, 'those oddly fascinating fronts which aped nothing Chelsea and yet seemed to breathe its atmosphere so intensely—gone!'[90] What the bombing started, redevelopment continued. In 1968 the Magpie and Stump was demolished, after a public local inquiry, the statutory procedure at that date, and a thoroughly specious decision by the Secretary of State. In its place now stands part of a block of luxury flats, wholly out of scale with the buildings in Cheyne Walk.

HOUSES IN CHIPPING CAMPDEN

When the Guild of Handicraft moved to Chipping Campden in 1902, the centre of gravity of Ashbee's architectural practice moved with it. He opened a second architectural office in Campden, and between 1902 and 1907 worked on sixteen buildings in and around the town. Campden joined Chelsea in the mythology of Ashbee's imagination, as a dream-village, rural, traditional, out of the hurry of modern industrialism and yet in touch with the essentials of life. But there was one important difference. His dream of Chelsea was vested chiefly in its literary and artistic traditions; that of Campden in the buildings themselves, in what Ashbee took to be 'perhaps the finest High Street in England'.[91] For this reason, Ashbee's work in Campden was much more a question of building in keeping than it had been in Chelsea.

By 1902 Ashbee had had some experience of architectural work with old buildings, and even advertised himself as a specialist in restoration work.[92] In the winter of 1897–8 he bought 118–19 Cheyne Walk, a couple of plain brick urban cottages of uncertain date in one of which J. M. W. Turner had lived and died, to save them from demolition, and restored them as a double house for his friends, Max

119. 118–19 Cheyne Walk.

120. (facing page). Izod's Cottage, High Street, Chipping Campden.

Balfour and Lionel Curtis (Plate 119).[93] He retained the carcase of the houses, restored the details of the façades, and restored such interesting fireplaces and panelling as had survived the attentions of tramps. But openings were made in the party wall, and internal walls were removed to provide a common hall, kitchen and dining-room, so that two small dwellings became one larger one, adapted to the tastes of a couple of middle-class bachelors. It may be that Turner's house would not have survived but for Ashbee's scheme; but one may equally ask in what sense the simple urban cottage in which Turner hid himself away did in fact survive this exercise in gentrification.

At the mediaeval church of Sts Peter and Paul, Horndon-on-the-Hill, Essex, Ashbee carried out a restoration scheme in 1898–1900, quite in accordance with the principles of the Society for the Protection of Ancient Buildings. Indeed, the most interesting aspect of the job is that Ashbee's survey reports showed that there was nothing basically wrong with the fabric, nor does there seem to have been a need for much more accommodation.[94] The new vicar, the Reverend S. W. Fischel, was put in touch with Ashbee by Mackmurdo, an early member of the SPAB, and it may be that his architectural tastes were of the scholarly-progressive kind that would sympathize with the Society.[95] At all events, the principal works carried out were the removal of plaster to reveal the timbers of the roof, the clearing away of encumbrances round the open timber structure at the foot of the tower, and the installation of a Gurney stove, of the kind approved by the SPAB; that is, chiefly, a clarification of the existing structure to reveal its archaeologically interesting features. With the addition of new church furniture by Ashbee, Fischel had, by the end of the day, a church of roughly the same size and effectiveness, but warm, academically correct, and up to the mark.

These preliminary examples are enough to show that working with old buildings in the 1890s was not as straightforward a matter as one would imagine from such stereotypes of conservation history as Morris and the SPAB defending the past against the ravages of over-restoration, or Ashbee the conservationist making his stand against greed and commercialism. There was something of the developer in Ashbee's attitude to Turner's house, and at Horndon-on-the-Hill it was SPAB orthodoxy which initiated change. In looking at Ashbee's work in Campden we will not assume that there is only one approved way of building in keeping.

Ashbee's first Campden job was Izod's Cottage of 1902, a new house built on the site of a couple of dilapidated cottages and using materials salvaged from them (Plate 120). It was in the High Street, though at its less glamorous end, and Ashbee clearly felt that he should keep close to the local traditions; the masonry and roofing slates were graded in size, there were mullioned windows with metal casements, and the only reticence was the recessing of the jambs of the windows in place of a drip-mould. The result was a pretty full essay in Cotswold vernacular, and there is little about the house today to distinguish it from an original cottage that has been carefully, if extensively, restored.[96]

In the next year he built a cottage in Sheep Street, for Lord Gainsborough, once

again on the site of an existing one and using old materials, and, like Izod's Cottage, providing accommodation for a member of the Guild (Plate 121). Here Ashbee took a simpler approach, using graded masonry and slates, but with plain oak lintels over the windows and wooden casements of the sort he used on all his small houses. He built the new cottage over the ground floor of the old one, giving a sheer and effective drop to the street, as well as keeping his new house dry. Ashbee could see the hard, stark side of Cotswold buildings and landscape, an insight which has been smothered by the saccharine images of twentieth-century tourism, and he caught some of this mood in the gauntness of his design.[97]

In 1904 he restored and added to a cottage for Paul Woodroffe, the stained glass artist, at Westington, an outlying hamlet of Campden (Plate 122). The original building he described as 'a somewhat melancholy Cotswold cottage' to which a low outhouse wing had been added; and it filled the view as the road curved out of Campden.[98] His addition was a shallow gabled wing containing a hall, staircase and bathroom (Plate 123); it was plain enough, but its place in the street view and the dimness of the original building made it the chief and most attractive feature of the house; someone who did not know its history would take the gable for old work and the outhouse wing for the twentieth-century addition.

121. Cottage for Lord Gainsborough, Sheep Street, Chipping Campden.

122. Westington, Chipping Campden. The cottage was altered and added to by Ashbee for Paul Woodroffe in 1904.

123. Woodroffe's cottage with Ashbee's additions.

The Woodroffe house raises one of the problems of adding to cottages according to SPAB principles. Ashbee wrote, 'As a general principle I have, in this matter of the repair of cottages and little buildings in the country, followed the lines of the Society for the Preservation of Ancient Buildings.'[99] And in detail this was probably true: the Woodroffe house, for instance, has gutters of two planks in a V-section, an SPAB recipe. But there were larger and more problematic issues involved in the Society's teachings, notably their view that additions to old work 'should be simple and unpretentious, of good material and workmanship, and frankly the production of the present day'.[100] This view had been worked out with reference to buildings of considerable age and architectural character, mainly mediaeval churches.[101] And it was clear how a vestry, for instance, added to a mediaeval church, could be made 'simple and unpretentious ... and frankly the production of the present day'. But it was not so clear how SPAB orthodoxy could be applied to cottages which were already and in themselves simple and unpretentious. In about 1902 Ernest Barnsley built himself a house called Upper Dorvel at Sapperton in the Cotswolds, by adding picturesque and characteristic cross-gabled wings at either end of a plain and unromantic existing cottage. Barnsley was an active member of the SPAB; but in his house it was the new work which seemed old and the old work which seemed simple and unpretentious.[102]

The converse of this point—the larger the original building and the more substantial its architectural character the more bearing SPAB principles will have—was well illustrated by Ashbee's work on the Norman Chapel at Broad Campden of 1905–7 (Plates 71, 124–5). When he surveyed the building in 1903 it was completely derelict.[103]. There was the nave of a Norman church, with north and south doorways and chancel arch surviving; in the fourteenth or fifteenth century this had been turned into a dwelling by the insertion of an upper room with a fine timber

263

124. The Norman Chapel, Broad Campden. Perspective drawing of the south or garden front by Philippe Mairet, 1907.

roof, now partly collapsed; and at about the same time two small two-storey domestic wings had been added, running out from the west end of the chapel and then south. It was a fascinating relic; Ashbee may have bought a ground lease at this date, and would have liked to restore it as his own house. But he had to wait for the arrival of a most sympathetic client in the person of Ananda Coomaraswamy.[104]

It was clear that the original building should be devoted to reception rooms so that they could be kept uncluttered; and in all stages of Ashbee's designs the fine room above the nave was planned as a library and the fourteenth- or fifteenth-century additions were thrown together as a dining-room. As for the nave, in his first scheme Ashbee treated it as a large hall, opened out the chancel arch to some extent, and put a staircase hall where the chancel would have been; and since the Coomaraswamys wanted a music room, he added a wing running south from the staircase hall with bedrooms above. This appears to have been designed in a rather stodgy Cotswold vernacular, and obscured part of the south wall of the nave.[105]

Coomaraswamy may have found this too expensive, for the final solution was less ambitious, and happier in its effect. The staircase was put in the entrance hall, and the nave was planned as a music room with the chancel arch treated as a window.[106] However, the ceiling over the nave had been laid so low in the late Middle Ages that it broke across the head of the chancel arch, and this had been

264

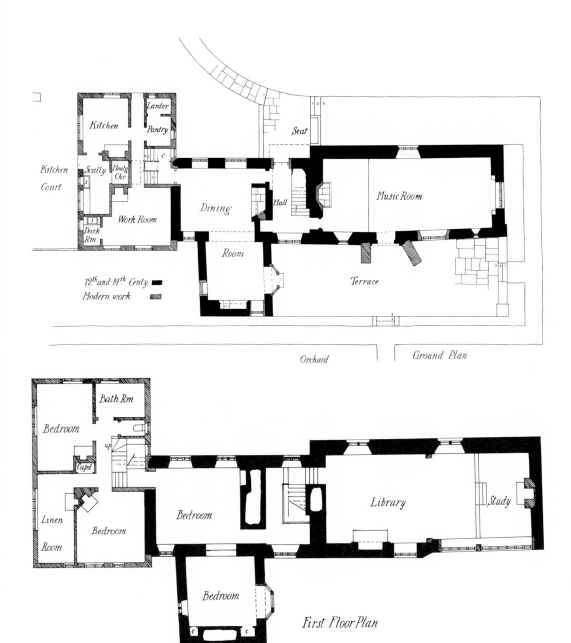

Kitchen

Larder

Pantry

Kitchen Court

Scully

Heat&
Chr

c

Work Room

Dark
Rm

Seat

Dining

Hall

Music Room

Room

Terrace

12ᵗʰ and 14ᵗʰ Centy.
Modern work

Orchard

Ground Plan

Bath Rm

Bedroom

up

Cupd

Linen
Room

Bedroom

Bedroom

Library

Study

Bedroom

First Floor Plan

125. The Norman Chapel, ground and first floor plans.

filled with masonry. Ashbee's solution was to leave most of the ceiling as it was, but to raise its easternmost bay a few feet; the change which this caused in the floor level of the library above was happily adapted to a dais which, curtained with Morris textiles, provided a splendid inner sanctum for the Singalese scholar (Plate 126). As for the rest of the building, Ashbee's final treatment was a model of sensitive enhancement. Where the walls of the nave were unstable they were rebuilt and buttressed; to let more light into the late mediaeval wing he built a two-storey bay of oak with roughcast spandrels and a handsome moulded bressumer to carry the gable; and at the north-west corner he built a new service wing

126. The library at the Norman Chapel in Coomaraswamy's time. The trestle table came from the workshop of A. Romney Green.

of roughcast brick with white-painted wooden casements, much like any of his humblest country buildings. He said that he built like that 'to harmonise and yet not compete with the stonework of the two earlier periods', sentiments of the purest SPAB kind.[107]

Though his original idea of a separate music room wing was not a happy one, and though he may have been deterred from it more by cost than by SPAB principles, Ashbee's executed scheme for the Norman Chapel was a triumphant demonstration of the value of the Society's approach when applied to buildings of some size and architectural character. Where his new work was considerable, it was different enough in treatment not to affect one's sense of the older buildings; while these buildings were left uncluttered in their turn. Craggy and exposed on its little hill, the Norman Chapel was both old and new. It was gentle and civilized in a modern way: you could sit on the terrace by some of its oldest stones and be sheltered from the wind (Plate 127). Yet much of its magic lay in its great age; it had on it what Ruskin called 'the golden stain of time', and the sense of tradition,

266

of a building adapting itself to changing uses and yet somehow staying the same.[108] And perhaps what fascinated Ashbee most was the simple fact that long ago it had been a church and was one no longer, and so bore witness to the story of men's shifting beliefs. Like Chelsea, it stirred his historical imagination, as his curious novel *Peckover* showed.[109]

Ashbee's Campden work can be conveniently compared with that which was

127. The terrace at the Norman Chapel.

being done at about the same time only a few miles away in the fashionable village of Broadway, at the foot of the Cotswold escarpment. In almost all cases, Ashbee's work was more reticent and austere, more nervous of adopting the obvious forms of seventeenth-century Cotswold vernacular, than the contemporary work of Guy Dawber, Andrew Prentice and C. E. Bateman in Broadway.[110] Yet, as we have seen, his work was not done in a doctrinaire spirit of unpretentiousness. It was various, sometimes academically correct, sometimes austere, sometimes picturesque; but always taking its cue from a refined sense of the place and of the neighbouring buildings.

COTTAGES AND LITTLE HOUSES

In 1906 Ashbee published *A Book of Cottages and Little Houses* which was partly a disquisition on the ethics, aesthetics and economics of building small houses in the country, and partly a presentation of his own work in this field; he hoped, perhaps, to give a boost to his practice in difficult times. There was a good deal of interest in the small house in the country around 1900; reforming landowners were building cottages for farm labourers and wanted to know what the basic standards and costs might be; middle-class city dwellers were finding that they could afford a weekend cottage or seaside home and that the railways could get them there; architects were looking for ways to protect architectural character and sensible planning within the tighter constraints of size and cost; and there was a growing literature on the subject.[111] Ashbee's book, and in a sense the houses themselves, were a contribution to this debate, and they ranged from an entry in the 1905 competition to build a cottage for £150 at Letchworth Garden City, to a detached middle-class house with four bedrooms; but most of them were either workers' cottages of the kitchen-scullery or kitchen-scullery-parlour kind, costing c. £200–£250; or small middle-class houses with a kitchen, dining-room, sitting-room and possibly one other small reception room, varying in price from c. £800 to £1200.

His first house of this kind was built in 1900 on a building estate in Orpington (Plate 128) for Henry (later Sir Henry) Fountain, who perhaps came to Ashbee because he had been to King's College, Cambridge. It was called The Shoehorn, probably because of the amount of accommodation Ashbee squeezed in, and is now 15 Station Road, Orpington. It looks as if Ashbee started with the idea that he would have an absolutely square plan with an almost unbroken perimeter, and a pyramidal roof with a central chimney stack. Into this box, 29 feet square, he managed to fit the basic middle-class reception rooms plus a study, by making the hall double as a dining-room and by the exercise of some very tight planning. It was not completely successful, doors and hearths were forced awkwardly close together, and it may be that some internal convenience was sacrificed for the sake of the external effect: a neat brick box under a neat tiled lid.[112]

Put like that, The Shoehorn sounds self-consciously pretty, but a closer look reveals a more robust character.[113] It was built of local bricks of standard dimensions, not the two-inch handmade bricks Ashbee had used on Cheyne Walk; all the windows were set in thick, all but unmoulded wooden frames; and on the ground floor they were spanned by segmental arches closer in character to industrial

128. The Shoehorn, 15 Station Road, Orpington.

than to domestic buildings. The treatment of the front door and flanking windows had a skeletal resemblance to a late seventeenth- or early eighteenth-century porch, but it was treated in a quite rudimentary way as a framing of six-inch wide planks under a *cyma recta* moulding, as if one were demonstrating the elements of post and beam construction to a child. At The Shoehorn one is aware, not just of neatness and sturdiness, but of a tense, negative feeling, of the many obvious elaborations which have been refused.

The Shoehorn is interesting because it tries so hard not to be; it is extraordinarily and deliberately ordinary. Many Arts and Crafts architects preached a gospel of plain, ordinary building, but often their work was more picturesque than their preaching warranted; it is refreshing to find Ashbee taking the argument literally. His comments on the building throw some light on his self-effacement: 'It was on a building estate that was being developed by others, and what I was asked to do was something that should be a little more restrained, quiet and restful than what was customary, and also be in very small compass.'[114] One has only to walk along Station Road, Orpington, today to see what he was avoiding, the scatter

269

129. Little Coppice,
Pinewood Road, Iver
Heath. (From a
drawing by F. L.
Griggs in C. R. Ashbee,
*A Book of Cottages and
Little Houses* (1906),
plate 11.)

of bays, half-timbered gables and clever porches which were the normal means
of articulation in late nineteenth- and early twentieth-century suburban housing.
In themselves such features seem versatile, and often pleasant today, but progressive
architectural opinion round 1900 censured them as fussy, inappropriate and the
enemies of a really architectural treatment:

Many bays, gables and wings generally cost more than their effect warrants, and if the
house is small will look small also. Breadth of effect is by no means impossible in a small
house, but the attempt to crowd into it all the features of a large mansion invariably ends
in disaster both to convenience and artistic effect.[115]

Ashbee designed The Shoehorn in this spirit, and though breadth of effect was
not its most obvious quality, it was to such refined and intangible architectural
effects that his attempt was addressed.

Ashbee was probably pleased with the compactness of The Shoehorn, for in
almost all his small houses he kept to a rectangular plan and avoided breaking its
perimeters with bays, outbuildings and the like. (Voysey had shown the way in
this at The Orchard, Chorleywood.) And a number of later houses also had
pyramidal roofs, though more often he adopted a simple system of cross-gables
with at least two stacks, which made their plans more relaxed. The most obvious
change after The Shoehorn was a superficial but important one; from 1902–3 he
generally used roughcast over brick for his external treatment, and his use of it
says a good deal about the character of his small houses.[116]

One of the first uses was at Little Coppice, Pinewood Road, Iver Heath, of 1903
(Plate 129).[117] Roughcast is a typical treatment in parts of Buckinghamshire, but
the design of Little Coppice, with its buttresses, suggests that Ashbee owed as much

270

to Voysey as to the local vernacular; and that is confirmed by later small houses, all roughcast, which are found in Gloucestershire, Hertfordshire and Sussex. Ashbee was using it, like Voysey and many other Arts and Crafts architects, as a standard treatment, irrespective of locality. Such a use is puzzling, considering the Arts and Crafts belief that architects should take their cue from the local vernacular when building in the country. After all, though roughcast itself had a respectable vernacular pedigree, as a covering for brick cottages it could not date back much beyond 1800, and since that date had been used quite widely throughout the country; in Arts and Crafts eyes, it must have lacked the glamour both of age and of locality.[118] The explanation of its popularity may have been partly that it was a cheap form of walling, a point of supreme importance in small houses; and partly that it was neat and unpretentious, had so neutral a character that you could expect it to fit in anywhere. It was this unpretentiousness that seems to have weighed most with Ashbee.

In 1907 he built a house called Byways at Yarnton, outside Oxford (Plate 130). The roof and chimneys were treated in a Cotswold way; but the rest of the house was given a simple coat of roughcast over brick, and Ashbee explained that it 'had been kept as simple as possible in design in order that it may harmonise with the

130. Byways, Yarnton.

131. Five Bells, Pinewood Road, Iver Heath.

building traditions of the district'.[119] He did not mean that the building traditions of the district were peculiarly simple, far less that they included roughcast on brick; but that his design and materials were so neutral and straightforward that they would not disturb those traditions. We have, of course, met this attitude before, in the service wing Ashbee added to the Norman Chapel. It is a measure of the reticence of his small houses that he should approach the design of a new detached house on the fringe of the Cotswolds with a reverence for local traditions worthy of the SPAB.

An architect who sets himself to build cheap houses without recourse to pretty features, and in so inoffensive a style that they will not seem out of place in any part of England, is forced back in the end on the simplest and most difficult of architectural effects, proportion. Of the £150 cottage at Letchworth the 'reductio ad absurdum of architecture' as he called it, Ashbee said: 'The principal thing to observe in so simple a piece of work as the £150 cottage must necessarily be proportion; obviously where every farthing has to be studied we cannot build with good scantling, and all our materials must be thin. But we can always have good proportion.'[120] Yet good proportion is something that his small houses often lack. The semi-detached houses called Five Bells, which Ashbee built in 1905 in Pinewood Road, Iver Heath (Plate 131), provide a useful illustration because they were similar in character to Baillie Scott's widely illustrated Elmwood Cottages at 7 and 7A Norton Way, Letchworth (Plate 132).[121] Both were designed as a semi-detached pair with cross gables to each end and a central recessed porch; but whereas the outline of Scott's pair was broken by recessions, outhouses, dormers and chimneys, Ashbee's presented an almost unbroken envelope; Scott's roof broke to a lower, more picturesque pitch over his scullery, Ashbee's kept to a supremely sensible forty-five degrees; where Scott had long low windows, Ashbee's were as high as they were wide; Scott decorated his porch with half-timber, Ashbee's only light relief was the odd touch of hanging five bells in the exposed metal joist which spanned the porch. Though Scott's pair were built and exhibited in the Cheap Cottage Exhibition of 1905, all his effects ran towards higher costs and more expres-

272

132. Design for Elmwood Cottages, Letchworth, by Baillie Scott.

sive proportions; all Ashbee's ran towards lower costs and boxy, reticent proportions. Like the late Mr Honeychurch in *A Room with a View*, he 'affected the cube because it gave him the most accommodation for his money . . .'.[122]

After his work in Chelsea and Chipping Campden, Ashbee's small houses are a disappointment. One can understand, and admire, his reason for building as he did, but it is difficult to get beyond a simply intellectual approval of the buildings. Their boxiness and reticence seem puzzling, almost perverse, when compared with the rest of his work, particularly that in Chelsea. On circumscribed urban sites he managed to introduce extraordinary varieties of plan and projection, but on open country sites everything was squeezed into a tight, rectangular box; his London façades were picturesque and elegant but all his small houses presented the same featureless wall of roughcast; his London houses were speaking designs, but his small houses were dumb.

THE SPIRIT OF THE PLACE

The answer lies in the puzzle itself. Ashbee needed the inspiration of a particular kind of setting. He had to have buildings around him to act as a cue for his designing, and he was perhaps unnerved by green field sites. If the buildings had history in them, and some strong tradition of the arts, architecture, literature and thought, the activities he prized most, then he was happiest. Chelsea and Chipping Campden had these in abundance; they were historic enclaves of culture and his imagination responded to them. Iver Heath had none of these things, and he built roughcast boxes. The secret of his best architectural work was a refined sense of place.

Three interesting and important designs, which have not been mentioned so far because they do not belong to any of the three principal groups, demonstrate this point. When Ashbee went to Budapest in 1905 to design a house for Zsombor de Szász, he was delighted with his client, with the atmosphere of the city and with the boys bathing in the Danube; but he thought the architecture of Budapest

273

133. House for Zsombor de Szász in Budapest. (From F. L. Griggs's drawing in the *Builder*, 1910, vol. 98, p. 326.)

was rotten.[123] Lacking a cue, he designed a long, low version of one of his roughcast houses, relying for effect largely on colour; white roughcast, green shutters and a red tiled roof (Plate 133). All his enjoyment of Budapest was poured into the statuary group 'The Spirit of Modern Hungary' which he designed for the hall; the architecture of the house remained bland and uncertain. Two years later he was asked to design a villa in Taormina for Colonel Shaw-Hellier, and we have seen what an impression the sun and stone and history of Sicily made on him when he and Janet travelled there in January 1907, how it healed and excited his spirit during the difficult times of the Guild. No place had ever made so strong an impression on him architecturally. 'I doubt', he wrote, 'whether there is anywhere else in the world such a record of stupendous building contained in so small a compass as here in Sicily . . . My time has been a good deal taken up with . . . the effort to give something of that wonderful Graeco-Sicilian in my Colonel's house.'[124] The conditions for one of his best buildings were here.

The Villa San Giorgio, as it was called (Plate 134), was different from anything he had built before, a large flat-roofed villa which fits readily into the fabric of Taormina. The walls of plastered stone, the architraves of the windows, the band of tufa inlay below the cornice, were all typical of buildings in the town, including the nineteenth-century ones; and at one end of the entrance front he built a handsome staircase very like that in the courtyard of the Palazzo Corvaia, one of Taormina's principal buildings. The plan was laid out more or less symmetrically around

134. Villa San Giorgio, Taormina: part of the entrance front.

135. Perspective sketch by Ashbee of his proposed hotel in Jerusalem, 1922.

a large two-storey *salone* with a chimneypiece at one end, inlaid with marble and tufa, and a richly carved organ gallery at the other, to indulge the colonel's rather uneven taste in music. In its succession of airy, columned spaces, white plastered walls and stretches of ornamental enrichment, it was like the interiors which Herbert Baker had built, and which Ashbee had admired so much, under the South African sun.[125] There is the feeling at the Villa San Giorgio, and it is one of the pleasures of the house, that two quite different traditions, that of Sicilian architecture and that of the English Arts and Crafts, have blended happily together. If it is not quite one of Ashbee's finest houses, not as expressive as his best on Cheyne Walk or the Norman Chapel; if there is a slight sense of quotation and of self-consciousness about the local details, it is perhaps because Sicily was all so new to him and he did not, as he did in Chelsea and Chipping Campden, reach an every-day acquaintance with the place.

In Jerusalem, finally, Ashbee did have time to let the city and its architecture grow upon him, and time to find an intellectual image of the place that would release the best in him as an architect. We have seen how he cared for the vernacular fabric of Jerusalem and for the image of the walled city standing distinct, the city of an idea. The sketch designs he made in 1922 for a large hotel for Thomas Cook

276

and Son (Plate 135) show what he might have done architecturally if his stay in the city had been longer.[126] He took the domed and arcaded vernacular of the Old City as his point of departure not because he was building pedantically in keeping—the hotel was well to the west of the Old City, across the valley—but because it was flexible. It allowed him to design a large building which would be almost monumental when seen from the Old City, and yet would tuck itself away, stepping back gently into the hillside, when seen from the proposed Ridge Road. It was the perfect site for Ashbee: he did not want to add to the Old City but to admire it; and he designed a hotel whose windows would be filled with the view of the great city walls, profiled against the light at the beginning of the day, warm from the sun at its close.

His ideas about architecture were often theoretical and ambitious; he was only too ready to interpret buildings in terms of the *Zeitgeist*. It is refreshing to find that his practice as an architect was inspired by something more down-to-earth and more properly architectural than such heady notions. When he evoked the atmosphere and traditions of Chelsea or Chipping Campden, when he tried to build his sense of Sicily into the Colonel's villa or of Jerusalem into Thomas Cook's hotel, he was responding, not to the Spirit of the Age, but to the Spirit of the Place.

CHAPTER ELEVEN
FURNITURE AND INTERIOR
DECORATION

DOMESTIC FURNITURE

When the Movement was at its height around 1900 there were few kinds of Arts and Crafts work more important than the making of furniture. It seemed to express the mood and ideals of the Movement so tellingly. Impressively solid and often austere, the tables and chairs, cabinets and mighty settles were a deliberate rebuke to the middle-class drawing-rooms of late Victorian England, with their close-packed mixture of plump upholstery, light movable furniture and elaborately painted and faceted cabinets; the frank construction and simply treated surfaces of Arts and Crafts furniture spoke of a preoccupation with honesty and natural materials. And somehow furniture seemed to resist the drift towards preciousness and whimsy which afflicted the more portable Arts and Crafts; it remained tied to use, 'stern use' as Ruskin would have said. Set in the context of an Arts and Crafts interior, it carried hints, not just of new ways in art, but of a new way of living.

The Movement continued a tradition of architect-designed furniture which went back to the eighteenth century, for almost all the leading Arts and Crafts furniture designers were architects: Mackmurdo, Voysey, Baillie Scott and, above all, Ernest Gimson and Sidney Barnsley. These last two seemed to typify so much of the spirit of the Movement, mixing the traditions of urban cabinet-making and country carpentry, taking the grain of woods and the necessities of construction, and making out of them a new and sophisticated style of furniture for a refined and country-loving upper middle class. In all this one would expect Ashbee to have a place, for furniture was always a large and important part of the Guild's output. Yet he does not enjoy a high reputation as a designer of furniture. To modern eyes his work seems uncertain in design and heavy in its proportions; accounts of the Guild tend to pass over it in favour of the more obviously successful metalwork and jewellery; and it has even been described as 'really very similar to the best trade work of the time', giving 'no indication of its Arts and Crafts background'.[1] In his own time, however, Ashbee's furniture was more readily and easily appreciated than it is now, and critics who had the chance to see it at close quarters at successive Arts and Crafts Exhibitions were not inclined to underrate its quality.

Furniture was probably made from the earliest days of the Guild, for C. V. Adams, one of the founder members, was a cabinet-maker; he was soon joined by R. G. Phillips and Walter Curtis, and by an apprentice, Charley Atkinson; and a good deal of furniture was produced before the move to Essex House in 1891, to judge from designs in the Guild Workshop Record Book.[2] These show that the Guild made very much the same types of furniture as trade cabinet-makers:

136. The Guild cabinet-makers at Chipping Campden.

there were occasional tables and chairs, cabinets of various kinds, sideboards, dining-tables and chairs, desks and writing tables, wardrobes and wash-stands. There were some omissions on grounds of taste: no many-shelved pieces like what-nots or over-mantels, and little all-over or buttoned upholstery, for when Ashbee did upholster, seat and back were usually treated separately, generally in plain leather boldly nailed down in the manner associated with the time of Cromwell.[3] Occasionally he allowed himself to be drawn by his admiration for old work into designing out-moded, antiquarian types such as a settle convertible into a table, designed in 1890, which was modelled on the early seventeenth-century type popularly known as a 'monk's bench'; or his standard trestle design for dining-tables, of which more later.[4] If there was a peculiarity in Guild furniture, it was a bias towards heavy or fixed pieces, cabinets and suchlike which go against the wall, with relatively few designs for tables and chairs. Until *c.* 1900 Ashbee seems to have been happy to supply chairs of the rush-seated type made popular by Morris and Company and Ernest Gimson, without putting his own stamp on their design.[5] The scope of the Guild in these early days was much like that of any small trade workshop; it did not specialize particularly, and made more or less what its clients wanted; and the prices of work seem comparable to those charged by such firms as Heal's and Harrod's in the middle-class market.

Style was a very different matter. Much trade furniture around 1890 was still touched by the enthusiasms of the Aesthetic Movement. Except perhaps in a heavy masculine room like a library, cabinets would be made up of slim, elaborately turned verticals, little shelves and nooks backed by rails of bobbins, panels of bevelled glass, and incised ornament picked out in gold. Ebonized woods made such pieces dark in appearance, though light and open in construction. Ashbee's early furniture was so different that it reads as a conscious reaction. It was unmistakably joiners' furniture, made of heavy members in explicit frame and panel construction; the usual woods were oak, basswood and walnut, the first two sometimes stained green. Cabinets were solid and enclosed rather than open in structure; and the detailing was traditional: frame and panel elements were usually moulded and fielded, legs were often bracketed, and cornices were normal. One is aware of sixteenth- and seventeenth-century exemplars, but in an uneven way, more in some pieces than in others, and more in isolated details, such as ball and claw feet and rather elaborate cornices of *c.* 1700, than in general character.[6] Some pieces were quite plain and others were painted, notably an oak cabinet for the New School at Abbotsholme whose doors were covered with a delicate design of undulating sprays of laurel interspersed with lines from Blake's *Auguries of Innocence*.[7] But Ashbee's favourite form of decoration was coloured and gilded gesso applied sparingly to the wood. On Mr Maxwell's cabinet (Plate 137), Ashbee and J. Eadie Reid have used gold and gesso and painting in an adaptation of the Renaissance motif of *putti* sporting among scrolling ornament; here they struggle playfully with the spheres which served Ashbee as an image of life's cyclical progressions. The general effect of these early pieces, compared with the trade furniture of the time, was of solidity, of character based on traditional construction, and of broad, restful surfaces.

From about the time of the move to Essex House early in 1891 until the mid-1890s, there is a gap in the story of Guild furniture. Only a handful of new designs can be firmly attributed to this period; and it is probable that less furniture was

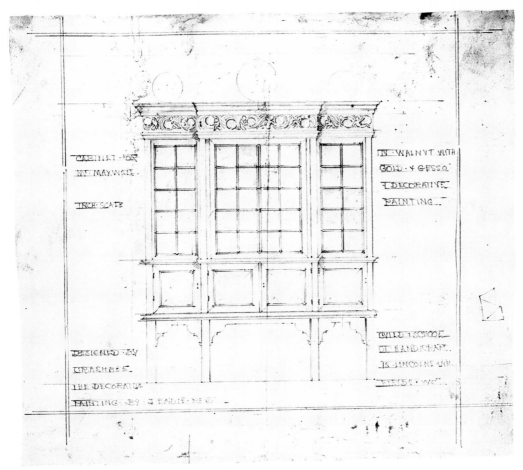

In the drawing (as labels):

CABINET FOR
MR MAXWELL

INCH SCALE

IN WALNUT WITH
GOLD & GESSO
& DECORATIVE
PAINTING

DESIGNED BY
C R ASHBEE
THE DECORATIVE
PAINTING BY J EADIE REID

GUILD & SCHOOL
OF HANDICRAFT
35 LINCOLNS INN
FIELDS WC

137. Design for a cabinet by Ashbee and J. Eadie Reid.

made, for the woodshop's four craftsmen were reduced to three in 1891; though they were four again in 1892, much of their time must have been taken up with interior decoration at Bryngwyn, Herefordshire, in 1892, and at the Magpie and Stump in 1893–4.[8]

These fallow years were, as it happens, critical in the development of Arts and Crafts furniture. During the 1880s furniture that could be clearly associated with the Arts and Crafts was confined, on the whole, to the severe designs of Mackmurdo and the Century Guild, decorated with vivid natural ornament, and to the work of Morris and Company which included two quite different kinds of furniture: fine cabinet-making on the one hand, often to George Jack's designs, and simple, sturdy pieces of joiner's work on the other, designed by Philip Webb or Ford Madox Brown.[9]

In 1890 five architects, all men of influence in the Arts and Crafts in their different ways, set themselves up to produce furniture under the style of Kenton and Company. Their work showed the same difference of emphasis. Reginald Blomfield and Mervyn Macartney generally designed pieces which showed their admiration for the manly elegance, as Arts and Crafts people would have put it, of late seventeenth- and eighteenth-century English furniture. W. R. Lethaby and Ernest Gimson produced some work of this kind, but they also designed oak furniture with obviously humble, even rustic, associations: chests by Lethaby with deliberately coarse inlay, a stark sideboard by Gimson with bold and playful chamfering along the back rail.[10] At this stage it seemed as if it was in the nature of the Arts and Crafts Movement that its furniture should follow two paths, the path of high cabinet-making with its preference for walnut, mahogany and veneers, refined techniques and exemplars of *c.*1700, and the path of deliberately humble furniture with its preference for oak, joinery techniques, and exemplars of varied date and vernacular origin.

The Arts and Crafts Exhibition of 1893 included work of both kinds by the architects of Kenton and Company; but it also included work by the Wood Handicrafts Society, which suggested a third path that the Arts and Crafts might follow. The central figure of the Society was probably Charles Spooner, who exhibited a sideboard and a writing cabinet in oak which were both plain and sturdy. But its most striking exhibit was a lady's work cabinet in green-stained oak by Voysey (Plate 138); striking for the broad, plain framing of the case, for the way it was slung between slim, tapering columns, for the bold openwork hinge decoration by W. Bainbridge Reynolds, and for its distance from, almost lack of, exemplars. It did not follow either of the established paths, for though it was simple it was neither massive nor crude, and it used vernacular exemplars, not as a source of rustic association, but as a starting point for something puritan in taste and modern in appeal, from which the period details had been stripped away. Most of Ashbee's later furniture was of this kind; he knew and admired Charles Spooner, who later taught a class in design at Essex House; and it is hard to believe, given the way his own furniture designs developed, that he did not look long and hard at the work of the Wood Handicrafts Society in 1893, and at Voysey's cabinet in particular.[11]

The Guild of Handicraft exhibited no furniture at all at that exhibition. Then, probably in the winter of 1893–4, the woodshop was dramatically enlarged from four to ten, and at the next Arts and Crafts Exhibition in 1896, they showed five pieces of furniture, one of which attracted considerable attention.[12] It was a music cabinet in oak, and quite different from anything Ashbee had designed before (Plate 139). The details were so far simplified as to be no longer traditional mouldings; the doors, sides and back were of frame and panel construction, but treated as flush surfaces, and it was quite undecorated, a classic piece of negative Arts and Crafts designing; by leaving out or smoothing away the expected features of traditional mouldings, frame and panel construction and ornament, it focused attention on the mass and surface of the wood. The *Studio* took exception to its nakedness and wrote of 'simplicity carried dangerously near triteness ... the pride that apes humility ...'; but the *Artist* thought 'There is no better piece of work on exhibition at the Arts and Crafts than the plain undecorated and untouched oak cabinet which the Guild show.'[13]

In the following year, 1897, Ashbee was asked to collaborate with an architect not well known in Arts and Crafts circles, but who had exhibited an interesting upright piano in the 1896 exhibition and written some romantic articles on interiors in the *Studio*, M. H. Baillie Scott. Ernst Ludwig, Grand Duke of Hesse, commissioned Scott to design furniture and interior decorations for the dining-room and drawing-room of his palace at Darmstadt in West Germany. Either at the Duke's suggestion or at Scott's, it is not clear which, Ashbee was asked to design the light

138. Lady's work cabinet of about 1893 by C. F. A. Voysey. (From *Dekorative Kunst* (Munich), 1898, vol. 1, p. [259].)

139. Music cabinet designed by Ashbee in about 1896.

fittings, and the Guild to make both fittings and furniture. In practice the collaboration was closer than such definitions of responsibility suggest, for Scott and Ashbee seem to have echoed each other's tastes. Scott's design for an upright chair with an embossed leather back for the drawing-room (almost the only item from the whole scheme to survive today) was based on a design by Ashbee which he had seen and admired at the Arts and Crafts Exhibition in 1890, and which was itself a simplified version of seventeenth-century chairs upholstered in leather; and it may be that two of his cabinets were inspired by Ashbee's music cabinet shown in 1896, for they have similar outlines.[14] As for Ashbee, there are many specific debts to Scott in the work he did after Darmstadt, tricks of design and details of decoration; but what is more striking is the way his furniture designs as a whole developed at this time, and along lines very similar to Scott's, towards more original furniture types, boxy, rectangular forms and clear, linear ornament. These are some of the essential elements in the mature style which Ashbee reached in 1897–8; they were all present in Voysey's work cabinet shown in 1893; but it seems that it was the experience of working on Scott's designs that finally settled the direction of his work.[15]

It was a squared-off style, full of right angles; cabinets were treated as boxes on legs; legs were more often than not square in plan and met the body without brackets; and almost all carcase furniture was built up of simple planks, from $2\frac{1}{2}$ inches to 6 inches wide, with surfaces planed to a clean right angle, and not worked or moulded any further, as if Ashbee wanted to keep a sense of the wood waiting to be used, piled up against the workshop wall. This scantling motif—the term is bizarre but appropriate—first occurred in the panelling of the dining-room at the Magpie and Stump, which had unmoulded stiles, and then in the dining-room at 73 Cheyne Walk in 1897. In the late 1890s it became general, as pilasters on either side of fireplaces, as rails at the back of sideboards and settles, and as balusters on staircases, grouped in twos or threes.

It was also, and perhaps most interestingly, used in the framing of doors and of carcase furniture. The Guild's usual method of frame and panel construction was to drop the panel into an open rectangular rebate cut into the inside edge of the frame, and then pin it into place with a moulding. (This was a normal practice in the furniture trade and different, for instance, from that of Gimson and the Barnsleys whose frame and panel construction was integral, the panel being let into a grooved rebate in the frame before it was joined together.) On early Guild furniture the moulding would go in the usual way on the outside of the frame, for all to see; all Ashbee did in the new style was to turn his framing inside out, and put the moulding on the inside, leaving the frame and panel on the outside to meet at a clean right-angle; a back-to-front device just as striking and abrupt as some of his houses on Cheyne Walk. And then, when he built up his frames from planks as much as six inches wide, with a panel not much wider in the middle, he enhanced the sense of geometry in his furniture, the sense of two planes of equal value, one recessed behind the other.

This kind of detailing can be seen in several ways. One can see the influence, for instance, of E. W. Godwin who had used it on his ebonized furniture of the 1860s and 1870s, and Ashbee may have been thinking of that, for the sideboards which he designed for the Magpie and Stump and 39 Cheyne Walk were in their upper parts open scaffolds of shelves and uprights, Arts and Crafts versions of Godwin's best-known design.[16] In Arts and Crafts circles such framing, or something near it, was used on panelling by Philip Webb and on pieces by Gimson, Spooner, Voysey and Scott already mentioned. It can be seen as a protest, a gesture against commercially produced furniture, for Arts and Crafts workers felt it was particularly distressing that complex and traditional mouldings should be made by machine. And perhaps there was also an element of workshop romanticism, of using materials not exactly in their raw state, but as they would be found just before use, before they were framed up, hammered out, printed on or woven.

The scantling motif was a matter of refining the forms of furniture and eliminating mouldings; the ornament of the mature style, on the other hand, was a new departure. Gesso was abandoned and painting used only occasionally; instead Ashbee made great play with metalwork and inlay. The hinges on his early furniture had been moderately discreet; now he attached to them long, and often generously wide, straps of wrought iron, pewter or steel, running across the face of his doors and ending with openwork in fleshy, natural forms of the sort he designed so well; drawer handles and lock plates were decorated with similar openwork.[17] We have already seen Voysey's ornamental hingework of 1893; Baillie Scott used equally wide strap hinges on a music cabinet for Darmstadt. The motif was essentially mediaeval in inspiration, and long, wide straps such as Ashbee used can be seen on a late fifteenth-century armoire at King's College, Cambridge, which he may have known.[18] In mediaeval buildings and furniture such straps were part of the structure of carpenter-made doors and helped to hold them together; the Voysey-Scott-Ashbee use raises the suspicion of ostentation, of an honesty that is only apparent, for such long straps were not as important to the structure of panelled doors as their prominence suggested.

For inlays, after various experiments, Ashbee used the simple motif of rectangular or lozenge-shaped panels, two or three inches across, each inlaid with a single plant design.[19] The flowers and plants were treated as flat, almost linear designs in combinations of pewter, satinwood, ebony, holly and coloured woods, and they kept close to the naïve character of flowers and plants inlaid on English oak furniture of *c*.1600; the pink was very much at home here and there was no attempt to emulate the cabbagey fullness of late seventeenth-century marquetry. These panels were most effective on plain pieces of furniture. At the head of a scantling pilaster on some austere oak chimney-piece, or in the centre of a door on a massive desk, surrounded by a frame of stringing, they would both relieve and enhance the puritanism of Ashbee's designs. Like the coloured stones which he placed so sparingly and effectively on his silver designs of this date, they show the value of what he called 'the concentration of live as against the distribution of dead ornament'.[20]

Some of the features of this new style can be seen on Ashbee's writing cabinet in mahogany and holly of 1898–9 (Plate 140). Here are the squared-off framing and the wide strap hinges, with beautiful, flamboyant openwork to the lock-plates; though there were also ornately inlaid tulips on the inner doors, coloured, gilded and carved in relief, an experiment perhaps inspired by some of Baillie Scott's designs for Darmstadt which Ashbee later abandoned in favour of the simpler, flush inlays.[21] This was possibly the most sumptuous piece of furniture Ashbee had designed to date and Tom Jelliffe, the Guild's most skilful cabinet-maker, worked on it; but there was more to it than mere embellishment.[22] There was a clever handling of effects of scale which was new in his designing. The great ball feet, the box-like proportions, the simple, thick framing and the bands of metal, create an insistent, almost mannered, sense of weight; in photographs it looks like a massive piece of furniture. To see it in the flesh and to realize that it is only four and a half feet high, is to appreciate its suppressed power and compact proportions.

This style was mature in more than just the trivial sense that it occurred at the height of Ashbee's career. It was as if he had found himself as a furniture designer; and though the elements of the style were few and simple, they furnished him with an inexhaustible source of designs, and with a style which lent itself to many different kinds of furniture. It is no accident that at about this time he stopped relying for light chairs on standard Arts and Crafts rush-seated designs and started

140. Writing cabinet of 1898–9. (Cheltenham Art Gallery and Museum.)

141. Chair in mahogany with inlay, of about 1900. (In the possession of the Ashbee family).

designing his own (Plate 141). The new designs were generally a skeletal version of early eighteenth-century English dining-chairs, with an upholstered seat and a broad central splat; the members were generally solid and squared, but their lines were often softened by a slight curve at the feet, at corners or on the top rails of the back; and the curve in the central splat both looked and was comfortable.[23] The fruitfulness of a style made out of simple elements is something we have seen already in Ashbee's buildings, and will see again.

There was a new independence in Ashbee's designs from around 1900; he was no longer content to produce austere or earthy versions of existing furniture types, and began to be deliberately unconventional, as his designs for piano cases show. He might have been expected to overlook the grand piano, it was so much an altar of Victorian middle-class drawing-room convention; but his mother and his wife were both good pianists, and besides, artists and architects of advanced tastes had been interested in reforming the design of piano cases for some time.

In 1879 Burne-Jones, helped by W. A. S. Benson, produced a design which replaced both the deep curves of the Victorian case (the result of technical developments towards greater range and power) and its three massive, independent turned legs with a treatment closer to the angular and vigorous lines of late eighteenth-century harpsichords and early pianos: a shallower curve, tapering at the end to an acute angle, and supports in the form of a light trestle stand. The case he designed in the following year for William Graham is well known.[24] It was made by John Broadwood and Sons, whose instruments were suited to such a shape, and decorated by Burne-Jones with scenes from the story of Orpheus and other themes. 'Reformed' or 'artistic' pianos provoked steady interest from now on; cases along Burne-Jones's lines were made by Broadwoods and decorated, sometimes by Morris and Company, sometimes by other artists; articles appeared with titles like 'Is the Pianoforte "A Thing of Beauty"?'; and Broadwoods, the manufacturers most closely associated with this movement, published their catalogue for 1895 under the title *Album of Artistic Pianofortes*.[25] Ashbee's pianos were part of this development.

The first of them, however, may have come as something of a shock (Plate 142). As a wedding present for Janet he designed a case for a Broadwood semi-grand piano in the form of a rectangular oak box, about 5 feet wide and 7 feet long, supported on a forest of legs. The materials—oak and holly—and the detailing were typical of Ashbee's mature style; the cabinet work was carried out by Broadwoods; and the Guild blacksmiths supplied massive wrought iron hinges decorated with Ash and Bee motifs.[26] When closed, the piano looked like nothing so much as an oversized cigar-box. The iron frame of the instrument was itself rectangular, but it was a most unusual design, being made of several castings bolted together. It was said that the design had musical advantages—the additional expanse of sounding-board and a stronger frame gave a fulness of tone equal to that of a concert grand—but these were not so compelling that such cases became common.[27] More probably, Ashbee was aiming at novelty for its own sake. He may have taken his cue from the fact that English pianos of the late eighteenth and early nineteenth centuries, when not of the harpsichord-like shape dignified by Sheraton and adopted by Burne-Jones, were in fact rectangular: the earliest surviving instrument by the first piano maker, Johannes Zumpe, now in the Broadwood Collection in the Victoria and Albert Museum, is of this shape; and in America in the mid-Victorian period such so-called 'squares' were the most popular kind of piano; though in either case they were normally wider than they were deep, unlike Ashbee's.[28] The idea of a rectangular piano, turned round, so to speak, and enlarged, gave Ashbee what he was looking for, a rugged table-like structure, a real departure from drawing-room convention. Hermann Muthesius (who thought the English the most unmusical race in the world) may have been thinking of this instrument when he criticized the Arts and Crafts men for believing that a case 'put together like a barn door' was suitable to a delicate instrument like the modern piano; the Sheraton tradition, he thought, offered greater possibilities.[29]

With the lid down, this instrument was a sombre thing; open, it revealed a bright and delicate scheme of decoration designed by Ashbee and painted by Walter

142. Semi-grand piano in oak and holly of about 1900. The piano now stands in the dining room at Toynbee Hall, and the partial restoration of Ashbee's decorative scheme of 1887 can be seen in the background.

Taylor, formerly an apprentice of the Guild and now working for Morris and Company (Plate V); such decoration was common on Broadwood pianos painted by Burne-Jones and others, but rare in Ashbee's mature furniture designs. It was based on a poem by Ashbee inscribed on the framing, a celebration of 'the Infinite' glimpsed through music, full of echoes of Keats and Blake:

> the music of all time
> Woke in my soul; and great grey poppies flung
> Their spell about me, and the gates stood clear
> Of ivory cities such as men pass through
> Who seek the infinite.[30]

The panels of holly between the oak framing of the lid were painted with images from the poem: a dreamer sleeping, three 'strange women' with musical instruments seated among poppies in the centre, and, above them, a Byzantinesque city

289

VI (above). Writing cabinet of ebony and holly, of about 1902. (Cheltenham Art Gallery and Museum.)

V. Painted decoration on a semi-grand piano of about 1900. (Toynbee Hall.)

of domes and spires with a great gold sun behind. This is 'The City of the Sun', one of Ashbee's favourite images of the ideal world.[31] The design is saved from the real danger of literalness partly by the way the darker oak framing breaks across it, leaving the scenes of vision floating on a plane behind; and partly by the delicacy of Walter Taylor's painting: the domes are only lightly drawn in outline, the poppies are not grey but soft blue and violet, oversized, commanding attention. This almost decadent scene conveyed an intense, introspective and personal sense of the power of music. It was quite different from the atmosphere that prevailed when the Guild held its Wednesday evening sing-songs, but it would have suited Janet, playing Beethoven or Brahms to herself in the big studio at 74 Cheyne Walk.[32]

The design date for this piano is a little uncertain. One would like to think, since it was a wedding present, that it was designed in 1898; but Broadwoods' records show that it only left their workshops on 3 November 1900, so perhaps that year is a more likely date.[33] It was followed by at least one more 'square' piano of about 1901, equally massive-looking and decorated more simply with panels of white holly painted with conventional ornament by Fleetwood Varley. Ashbee seems to have collaborated on this design with an architect called T. M. Shallcross.[34] The case of upright pianos was also the subject of experiment at this time, and the most radical design came not from Burne-Jones but from Baillie Scott, who exhibited his so-called 'Manxman' upright, made by Broadwoods, at the Arts and Crafts Exhibition in 1896.[35] Thinking the projecting keyboard an excrescence, Scott ran the top and sides of the piano out to the front of it and then closed it all in, cupboard-like, with boldly hinged doors; he got the idea, it seems, from an Elizabethan strong-box.[36] The furniture made for the Grand Duke of Hesse included a piano of this design; and Ashbee, already much taken with the boxiness of Scott's work, followed suit when he made designs for Broadwood uprights, which he did on at least four occasions.[37]

The mature style served Ashbee for the rest of his career as a furniture designer. In the Campden period there were perhaps as many as fifteen craftsmen working in the woodshop, and they produced a stream of wash-stands and bookcases, writing tables and chests of drawers, with squared-off details, decorative metalwork and inlays; the only specifically new feature was the occasional use of carving after Alec Miller and Will Hart joined the Guild in 1902. There was some high cabinet-making among this work, set pieces which shone at Arts and Crafts Exhibitions; and a second sumptuous writing cabinet veneered in holly and ebony and first exhibited in 1902, which is also now in Cheltenham Art Gallery and Museum, will serve as an illustration of Ashbee's furniture design at its most ambitious (Plates 143, VI).[38] Based loosely on Spanish cabinets then known as *varguenos*, a popular type in late nineteenth-century artistic circles, it looks heavy and severe when it is closed, thanks to the dark, close-grained ebony veneer, and the right-angled reveals seem particularly sharp; the darkness of the wood is only relieved by narrow bands of stringing. Opened, it reveals an expanse of light holly veneer inlaid with simple flower motifs, and a bank of little drawers whose silver-plated handles have spots of crimson leather showing through their openwork mounts, a note of colour which is picked up in the painted feet, carved in the form of grotesque dragons. It is a sophisticated piece which does not offer the obvious satisfactions of Arts and Crafts furniture: it is not appealingly simple; it has a richly textured grain

143. Writing cabinet in ebony and holly, of about 1902, now in Cheltenham Art Gallery and Museum.

to the wood, but no very evident construction; it is neither homely nor rustic in its associations. And yet it is, above all, interesting, an intense and difficult design which challenges enquiry.

It is interesting for the sense of exploration and intricacy it encourages. Baillie Scott enjoyed the game of concealing a bright and colourful interior within a sombre case; but before he knew of Scott's work Ashbee had written (by way of illustrating an educational point):

You know those beautiful cabinets in the South Kensington Museum, made by the Italian and Flemish craftsmen of the Eighteenth Century, they are among the finest pieces of

293

workmanship we possess. There is, first of all, a stately structure with solid doors, delicately moulded and carved. In the centre is a golden key; you turn it, and open the doors, when, within, you see the panels still more beautifully wrought, sometimes with colour and gesso, and a miracle of workmanship in the many drawers and recesses. The best work is within.[39]

On the Cheltenham cabinet the doors open to reveal a sparkling interior and a honeycomb of drawers; when the writing slab is pulled out, hidden compartments are revealed; and there are some elegant deceptions involved in the fact that the slab is part of the carcase, but the slides which draw it out are part of the base.

It is interesting for the way veneers, so closely associated with the development of elegant cabinet-making at the end of the seventeenth century, are here applied to framed and panelled surfaces which derive so obviously from the earlier joinery tradition. Ashbee is revelling in paradox and perversity; paradox because the crispness of the veneers actually gives a more pronounced character to his favourite motif of clean, right-angled 'joinery' reveals, they give a sharper flavour to his style; perversity because to veneer over frame and panel construction is difficult and unnecessary. It is as if Ashbee was translating the 'vernacular' forms of his mature style into the language of high style, just for the fun of it.

And it is interesting for the deliberate oddities and unresolved elements in the design. It is odd that the cabinet work should be finer than usual in Ashbee's work, but that the wrought iron fittings should be coarser; it is odd that the rear pairs of carved and painted feet—a surprise in themselves—should be turned through ninety degrees; it is odd that within the dark clustered columns of the legs there should be an additional leg of a quite different character, in fluted holly, though some early seventeenth-century furniture, notably the Great Bed of Ware, offers a precedent for this. These are not the *gaucheries* of an inexperienced designer; Ashbee had handled all these details in a more consistent way before; they are part of an attempt, not altogether successful, at a more ambitious and indeed mannered way of designing furniture than he had found possible within the puritan mainstream of the Arts and Crafts.

It was a summary of much of Ashbee's furniture, for the intricacy, and veneers on frame and panel construction, can both be found scattered among earlier pieces. But it was also a point of departure, towards a more mannered and formal style; and a Viennese critic saw its colour, interestingly, in the starkest terms, 'black, white and red'.[40] If the ambitions it suggested had been realized, Ashbee would have grown in stature as a furniture designer in the Arts and Crafts. As it was, he fell short of the first rank. He could not match Voysey's careful elegance or the expressiveness of Ernest Gimson and Sidney Barnsley; his ornament was not as assured or as colourful as Baillie Scott's. Historically he did not play an important part in Britain, for he arrived at a distinctive style later than other Arts and Crafts designers, and with their help. But that distinctive style is a part of the story of Arts and Crafts furniture. It was versatile, personal (it is not easily confused with anyone else's work) and it provided another variation on the mixture of simplicity and sophistication which is such a theme in Arts and Crafts work.

Like Voysey and Baillie Scott, Ashbee designed principally for the middle-class town house and suburban home, and if he had favourite furniture types they were the writing cabinet and the piano, the furniture of intellect and culture. In this respect comparisons with the archetypal Arts and Crafts furniture designers, Gimson and the Barnsleys, are unhelpful for Ashbee made no cult of the mighty, homely table or of the all-gathering hearth; and whereas their detailing was shaped and chamfered in a way that looked obviously hand-made, much of his was straight-forwardly and precisely machined. His aim was to bring reasonableness and sim-plicity to a more conventional and more urban type of furniture; he took suggestions from the trade and from historical exemplars, but his designs were almost always simpler than either; and he placed his ornament judiciously. The simplicity of his work does not seem remarkable today, but at the time it was keenly felt; and when he showed his austere and rectilinear furniture in quantity at the Vienna Secession in 1900, the Viennese were very interested; for it was the perfect embodiment of that unpretentiousness in English Arts and Crafts of which they had heard so much.[41]

CHURCH FURNITURE

Ashbee was always something of a modernist in Church matters, insisting that the Church should come abreast, as he would put it, of modern life. Church furniture did not figure largely in the Guild's productions, but one would expect such as there was to have a rather up-to-date and secular flavour. The great *Prayer Book of King Edward VII* which he printed at the Essex House Press had just this character, and so did some of the most original church work of other Arts and Crafts designers; at St Nicholas, Saintbury, where Ashbee worshipped in the Campden years, there was a side-chapel screen by Ernest Gimson, a big, thick thing with a curved profile like the back of a country wagon, quite unecclesiastical, but somehow apt in a country church. Yet surprisingly, Ashbee's church furniture remained, for a good part of his career, within the late Gothic tradition so well handled by his master Bodley. In 1896 he designed a screen for the chapel of The Wodehouse at Wom-bourne, and in 1897 another for the tower at the west end of St Peter's, Seal, in Kent, the gift of Janet's father; both of them were of a standard fifteenth-century type with little touches of modernity in the details; but neither suggested that he felt at home in this kind of work.[42] Their Gothic details were thin and hesitant, and while they were generally cast in the Bodley mould they showed none of the refined and full-blooded enjoyment of late Gothic foliage, none of the sensuous delight in the ogee curve, which was such a feature of Bodley's work.[43] It was as if Ashbee felt a sense of propriety, that he should use a modernized Gothic for church work which he would not have thought of using elsewhere.

The simpler, squarer style of his domestic furniture in the late 1890s appeared briefly in his church work and gave it something of the freer, more obviously modern character one would have expected. In 1898–9 he designed a very geometri-cal lectern for Sts Peter and Paul, Horndon-on-the-Hill in Essex, an open structure of oak columns, copper work and enamel which combined spheres, hemispheres, octagons and squares; and a reredos and sturdy rectilinear stalls for St Stephen's, Shottermill, in Surrey in 1900 (Plate 144).[44] When it is open, this reredos reveals faintly Gothic cusping, and sparse and vibrant figures carved in decorative low relief by Edward G. Bramwell; but its special feature is that Ashbee designed each of the panels to be about seven inches deep, so that when it is closed it looks like

144. Reredos, St Stephen's church, Shottermill.

a big box, as his cabinets did, and it is held together by his usual massive hinges.[45]
If Ashbee had had a good deal of church work to do, this kind of treatment might
have been interestingly developed; but as things turned out these were isolated
examples; and his most successful church work actually belongs to the period
1907–9, when he was influenced by more academic precedents.[46]

At the church of St Mary the Virgin, Calne in Wiltshire, he designed a reredos
in 1907 for a chapel on the south side of the nave.[47] It was an Epiphany scene
set in an open framework of late Gothic carving and tracery, so that one could
see through the reredos to what Ashbee called 'the beautiful Inigo Jones work of
the chancel'; the interest of the design lies in the pensive naturalism of Alec Miller's
carving.[48] The chancel was indeed rebuilt in the mid-seventeenth century, and its
arcades were carried on simple Tuscan columns with broad *abaci*; the rest of the
church is mediaeval, so that is has an interesting mixed character, which perhaps
acted as a cue in the next stage of Ashbee's work.

The organ at St Mary's is on a lavish scale for a parish church and had, until
recently, the romantic luxury of a little echo organ high up in the north transept.[49]
It seems that when Ashbee was brought in the instrument had already been built
by Peter Conacher and Company of Huddersfield.[50] So his job was simply to wrap
a case around it, and he attempted no cornice or cresting to make it more coherent
architecturally (Plate 145). As a whole his case, with its plain and rudimentary framing, was not very different from many that could be seen in organ builders' catalogues of this date, and he may simply have followed an arrangement suggested
by the builders. His attention was concentrated on the carved and gilded detail,
and particularly on the open-work of the pipeshades, scrolling foliage inset with
angels and birds, a peacock and a bird of paradise. Some of the inspiration for
this work came from later Byzantine and Romanesque carving and mosaic: such
foliage details and some of the interlaced squares and circles that Ashbee used can
be found on the walls and pavement of St Mark's in Venice, and Ashbee was perhaps
thinking particularly of the Norman work he saw in Sicily at just this time, while
working on the Villa San Giorgio in Taormina.[51] Two of the panels used at Calne
were also used on the organ gallery at the Villa San Giorgio. But there were also
echoes of seventeenth-century carving and woodwork, presumably suggested by
the date of the chancel arcade within which the organ stood.[52] Ashbee did not

145. Part of the organ case at the church of St Mary the Virgin, Calne.

draw particularly on the decorative traditions of English organ building; so his treatment was novel, and thoroughly successful as far as the detail was concerned. Carefully poised between Gothic and classical exemplars, it was apt to its setting; and Alec Miller's fresh and vigorous carving, interpreting small and sketchy indications by Ashbee, had much of the linear force and luxuriance of a pattern by William Morris.

INTERIOR DECORATION

Much the most interesting of Ashbee's interiors was the one he designed for the Magpie and Stump in 1893–4. This was destroyed in 1968 and though some of the fittings were given to the Victoria and Albert Museum, it can now only be reconstructed in words and pictures.[53] It was a complicated interior, and it may help to explore it room by room, as if in the company of a dinner guest.

Having passed the disturbing door-handles in the form of naked boys one would

297

enter the hall, a bare reddish room with little to catch the eye except the chimney-piece on the far side of the room (Plates 146, VII). This is a panel of what appear to be dull green tiles with spots of colour on them glinting in the light from the bay window. On closer inspection they turn out to be tile-sized plaques of copper, some plain, some decorated with repoussé work, others with enamels in crimsons, dull pinks, purples and sandy gold.[54] Even to the *cognoscenti* of Chelsea, this panel must have been puzzling; it looked a bit like those big flat seventeenth- and eighteenth-century tiled chimney-pieces in Holland, but the decoration was odd. It consisted of some squares on which the enamel colour had simply been sprinkled to form cloudy and speckled abstract patterns; others had red enamel globes of various sizes, and others again repoussé motifs which, though fairly crisp and explicit, still left one wondering why they, rather than others, had been chosen.

A guest who knew something of the Guild of Handicraft might have begun to decipher the imagery. There were the usual emblems, the Craft of the Guild, the sun, the pink; and there were Tudor roses and 'slips' which recalled the rich field of imagery in sixteenth- and seventeenth-century woodcut and embroidery from which the pink derived. More surprisingly, there were biographical images such as the coat of arms of King's College, Cambridge. And at the bottom left hand corner the work was signed '.C.R.A. .DES. .A.C. .EX.' and dated in the other corner 1893. This gave a kind of clue for in 1893 Guild enamelwork was in its infancy, and the craftsman responsible, Arthur Cameron, was only eighteen. Ashbee had chosen as the centre piece—and, he no doubt hoped, the talking-point— of his mother's hall a display of technical experiments; hence the simple forms and the abstract scatter of enamel—to pepper on the enamel powder in this manner was an obvious way of exploring the effects of colour and texture, which are fixed irretrievably in firing.[55] It was appropriate that this work should be presented almost at random, that it should be mixed up with symbols of the Guild and of Ashbee's career. It was a report of work in progress—from Mile End to Chelsea— and it is typical of Ashbee that he should have chosen to decorate the Magpie and Stump in this way.

The back wall of the room was covered with an expanse of embossed leatherwork (Plate 147), and the stairs ran up against this under an arcade. Ashbee had started experiments in leather in about 1890, believing that this kind of work was no longer practised in Britain and was 'almost exclusively in the hands of the Germans'.[56] This was something of an exaggeration, for Walter Crane and others had exhibited such work at early Arts and Crafts Exhibitions, often executed by Jeffrey and Company, and work on a small scale, for blotters, purses and the like was very popular with the Home Arts and Industries Association.[57] But the general practice of embossing leather had lapsed towards the end of the eighteenth century, and its revival in Germany in the late nineteenth century was on a much larger scale than in Britain. Four or five artist-craftsmen were involved, of whom one, Georg Hulbe, employed as many as two hundred people in his Hamburg workshops in the 1880s and 1890s; another, Hartwig Jacobsen, came to England in about 1890 to promote the craft. Ashbee bought tools from Germany, perhaps from Hulbe of whom he was certainly aware, and studied German techniques; and soon Bill Hardiman, the best modeller in the Guild, was carrying out designs for chair backs and friezes.[58] The wall coverings at the Magpie and Stump were possibly the most ambitious

146. The chimney-piece in the hall at 37 Cheyne Walk;
it is now in the Victoria and Albert Museum.

147. Embossed leatherwork in the hall, 37 Cheyne
Walk.

scheme to date, an undulating pattern of briar-like plant forms crowned by a frieze of Tudor roses and emblems of the wheel of fortune; the chestnut-coloured oxhide kept its soft, bulgy quality under Hardiman's incising, modelling and gilding. This was something different from the sumptuous interiors by Shaw and Ernest George and Peto, where the walls were covered either with Spanish and Dutch leatherwork of the sixteenth and seventeenth centuries or with modern stamped leather papers of traditional design. Ashbee was aiming at the revival of the traditional craft in the spirit of his own time; Hardiman's energetic modelling of his design, in which the breadth of the Arts and Crafts mingles with the linear excitement of Art Nouveau, went some way towards this.[59]

The stairs led up to the drawing-room on the first floor, which spread across the whole of the front of the house with views out across the Thames (Plate 28). It was furnished comfortably with an easy mixture of antique and modern furniture, 'a room', the *Studio* reported, 'which is not at first sight conspicuously unlike many another modern salon in the abode of people of taste'.[60] Mrs H. S. Ashbee's preferences are felt here, one imagines, as much as her son's. The walls were covered with a paper in two tones of peacock blue (a favourite Aesthetic colour), which was probably made by Watts and Company, for whom Bodley provided many designs.[61] At the end of the room facing the bay window, there was a massive teak beam supported on stone brackets, carved with perky musical *bambini* and the Ash and Bee motif, the surface of the stone left rather obviously rough. It spanned the entrance to the music room which ran far back towards the garden and out of whose depths a copper chimney-piece gleamed with jewel-like effect: plain expanses of metal round the fire itself, and then copper open-work above in a bold pattern with stained wood showing through, the whole framing a sixteenth-century Italian painting said to be by a pupil of Giulio Romano.

Of a quite different character, and not obvious at first because it was painted in a range of colours close to the peacock blue of the wallpaper, was the painting on the drawing-room chimney-breast, by Roger Fry (Plate 148). It was a sophisticated piece of work, a formal landscape garden with a narrow canal vanishing abruptly into the centre of the picture; it made much of the sweeping contrary curves of a dark hedge and lighter, taller, poplars behind. Fry was much taken up with the New English Art Club at this time, and his painting has some of the purely ornamental character of Charles Conder's decorative work, though it is not gay, not like Watteau, as Conder could be.[62] Here was another new note. Given the local allusions which Ashbee built into the Magpie and Stump, one might have expected this to be a local scene, Cremorne perhaps, the famous Chelsea pleasure gardens; but it was not, nothing so comfortably intelligible. It encouraged rather a lonely and disturbing mood: the park was dotted with people, but they were dwarfed by the formal lines and violent perspective of the scene, and surrounded by the haunting presence of tall, pale term figures.

The room was lit by electric light from a large corona hanging in the centre, one of many fittings throughout the house which were obviously not from the trade.[63] The proper decorative treatment for electric light had been much discussed since its introduction in the early 1880s and some Arts and Crafts designers, notably W. A. S. Benson, had devised simple and apt solutions; but it was still new enough in the mid-1890s for Ashbee to want to preach about it, about treating electricity

149. Light fitting, 37 Cheyne Walk.

148. Painting by Roger Fry on the chimney-breast in the drawing-room, 37 Cheyne Walk.

for what it was and not as gas. 'Our designers for electric light', he wrote, 'have for the most part, not yet made the discovery that electric light *falls* . . .'[64] His own fittings were simple combinations of flexible wires and metalwork; he made much of the electric flex and hung all but his most elaborate fittings from that alone; upright bulbs, he thought, were really only proper in low table lamps.[65] But it was the decorative metalwork of his fittings more than their functional honesty which gave them their special quality, for he drew here on the special skills of the Guild. Copper and pewter were the normal materials, fashioned by W. A. White and the other silversmith-metalworkers; Ashbee liked to cover up the usual, utilitarian porcelain ceiling rose, and repoussé metalwork lent itself to this (Plate 149); the fittings were decorated with enamels, red and grey on copper, blue and green on pewter; and little glinting coloured beads of coral or gemstones

301

150. The dining-room, 37 Cheyne Walk. (From *Kunst und Kunsthandwerk* (Vienna), 1901, vol. 4, p. 464.)

were sometimes hung from the silk bags that Ashbee used to veil the bulbs. One particularly fine square rose in the drawing-room at the Magpie and Stump had a green enamel centre with four peacocks embossed around it and green lacquer eyes on their tails.[66] A journalist in the *Studio* made the apt comment that the light fittings and other architectural metalwork at the Magpie and Stump were like jewellery on a large scale.[67]

The company would go down stairs again to dinner, into a long room underneath the music room, with an austere atmosphere which the cooking could not always be relied upon to relieve (Plate 150). One sat in light, ebonized rush-seated chairs at trestle tables so narrow it was almost embarrassing to look the person opposite in the face. These tables, which had been produced since the early days of the Guild, were of simple construction; X-frame legs with a stretcher passing through them and held in place with pegs; on this rested four planks screwed to a pair of battens.[68] Like mediaeval trestle tables they could be dismantled, but they were modelled on seventeenth- and eighteenth-century vernacular types that were lighter and more convenient than mediaeval examples (and less romantic in the Arts and Crafts way). The walls of the dining-room were panelled in wood painted a light colour with plain unmoulded stiles and simple fielding; the frieze above was painted at first by Agnes Ashbee with a pattern of stylized windswept trees along the two long walls; later naked boys sporting with woodland deer were added among the trees,

VII. Detail of the chimney-piece from the hall at 37 Cheyne Walk. (Victoria and Albert Museum)

apparently by Walter Taylor; on the short wall by the door a couple of handsome peacocks were painted in a casual, country garden pose.[69] Underneath them there was an inscription about 'fop and fashion peacocking', a teasing and self-conscious allusion, perhaps to the life of London's artistic quarter, a life Ashbee had chosen for himself in setting up as the dandified Whistlerian designer.[70]

The house was, a guest might have felt, interesting; but somehow it did not hang together and there were so many things that needed to be explained. The conversation at the dinner table would go this way and that, Mr Shaw's latest play, the situation in South Africa, the new cathedral at Westminster . . . It would be surprising if some of Ashbee's favourite topics did not come up, the craftsman and the machine ('King Charles's Head'), the emptiness of teaching in the new polytechnics, the revival of jewellery as an art; surprising if one was not made aware of Ashbee's interesting experiment with all those poor boys out in the East End. By the end of the evening it might have been possible to look at the house in a new light. Not that it was any less puzzlingly eclectic than before; but now one could see that it was not meant to make sense visually. It was biographical, a gathering of the endeavours of which he spoke so enthusiastically, and those of his friends; it looked as it did because there was a cocky young enameller in Bow called Arthur Cameron; and one of Ashbee's closest friends was a rising artist in Chelsea; and the leather industry had somehow to be got out of the hands of the Germans.

Such a loose and eclectic approach to the furnishing of a house was not foreign to the Arts and Crafts, indeed the Movement specifically encouraged the idea of individual artists and craftsmen collaborating on a single building. At 15 Stratton Street, off Piccadilly, for instance, a town house of 1895, a number of the most distinguished members of the Art Workers' Guild were employed in this kind of collaboration. W. H. Ansell, who was working at the time for the architect C. J. Harold Cooper, recalled the decoration:

The staircase was of English oak, with a balustrade of trees and little boys, carved by Stirling Lee and W. S. Frith; the windows were Image's. The billiards room had low cupboards in unpolished mahogany, with a green morocco-lined wall above, and a beaten dull copper frieze by Nelson Dawson. The fireplace had a bronze panel of racehorses at the start of a race, modelled by Arthur Walker . . . The stained glass in this room was by Christopher Whall and the door furniture Nelson Dawson's. The panelled satinwood drawing room had marble fireplaces carved by Pomeroy, and really delightful silver finger-plates of Dawson's.[71]

The quality of the work at 15 Stratton Street was probably higher than that at the Magpie and Stump, and the atmosphere a little more precious, but the intention was not very different. It was not a question of orchestrating the different artist-craftsmen so that the decoration of 15 Stratton Street had a unity of style. The experiment was more ambitious, more social in nature than that, and the effect was more various: each artist-craftsman contributed according to his lights, and the hope was that by working together they would achieve a broader unity, the Unity of Art which the Art Workers' Guild took as its motto.[72]

After the Magpie and Stump Ashbee developed a style of interior decoration that was simpler than that early experiment; this went hand in hand with the same development in his designs for furniture. He used this style in his houses on Cheyne

151. The hall, 39 Cheyne Walk.

Walk round 1900, in many of the small middle-class houses he built in the country and in the (very few) cases where he designed interiors for existing buildings.[73] And yet, oddly enough, the basic elements of the style, the treatment of the walls and of the hearth, can both be traced back to the eclectic interior of the Magpie and Stump.

Where possible, Ashbee liked to cover walls with panelling up to picture-rail height, dividing it vertically, as in the hall at 39 Cheyne Walk (Plate 151), or once or twice horizontally as well. The panels would be unfielded and the stiles unmoulded; the 'scantling' motif, first seen in the dining-room at the Magpie and Stump, became general in Ashbee's panelled interiors as in his furniture. If he could not panel he would simply paint, and he scarcely ever used wallpaper after the Magpie and Stump. Phoebe, his faithful secretary, recalled many years later how zealously she imposed what she took to be Ashbee's tastes on her family: 'NO wallpapers, every room had to have distempered walls, all doors and woodwork were painted green.'[74] For the frieze he liked original decorative painting with a theme to it, like the streetscape of Cheyne Walk at number 39, or the painting of Queen Victoria's Diamond Jubilee Procession, which Max Balfour began for the little white dining-room at Number 74; if that were not possible, he would sometimes use plasterwork modelled in low relief, but never flat coloured pattern; often he left the frieze blank.[75] As for the hearth, Ashbee only designed one or two of the kind so closely associated with the Arts and Crafts, broad, homely and intimate, with big settles drawn up to its edge; reforming ideas about fire-places

305

were, in any case, encouraging smaller hearths in the 1890s. Ashbee's typical treatment was austere, vertical, and rather unhomely.[76] He would often do without a mantelshelf; he would treat the hearth in an unexpensive way; and then he would make the chimney-piece the visual focus of his decorative scheme by concentrating attention on a particular ornamental, and often emblematic, feature. The chimney-pieces at the Magpie and Stump were the start of this; it continued in his later London houses; at Woolstaplers' Hall and at the Villa San Giorgio he used a roundel of St George and the Dragon, carved by Will Hart, over the fire-places; and in the de Szász house in Budapest it was that enigmatic statuary group, *The Spirit of Modern Hungary*.[77] This was an example of his common practice, the concentration of live ornament on a single point: he used the hearth and its emblem to set the tone of his interior, directing attention away from warmth, conviviality and comfort, domestic virtues, towards more intellectual ones; it was his temperament to do so, for though his work in interior decoration was almost all domestic, he found little satisfaction in domesticity.

The same quality of reserve can be found in the cast iron fire-places which Ashbee designed for the Falkirk Iron Company in 1897; one of them can be seen in the hall of 39 Cheyne Walk.[78] But the explanation in this case lay mostly in Ashbee's sense of the material, for cast iron ornament had been taken to such an extent of elaboration in the nineteenth century as to encourage caution. In the Arts and Crafts Lethaby was a particular advocate of the material, and of delicate mouldings in an eighteenth-century spirit, and there were several sympathetic manufacturers, such as Longden and Company and the Coalbrookdale Company; but one critic was still surprised when Lethaby showed some cast iron grates at the Arts and Crafts Exhibition in 1896, such was the material's reputation.[79] Lethaby's grates were decorated with simple motifs, and Ashbee's ornament followed the same lines: natural forms and patterns of reeding treated with soft and indefinite modelling and no undercutting; he said he followed 'the lead casting of the Adams period, without in any way slavishly copying'.[80] Yet even here he still liked to concentrate attention on a single ornament, and on one design (Plate 152) he modelled 'a cluster of little bats hanging under the mantelshelf with a suggestion of webs falling from their wings'.[81]

Such austere interiors as Ashbee's may seem to amount to something less than interior decoration. They do not have the rich textures that were common in interiors of advanced taste in the 1870s and 1880s. A commercial firm of furnishers and decorators round 1900 would have provided something more elaborate; and a client may have felt that they offended against propriety, against the expectation that rooms should be decorated to a certain level and in certain ways. They differ too from the work of the two best-known architect-decorators associated with the Arts and Crafts. Ashbee did not seek, like Baillie Scott, to create a warm and mythically mediaeval atmosphere, wrapping his interiors round with colours and patterns of his own design. Nor did he create, like Mackintosh, subtle formal compositions in line, colour and space which extend the visual rules to every detail of furniture and decoration: it matters, in a Mackintosh interior, where every Mackintosh chair is put. But this is not to say that interior decoration was something that lay outside Ashbee's skills or interests, or that his interiors were exceptional in their austerity. In Britain it was Mackintosh and Baillie Scott who were unusual

152. Cast iron fire-place designed by Ashbee for the Falkirk Iron Company.

in seeking to extend the architect's control to the whole interior with all its decorative details, an attitude which they shared with J. M. Olbrich and Josef Hoffmann in Vienna; and which was brilliantly satirized in Adolf Loos's parable of 'The Poor Rich Man' with his architect-designed slippers.[82]

Ashbee's interiors belonged to the mainstream of the Arts and Crafts in England, with the work of all those architects who designed reserved, light interiors where the character was given by panelling, a little plasterwork in low relief, and the careful handling of the chimney-piece; interiors which did not create an intense and separate atmosphere, but were continuous with the architecture; interiors which provide a background for furniture without determining its character. The names of Voysey and Lethaby come to mind, but there were so many architects working in this way that they cannot all be named; few will be missing, though, from the membership roll of the Art Workers' Guild and the pages of Lawrence Weaver's *Small Country Houses of To-Day: Volume One*.

Ashbee's very intellectual treatment of interiors may explain the success of the work he did in the library at Madresfield Court, a country house of mixed and in large part Victorian date in Worcestershire. The tastes of Ashbee's clients, William, seventh Earl Beauchamp and his wife Lettice, were very much for the Arts and Crafts: there are light fittings by the Birmingham Guild of Handicraft scattered throughout the house; while Ashbee was working on the library, the chapel was being transformed by artists and craftsmen, also from Birmingham, into an exquisite casket of High Anglican devotion, painted and jewelled, glazed and gilded; and the books they were adding to an established aristocratic library were of just the sort to inspire confidence: the big architectural folios from Batsfords, the products of the private presses.[83] There was a dilettante note about their work

307

153. Detail of one of the library doors at Madresfield Court.

154. (facing page). The library at Madresfield Court, showing the carved bookcase ends, with the Tree of Life nearer the camera.

on the house, a sense of decorative work done for its own sake, and it was characteristic that they should ask Ashbee to work on a room that was already furnished with the full complement of bookshelves that it has today: his work was essentially embellishment.[84]

He worked in two stages. In 1902–3 he installed two single and one pair of double doors in oak, connecting with the neighbouring rooms. On their library side they were framed up in Ashbee's usual way, and scattered among the panels were scenes appropriate to the library, carved in low relief by Alec Miller: a monkish scholar in his cell, a farmer reaping, a musician, a doctor, a pilgrim leading a Puritan family towards the light (Plate 153). It was a delicate scheme of imagery, attractively wide in its allusions: there are so many ways to wisdom, so many kinds of knowledge. It avoided the traditional allegorical figures, the emblems of the Arts and Sciences, which so often underline the fruits and benefits of knowledge, the completeness of the cultural system. Ashbee's imagery was tentative and austere, a scatter of insights so to speak, a sense of knowledge not as power, or even wisdom, but as searching. Such modern notions were typical of Ashbee (less so, one imagines, of his client) and he seems to have been at home in the library at Madresfield. These doors, though few in number and partial in effect, were his most successful scheme of interior decoration; the things which he (and Alec Miller) did best are concentrated here: the contrast between the broad framing and the carved panels; the vivid ornament on the pewter door furniture; the delicacy of Alec Miller's carving when he catches a flock of birds brawling and tumbling as they fly into the sun.[85]

The second stage, which was carried out in 1905, was to decorate the ends of two free-standing bookcases with carving (Plate 154).[86] On one was carved an image of the Tree of Knowledge with Adam and Eve on either side (looking unmis-

308

155. Detail showing the roots of the Tree of Knowledge in the library at Madresfield Court.

takably modern despite their nakedness): on the other the Tree of Life rising among the towers of the Heavenly Jerusalem. Ashbee enjoyed having to squash his design into such a narrow format—the trees are elongated in a typical turn-of-the-century way; he may not have been so happy with the traditional and explicit symbolism of this contrast between sacred and profane learning; but he managed to turn it to account. The central parts of his images, Adam and Eve and the Heavenly Jerusalem, are treated in a pedestrian manner; the upper part, the branches of the tree loaded with fruits and a squirrel, an owl, a peacock and other birds, are better; the lower parts best of all. The roots of the Tree of Life flow out in a smooth and abundant torrent for they are also, by virtue of a traditional ambiguity, a river; in the current of Ashbee's design leaves and fishes float up and down indiscriminately; there are eddies in the flow of the water which are also knots in the wood of the tree. The lines of the design are liquid, the modelling crisp; and it is a fine example of English Art Nouveau. But that is only a stylistic description; the excellence of his design is that it has a meaning, and that his liquid curves convey the sweet abundance of the River of Life.

Ten feet away, the roots of the Tree of Knowledge are thick and heavy, twisted in upon themselves in telling contrast (Plate 155). Among them clamber underground and underwater creatures, an otter, a mouse, a frog. But there is also, burrowing in their company, a little crooked old man with a top hat, an umbrella and a hefty tome under his arm. There is, so far as I know, no parallel in Ashbee's work to this humorous and unexpected figure of the purblind scholar—Teufelsdrockh on a day when the Divine Light did not illumine his researches.

CHAPTER TWELVE
METALWORK

In October 1888 the infant Guild of Handicraft exhibited seventeen items at the first show organized by the Arts and Crafts Exhibition Society. All of them were metalwork, and apart from a 'Specimen of painting in enamel' which remains a mystery, they were all examples of repoussé work, big dishes, bowls and plaques, mostly in copper, decorated with ornament beaten up in relief.[1] It was an impressive exhibit, considering that the Guild had only been in existence for about three months, and *The Sunday Times* found it 'wonderfully good'.[2] The curious fact about the Guild's exhibit was that fifteen of the items were designed by John Pearson, the senior metalworker of the Guild, and one by his shopmate, John Williams. None of them was designed by Ashbee. Though Ashbee's reputation as a designer rests chiefly on his metalwork and jewellery, it was not he but Pearson, a craftsman of distinct style and independent character, who played the largest part in the Guild's metalwork for the first few years. The fact that many of the pieces of Guild metalwork which survive from this period are marked with Pearson's name or initials, and not with those of the Guild of Handicraft, may be taken as an emblem of independence in the metal shop.[3]

In repoussé work the metal is held against a firm but giving surface, usually pitch; the ornament is beaten up from behind and then finished off with fine tools from the front. The technique was used by virtuoso silversmiths in the mid-Victorian period, to create delicate effects of pictorial realism; but the copper and brass wares of the 1880s were often of a different kind, bold and vigorous, decorative and naïve. In the amateur craft classes fostered by the Home Arts and Industries Association, repoussé work was only less popular than woodcarving, and a number of such amateur metalworkers exhibited alongside the Guild at the Arts and Crafts Exhibition in 1888.[4] Trade metalworkers also exhibited repoussé wares there, for they were a saleable feature of some richly decorated artistic interiors of the 1880s. Sconces and finger plates, dishes and plaques in brass and copper added to the texture of such interiors with their broad ornament and glinting surfaces, the dishes propped on sideboards and rarely used, for the central reserve was usually decorated with embossing as well as the rim. They struck an eclectic note, gave a hint of the Netherlands and of the Near East; indeed, genuine old brass work and new work in the old style could be had from Bruges and from Damascus.[5] There was thus a distinct, if specialized, market for the Guild's first wares.

Pearson decorated them with stylized flower and plant forms, and a number of favourite motifs (Plate 157): grotesque birds and animals, galleons of the sort

156. The metalworkers of the Guild of Handicraft, in about 1901.

Ashbee adopted as the Craft of the Guild, and a species of fat and hopeful-looking fish, all rendered with a vibrant technique in which the working of the separate tools and processes can be clearly read: the sharp spines and outlines of the chaser, the soft domed surface of the body of the design from the bossing tool, and finally the background matted with punches. Like the Martin Brothers with their grotesque pottery figures, Pearson seemed to be a craftsman of primitive and vigorous talent of the sort the Arts and Crafts liked to idealize, though he could also produce work of some refinement. An article published in the *Studio* in 1897 explained something of his earlier history:

In his peregrinations in the East End, Mr. Ashbee came upon a workman who had at one time been employed in De Morgan's tile works. This man, broken down in health and out of any regular employment, had carefully examined in the British Museum the Repoussé copper of the Middle Ages. With the spirit of emulation he employed himself in imitating or adapting De Morgan's tiles in beaten copper. Mr. Ashbee secured his services, and this man continued the execution of this class of work, and laid the tradition which has been carried on at Essex House.[6]

This was written some years after Pearson had left the Guild, presumably from information supplied by Ashbee, and it calls for some commentary. The reference to De Morgan throws light on Pearson's choice of motifs, for his grotesques, galleons and fish amount almost to versions of De Morgan in metal; but his employment cannot, it seems, be verified now for lack of surviving evidence.[7] As for repoussé copper of the Middle Ages, there was in fact little of that in the British Museum in the 1880s that could serve as an exemplar for Pearson's work, but he may have studied German brass dishes of *c*. 1400–*c*. 1650, whose motifs, though not identical to his, have the same scale and coarseness; ironically, these were generally stamped work, not repoussé.[8] The arrangement of his big dishes, with an embossed central reserve and a broad rim decorated with scrolling and interlaced plant forms and gambolling creatures recalls English repoussé silver dishes of the 1660s, which he could have seen at South Kensington or at the British Museum. The *Studio*

157 (facing page). Repoussé brass charger designed by John Pearson and executed by John Pearson and John Williams, 1889. Diameter 62.3 cms. (Private collection).

158. Biscuit box in gilded brass of about 1890, probably designed by John Williams. Height 12.8 cms. (In the possession of the Ashbee family.)

says nothing about how Pearson acquired his practical skills, but Shirley Bury has suggested that he may have attended classes run by the Home Arts and Industries Association—repoussé work was taught in their central training studios in Langham Place in London—or from one of the manuals written by C. G. Leland, the energetic American propagandist for craft work in education, who was a guiding light of the Association.[9] The specimen designs in Leland's *Art Work Manual No. 8: Repoussé Work or Embossing on Sheet Brass*, published in New York in 1883, are not unlike Pearson's ornament, though dry and wiry in comparison with his executed work.

Pearson's work had such a distinct character, and his position as the first skilled metalworker in the Guild was so influential, that it is not surprising that he should have started a decorative tradition, as the *Studio* said. The early metalwork of the Guild tells the story of a process of diffusion, Pearson's style of repoussé becoming more firmly established among Guild products as his personal contribution grew less. Ashbee began designing metalwork himself in the summer of 1889 if not before, and at the Arts and Crafts Exhibition in that year he contributed eight items of metalwork to the Guild's exhibit, alongside twenty-three by Pearson.[10] His early designs were clearly derived from Pearson: he used wrought iron, an outside craftsman called R. Underhill being employed for this, but repoussé work in copper and brass was its principal feature.[11] A typical design was a coal scuttle consisting of a shallow copper bowl cradled by three wrought iron arms, the bowl decorated with an all-over pattern of Pearsonian repoussé flowers.[12] In the following year, 1890, Pearson seems to have withdrawn rather from Guild metalwork: in the autumn he was almost expelled for making and selling his wares outside the Guild, and at the Arts and Crafts Exhibition he only contributed six items.[13] But by this time the style which he had introduced had become independent of him: the biscuit box which Ashbee's mother gave to her daughter Frances for her birthday in February 1891 (Plate 158), was decorated with a frieze of pinks very much in his manner, but the designer seems to have been John Williams.[14]

315

In a puzzling episode in the summer of 1892, Pearson and Williams resigned from the Guild within three days of each other.[15] But there was little loss of continuity in the Guild's metalwork; there were other craftsmen by this time, able to continue the style, and big dishes and coal scuttles, bowls and finger-plates, remained a staple of the Guild until about the turn of the century, when sales seemed to dry up; Ashbee blamed this on competition from commercial brasswork, much of it stamped out in imitation of repoussé.[16] Pearson's grotesques went with him, but other motifs and the naïve and powerful treatment remained; one element in the workshop tradition Ashbee sought to cultivate had been established.

On his own once more, Pearson went on producing his repoussé work for another ten or fifteen years, with little variation in type or style; for a time he helped in the metalwork classes run by J. D. Mackenzie, one of the colony of *plein air* artists in the Cornish fishing port of Newlyn, to occupy the younger fishermen in their spare time.[17] Williams too was involved with amateur classes in the 1890s, and one can see the legacy of Guild metalwork in the embossed fishes, peacocks and pomegranates which came from his classes at Newton, Cambridgeshire and Fivemiletown, County Tyrone.[18] But his later career was more ambitious than Pearson's, thanks partly to his years of teaching in the School of Handicraft; at about the turn of the century he was appointed principal of the Artistic Crafts Department at the Northampton Institute in Clerkenwell, London's silversmithing district; and in 1904 he was elected to the Art Workers' Guild.[19] It is a good question which of them reflected most accurately the direction of the Arts and Crafts, Pearson the plodding craftsman, or Williams the teacher and administrator.

A GUILD EXPERIMENT 1890–1896

With Pearson and Williams we have run rather ahead of other developments and must go back to 1890 or so to understand a different and overlapping phase in Guild metalwork. Striking repoussé work had helped the Guild to make its mark at the beginning, but must have seemed too limited to Ashbee; within eighteen months he had begun to enlarge the scope of the metal shop and to bring its practices closer to his Guild ideal. These were years of exploration: he introduced new craftsmen, new techniques and new materials; he encouraged a spirit of collaboration in the shop: he learnt to make metalwork himself, and helped his budding craftsmen to design for themselves, nurturing the habits and freedom which alone, he believed, could produce a Guild style. In some ways this period parallels the fallow years of Ashbee's furniture design, for if one sets the Guild light fittings on one side, the actual output between 1890 and 1895 was probably small and it was uncertain in design.[20] But in this case Ashbee was deeply involved in the working of the metal shop; the uncertainty was part of an ambitious experiment; and it is not the quality of the work which gives this period its interest, but the story, the stages by which the Guild reached its own kind of proficiency.

Two new craftsmen joined the metal shop in 1890, W. A. White in February, Bill Hardiman in June; they came, as Ashbee wanted, unsullied by trade experience, having shone in the metalwork class at the School of Handicraft, the first fruits of his efforts to create whole craftsmen rather than the narrow specialists of the trade.[21] In that year, and in the next two, he was able to publicize these efforts at a series of exhibitions of art metalwork organized by the Armourers' and Brasiers' Company at which many firms from the top end of the trade and some budding Arts and Crafts metalworkers exhibited; an original design by Hardiman won a prize in 1890 and one by White in 1892.[22] These two were joined in November 1891 by Arthur Cameron who had been Ashbee's office boy in Lincoln's Inn Fields, and, after three or four years, by Jack Baily.[23] All four worked for the Guild for many years: White and Hardiman until 1906, Cameron until liquidation at the end of 1907, Baily beyond; they became the nucleus of the shop, remained that when other craftsmen were added, and gave a basis for continuity and collaboration.

Hardiman had a particular talent for modelling. 'He came to the School of Handicraft in the evenings', Ashbee wrote, 'and I was struck with the extraordinary fidelity and feeling with which he made a copy of the St. Cecilia of Donatello.'[24] Ashbee also had some experience of modelling, and he liked Hardiman; and so the Guild struck out on a new path, impelled not so much by considerations of their market or by technical necessity as by the frail motives of talent and workshop sympathy.[25] Modelled and cast work became a regular feature of their metalwork from now on, though not necessarily a prominent one, for it was most often used for details such as feet, finials and brackets. The earliest evidence of this was at the Armourers' and Brasiers' exhibition in May 1890 which included models in wax for a door-knocker and bell-pull, designed and made by Hardiman: 'we often worked on the wax or the metal together', Ashbee recalled, 'after I had completed the design, but his touch was much more delicate and sure than mine'.[26] Ashbee was referring to the process of lost-wax casting, in which the design is modelled in wax and a mould formed round it; the wax melts and runs out when the mould is baked, and a casting is made by pouring molten metal into the resulting cavity. Many Guild castings were made in this way, though perhaps not all, and when designs were to be used repeatedly, such as the tiny terminal figures which serve as brackets on his cups, an intermediate casting would be made, perhaps in bronze, using the lost-wax process; from this all later versions could be sand-cast.[27]

The technique was a subject of intense interest at this time among the most advanced English sculptors, those who had trained at Lambeth and in France, for whom Renaissance Florence embodied the peak of expressiveness in sculpture, and whose ambition, under the aegis of the Art Workers' Guild, was to explore the boundaries of their art where it merged with architecture and the crafts. Alfred Gilbert, helped by Stirling Lee and Onslow Ford, experimented with lost-wax from about 1885, and so did Harry Bates; they were attracted by its immediacy, by the way it could preserve the delicacy of their modelling, and allowed them to do the casting themselves, instead of relying on the often clumsy services of British foundries. As Susan Beattie has said, 'the cause of lost-wax casting was taken up with missionary fervour, not only by Gilbert and other sculptors such as Ford, Lee and Bates in lone experiments, but in open discussion in schools and societies'.[28] And in 1888, John Sparkes, who had made the South London Technical Art School a nursery for such sculptors, saw 'The question of reviving the cire perdu method rapidly coming to the front ...'.[29] Interest in lost-wax casting was perhaps at a peak around 1890 when Ashbee was beginning his experiments, and he was certainly aware of it, and in touch with what came to be known as the New Sculpture movement; for Stirling Lee gave 'A Talk on Sculpture' to the School of Handicraft on 24 April 1890; and Arthur L. Collie, who set himself up in 1889 as a publisher of limited editions of statuettes by these sculptors, seems to have been on the committee of the School of Handicraft in 1889–90.[30] In the next chapter we shall see how much Ashbee's early experiments in jewellery owed to the movement. It seems obvious that his interest in lost-wax casting was inspired by the New Sculpture; that in seeking to enlarge the repertoire of the Guild beyond repoussé work, so closely associated with amateur metalworkers, he turned not to the trades but to those sympathetic practitioners of the fine art of sculpture who were reaching out towards the decorative arts.

1890 saw Ashbee using silver for the first time, as well as casting methods. Both were actually more prominent in jewellery than in metalwork, and it was jewellery which held his creative attention at this time; part of the story therefore has to wait until the next chapter. The picture of Ashbee's first five years of silverwork is, in any case, unclear.[31] There is one example of silverwork which can be dated to about 1890–1, a small spoon with an ivory handle, which belonged to Emily, wife of Ashbee's Birmingham friend, Arthur Dixon; it is inscribed 'IN. MIND-FULNESS. OF. A. REBUKE. SEP. 26. 90.'[32] (26 September was the date of the inaugural meeting of the Birmingham Guild of Handicraft at which Ashbee spoke, but history does not record who was rebuked or by whom.) After that, all is uncertainty. The Guild exhibited a 'Case of Silverwork' at the New English Art Club in November 1892, but there is no record of what it contained; a few pieces of early 1890s silver are known to survive, but none are precisely datable; and periodical illustrations are of little use since they rarely distinguish between silver and the other materials Ashbee used.[33] It is not until 1896, when Guild silver exhibited at the Arts and Crafts Exhibition can be clearly identified, that one can begin to speak with confidence of silverwork rather than metalwork in general.

The executed metalwork of this period falls into four groups, two of which we have already seen, repoussé work and fittings for electric light; the third is a series of cups (Plate 159). This seems to have been developed fairly early for there is a design for two of them dated August 1892, and two more were exhibited in 1893; others were illustrated in a Guild catalogue of about 1895.[34] The basic design was a bowl set on a narrow stem and spreading foot; it might be made of silver, bronze or gilded metal; usually the bowl would be raised work, but the stem, foot, handles and brackets could be cast, Ashbee making use of his new technique. He was also making use of the South Kensington Museum, for there are echoes here, in the domed bosses of the feet, the narrow cast stem and the brackets, of German and Dutch ceremonial drinking cups of the sixteenth and seventeenth centuries, though Ashbee's designs are much simpler and less fantastic; the South Kensington Museum had acquired a good deal of such German silver by this date.[35] The brackets themselves were sometimes thick wires, sometimes cast terminal figures, scaled down versions of the handles on seventeenth- and eighteenth-century cups and bowls; and other cups were decorated with neo-classical festoons. The effect is the same as on some of Ashbee's early furniture: there is more force in the eclectic antiquarian details than in the design as a whole.

One of these pieces, a silver cup and cover, had a plaque of plain red enamel on the cover, but this seems to have been Ashbee's only use of enamel on small

VIII. Bowl and cover in silver and enamel, the finial set with a coloured stone. Height 13 cms. (Victoria and Albert Museum)

159. Guild metalwork of the early 1890s: a sporting cup in gilt metal of about 1895, height 11.1 cms.; a silver mustard pot of about 1893, possibly made for Mrs H. S. Ashbee, height 8.8 cms.; and a silver two-handled cup hallmarked 1903 but reproducing a design of the early 1890s, height 16.5 cms. (All three in Cheltenham Art Gallery and Museum).

metalwork at this date.[36] The fire-place and light fittings at the Magpie and Stump were one prominent early use of enamel, jewellery was another; but for Ashbee's characteristic combination of enamel with silverwork we have to wait until the second half of the decade.

Some, perhaps most, of these cups, were challenge cups, trophies, or prizes for sports, and Ashbee designed them partly because he liked to see young men run and swim, and partly because he thought commercially manufactured trophies an insult both to Art and Athletics. When the London Schools Swimming Association was founded in 1893 he presented it with a cup and cover of his own design, decorated with young men poised to dive (the Fabian Society gave a shield designed by Walter Crane).[37] A few years later he wrote an article which applied to trophies his drastic antithesis of Art and Commerce.

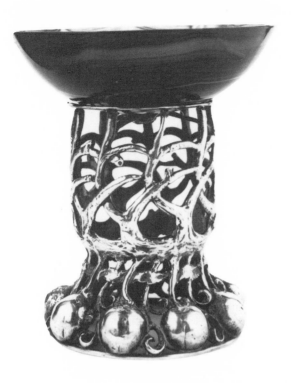

160. Salt-cellar in silver with an onyx bowl, of about 1893. Height 8.9 cms. (In the possession of the Ashbee family).

Henley, Bisley, Epsom, Oxford and Cambridge, the public Schools, the Board Schools, and every swimming, football, cricket, racquet, and tennis club in England, might hand down an honourable name for itself if it devoted its few sovereigns in varying degrees to the making of a work of Art rather than to the purchasing of a piece of mere ugly bullion.[38]

In point of fact, Ashbee's cups follow the general outline of many trade trophies, and if they were put on the familiar black plinths they would not look so different except in one respect: the trade trophies would be smooth and shiny, Ashbee's just a little rough from the hammer or the modeller's touch. The difference between art and bullion, it seems, lay in this surface quality, the human imprint of the craftsman.

The fourth group consists of tableware. Some of it—perhaps all, for there do not seem to have been many pieces—was designed for Ashbee's mother; and though none of it can be precisely dated, the fitting out of her new home at the Magpie and Stump suggests a date of 1893–4. There was a large soup tureen of plated copper and brass which can be seen at the back of the dining-room at the Magpie and Stump; there was a little silver cup supported by five bears, probably modelled by Hardiman; several silver spoons, one of sixteenth-century pattern; and small silver bowls on short cast legs ending in rudimentary ball and claw feet: these were salt-cellars and mustard pots and one of them, or a virtually identical example, is now in Cheltenham Art Gallery and Museum (Plate 159). The learned allusions and the awkwardness of the challenge cups are found here too.[39] The happiest piece, which still survives in the Ashbee family, is in some ways the simplest, a salt-cellar made out of a shallow onyx bowl, resting on a delicate cylindrical cage of cast silverwork (Plate 160); a decorative exercise almost, uncomplicated by practical difficulties or historical example. The open-work is formed into a pattern of branches and the solid base is decorated with a succession of bosses; perhaps surprisingly in so slight a thing, Ashbee has taken up the emblems of circles and trees, the themes of struggle and progression which he had first used in his Dante illustration of 1889.[40]

The early history of Arts and Crafts metalwork echoed the experience of the Guild, especially in the way interest spread, slowly, from base metalwork into silverwork, and also into enamelling. At the first three Arts and Crafts Exhibitions, in 1888, 1889 and 1890, a good deal of metalwork was exhibited, but it was almost all in copper and brass: there was W. A. S. Benson showing bowls, lamps and light fittings, as he was to do so for the next twenty years or so; there were the repoussé workers, amateur and trade, whom we have already met; and there were architectural metalworkers like Longden and Company, J. Starkie Gardner, and J. W. Singer and Sons who were the pioneers of commercial lost-wax casting: there were fewer tensions between the Arts and Crafts and the trades in architectural metalwork then in some other areas, and Henry Longden, Herbert Singer and Starkie Gardner were all members of the Art Workers' Guild from an early date. Of silver or enamels, on the other hand, there was very little and almost nothing that suggested any consistent development in the Movement: a 'Silver Loving Cup' by George Simonds, sculptor and first Master of the Art Workers' Guild, in 1888; three Limoges enamels by Rosa Wallis, from The Residences at South Kensington, in 1889, and a case of silver in the same year by William Smith of 150 Crown Street, Liverpool, not a name to conjure with in the Arts and Crafts; only the vases of Clement Heaton in cloisonné enamel were part of a lasting development.[41]

Between the third and fourth exhibitions there was a gap of three years. In 1893 the exhibits of silver and enamels were not much larger than before, but they were the first fruits of Arts and Crafts experiments of some importance. The Guild of Handicraft exhibited a case of 'hammered hollow ware in different metals'; it is not clear how much of this was silver.[42] Another case contained silver by Arthur Dixon, Jessie Newbery and Robert Catterson-Smith, and enamels by Constance Blount, Alexander Fisher and several students at Finsbury Technical College, including Nelson Dawson.[43] Here were some of the influential names in early Arts and Crafts silverwork and enamelling. The first Arts and Crafts silversmith was perhaps Gilbert Marks, who started producing repoussé silverwork in the late 1880s, but he was not much involved in the Movement personally.[44] Ashbee and Dixon were to count for more as designers of simple, useful silverwork, while Fisher and Dawson stood for a more luxurious tradition of pictorial enamels combined with various metals.

The Arts and Crafts Movement was predictably attracted to enamelling, a traditional craft which lent itself, like wood engraving or tapestry, to treatments at once pictorial and decorative. Two of the principal enamelling techniques, champlevé and cloisonné, in which the design is created by separate cells of enamel divided by strips of metalwork, were both practised in the trade, the more delicate cloisonné being preferred, and both were adopted with equal enthusiasm by the Arts and Crafts; a third technique, properly known as painted enamels, in which the enamel is applied directly to a level and undivided metal plate, was less well known in England in the late nineteenth century. Alexander Fisher, originally an enameller on pottery, became interested in this technique while a student at South Kensington in the 1880s; after visiting France he developed his own technique in about 1890, and then taught a class at Finsbury Technical College, with results which we have seen at the Arts and Crafts Exhibition in 1893. This kind of enamelling was known as 'Limoges', though the range and translucency of late nineteenth-century colours was much greater than those of the fifteenth- and sixteenth-century work from which they took their name; and Fisher's example seems to have stood behind much Arts and Crafts enamelling of this kind.[45] One might have expected Ashbee to send Arthur Cameron to Fisher's classes, but in fact he did not, and early Guild of Handicraft enamelling was independent of Fisher's influence; indeed, it was so plain and simple that it scarcely counts as painted enamels.[46]

That early Arts and Crafts Exhibitions could only display large quantities of base metalwork, and that work in silver and enamel was slow to emerge, was partly due to the fact that the Arts and Crafts viewed the precious metals trades, whether in their London centres of Hatton Garden or Clerkenwell, or in Birmingham or Sheffield, as irredeemably philistine. Setting themselves apart from the trades, they could only learn their skills by slow and lonely experiment; and they did not invite trade silversmiths or jewellers to exhibit at the Arts and Crafts Exhibitions in any numbers. There is an interesting contrast with architectural metalwork here: the expectations of craftsmanship among Gothic Revival architects since Pugin, notably Street and Sedding, and the response of firms like Longden's, Singer's and Starkie Gardner's, had prevented the distrust which seemed so automatic to the Arts and Crafts from taking hold.

A less jaundiced view of the precious metals trades and of the silver trade in particular shows them more prosperous in the 1890s than they had ever been; discoveries in Nevada, Colorado, Australia and Asia brought the price of silver steadily down; more and cheaper wares were produced and more men were employed. Mechanical processes, notably rolling mills, die-stamping, engine-turning and electro-plating, were well established; but handwork was still essential to many stages of production, particularly in wares of high quality; the principal craftsmen were an aristocracy of labour, known for their skill. Design was on the whole unadventurous; catalogues of c. 1900 reveal a whimsical naturalism popular at the mid-century lingering on, but the most popular manner, especially in tableware, was an approximation to Georgian styles; not the austere and functional Georgian popular in the 1930s, but something closer to rich, late Victorian taste, with much fluting and gadrooning. On the edge of the trade, as in other late Victorian art manufactures, was the South Kensington system of art training, promoting improvement in taste and design; the most ambitious designs from schools of art such as those in Birmingham and Sheffield in the 1880s tended to be in a Renaissance manner influenced by Alfred Stevens.[47] For all this many members of the Arts and Crafts, and certainly Ashbee, had nothing but scorn; silverware was, he said, 'that most degraded of all English crafts', and the trade inspired some of the most quotable passages in his writings; on style: 'the last degraded leavings of Lamerie and Adam . . .'; on technique: 'a thing . . . of a hundred subdivisions, fanned into existence by a hundred callous machines . . .'; on workshops: 'some filthy phthisical cubby hole in a black, back street in the model city of Birmingham . . .'.[48] The invective is fierce and indiscriminate; it was also the inspiration for much of his, and other Arts and Crafts experiments in silverwork.

At the Arts and Crafts Exhibition in 1896 the Guild exhibited two cases of metal-

161. Part of the Guild of Handicraft's exhibit at the Arts and Crafts Exhibition, 1896. (From the *Magazine of Art*, 1896–7, vol. 20, p. 67.)

work and jewellery, each containing perhaps as many as forty items. A photograph of one of the cases, published in the *Magazine of Art* (Plate 161), shows a repoussé copper dish, some jewellery, a large number of presentation cups, and some tableware; quite a number of the pieces seem to have been made of silver.[49] The catalogue, which at these exhibitions was careful to attribute work fairly to the designer and the craftsman, said of both cases that they were designed by Ashbee 'assisted by W. Hardiman, W. A. White, A. Cameron and J. Baily'.[50] That probably expressed quite accurately the state of design in the metal shop, with Ashbee in the leading role, all four principal craftsmen associated with him, and no further distinction between them. The exhibition seemed to catch the Guild's metalwork at a critical point, summing up the collaborative experiment of the past five or six years, and heralding developments in silver and tableware in the next phase. The Scottish architect Robert Lorimer wrote to a friend that he had been to the exhibition and had not found much to like, apart from 'some really delightful simple jewellery and silver things from Ashbee's place, he's really coming at it now . . .'.[51]

BEAUTY AND USE 1896–1902

The next six years or so saw the flowering of Guild metalwork. By the time they moved to Campden in 1902 a new, simple and distinctive style had been established, and it is a measure of its maturity that the same pieces appeal to the connoisseur, who likes to handle a fine object, and to the historian who is interested in what is typical of Ashbee and the Guild.

It was a flowering of work in silver rather than in any other metal. From 1897 onwards, the metal shop was expanded from its nucleus of White, Hardiman, Cameron and Baily, up to nine workmen in 1899, fourteen in 1901, dropping to about ten in 1902 with the move to Campden, and rising again after that. More than half the newcomers seem to have been trade craftsmen, the rest apprentices; and almost all were listed as silversmiths.[52] As the workshop expanded more silver was made, and a graph of its production would match the growth of the shop, rising steeply from 1899 to 1901, dropping in 1902 and recovering again in 1903.[53]

324

Since the Guild found it difficult to sell repoussé work in the early 1900s, there must have been a real change in the output of the metal shop. It is no accident that the hall-marking of Guild silver dates from this period: Ashbee registered his first mark at Goldsmiths' Hall in London on 29 January 1896, the letters  in a shield; after registration as a Limited Company, he registered a second mark,  in a rectangle chamfered at the corners; round 1900 both marks were used concurrently but there does not appear to be any significance in the use of one or the other.[54]

The enlargement of the workshop and the shift to silver were accompanied by a new emphasis in the kind of work produced. Presentation cups remained a part of the Guild's repertoire and miscellaneous pieces like trinket boxes were also made. But much the largest part of the increased output was tableware (Plate 162). Gone was the sketchy production of the early 1890s; tureens and breakfast dishes, salt-cellars and pepper-pots, butter dishes and decanters, knives and forks, were now produced in quantity; gradually the range of Guild tableware was expanded to provide an almost complete service; almost all of the pieces in the Goldsmiths' Alliance advertisement (Plate 163) can be matched in the work of this period, though Guild wares were generally more miscellaneous in design, not presented as distinct sets with matching ornament. Indeed so closely did they follow the types of trade tableware that one begins to wonder whether Ashbee's attention to Georgian exemplars at this time did not reflect fashions in the trade, paradoxical though that may seem.

These wares were part of Ashbee's aesthetic of the dinner table; the essentials were colour and form, not wealth and display.

162. A setting of silver tableware by the Guild of Handicraft. From the top: (1) dish of 1902; (2) decanter of 1903; (3) pepper-pot of 1901; (4) three-handled mustard pot and spoon of 1901; (5) salt-cellar of 1901; (6) pepper grinder of 1906; (7) napkin ring of about 1905; (8) fruit knife and fork of 1901; (9) sugar sprinkler of 1900; (10) butter knife of 1900, and (11) electric bell of 1901. (4, 5, 8, 9 and 10 Victoria and Albert Museum, the others private collections).

163. Advertisement from the *Illustrated London News*, 1891, vol. 99, p. 716.

I have purchased in the back streets of Milan and in the King's Road in Chelsea, little pieces of pewter and little halfpenny dishes which my good housekeeper has told me she considers eyesores when guests come, but which nonetheless are more beautiful objects than some of the best Minton and Wedgwood of the modern make.[55]

For china he recommended:

A plain white stoneware service of the old Wedgwood form without any pattern upon it, such as are still to be had by application to the Wedgwood Works, at Etruria, from the designs of the old Josiah ... With white service on the white cloth, or if you prefer a sage-green cloth, you can put some green Powell glass and some few pieces of silver, but not too many ...[56]

And for cutlery:

I often myself pick up pieces of old bone and ivory, old Turkish cigarette mouthpieces and odds and ends that any jay would envy me for, and I make designs for the treatment of these as knife and fork handles ...[57]

It was a pleasant and simple taste, setting itself rather deliberately against the elaborate table decorations of the time; and it would have made an excellent setting for food, though Ashbee was probably less interested in that than in waging his holy war against the philistine board loaded down with ostentatious plate.

At the back of these changes was another, less easy to define. In the early 1890s the metal shop had been small and introverted, concentrating on technical experiments and working together; saleable wares were produced but it was as if they were made, in Ashbee's terms, more for the producer than the consumer; on one occasion in 1895 Lord Leighton visited Essex House and wanted to buy a little silver mustard pot that Hardiman had made for Ashbee; Ashbee would not let him have it because 'it was a gift for love'.[58] In the second half of the decade the workshop became more outward-looking and things were made less for love. Production expanded, trade workmen were employed, and the presentation cups were displaced by tableware in silver, for which there was a larger market. It is hard to say whether this was a matter of deliberate policy. Like the registration of the Guild as a limited company in 1898, and the opening of a West End shop in 1899, it made the Guild more businesslike; perhaps Rob Martin Holland, the friendly banker, encouraged it. Ashbee, one imagines, viewed it with mixed feelings.

If he did, that did not affect the designs of this period which, with the shift towards silver and tablewares, gained an assurance and clarity not found in the tentative and sometimes clumsy work of the early 1890s. The new manner, like Ashbee's furniture designs of the same date, was a matter of a few elements, but remarkably versatile.

Most of the new wares were austere by the standard of the day. Ashbee would generally concentrate his ornament in one part, leaving the others plain, and on his bowls, cups and dishes there could be quite an expanse of naked silver. Not that he was less interested in these parts; he left them plain so as to draw attention to them, to the metal itself and the way it was worked. The traditional method of finishing hand-raised silver, known as planishing, is to work over the surface with a round-faced hammer, leaving a rippling pattern of small but quite visible marks. Nineteenth-century trade silver, by contrast, was generally given a smooth surface by spinning on a lathe and then polished to a brilliant shine.[59] Ashbee set great store by planishing, both because it produced a soft sheen which he felt was more natural to silver, and because it showed that the work was handmade, the hammer-marks providing a Ruskinian guarantee of its human value.[60] All his mature silver has this surface texture, an almost tactile quality which, like the grain in Arts and Crafts furniture, makes you want to reach out and touch it.

The elegant use of wirework on Guild silver also dates from this period. Ashbee used it in the early 1890s for light fittings and jewellery, but on his cups of that date the handles were probably cast.[61] In 1896 he exhibited a biscuit-barrel resting in a cradle of five C-curved wires, and a silver dish cover with a handle of snake-like intertwining wires.[62] The most characteristic and successful uses emerged in the next few years: wires twisted together to form the grip of a handle (c. 1897): an open arcade to support a bowl (1899) (Plate VIII); best of all, a loop handle formed of two wires soldered together, sweeping out in a graceful and mannered curve, just that much larger than was strictly called for by the shallow dishes to which they were attached (1900) (Plates 167–9).[63] The wires were slightly flattened at the tips where they were to be soldered on, but otherwise they were used just as they came from the bench, recalling the 'scantling' motif on Ashbee's furniture. In their elegance they were both construction and ornament, beauty and use.

Silver balls were incorporated into these designs in an equally straightforward way, usually as feet; they were either attached to the base at an angle, in a way that recalls English, Dutch and German silver of the seventeenth century, or, most effectively, the spreading foot of a cup or bowl was floated over a circle of balls. Even more than wires, the balls could be incorporated directly into designs, for they were simply components of which a stock would be kept in the workshops, and their exact placing was something Ashbee could leave to the judgement of his craftsmen. Both wires and balls were often used in trade silver, almost always for the humblest purposes on cheap and plated wares: Ashbee's use was perhaps an example of the bravura with which Arts and Crafts designers liked to invert the order of things and make some plain and unregarded element a feature of prominence and style.

For colour, one of the most attractive and original features of these new wares, Ashbee used coloured gemstones (Plate X) and enamel. In the early 1890s he had experimented with such stones in his jewellery, but used them only occasionally in metalwork, and then in obvious places such as finials. Now he used them more freely, circling the bodies of his wares with them, placing them where they would highlight his ornament or relieve the masses of his silver. The stones were, like those he used in jewellery, cheap, colourful, and despised by the trade, with the pert green chrysoprase perhaps the favourite and mother-of-pearl the subtlest, its milky gleam echoing the sheen of his silver. He was in effect treating his metalwork with the freedom of jewellery, and the *Studio* commented on his 'most happy knack' of setting stones in unexpected places.[64] The church plate of the Middle Ages and the Gothic Revival is rich in precedents for such use of coloured stones, and enamels; domestic plate is less so; the secular plate of Pugin and Burges was decorated with gemstones and was probably known to Ashbee, but it was more sumptuous and learned than his.[65] He did not emulate the richness of chalices and ciboria, or ceremonial drinking cups, in his domestic wares; his use of stones was sparing, aesthetic, secular and thoroughly untraditional. It was so simple and effective it is surprising that nobody had thought of it before; after Ashbee showed the way, others followed.

Enamels, which had rarely been used in early Guild silver, now became one of the chief attractions. In 1899 several silver bowls and boxes were made, and their lids were inset with enamel plaques probably by Arthur Cameron. Some were of a single, almost pure colour, as on the bowl and cover illustrated (Plate VIII); others were of a single colour but with more of what the *Studio* called a 'subtle and cloudy, marble-like effect'; and others again were painted with a design in several colours.[66] The few known examples of the last kind are strong in colour but amateurish in technique.

Guild enamelling became more skilful when Fleetwood C. Varley and William Mark joined in about 1900.[67] Varley was a water-colour artist from Chelsea, and it is not clear where he had learnt enamelling; he was often his own designer and painted innumerable plaques of misty landscapes which were set in the top of cigarette boxes and the like.[68] Mark was Australian and had worked for Nelson Dawson; his work has superb colour, delicacy of touch, and sparkle, but, as Ashbee wrote, 'His drawing is not good. His most successful work has been to render in colour the drawings of others.'[69] Both worked chiefly in painted enamels of the Limoges sort, though other techniques were sometimes used, and they changed the complexion of Guild enamelling.[70] The lids of dishes and boxes were now decorated with pictorial enamels which drew attention to themselves as pictures, overshadowing the metalwork; Varley and Mark would often sign these plaques themselves, something rare in the Guild since the days of Pearson. Arthur Cameron, who had been in the Guild longer but was less skilful, seems to have learnt from the other two, and began to sign his enamels likewise. (Plate IX).

At the same time Ashbee began to include smaller enamel plaques in his silver-work, usually painted with some slight decorative motif, such as a single flower; they worked in rather the same way as his gemstones, punctuating the metal (Plate XI). They were perhaps more consistently attractive than the larger plaques, for they were subtler, being part of a larger design, and the thick, glinting ill-defined medium perhaps lent itself more easily to decorative than to pictorial effects. Large pictures in enamel are something of a *tour de force*, such as an Alexander Fisher or a Phoebe Traquair could carry off; Varley and Mark were more effective on less ambitious ground.

The elements of Ashbee's mature style were simple, striking and untraditional; like other Arts and Crafts designers, he wanted to speak in the language of his own day, and they provided him with a strikingly modern vocabulary. The fresh-ness of his style can only be fully appreciated, however, in the context of his tradi-tionalism. The past is present in his mature work in a way that is both subtle and uneven; uneven because in some pieces there is no reason to suggest an exemplar at all, while in others he continued to use the traditional motifs of his early metal-work, bosses and cast terminal figures, even though he now had alternatives to them; subtle because in other pieces again an exemplar is felt, not in the motifs or technique, but in the form or type of the piece.[71] The cup and cover, for instance, which he designed for Harris Heal to present to the Painter-Stainers' Company in the City of London (Plate 164) clearly and deliberately evokes the tradition of

IX. Three silver boxes of 1903, decorated with painted enamels: top, enamel signed by Arthur Cameron, diameter of box 10cms.; middle, enamel signed by F.C. Varley, width of box 14.7 cms.; bottom, enamel signed by William Mark, width of box 13.8 cms. Mark's design is based on an engraving by Dürer, *St George on horseback*, of 1505–8. The boxes are in the collection of the Österreichisches Museum für angewandte Kunst in Vienna, and were acquired in November 1903.

164. (right). Cup and cover in silver, turquoises and enamel, 1900. Height 45 cms. (Victoria and Albert Museum).

165. (far right). Silver table basket, 1899. Diameter 17.6 cms. (Private collection).

English standing cups of *c.*1660; and yet, with its mannered and naturalistic frieze of tulips, its stones set in the cover along with an enamel plaque, and its delicate wirework finial, it belongs equally clearly to Ashbee and 1900. This trueness to past types was not confined to presentation and church silver; the silver table baskets which the Guild produced from 1896 onwards, their sides formed from curved panels of solid silver alternating with sprays of flowers in open-work, recall mid-eighteenth-century examples (Plate 165); Ashbee's beakers and vases are of seventeenth-century inspiration; his pear-shaped teapots simplified versions of Queen Anne; other echoes can be found among his classic designs.[72] It was just because his mature style was so fresh, assured and versatile that he could afford to commit himself to tradition.

SOME CLASSIC DESIGNS

Among the silver designs of this period there are a handful which stand out both because they are successful in themselves and because they seem to have been very popular. There is little in the records of the Guild to show which designs sold best, but these turn up so often in the decorative art market as to suggest that they sold well at 16A Brook Street and were made in quantity; indeed there are so many loop-handled dishes that they can only provoke yawns at Sotheby's and Christie's nowadays. It is remarkable, though, that even in this case, where the Guild seems to have approached its own kind of mass-production, one rarely finds two identical pieces; the choice of a coloured stone, the outline of a handle, the form of a knob or a finial, will almost always set them apart.

The first of these designs has a curious underground origin (Plates XII, 166). When the building site for the Magpie and Stump was being cleared in 1893, fragments of pottery and glass were unearthed, including three broken, fat-bellied

330

166. Three decanters, from left to right: 1901, height 20.5 cms.; 1904, height 25.3 cms.; 1903, height 21 cms. (The first and third in private collections, the second in the Victoria and Albert Museum).

bottles of thick green glass.[73] Ashbee, who took a romantic interest in the archaeology of Chelsea, kept them, and about four years later James Powell and Sons of Whitefriars, London, the manufacturers of table glass most favoured by the Arts and Crafts, made a new version in thinner green glass, refining the outline slightly.[74] Ashbee took the new bottle, grasped it firmly round the neck with a silver collar, and threw a slim cordon of wires around the body, cradling the fulness of the glass without disturbing its form; to pick up one of these decanters, especially when it is full, is to experience a slight feeling of panic, a fear that so slight a structure cannot support or protect the heavy, fragile glass. The design was a version of ordinary late Victorian glass claret jugs with silver or plated mounts, but for Ashbee it had rougher and more vivid associations: 'it was doubtless bottles of that shape,' he wrote of his Chelsea finds, 'good solid glass, from which Falstaff and his worthies drank their sack'.[75] The first design was produced in 1897 or 1898, and many variations followed.[76] In nearly all of them, and especially in the 1904 example with its stylish finial, Ashbee was designing at the top of his bent; if one had to take a single piece of his work to a desert island, this would be it. The cost of these elegant objects was only £3 or £4, for little silver was used.[77]

The second classic was a circular dish and cover, eight to nine inches across, designed in about 1900 (Plate XIII).[78] It was advertised in Guild catalogues as a muffin dish, the high cover accommodating a stack of muffins, and as a breakfast dish. (Quite separate designs were produced to match the low, flat-topped, oval or rectangular vegetable or entrée dishes which were common in the late nineteenth

331

X (following page). Dish in silver, the foot set with chrysoprases. Height 8.2 cms. (Private collection).

XI (page 333). Fruit stand in silver decorated with painted enamels, 1905. Height 15.4 cms. (Collection of John Jesse).

167. Silver dish with one loop handle, 1900. Overall width about 19.5 cms. (Victoria and Albert Museum).

168. Silver dish on a foot with two loop handles, 1901. Overall width about 25.2 cms. (Victoria and Albert Museum).

169. Silver dish with two loop handles and an enamelled cover, the finial set with a coloured gemstone, 1900. Overall width 27 cms. (Victoria and Albert Museum).

century, but they do not seem to have survived in the same quantity.[79]) Most of the muffin dishes known to survive are made not of silver but of silver plate, and among Guild wares these designs, entrée dishes, soup tureens, larger dish covers and clock cases were commonly advertised as plated. It is not clear why these articles should have been chosen for cheaper production; nor is it clear just what the standing of plating was in the Arts and Crafts Movement, which was such a champion of 'honesty'.[80] At all events, the muffin dishes, whether plated or silver, depended for their effect on the surface treatment of the metal, on outline, and on isolated points of colour, as in the finial; sometimes a stone of solid colour and unreflective quality would be chosen and mounted rather high on a finial of snake-like wires, an excellent refinement. A circular dish and cover in plate to the standard design would cost £2 5s., depending on its size, or £3 5s. if it had a hot-water jacket in the base.

The so-numerous loop-handled dishes also date from about 1900. Properly speaking there are three separate designs which all appeared at about the same time.[81] The simplest design is a shallow circular dish, about four inches across, with a single handle (Plate 167); then there is a similar dish set on a spreading foot with two handles whose wires are attached to the bowl at the top and to the foot at the bottom (Plate 168); finally, a dish on a foot with two handles and a cover enriched with an enamel panel and a knob or finial (Plate 169); in the first two designs a coloured gemstone is usually set at the point where the wires of the handle part

to join the bowl.[82] To present the designs in this way is rather to suggest that they evolved in this sequence; in fact, it is not clear which came first; equally it suggests that they are variations on a single theme; in fact, they have different moods: the first low, solid, puritan and useful, as much a matter of the dish as the handle, the second linear and expansive, tempting one to ceremonious gestures, more handle than dish; the third compact, luxurious and secretive. It is also to overlook the flexibility of the designs, the fact that the curve of the handles and the colour of the gemstones and enamel are capable of, indeed seem to call out for, many variations.

The writers of catalogue entries and of captions have been understandably puzzled to know how to describe these dishes and have either chosen the neutral 'loop-handled dish', or guessed at uses, such as 'cup', 'porringer' or 'sweet dish'. No doubt they lent themselves to many uses, but in Guild catalogues they are referred to as jam or butter dishes, a use which underlines the importance of the green glass liner.[83] Some of them at least were intended to stand in place of the Georgian-style scallop shells on which late Victorian butter often sat, or of glass leaves for jelly and jam. Ashbee's alternative was a simple, general purpose dish, at the opposite extreme from naturalism. In developing it he may have been thinking of the workshop, for the designs are technically straightforward, can be assembled out of more or less standard parts, and yet leave room for the craftsman's choice. He may also have been thinking of the several kinds of low, one- or two-handled dishes in the history of silversmithing which have some kinship with his design; of wine tasters, porringers and so-called bleeding bowls; of such dishes in seventeenth- and eighteenth-century Scandinavian silver: the South Kensington Museum received an important gift of this kind in 1898, and Ashbee shows debts to it elsewhere; of the Scottish quaitch, a dish of comparable simplicity.[84] But if he was, it was only in the most general way, for his simple bowl, with its original handle, owes no specific debts.

The attribution of these designs raises a problem. They are so central to Ashbee's reputation and so typical of his work that it seems impertinent to attribute them to anyone else. However the Arts and Crafts Exhibition Society's catalogue for 1903, a specific and usually reliable source, attributed a single-handled dish to Arthur Tuckey, who looked after the Guild shop at 16A Brook Street, and a two-handled bowl and cover to W. A. White.[85] No drawing in Ashbee's hand exists, and it begins to look as if his best-known design was not in fact his after all. One solution to this problem, which has the merit of being simple, not improbable, and reflecting credit on all concerned, would be to suppose that Ashbee was the author of the original designs in about 1900; that, having committed them to the workshop, he carried his encouragement of the craftsmen so far as to attribute variations on his designs to them alone; and that a pedantic and less generous attribution of the two dishes would read 'Variations by A. S. Tuckey and W. A. White on a theme by C. R. Ashbee'. A single-handled dish with its green glass liner cost £2 5s. in 1906, the two-handled version £2 15s.[86]

The last classic design takes us into the Campden period, for it dates from about 1904 (Plate XI). It consists of a shallow, circular dish on a hexagonal stem of open-work and a circular or hexagonal base with ball or cushion feet; plaques of decorative enamel are set around the stem or on the slope of the base.[87] Its several aspects

XII. Silver-mounted decanter, the finial set with a chrysoprase, 1904. Height 25.3 cms. (Victoria and Albert Museum).

170. Silver spoon warmer designed by Bill Hardiman, about 1902. (From the *Art Journal*, 1903, p. 152.)

171. (facing page). Silver kettle and stand, 1906. Height 29.2 cms. (Private collection).

are best understood by way of the different names it has been given. In Guild catalogues it was called a fruit stand, which suggests a straightforward use but is misleadingly utilitarian. In museums and sale rooms it would be catalogued as a tazza, for that is the historical type to which it conforms. Ashbee called it an epergne, a word which more often refers to an elaborate structure with many arms, each supporting a dish, the kind of thing which acted as a centre-piece for a formal table setting.[88] Ashbee's word is actually suggestive: in contemporary trade catalogues fruit stands were referred to as epergnes, and these pieces were meant for just such a showy, formal role; they were more luxurious and expensive than other Guild tablewares and they could be large.[89] Though the example illustrated is only six inches high, others rose to a foot or more, a size at which, piled high with fruit, they could dominate many dinner-tables, and a stand of average height, around nine inches, would cost as much as thirteen guineas.[90] Victorian epergnes were often decorated with naturalistic or loosely classical ornament; Ashbee recast the type in his own decorative language: the vigorous natural forms of his openwork are structurally expressive, making the stem light but strong; the enamels serve for enrichment; and the success of the design depends on the bold and graceful way in which the shallow dish spreads out from the narrow stem: two designs of 1903, with deeper dishes and thicker stems, have none of its linear elegance.[91]

SILVER OF THE CAMPDEN PERIOD 1902–1908

When the move to Campden was debated by the Guild, the metalworkers were uncertain about it, and in the event some silversmiths chose to stay in London; they were mostly recent recruits, nervous perhaps of working far from the centre of their trade. (George Colverd, on the other hand, an apprentice silversmith and keen footballer, came down to Campden and then went back to London again because he did not want to lose the chance of a place in the Millwall Reserves.[92]) The nucleus remained, though by now Hardiman was becoming hopelessly insane. He thought that Ashbee, White and Osborn, the Guild manager, were persecuting him; and though he continued to be employed by the Guild, almost until his death in 1906, he worked now on his own; the silver spoon-warmer, exhibited in the autumn of 1902 (Plate 170), is a good example of his skill as a designer and model-

ler.[93] By 1903, the shop was back at its former strength with a mixed bunch of new-comers, including George Hart, virtually an amateur whose work Ashbee had seen when judging an Arts and Crafts exhibition in Hitchin; Fred Partridge and Arthur Penny from Birmingam Municipal School of Art, Partridge, skilled, romantic and wayward; Penny, a good modeller though deaf; and Stanley Keeley, a boy in his teens from Campden.[94]

By and large Guild silver at Campden maintained the standards and the character of earlier work, though the volume of work seems to have fallen off from 1904. We have already seen one important new design of this period, the fruit stand, and the handsome tea-kettle of 1906 (Plate 171) displays familiar qualities, an expanse of hammered metal, unmistakably modern ornament, the sense of an exemplar as the frieze of ornament takes the place of fluting.[95] However, in about 1905 the Guild issued an eighty-page catalogue, illustrating about a hundred and twenty examples of Guild metalwork, old and new, and about seventy of jewellery.[96] Some of the designs in the catalogue struck a new note: there were teaspoons of Guild character, but stamped, not wrought; Celtic interlaced ornament; trinket boxes of commonplace design—excuses for the enamel picture on the lid; photograph frames and menu stands decorated with whimsical frogs and butterflies; repoussé ornament in a fluid style, melting into the background metal in the Art Nouveau manner.[97] Round 1900 Guild metalwork had addressed itself to the market and become more business-like; in these designs it seemed to go one step further, and addressed itself to the fancy goods and Christmas trade. Were these the wares to which Ashbee referred when he said of work done at Campden 'A great deal of it indeed was work in trifles, little work, and work of which we were not particularly proud.'?[98]

The Guild was in an impossible situation. Their simple silver, and that of other Arts and Crafts metalworkers, had struck a fresh and interesting note in the late 1890s, and it was successful enough to be taken up by commercial manufacturers and retailers. William Hutton and Sons of Sheffield were the first, and in 1899 Liberty's launched their 'Cymric' range, which developed into an impressive collection of silver tableware, jewellery and fancy goods over the next few years.[99] In style the Cymric wares were a rich blend of Arts and Crafts and Art Nouveau, for many designers were employed, with Archibald Knox contributing distinctive ornament of Celtic inspiration. Very few of these wares could be confused with the less sophisticated products of the Guild, but very many of them used the same elements of design, stretches of plain silver, concentrated ornament, enamels and coloured stones, particularly turquoises, and flower and plant forms in conventionalized repoussé work. Aymer Vallance, reviewing the Cymric range's claim to novelty in 1901, commented that 'the Guild of Handicraft has for some years been producing work which seems to possess not dissimilar properties'.[100]

Later on, Ashbee told the story of how a sprightly young man once bought a silver brooch at the Guild's shop, and how it appeared six weeks later, with twenty others like it in the window of 'Messrs. Nobody, Novelty and Co.'—a pseudonym which revealed more than it hid.[101] But Liberty was not a plagiarizer and the threat was not so much from close copies as from the general character of Cymric wares, which offered an alternative to those of the Guild: 'the work is all hand-hammered', Liberty's announced in a catalogue of 1899–1900. 'In this feature of the work ...

there is an echo of those more leisured days when the craftsman not only loved his art for its own sake, but was able to devote his life to it with comparative indifference to the pecuniary result of his labour of love.'[102]

These were just the qualities and associations which Ashbee claimed for his work, perhaps with more justice, and certainly in less glutinous prose; and for him the situation was thick with irony; for the success of his wares had created an opportunity for a competitor with greater flair and more stylish designs, a competitor who was the very embodiment of that commercialism against which Ashbee fought all his life. And now, to make the irony more painful, the Guild was trying to compete against Liberty's, and imitate their wares, in order to survive.

It was a brave attempt, but the most likely outcome was that the Guild would lose some of its integrity and gain no more business; and that is what seems to have happened. In 1906 the metal shop was reduced from fourteen men to ten, and one of those to go was W. A. White, the craftsman of longest standing and the most prolific designer among them; he went, ironically, because of 'the need for cutting down expenses in the design department'.[103] At the clearance sale of the Dering Yard gallery that spring muffin dishes were offered at £1 2s. 6d., and a silver-plated challenge cup mounted on ebony elephants was reduced from £10 0s. 0d. to £7 15s. 6d.[104] One sad measure of Ashbee's desperation at this time is a handful of designs which are little more than reproductions, uninventive copies, of traditional types, and especially of late seventeenth-century and eighteenth-century English silverware, as if he was fishing for customers in the rising Georgian taste.[105]

It would be neat and easy to end the story of Guild metalwork on this note, the uncertainty of style echoing the economic troubles of the Guild. But it did not end like that. Surrounded by the business worries of the years round 1906, Ashbee began to produce designs of a new and thoroughly convincing kind.[106] Their characteristic features were ropework in emphatic horizontal layers; coloured stones, especially mother-of-pearl, set close together between the ropework; and modelled figures. Alec Miller took Hardiman's place as the Guild's modeller and produced groups of small figures and caryatids; other figures may have been modelled by Ashbee himself.[107] The new work was quite different in style from the tableware of c. 1900, restful where that was dynamic, rich where that was austere, monumental where that was humble. It combined features from mediaeval and neo-classical metalwork with skill and ease; it was both more explicit in its traditionalism than the work of c. 1900, and more coherent than that of the early 1890s; it was a welcome demonstration of Ashbee's range as a designer, and a complete surprise. In 1906 some fine pieces of this sort were designed for Count Lionel de Hirschel de Minerbi of the Palazzo Rezzonico in Venice (Plate 172); when Ashbee showed him a tureen nearing completion, the Count said he wanted something 'more in the manner of "L'Art Nouveau"'.[108] Ashbee, to whom those words were distasteful, refused, and the piece was melted down. Pity the poor Count. He may have wanted swirling maidens and snake-like coils; but he may simply have been expecting something less monumental, one of the Guild's pieces of plain and striking silver which had seemed so fresh and new round 1900, and with which Ashbee's name was so closely linked.

172. Tureen for Count Lionel de Hirschel de Minerbi, as published in C. R. Ashbee, *Modern English Silverwork* (1909). The original stood 44.2 cms. high.

MODERN ENGLISH SILVERWORK

In 1909, when his days as a designer of metalwork were almost over, Ashbee published a retrospective collection of his executed silverwork, some hundred and fifty designs on a hundred lithographed plates. They were only a quarter, perhaps, of his designs, and selected at random; but they gave a broad impression of his work.[109] Here were the gawky cups of the early 1890s, and the Venetian Count's unsatisfactory soup tureen, the many varieties of mustard pot and salt-cellar, and a crucifix made for the high altar of Lichfield Cathedral, where it still stands.[110] Philippe Mairet executed the drawings in a spare and precise style which captured the linear quality of Ashbee's work round 1900, and some of the plates were touched with water-colour, for coloured stones and enamel. Ashbee gave it one of those large and suggestive titles he chose so well, *Modern English Silverwork*, and dedicated it, in a barbed and theatrical gesture, 'to the Trade Thief, desiring him only—if indeed he have any aesthetic honour, thieves sometimes have!—to thieve accurately'.[111] It was as if he was rounding off fifteen years or more of silverwork, mocking but philosophical, reflecting on the exploitation of his style by others, and on the fact that the metal shop had seen his greatest successes and, more recently, compromise and defeat.

By the time *Modern English Silverwork* was published the metalwork of the Arts and Crafts Movement had changed a good deal from the hammered copperwork and tentative silver of the early 1890s. The silverwork of Henry Wilson, at once monumental and organic, now rather set the tone, and there were many new silversmiths and enamellers of much the same temper; John Paul Cooper, Edward Spencer, Ramsden and Carr, Harold Stabler and Phoebe Traquair, to name only the best known, all started working in precious metals in the late 1890s or early 1900s; and the Arts and Crafts Exhibitions were increasingly full of the work of talented students from the schools of art, especially in London and Birmingham. This new work was probably more skilled than that of the early 1890s, and certainly more sumptuous: there was a liking for intricate ornament and exotic materials, for presentation and dilettante wares, caskets and christening cups, maces and mazers. The simple tableware of *c.* 1900 with which Ashbee had made his name must have seemed crude by comparison, and it may be that his richer and more monumental work of *c.* 1906 was a response to this change.

He need not have been so anxious to keep abreast of things. His reputation as a designer of Arts and Crafts metalwork rests securely on the simple tableware, and large claims can be made for it. They may be qualified when the history of Arts and Crafts metalwork and studies of individual designers come to be written, but for the moment they are, that he was the pioneer of silver tableware in the Arts and Crafts: the flow of designs which began between the Arts and Crafts Exhibitions of 1893 and 1896 and continued for the next ten years or so was preceded only by occasional designs from other hands; that his tableware was the most comprehensive in the Movement, matching the types of trade silver at very many points; and that this work was a perfect expression of one strain in the Arts and Crafts, in the way it addressed itself to the needs of everyday life, in its preoccupation with materials, in its simplicity and its sense of tradition. Only the work of Arthur Dixon and the Birmingham Guild of Handicraft bears comparison, and that, though it was even simpler than Ashbee's and more consistent, was begun at a slightly later date, and seems to have had a narrower range.[112]

These wares have earned Ashbee a wider reputation; they, more than any other of his designs, have made him a part of the genealogy of the Modern Movement, reaching out on the one hand to the radical metalwork of Christopher Dresser, and on the other to the novelty of Art Nouveau. One of Ashbee's loop-handled dishes is illustrated in histories of modern design with unfailing regularity. The comparison with Dresser is apt, for both men designed silver tablewares simpler than most trade work, proud of their plain surfaces and evident construction; but Dresser was thinking of semi-industrial processes and of geometry, Ashbee of gentle, traditional shapes and the skills of his craftsmen. To a modern eye both Dresser and Ashbee seem to stand apart from the work of their contemporaries; but they were not necessarily alike for all that. As for Art Nouveau, some of Ashbee's handles would not have been so generously looped, his organic ornament so sinuous, or his handles sometimes fixed with such serpentine curves, if he had not been aware of developments in Belgium, France and Germany; the influence is palpable. But to compare his metalwork with the fluid, sometimes precious, semi-sculptural work of Guimard, Lalique or van de Velde is to feel how sober it is.[113] The story of the origins of the Modern Movement traced by Pevsner and others moves fast and selectively over the landscape of the turn of the century, linking one architect or designer with another and moving on; Ashbee properly has a place in this chain, and the argument holds; but it does not throw much light—it was not meant to throw much light—on his work in itself.

It is more enlightening to see Ashbee's work alongside silver of an earlier date than in the rarified and miscellaneous company of classics of modern design; not because this shows Ashbee as a traditionalist, though he was that; nor because it shows him as a modernist, adapting and updating exemplars, though he did that too; but because it shows how radical his silverwork was. It is not a question of style but of splendour. So much of the history of metalwork shows obedience to the principle that metals of the highest value call for the highest workmanship; mediaeval chalices and gospel covers, Renaissance drinking cups, things to which Ashbee attended, demonstrate this; and yet he attempted little high craftsmanship; his silver makes a show of plain surfaces and simple, even crude, construction; it was puritan in taste, reduced to a few elements which, by virtue of that reduction, came to be seen as essentials. And his intentions, his theoretical attitude to silver, were positively paradoxical. For he chose to specialize in work whose *raison-d'être* has always been that it is worth a lot of money, while insisting that his own work was a matter of art, in which money values did not enter. It was as if he proposed, single-handedly, to redefine the tradition of working in the precious metals.

There is one last context in which Ashbee's silver should be seen, and that is the workshops of the Guild. To have set the pattern for the silver tableware of the Arts and Crafts, to have been a pioneer of modern design, to have attempted the redefinition of precious metalwork, was much; to have created a workshop tradition, a Guild style, was more. There were several elements in the Guild style, as Ashbee understood it, some simple, others more ambitious. It was a matter of repeating certain motifs: Pearson's work had started a store of these and Cameron was good at 'Jolly Art Fishes' as the Guildsmen called them.[114] It was a matter of Ashbee sitting down with Hardiman and others and learning to make castings and hollow ware by experiment. It was a matter of designs so simple that any craftsman could execute them and introduce his own variations. It was a matter of craftsmen staying long enough with the Guild to form a real group, as White, Hardiman, Cameron and Baily did. Ashbee thought that the metalworkers of the Guild had vindicated his belief that the origins of style lie in the social relations of men to men, and in the introduction to *Modern English Silverwork* he wrote,

So it comes that when a little group of men learn to pull together in a workshop, to trust each other, to play into each others' hands, and understand each others' limitations, their combination becomes creative, and the character that they develope in themselves, takes expression in the work of their fingers. Humanity and Craftsmanship are inseparable.[115]

XIII. Muffin dish in silver, the flange set with chrysoprases and the finial with a dark green stone, 1900. Height 15 cms. (Victoria and Albert Museum.)

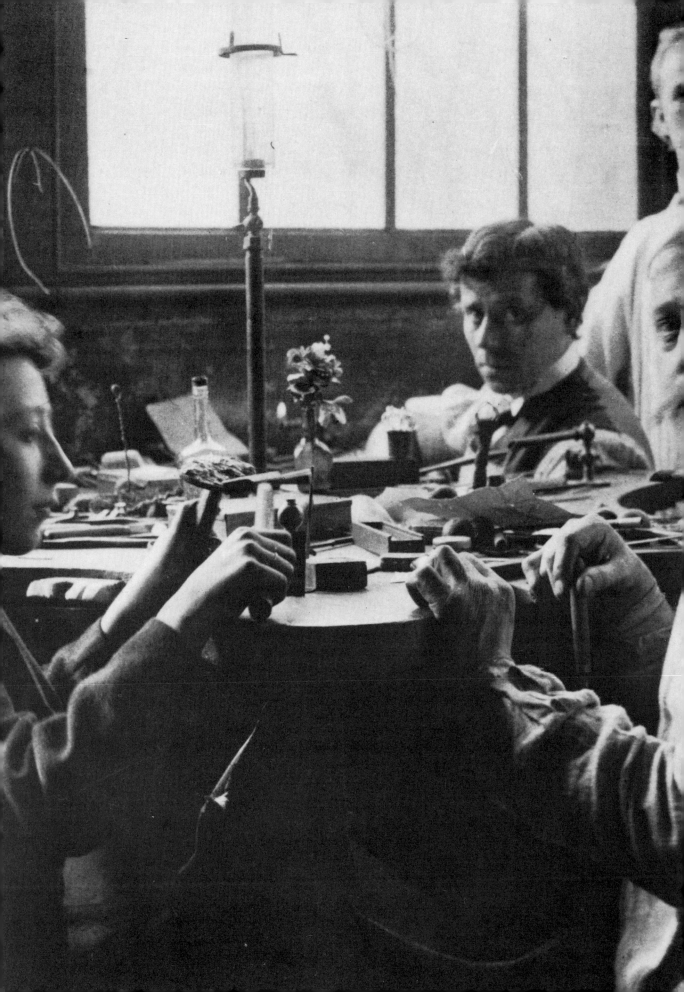

CHAPTER THIRTEEN
JEWELLERY

LET US LOOK TO THE CINQUECENTO

In 1890, when Ashbee started designing jewellery, the *Young Ladies' Journal* told its readers:

Fancy jewels are more fashionable than ever; pins and brooches of all styles—flowers, birds, emblems, animal's heads, beetles, dragon-flies, etc. It is the fashion to stick pins, the head of which is a jewel, here, there, and everywhere—in the hair, in the draperies of the bodice, in folds of lace or bows of ribbon, and even in bonnets and hats.[1]

Most of the things which Ashbee designed, his houses and furniture, metalwork and books, were useful and sometimes rather serious things. But in this chapter we seem to breathe a different air, we find ourselves in a world in which ornament and display, luxury and the nuances of etiquette play the largest part, a world of women's fashions only less changeable than that of dress itself. One wonders what a member of the Arts and Crafts Movement, which held the quality of usefulness so dear, was doing there.[2] One wonders particularly what Ashbee was doing there, who was not often stirred by women's beauty, and whose favourite women were wise, and unconventional, and usually old.

The truth is that he was not 'there' at all. He was in the sunlit streets of fifteenth-century Florence, a city instinct with ideas and art, among the *botteghe* of the artist-goldsmiths; there were no fancy jewels there, no folds of lace or bows of ribbon. 'Well, we live in an ugly time,' he wrote, 'and jewellery is not the least of the lost children of Art . . . let us look to the Cinque-cento.'[3]

He admired the fifteenth-century Italians because he believed that they practised jewellery as an art. He did not mean that they treated it like sculpture or painting. 'Jewellery is, before all others, an art of limitations. An artist cannot but put less of himself into a gem than into a statue, he is necessarily more cabined.'[4] He meant that jewellery was treated as one among other arts in the fifteenth century; painters and sculptors were no strangers to the *bottega*: Donatello and Ghiberti, Brunelleschi and Schongauer and Dürer were all goldsmiths; and the craftsmen of the day moved easily among the different branches of their art, from the minutest gem-setting to the founding of statues. 'The arts and crafts were one and indivisible.'[5] It was all very different from the commercialism into which the making and the wearing of jewellery had sunk in his own day.

Our modern ladies have little or no understanding of how jewellery should be worn, or what relation it should have to the person or to costume. Their jewellery is vulgar and tawdry, showy or mean, and is usually treated as a fashionable adjunct rather than as the

173. The Guild jewellers at Essex House, in about 1901.

final point up to which the whole costume should lead; it is almost always a commercial article and scarcely ever a work of art. The ladies of the Cinquecento, or the men too, and the artists who painted them, knew better.[6]

He admired the prominence of Renaissance jewellery, whether in fifteenth-century Italy or elsewhere. In the still bright air of late fifteenth- and sixteenth-century portraits, he saw jewellery worn with pride, the focus of dress and not a mere accessory; they showed him that 'The interest in jewellery must not be broken up and divided, it must culminate. The culminating point is the final folding of the robe, the favour in the hat of the man, the precious gift in the breast of the woman.'[7] He was not arguing for less jewellery necessarily; it was an aesthetic not a sumptuary law, and Holbein's Henry VIII stitched fat with pearls might pass Ashbee's test if his jewellery 'culminated'. But in the 1890s, when he saw women scatter themselves with trivial ornament, he was inclined to play the Puritan. Phoebe Haydon recalled taking down a letter in which he told a client for whom he was designing jewellery, 'that a lady should only wear jewellery on high days or holidays, and that it should then be a large and good piece of jewellery, and not a number of little "cracker toys"'.[8] Phoebe, who was wearing a pearl necklace and three little enamel brooches strung together with fine gold chains, on which she rather prided herself, blushed, and reduced her jewellery accordingly.

And he admired it for its colour.

We nowadays have lost all understanding of the colour of jewellery. We use certain conventional stones, diamonds, rubies, sapphires, white pearls, the stones that are in the market, and we set them uniformly in gold as the most expensive of metals; the rest are 'fancy stones,' and don't concern us. To the Cinquecento jeweller no stones were fancy stones . . .[9]

He looked closely at examples in the South Kensington Museum and possibly also in the Louvre and the Kunsthistorisches Museum in Vienna, and was delighted with their bold conjunctions. Renaissance figurative pendants in particular, birds, ships and the like, and the earlier *enseignes* with narrative scenes on them, are made of rich enamel, gold and coloured stones, set down, modelled and pierced as a vivid and miniature realism requires; the colours do not belong to a single material or rest in a single plane; there is no harmonious system of polychromy. Ashbee liked that, liked it when one colour against all expectations brought out another: 'the red garnets of the border marry with the "rosso clero" background of the Crucifixion', he wrote of an enamelled pendant.[10]

This was a serious taste, as much concerned with how jewellery is used as with what it looks like. Ashbee was well aware that much Renaissance jewellery was made for men; and he hinted at the importance of symbolism in jewellery and of 'barbaric splendour', as if he regretted the passing of the days when rings were worn to ward off sickness and men wore *enseignes* in their hats as favours.[11] Such ideas could not easily be brought to bear on the jewellery of his own time, were perhaps a reaction against its 'mere' prettiness.

His particular hero in all this was Benvenuto Cellini. Since the eighteenth century, when his *Vita* was first published—and translated by Goethe among others—Cellini had been celebrated as the embodiment of the Renaissance spirit, its artist-craftsman *par excellence*, with the result that virtuoso metalwork of the sixteenth century was indiscriminately attributed to him, and much Victorian metalwork of Renaissance character was said by the trade to be in 'the Cellini style'.[12] Ashbee's enthusiasm was thus not without precedent, though by his time a more informed sense of Renaissance metalwork prevailed. He was introduced to Cellini by John Addington Symonds's impressive translation of the *Vita*, published in 1887, and was probably struck then by Cellini's thrilling account of the casting of his *Perseus* by the lost-wax method. He then went on to read *I Trattati dell'oreficeria e della scultura*, which had been published from the original Italian manuscript in 1857.[13] This was in the early years of the Guild and one can imagine his sense of discovery: here were not only the gossip and rivalries of the Renaissance workshops, their little human pictures, but also techniques of jewellery and precious metalwork described in a disorderly but not impractical way; in the Guild's metalwork experiments of *c.* 1890 it could be used as William Morris used Hellot's *L'Art de la teinture* in his dying experiments, as a guide to the old techniques, unsullied by contact with the trade.

Ashbee thought that a translation of the *Trattati* was needed as a workshop handbook, and he nursed the idea during the 1890s.[14] He was not alone in this, for when he started working on a translation himself in the late 1890s, he found that two other metalwork enthusiasts, G. B. Simonds, the sculptor, and Antonio de Navarro, a wealthy connoisseur, had had the same idea.[15] Both courteously gave way to him and *The Treatises of Benvenuto Cellini on Goldsmithing and Sculpture* were fittingly printed and published in 1898 as the first production of the Essex House Press. Ashbee's vivid translation caught the tumbled vulgarities of Cellini's speech better than Symonds's smoother *Life* had done—he wrote 'bum' when the text required it; and it was a practical handbook, dedicated 'To the metal workers of the Guild of Handicraft, for whom I have set my hand to this work, and to whom I look for the fruit it is to bear'. Ironically, this was just the time when silversmiths and jewellers from the trade, who could learn least from Cellini, were beginning to be recruited to the Guild; and one wonders in general whether such a handsomely produced book—it cost £1.15s.— was much used in the workshops of the Arts and Crafts Movement. Henry Wilson would not have recommended it, for he thought Cellini 'an amazing blackguard', and the arcane *Diversarum Artium Schedula* of the eleventh-century monk Theophilus a more wholesome treatise; on the other hand, the library copy at Birmingham Municipal School of Art, where much good Arts and Crafts metalwork was done, is exceedingly well thumbed.[16]

The colour, pride and human drama of Cellini and the Cinquecento—Ashbee did not distinguish much between the two—had the force of a myth in Ashbee's ideas, light against his dark image of contemporary metalwork, the 'filthy phthisical cubby hole' in the back streets of Birmingham.[17] That was an image for the precious metals trades in general, of which jewellery is a part; much of what was said in Chapter 12 about these trades also applies here; there was the same prosperity, the same dependence on the skilled hand and the machine. There were, however, important developments that were peculiar to the jewellery trade from about 1870 onwards, which have a bearing, almost always a negative bearing, on Ashbee's work. The fine jewellery of the late Victorians was dominated by diamonds; they had been fashionable throughout the nineteenth century, but from 1868 they came onto the market from the newly exploited South African mines in quantities unprecedented in the history of fine jewels; by the late 1870s they were displacing the coloured jewels popular with the mid-Victorians and by 1890 they were universal; it was the fashion to set them close together, the mount scarcely visible, and accompanied by other pale stones, pearls, moonstones or opals. At the same time, the production of cheap jewellery, made with mass-produced, die-stamped parts and cheaper stones, expanded greatly in these years. And finally there was an enduring taste for literal and often whimsical motifs in jewellery as the *Young Ladies' Journal* showed; they might be natural (roses, butterflies), sentimental (hearts and lovers' knots), or, very often, sporting (golf clubs, horseshoes, a fox's head); but they were always lifelike. These were Ashbee's 'cracker toys'.[18]

Ashbee was as dismissive of the jewellery fashions of the time as he was of metalwork: 'all this manifold production of rubbishy trinkets,' he wrote, 'useless ornaments, and things made for "the Market," . . .'.[19] But it would be wrong to assume that there was nothing in contemporary jewellery that could meet his expectations. The tastes of an artistic and scholarly minority in the 1870s and 1880s to some extent prepared the ground for the jewellery of the Arts and Crafts. Women who wore flowing, generously gathered, artistic dresses took a critical view of jewellery and for a time in the 1880s would only wear a string of amber beads—colour and prominence indeed. There was an interest in Indian jewellery and in the local and traditional work of European countries—'peasant jewellery' as it was evocatively known—whose loose structure of repeating motifs, in which the metal counts for more than the stones, was in telling contrast to the rigid and gem-encrusted jewels of modern western fashion. The collections of the South Kensington Museum were rich in such things, acquired for the lesson of simple taste which they taught; and Indian jewellery could be bought from the importers Procter and Company of Oxford Street. Jewellery in the 'antiquarian style' was also popular in these circles, particularly that made by Alessandro Castellani in Naples and later by Carlo Giuliano in London, in scholarly imitation of Ancient Greek, Etruscan and Roman originals. Arts and Crafts jewellers would not have approved of their close copying,

174. Silver clasp, 1890. Width 14.6 cms.

350

175. Silver medallion with a portrait of Cecil Langham, 1892. Diameter 7.7 cms. (In the possession of the Ashbee family).

but this kind of work and the artistic taste for old, loosely constructed metalwork jewellery as a whole, prepared the ground for the Arts and Crafts.

JEWELLERY OF THE 1890S

The origins of Guild jewellery in the early 1890s can be found in two quite precise and rather unexpected circumstances. The earliest datable piece is a cloak- or belt-clasp, made for Ashbee's mother, consisting of two cast silver discs, one bearing a portrait of Mrs H. S. Ashbee in near profile and the date 1890, the other a stylized Tudor rose (Plate 174).[20] (The fact that the open-work borders do not match suggests that the right hand disc may not be original; one might have expected an answering portrait of Ashbee's father here, for his parents were not separated until 1893.) The next datable piece belongs to 1892, a cast silver medallion with a portrait head of Ashbee's baby nephew, Cecil Langham (Plate 175); rays of light, a blend perhaps of Wordsworthian and Platonic imagery, stream from behind his head and the border is decorated with settings, according to Ashbee, of eighteenth-century grey paste.[21] It is a large and heavy thing, about three inches across, and it is not clear whether it was meant to be worn or not. The decoration of the border associates it with Renaissance medallions, several of which Ashbee must have known as being speculatively attributed to Cellini and illustrated in Eugène Plon's *Benvenuto Cellini, orfèvre, medailleur, sculpteur*.[22] He himself called it a medallion brooch, suggesting he meant it to be worn; but on the other hand it has no hook or pin.

The clasp and the medallion are the incunabula of the jewellery of the Guild of Handicraft, and indeed of its silverwork. The clasp is the first dated evidence of Ashbee's use of silver and of casting; and they both reveal the enthusiasms and experiments of the under-documented years of the early 1890s.

351

176. Clasp by Hamo Thornycroft, formed from two medallion portraits of his children, 1888–9. (From the *Magazine of Art*, 1896, vol. 19, p. 236.)

They reveal an interest in portrait medals which is easily understood, for the art of the medal, coming quickly to birth in mid-fifteenth-century Italy, was always associated with the Cinquecento Ashbee so much admired; there was a growing interest in the art in the 1880s and the British Museum put a selection of its Italian medals on permanent exhibition in about 1879; Ashbee would have studied them there and at the South Kensington Museum.[23] They also reveal another facet of Ashbee's debt to the New Sculpture movement; for the fashion for making modern portrait medals in the Renaissance manner, started by Alphonse Legros, was taken up by Alfred Gilbert, George Frampton, Hamo Thornycroft and Onslow Ford in the 1880s; it was, like their interest in statuettes, a small-scale and particular application of the sculptor's art.[24] How closely Ashbee followed them can be judged from a bronze cloak-clasp by Hamo Thornycroft, of which a wax model was exhibited at the Royal Academy in 1889. It consisted of two medallion-like discs, each carrying a portrait head of one of his children (Plate 176).[25] Ashbee's clasp for his mother followed Thornycroft's idea, and much of his detailed treatment. And his portrait of Cecil Langham was closely modelled on the head of Oliver Thornycroft, which was also cast as a medallion, thus pointing up the similarity of Ashbee's design.[26] One has a distinct sense here of where Ashbee stood, of whom he took to be his peers.[27]

These two pieces are something of a prelude; a few other portrait clasps were made, but no other medallions are known. The main stream of Guild jewellery in the 1890s was of a different kind, more exclusively decorative in design. Its origin lay in the second of these surprising circumstances. In the summer of 1891 Ashbee announced that he planned to start teaching gold- and silversmiths' work in the School of Handicraft 'with a view to accepting the offer made by a client of the Guild, for the use by the guild and school, for artistic purposes, of one of the finest private collections of gems in England . . .'.[28] A year later he proposed to make small gifts of Guild work to those who subscribed five pounds or more to the School; these might include 'jewellery and silver-work, with small gems from the Booth collection'.[29] The starting date for the main stream of Guild jewellery, and perhaps also something of its inspiration, can be found in these two announcements. Abraham Booth was a Gloucester timber merchant in his late fifties, whose collection of gemstones, formed 'as an object of interest and enjoyment', was described by A. H. Church, the leading expert on the scientific and artistic aspects of gemstones, in a pamphlet published in the mid-1880s.[30] It consisted to a large extent of finely-cut cameos in a classical style and of pieces of amber with insects or plants preserved in them, reflecting mid-Victorian tastes. It is not clear whether Booth

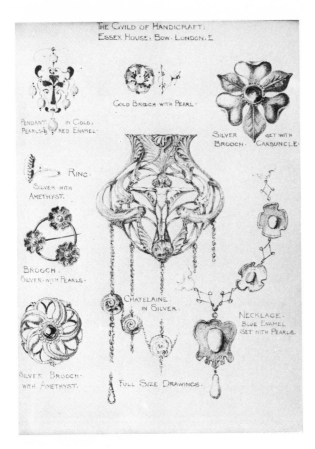

THE GVILD OF HANDICRAFT:
ESSEX HOVSE: BOW-LONDON-E

GOLD BROOCH WITH PEARL·

PENDANT · IN GOLD,
PEARLS-& RED ENAMEL·

SILVER
BROOCH·
SET WITH
CARBUNCLE·

RING·
SILVER WITH
AMETHYST.

BROOCH·
SILVER·WITH·PEARLS·

CHATELAINE·
IN SILVER·

NECKLACE·
BLUE ENAMEL·
SET WITH PEARLS.

SILVER· BROOCH·
WITH · AMETHYST.

FULL SIZE DRAWINGS·

177. Page from a Guild catalogue of about 1895.

shared Ashbee's enthusiasm for colour and aesthetic qualities in stones and he does not seem to have had other contacts with the world of the Arts and Crafts. But at all events the Guild's first work with gemstones seems to have been partly at his initiative and he remained an important source for Ashbee's stones.[31]

The first clear evidence of Guild jewellery of this sort is an illustration in the *Art Journal* for December 1893, which shows two brooches in silver and gold and a silver chatelaine, all lost-wax castings, and a brooch in wrought silver.[32] At the Arts and Crafts Exhibition in that year the Guild showed a case of jewellery for which no illustrations seem to survive; the designs here were attributed mainly to Ashbee, but partly also to Hardiman.[33] The execution of the work was attributed mainly to Hardiman and A. Schonwerk, who may have been a trade jeweller employed to deal with the setting of stones; Arthur Cameron, and probably also W. A. White also made jewellery, so that to a large extent jewellery in the 1890s was made not by experienced jewellers but by the Guild's self-taught metalworkers, as the character and the construction of the settings show.[34] Some pieces were cast, others appear to have been built up out of wrought gold and silver, short lengths of wire and small, presumably cast, beads. Almost all pieces were set with stones, and some with enamel but, in contrast to the contemporary fashion, the metalwork setting was not overshadowed by the stones.

A page from the Guild's first catalogue (Plate 177), issued in about 1895, shows the variety of jewellery designs in the first few years. Some are derivative, as one might expect. The silver chatelaine, one of the most elaborate pieces of the decade, recalls the fluid neo-baroque chain which Alfred Gilbert designed for the Mayor

353

and Corporation of Preston, of which a sketch model was exhibited at the Royal Academy in 1888 and the chain itself in 1892.[35] The smaller silver brooch with pearls is based on mediaeval and later examples set with rosettes. In the profile of the pendant in gold, pearls and red enamel one might hear echoes of the Renaissance, but it is noticeable in these years how Ashbee drew only occasionally on the jewels of the epoch he so much admired, and then in the most skeletal way. The common inspiration in these pieces was as much the rejection of modern jewellery as the emulation of old work; many things would have set them apart in the 1890s: their size, the use of coloured stones instead of diamonds, the frequent use of silver, which was not fashionable in the 1890s, a poor substitute for gold, the prominence of the metalwork settings, and their lack of intricacy and refinement.

The designs on this page which endured, and which are most characteristic of the growing jewellery repertoire of the 1890s are the silver brooch at the top right hand corner and even more that at the bottom left. Roughly circular brooches or clasps designed on the theme of flowers and leaves were among the most numerous and most satisfying of Ashbee's designs at this stage. Sometimes they were roses like that on the clasp of 1890, following the conventions of the Tudor rose. But sometimes they were more generalized, a coloured stone or stones in the centre with silver petal- or leaf-like forms in open-work around it. Natural forms were conventionalized in the simple linear way that was typical of Ashbee's early decorative work in repoussé, leatherwork, gesso and the graphic ornaments in the early publications of the Guild; nature and ornament were evenly balanced. The brooch worn by Jane Whitehead (Plate 181) is perhaps the epitome of the early jewels of this kind, in its size and boldness, in the prominence of its silverwork, and in the way the formal motif, the spiral which meant so much to Ashbee, has almost submerged the natural forms.[36] Here, and in a number of other spiralling and flower-like pendants and brooches Ashbee seems to have been thinking of India, and perhaps as much of the medallions which are a general feature of Indian decorative art as of Indian jewellery in particular.[37]

The other favourite naturalistic theme of this period is particularly difficult to describe because its essence is ambiguity. The brooch or pendant consists of a central stone and anything between two and five pieces of silver or gold which are leaves or wings; it is longer than it is wide. At one extreme, with five leaves and a compact shape it is a pansy.[38] At the other, with a looser shape and two bony wings, and little wire antennae, it is a bat, as at the Arts and Crafts Exhibition in 1896.[39] In between there are all sorts of subtle gradations between flowers and insects, bees and butterflies. The beautiful rusty red enamel pendant (Plate XIV) is perhaps closer to a butterfly than a flower; but part of its beauty is that it suggests them both. Ashbee may have been influenced by contemporary fashions here, for all sorts of flowers and insects, bats, beetles, butterflies and dragonflies were popular motifs, especially on the little pins it was fashionable to wear in the 1890s. But they were always made as lifelike as possible, and in choosing the same motifs but treating them in a deliberately stylized and ambiguous way, Ashbee may have been trying both to meet and to correct the taste of his time.

Not all the jewellery of these years was naturalistic. There were some pieces—not many, to judge from surviving evidence—which could be described as formal if they were not so slight and simple, so absolutely lacking in pretension. Ashbee

XIV. (facing page top). Pendant of about 1899, made of gold, enamel, garnets, amethysts and pearls. Height 10.5 cms. (Private collection).

Jewels for Lady Pollock

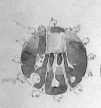

a pendant or
brooch
in blue enamel
with pearls.

pendant or brooch
in red enamel
& pearls

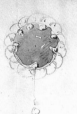

pendant
or brooch
in aquamarine
red, gold
& pearls

a pendant or
brooch
in blue enamel
with Chrysoprase

buckle silver
with obsidian
or carbuncles

Clasps
in gold
or silver

C. R. Ashbee del.
Jan 97.

GUILD OF HANDICRAFT

would take a largish coloured stone or a plaque of Arthur Cameron's plain enamel and surround it with pearls or other stones set in light wirework, or hanging from little chains. He gave Janet such a pendant as an engagement present in 1897, an oval garnet surrounded by amethysts, and the pendants or brooches which he designed for Lady Pollock in the same year were of this kind (Plate XV).[40] These show his skeletal recollections of Renaissance jewellery; the larger circular brooch, which is in blue enamel, has a rim set with pearls just as on the sixteenth-century medallion of Phaeton driving the sun chariot in the Musée Condé at Chantilly, which was among those attributed to Cellini by Plon, but otherwise it is an abstract design of the 1890s; the others reproduce the scale of setting and relationship between stones which can be seen in the pendants and brooches of Renaissance portraits, but in Ashbee's work the materials are often humble and the settings light and open.[41] The appeal of these designs rests in little more than the intrinsic colour of enamels and stones and their combinations; and that, in Ashbee's eyes, was quite enough.

He enjoyed gemstones more than any other materials which came his way as a designer, more even than silver. In 1894 he wrote an article 'On the Setting of Stones' in the *Art Journal*, a happy practical, particular piece of writing, which shows how much he enjoyed them.

I like to work in one of three ways—either with the pencil, painting curves in plan, section and elevation on a piece of paper till I feel the lines I want, the main curves and the big central stone shot forward into prominence; or with a piece of wire shaping curves that flow from one plane into another, and object to paper renderings; or with a piece of wax that will let itself be lovably pinched and petted, and holds the stones affectionately as you develop your work.[42]

He was lively, relaxed and just a little precious, writing about stones without wanting to draw them into the service of a larger argument.

Get to love your stones, handle them, finger them, play with them, dip them in the water, get to know them intimately in various lights, carry them about in your pocket, look at them at odd moments, look at them on Friday evenings, come and peep at them again on Saturdays, have them out once more on Sundays after dinner . . . I like to think of my stones in the dark, and construct my colour compositions mentally; indeed, make little *mariages de convenance* for them without their knowledge—the fiery ruby with the passionate blue sapphire; the pale amethyst with the twinkling crystal; the dreamy moonstone on its bed of dark grey silver, the milky obestine in its trembling cup of hammered metal; the fairy carbuncle, which nobody will wear because it is so cheap . . . the green prismatic olivine, with the rainbow lights in it on its field of blue enamel, and the glorious opal of a thousand tints . . .

Mr. Abraham Booth, from whom most of my best stones come, sits, I believe, for hours in the sun looking into the infinite abysses of his opals . . .[43]

Ashbee's own practice in setting stones was not, so far as the evidence goes, as rainbow-like as these lyrical passages suggest, at least in the early 1890s. He rarely used the stones then classed as 'precious' (diamonds, rubies, emeralds, sapphires and fine pearls), and of the 'semi-precious' stones he only occasionally used the cheapest, such as moonstones, or those of variable colour and texture, such as turquoises, both of which were to be popular in Arts and Crafts jewellery of the early 1900s.

XV. (previous page bottom). Designs for jewels for Lady Pollock, January 1897.

He held a middle ground. His favourite stones were violet amethysts and wine-dark garnets, which he would usually set in silver, and pearls which went with grey-blue, blue or red enamel. These were simple combinations, for pearls and silver have, in their different ways, more sheen than colour, and it was only perhaps in the second half of the 1890s that he regularly practised the *mariages de convenance* of which he wrote, mixing stones of different colour with each other and with enamel. The butterfly pendant of 1899 (Plate XIV) is a superb example of his mature and rather peculiar colour sense: he seems to be playing a bold game of distances in colour, the garnets, amethysts and rusty red enamel so close in colour as almost to fight, and the big cool pearl in the centre far away, aloof, balanced against them.

The pendent pearls in this design, and almost always in Ashbee's jewellery of the 1890s are irregular, what he called 'the long, grey, unfinished pear-shaped pearls, so favourite a stone through the Middle Ages and the Renaissance'.[44] Late Victorian fashion, it need hardly be said, favoured pure white pearls of perfect roundness, no veins of colour, no craggy accidents of shape. There are also differences in the cutting of the stones, the amethysts being faceted so as to reflect the light brilliantly, the garnets cut *en cabochon*, that is, cut to a curve and polished so that they hold the light in a quiet, steady way; garnets treated in this way are known as carbuncles, the word Ashbee normally used. The Arts and Crafts had special views on the cutting of stones. Ruskin had said, with typical dogmatism, that no stone should be faceted; mediaeval examples could be brought to support the case for cabochon; and the Arts and Crafts favoured it because it enhanced the solidity and subtlety of colour in stones as against mere flash and brilliance.[45] Ashbee shared this enthusiasm, and probably the majority of his stones were finished in this way; but he was not dogmatic. The sherry-coloured topaz he would always facet, amethysts only sometimes; in the butterfly pendant the faceting of the amethysts helps to stiffen up the tension between the stones; the cutting of stones was for Ashbee a matter of character and setting.[46]

It must have been obvious to the small number of people who had seen and handled Ashbee's jewellery, and to the many who had seen it illustrated in the *Studio*, the *Art Journal* and *Dekorative Kunst*, that he had created an entirely fresh kind of informal jewellery by the end of the decade. It was simple and versatile, like his most successful designs in other media; he only used a coloured stone, a few pieces of metal and wire, and two or three decorative motifs, and yet he did not become repetitive. It was relatively cheap especially when made of silver rather than gold: Ashbee sold 'rosettes' at the Arts and Crafts Exhibition in 1893 for 2s.6d.; and the average price for a silver brooch set with a stone was probably £2 or £3.[47] And it was modern, in the sense that it owed no very obvious debt to the past and took its motifs so often from nature, the only source of inspiration that is at once old and always new. But it was quite different from the cheap modern jewellery produced in such quantities in Birmingham at this time. There was no array of whimsical motifs, no realism in precious metals, the fox's head as much like life as possible, the horseshoe studded with pearls. Ashbee's jewels were decorative and conventionalized, and subtle in their allusions; they hovered between insect and flower, wing and petal; and they also hovered between petal, wing and metal, for the wave-like forms and gentle curves were always minimally worked, as if to keep a sense of the materials themselves. Rejoicing in coloured stones for their

own sake and not for their cost, bold in their size and execution, subtle in their naturalism, moderate in their price, they were just the kind of jewellery you would expect from the Arts and Crafts.

In fact, Ashbee was a pioneer of Arts and Crafts jewellery, just as he was of simple silver tableware. None of the major jewellers of the Arts and Crafts was working as early as 1892, unless it was Alexander Fisher; and as for the Arts and Crafts Exhibitions, it was 1899 before jewellery figured largely, with contributions from Nelson Dawson, Henry Wilson and the Gaskins, as well as Ashbee. So Ashbee was more or less first in the field; and he was also influential; not many Arts and Crafts jewellers adopted his style but many adopted his taste and principles. In 1901 Aymer Vallance wrote an account of modern British jewellery which underlined Ashbee's importance.[48] He spoke of a widespread movement during recent years for the production of jewellery on true aesthetic principles, whose common characteristics were, the importance given to metalwork in jewellery as distinct from stone-setting; the choice of stones for their aesthetic rather than their monetary value; the use of enamelling and unsought-after stones; and the fact that this jewellery appealed, not to the very rich, but to 'those of quite moderate means'.[49] This could stand almost unaltered as a description of Ashbee's jewellery to date, and Vallance recognized his importance:

Among pioneers of the artistic jewellery movement, Mr. C. R. Ashbee holds an honourable place. He stood almost alone at the beginning . . . Novel and revolutionary as were, at its first appearance, the principles underlying Mr. Ashbee's jewellery work—viz. that the value of a personal ornament consists not in the commercial cost of the materials so much as in the artistic quality of its design and treatment—they became the standard which no artist thenceforward could wisely afford to ignore . . .[50]

THE POOR PEACOCK OF THE ARTS AND CRAFTS

During a period of two years or so round 1900 the Guild took on almost a dozen more jewellers, and the arrival of the enamellers Fleetwood Varley and Bill Mark also belongs to this period.[51] Little is known about many of the newcomers but it is likely that some of them were experienced craftsmen from the trade; Ted Horwood, for instance, who joined in 1899, was about twenty years old, had four and a half years' work behind him and was, according to Cyril Kelsey, 'supposed to be pretty smart'.[52] The jewellers were changing as the metalworkers had changed a year or two before, and the original team of self-taught jeweller-metalworkers was being augmented by more specialized skills. At the same time Ashbee's ambitions grew. Having confined himself for the most part to inexpensive jewellery that could be worn during the day, he now began to design grand and formal pieces that were suitable for wearing in the evening. And having spent many years skirting the specific example of Renaissance jewellery, he now began to acknowledge it in his designs. One can even catch, in these years, the pale flash and brilliance of diamonds in his work.

In about 1900 he designed a brooch for Janet in the form of a peacock (Plate XVI); it was possibly a present from her father.[53] The body of the bird was made of gold with a large pearl in its breast; the tail began as a series of broad silver

XVI. Brooch of gold, silver, pearls and diamonds, with a ruby in the peacock's eye, of about 1900. Height 14 cms. (On loan to the Victoria and Albert Museum from a member of the Ashbee family).

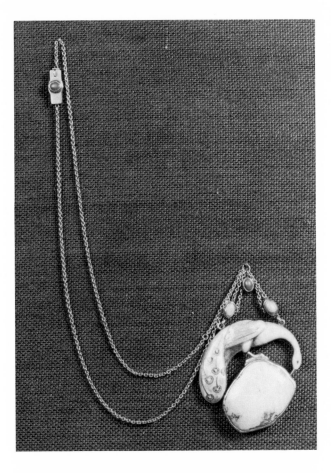

178. (facing page). Pendant and chain in gold, silver, diamonds and pearls, with a demantoid garnet in the peacock's eye, 1901. Height of the pendant 10.5 cms. (Victoria and Albert Museum).

179. Pendant and chain in gold, enamel and turquoises, of about 1901. The design was probably more complex originally, with more stones and linking chains above the pendant. Height of the pendant 5.7 cms. (Victoria and Albert Museum).

plates studded with diamonds, and then changed to narrow, overlapping fins of gold set with blister pearls and interspersed with silver rods carrying star-like discs. The metal was worked over with ridges and hatching, and there was a solitary ruby in the peacock's eye. The whole thing was large—over five inches from top to bottom—stiff, and heavy, and must have been difficult to wear. It was not what Ashbee's admirers would have expected of him either in its grandeur or its paleness. In nature the peacock spreads its fan-like tail and every feather is marked with a brilliant blue-green eye; few images could be more aptly rendered in coloured stones or enamel. During the 1890s Ashbee had made himself the champion of these things. And yet here he washed almost all colour from the peacock's tail, and reconstructed it of gold and silver, giving it a barbarous and wholly artificial splendour. It was a carefully judged departure from his earlier practice. In January 1901 he designed a pendant in the form of a peacock which differed in its detailed treatment, but the materials were just the same—gold and silver, diamonds and pearls—the tonality just as pale (Plate 178).[54]

He was obviously attached to the peacock motif, and designed about a dozen brooches and pendants on this theme in the early 1900s.[55] Some were smaller versions of the first and grandest, with proud tails rendered by stiff fins, others were more informal, like the bird pecking at a turquoise matrix (Plate 179); some use colour more than others, but all more than the first and grandest, in which Ashbee briefly abandoned his preoccupation with colour and came closer to the fashions of the day.[56] It would be too much to say that he also abandoned his preoccupation

361

180. Detail of a pendant and chain in silver, gold, enamel and pearls, designed and, at least in part, executed by Ashbee in about 1901. Height of pendant 10.5 cms. (John Holden Gallery, Manchester Polytechnic).

with jewellery as an art and designed in a way that is at once less high-minded and closer to the mainstream of European jewellery, working with an eye to splendour and display, the sumptuousness of the goldsmith's artifice, the sheer weight of gold and precious stones; but in the first of these two peacocks he came close to that.

There were other jewels made at this time which should be counted alongside the peacocks, for they were intricate in craftsmanship, and figurative in design, and they cost a good deal more than two or three pounds: a squirrel pendant in 18-carat gold, *plique-à-jour* enamel, pearls, sapphires and peridots was advertised at ninety pounds at the Arts and Crafts Exhibition in 1903, the highest recorded price for Guild jewellery.[57] They include several pendants in the form of a ship, of which the Victoria and Albert Museum owns two; one has a sail of opal so brilliantly streaked with pinky purples, greens and blues that it seems to be sailing into its own Mediterranean sunset. (Plate XVII).[58] On another, whose whereabouts are now unknown, the tiny modelled figure of a boy sits on a big and boat-shaped blister pearl, surrounded by intricate rigging of delicate golden wires; if found, this might turn out to be the most exquisite Ashbee jewel of them all.[59] There were also a few pendants incorporating the human figure. The most ambitious has an inch-high winged and haloed figure—angel or saint?—cradling a sphere under a disc-like canopy of blue enamel with golden wires swirling round about (Plate 180).[60] The ambition is not in the technique—the cast figure was left rough and unexpressive from Ashbee's modelling—but in the symbolism of the figure in its spiralling golden cage; in Ashbee's hope that he could express in this piece of jewellery, as in the salt cup illustrated in Chapter 9, his sense of the spiritual values of imagination and change.[61]

In all this work one feels the direct influence of Renaissance jewellery, so long skirted by Ashbee, and of Renaissance pendants in particular. It can be seen in its figurative character: pendants and brooches are like one thing or another, ships and squirrels, decorative but unmistakable; there is no ambiguity as in the 1890s. (One of the paradoxes of this work is that it brought him nearer to the lifelike jewellery of commercial production; but the distinction between figurative and lifelike remains.) It can be seen in the ensemble of chains, enamelled gold and pendent pearls, and in the trick of making creatures out of blister pearls and other stones of strange and suggestive shape; a Guild catalogue of c. 1905 has a fine cock made out of two such pearls.[62] Ashbee would have known the pendants of this kind which came to the British Museum in 1898 as part of the Waddesdon Bequest, for some of them were associated with Cellini by Plon.[63] And the South Kensington Museum had a collection of late sixteenth- and early seventeenth-century pendants from Spain, which he knew and admired; the bird pendants among these may have helped with his peacocks.[64]

But Renaissance influence did not greatly affect the final point, the choice of a motif. Ships, it is true, are commonly found on Renaissance pendants, but here they can also be read as the Craft of the Guild; the shrouded, angelic figure was particularly personal and modern; and as for the peacock, few birds are more resplendent or have a better pedigree in the decorative arts; and yet they were not used in Renaissance pendants or, oddly enough, in sumptuous European jewellery until the nineteenth century, only in Indian and 'peasant' jewellery. When Ashbee used it so often he was not looking to the Renaissance but making an emblem for himself in that stagey spirit, at once self-deprecating and defiant, which we have explored in Chapter 9 and seen on the walls of the dining-room at the Magpie and Stump. He knew that colour and finery and lavish craftsmanship were part of the protest of the Arts and Crafts, else why make jewellery at all? And he knew that the richer the colour, the more redundant the finery, the more the Arts and Crafts stood out, like the peacock 'all eyes and pride' in a grey and hostile world. On the flyleaf of the binding which D. S. MacColl designed for him in 1892 he wrote, 'The poor peacock of the Arts and Crafts with his proud tail exploding in fireworks'.[65] His peacock brooches and pendants belong to the same train of thought, in which 'poor' may also be read as 'proud'.

LATER JEWELLERY

The costly figurative pieces were exceptional, and most of the Guild's jewellery in the early 1900s was, like that of the 1890s, informal, decorative and fairly cheap; but there were developments. There was probably much more of it, more craftsmen being employed; and Ashbee changed his palette; enamels and rough pearls were even more popular than before; amethysts were still used but garnets were almost disregarded, and the favoured stones were the many-coloured opal and turquoises of the fissured and irregular kind.[66] Brooches and pendants were still the commonest type, but there was a slight broadening of range, more necklaces for instance. Ashbee never attempted to produce a complete range of jewellery as he did of tableware, and it is interesting to see what he did not design: no parures (sets of

181. Jane Whitehead
and her son Jeffrey
photographed by Eva
Schütze-Watson in
1904. The brooch she is
wearing is a
characteristic Ashbee
design of about 1893–4.

matching jewellery), no dog-collar necklaces, few bracelets and bar-brooches, all of which were fashionable, very few earrings which were not, and few finger rings which, for some reason, he thought luxurious and improper; he called them 'Jezebel'.[67] What he did design probably went well enough with the clothes of his clients, whom one pictures as women of the middle class with artistic interests and maybe independent views. Few women could hope to wear Ashbee's jewellery as sympathetically as the beautiful and care-worn Jane Whitehead of the Byrdcliffe Colony at Woodstock, one of the centres of the Arts and Crafts in New York State (Plate 181); she is so full of high thinking and simple living, and Ashbee's brooch is so obviously the culminating point of her loose-fitting artistic dress. But even without such dresses Ashbee's clients would probably have shown in their clothes how the principles of dress reform had penetrated fashion by this date: a comfortable shirt-like blouse for daytime wear, with a straight full skirt belted at the waist. One can see Ashbee's jewels in this setting as well, his neat brooches at the neck of the blouse, a light, flexible necklace, and a strong but decorative clasp for the belt.

Enamelling played a more varied part in Guild jewellery of these years. Arthur Cameron's plain enamels had been used to good effect in the 1890s, as elements of colour pure and simple. Varley and Mark introduced more sophisticated techniques of which the vivid and graceful design of a bird executed by William Mark in *plique-à-jour* enamel is an outstanding example (Plate XVIII).[68] In this technique the design is made up of metal cells filled with enamels, as for *cloisonné* work, but after the enamels have been fired the metal backing is removed, leaving a fragile honeycomb of colour for the light to pass through. It is a delicate and risky process which Cameron would scarcely have attempted in the 1890s. Only a few examples of this technique are known in the jewellery of the Guild, and the commonest—and most appealing—use of Varley's and Mark's skills was in little plaques of painted enamel which were set in mounts of gold or silver wire, with two or three stones hanging from them, to make pendent miniatures of a sort popular throughout the nineteenth century(Plate XIX).[69] The pictures on the plaques were usually of flowers or a peacock or some figure from mythology or romance, rendered in the lustrous and slightly indefinite technique of painted enamels; these pendants are modern, graceful, unambitious things, and like the brooches of the 1890s, which they do not in the least resemble, they depend for their effect on colour and the suggestion of natural forms.[70]

The necklaces which Ashbee now designed in some numbers show his feeling, found also in other Arts and Crafts designers and in Liberty's jewellery, for an easily overlooked element, the chain, and its capacity for graceful linkages and swinging movement.[71] In one favourite type of design he would take half a dozen or so stones or enamel plaques of moderate size for the principal curve of the necklace and a large stone or plaque for the pendant; and then, with many little stones of another kind and short lengths of chain, he would weave a web between the principal points using the little stones at junctions; some chains would be taut with the weight of the stones, others would hang in loose and gentle curves.[72] In another type he would have great lengths of chain hanging from a pendant and set with stones to give them weight and swing. He designed an elaborate necklace and pendant along these lines in November 1901 for Miss Tree, probably the daughter of the actor-manager Beerbohm Tree; it had a punning pendant of a tree in open-work, and three long chains set with seventy-one stones strung between panels of open-work; in other designs the chains swing free with a cluster of spherical stones at the end(Plate 182).[73] Flexible and free in comparison with the encrusted jewellery of fashion, apt to the clothes encouraged by artistic tastes, these necklaces perhaps took their cue from the local and traditional jewellery of European countries.[74]

The brooches and pendants in these years stayed much the same in type, cost and style (Plate XIX): the formula of flower-like forms spiralling round a central stone seems as fruitful in the pearl and opal brooch as it had been in the 1890s; if there was a shift it was towards a slightly more literal naturalism, as in the little pendant with a tree; and that again meant a slight *rapprochement* with commercial jewellery.[75] More change can be seen in the cloak- or belt-clasp which shows Ashbee's later informal jewellery at its best (Plate XIX). The bee-like insect is like those

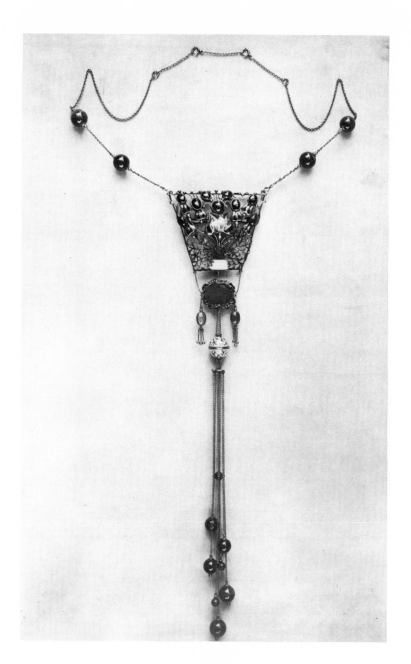

182. Pendant and chain
of the early 1900s.

he designed in the 1890s, but there is more expertise here, in the construction of
the different layers and the flower disc of painted enamel; there is more naturalism
in the hovering of the insect; and there is a stronger sense of line, a more vigorous
and original style in the spear-shaped mounts of silver open-work. This design was
repeated in several variations, and rightly.[76]

When Janet Ashbee boiled over with frustration in the spring of 1904 at the
difficulties of competing against Liberty's, she spoke of the Guild as 'potboiling
with vile brooches'.[77] There was a broad enough similarity between Cymric jewellery and the Guild's to explain Janet's anger, just as there was in silverware, but
it is odd that she should talk of the Guild responding with vile brooches, for the
jewellery of the early 1900s shows less clear signs of competing with Liberty's than

366

did its silverware.[78] The most characteristic motif produced by Liberty's, Murrle, Bennett and Company, and others in the wake of Arts and Crafts jewellery was a brooch or pendant of interlaced form, carefully poised between abstract and natural forms, and usually set with enamel or turquoises.[79] In the large Guild catalogue of *c.* 1905, which illustrates about seventy pieces of jewellery, there is only one that comes close to this type and even that turns out to be quite different in the hand, being more three-dimensional.[80] As the difficulties of the Guild increased in 1906 and 1907, however, the proportion of vile brooches increased; a bright and plausible catalogue entitled 'Christmas Season, 1907' illustrated nine pieces of jewellery most of which would have been vile in Janet's eyes, particularly a lifelike green enamel lizard, crawling about free from any decorative control.[81]

The sadness of the Guild's collapse has a particular force here, for it was just in these years that Arts and Crafts jewellery flourished most. As in metalwork, it was not only a question of outstanding talents—the delicate arabesques and hedgerow naturalism of the Gaskins, John Paul Cooper's tiny pendent pictures in silver and gold and coloured stones, the massy jewels of his master Henry Wilson— but also of fine work by many hands. If there was any doubt that the Arts and Crafts might be too puritan, too serious a movement to take up jewellery, the Arts and Crafts Exhibitions of 1906 and 1910 would have dispelled it. And it was Ashbee who had started it all with his simple brooches and his preaching about the Renaissance; whose handsome peacocks had shown the range of his tastes and talents; and who so clearly enjoyed, for all his high-minded talk of art, the trivial intricacies of bending little bits of wire. No other craft for which he designed gave him so much pleasure, unless it was that one so far removed from jewellery and so full of the necessities of life, architecture.

XVII (right). Pendant in the form of a ship, made of gold, enamel, opal, diamond sparks and tourmalines. Early 1900s. Height 8.5 cms. (Victoria and Albert Museum.)

XVIII (below). Finial made of gold and silver, *plique-à-jour* enamel, moonstones, pearls and a topaz. This design ·was originally the finial of a hair-comb and has since been re-set as a brooch. Early 1900s. Height 8.5 cms. (Private collection.)

XIX (facing page). Four pieces of Guild jewellery of the early 1900s: top left, a pendant in gold and enamel with aquamarines and citrines, height 7 cms.; top right, a pendant in silver, enamel and pearls, height 4.1 cms.; middle, a brooch in silver, pearls and an opal matrix, width 5.4 cms.; bottom, a clasp in silver, enamel and turquoise matrix, width 14 cms. (The first three in the collection of Gerald and Celia Larner, the fourth in a private collection.)

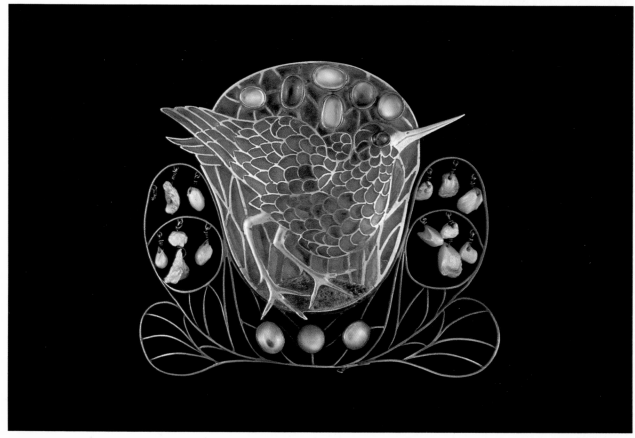

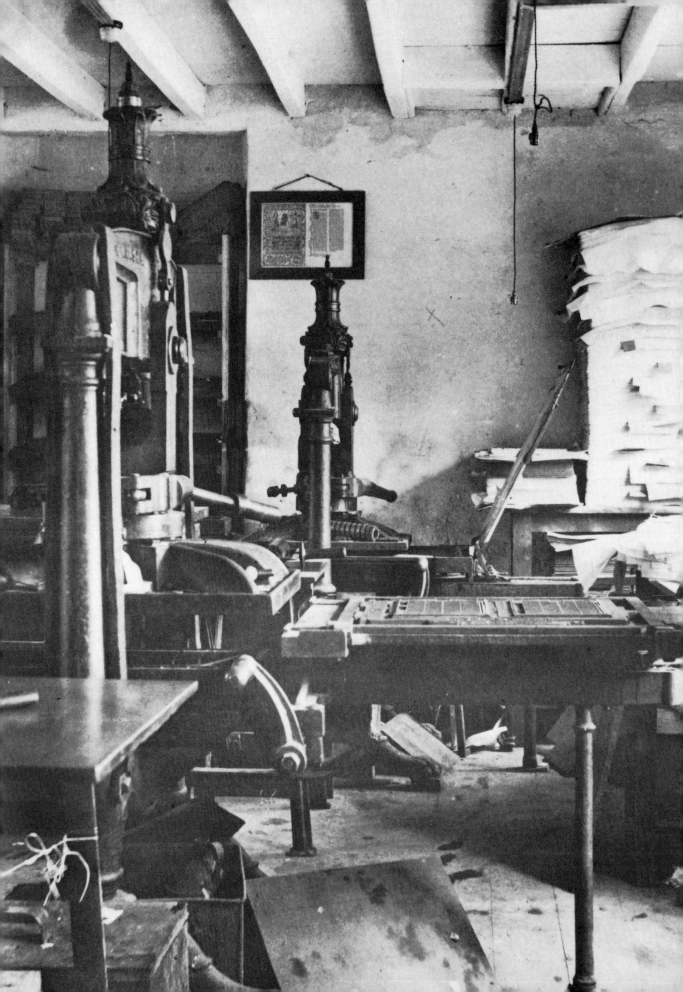

CHAPTER FOURTEEN
THE ESSEX HOUSE
PRESS

ANTIQUE PRINTING

Among Ashbee's papers in the Library of the Victoria and Albert Museum is a stout, oblong album indexed as 'Letters from William Morris' and others. It is a record of the earliest years of the Guild from 1887 to 1891, and it contains a mixture of newspaper cuttings, letters from public figures and printed matter intended to promote Ashbee's fledgling workshop. There are tickets for lectures at the School of Handicraft, fly-sheets advertising the skills of the Guild's craftsmen, pamphlets printed up from talks Ashbee had given. His first experience of printing, of different typefaces and papers, of the laying out of a page and of illustration, was in the production of these ephemeral items.

It is here, for instance, that one finds the first and clearest examples of the emblems which were so important to him. The image of Los and Golgonooza became the letter-head of the Guild (Plate 95); the Craft of the Guild appeared in a flatter, more decorative style in about May 1889 (Plate 97); and the text of a lecture by Ashbee, printed in November or December 1889, carried a striking image of an ash tree with a bee superimposed on it, in a style reminiscent of early printers' marks (Plate 184).[1] This had a specific meaning, for it was a rebus like that on Ashbee's father's book-plate; but it also had a general meaning, the background suggesting the ash tree Igdrasil.[2] This resonant device served Ashbee well on his own letter-heads and as a book-plate, for many years.

The pink made its appearance in 1890, and an early version can be seen on the circular letter from the Guild of September 1890 illustrated in Chapter 9 (Plate 96). This letter is also a good example of the printing style of early Guild ephemera. Printed in black and red, with traditional printers' ornaments used to fill out the paragraphs and 'V' substituted self-consciously for 'U', it breathed a distinctly old-fashioned air; the typeface was 'Old Style', a design introduced in about 1860 as a compromise between nineteenth-century tastes and the early eighteenth-century typefaces of William Caslon. A quite specific taste in printing pervades the whole sheet, as we shall see.

At the end of 1890 Ashbee published a complete book from the Guild, called *Transactions of the Guild & School of Handicraft. Vol. I.*[3] This was the time when Ashbee stood alone, having parted company from Llewellyn Smith and others on the School committee, and he perhaps wanted to make a brave show of things.[4] He dressed it up in a distinctive style. There were covers of coarse brown paper—'grocer's sugar paper' the *Builder* called it derisively—on which the title and Guild pink were printed with careful asymmetry; the titling throughout the book was

183. Two Albion presses in the Guild's workshops at Chipping Campden.

184. (above). Ashbee's rebus, 1889.

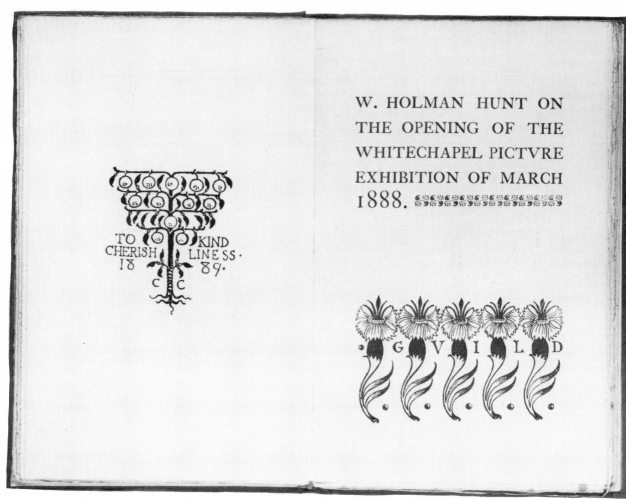

185. C. R. Ashbee (ed.), *Transactions of the Guild & School of Handicraft. Vol. I.* (1890). Page height about 22.3 cms.

set in Caslon Old Face, a full-blooded revival from the early eighteenth century; the text was in Old Style, and the paragraph endings were filled out with printers' ornaments.[5] The black and white illustrations to the lectures were necessarily various in character, but the preliminary matter, chapter headings and Ashbee's history were illustrated in a consistent style with emblems, notably a striking row of five pinks with the word 'GVILD' between them (Plate 185), and narrative drawings such as those illustrated in Chapter 2 (Plates 14–15); they were rendered in rough ink lines, areas of solid black, and a flat, frieze-like composition. Some of them were by J. Eadie Reid, and presumably the others, including the pinks, were by Ashbee, though there is no documentary evidence of this.[6] 750 copies were printed in a standard format, but book-lovers were to be tempted by a further 250 large paper copies and 200 sets of the illustrations separately printed on Japanese vellum.[7]

The whole thing was redolent of artistic book production in the 1880s; the brown paper covers with their Guild emblem and asymmetrical layout recalled Whistler's books and exhibition catalogues, and the typography and illustrations showed the influence of the odd, late Victorian fashion for 'Antique Printing' which was led by Andrew Tuer at the Leadenhall Press in Leadenhall Street, E.C.[8] Following this fashion printers, and particularly jobbing printers, would sprinkle their texts with supposedly Chaucerian language: 'Ye Olde' this and that; they would set it in Caslon Old Face or Old Style, with archaic typographical features to match those of the language, particularly a long 's', and a liberal use of printers' ornaments of the sixteenth and seventeenth century. Few 'Antique Printers' took their exemplars seriously; it was a matter of old-world atmosphere rather than of design. Andrew Tuer created the most enduringly attractive products of the fashion in the books of old ballads, street cries and suchlike which he published in the early 1880s illustrated with crudely worked, dense, black, humorous and marvellously expressive woodcuts by the Newcastle artist Joseph Crawhall.[9] Ashbee's printing was seen to be of this kind: one correspondent thanked him for a prospectus 'printed on semi-medieval paper' and the *Manchester Examiner* admired the *Transactions'* 'antique simplicity, the old style letterpress and illustrations smiling forth quaintly in red ink and black from the surface of the best and quaintest looking hand-made paper'.[10]

It was necessarily a collaborative affair, for Ashbee did not have a press of his own, and an important contribution to it was made by Penny and Hull, printers, of 53 Leman Street, just across Whitechapel High Street from Toynbee Hall; they printed *Transactions* and probably also most of the Guild's advertisements and pamphlets.[11] Theirs were the Caslon Old Face and Old Style types, the old-fashioned ornaments, and a printing style close to Tuer's. Ashbee gradually refined their practices—the circular letter of September 1890 is more austere than their earliest work for the Guild, and recalls the style of the *Century Guild Hobby Horse*; and he also supplied his own decorations and illustrations which were wholly in keeping with their work, for in choice of motifs, drawing, and placing on the page, they were just like those of Joseph Crawhall.[12] The result was a version of Antique Printing free of mock-antique language but not of antique typography ('V' for 'U' is common, though there are not many examples of long 's'), sympathetically illustrated, and appropriate to the ideals and activities of the Guild. When supporters of the Guild and School opened their complimentary copies of *Transactions* they could tell that this was an organization which set its ideals above and apart from the ordinary run of modern commercial workshops.

Three years later, Ashbee produced *A Few Chapters in Workshop Re-Construction and Citizenship*. Like *Transactions* it was published by the Guild, and it was probably printed by Penny and Hull; it used Caslon Old Face for the title page and Old Style for the text, as before, but there was no mixture of red and black, the paragraphs were not filled out with ornaments as before, and decoration was mainly confined to head- and tail-pieces to each chapter; it was purged of the more obvious features of Antique Printing, lighter, simpler, and easier to read. Many of the head- and tail-pieces seem to have been designed specially for the book (Plate 186), and they showed developments in drawing style and in the character of the imagery. In *Transactions* and before, Ashbee had used a thick, rough line suitable for wood engraving (not that his designs were necessarily printed in that way); now, alongside dense areas of black, he used fine lines which could more reliably be printed from the stronger, metal process blocks which began to be widely used in the 1880s. We know that Aubrey Beardsley exploited the new technique in this way and Ashbee may have been following his example; he might well have seen Beardsley's

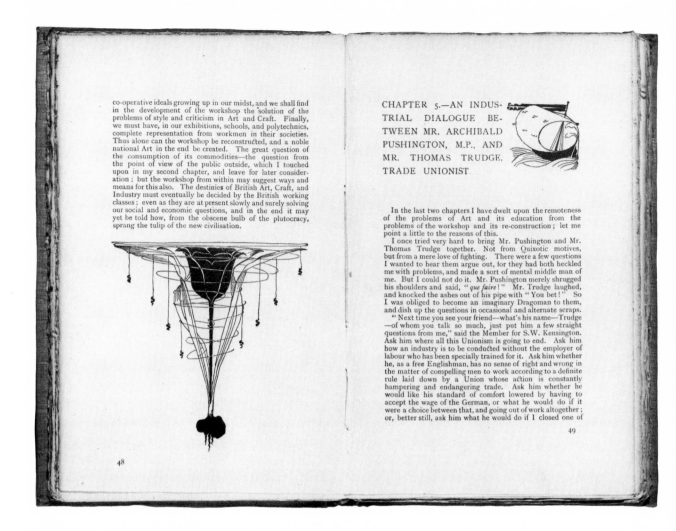

co-operative ideals growing up in our midst, and we shall find in the development of the workshop the solution of the problems of style and criticism in Art and Craft. Finally, we must have, in our exhibitions, schools, and polytechnics, complete representation from workmen in their societies. Thus alone can the workshop be reconstructed, and a noble national Art in the end be created. The great question of the consumption of its commodities—the question from the point of view of the public outside, which I touched upon in my second chapter, and leave for later consideration; but the workshop from within may suggest ways and means for this also. The destinies of British Art, Craft, and Industry must eventually be decided by the British working classes; even as they are at present slowly and surely solving our social and economic questions, and in the end it may yet be told how, from the obscene bulb of the plutocracy, sprang the tulip of the new civilisation.

48

CHAPTER 5.—AN INDUS-
TRIAL DIALOGUE BE-
TWEEN MR. ARCHIBALD
PUSHINGTON, M.P., AND
MR. THOMAS TRUDGE,
TRADE UNIONIST.

In the last two chapters I have dwelt upon the remoteness of the problems of Art and its education from the problems of the workshop and its re-construction; let me point a little to the reasons of this.

I once tried very hard to bring Mr. Pushington and Mr. Thomas Trudge together. Not from Quixotic motives, but from a mere love of fighting. There were a few questions I wanted to hear them argue out, for they had both heckled me with problems, and made a sort of mental middle man of me. But I could not do it. Mr. Pushington merely shrugged his shoulders and said, "*que faire!*" Mr. Trudge laughed, and knocked the ashes out of his pipe with "You bet!" So I was obliged to become an imaginary Dragoman to them, and dish up the questions in occasional and alternate scraps.

"Next time you see your friend—what's his name—Trudge —of whom you talk so much, just put him a few straight questions from me," said the Member for S.W. Kensington. Ask him where all this Unionism is going to end. Ask him how an industry is to be conducted without the employer of labour who has been specially trained for it. Ask him whether he, as a free Englishman, has no sense of right and wrong in the matter of compelling men to work according to a definite rule laid down by a Union whose action is constantly hampering and endangering trade. Ask him whether he would like his standard of comfort lowered by having to accept the wage of the German, or what he would do if it were a choice between that, and going out of work altogether; or, better still, ask him what he would do if I closed one of

49

illustrations to *Le Morte d'Arthur*, published in 1893, and must surely have seen the first version of Beardsley's drawing 'Salome with the Head of St John the Baptist' which was published in the *Studio* in 1893.[13] As for imagery, in his early emblems such as the World Tree, Ashbee had adopted and extended traditional and indeed arcane meanings; now, starting from the same point, he drew pictures whose meanings were clearer and more of his own time; the roots-and-all drawings in herbals probably suggested the 'tulip of the new civilisation' bursting from 'the obscene bulb of the plutocracy'; while from Blake, perhaps via Walter Crane's *Flora's Feast* of 1889, came the drawing of a naked youth rising from among the leaves and petals of a flower; both these images worked in terms of page design, spreading outwards and upwards to meet the text above, and in terms of Ashbee's meaning, expressing hopes for the growth of a new spirit in the workshops of the 1890s, which was the burden of his text.[14]

For the cover of *A Few Chapters* Ashbee abandoned Whistlerian brown paper in favour of boards covered in pink cloth on which was blocked the most interesting image of the whole book (Plate 187).[15] The little Craft of the Guild sailing out of the bay of industrialism was familiar from his earlier work; but the black, smoking factory chimneys showed a real, rather than an ideal, world for the first time among his emblems; and then, as the smoke rose, it was translated into an abstract

186. (facing page). C. R. Ashbee, *A Few Chapters in Workshop Re-Construction and Citizenship* (1894). Page height about 22 cms.

187. The cover of *A Few Chapters in Workshop Re-Construction and Citizenship* (1894). Height 23 cms.

pattern of swirling lines which quite belied its sooty origins. The influence of continental Art Nouveau, then in its infancy, seemed to combine here with Ashbee's thoughts on the beauty possible in 'factory chimnies fuming into cloud' of nine years earlier; they produced an image subtler and richer than any that had gone before, bringing together the real and the ideal, and apparently happy to rest in uncertainty.[16] *A Few Chapters* is a point of maturity in Ashbee's work as a graphic designer: he could now lay out a simple page of type without affectation, and could draw in a way that filled out the sense of his own writings; though he had not yet tried to illustrate anyone else's. He could have gone on in this way, working with a trade printer and illustrating his own work, and the results would certainly have been interesting.[17]

A PRIVATE PRESS

When William Morris died in October 1896 it fell to his former secretary, Sydney Cockerell, and F. S. Ellis, his bookseller friend, to settle the future of the fine library at Kelmscott House in Hammersmith and of the Kelmscott Press. On 10 December 1896 Laurence Hodson came to see the library, thinking perhaps of buying all or part of it; nothing came of this but he probably wrote to Cockerell several times in the following year and on 20 December 1897 he came again, to look at the Kelmscott Press; on 5 January 1898 Cockerell wrote in his diary that the Press was about to close, and seemed to feel that its affairs were settled.[18] There is nothing to suggest that Ashbee was involved in any discussions that may have taken place. It seems that Hodson suggested to Cockerell in December that he might take over the Press and carry on its traditions. This would not be surprising, for among the remarkable collections of late nineteenth-century fine and decorative arts of 'our little masterful brewer', as Ashbee called Hodson, the arts of the book as understood and practised by Morris and others had a special place.[19] His collections included original drawings for book illustration by Laurence Housman and Aubrey Beardsley, Arthur Gaskin and Bernard Sleigh, bindings by Cobden-Sanderson, drawings by Burne-Jones for the Kelmscott Chaucer, designs for an illuminated manuscript of *The Aeneid*, on which Morris and Burne-Jones worked abortively in 1874, probably the largest collection of literary manuscripts written by Morris himself, and of course Kelmscott Press books; Morris had shown him over the Press several times.[20] Hodson presumably approached Ashbee early in 1898 with a proposal that the Guild should take over the Kelmscott Press; in March he agreed to take out shares in the proposed Guild of Handicraft Limited to finance the project, and by the end of the month the decision had been taken.[21]

Hodson's proposal was attractive to Ashbee, for he was a very bookish person. He had thought of starting a press at the Guild as early as 1891, and they had done some wood-block printing at about that date; now, when the Guild was buoyant and taking on men in the other shops, he had the chance to take over the press of the 'master-craftsman'; and besides, there was his translation of Cellini's *Trattati* in manuscript, waiting to be printed.[22] The title 'The Essex House Press' came readily to hand. One wonders whether Ashbee saw all that was implied in it. For ten years he had printed and published as occasion demanded, and because he had something to say, using a commercial printer. Now he would have printers of his own, who would have to be kept continuously in work; and with the presses from Kelmscott came a new, specialized, and aesthetic idea, of printing for its own sake, of the Book Beautiful. He would need to make room now for this aesthetic motive, alongside his normal instinct for didactic publishing.

There have been many private presses in the history of printing, so called because they print to satisfy their owners, rather than commercial interests. Some have been antiquarian, others political or literary. The private press movement of the 1890s was concerned with printing itself, with the quality and character of types, the layout of the page and the way the paper takes the type and ink, with how a book is bound and built up together. A convenient, if arbitrary, starting date for the movement would be November 1888, during the first Arts and Crafts Exhibition, when William Morris's friend, Emery Walker, gave a lecture on 'Letterpress Printing and Illustration' illustrated by lantern slides. Morris, who had experimented over several decades with typography and illustration in the publication of his own writings, was astonished and excited to see the letters of the early Italian printers enlarged on the screen, and went home determined to try his hand at type design. From this developed the Kelmscott Press which, between 1891 and 1898, produced fifty-two titles in a style quite unlike the book production of the time. In artistic circles there began to be talk of a revival of printing, and other private presses were set up. D. B. Updike and B. G. Goodhue started the Merrymount Press in Boston, Massachusetts in 1892, and printed *The Altar Book*, Morrisian in its mood and sumptuousness. Charles Ricketts who lived in Beaufort Street, Chelsea, ran the Vale Press from 1896; his books were more various than Morris's in design, some of them lighter, many drawing on Renaissance and also arcane sources for their imagery; they were printed commercially, but they were designed from cover to cover to satisfy Ricketts's aesthetic standards. In 1894 Lucien Pissarro started the Eragny Press in Hammersmith, specializing in colour printing from wood blocks, and St John Hornby started his Ashendene Press at his home in Hertfordshire in 1894, very much as a private hobby, and moved it to Chelsea in 1899; his early books were printed in Caslon and the Oxford University's lively, archaic Fell types. These were the presses whose ranks Ashbee aspired to join in 1898; the famous Doves Press run by Cobden-Sanderson and Emery Walker, followed soon afterwards.

They worked, generally, along the same lines. Their artist-proprietors usually designed several typefaces specially for the press, in contrast to the centuries-old practice of the trade, where printers simply used available faces. Apart from Ricketts they printed 'by hand', using iron presses such as the Albion, developed in the early nineteenth century, superior versions of the wooden presses used since Gutenberg. They printed slowly, producing editions of several hundred copies at a time when comparable commercial editions would be in the region of a thousand; these would be sold as 'limited editions' of the sort book-collectors liked to own, no further copies being printed. (The need to sell the books once they were printed was actually less urgent in some presses than in others, depending on the private wealth of the printer.) The titles printed varied with tastes and circumstances, but almost always included a selection of 'great literature' (the Bible, Dante, Shakespeare), and of modern Romantic literature (Coleridge, Shelley, Keats and Rossetti). Matthew Arnold's sense of culture seems to lie behind this preference for reprinting literary landmarks, and so does the idea that private presses should give a monumental form to works of genius. 'Great thoughts', Cobden-Sanderson wrote, 'deserve and demand a great setting . . .'[23] Books printed in this spirit run the risk of being fingered and admired more often than they are read, and in the solemn world of the Kelmscott Chaucer, the Doves *Bible* and the Ashendene Dante one has to remind oneself that the only physical description of a book worthy of the works of genius is that it is legible and well thumbed.

The design of private press books was partly inspired by what they saw as the defects of the commercially printed book: poor materials weakly bound, the page of type centred, lightly inked and widely spaced, producing an overall scatter of grey on the paper, and the illustrations planned without consideration of what the type looked like. By contrast, the private presses used handmade paper because it was strong, and because, when damped down and printed with the right ink, it gave a peculiarly dense black with a little sparkle in it. In the layout of the page they generally followed Morris, who believed that the unit of a book is not a page but two pages, an opening; accordingly he grouped the two pages of type close together, with narrow margins in the gutter between, 20% wider margins at the top, 20% wider again on the outside, and so on. (There is a difference here between a designer's way of looking at books and a reader's: you can look at an opening and admire its proportions, but you can only read a page.) Morris liked his type to look black on the page, so he spaced as little as possible between words and lines, and designed thick letters for his typefaces which sit down close together; few others produced a page as dense as his, but all were blacker than the commercial norm. In the catalogue of the first Arts and Crafts Exhibition, Emery Walker wrote that illustrations should be designed so as to harmonize with the page of type, and this became a principle of the private presses, best observed by using the strong black and white lines of wood engravings, which thus acquired a new life as they disappeared from trade practice.[24] Finally, they would decorate a few important pages with ornamental initials and elaborate scrolling borders, a fashion in which Morris led the way and which, like the crisp, handmade paper, sticks in the memory.

All these practices were modelled on German and Italian books of the first fifty years of printing. Morris's paper was based on a Bolognese example of c. 1473, St John Hornby's proprietary typeface on that used by Sweynheym and Pannartz from 1465, and some of Ricketts's illustrations were inspired by the beautiful outline style of fifteenth-century Italian woodcuts. They produced books which seem bizarre by comparison with most printing of the nineteenth century, and indeed of the twentieth. In the context of the Arts and Crafts Movement on the other hand, they are just what one would expect. Though printing historians have tended to treat the private presses as something slightly apart from the Arts and Crafts, there is no good reason for this. The principal actors and the attitudes were the same; the private presses were the Arts and Crafts applied to printing.[25]

Morris and others were scornful of contemporary book production, in the usual Arts and Crafts way; and this was in part understandable. The achievements of Victorian printing lay not so much in book typography as in techniques of reproduction, particularly chromolithography, and in a range of decorative display faces whose force and liveliness have kept them in favour through the darkest hours of anti-Victorianism. Neither of these achievements would have recommended themselves to people of Morris's taste; and when it came to printing the text of books, the Victorians had remained wedded to the so-called 'modern faces' made fashionable by Baskerville and Bodoni at the beginning of the nineteenth century, with their cool and rather geometrical precision, supplemented only by Old Style in general book production from the 1860s; a typeface must be reasonably familiar to be successful, but by 1890 modern faces had become stale through constant use.

Arts and Crafts men tended to assume that the only alternative lay with Kelmscott and the return to incunabula. But in fact the tastes, skills and types needed for a more vigorous and traditional typography had been available throughout the Victorian period, at the Chiswick Press in Tooks Court, off Chancery Lane. It was here that Caslon Old Face was revived as early as the 1840s in an antiquarian spirit. (Antique Printing was the illegitimate offspring of this revival.) It was to Chiswick that Morris turned in his experiments with book production before Kelmscott, and there that Mackmurdo, Selwyn Image and Herbert Horne had their *Century Guild Hobby Horse* printed, in a way that showed, before Morris said it, that a book could be 'beautiful by force of the mere typography'.[26] At the first Arts and Crafts Exhibition the Chiswick Press had the largest exhibit of books, examples drawn from the range of their production over the past forty years.

Without being uncommercial, Chiswick provided an alternative to the pallid moderns of the average printer; and so, by 1890, did R. and R. Clark and T. and A. Constable, both of Edinburgh.[27]

As if to bring home this point, there was a brilliant flowering of commercial book design just at the time when Morris was running his Kelmscott Press. It was promoted by a group of publishers of *belles-lettres*, chiefly John Lane, Elkin Mathews, Grant Richards, Fisher Unwin, and Ashbee's old friend, Charles Kegan Paul; Lionel Johnson, Richard le Gallienne, Francis Thompson and W. B. Yeats were among their prize authors, writers influenced by France and symbolism, and moving in circles cruelly in the public gaze during the trial of Oscar Wilde. At the same time, and in some of the same books, Lane and others published many book illustrators, of whom Beardsley was only the most notorious. 'A brilliant band of illustrators and ornamentists have appeared . . .', Walter Crane wrote in 1896, 'and nearly every month or so we hear of a new genius in black and white who is to eclipse all others.'[28] There were decorative illustrators such as Anning Bell, Arthur Gaskin, Sturge Moore, Laurence Housman, Charles Ricketts and Heywood Sumner, who admired earlier phases of wood-block illustration, the German and Italian woodcuts of the fifteenth and sixteenth centuries, Blake and Calvert, or the crowded intensity of Pre-Raphaelite wood engravings of the 1850s and 1860s; there were open air and topographical draughtsmen, such as Joseph Pennell, E. H. New and Herbert Railton, artists of character and incident, such as Hugh Thomson and E. J. Sullivan, and illustrators of children's books including Georgie Gaskin, Arthur Rackham and Charles Robinson; the quantity and range of talents was extraordinary.[29] Most of the books they produced were less dependent on revived typography and hand printing than those of the private presses, more varied in design, more simply pretty. But they were decently printed and bound, and the artists gave as much care to the design of the binding, title-pages and layouts as to the illustrations; these books were almost as well built as those of the private presses, and they did not obtrude the fact. The two schools of book production actually had much in common; they shared a taste for Romantic literature and limited editions; the decorative artists, particularly Ricketts, were equally at home in both; they were complementary. It is arguable that the private presses and the *belles-lettres* publishers between them made the 1890s and the early 1900s the golden age of British book production.

The staff and equipment which were transferred from Hammersmith to Mile End in the spring of 1898 amounted only to a skeletal printing shop. Morris's types were retained by Cockerell and Ellis as executors; and the wood blocks for illustrations, borders and decorative initials went to the British Museum.[30] Ashbee seems to have acquired the empty type cases and other equipment, two Albion presses and possibly a small proofing press. With them came three of Morris's printers, Thomas Binning and J. Tippett, compositors, and Stephen Mowlem, pressman.[31]

In order to start printing, Ashbee bought several founts of Caslon Old Face, chiefly in 14 point, which he used as a general text face, and capitals in 24 point for chapter headings in the larger books; it was the obvious choice for someone of Arts and Crafts sympathies; at the same time he announced his intention of designing a typeface himself.[32] For most other materials he went to the suppliers Morris had diligently searched out: Joseph Batchelor and Sons of Little Chart in

Kent supplied a paper like Morris's, water-marked with the Guild pink and the dates 1888 and 1898, and ink and vellum came from Morris's sources.[33] From the first Edward Arnold of 37 Bedford Street, Strand, was the publisher of Essex house Press books; he held the stocks, it seems, and supplied to booksellers.[34] At the same time Ashbee would advertise the books by means of a prospectus, inviting customers to order directly from the Guild or from his architectural office, and presumably passing the orders on to Arnold.[35] There were no American publishing arrangements until December 1900 when Wilfred Buckley, a partner in the English general merchant's firm of Samuel Buckley and Company, which had a branch office at 100 William Street, New York, agreed to publish Essex House books in the United States.[36] The first of the prospectuses gave notice of the books which Ashbee intended to print. They included *Pilgrim's Progress, Piers Ploughman* and Froissart's *Chronicles*, all of which Morris had planned to print at one time or another; pages of the Froissart had been standing in type for several years, and Morris had planned it as a great work, a companion to the Chaucer.[37] Ashbee's aim, it seemed, was to carry on the traditions of good printing which Morris had revived.

TYPE, ORNAMENT, LAYOUT AND ILLUSTRATION

The first book printed at the Essex House Press was Cellini's *Treatises*, published in December 1898. It did not have Morris's types and ornaments, but it still had the feel of a Morris book; the materials were the same, the pages were laid out according to his canons, and Caslon printed almost as black as Morris's roman face, Golden. It showed the technical skill of the Kelmscott printers, as do almost all Essex House books. Printers, for instance, worry about presswork, whether the type prints clearly and evenly across the page and throughout the book, not black here and grey there; the presswork of the Cellini is good. It was a handsome book, designed to be used and read.[38]

But private press tastes looked for more than the austere satisfactions of good materials, proportions and presswork, and in 1899 Ashbee designed a set of decorative initials with which to ornament his page; he called it the alphabet of pinks (Plate 188).[39] White letters on a black background such as these, with conventionalized natural ornament wreathed around them, belong to a tradition of decorative initials which goes back to the German printers Gunther Zainer and Erhard Ratdolt in the fifteenth century; in Ashbee's alphabet, however, it is the departures from tradition that are interesting. In most initials of this kind the ornament is flat and conventionalized, white on black, and it is bounded by the straight sides of a rectangle; many of Morris's were like that. Ashbee's pinks grow closer to nature, and the intermediate grey tone of their striped leaves, wreathing sinuously and impertinently among the letters, gives depth and a greater sense of movement, though in the smallest size they are rather cramped; the outlines of the initials, though broadly rectangular, are bumpy and organic, formed by the letters and the flowers themselves as they swell out against a notional frame; these are among the most Art Nouveau of Ashbee's designs in any medium. They are more lively and less elegant than initials more obviously descended from Ratdolt; and they

the Courtier ought to practise his good condicions and quali-
tyes, and those other thinges which the Count hath said are
meete for him.

HEN Sir Friderick: Madam (quoth he) where ye will
sever the sort, the time and the maner of good condicions and qualytes and the well practisinge of the
Courtyer, ye will sever that can not be sundred: for it is these
thinges that make the condicions and qualytes good and the
practising good. Therfore sins the Count hath spoken so much
and so wel, and also said somwhat of these circumstances, and
prepared for the rest in his minde that he had to say, it were but
reason he should go forward untill he came to the ende.

HE Lady Emilia aunswered: Set the case you were
the Count your self, and spake that your mind geveth
you he would do, and so shall all be well.

HEN said Calmeta: My Lordes, sins it is late, least
Sir Friderick should find a scuse to utter that he know-
eth, I beleve it were wel done to deferre the rest of the
communication untill to morowe, & bestowe the small time
that remayneth about some other pastyme without ambicion.
The which being agreed upon of all handes, the Dutches will-
ed the Lady Margaret & the Lady Constance Fregosa to shew
them a daunce. Wherefore Barletta immediatly, a very plea-
saunt musitien & an excellent daunser, who continually kept
al the Court in mirth and joy, began to play upon his instru-
mentes, and they hande in hande, shewed them a daunce or
twoo with a verye good grace & greate pleasure to the lookers
on: that doone, because it was farre in nighte, the Dutches
arrose upon her feete, and so every man taking his leave rev-
erentlye of her, departed to his reste.

90

THE SECOND BOOKE OF THE COURTYER OF COUNT BALDESSAR CASTILIO UN-TO MAISTER ALPHONSUS ARIOSTO.

OT without marveile many a time
and often have I considered wyth
my self howe one errour should
arise, the which bicause it is gen-
erallye seene in olde men, a man
may beleave it is proper & natur-
all unto them: and that is, how (in *An errour*
a maner) all of them commend the *in age*
times past, & blame the times present: dispraising our doinges and
maners: and whatsoever they dyd not in their youthe: affirm-
ynge moreover every good custome and good trade of lyving,
every vertue, finally ech thing to declyne always from yll to
worse. And in good sooth it seemeth a matter yery wide from
reason and worthye to be noted, that rype age whiche with
long practise is wont to make mennes judgementes more per-
fecte in other thinges, should in this behalf so corrupt them,
that they should not discerne, yf the world wexed worse and
worse, & the fathers were generally better then the children,
we should long ere this tyme have ben come to that utmost
degree of yll that can not wexe worse. And yet doe we see not
onely in our dayes, but also in tymes past that this hath al-
waies ben the peculier vyce of that age. The which is to be
manifestlye gathered by the writynges of manye most aunti-
ent aucthours, & especyally comedy writers, whiche expresse

91

188. Baldassare Castiglione, *The Courtyer* (1900). Page height about 22.5 cms.

should be seen embedded in a page of Caslon, not because they harmonize with
the type, but because they contrast with it, their dense blacks and vibrant patterns
punctuating and enlivening its even texture; Ashbee did not often use them in
other combinations.[40]

The typical dress of early Essex House books, Caslon, good presswork, and occasional ornament, made good reading copies and allows one to enjoy Ashbee's individual literary tastes. In October 1900, for instance, he published *The Courtyer* by
Baldassare Castiglione, a thick quarto decorated only with the alphabet of pinks,
and edited by Janet from the 1561 translation by Sir Thomas Hoby. (It was a happy
consequence of Ashbee's new printing venture that it gave Janet an entrée into
the work of the Guild, and she edited several of its titles.[41]) This symposium of
scholars and nobles at the court of Urbino, discoursing on the attributes of the
perfect courtier, was a classic of the Italian Renaissance, and Hoby's translation was
a classic in its way also: an edition of it was published in the same year as Janet's,
in David Nutt's Tudor Translations series. Ashbee's affection for it, as for many
of the books he printed at the Essex House Press, was a curious mixture of literary
taste, intellectual sympathy—he appreciated *The Courtyer* as a treatise on manners—
and a sense of history; for him *The Courtyer* belonged to a golden moment. In
the humanism of the Italian neo-Platonists, in Rabelais, Erasmus and Thomas More,
he found the origins and touchstones of modern thought, 'the Spirit of the Renaissance,' as he put it, 'at which our modern, mental freedom may catch with delight
. . .'.[42] One wonders why he did not reprint More's *Utopia*. He particularly enjoyed
reading such texts in sixteenth-century English, and his reprinting of Hoby was

381

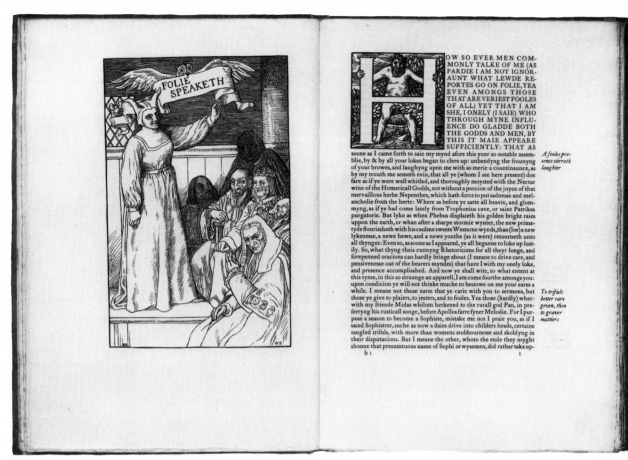

189. Erasmus, *The Praise of Folie* (1901). Page height about 29.5 cms.

done, the colophon said, 'in honour of the great Elizabethans'; he thought the England of Elizabeth the most golden moment of all, and her authors the founders of English prose.[43] Morris had seen the rougher English of his Caxton reprints in the same light.

Erasmus's *Praise of Folie*, which Ashbee printed in 1901 from the 1549 translation by Sir Thomas Chaloner, belongs with *The Courtyer* (Plate 189). The text was printed without interruption, apart from three illustrative borders, two tail-pieces, and a decorative initial and frontispiece shown here, all by Willie Strang. Erasmus's complex rhetorical game does not lend itself to illustration; it was linked by tradition with the genius of Holbein; and it was an unusual artist who would attempt the task. Strang's work, stark and sometimes macabre pictures of vagrants and bony-faced, expressionless peasants, enjoyed a surprising vogue in the 1890s with John Lane and other publishers of pretty books, and revealed an artist who looked at life in a large, bleak and kindly way, which is perhaps why Ashbee chose him.[44] The earthy features of his king and judge put them on a level with the peasants, and reveal the skull beneath the skin; but treat them kindly too. Strang's drawings caught some of the paradoxes of Erasmus, if not his nimbleness.

Another attractive group among the early books is the three Puritan titles, Bunyan's *Pilgrim's Progress* (1899), Woolman's *A Journal of the Life and Travels of John Woolman in the Service of the Gospel* (1901) and William Penn's *Some Fruits*

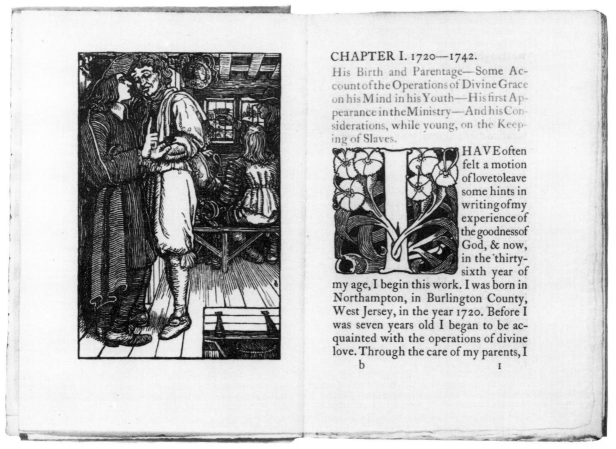

The facing page reads:

CHAPTER I. 1720—1742.

His Birth and Parentage—Some Account of the Operations of Divine Grace on his Mind in his Youth—His first Appearance in the Ministry—And his Considerations, while young, on the Keeping of Slaves.

I HAVE often felt a motion of love to leave some hints in writing of my experience of the goodness of God, & now, in the thirty-sixth year of my age, I begin this work. I was born in Northampton, in Burlington County, West Jersey, in the year 1720. Before I was seven years old I began to be acquainted with the operations of divine love. Through the care of my parents, I

b   1

190. *A Journal of the Life and Travels of John Woolman in the Service of the Gospel* (1901). Wood-engraved frontispiece by Reginald Savage. Page height about 15.0 cms.

of Solitude (1901). They each had a wood-engraved frontispiece (Plate 190) and all three were printed in the same 16mo format, making them roughly six inches high by four wide. The private presses did not normally make much of format, taking it for granted, and there is a quite distinct flavour, pleasantly bookish and old fashioned, about these fat little volumes; Ashbee called them 'a series of little dumpy Puritans'.[45] The Bunyan was an obvious title, the two Quakers less so. Though he usually had little to say in praise of Puritanism and its effect on English life and culture, Ashbee admired the Quakers in his own argumentative way, as the guardians of morality in business; and Woolman and Penn appealed to him, not so much for their literary qualities or their spirituality, as for their historical and intellectual significance; he saw them as precursors.[46]

The New Jersey Quaker was the first man who directly applied Christian Ethics to industrial conditions. He is the first Socialist of the age of Industrialism. He came at the beginning of it all, and he foresaw. He discovered the tendency of machinery, he condemned cheap labour as unchristian, and he weighed up to a nicety the growing materialism of his time and ours, he weighed it up and found it worthless.[47]

This passage explains why Ashbee reprinted Woolman, though it is an odd reading and a classic example of his preoccupation with 'the Machine'. Woolman certainly brought his earnest spirit to bear on everyday and economic life, and he preached

383

the virtues of simple, unostentatious living. But there was no question of machinery. The social evil of his time, with which he was constantly concerned, was the buying and selling of negro slaves, and Ashbee seems to have read the whole book in the light of an analogy.

The first important departure from the style of these early books was an edition of Shelley's *Adonais* published in March 1901: it was printed on vellum and offered as the first of a series of 'Great Poems of the Language'.[48] Future poems in the series would probably not exceed twenty, it was announced, starting with Keats's *The Eve of Saint Agnes* and Gray's *Elegy written in a Country Churchyard*; each would have a frontispiece, and work had been promised by various artists.[49] In the event fourteen 'great poems' were printed in a more or less uniform treatment: a short poem would be chosen, with initial letters drawn in and coloured by hand; a frontispiece engraved on wood and also coloured by hand; and a vellum binding blind-stamped with a handsome design by Ashbee eloquent of his neo-Platonism, a rose flanked by the words 'Soul is Form' from Spenser's *An Hymn in Honour of Beauty*:

> For of the soul the body form doth take;
> For soul is form, and doth the body make.[50]

Usually a hundred and twenty-five or a hundred and fifty copies were printed, and they were not cheap: one of these slim volumes could cost two or three guineas, as much as one of Ashbee's more substantial books printed on paper.[51] The titles chosen reflected Ashbee's tastes, but with less of that personal flavour that we have seen; many of them had been published repeatedly by John Lane and others in the 1890s, in different pretty treatments, and *The Ancient Mariner* and Wordsworth's *Ode on Intimations of Immortality*, which Ashbee printed, were only less published in this way than *The Rubaiyat of Omar Khayyam*. It seems as if, in this series, Ashbee had an eye on a particular market.

It was the printing on vellum and decoration by hand that claimed attention, features which recalled mediaeval manuscripts and early printed books, and so lent an air of individuality and archaic glamour. Unfortunately neither was a great success. Morris had revived printing on vellum at Kelmscott, and it was common among private presses to run off five or ten special copies of a title on vellum, in addition to the full edition on paper. But vellum is not always easy to print on. Made from the skin of young calves, its two sides have rather different surfaces: the hair side is apt to be rough and take the ink patchily, while the inner side is smooth with black, glossy presswork. Openings where a hair side faces an inner side, of which there are many in the 'Great Poems' series, expose the difference. Ideally, each sheet of vellum should be treated individually; that would have been easier at Essex House if they had confined themselves, as other private presses did, to five or ten copies, instead of the 125 or 150 of the 'Great Poems' series.[52]

As for the hand-drawn initials they were, on the whole, weakly done. The first two books were decorated by an unknown hand in an amateurish and stylized version of late mediaeval initials with long, looped serifs; in the third book, Gray's *Elegy written in a Country Churchyard*, something went wrong and the anonymous illuminator's work had to be completed by Florence Kingsford, who had studied lettering at the Central School of Arts and Crafts in London.[53] She completed six more titles in the series, using the Carolingian-derived letters taught by Edward

Johnston at the Central School, which were an improvement, though not as strong as her work for St John Hornby, on *The Song of Songs* (1902), for instance.[54] Ironically, the most successful initials in the series were those for Whitman's *Hymn on the Death of Lincoln* and for *The Flower and the Leaf*, a title then attributed to Chaucer, which were not drawn by hand at all but engraved on wood, printed, and then coloured by hand.[55]

The wood-engraved frontispieces were drawn by eight different artists, most of whom were illustrators of some reputation and experience, and they reflect some of the styles in contemporary book illustration.[56] Some were in a simple outline style of the sort found in contemporary children's books, which could be easily and tellingly enriched with colour. Edith Harwood's *The Flower and the Leaf* and the three frontispieces which Ashbee contributed were of this kind. The light, tense drawing which Ashbee used in his pencil and water-colour sketches, for jewellery for instance, here acquired a (not inappropriate) naïveté when translated into the heavy line of wood engraving.[57] Some of the other illustrators, Laurence Housman, Reginald Savage, and Paul Woodroffe, were of the decorative school for whom the textures of earlier wood engraving were important; hand colouring added less to their work. Willie Strang's two frontispieces in a coarse woodcut style were rightly left uncoloured; and perhaps the best frontispiece of the series was Paul Woodroffe's clever drawing of Browning's Duchess, poised between portrait and incident, which depends chiefly on decorative composition and texture, and is only lightly enhanced with colour (Plate XX).

The most characteristic illustrator of the Essex House Press was Reginald Savage; he illustrated four of the Great Poems series, and completed a fifth for Tennyson's *Maud* which Housman had not been able to finish; and he also illustrated five important titles among the ordinary books.[58] He had not done much book illustration before Ashbee asked him to illustrate *Pilgrim's Progress* (1899); but there had been a number of illustrations in the *Dial*, edited by Ricketts and Shannon, which showed an exotic imagination of great intensity and a command of different techniques and styles.[59] So far as his work went, he belonged to the circle of Ricketts and Shannon, Sturge Moore and Pissarro, though he lived, apparently, in a less charmed quarter than Chelsea or Bloomsbury.[60] '"I never found him very interesting as a *man*,"' Janet reported Laurence Housman as saying, '"but his drawings are delicious. Have you ever looked him up? He must live in a queer place I should think." "Yes, at the back of Beyond," Charley put in "awful Philistine place, lodging house sort of thing—".'[61] It seems that he had a lot of aunts and sisters to support. Savage had a strong feeling for the medium of wood engraving and cut some of his blocks for the Essex House Press himself; the result was illustrations which have some of the Pre-Raphaelite intensity with a coarser, more primitive line, such as Arts and Crafts people liked. They were full of the fabric of clothes, and the grain of wood, and thick, Pre-Raphaelite hair, rendered in strong, undulating white lines on black: 'he does hair so beautifully', Housman had said, '—don't you like his hair? You know I really got *my* hair from him . . .'[62] It was a style that matched the weight of a private press type page, and though Ashbee never gave him titles that exploited the bizarre and exotic strain in his work, he could handle many different moods—Pre-Raphaelite luxuriance in Spenser's *Epithalamion* (1901), caricature in Thomas Hood's *Miss Kilmansegg and her Precious Leg* (1904) or commonplace incident in Woolman's *Journal* (1901) (Plate 190). It was lucky for the Essex House Press that Ashbee had seen his talent and that his sisters and aunts kept him so constantly at work.

In April 1901 Ashbee published the first book in his new type; it was his own *An Endeavour towards the teaching of John Ruskin and William Morris*, and the type was named after it; a photograph of June 1900 shows the design on a large scale while Ashbee was still working on it (Plates 191–2).[63] It was a complete fount of 12 point roman, and as the type of the Essex House Press it took its stand alongside the types of Kelmscott, Vale, Eragny, Doves and Ashendene.[64] Of this design, and of his 'Prayer Book' typeface, an altered version in 18 point, Ashbee wrote:

In the design of these founts I sought to follow upon the lines laid down by Morris. Developments appeared possible in the direction of combined letters, and my bias was towards a black (in preference to a grey) page and the introduction of a rather Gothic and perhaps uncial feeling into the roman character.[65]

It is simplest to take these points in order. Ashbee's design was broadly based on Morris's Golden; it has the same thickness in the letters, and they sit as close together, printing black and heavy; and Ashbee made more pronounced the thick slab serifs set at sharp right angles which Morris had grafted onto his exemplar, the fifteenth-century types of Nicolas Jenson; with the heavy inking of Kelmscott and Essex House, fine serifs made little sense.[66] When it came to developing combined letters, Ashbee altered the usual practice of only combining lower case 'f' with 'l', 't' and

191. A draft of the Endeavour typeface. The distinctive descenders on 'h', 'm', and 'n' do not yet figure in the design.

VIII. THE ESSEX HOUSE PRESS.

OMING now to the Guild's latest venture, the Printing Press, a special word is needed. It had long been my desire to do work in this direction, but, rather than not go into the matter thoroughly, I felt it would be better to leave it alone, and with the beautiful work of the Kelmscott & Vale Presses before me, any new attempt in this direction almost seemed an impertinence. Such publications, therefore, as we had so far produced from Essex House had been printed in the ordinary commercial manner in Whitechapel. ∴ But when William Morris died, and the Kelmscott Press came to be broken up, the problem of a Press at Essex House presented itself in a new light. The Guild, however small so far the yield of its collective craftsmanship, had established a workshop tradition of its own, and as an organization it justified the hope that it might become the home of such traditions as it would be difficult for private individuals, without the marvellous power and versatility of Morris, to carry through single-handed. With the aid of my friend Laurence Hodson, to whose literary & typographical scholarship I am much beholden, and without whose assistance I should have been unable to enter into the undertaking,

∴ See separate list of the Essex House publications.

192. C. R. Ashbee, *An Endeavour towards the teaching of John Ruskin and William Morris* (1901). Page height about 21.5 cms.

THE FLIGHT OF THE DUCHESS.

YOU'RE my friend:
    I was the man the Duke spoke to;
I helped the Duchess to cast off his yoke, too;
So here's the tale from beginning to end,
    My friend !

OURS is a great wild country:
    If you climb to our castle's top,
I don't see where your eye can stop;
For when you've passed the cornfield country,
Where vineyards leave off, flocks are packed,
And sheep-range leads to cattle-tract,
And cattle-tract to open-chase,
And open-chase to the very base
Of the mountain where, at a funeral pace,
Round about, solemn and slow,
One by one, row after row,
Up and up the pine-trees go,
So, like black priests up, and so
Down the other side again

3

XX. Frontispiece by Paul Woodroffe to Robert Browning, *The Flight of the Duchess* (1906). Page height about 19 cms.

XXI. *The Psalter* (1901). Page height about 29.5 cms.

to marcke what is done amysse, Oh Iærde who maye abyde it? For there is mercy wyth the, therfore shalt thou be feared. I loke for the lord, my soule doth wayte for hym, in hys worde is my trust. My soule fleythe vnto the Lorde, before the mornynge watche, I saye, before the mornynge watche: O Israel trust in the Lorde, for wyth the Lorde there is mercy, and with hym is plenteous redempcyon. And he shall redeme Israel, from all hys synnes.

PSALME CXXXI.
DOMINE NON EST EXALTATVM.
DAVIDS SONGE OF THE STAYRES.

 LORDE, I am not hye mynded, I haue no proude lookes. I do not exercyse my selfe in greate matters, which are to hye for me. But I refraye my soule and kepe it lowe, lyke as a chylde that is weaned from hys mother: yee, my soule is euen as a weaned chylde. O Israel trust in the Lorde, from thys tyme forth for euermore.

PSALME CXXXII.
MEMENTO DOMINE DAVID.
A SONGE OF THE STEARES.

 ORD, remembre Dauid, and all his trouble. Howe he swore vnto the Lorde, and vowed a vowe vnto the almyghtye God of Iacob: I wyll not come wythin the tabernacle of my house, nor clyme vp in to my bedd. I wyll not suffre myne eyes to slepe, nor myne eyelyddes to slomber, nether the temples of my heade 78

to take anye rest. Vntill I fynde out a place for the temple of the Lorde, an habitacion for the myghtie God of Iacob. Lo, we hearde of the same at Ephrata, and founde it in the wood. We wyll go in to hys tabernacle, & fall lowe on oure knees before hys fote stole. Aryse, O Lord, into thy restynge place, thou and the arcke of thy strength. Let thy preastes be clothed wyth ryghteousnesse, & let thy saynetes synge with ioyfulnesse, Fr thy seruaunt Dauids sake, turne not awaye the presence of thyne anoynted. The Iærde hath made a faythfull othe vnto Dauid, and he shall not shryncke from it: Of the frute of thy body shall I set vpon thy seate. If thy chyldren wyll kepe my couenaunt, and my testimonyes that I shall lerne them: theyr chyldren also shall syt vpon thy seate for euermore. Fr the Lord hath chosen Sion, to be an habitacion for him selfe hath he longed for her. This shalbe my rest for euer, here will I dwell for I haue a delyte therin. I wyll blesse her vytaylles wyth increasse, & will satisfye her poore wyth bread. I will decke her Preastes with health, & her saynetes shall reioyse and synge. There shall I make the horne of Dauid to floryshe, I haue ordened a lanterne for myne anoynted. As for hys enemyes, I shall clothe them wyth shame, but vpon hym selfe shall hys crowne floryshe.

PSALME CXXXIII.
ECCE QVAM BONVM.
A SONGE OF THE STAYRES OF DAUID.

 EHOLDE, howe good & ioyfull a thyng it is, brethren to dwell together in vnitye. It is lyke the precyous oyntement vpon the heade, that ranne downe vnto the

beerd: euen vnto Aarons beerd, & wente downe to the skyrtes of hys clothynge. Lyke the dewe of Hermon, which fell vpon the hyll of Sion. For there the Lord promised hys blessynge, and lyfe for euermore.

PSALME CXXXIV.
ECCE NVNC BENEDICITE.
A SONGE OF THE STAYRES.

 EHOLDE, nowe, prayse the Lorde, all yee seruauntes of the Lorde, yee that by nyght standeth the house of the Lorde, euen in the courtes of the house of our God. Lyft vp youre handes in the sanctuary, & prayse the Lorde. The Lorde that made heauen and earth, gyue the blessynge out of Sion.

PSALME CXXXV.
LAVDATE NOMEN DOMINE.

 PRAYSE THE Lorde laude ye the name of the Lorde, prayse it O ye seruauntes of the Iærde. Ye that stande in the house of the Lorde, in the courtes of the house of oure God. O prayse the Lorde, for the Lord is gracious: O synge prayses vnto hys name, for it is louely. For why? the Lorde hath chosen Iacob vnto hymself, and Israel for hys awne possessyon. For I knowe that the Iærde is greate, and that oure Iærde is aboue all Goddes. Whatsoeuer the Lorde pleased, that dyd he in heauen and in earth, in the see, & in all deape places: He bringeth forth the cloudes from the endes of the worlde,

and sendithe forthe the lyghteninges with the rayne, brynginge the wyndes out of hys treasuryes. He smote the fyrst borne of Egypte, both of man & of beast. He hath sent tokens and wonders into the myddest of the, O thou lande of Egypte, vpon Pharao and all hys seruauntes. He smote dyuerse nacyons, & slewe myghtye Kynges. Sehon Kynge of the Amorytes, & Og the kinge of Basan, and all the Kingdomes of Canaan. And gaue theyr lande to be an heritage, euen an heritage vnto Israel his people. Thy name, O Iærde, endureth for euer, so doth thy memorial, O Lorde, from one generacyon to another. For the Lord wyll auenge hys people, and be gracyous vnto his seruauntes. As for the ymages of the Heathen, they are but syluer and golde, the worcke of mens handes. They haue mouthes, & speake not: eyes haue they, but they se not. They haue eares, and yet they heare not, nether is there any breth in theyr mouthes. They that make them, are lyke vnto them, and so are all they that put theyr trust in them. Prayse the Lorde ye house of Israel, prayse the Lorde ye house of Aaron. Prayse the Lorde ye house of Leui, ye that feare the Lorde, prayse the Lorde. Praysed be the lord out of Sion, which dwelleth at Ierusalem. Halleluiah.

PSALME CXXXVI.
CONFITEMINI DOMINO.

 GEUE thankes vnto the Iærde, for he is gracyous, & hys mercy endureth for euer. O geue thankes vnto the God of all goddes, for hys mercy endureth for euer. O thanke the Lord of all Lordes, for hys mercy endureth for euer. Whych 79

'i'; instead he designed two 'f's, one so upright it was compatible with the normal form of 'l', 't' and 'i', the other with a long and script-like curve at the top which he combined not only with 'l', 't' and 'i', but also with 'a', 'e', 'r' and 'u'; he linked 't' to 'h', 'l' to 'l', and the tail of 'y' to 'l' and 'e'. The use of many combined and compressed letters had been a feature of the first fifty years of printing, and Ashbee may have meant his Endeavour typeface to recall such practices.[67] His oddest archaism of this kind was to put lower case letters into the arms of upper case, as F, lo, RS and LY.

Ashbee's reference to 'a rather Gothic or perhaps uncial feeling' is confusing and, strictly speaking, self-contradictory since uncial and Gothic scripts are very different. But there are five letters which show what he meant. Upper case 'G' and 'U' and the curved forms of lower case 'h' and 'm' recall uncial and half-uncial scripts used in the fourth to the eighth centuries; while the striking fact that the curved strokes on lower case 'h', 'm' and 'n' fall below the line as descenders seems to come from a quite different source, the Gothic typefaces known as *lettres bâtardes* used for vernacular printing in France and the Netherlands in the fifteenth century. Indeed the first type used by Caxton when he printed at Bruges with Colard Mansion in about 1475 had these features. Ashbee may well have known of this from William Blades's detailed study of Caxton published in 1877; and a replica of Caxton's fourth type, which has curved descenders on the 'h' and 'm', had been cast in the mid-nineteenth century, and was used by William Morris experimentally, though never in a published book.[68] It may be that the most curious features of Ashbee's Endeavour were intended to echo and acknowledge England's first printer.

Endeavour is livelier than other private press types, thanks to its more eccentric letters, and it prints a page of solid black as Ashbee wanted. But it lacks consistency. The individual letters follow no regular principle, either in the handling of the serifs or in the alternation of thick and thin on which the character of a typeface so much depends. In a page of continuous prose the descenders of 'h', 'm', and 'n', abetted by the slightly more orthodox 'y', create a curving movement which distracts the eye. And the face as a whole shows obvious signs of the different sources from which it is derived: in the lower case the 'Gothic' and 'uncial' letters stand apart from the more roman rest; in the upper case 'G' and 'U' have a Gothic or uncial character, 'L' and 'E' are roman capitals like those of Caslon coarsened in the serifs, while many of the other upper case letters have more in common with the free and individual lettering of 1890s ornament and display, especially under the influence of Art Nouveau, than with book typography. The low junction of the diagonals in 'B' and 'K', the high crossing in 'H', the cusp-like diagonals in 'M', the generously full loops to 'P' and 'R' can all be found in the 1890s carved in stone or embossed in metal, printed on posters or drawn, most fancifully of all, in the titling of architects' drawings, rather than in the typography of books.[69] There is nothing wrong with eclecticism in typography, but in Endeavour the different influences were not fully digested. In his enthusiasm to provide the Essex House Press with its own typeface, Ashbee perhaps did not appreciate how specialized and exacting is the discipline of designing book types, and produced instead a design which has the easier and more atmospheric virtues of display.

The most expensive and ambitious book to come from the Press so far was an edition of *The Psalter* according to the 1540 text often called 'Cranmer's Bible', published in October 1901 (Plate XXI). It cost four guineas and the Psalms were set out in two columns of Endeavour with the verses divided by an ornament in red, an arrangement which involved a tricky second printing, but increased the effect of sumptuousness. Ashbee's rather individual attitudes to the texts of the Church were much in evidence. He followed the spelling as well as the language of the 1540 edition, so attached was he to the literature of that great age which he loosely termed 'Elizabethan'; the book has an archaic flavour as a result. But on the other hand he designed for it a new series of sixty-one initials decorated with pictorial scenes which, though they echoed the pictorial initials of Holbein and his contemporaries, were generally very personal and up to date.[70] They were designed to illustrate, where possible, the psalm they accompanied, and so we have the visual wit of a lion pacing through the letter 'H' for Psalm 17 ('Lyke as a Lyon that is gredy of his Praye . . .') and the comic embrace of Psalm 133 ('Beholde, how good & joyful a thing it is, brethren to dwell together in vnitye'). Some have a humanist air about them, for the naked male figure was for Ashbee an emblem of the soul, others were devotional in theme, others again were down to earth, close to grotesque.[71] There was little of the tradition of Church service books here, no sixteenth-century ornament to match the language, no Gothic type; Ashbee's *Psalter* was thoroughly unecclesiastical. In its sumptuousness; in its sense of the Church of England as a literary inheritance; in its very personal churchmanship, *The Psalter* was a foretaste of the *magnum opus* of the Essex House Press.

THE PRAYER BOOK OF KING EDWARD VII

At the beginning of 1901 the old queen died, and was succeeded by her portly and unsatisfactory son; it was a long time since there has been a new monarch. Ashbee, whose patriotism distinguished between the throne and its occupant, decided to print a special edition of the *The Book of Common Prayer* as a memorial of the new reign; that and the Bible were, he believed, 'perhaps the two greatest standard works in the English tongue . . .'.[72] His edition aspired to rank in importance with *The Book of Common Prayer* of 1549, printed by Grafton and by Whitchurch, and sometimes known as *The First Book of Edward VI*; and the king gave permission for it to be called *The Prayer Book of King Edward VII*.[73] Ashbee designed a new type for it, called Prayer Book, damaging his eyes in the process; it was a variation on Endeavour in 18 point with some of its eccentricities removed and more of a curve in 'v', 'w', 'x' and 'z'.[74] He prepared some hundred new designs for engraving on wood, including several full-page and double-page illustrations, many frames and borders, fifteen head-pieces, twenty-one special pictorial initials, a new set of initials decorated with trefoils and another plain set of initials.[75] It was to be a folio, bigger than anything the Press had printed before. Printing began in 1901 and took two years to complete; it was issued in the autumn of 1903, in standard bindings of white vellum or oak boards.[76] Four hundred copies of this 'sumptuous and magnificent Edition', as a prospectus described it, were offered to the public at twelve guineas each; ten copies were printed on vellum at £40 each, and the first of these was presented to the king.[77]

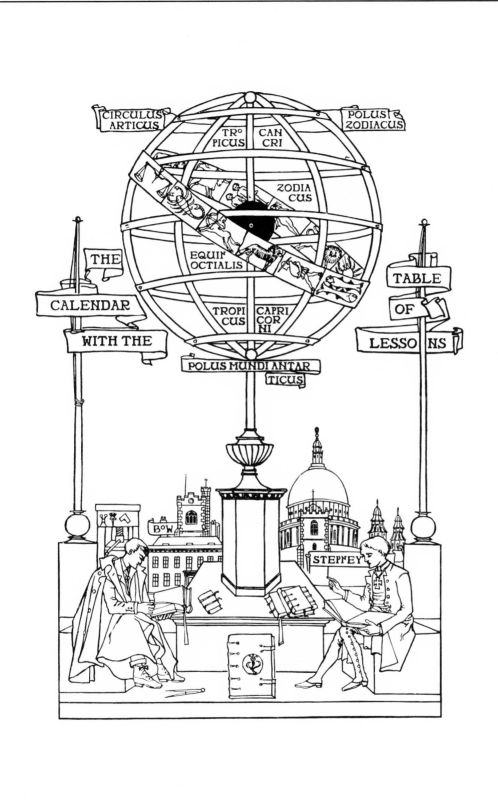

193. *The Prayer Book of King Edward VII* (1903), the first page of the Calendar. Page height about 35 cms.

A COMMINATION,

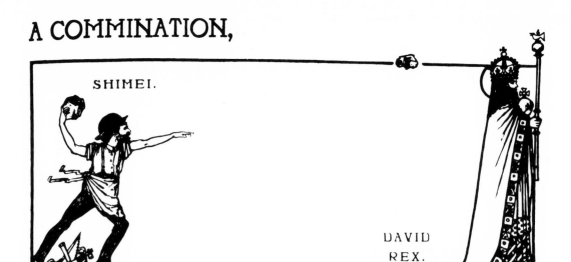

SHIMEI.

DAVID
REX.

OR DENOUNCING OF GOD'S ANGER AND JUDGMENTS AGAINST SINNERS,

194. *The Prayer Book of King Edward VII* (1903), the Commination prayers.

Apart from the collects, epistles and gospels to be read throughout the year, and the Psalms, the matter of *The Book of Common Prayer* is various typographically, and this is particularly true of the preliminary matter. When Ashbee laid out his *Prayer Book* he emphasized and exploited this variety, and the richness which comes with printing the instructions to the clergy and laity in red. He used two typefaces, Endeavour and Prayer Book; he used two sets of initials with Prayer Book where he could have used one; his head-pieces and other decorations were as different from each other in format as could be, though similar in style; and he laid out each section of the book in a different way. To leaf through the pages of *The Prayer Book of King Edward VII* is to be impressed by the wealth of designs; the pages are not all sumptuous visually as some of Morris's were, for the illustrations and decorations were often austere in style; but there is a sumptuousness of effort, a sense of individual design lavished on each of the many parts. And this was, no doubt, what Ashbee intended.

All the illustrations in *The Prayer Book* were by Ashbee; he did not seek the help of any other artists. And though there were not many more new designs than in *The Psalter*, they were much more ambitious. The original drawings were in pencil and probably in the light and sketchy style already referred to; some of them were worked over in ink by Robert Catterson-Smith, to adapt them to the simpler tones of wood engravings; he had done the same with Burne-Jones's delicate pencil drawings for the Kelmscott Chaucer.[78] The result was a simple style of drawing, clear and occasionally stiff, which when it came close to outline drawing, recalled the graceful and symbolic-seeming illustrations to Francesco Colonna's *Hypnerotomachia Poliphili* (Venice, 1499), of which a facsimile was published in London in 1888. Colonna's text is dull and mildly pornographic, but the illustrations were something of a cult in the Arts and Crafts, and to Ricketts it was 'that most vital of old Italian decorated books'.[79] The deliberately gauche perspective in which Ashbee drew St Paul's on the title-page and the first page of the Calendar in *The*

Prayer Book may owe something to the *Hypnerotomachia* (Plate 193).[80] In Ashbee's hands this strong and simple line lent itself to flat and decorative illustrations. The Commination head-piece (Plate 194), one of the best designs in the book, is so flat and linear, so much a matter of movement across the page, that the distinction between the illustration and its frame is at some points effectively and wittily dissolved. Ashbee's talent as an illustrator was for this kind of specialized decoration and not for full-scale pictorial work.

The sight of a carpenter in bowler hat and braces hurling rocks at King David is not expected in *The Book of Common Prayer*; but it is of the essence of Ashbee's edition. He believed that the Church of England should be the embodiment of the spiritual life of the English people; it should be large, inclusive, modern, serious. (We have seen him arguing this case with Laurence Hodson in 1902, in a debate sparked off by *The Prayer Book*; it must have irked Hodson to find himself supporting such 'hopelessly uncatholic' work.[81]) On this view, *The Book of Common Prayer* should express that life, and though its sixteenth-century texts were vital as tradition and as the expression of a great age, it should also be modern, and should reflect a more than merely ecclesiastical spirituality. Hence the carpenter; for the denunciations of our own time, Ashbee wrote, 'are best gathered from the lips of Socialistic workmen'.[82] Hence also the procession of 'great men and women who have influenced the Church of England' which marches across eight successive contents pages (Plate 195). Newman was there, rubbing shoulders uncomfortably with Kingsley, and Cranmer with Mary Tudor; Darwin and Huxley were considered for modern science, but in the end Isaac Newton went in. F. Crawford Burkitt, whom Ashbee consulted on the theology of his illustrations, protested at the inclusion of Sir Thomas More as 'too absurd . . . his whole life was a protest against the prayer book'.[83] Ashbee was unmoved in his relativism. For him, clearly, history was a force of greater spiritual import than the Church.

In this procession and in other illustrations, Ashbee's *Prayer Book* was not only a consciously modern book but also a very personal one, even though it was designed for public worship.[84] In his design for the first page of the Calendar (Plate 193), a bishop sits beneath the orrery instructing a layman. This is publicly intelligible. In the background is St Paul's, a house, a printing press and two churches labelled Stepney and Bow. These are not so clear. Only Ashbee and a few of his friends would know that the layman was Ashbee, the house Essex House, the press that on which the book was printed, and the bishop the youthful Winnington Ingram, Bishop of London when *The Prayer Book* was published, whom Ashbee first met when he was repairing St Mary's, Stratford-le-Bow, and recording St Dunstan's, Stepney for the Survey Committee. Mediaeval patrons had themselves included in altar-pieces in this way, but they brought less private imagery with them.

There were not many prayer books like Ashbee's at the turn of the century. The tradition of finely printed prayer books, to which the Chiswick Press was the principal contributor in the nineteenth century, belonged to a more orthodox Churchmanship; and it was strengthened in the late nineteenth century by a revival of liturgical scholarship which set great store by the English traditions of Anglican worship, its roots in the mediaeval liturgy and particularly the Sarum rite; it was, broadly speaking, a High Church movement. (One of the leaders of this revival

Q. ANNE
HOADLEY
BERKELEY
SIR ISAAC NEWTON
J. WESLEY
BUTLER

195 a and b. *The Prayer Book of King Edward VII* (1903), the procession of the 'great men and women who have influenced the Church of England'.

was Henry Bradshaw, the University Librarian at Cambridge who had been, oddly enough, something of a father-figure to Ashbee in his undergraduate days.[85]) As it happens, two other finely printed prayer books were published in 1903, both High Church in their inspiration; and they reveal by comparison the peculiar qualities of Ashbee's Churchmanship and design. *The English Liturgy* was edited by W. H. Frere, Percy Dearmer (who was one of the strongest links between the High Church movement and the Arts and Crafts) and S. M. Taylor, and it was printed in black and red by T. and A. Constable.[86] It was, by comparison with Ashbee's layouts, a very orderly book which relied for its effect almost entirely on a heavy typeface, one of the many descendants of Morris's Golden, and on a few interlaced decorations by Laurence Housman; there were no illustrations. And in being orderly it was also impersonal, a book of the Church and not, like Ashbee's, one man's book. *The Altar Service Book*, on the other hand, was edited by Dr Vernon Staley and printed by the De La More Press, specialists in fine liturgical printing. The text was set straightforwardly in Caslon, and at important points there were illustrations by Blanche McManus set in Morrisian frames of scrolling foliage. If one could imagine the often mawkish piety of early twentieth-century Roman Catholicism rendered in the black and white drawing style used by Walter Crane in his socialist propaganda, one might be prepared for Blanche McManus's designs.

Ashbee shared with these Churchmen an admiration for the traditional service book of the Church of England, and wanted to see it finely handled. 'There is nothing quite so beautiful', he once wrote, 'as a Church of England service in all its Elizabethan glory.'[87] But this was an admiration founded on aesthetics, literature and history, not on doctrine; and it was combined with a broad and modernist

view of the Church's social and spiritual role not often found in finely printed prayer books. Compared with *The English Liturgy*, *The Prayer Book of King Edward VII* has a mongrel and aggressively personal character. Compared with *The Altar Service Book*, it is vivid and thoughtful and, unlike Blanche McManus's, its illustrations have stood the test of time.

THE LAST PHASE

The *Prayer Book* was a commercial success, and J. Pierpont Morgan bought a dozen copies to give away to the American bishops; Ashbee was encouraged to plan an even more ambitious book, and a religious one again: a two-volume folio Bible decorated with about sixty wood engravings by Willie Strang and costing 45 guineas for copies on paper, 175 guineas on vellum.[88] But recent titles apart from *The Prayer Book* had not sold well, and the Press could not sustain the risk of such a project, with the Guild in straitened circumstances; so three hundred subscribers were sought before printing began.[89] The Press was put on short time in the summer of 1904, perhaps with the idea of waiting on the Bible project, and the books published during the next two years consisted only of the last of the 'Great Poems' series, a few minor titles and work apparently brought by Ashbee and his friends to keep the printers in employment. The publishing arrangements with Arnold, and Buckley in New York, seem to have ended at this time.[90] The *Bible* would have put them back on full time, but the 300 subscribers could not be found, nor 200, nor 100; only 40 people wanted to order it.[91] In the summer of 1906 the

Press was closed down as part of the survival plans for the Guild; Ashbee hoped it was only temporary. On 31 August he went down to the workshop to help Binning with the inventory.

As for the racks, and the making up frames, and the 24 brass tube quarto galleys, and the wide slips and the chases and the demy folio chases and the quotations and the leads and the reglets and the super Royal inking table and the expanding roller frames, I got so confused among the detail that I had to chalk my own numbers on them to the old man's disgust. 'You ought to have known all their names' his look seemed to say 'after producing books upon them for 10 years' but then I was thinking of the books while he was thinking of the tools and the honour and dignity of the tools.[92]

As things turned out, the closure was temporary. In the spring of 1907 Ananda Coomaraswamy moved in to the Norman Chapel in Broad Campden, bringing with him the materials for a book on the Arts and Crafts of Ceylon, and he took over one of Ashbee's presses and the Caslon type to print this work; Morris was one of his heroes, and the association seemed perfectly apt.[93] Only a small staff was employed and the Essex House printers were not all recalled; but in this reduced form the Press continued for another three years, outlasting much of the rest of the Guild. Coomaraswamy's *Mediaeval Sinhalese Art* was published in December 1908, and Ashbee designed a big printer's mark for it, weaving together allusions to Kelmscott and Essex House and the Norman Chapel.[94] Coomaraswamy also wrote and printed about a dozen short studies and pamphlets campaigning for a better understanding of Indian art; both these and *Mediaeval Sinhalese Art* were printed to a workmanlike standard, but little more: a pulpy machine-made paper was often used, through which type knocked rather heavily. During these years there was an arrangement whereby Ashbee also used the Press, and he printed several books including *The Private Press: A Study in Idealism* in which he looked back over his work as a printer and suggested, characteristically, its larger meaning. *The Private Press* was not meant to be valedictory—he hoped to go on printing—but it was. In the summer of 1910 Coomaraswamy put in hand the printing of his last few books, and sailed for India.[95] In October *Two Drawings by Hok'sai*, with an introduction by William Rothenstein, appeared, the final production of the Essex House Press.[96]

Since 1898 the Essex House Press had printed more than ninety titles. There were more than just the outstanding titles we have looked at; there were small items of private printing, books, pamphlets and ephemera connected with Ashbee's many activities, monographs for the Survey Committee, reports on the Campden School of Arts and Crafts.[97] All were printed to the same high standard, whether they were Shakespeare or notices of a shareholders' meeting: apart from the 'Great Poems' series, and the books printed by Coomaraswamy, where the standard drops a little, the technique of the Essex House Press is a constant source of pleasure. It is hard to be equally enthusiastic about Ashbee's work as a designer. He was more successful in decorative designs, of which he had had some experience in the 1890s than in designing type or laying out *The Book of Common Prayer*. As the *magnum opus* of the Essex House Press, *The Prayer Book* begs comparison with the Kelmscott Chaucer, and Ashbee saw the American bibliophile W. K. Bixby treat either volume with equal reverence; but few would agree with him.[98] As

196. Essex House Press books on the shelf.

for Endeavour, it has not lacked distinguished critics. 'The private press movement produced no more inglorious achievement than Mr. Ashbee's Endeavour . . .', wrote Stanley Morison, and D. B. Updike called it 'obscure and dazzling', a simple but damning paradox.[99] More recently, Colin Franklin has argued that Endeavour should not be judged by the scholarly standards of other private press types and that it was a brave experiment, which we can appreciate for its turn-of-the-century flavour, an art nouveau letter conceived without reference to tradition.[100] It certainly has such a flavour, for there are elements of display lettering in it; but there are, by Ashbee's own admission, scholarly elements too—that 'rather Gothic and perhaps uncial feeling'. It is a mongrel face, like Ashbee's designs for furniture and metalwork in the early 1890s, derivative in the parts, not yet coherent in the whole. In furniture and metalwork it took Ashbee eight or ten years to arrive at a simple and mature style; yet he hoped to become a typographer in two. Perhaps, in his enthusiasm for carrying on the Kelmscott tradition, he threw himself into printing and all its technicalities with careless enthusiasm; perhaps Binning's disapproving look was deserved.

Which is not to say that there is little to admire in the books of the Essex House Press. The best way to look at them is all together on a shelf (Plate 196); that shows how various the titles are, how they reflect a real and attractively personal taste. There are some of the classic private press titles, chiefly among the 'Great Poems' series, but you can also laugh at Thomas Hood's *Miss Kilmansegg and her Precious Leg* (1904), cast bronze with Cellini, follow Woolman's life and travels through his clear-as-water prose, or argue with Ashbee about *Socialism and Politics* (1906). The serious and rather exclusively literary taste of other private presses is attractively diluted here. The physical variety of the books is obvious on the shelf; they range from the big *Prayer Book* to the little dumpy Puritans, with all sorts of things in between, including *The Masque of the Edwards of England* (1902), in an oblong

397

197. Two versions of *The Essex House Song Book* (1903–5), bound and in parts. Page height about 23 cms.

picture-book format and partly printed by chromolithography on grey paper; or *The Essex House Song Book* (1903–5) which came either as a bound volume or as loose parts, which sit conveniently on the piano (Plate 197); Ashbee thought this the best book issued by the Press, apart from *The Prayer Book*.[101] The uniform formats of the Doves Press books are fearfully serried by comparison, 'typographical Tiller girls' as Francis Meynell called them.[102]

If Ashbee would not have made an expert printer, he might have made an interesting publisher; a bibliography of the Press, if it were seen simply as a publisher's list, would be very attractive. And he knew how to promote other people's talents.[103] The Essex House books were the richer for his patronage of Reginald Savage; and by Strang, whom he admired enormously, he published not only book illustrations but also a portfolio of big, harsh two-colour wood engravings, *The Doings of Death* (1901).[104] All that is best in Essex House Press books can be found in Ashbee's selected edition of the *Parentalia* of Sir Christopher Wren (1903) (Plate 198). Here are pages of Caslon beautifully worked by the Essex House printers; observant, atmospheric drawings of Wren's City churches by E. H. New, one of the best topographical artists of the day, perfectly balanced against the type; and always the driving, genuine spirit in which Ashbee put his books before the world. This was no academic exercise, but part of a campaign against the destruction of Wren's churches in the City of London; in flaming conservation rhetoric Ashbee warned London of 'the greed of new railway exploiters, the apathy of her citizens and the indifference of her churchmen for the beautiful things they still possess . . .'.[105] He knew what books could be about and his are meant to be read, not just fingered and admired.

XI. St. Bennet's Paul's Wharf Church, situated on the North-side of Thames-street, in the Ward of Castle-Baynard, was rebuilt in 1683, of Brick and Stone, ornamented on the Outside with Festoons carv'd in Stone round the Fabrick; the quadrangular Roof within is supported by four Pillars and Pilasters of the Corinthian Order, with their Architrave, Friese, and Cantaliever Cornice; the Length within is 54, Breadth 50, Height 36 Feet; the Steeple (which is of Brick and Stone, as the Church) consists of a Tower, Dome and Turret, the Altitude about 118 Feet.

S^T BENNET'S

XII. St. Benedict's (vulgò St. Bennet) Fink-church, situated on the North side of Thread-needle-street, in the Ward of Broad-street, was built in 1673, of Stone, and is a fine Piece of Architecture; the Body of the Church within is a compleat elipsis, (a very commodius Form for the Auditory) and the Roof is an eliptical Cupola, (at the Center of which is a Turret glaz'd round) environ'd with a Cantaliever Cornice, & supported by six Columns of the Composite Order; between each of which is a spacious Arch, and six large light Windows, with strong Munions and Transums: The Length (or greater Diameter) of the Church is 63, the Breadth, (or lesser Diameter) 48, the Altitude 49 Feet. The Steeple consists of a square Tower, over which is a large Cupola, and above that a Spire, which are together above 110 Feet; and the Tower is adorn'd with Fresco-work of Festoons &c.

XIII. St. Bartholomew's Exchange (or the Little) Church, situated on the East-side of Bartholomew-lane, and near the Royal Exchange, in the Ward of Broad-street, was rebuilt in 1679; 'tis a strong Building, the Roof flat, adorn'd with Fret-work, and supported with Columns of the Tuscan Order, and large Arches. Here are three fine Door-cases, on the N. S. and W. Sides of the Church, whose Pilasters, Entablature, & Pediments are of the Corinthian Order, adorn'd with Cherubims, Shields, Festoons, &c. that towards the South being more particularly spacious and fine: The Length is 78, Breadth 60, Height 41; and that of the square Tower, about 90 Feet.

198. Christopher Wren, *Life and Works of Sir Christopher Wren* (1903). Page height about 29 cms.

The standard bindings for most of the Essex House Press books were made of plain limp vellum or of paper-covered boards, in the deliberately unostentatious manner of the private presses. The principal exception was the standard binding for *The Praise of Folie* for which Ashbee designed a suitably motley vellum cover in cream and red. Some of these bindings, perhaps all, were carried out by J. & J. Leighton, who had worked for the Kelmscott Press.[106]

From an early stage Ashbee advertised the fact that special bindings of Essex House books would be carried out by Douglas Cockerell, who taught bookbinding at the Central School of Arts and Crafts.[107] Then, in the summer of 1902, a bindery was established in the Guild, under the direction of Annie Power, who had been a pupil of Cockerell's; she was helped by Edgar Green and two Press wives, Nellie Binning and Lottie Eatley.[108] A number of lavish and very individual bindings were produced by this workshop, including a *Pilgrim's Progress* with an enamel plaque on the front mounted in silver, and others of the same title carved in rosewood, holly and ebony by Alec Miller. The more characteristic leather bindings of these years were restrained and conventional: full leather, tooled on the front and back in gold with a pattern of intersecting lines creating panels which echo the proportions of the boards; some of the panels would be filled sparingly with leaf ornament or figures taken from the decoration of the text; if these were designed by Ashbee they show, nevertheless, a strong influence from Cockerell.[109] The bindery seems to have closed down when Annie Power got married in 1905.[110]

PART THREE

CHAPTER FIFTEEN
REPUTATION AND INFLUENCE

Much the best photograph of Ashbee was taken just before Christmas 1900 in Chicago (Frontispiece). It shows him at the height of his career and much as he would want to be seen, carefully but not theatrically posed. The storm and stress of Chicago, the bracing, eloquent company of Frank Lloyd Wright, who is taking the photograph, have perhaps thrown him into a prophetic mood, and he sits like some Whitmanic seer, gazing into the future, gauging the prospects of the twentieth century. Yet his gaze is intent, and his grey-brown, hazel, heavy-lidded eyes, which counted for much in people's sense of him, will swing, slowly and watchfully, if you challenge his attention, to transfix you. In this pose he is neither a public figure nor a private friend; he meets you on his chosen ground, the ground of ideas.

He was an odd, unclassifiable figure, overlapping conventional boundaries; architect and designer, businessman, journalist, schoolteacher and publicist. People were apt to take him as one thing or another, rarely in the round. And though he wrote a lot, it was not easy to say where he stood, for he would not accommodate his ideas to those of any larger movement, insisted on seeing things in his own way. He was a solitary idealist, and it was not surprising that journalists did not always get his drift. But it was impossible to overlook him. Thanks to King's College, Cambridge he felt that he belonged to an intellectual élite and it came naturally to him to proclaim his views and promote his work. If there was egotism in his lonely crusade, it was indistinguishable from zeal.

It was in the Arts and Crafts Movement that his particular talents were most at home, and this was the immediate setting of his work. The artists, architects and designers of the Movement were his peers; he was a long-standing member of the Art Workers' Guild and eventually its Master, and an active committee member of the Arts and Crafts Exhibition Society; to the historian he appears as one of the Movement's most original and important figures.[1] And yet he stood a little apart from his colleagues. There were informal but influential Arts and Crafts groups in London, based on friendship and common haunts, such as that round Mackmurdo's house at 20 Fitzroy Square in Bloomsbury, or around Gray's Inn Square in Holborn and the barrack-like Raymond Buildings, where Lethaby worked and Philip Webb was held in reverence. Ashbee never penetrated these circles and never, socially, reached the heart of the Movement. The circle of artists which he cultivated in Chelsea, though it did not exclude the Arts and Crafts, had a different, less ostentatiously wholesome, tone. In the Art Workers' Guild, and among the élite of the Arts and Crafts, Ashbee's achievements in creating and running the Guild of Handicraft were no doubt admired; and yet some people looked askance at him.[2]

Voysey read twelve chapters of *Craftsmanship in Competitive Industry* and had not the patience to finish it, for his individualism was offended by Ashbee's call for legislation to protect the craftsman. 'And after all no legislation or organization is going to make me like Ashbee's work,' he wrote.[3] Morris's family and close friends did not look kindly on him, feeling that he aped Morris too much and posed as his successor; that was scarcely fair. Journalists encouraged this idea because it made good copy; but Ashbee did not. Only in setting up the Essex House Press did he deliberately adopt the mantle of Morris; and when Sydney Cockerell said he thought Ashbee was a fraud, it was probably because he felt that the work of the Essex House Press had compromised the Kelmscott traditions that he held so dear.[4] Ernest Gimson never had much to do with Ashbee partly because Ashbee talked a great deal, and Gimson believed in 'Work, not words . . .'.[5] And when Ashbee published *Should We Stop Teaching Art* in 1911, his colleagues poked gentle fun at it at the Art Workers' Guild Revels, parading a big book called *Should Ashbee Stop Teaching Us*; Ashbee was much amused.[6] Perhaps part of the difference between Ashbee and his colleagues was that he ranged so widely in his ideas, brought so many issues into the discussion.

Ashbee was not the only one in the Arts and Crafts who taught and talked a good deal, Lethaby was another; and Lethaby invites comparison for he and Ashbee were the most challenging figures, intellectually, of their Arts and Crafts generation. They seemed at times to think in parallel: round 1890 it was symbolism that interested them, round 1910 it was cities, the reorganization of the Arts and Crafts, the example of Germany. Both men wanted to make art more like work and work more like art; but they did it in different ways. Lethaby talked about art as if it was just another kind of making or doing, like cooking or playing games; it was a gentle, coherent, very takeable point of view, and expressed in a homely, aphoristic style; he would demonstrate that architecture, for instance, is something that people do, a various, practical, human activity, not style; though at times he was so ready to cut through all the art nonsense that he ran the risk of confounding art and work completely. He became the wise old man of the Art Workers' Guild and, in a sense, of English art education as a whole; and part of the reason was that he was so much in tune with English anti-intellectualism. Ashbee, as we have seen, could not fit into any schools or institutions, unless they were his own. And while Lethaby talked reassuringly about cooking omelettes or playing tennis, keeping his eye on art, Ashbee in his plural, opportunist, slightly over-educated, baffling and intensely eager way, would talk about all the different social and intellectual movements of the day, dissipating art, his Arts and Crafts colleagues may have thought, in his restless intellectual search for the social formula that would make it new. At a conference of architects in 1917 Lethaby said:

We really all agree in very much but we are so eager for word arguments that . . . we raise confusing other questions in philosophy or politics; questions about freedom or tariff reform or education, or the leasehold system or the theory of aesthetics; but all the time we must agree that our institutions and thoughts being what they are we must, as architects, at least aim at order in our cities and towns. We cannot solve all the bordering questions . . .[7]

That list of topics could almost have been taken from the contents page of one of Ashbee's books; it was always the bordering questions that interested him.

In the wider, more impersonal world of exhibitions and the art press, Ashbee enjoyed a better reputation. He was an energetic exhibitor and the Guild's work could be seen at all the shows organized by the Arts and Crafts Exhibition Society up to 1916. He showed as far afield as Stockholm and New Zealand, and could be seen as often at small amateur shows in Falmouth or Carlisle as at the big, international exhibitions.[8] The artistic monthlies gave him much the same kind of attention as they gave to other leading figures in the Arts and Crafts. In the mid-1890s the *Art Journal* asked him to write several articles on jewellery and metalwork which, at this early date, probably served to promote his ideas about the artistic treatment of precious metals as much as his work itself did.[9] The *Studio*, founded in 1893, allied to the Arts and Crafts, and apparently enormously influential outside Britain, was consistently enthusiastic about his work, and in 1897 published an article on 'The Guild of Handicraft: A Visit to Essex House.'[10] It made much of the Guild's special qualities, the co-operative partnership, the way the life of the craftsmen spilled over into Wednesday suppers and communal singing; particularly helpful were George Thomson's drawings of the Guildsmen at work (Plate 199), which encouraged the sense of an intriguing social experiment being carried on in Mile End, far from the usual haunts of *Studio* readers.[11]

There was a consensus in the art press, with which the preferences of this book coincide, that the most interesting aspects of the Guild were the communal spirit of its workshops, and its silver and jewellery. And it was in these areas that Ashbee was most influential in Britain. He was, as we have seen, the pioneer of silver

199. Jack Baily (left) and Arthur Cameron at Essex House in about 1897, working on table baskets of the sort illustrated in plate 165. (From George Thomson's drawing in the *Studio*, 1897–8, vol. 12, p. [29].)

tableware and jewellery in the Arts and Crafts, and though his style was not so striking and consistent that it was widely copied, he exercised a subtle and constructive influence: Arts and Crafts metalworkers and Liberty's designers took their cue from him, working with simple forms and plain expanses of silver studded with enamel and coloured stones.[12]

As for the Guild, we have seen that one workshop, the Birmingham Guild of Handicraft, was closely and consciously modelled on it, in its mixture of craftsmanship and philanthropy, its scorn of the trade, and its early, simple metalwork.[13] And there were many other Guilds of Handicraft scattered throughout the country round 1900, so that Ashbee's influence seems all-pervading: the Lambeth Guild of Handicraft, the Gentlewomen's Guild of Handicraft, the Guild of Crediton Handicrafts, and so on.[14] The Scottish Guild of Handicraft, for instance, was started in Glasgow in about 1900; it was run on co-operative lines, with the members holding shares and being controlled by a committee; and when it moved to Stirling in 1906 the *Studio* was reminded of its namesake's move to Campden; but these echoes of Ashbee's Guild are a little deceptive, for the Scottish Guild was essentially a federation of independent craftsmen formed to sell and exhibit their work; the workshop element so vital to Ashbee was there, but it was less important.[15] The word 'Guild' did not always mean the same thing in the Arts and Crafts, and some of these Guilds of Handicraft were more of a tribute to Ashbee's knack of choosing a name than to the workshop he ran. The largest and most important of them, the Clarion Guild of Handicraft, was again a federation, not a workshop, a mass of amateur craftsmen and craftswomen co-ordinated through the women's page of the *Clarion* newspaper.[16]

To see Ashbee in the context of the country as a whole, of the art-loving public at large, is to see him in a different and more favourable light. His colleagues at the Art Workers' Guild may have found him a little tiresome, but in more distant circles, among art students and amateurs who took the *Studio* and the *Art Journal* as their guide, Ashbee and the Guild were names to conjure with.

In rather the same way—distance lending enchantment—Ashbee enjoyed a considerable reputation in Europe and America: his work was widely exhibited and publicized in books and articles. This popularity was a part of the enthusiasm for British architecture and design which was widespread in Europe and America at the turn of the century, enthusiasm for the homely, unostentatious quality of British domestic architecture, and for the simple, unacademic elements in the work of the Arts and Crafts Movement. It was a more catholic, less exclusively progressive taste than has sometimes been suggested, as much concerned with domestic comfort as with originality of style; Voysey and Mackintosh were not its only heroes, and in the pages of German magazines, for instance, one finds illustrated not only their work, and Ashbee's but also that of Ernest Newton and Guy Dawber, architects of a more traditional mould.

In the United States, interest in Ashbee's work grew as the Arts and Crafts Movement itself developed during the second half of the 1890s, a decade or so after the Movement in Britain. Interest seems to have been strongest in Chicago where the Movement drew particular strength from the craft workshops at Jane Addams's Hull House and from the young and adventurous group of Prairie School architects, including Frank Lloyd Wright, who worked at Steinway Hall on East Van Buren

Street.[17] It was in Chicago that the *House Beautiful*, an architectural magazine with Arts and Crafts sympathies, began publication in December 1896; its first number included illustrations of work by Morris, Crane, Voysey and Ashbee, and in January 1897 it carried a long and appreciative review of *A Few Chapters in Workshop Re-Construction and Citizenship*.[18] From 1897 the *Studio* was published in the United States as the *International Studio*. The Chicago Arts and Crafts Society held its first exhibition in the Art Institute in the spring of 1898 at which Ashbee showed jewellery, much of which was bought by Mrs Coonley, mother of Wright's client, Avery Coonley.[19] Also in 1898 he sent an exhibit to the T Square Club in Philadelphia, which then moved on to the Chicago Architectural Club.[20] At the T Square Club again in 1899 he showed designs for silver, jewellery, fire-places and furniture, along with views of his work on the Wodehouse at Wombourne and two of his houses on Cheyne Walk; the *Inland Architect*'s reviewer singled out his work for praise.[21] The annual exhibitions of the Chicago Architectural Club, held at the Art Institute, were largely selected in these years by the Steinway Hall group, and in 1900 nineteen English architects and designers were represented, with Ashbee showing fourteen items.[22] By the time he arrived personally in Chicago in December 1900, his reputation there was well established; it was ironic that it should have been at a meeting of the Architectural Club, which prized his work, that he should have made his unfortunate and clumsy remarks about a 'Nameless City'.[23]

What Ashbee valued more than his designs—the Guild idea, his hopes for the remaking of industrial life—reached Chicago through his own writings and particularly through the advocacy of Oscar Lovell Triggs, who taught literature at the university there. Editor of Whitman, admirer of Morris, socialist and fervent educator, Triggs was a kindred spirit. Like many people in the American Arts and Crafts, and especially in Chicago, he looked for the growth of a distinctly American and democratic culture through the Arts and Crafts. Though not a designer or craftsman himself, he founded the Industrial Art League in 1899 as a voluntary association to foster Arts and Crafts workshops in the Chicago area; it soon had a large and influential membership.[24] In 1902, Triggs published *Chapters in the History of the Arts and Crafts Movement* in which, having discussed Carlyle, Ruskin and Morris as mentors of the Arts and Crafts, he devoted one chapter to 'Ashbee and the Reconstructed Workshop' and another to the Rookwood Pottery.[25] There was nothing to suggest that he knew Ashbee or had visited the Guild; the chapter was largely made up of quotations from Ashbee's writings as if Triggs endorsed his every word; and yet his selection of passages was interesting. As an educator, he was less concerned with Ashbee as a designer or with the Guild as a practical workshop, than with Ashbee as an Idealist. Uniquely among those who admired or wrote about Ashbee and the Guild, he chose to emphasize comradeship in the workshop as the basis for a sound, new art, the mingling of school and workshop at Essex House, themes very close to Ashbee's heart; and he called the Guild 'another milestone on the road to Industrial freedom . . .'.[26] In the following year, Triggs's book was reviewed by Horace Traubel, editor of the *Artsman*, the journal of the Rose Valley Association in Pennysylvania:

Triggs writes what is in part chronicle, in part biography and in part prophecy. He talks in words his own. He talks in the words of others. Of Morris, of Ruskin, of Carlyle, of Whitman. And in words of Ashbee. Ashbee so far is not much known on this side of the Atlantic. But he deserves suffrage and will get it. Not only for his shop, which is germinal, but for his written speech, which strikes fire way up where men dream and way down where men root.[27]

It is easy to see why Ashbee should have appealed to Arts and Crafts people in America. He was better able than most of his British colleagues to appreciate the temper of the Movement there which was, broadly speaking, more interested in making plain and ordinary objects for the use of a universal middle class: British Arts and Crafts could seem precious and over-exquisite by comparison. Ashbee's belief in Whitmanic democracy and the unambitious character of many of his designs would have struck a chord. Also, he wrote a good deal, and books travel well; some American Arts and Crafts magazines liked to dot their pages with free-standing quotations from Ruskin, Emerson and other sages; passages from Ashbee's writings were used in this way.[28] And then he had such an appetite for things American; he came to the United States again and again, preferred Chicago to Anglophile Boston, and once wrote that if he could be born again he would choose to be an American.[29] With his constant lecture tours, his visits to so many centres of the Movement in America, he was almost the transatlantic ambassador of the Arts and Crafts.[30] It would be hard to imagine some of the more insular and tweedy figures of the Arts and Crafts in Britain, Ernest Gimson for instance, relishing the vital forces of Chicago as Ashbee did.

And yet there were aspects of the Movement in America which were at odds with his attitudes. It was not scornful of business methods and business success as he was, and less seemingly negative about 'the Machine'. In 1903 *Handicraft*, the magazine of the Boston Society of Arts and Crafts, published a long and enthusiastic article about the Guild which presented Ashbee as a masterful, pragmatic figure, pursuing his ideals step by step as conditions allowed, and the Guild as a successful marriage of idealism and business success.[31] Neither point was completely untrue, but somehow the crazy, quixotic element in Ashbee's work had been expunged, accommodated to the standards of the American movement. An article in the same magazine two months later criticized the Guild for 'leaving the machine out of account almost altogether'.[32]

It is not so easy to see what influence Ashbee exerted in America, to distinguish his contribution from that of British Arts and Crafts as a whole. In architecture it was Voysey and Baillie Scott who probably counted for most, in printing Morris; in furniture, which was so characteristic of the American Arts and Crafts, Voysey again was probably the principal influence.[33] The sturdy 'Craftsman' furniture made by Gustav Stickley at Eastwood near Syracuse from 1899, and that produced by Elbert Hubbard's Roycroft Community at East Aurora from about 1901, both in Upstate New York, was very like some of Ashbee's plain, rectilinear designs of 1897 and after, remarkably so during the short period in 1903 when Harvey Ellis graced Stickley's furniture with delicate inlays in wood and pewter.[34] But many Arts and Crafts furniture designers worked in this way and it would be invidious to single Ashbee out; and besides, the dating of his individual furniture designs is so imprecise at present that it is often impossible to argue for their priority; it may be that things worked the other way about and Ashbee was influenced by Stickley and Harvey Ellis. One would expect to find Ashbee's influence strongest

200. A silver dish with two loop handles, sold by Shreve, Crump and Low of Boston. (The Art Institute of Chicago, Gift of Mr and Mrs Robert A. Kubicek).

in the silver and jewellery of the American Arts and Crafts, and the work of the Kalo Shop, Chicago's largest and most distinguished producer of Arts and Crafts silver, certainly shows it. In Boston, where Arts and Crafts silver and jewellery flourished, one actually finds the prestigious department store of Shreve, Crump and Low selling a silver loop-handled dish, sometime between 1902 and 1914, which appears to be identical to those produced by the Guild, though it has no English assay marks (Plate 200). One would like to know more of the circumstances here, for Shreve, Crump and Low were a reputable firm not likely to copy a designer's work without giving credit; but work of this kind is only beginning to be investigated.[35] We do not know enough either about the origins of American Arts and Crafts workshops to be sure that any of them was specifically modelled on the Guild of Handicraft. Research into the Arts and Crafts Movement in America, which has developed remarkably following Robert Judson Clark's pioneering exhibition at Princeton in 1972, will settle these questions gradually.[36] In the meanwhile, one has to rest content with the tribute paid by the greatest architect and designer of the American Arts and Crafts, Frank Lloyd Wright, who told Ashbee enigmatically, 'I have learned much from you already in ways you little suspect—and will learn more.'[37]

In Europe, as in America, it was Anglophile interest in the Arts and Crafts which drew attention to Ashbee's work, and that was perhaps strongest at first in Belgium. Morris and English Arts and Crafts inspired the Belgian architect Serrurier-Bovy to become a decorative artist in the 1880s, and the painter van de Velde in the 1890s; Walter Crane, the most celebrated English example of the artist who had escaped from the confines of easel painting, exhibited in Brussels in 1891; and in 1894 the *avant-garde* group of artists known as Les Vingt re-formed themselves as La Libre Esthétique with a new commitment to the decorative arts. French symbolism and post-impressionism, socialism, the flowing natural ornament of Morris and the Century Guild, sturdy English furniture, artists taking up the crafts, all con-

409

tributed to the mood of artistic Brussels in the mid-1890s.[38] The first exhibition of La Libre Esthétique, at Brussels in 1894, was also the first occasion on which Ashbee exhibited in Europe; in the following year he showed with them again, and with L'Oeuvre Artistique in Liège.[39] Gauguin, Toorop, and Puvis de Chavannes were among the other exhibitors at Brussels, and from Britain, Morris, Watts, Beardsley, George Frampton (who showed his disturbing symbolic bust *Mysteriarch*) and luminaries of the Arts and Crafts Exhibition Society such as Crane, Cobden-Sanderson and Heywood Sumner.[40] The Guild's work, which perhaps included silver, probably appealed, at that date and in that company, more for its simplicity and the suggestion of spirituality in its decorative emblems, than for elements of Art Nouveau; on one of these occasions examples of the Guild's metal-work were bought by one of the Belgian museums.[41] In France, on the other hand, where sympathy for the English Arts and Crafts was less strong, Ashbee seems to have made little impression.[42]

In Germany, architects and designers had looked to England for guidance towards a simple, domestic manner since the late 1880s; in 1897 the magazines *Dekorative Kunst* and *Deutsche Kunst und Dekoration* started publication, their titles showing the new preoccupation with applied art. In 1897 Arts and Crafts workshops were started in Munich by artists and designers connected with the Secession there and in 1898 in Dresden by Karl Schmidt, though both these were more open to business and industrial methods than their English counterparts.[43] Ashbee's part in decorating the Grand Ducal Palace at Darmstadt, though not large, was timely, and marks the beginning of interest in his work.[44] He exhibited in the prestigious showrooms of Keller and Reiner in Berlin in the winter of 1897; and a scatter of references to his work in the early numbers of *Dekorative Kunst* was followed by a substantial article on the Guild by Hermann Muthesius in May 1898.[45] Muthesius was technical attaché at the German Embassy in London, and could study the Guild at close quarters; but his view of its workshop structure was coloured by his distrust of anything that smacked of anti-capitalism. He wrote with great sensitivity about Ashbee's silverwork and jewellery, but he chose, like *Handicraft*, to present the Guild as a successful business enterprise:

It has been reserved for the Englishman, who in all that he does stands in the first rank of businessmen, to find in the Guild system a form which combines real commercial management with the best artistic standards so eliminating the middleman and providing artistic goods and faultless craftwork at reasonable prices. On these grounds more than on any other are these Guilds worthy before anything else of the most earnest consideration in Germany.[46]

Such praise, though warm, distorted the idealism of the Guild, and Ashbee took issue with Muthesius for saying that 'stripped of its glamour' the Guild was merely a business enterprise.

There is something in the glamour that Herr Muthesius missed. There are many of us in the Guild—I for one—who, if it was a mere business enterprise, would have no further interest in it. Mere business we could pursue more profitably elsewhere and unencumbered with altruism . . . the Guild is a protest against modern business methods, against the Trade point of view, against the Commercial spirit.[47]

Later German-language articles, particularly those written in Vienna, were more ready to see the Guild as Ashbee saw it, enthusiastic about its workshop democracy and its collaborative designing.

It was in Vienna, of all European cities, that Ashbee was most enthusiastically received. The most important German-speaking city of long standing, Vienna was nevertheless culturally parochial, a city in which tensions between young, progressive artists, writers and musicians on the one hand—the café groups—and the cultural establishment on the other, were stronger than usual. But in the 1890s the progressives were gaining ground, even within the city's institutions. In 1897 the younger members of the established exhibiting body, the Künstlerhaus, broke away to form the Vereinigung Bildender Künstler Österreichs, which was familiarly known here also as the Secession; they hoped to bring Vienna into the mainstream of progressive European art. They built themselves arresting exhibition rooms in the Friedrichstrasse and inscribed over the entrance the legend of their modernity and aestheticism, 'To every age its art, to art its freedom'. Their early exhibitions, in which German, French, Belgian and English artists figured, were a success. At the same time, Arthur von Scala, an orientalist and an Anglophile, was appointed director of the Österreichisches Museum für Kunst und Industrie; attached to the museum was the Kunstgewerbeschule, and here the Secessionist Felician von Myrbach was appointed head; the architect Josef Hoffmann and the designer Kolo Moser joined his staff in the late 1890s. Both were prominent members of the Secession and admirers of English applied art; the mood in the world of Viennese applied art around 1900 was Anglophile and progressive.[48]

Von Scala quickly showed where his sympaties lay: in the winter of 1898–9 he put on an exhibition of furniture and decorative arts which included 'modern furniture of quite recent date' from England and America; and in December 1898 he bought a sweet dish, a presentation cup, a bowl and a vase from the Guild of Handicraft, all in base metal.[49] But he was not quick enough for Hoffmann, who felt that there was still too much English antique and reproduction furniture in von Scala's exhibitions, and planned to devote the Secession's winter exhibition of 1900 to European applied art of the most up-to-date kind. (Vienna looked to Holland and Belgium, as well as to England, at this time.) In April 1900 he wrote to von Myrbach,

Surely, *Herr Baron*, you intend to visit the 'Guild of Handicrafts' in Essex House in the East End of London. C. R. Aschbee works there . . . May I ask you, *Herr Baron*, to negotiate if possible with Aschbee with regard to the exhibition. To be able to show real English art and craft in Vienna would be worth the trouble and would hit the museum hard.[50]

Von Myrbach went to see Ashbee in London and it was agreed that the Guild should exhibit.[51] As it happened, the large collection of furniture, jewellery and metalwork which Ashbee had designed for Gyula Mandello, the Hungarian economist, was standing ready in the workshops, and he decided to show it in Vienna on its way to the client. When the eighth exhibition of the Secession opened at the beginning of November 1900, the largest single exhibition was La Maison Moderne from Paris; but the Guild came next with fifty-three items worth over £1,200, Mandello's collection accounting for £565 of this; and Ashbee's mahogany writing cabinet now in the Cheltenham Art Gallery and Museum was given a place

411

of honour in the middle of the central hall (Plate 201). Among foreign exhibits, the talking-point was the room furnished with the work of C. R. Mackintosh and the other members of the Glasgow Four, whose colours, elongated proportions and hints of symbolic depth were a new and exotic experience for the Viennese. The designs of Hoffmann and Moser, who also exhibited, were refined, unfussy and original in form, and very obviously conscious of questions of style; while their mentor, the architect Otto Wagner, exhibited furniture sumptuously enriched with stained glass and mother-of-pearl.[53]

Alongside this work, Ashbee's furniture seemed very sober and down-to-earth; to the eloquent Viennese critic Ludwig Hevesi it was 'like a bite of black bread after a Lucullan menu', a necessary and healthy antidote to Viennese luxury, but not easily digestible.[54] He liked Ashbee's little flower-like brooches, and the hammered silver muffin dishes, but the furniture seemed to him as if it came 'from a rectangular planet, inhabited by stoutly built peasants. Everything is upright, angular, at ninety degrees.'[55] He felt uncertain about it. He could not quite bring himself to approve of it and said it left the Viennese 'with a few exceptions', rather cool. At the same time he obviously relished writing about it: 'bomb-proof' is how he described an armchair with high, solid sides, a chair so massive a man could well withdraw into it 'as into a hermitage . . .'; cabinets of dark wood sparingly inlaid with small panels of pinks reminded him of 'some London suburbanite who wears his sober flannel suit year in, year out, and only changes the carnation in his buttonhole on Sundays'.[56] The analogy of clothes recalls the point of view of Adolf Loos, most acute of Viennese critics and scourge of Arts and Crafts preciousness. Loos may have admired Ashbee's furniture, for he was an advocate of 'pure and simple construction, straight lines, right-angled corners'; but if he did, the situation was ambiguous, for he thought 'this is how the craftsman works who has nothing in front of him but his materials, his tools and his predetermined objective'.[57] No artist leading him from above, Loos meant, and no Ruskinian ideas of personal expression. Ashbee's craftsmen were not like that.

In fact, Hevesi seems to have misconstrued the Viennese response to Ashbee's furniture, for the Guild exhibit sold very well; Ashbee received a number of fresh orders for furniture, duplicates, presumably, of his designs for Mandello, and the Cheltenham writing cabinet was bought by a Viennese family; Hoffmann himself bought a salt-cellar and spoon, and the Österreichisches Museum four pieces of silver tableware. Ashbee had made his mark, like the Glasgow Four, though in a less dramatic way; and as for the Anglophile designers of Vienna, the black bread of his furniture was just what they wanted. The Viennese architect, Robert Örley, and perhaps also Kolo Moser, show its influence; while for Hoffmann it provided a welcome confirmation of the way his own work was going, away from the influence of J. M. Olbrich and Art Nouveau, towards a simple rectilinear style. In the years immediately following the eighth exhibition, the magazine *Kunst und Kunsthandwerk*, which was the official organ of the Österreichisches Museum, published three substantial articles on Ashbee, presenting him as the chief English inheritor of the Ruskin–Morris tradition, his houses on Cheyne Walk as pragmatic interiors full of light, their functional arrangement showing on the face of them, and the Guild as an artistic yet practical workshop—familiar views by now.[58]

The Secession suffered a split in 1904–5, between the decorative artists, including

201. The central hall at the eighth exhibition of the Vienna Secession. (From the *Studio*, 1901, vol. 22, p. [265].)

Hoffman and Moser, and those more exclusively concerned with painting; and the decorative artists withdrew. Ashbee, however, stayed on good terms with both parties, and he exhibited work with the Secession in 1902, 1905 and 1906 (when he showed fifty-eight items) making up a record of exhibits with the Secession far greater than that of any other British artist or designer.[59] Hoffmann, Moser and their friends now exhibited under the title Kunstschau, and Ashbee, together with Baillie Scott, Ernest Newton, Mackintosh, John Paul Cooper and the Artificers' Guild, showed with them in 1909; Van Gogh, Gauguin, Munch and Matisse were also included in what amounted to a comprehensive review of *avant-garde* painting.[60] If the Viennese were obviously charmed by Mackintosh in 1900 and fêted him in the streets when he visited the exhibition (Ashbee was in the United States at the time), they were also, and consistently, interested in Ashbee.

In the early 1900s Hoffmann and Moser were thinking of setting up workshops in Vienna, and in December 1902 Hoffmann was in Britain with von Myrbach, visiting art schools; he saw Mackintosh in Glasgow and may have been to see Ashbee on this occasion.[61] In the early summer of 1903 he and Moser started the Wiener Werkstätte, Produktiv-Gemeinschaft von Kunsthandwerkern with the backing of Fritz Wärndorfer, a wealthy Viennese businessman, and it is said that these workshops were modelled on or inspired by the Guild.[62] There were workshops for furniture and joinery, bookbinding and leatherwork, metalwork including gold and silver, and jewellery; and also an architectural office; Hoffmann and Moser were the only designers at first and fashionable circles in Vienna took readily to their striking wares, simple and geometrical in shape, but enriched with exquisite ornament and generally rather expensive. The *Arbeitsprogramm* which they issued in 1905 was a thoroughly Arts and Crafts document, championing everyday objects, fine workmanship, and applied as against fine art; and of jewellery they wrote:

We shall use many semi-precious stones . . . because in our eyes their manifold colours and ever-varying facets replace the sparkle of diamonds. We love silver and gold for their sheen and regard the lustre of copper as just as valid artistically. We feel that a silver brooch can have as much intrinsic worth as a jewel made of gold and precious stones. The merit of craftsmanship and artistic conception must be recognized once more and valued accordingly.[63]

This was the gospel of artistic jewellery according to Ashbee in its purest form.

To see the early products of the Wiener Werkstätte alongside those of the Guild is to see how simple, solid and almost naïve Ashbee's designs were, and at the same time how that very quality appealed to Hoffmann and Moser; it is to see how particular Ashbee motifs were popular in Vienna: the use of coloured stones, and hammer-marks left on the metal; even the massive ball feet of Ashbee's writing cabinet exhibited in 1900 reappeared in a design for a dressing table of 1904 made by the Wiener Werkstätte (Plate 202).[64] But it is also to see how much more sophisticated Hoffmann and Moser were; modest features of Ashbee's work, valued for their associations and the way they heightened the sense of usefulness, were dramatized and overstated as part of a more precious and purely visual style; the coloured stones were used in tight, luxurious profusion, the hammer-marks were deeper, more precise, the obsession with right-angles so strong that it earned the nickname '*Quadratlstil*'. One is not surprised to learn that the workshops and office

202. Dressing table made by the Wiener Werkstätte, and possibly designed by Kolo Moser, 1904. (Private collection).

ledgers at the Wiener Werkstätte were painted in matching colours, blue for woodwork, grey for bookbinding and so on, a refinement which no doubt served the purposes of art as much as of business efficiency.

By about 1905 Ashbee had a small but enthusiastic European following, largely in German-speaking countries. He was an honorary member of the Vienna Secession, and of the Munich Akademie.[66] He had important clients in Hungary, Gyula Mandello and Zsombor de Szász; and though he did not exhibit in Budapest like some British Arts and Crafts designers, he was the subject of a long article in *Magyar Iparművészet* in 1910.[67] The Kunstgewerbemuseum in Zurich bought his work in 1903; the museum in Vienna bought four more pieces of metalwork, including a big silver altar cross, from the Secession exhibition in 1906; and he was awarded a *Diplôme d'Honneur* at the Esposizione Internazionale in Milan the same year.[68] In 1910 the Museum für Kunst und Gewerbe in Hamburg bought three books from the Essex House Press and, perhaps not surprisingly, Ashbee's work as a graphic designer was appreciated in German-speaking countries: he was also an honorary member of the Deutsche Buchgewerbe Künstler. His influence as a designer was not confined to Vienna though it was strongest there, and craft jewellery in Germany and Austria commonly followed the very general principles which Ashbee had been the first to suggest in the early 1890s: the prominence of metalwork, the use of silver and of cheap and colourful stones. Even though German craft jewellery as a whole owed few stylistic debts to England, there were echoes of Ashbee's jewels in the work of Hermann Hirzel of Berlin, and in the early work of H. E. von Berlepsch-Valendas and Karl Rothmüller, both of Munich.[69]

415

We have met Hans Eduard von Berlepsch-Valendas already, waxing lyrical on a visit to Chipping Campden; and other continental designers and critics beat a path to Ashbee's door.[70] In November 1904 Heinrich Waentig, a professor of economics and political science, paid a visit. 'A titanic Teuton has descended upon us', Ashbee wrote,

One Prof. Waentig of Munster—or as Carlyle might have called him Teufelsdruck Waentig. He is writing a book—*cela va sans dire*—on Handicraft in the modern social scheme of things and having a holiday he came in a Bee line from Munster to Campden . . . my word how he talked! German or English indifferently amazingly—wonderfully! He set up his verb in the remote distance and then stalked it, so to speak through mountains of nouns, adjectives, participles relatives and grammatical compounds . . .[71]

Ashbee asked Will Hart to take charge of the professor, Alec Miller and Archie Ramage talked socialism to him, and the professor was impressed. For Waentig was no mere lightweight enthusiast for the decorative arts. He had a serious thesis to research; he wanted to know whether one had to follow Morris from capitalism into socialism in order to have well designed goods for all.[72] The Guild appeared to him to be at least one kind of practical alternative to social revolution, and though by the time his book, *Wirtschaft und Kunst*, came out in 1909 he had to recognize sadly that the Guild had 'fallen victim to a depression in the trade cycle', he was still full of enthusiasm:

I have wandered through their workshops and listened to them at their work, slept in the guest house and made friends with the workmen over meals. It has been an unforgettable experience for me. One knows that this solution to the socio-political problems of our age will not be a solution for all, or even for many, but yet the sense of practicality in it all shines out for me as a truly significant fact.[72]

On a busy day in Campden, Ashbee could joke about Teufelsdruck Waentig; but he had considerable respect for the Arts and Crafts work being done outside Britain, especially after 1900. 'The principles of the movement', he wrote in 1911, 'are now more consistently and logically studied in Germany and America, and also in some of the smaller countries of Europe . . .'[74] He was thinking of collaboration between technical schools and local industry in Germany; of experiments in Belgium and Denmark; of Frank Lloyd Wright and Greene and Greene.[75] He may have felt that the Arts and Crafts designers who exhibited alongside him in Brussels or Vienna were a little precious, less ready to tolerate technical or artistic defects than he was, for the sake of the human experiment; but they were kindred spirits. In 1911 he listed J. M. Olbrich, Hoffmann, Moser, Bruno Paul and Bruno Mohring as architects ranking with the best of the progressive spirits in the English Arts and Crafts.[76] It would be interesting to know what he thought about the Deutscher Werkbund which was set up in 1907 to reform standards of design in German industry through an alliance of artists and industrialists.[77] It drew on the standards and experiences of German Arts and Crafts workshops; it pitched its ideals high, in the way he liked: the purification of national taste, the model of the simple, honest, modern German home; and it did not, thanks partly to the influence of the liberal politician Friedrich Naumann, overlook the dignity of labour, the joy of the craftsman; one would expect Ashbee to be sympathetic. At the same time, there was a strong pro-machine element in the Werkbund's ideas, and this may have influenced the change of tone in Ashbee's later writings. If he had been present at the famous debate between artistic freedom and *Typisierung* which took place at the Werkbund's Congress in 1914 he would certainly have spoken up, and added to the intellectual melée, for he believed that he had resolved this issue (or one very like it) in defining the relationship between 'standard' and 'standardization' three years earlier. But this is speculation. There seems to be no evidence to show what Ashbee thought of the Werkbund, and he was not among the original members of the Design and Industries Association, the English organization modelled on it.[78]

During the First World War and the 1920s, interest in Ashbee's work seemed to wane in Britain and in Europe, at least so far as published references go. He was not mentioned, for instance, in Charles Marriott's thorough account of *Modern English Architecture* (1924), though Voysey, Lethaby, Prior, Baillie Scott, Mackintosh and Parker and Unwin were. But interest revived in the late 1920s and 1930s, and by this time Ashbee was being looked at historically. In 1929 the visionary German architect Bruno Taut, while staying by the sparkling waters of Lulworth Cove in Dorset, wrote *Modern Architecture*, an early popular account of the Modern Movement; he traced the origins of the Movement to the nineteenth-century engineers, and to British domestic architecture at the turn of the century, particularly that of Ashbee and Mackintosh. For Taut, the Modern Movement was a reaction against exaggerated Romanticism and sentimentality in building, and Ashbee's reticent houses on Cheyne Walk seemed to him thoroughly unromantic: he called Ashbee 'that austere, neat protagonist of brick'.[79] The phrase was apt; the interpretation was understandable, but not quite so apt, considering the Romantic sense of Chelsea and its past which went into the designing of Ashbee's houses. Arts and Crafts simplicity was often ambiguous in this way: Romantic admiration for the vernacular and Rationalist stripping down to essentials could produce the same simplicity; and this ambiguity was part of the relationship between the Arts and Crafts and the Modern Movement.[80]

In 1935, as we have seen, Ashbee read the draft of an article on '*William Morris, C. R. Ashbee und das zwanzigste Jahrhundert*' by another German apologist of the Modern Movement in England, Nikolaus Pevsner; and in the following year Pevsner published *Pioneers of the Modern Movement*.[81] Ashbee figured most prominently in the first chapter of this book, which dealt with theories of art and design, and set out the basic thesis, that 'the phase between Morris and Gropius is a historical unit . . .'.[82] For Pevsner, the important part of Morris's teaching was that artists should turn their attention to the decorative arts; he was uneasy with the Romantic element in Morris's socialism, and deprecated what he saw as Morris's inability to come to terms with 'the Machine'. He thought Ashbee was probably the most original thinker of the next generation, and he gave him a transitional role in the story. Some important aspects of Ashbee's work, notably the Campden experiment, seemed to Pevsner even more mediaevalist than Morris, but others were progressive. He saw a shift of conviction in Ashbee's writings which lent itself elegantly to the argument: having stood at first, like Morris, against the machine, Ashbee had come to a new, more realistic and progressive position; having battled hopelessly in the Guild against the industrial system, he reached a point where he could write, in the first axiom of *Should We Stop Teaching Art*, 'Modern Civilisation rests on Machinery, and no system for the endowment, or encouragement, of the teaching of art can be sound that does not recognise this.'[83] 'In pronouncing this axiom,' Pevsner wrote, 'Ashbee has abandoned the doctrine of the Arts and Crafts and adopted one of the basic premises of the Modern Movement.'[84] Pevsner's book, and its various later editions revised under the more ambitious title *Pioneers of Modern Design*, has done more to shape Ashbee's reputation today than any other.

Since the Second World War, other sides of Ashbee's work have attracted attention. Historians and collectors have changed their minds about Victorian and Edwardian architecture and design; Art Nouveau was all the rage in the 1960s; and so we have Ashbee the architect and designer of simple and telling silver, closer than the Arts and Crafts usually came to Art Nouveau. The Campden episode has always been memorable, and Fiona MacCarthy's *The Simple Life: C. R. Ashbee in the Cotswolds* (1981) is a beautifully observed and sympathetic account of six romantic years, a portrait of Ashbee as the tireless, endearing, eccentric idealist. Yet Pevsner's picture of the hesitant 'Pioneer of the Modern Movement' is still the most influential, and in general histories and biographical dictionaries it is almost universal.[85] In *The Arts and Crafts Movement: a study of its sources, ideals and influence on design theory* (1971) Gillian Naylor gave a thoroughly sympathetic account of Ashbee's career, rounded it off by describing Axiom 1 of *Should We Stop Teaching Art* as a 'radical reappraisal' of his assumptions, and added a further twist to the argument by suggesting that Frank Lloyd Wright may have helped Ashbee to come to terms with the machine.[86] For Gillian Naylor and for many others, the interest of Ashbee and the Arts and Crafts Movement lies in the way they look forward to the twentieth century.

There is much in Ashbee's work, career and attitudes to support this point of view, for he always thought of himself as a modernist, responsive to the spirit of his age, marking his work off by its deliberate simplicity from sources in the distant past. He admired the architecture of the American Middle West and the Pacific Coast, and the work of American engineers, because there 'orders, columns, cornices, all flummery stuck on, was pruned away; a real structural form, true architecture in the Greek or Mediaeval manner, was once more evolved . . .'.[87] And he did change his mind in about 1910, about machines among other things. The story of his travels and contacts in Europe and America is a veritable Baedeker of early Modernism. Is there a new art to be developed in a German duchy? He is there, making the Grand Duke's furniture. Are craft workshops to be set up in Vienna? The Guild is their model. Is there a native American genius at work in Chicago? It is Ashbee who will seek him out and introduce him to Europe. In the Pevsnerian view, the Arts and Crafts Movement was transitional, looking back to the Romanticism and traditionalism of the nineteenth century, and forward to the hard, clear, rational world of modern technology. In a way, Ashbee seems to fit this picture exactly.

But in the end, the Pevsnerian view, the view which concentrates attention on the 'forward-looking' elements in Ashbee's work, is inaccurate, unbalanced and unsympathetic. It is inaccurate because Ashbee did not change his fundamental convictions in 1911; there was no abandoning of the Arts and Crafts, no adopting of the Modern Movement at that time; and if advocates of this view would take the trouble to read the first chapter of *Should We Stop Teaching Art* from which they so regularly quote, they would see that in pronouncing the axiom, 'Modern Civilization rests on Machinery . . .', Ashbee, so far from abandoning the Arts and Crafts Movement, was actually stating its *raison d'être* as clearly as he could.[88] The changes in his last books were changes only in tone, scope and tactics. Long before 1911, he had acknowledged that modern civilization rests on machinery; how could he overlook so bland a statement of the obvious? As early as 1894 he wrote of 'the Machine' as 'the basis of social re-construction', which is if anything a stronger statement than his later one.[89] And, on the other hand, he continued, long after 1911, to be almost as hostile to 'the Machine' as he had always been. It is true that he was keener to acknowledge that goods made by machine could be beautiful; but in Ashbee's writings 'the Machine' was a word of shifting and elastic meaning, which could refer both to particular machines and to the system of mechanical industry as a whole. 'We know that beautiful things can be made by mechanical power. It is the system as a whole we have to consider . . . We must free the human spirit again . . . We have to free it now from the incubus of mechanism—of power, misunderstood, misapplied, miscontrolled.'[90] These words were published in 1917, and the theme runs through his later writings:

Machinery untamed . . . that is the barbarism we have now to fight . . . the accursed conditions of industrial machinery in which we live . . . the tyranny of mechanism . . . we know that the great mechanical interests, the large factory organisations . . . are against us . . . the slavery of the machine . . . the corrosive influence of mechanical power . . .[91]

There was no shifting from the Arts and Crafts here, no kinder view. Throughout his career Ashbee preached 'the limitation of machinery', and that was his first and last word on the issue. The most important task facing an industrial society was to distinguish between those things which are best made by hand and those which are best made by machine. Until that distinction was made, he could and would approve of individual machines and designs, but he could not make peace with industrialism.

The Pevsnerian view is unbalanced just because it concentrates attention on some aspects of Ashbee and not others. In his designs, for instance, it prizes freedom from the influence of the past, and treats traditional elements as passive and uninteresting, a point of departure at best; whereas it is clear that the quality of his work, taken in the round, often depends on the recollection of exemplars: the village sense in Chelsea, English furniture in its late seventeenth-century transitional phase; the jewellery of the *bottega*, the aura of Caxton. It is impossible to give a sympathetic account of his work as a designer while concentrating only on those elements which look forward to the Modern Movement. In Pevsner's *Pioneers* that was a legitimate approach in so far as he was tracing the pedigree of the Modern Movement; in studies which set out to present architecture and design at the turn of the century in their own right, it is more or less misleading.

It is unsympathetic partly because it interprets Ashbee, whose inspiration was largely Romantic, in a rationalist spirit; and partly because it is so academic. *Pioneers of the Modern Movement* was an intensely polemical book, written in the service of an architectural crusade; yet its argument scarcely reached beyond the lecture room and the terms of reference of art history. The ideas that the twentieth century

419

is an age of technology (a crude enough stereotype) and that particular forms and materials will express that character, are simply the working concepts of a particular tradition of art history, style, and the 'Spirit of the Age'; they are tools for interpreting the past, no more. How much fresher, how much larger, is the world to which Ashbee belongs, with its themes of work, friendship and the fruitfulness of ordinary experience?

It is interesting to play with the word 'Modern' here. Art historians use it to refer, among other things, to styles and attitudes in the twentieth century which have made some complete break with the past. Since the Second World War, social scientists have used 'modernity' and 'modernization' to describe the whole process which Western countries underwent in the nineteenth and early twentieth century; a developing economy, industrialization, the growth of cities, the dominance of the urban bourgeoisie, secularism, parliamentary democracy. If this is modernization, what is Ashbee with his little band of mediaevalizing craftsmen, his retreat to the country? Ashbee, who, against the culture, individualism and economic life of the bourgeoisie, joins hands with the artists of Bohemia and the workmen of Mile End? He is no less than a full-blown, drastic, Romantic anti-Modernist, shaking his cultured first at the birth of the modern world. The interpretation may be pretentious, but it probably touches Ashbee at more points than does Pevsner.

CHAPTER SIXTEEN
CONCLUSION

Ashbee's basic convictions did not change much during his adult life. He once put them very clearly in a letter to Laurence Hodson. He said that what he had always admired in William Morris was his 'creative splendour'; Morris showed what you could do.

I don't mean that every Tom, Dick and Harry had Morris' genius, but that the great neglected power for creation lay in men's hands under the inspiration of the arts and that this was demonstrable from tradition, more especially mediaeval tradition.

My life's work has as you know been to try and put this into practice.[1]

He believed that ordinary, everyday life can be creative; that imagination is as much a part of the lives of ordinary people and their surroundings as it is of art; that in work and play every man and woman can be their own kind of artist; and that if they are not, in modern society, they are reduced to puppets twitched, by the industrial system, between drudgery and sensationalism. This conviction took hold of Ashbee at Cambridge and remained with him for life. It was the inspiration of the Guild of Handicraft, and though there were problems enough in the running of the Guild, he never suffered the pain and embarrassment of ceasing to believe in the organization he had created.

It was a conviction born in and of the intellectual climate of late Victorian England. It had a lot in common with Matthew Arnold's sense of the ennobling influence of culture, and with the way literature, music and the arts were used in the late nineteenth century as vehicles for social reform, spreading sweetness and light among the working classes. It was in this spirit that free libraries, art galleries and museums were opened throughout Britain, and that Canon Barnett held his picture exhibitions in Whitechapel. The element of culture is not uppermost in the workshops of the Guild, for Ashbee would insist, and rightly, that they were about craft and earning a living, and not, like an art gallery, about works of art and improving leisure. But essentially the Guild was an attempt to enrich the lives of working men through the values of art in the broadest sense. The idea surfaced in the Guild sing-songs and Elizabethan plays; in Ashbee's more peripheral activities such as University Extension lecturing, when he grafted the humanistic on to the technical; and in the Watch Committee whose priority was to preserve some dignity and architectural quality in the everyday fabric of London's suburbs, starting with the East End. There was certainly an element of palliative in Ashbee's use of art as a vehicle of social reform, as there had been in Arts and Crafts attitudes from Ruskin onwards, an anxiety to divert energies which would otherwise take the form of political action and class hostility. 'Where ten men work continuously together in one shop', Ashbee wrote, 'they may become genuinely interested in their craft, where fifty work together they are more likely to be primarily interested in politics and social questions . . .'[2]

It is part of the complexity of Ashbee's ideas that they were also related to the socialism of the day, if rather one-sidedly. He was not a socialist in the straightforward political sense, and it would be hard to say how he voted.[3] He wrote 'there is no real antagonism between capital and labour . . .'.[4] Class for him was not a political concept but a problem, a gulf to be bridged with a firm handshake and the mysterious power of comradeship. But in the 1880s, before socialism became closely identified with parliamentary politics, it seemed to him the one thing that could re-make British industry, large enough in its sympathies to embrace his doctrine of comradeship and the collaboration with artists which his plans required. He really could believe at that stage that trade unions could act as he thought mediaeval guilds acted, regulating their work in the name of aesthetic standards; later he found modern socialists so ready to accept, indeed to assume, the factory system that he could no longer count himself among them. But he always said that the socialist movement was one of the original sources of inspiration for the Guild.[5]

Most of all, Ashbee's convictions belong to the Romantic critique of industrial society. It was Ruskin who had set up the standard of the craftsman's happiness; and it was Morris who had recalled the Middle Ages 'when imagination and fancy mingled with all things made by man . . .'.[6] Morris also said that the leading passion of his life was a hatred of modern civilization; and these Romantics were antithetical to the modern world, almost of necessity, setting the past against the present, handwork against machine-work, the country against the town. The world of industry seemed to concentrate in itself all that they hated; it was a foul, belching demoniac presence to Ruskin, mere drudgery and misapplied ingenuity to the stout and dismissive Morris. And so they drew apart into a world of Romantic values, nature, art, history. And the distance which they set between themselves and industry encouraged powerful and ill-informed stereotypes: they hated the world of industry not because they lived and worked in it and knew it well, but because they did not. And Ashbee was of their camp. His life's work, as he understood it, was an endeavour towards the teaching of John Ruskin and William Morris. The whole *raison d'être* of the Guild was that it should develop ways of working that would be both new and old, but not those of commerce and industry.

The Romantic critique was, broadly speaking, literary and literary historians have ranged its chief exponents among the Victorian 'sages'. Ashbee did not want to be a sage. It was enough for him that Carlyle, Ruskin and Morris had set out certain truths. He called himself a 'Practical Idealist', and his task was the humbler one of putting these truths to the test, working out their bearing in the everyday world. The Guild of Handicraft was one way of doing this, a small, thoroughly idealistic experiment. The books he wrote were another; in these he explained the change of heart and the adjustments to existing institutions which would be needed to give his Romantic ideals a place in industrial society as a whole.

Humble it might be, but it was also a difficult, and perhaps an impossible task, for the Romantic critique did not lend itself to being put into practice. Some of Ruskin's fiercest invective was reserved for British industry; and Morris became a revolutionary socialist and looked forward with a savage delight to the tearing down of the whole rotten fabric. These were not the men to encourage patient, practical endeavour. To be practical in pursuit of their ideals was to face two equally unwelcome possibilities. Ashbee could stand by the radical, anti-industrial character of the tradition (as he did in the Guild) and be dismissed as a crank; even if he had some measure of success, it would be meaningless, for how could a band of Ruskinites demonstrate their practicality except in terms of a commercial success which they despised? (The story of the Guild is heavy with this irony.) If, on the other hand, he set out to be eirenic, as he did in his books, to build bridges between the Romantic tradition and the everyday world, he would dilute the tradition.

His proposals for the limitation of machinery, which were the core of his ideas for the re-shaping of industry, illustrate the point perfectly. He looked for the protection of traditional craft industries within the industrial system as a whole. From the point of view of Ruskin and Morris that was too bland, a compromise. From the point of view of the practical man it was entirely quixotic, for it required the recasting of the whole system of industry, commerce and consumption, and the attitudes that went with it; and there was little in the industrial circumstances of early twentieth-century Britain to encourage such a development, no real social or political weight, for instance, behind this kind of anti-industrialism, as there was in Germany among the master-craftsmen in the late nineteenth century.[7] Ashbee himself believed that the fabric of mechanical production was being undermined, and that all sorts of forces were working towards the limitation of machinery. The development of Guild socialism before the First World War was almost the last of many movements that lent colour to his view; and it started with *The Restoration of the Gild System* (1906) written by A. J. Penty, an Arts and Crafts architect.[8] But Guild socialism, as it turned out, offered no more challenge to the factory system than the parliamentary and municipal socialisms in which Ashbee had already lost faith; in the end there was only the Arts and Crafts Movement which valued craftsmanship as he did, and that was too dilettante and peripheral an affair to be of much help in his larger purposes.

In the end, his various schemes for the limitation of machinery, the transformation of art schools into productive guilds, the Art Institute as a civic powerhouse of creative life, though plausible, detailed and zealous, were not quite what either the visionary or the practical man wanted to hear; and his books, in which he developed these schemes with such care, though often interesting and full of striking passages, were the least successful aspect of his work. Ever since his Cambridge days, when he had been taught history as a preparation for public life, he had relished a certain intellectual sweep, an educated outlook over the political, social and economic life of his time; and it was important to him to write, and to develop his ideas on a national scale. But it was actually when he dropped this discursive intellectual stance, stepped down from the larger stage, and was personal, practical and no less passionately idealistic, that he was most impressive.

The Guild of Handicraft counted for much; it was, in a way, his life's work and he gave more of himself to creating this 'cell of good living'—the phrase is

Eric Gill's—than to anything else. It was not always as harmonious as his rather theoretical accounts of workers' co-operation and profit-sharing suggested; he could be masterful, inspiring respect, and even fear, as well as affection; if the Guild was democratic, it was to some extent at his prompting. But it was a generous experiment nevertheless, a workshop where men had time and leisure, where the work itself counted for more than the system of production or quantity of output or profits. His imaginative way of recruiting men for their character not for their skill; the decision to sit down in the early 1890s and work out the Guild's own kind of metalwork by tentative, stumbling experiment; the time spent on awkward young misfits of the Arts and Crafts like Cyril Kelsey; the plays and songs, the Wednesday suppers and the river trips; all these made the Guild the most radical workshop of the Arts and Crafts, the one which came closest to a social sense of the arts and crafts, not taste, not exquisite design, not virtuoso craftsmanship, but work and the stuff of ordinary life.

It was perhaps at its best in the 1890s when it was small, full of hope and defiance, and working out something new in the unlikely setting of Whitechapel and Mile End; round 1900 it seemed to hold business success and idealism in the balance and the ambiguity of the situation was not lost on Ashbee; Campden was idyllic, the fulness of the Romantic ideal, and perhaps a little overripe. The Guild failed of course, but we have seen how meaningless it is to say so, for there was no kind of success in the world of business that they could accept without compromise, and it was perhaps better that they should have gone out as they did. Right at the beginning of his career, in 1887, Ashbee had written enigmatically: 'There are two sorts of failure, of which the higher is success.'[9]

Scattered among Ashbee's papers of the 1920s and 1930s are occasional letters from former Guildsmen, looking back on the time they spent in the workshops. Fred Hubbard, one of the founder members, wrote from Hampstead Garden Suburb in 1933 paying tribute; seventy-four and half-blind, he had had a visit from John Williams, in whom more than anyone else the early ideas and achievements of the Guild were embodied, 'and we agreed—well, we agreed that those early years were wonderful, and you filled them'.[10] In 1939 Ashbee heard from William Cameron, son of Arthur the Cockney enameller, who was now grown old, withdrawn and cynical; his son wrote to excuse his silence: 'the collapse of the Guild was *his* collapse too. He was never the same again, and he was unable to discuss his trade without flavouring his words with bitterness regarding conditions in the trade shops. It was, in your own words, nearer to Utopia than any of you realised at the time.'[11] And if these memories seem a little rosy, there are the recollections of Ashbee's secretary, Phoebe:

I have read *hundreds* of letters from young people (now grown old) thanking him for the way he influenced their lives and opened their eyes to the beauty of things. Many of these letters were from people whom I *know* hated and feared him in their youth, but in later years realized how much they owed him, simply by living near, or working for him or with him.[12]

There were times, of course, when ideal and reality were very far apart, and no one was better placed to feel that than Alec Miller, the most idealistic of Ashbee's craftsmen. 'The "Guild" was never a real Guild since it became a company,' he told Ashbee in 1911,

had you been a man in the shops and known the men who composed the Guild not only as men but as workmen and co-operative partners you would have seen that there was no real Guild, at least since I knew it in 1902. Most of the Guildsmen as I saw to my disgust very quickly after I came . . . regarded the 'Guild' as a nuisance—and indeed many said it was a kind of myth to keep up which the office deducted the percentage every wages day.[13]

Perhaps he was right; success and numbers probably did blur the idealism of the Guild after 1900. But when Miller took a longer view, writing his account of Ashbee and the Guild during the Second World War, he saw things differently.

Freedom has been described—was it by Tawney, or Graham Wallas?—as 'the opportunity of continual personal initiative in the service of the community'. Well, the Guild seemed to me to be the home of just this kind of freedom, freedom and pleasure in one's work, and idyllic and beautiful surroundings; what more could one desire or hope for? There was presently opened to me in the Guild an entrancing and wholly new kind of life, in which it is now difficult to separate the various elements—the strange and romantic beauty of the Cotswolds, the absorbing interest of work, the widening intellectual life into which we of the Guild were introduced, the sense that we were a group enthused by a common aim, and directed by one who though in complete authority over our working days was yet approachable and with whom it was easy to be on friendly and even affectionate terms. This sodality was something entirely new in my life, and the sense of it remains as the greatest gift of the Guild, a gift which went beyond Guildsmen and left a permanent impression on a generation.[14]

Ashbee's work as a designer should be seen in this Guild context first of all, as part of the workshop, for he was always more interested in the life of the Guild than in the wares they produced, and sometimes spoke as if the value of those wares lay not in their usefulness or their beauty, but in the fact that they came from the hands of his craftsmen. Like other Arts and Crafts designers, he left the hammer-marks on his metalwork partly to give this suggestion. Some of his emblems were meant to show it too: the pink most obviously and the Craft of the Guild (its voyage of exploration), the winged youth (image of the imagination) and the Fair Tree of Human Art. The simplicity of some of his butter dishes and decanters was probably dictated as much by workshop considerations as by taste: the newest recruit could show himself proficient with them. Ashbee's designs lent themselves, in these respects, to his larger purposes, and the two sides of his endeavour, the social and the aesthetic, converged at these points. Even some of the puzzling and unsatisfactory aspects of the Guild's work, such as the variety of its designs and their unevenness in quality and execution, have a value as documents of his social experiment. It is not that Ashbee was always careless of technique or design; it was just that he was interested in growth and experience, and the tentative efforts of a new apprentice meant as much to him as the finished work of a skilled craftsman; he was happy to present both as the work of the Guild. The humble beaten copper bowl had its own story, just as much as the intricate, exquisite pendant; this was, or hoped to be, human and expressive craftsmanship such as Ruskin had seen on the carved capitals of Venice, with all their imperfections.

We have watched him change and grow as a designer in different lines of work; and a common pattern has emerged. At first his work was awkward in its proportions, and he had no settled direction, not surprisingly, for he had no apprenticeship in design; the influence of exemplars was obvious in his details and he depended a good deal on the work of others. The Magpie and Stump inside and out, repoussé copperwork including Pearson's, and the silver portrait medallions, are good examples of this phase, and it had as much in common with the taste of the 1880s and the Aesthetic movement as with the Arts and Crafts. Then he narrowed his choices, limited his designs to a few elements, and found his true direction. It happened first in jewellery in the early 1890s, with the unambitious brooches and pendants; in other cases it happened in the mid- to late 1890s, with the country materials and treatments in his houses on Cheyne Walk, the squared-off joinery, metalwork and inlays in his furniture, and the plain hammered silver, enamels, coloured stones and wirework in his tableware. In this phase the exemplars are felt less in the details than in the overall character of the designs and their associations (vernacular townscape behind his Chelsea houses, *varguenos* behind his desks). This mature phase produced a large number of distinctive designs despite, or perhaps because of, the fewness of their elements; and it suggests that his was the kind of talent which thrives on austerity and a set of limitations. It continued into the Campden years, and in some, though not all, cases it was followed by a third and rather academic stage, as in the houses for Cheyne Walk influenced by English Renaissance and his more massive and learned silver of c. 1906. It need hardly be said that scarcely any of these phases apply to Ashbee's printing.

The best of Ashbee's designs rank with the best of the Arts and Crafts Movement as a whole; and they claim no other standing. Like most Arts and Crafts objects, their appeal was not narrowly aesthetic, not just a matter of formal values; they were expressive. The strength of his architectural work lay in its sense of place, the way it drew on and transposed the historical mood of its surroundings; on Cheyne Walk it is remarkable how the meanings crowd together: the affectation of anonymity, the recollections of riverside Chelsea before the Embankment, those clever, enigmatic facades which seemed to have grown out of the past, and out of necessity. In his silver tableware he addressed the everyday business of eating and drinking, evoked a particular quality in the silver, sheen not sparkle, and placed his ornament just so, sparing and effective. These are classic Arts and Crafts virtues, to which he added, in the slightly mannered lines of his classic designs, a sophistication of his own. Most of his jewellery was slight and simple; but with silver and coloured stones he could conjure up delicate images hovering between insect and flower, and he could rebuke the philistine rich at the same time; the slightly chiding quality in his jewellery was very influential. It would have been enough in the career of any man to have reached this kind of expressive mastery in one medium alone; Ashbee designed for half a dozen or so, and excelled in several. And all the time designing was only one of the things he did, a responsibility squeezed in, heaven knows how, between singing and swimming, lecturing and travelling, writing poetry and sitting on committees, dining out in Chelsea and long winter evenings spent writing up the Journals, a bird's-eye view of the spreading country of his mind, well stocked with incident.

The range and variety of his activities were one of the most impressive things about him. Simply from the point of view of the historian, it is remarkable how he touched on so many different sides of British cultural and intellectual life at the turn of the century; he is of interest to the historian of architecture and of design, of social reform, technical education, homosexuality, conservation, the folk-song revival, University Extension, 'Back to the Land', pacifism, town planning, Jerusalem under the British Mandate and America seen through English eyes. Some of this was accident, much of it was the result of his continual, obstinate and important resistance to the pressures of specialization, his protest against people and institutions who pursue limited goals without thought of their wider consequences, and particularly against that arch-specialization, the belief that the end and aim of economic life is making money. He saw the connections between things. He would not just be an architect, he would also be a builder. He could not accept that he had no more to do with the craftsmen of the Guild of Handicraft once the workshops had closed for the night. And he could not lecture to just any University Extension audience, could not bear to be parcelled up as 'culture'. There were dangers, of course, in his many-sidedness. He could overstretch himself as a designer, as he did in the Essex House Press, could be Jack-of-all-trades and master of none; and he could be muddled and pretentious as a writer.[15] One does not always feel with Ashbee, as with comparable figures of great versatility, like William Morris or Eric Gill, that there was a driving inspiration, a single point of view which makes sense of all his manifold activities.

But there was such a point of view, not easy for Ashbee to express, not easy for others to grasp, in which the craftsman and his work are inseparable. He came close to expressing it clearly in 1890, when he wrote of the School of Handicraft:

Our object is not to create a *dilettante* and ephemeral School that shall be pretty and winning, and be supported on the passing charity of West End culture; its existence determined by the margin of spare time which we, and our friends looking kindly on us, are enabled from the more earnest calls of life to yield it—*the School of a hobby*; our ideal is to create a School whose life shall depend upon what is the only living thing—the Life of Workmanship . . .[16]

That is what makes his work of lasting interest, the sense that the sources of creativeness are in ordinary life and in work. It was the experience of the craftsmen which mattered in the Guild; it was the life of the citizens which should be expressed in a town plan, as Ashbee understood it; he cared about the people for whom historic buildings were to be saved, not just the buildings. And he did not care if Ben Jonson's verse was crucified on the lips of his apprentices, so long as they saw things in a fresh light after the performance. Ideas of life, work and art were neighbours in Ashbee's mind, and he made connections between them, simple and important connections.

He lived his life in the service of these ideas, always wanting to make the world a better place. That was a kind of mental armour that he had put on at Cambridge, perhaps to protect himself against things he could not face or understand; and gradually it came to fit him easily and could not be taken off; it became a part of his character. At dinner parties and at committee meetings he was apt to be a little stagey, and so sometimes seemed obsessive, even arrogant, to colleagues and acquaintances, people who did not know him very well. To his family, close friends and comrades, he showed another side, generous, undogmatic, even elusive. He had an extraordinary power of getting to know people, particularly the young, of drawing them out, and making them feel, however great the gap of age or circumstances, that they were worth listening to. In small, close, chosen circles, in the East End more easily than the West, among the Guildsmen more easily than among professional colleagues and the middle class, he was relaxed and happy, an inspiration to his friends.

If he wanted to protect himself it was partly because of the difficulties of his emotional life. We do not know what happened in that mysterious passage of arms between Ashbee and his father in 1882; but however much support he may have received from his mother and Charles Kegan Paul it cannot have been easy. A few years later he faced the strangeness of his own homosexuality, and made an honest place for it despite the intense pressures of society. He was, morally speaking, a self-made man. And then, in those honest and frighteningly cool letters to Janet of 1897, he began to take another path. The note his wooing struck was surely false, but his instinct in choosing her was true. Janet, with her more robust intelligence, could qualify his egotism; he knew it and he welcomed it almost despite himself. In the end he allowed himself to be made over by her need for love. Though there were frustrations for him in those years before and during the First World War, when his schemes seemed to be getting nowhere and babies had usurped his hearth, he was better with Janet than by himself, more tender, less precious.

His energy and optimism were extraordinary and there was always a kind of undergraduate spring to his life. His success in starting a new, original and ambitious little organization in 1888 was perhaps due to the energy of youth. But twenty years later much of that experiment was in ruins; he sat down and within six months had written a book explaining the problem and its solutions, turning his difficulties to polemical account; and within another three months he had worked out a scheme for smallholdings that would put the Guildsmen back on their feet; that was extraordinary. The First World War put paid to this and all his other schemes; he could have given up that stage without reproach. But there he was, in the spring of 1919, aged fifty-six, sailing out to Jerusalem to begin all over again, his intellectual nerves a-tingle at the prospect of work and idealism.

One of the last images of Ashbee is a small water-colour drawing made by the artist and writer William Gaunt in 1937 (Plate 203). Gaunt had gone with John Betjeman to the Art Workers' Guild to hear Ashbee lecture on 'The Dartington Hall Experiment'. In his drawing, some of the Guildsmen seem to have nodded off, but Ashbee was alive, irrepressible, arguing no doubt for the continued relevance of his own ideas. The high brow and the little beard, the unquenchable idealism, suggested an idea to Gaunt and he made the lecturer's pointer a little longer, like a lance.[17] This is Ashbee at seventy-four, as Don Quixote, old, a little feeble, but undaunted.

203. Ashbee lecturing; a detail from *Art. Workers Guild Meeting, May 1937,* a drawing by William Gaunt.

NOTES TO THE TEXT

ABBREVIATIONS AND CONVENTIONS

The place of publication is London, unless otherwise specified.

Where a footnote to a quotation contains several references, the first reference is to the source of the quotation.

The Ashbee Journals have recently been rebound by King's College Library, Cambridge, and are now for the first time fully paginated. Unfortunately, my research was done too early to take advantage of this, and I have had to refer to items in the Journals by date. The Journals are arranged in a workable but not always exact chronological order; and the system of referring by date is therefore sometimes imprecise. Also, some items in the Journals are dated, and others are not; simple references by date are therefore ambiguous, sometimes serving to *identify* an item with that date on it, sometimes serving only to *locate* an item at that point in the chronological sequence. I apologize in advance to anyone who has difficulty in tracing the passages I have referred to.

The various sets of 'The Ashbee Memoirs' are not identical. My references are to the set in the Library of the Victoria and Albert Museum.

The Library of the Victoria and Albert Museum contains a set of four photograph albums formerly belonging to Ashbee, known as 'The Ashbee Collection'. They are not numbered in a sequence, but I have referred to them as volumes 1–4, and this numbering relates to the Library's accession numbers as follows: vol. 1: x.716. 64—1959; vol. 2: x.716. 65—1959; vol. 3: x.716. 66—1959; vol. 4: x.716. 67—1959. Volume 3 is not paginated; volume 4 is only partly paginated.

Objects shown at the exhibitions organized by the Arts and Crafts Exhibition Society are identified by the abbreviation A&CES, followed by the year of the exhibition, followed by the catalogue number, thus: A&CES:1888:454.

Objects which have passed through the sale rooms recently are referred to by the name of the auctioneers, followed by the date of the sale, followed by the catalogue number, thus: Sotheby's Belgravia 7 Dec 1979: no. 127.

The following abbreviations have been used for sources referred to often in the notes:

A	*The Architect*
A&CES	The Arts and Crafts Exhibition Society
AJ	*The Art Journal*
American Sheaves	C. R. Ashbee, *American Sheaves and English Seed Corn* (London and New York, 1901)
AR	*The Architectural Review*
Ashbee Collection	A set of four photograph albums known as 'The Ashbee Collection', V&A Library
B	*The Builder*
BN	*The Building News*
Chapters	C. R. Ashbee, *A Few Chapters in Workshop Re-Construction and Citizenship* (1894)
Cheltenham	Cheltenham Art Gallery and Museums, *C. R. Ashbee and the Guild of Handicraft* (Catalogue of an exhibition 1981)
CMAF	*The Cabinet Maker and Art Furnisher*

Cottages	C. R. Ashbee, *A Book of Cottages and Little Houses* (1906)
CPL	Chelsea Public Library, London
Craftsmanship	C. R. Ashbee, *Craftsmanship in Competitive Industry* (London and Chipping Campden, 1908)
CT	Drawings, etc., in the possession of the Campden Trust
DES	Department of External Studies, Oxford University
DK	*Dekorative Kunst* (Munich)
DSR	District Surveyor's Returns for South Chelsea, Greater London Record Office
Endeavour	C. R. Ashbee, *An Endeavour towards the teaching of John Ruskin and William Morris* (1901)
FA	Papers in the possession of Felicity Ashbee
FA Jerusalem	Papers in the possession of Felicity Ashbee relating to Ashbee's work in Jerusalem
GLRO	Greater London Record Office
'Grannie'	C. R. Ashbee, 'Grannie': A Victorian Cameo (Privately printed, 1939)
GWRB	'Guild Workshop Record Book Sept. 89', an album of drawings and photographs, V&A Library
HSA	The Diaries of Henry Spencer Ashbee, in the possession of Felicity Ashbee
J	The Ashbee Journals, King's College Library, Cambridge
Jerusalem 1918–1920	C. R. Ashbee (ed.), *Jerusalem 1918–1920: Being the Records of the Pro-Jerusalem Council during the Period of the British Military Administration* (1921)
Jerusalem 1920–1922	C. R. Ashbee (ed.), *Jerusalem 1920–1922: Being the Records of the Pro-Jerusalem Council during the First Two Years of the Civil Administration* (1924)
JJ Coll	The John Johnson Collection of Printed Ephemera, Bodleian Library, Oxford
KCC	The Library, King's College, Cambridge
K und K	*Kunst und Kunsthandwerk* (Vienna)
LCC	London County Council
'Letters'	'Letters from William Morris, Walter Crane . . ., etc.', V&A Library
LSC	Archives of the London Survey Committee, Greater London Record Office
MA	*The Magazine of Art*
MDR	The Middlesex Deeds Register, Greater London Record Office
'Memoirs'	'The Ashbee Memoirs' (Typescripts, *c.* 1934), V&A Library
MES	C. R. Ashbee, *Modern English Silverwork* (1909)
MGH	Minutes of the Guild of Handicraft, V&A Library
Miller	Alec Miller, 'C. R. Ashbee and the Guild of Handicraft' (Typescript, *c.* 1941) V&A Library
MSH	Minutes of the School of Handicraft, V&A Library
Palestine Notebook	C. R. Ashbee, *A Palestine Notebook 1918–1923* (1923)
PRO	The Public Record Office, London
'Rachel'	Janet Ashbee, 'Rachel' (Typescript, *c.* 1908) in the possession of Felicity Ashbee
Report	C. R. Ashbee, *A Report by Mr. C. R. Ashbee to the Council of the National Trust . . . on his visit to the United States* (1901)
RIBA	The Royal Institute of British Architects, London
S	*The Studio*
SWS	C. R. Ashbee, *Should We Stop Teaching Art* (1911)
Transactions	C. R. Ashbee (ed.), *Transactions of the Guild & School of Handicraft. Vol. I.* (1890)
Treatises	C. R. Ashbee (trans.), *The Treatises of Benvenuto Cellini on Goldsmithing and Sculpture* (1898)
V&A	The Victoria and Albert Museum, London
WGC	C. R. Ashbee, *Where the Great City Stands: A Study in the New Civics* (1917)

The various catalogues and brochures issued by the Guild of Handicraft are referred to by an alphabetical sequence, catalogue A, catalogue B and so on, as follows:

A   *The Guild of Handicraft, Essex House, Mile End Road, Bow, London, E. Illustrations of some of its works* [c. 1895]. 16 pages.

B   [Illustrated catalogue 1897]. 4 pages.

C   *A Set of Illustrations of the Works of the Guild of Handicraft, Limited, at Essex House, Bow, E.* [c. 1898]. 14 pages.

D   *A Few Examples of the Guild's Work* [c. 1903]. 32 pages.

E   [A brochure concerning *The Prayer Book of King Edward VII* and the work of the Guild] (1903), 4 pages.

F   *A Few Examples of the Guild's Work* [1904–5]. 72 pages. An enlarged version of catalogue D.

G   [Catalogue of architectural work, interior decoration, furniture, church furnishing and architectural metalwork etc. 1905–6.] 84 pages.

H   [Catalogue of silverwork, jewellery etc. 1905–6.] 80 pages.

I   *Stocktaking sale* [1906]. 16 pages.

J   *Arts and Crafts at Campden* [1906–7]. 20 pages.

K   *Christmas Season, 1907.* 4 pages.

Copies of all these catalogues can be seen in the Library of the Victoria and Albert Museum.

NOTES

CHAPTER ONE
CITIES OF YOUTH AND THOUGHT
1863–1886

1   'Grannie', p. 4.
2   Ibid., p. 7.
3   Ibid.
4   Ibid., pp. 7–8.
5   *Palestine Notebook*, p. ix.
6   'Grannie', pp. 46–7.
7   Kelly and Co., *Post Office London Directory, 1862*. For H. S. Ashbee generally, see *Dictionary of National Biography Volume 22 (Supplement)* (1909).
8   Ms diaries, in two volumes covering the period 1854 and 1873–88, and four volumes devoted to his journey round the world in 1880–1, FA.
9   Birth certificate for C. R. Ashbee.
10 *Dictionary of National Biography*, loc. cit.; for H. S. Ashbee's father's books, see a passing reference in J, 25 Dec 1901.
11 *River Scene with Ruins* is now attributed to Nicholas Thomas Dall.
12 'Grannie', p. 19.
13 HSA, 24 Dec 1874, 20 April and 4 Aug 1876.
14 'Grannie', p. 31.
15 C. R. Ashbee, 'Trivialities of Tom' (Typescript 1940–1), pp. 7–8, V&A Library.
16 For Turle, HSA, 26 Feb 1875; for Reid, 8 June 1875, for Gomme, 7 April 1882; for Graham, with whom Ashbee published *Travels in Tunisia* (1887), 5 Nov 1883–12 Jan 1884; for Crossland, 19 June 1886.
17 'Grannie', p. 50; for Turner see HSA, 29 Nov 1873; for Jefferson, J, 25 Dec 1901.
18 For the Paris branch, see Guy Langham, 'Grandpapa at Hawkhurst' (Typescript, n.d.), p. 50. This is an edition of the diaries of H. S. Ashbee, formerly in the possession of the late Capt. Langham. For visits to bibliophiles in France, see HSA, 8 Nov 1873, 15/25 Sept 1875 and *Dictionary of National Biography*, loc. cit.
19 HSA, 23 July 1877.
20 For the Paris family, information from Felicity Ashbee; for *My Secret Life*, G. Legman, *The Horn Book: Studies in Erotic Folklore and Bibliography* (New York, 1964), pp. 26–45. The slight indications of dates and external circumstances in *My Secret Life*

do not tally with what is known of H. S. Ashbee's life; if *My Secret Life* is true, Ashbee cannot be its author; if it is not true, his authorship can scarcely be inferred from internal evidence. See also Steven Marcus, *The Other Victorians* (1966), pp. 87–97.
21 'Grannie', *passim*. See also J, 25 Dec 1901.
22 HSA, 21 and 27 June 1875.
23 J, 5 Dec 1884; HSA, 7 Jan 1876.
24 HSA, 14 June 1875, 28 Sept 1884, 22 Feb 1885. Ashbee's will refers to books at 4 Gray's Inn Square.
25 'Grannie', pp. 61–2.
26 H. Thomas, 'The Cervantes Collection in the British Museum', *Library*, 1908, vol. 9, pp. 429–43.
27 *Dictionary of National Biography*, loc. cit.; *Notes and Queries*, 1900, vol. 6, pp. 121–2.
28 'Rachel', p. 40.
29 Typescript in the V&A Library.
30 David Newsome, *A History of Wellington College 1859–1959* (1959), Chapter VI.
31 Information from Wellington College archives kindly provided by Mark Baker, archivist; letter from W. Goodchild to Mrs H. S. Ashbee, 16 May 1880, FA.
32 J, 27 June 1886; HSA, 24 Nov 1882. Janet Ashbee gave a broad account of this episode to Sir Nikolaus Pevsner on 25 Nov 1958, see notes of that date among Sir Nikolaus's papers. See also *American Sheaves*, pp. 122–3.
33 'Rachel', p. 41. J, 5 Dec 1884 appears to confirm that C. R. Ashbee was not supported by his father.
34 Dennis Proctor (ed.), *The Autobiography of G. Lowes Dickinson* (1973), p. 65. For the reform of late Victorian Cambridge, see Sheldon Rothblatt, *The Revolution of the Dons: Cambridge and Society in Victorian England* (1968); and for Browning, Ian Anstruther, *Oscar Browning: A Biography* (1983), particularly pp. 85–7.
35 J, 13 June, 31 July and 1 Oct 1884. There are copies of the *May Bee* in the V&A Library.
36 Proctor, op. cit., p. 66. For the article, see J, 31 July and 9 August 1884, and *BN*, 1884, vol. 47, pp. 200–1, though the article is signed 'C.B.A.'.

37 Proctor, op. cit., p. 63; Mark Girouard, *Sweetness and Light: The 'Queen Anne' Movement 1860–1900* (1977), p. 38; for Berry, see *Times*, 19 Aug 1929; for Grant, *Times*, 1 June 1948; and for Headlam, *Dictionary of National Biography 1922–30* (1937).

38 J, 17 Feb 1885.

39 Proctor, op. cit, p. 66.

40 Ibid., p. 68.

41 Ibid., p. 67.

42 C. R. Ashbee, *Socialism and Politics: A Study in the Readjustment of the Values of Life* (1906), p. 4.

43 E. T. Cook and Alexander Wedderburn (eds.), *The Works of John Ruskin* (1903–12), vol. 10, p. 193.

44 J, 13 Sept 1914 and *WGC*, pp. 29–30.

45 May Morris (ed.), *The Collected Works of William Morris* (1910–15), vol. 22, p. 43.

46 Martin J. Wiener, *English Culture and the Decline of the Industrial Spirit 1850–1980* (Cambridge, 1981), *passim*.

47 Letters to Oscar Browning, 7 and 22 Nov 1884, in the Oscar Browning Papers, Hastings Public Library; J, 17 Feb 1885.

48 G. Kitson Clark, 'A Hundred Years of the Teaching of History at Cambridge, 1873–1973', *Historical Journal*, 1973, vol. 16, pp. 535–53; Jean O. McLachlan, 'The Origin and Early Development of the Cambridge Historical Tripos', *Cambridge Historical Journal*, 1947, vol. 9, pp. 78–105; Deborah Wormell, *Sir John Seeley and the Uses of History* (Cambridge, 1980), *passim*.

49 'Trivialities of Tom' (Typescript, 1940–1), p. 2, V&A Library.

50 J, 16 April 1885.

51 Proctor, op. cit., p. 71.

52 Rothblatt, op. cit., p. 226; Sheila Rowbotham, 'The Call to University Extension Teaching 1873–1900', *University of Birmingham Historical Journal*, 1969, vol. 12, pp. 51–71.

53 For School Board elections and Stepniak, J, 1 Nov 1885; for Felix Cobbold, prospective MP for North-West Suffolk, J, 19 Oct 1885.

54 On Carpenter and the socialism of the 1880s, see Sheila Rowbotham and Jeffrey Weeks, *Socialism and the New Life: The Personal and Sexual Politics of Edward Carpenter and Havelock Ellis* (1977).

55 J, 14 May 1885.

56 J, 9 Dec 1885.

57 J, 11 Dec 1885.

58 J, 12 Dec 1885.

59 J, 14 Dec 1885.

60 J, 15 Dec 1885.

61 J, 4 Jan 1886.

62 For Fry, see Frances Spalding, *Roger Fry: Art and Life* (1980).

63 J, 26 June 1886.

64 J, 30 March 1886. The works appear to have been those of J. and J. Beal, manufacturer of spring and butchers' knives, Red Hill Works, Sheffield.

65 J, 31 March 1886. The foundry was that of John Brown and Company, Atlas Steel and Iron Works, Sheffield.

66 J, 18 Sept 1885.

67 J, 29 Sept 1885.

68 For Henrici, see Thieme-Becker, *Allgemeines Lexikon der Bildender Künstler* (Leipzig, 1923), vol. 16.

69 J, 1 April 1886.

70 J, 7 April 1886.

71 J, 27 June 1886.

72 J, 8 July 1886.

73 J, 25 July 1886.

74 In September 1885 he was staying with Arthur Laurie's family in Edinburgh and wrote, apropos of Laurie's sisters, 'I am not very susceptible to the charm of sweet womanhood (or girlhood)—suppose I have not developed yet!' (J, 23 Sept 1885.)

75 Proctor, op. cit, p. 90.

76 Jeffrey Weeks, *Coming Out: Homosexual Politics in Britain, from the Nineteenth Century to the Present* (1977), pp. 1–83. Carpenter preferred to use the word 'homogenic' rather than 'homosexual' because both halves of the word came from a Greek source; Ashbee preferred 'homogenic', and the word perhaps carried for him the special association of comradeship as preached by Whitman and Carpenter.

77 J, 29 July 1886.

CHAPTER TWO
EAST LONDON
1886–1891

1 J, 5 Sept 1886.

2 Ibid.

3 J, 18 Sept 1886.

4 J, 29 Sept 1886.

5 J, *c.* Oct 1886.

6 David Verey, 'George Frederick Bodley: climax of the Gothic Revival' in Jane Fawcett (ed.), *Seven Victorian Architects* (1976), pp. 84–101; J, 8 April 1902.

7 J, Dec 1886.

8 Ibid.

9 Ibid.

10 Morris quoted in Gareth Stedman Jones, *Outcast London: A Study in the relationship between classes in Victorian Society* (Oxford, 1971), p. 294.

11 Arthur P. Laurie, *Pictures and Politics: A Book of Reminiscences* (n.d. [1934]), p. 73.

12 Melvin Richter, *The Politics of Conscience: T. H. Green and his age* (1964).

13 Dame Henrietta Barnett, *Canon Barnett: His Life, Work, and Friends* (1918), vol. 1, pp. 302–11; see also Asa Briggs and Anne Macartney, *Toynbee Hall: The First Hundred Years* (1984).

14 Ibid., p. 301.

15 Ibid., p. 225.

16 Ibid., p. 151.

17 Charles Booth, *Life and Labour of the People in London* (1902), First Series, vol. 1, p. 66.

18 J, 27 June 1886.

19 J, *c.* Oct 1886.

20 Proctor, op. cit, pp. 76–7, 139.

21 J, 15 Nov and 14 Dec 1886.

22 Fourth Annual Report of the Universities' Settlement in East London, 1887, p. 15, GLRO.

23 J, 22 Nov 1886.

24 J, 7 Dec 1886.

25 See, for instance, an undated report of a similar lecture in *Thames Valley Times*, J, 9 Jan 1887.

26 J, 15 Jan 1887.

27 *Endeavour*, p. 2. J, 16 Feb 1887 refers to a Ruskin society and a Ruskin club; it is not clear how these relate to the class.

28 See *Ruskin Reading Guild Journal*, 1889, and *Igrdasil: Journal of the Ruskin Reading Guild 1890–92*; and Brian Maidment, 'Interpreting Ruskin 1870–1914' in John Dixon Hunt and Faith M. Holland (eds.), *The Ruskin Polygon* (Manchester, 1982), pp. 159–70.

29 Undated 'Proposal for the Establishment of a Technical and Art School for East London' at the beginning of 'Letters'. I assume that Ashbee designed the scheme, though there are intriguing references to a burlesque treatment of the story of evolution by Roger Fry, perhaps intended for this scheme; see J, June 1887, Fry to Ashbee; and Ashbee to Fry, 20 July and July 1887, in the Fry Papers, KCC.

30 I know of no drawing or photograph of the scheme. As a preliminary to a recent and sensitive redecoration of the dining-room for Toynbee Hall's centenary, which has partly reinstated the colours of Ashbee's scheme, test strips were taken to investigate the earliest layers of paint. These suggested that the medallions were originally surrounded by leaves, and perhaps also by branches, in crimson on a brownish-red background; and that the medallions were gilded. (See a Conservator's Report of Aug 1984 by Caroe and Martin, architects.) But a full investigation was not possible for lack of funds, and the design of the scheme as a whole is still unknown. One possibility is that the wall was covered with a design of trees in whose branches the medallions hung, as on the cover of GWRB. (Plate 98)

31 'Letters', undated 'Proposal'.

32 J, Jubilee Day 1887.

33 J, 7 July 1887.

34 HSA, 10 July 1887.

35 Ibid., 31 Dec 1887.

36 J, 8 Sept 1887.

37 J, Aug 1887.

38 J, 9 Oct 1887.

39 J, 4 Dec 1887.

40 'Letters', undated 'Proposal'. A letter in the same album from Canon Rawnsley, apparently in answer to this Proposal, suggests that it was printed by December 1887 at least; but most copies seem to have been sent out early in 1888.

41 J, 20 March 1888; cuttings from *Daily Telegraph*, 4 April 1888, *Times*, 9 April 1888, and others in 'Letters'.

42 'Letters', 28 March 1888.

43 *Times*, 25 June 1888 which misquoted Ruskin and, one imagines, the beams.

44 'Letters', advertisement sheet for the School and Guild of Handicraft dated June 1888, List of Subscriptions and Donations, Feb 1889, and List of Subscriptions and Donations, 1890; compared with lists of committee members, associates and subscribers to Toynbee Hall in Third Annual Report of the Universities' Settlement in East London, 1886, GLRO.

45 Barnett, op. cit., vol. 1, pp. 289, 299.

46 Jeremy Blanchet, 'Science, Craft and the State: A Study of English Technical Education and Its Advocates, 1867–1906' (D. Phil. thesis, Oxford University, 1953), pp. 60–92; Gordon Millar, 'Art Schools in England from c. 1864 to 1911' (M.A. thesis, University of East Anglia, 1975), *passim*.

47 'Letters', undated 'Proposal'.

48 Quoted in Gillian Naylor, *The Arts and Crafts Movement* (1971), p. 117.

49 'Letters', prospectus of June 1888; C. G. Leland, 'Education in Industrial Art', *AJ*, 1885, p. 137; and Alfred Harris, 'Home Arts and Industries' in *Transactions of the National Association for the Advancement of Art and Its Application to Industry: Edinburgh Meeting 1889* (1890), pp. 421–31.

50 Minutes of the A&CES, 25 Aug 1887, V&A Library.

51 J, Jan/Feb 1888.

52 *Endeavour*, pp. 1–3 and 15; Ashbee's account does not include Williams among the founding members of the Guild because he assumed that it started in May 1888.

53 J, 9 Feb 1887.

54 *A*, 1889, vol. 42, p. 325—'so dexterous a craftsman as Mr. Pearson'—and *B*, 1889, vol. 57, p. 254 and 1890, vol. 58, p. 373.

55 J, end of Dec 1889. On Pearson and the School of Handicraft, a Circular dated Sept 1890 in 'Letters' lists him as an instructor, but he does not appear in the reports on classes in the Annual Reports of the School for 1888–9 or 1889–90, V&A Library. For working outside the Guild, see MGH, 16 Oct 1890.

56 J, July 1888.

57 See pp. 315–16.

58 Ashbee to Janet Forbes, 7 Oct 1887, FA. Adams was Secretary of the Cabinet Makers' Union in 1890, see a cutting of 30 Sept 1890 in 'Letters'.

59 J, 18 Aug 1888.

60 'Letters', 10 May 1888; Barnett, op. cit., vol. 2, p. 164. The picture and its frame are now in the possession of Manchester City Art Gallery.

61 'Letters', 17 Oct 1888.

62 See GWRB. None of the Guild work appears to survive at Riseholme Hall, which is now used by Lindsey College of Agriculture.

63 MGH, 23 Jan, 11 Feb, 18 March and 1 April 1889.

64 MGH, 12, 6 May 1892.

65 Booth, op. cit, First Series, vol. 1, p. 112.

66 See his response to a Board of Trade enquiry into profit sharing, MGH, 1 Sept 1897, and *Endeavour*, pp. 13–14.

67 'Letters', 19 May 1889. The painting is now in the Lady Lever Art Gallery, Port Sunlight. For the smaller study, now in Birmingham Museum and Art Gallery, Hunt designed a circular frame which was made in repoussé copper by Williams, see *B*, 1890, vol. 58, p. 397.

68 For Phillips going to Abbotsholme, see advertisement sheet of Sept 1889 in 'Letters'; for difficulties, MGH, 2 Jan, 10 April, 1 May and 10 June 1890; Phillips left Abbotsholme in August 1891 and was to be replaced by the metalworker W. A. White; it is not clear how long White was there for. For Ashbee's meeting with Reddie, see J, Oct 1888.

69 As Sir Nikolaus Pevsner noted in *Pioneers of the Modern Movement* (1936), p. 145.

70 *Transactions of the NAAAAI: Edinburgh Meeting 1889* (1890), pp. 451–2, 455, 460. This lecture was also printed as a pamphlet and as part of *Chapters*, see Appendix 4, no. 3.

71 'Letters', 3 Dec 1889.

72 MGH, 21 Nov 1889.

73 *Craftsmanship*, p. 214; J, 30 Jan 1903. When he first joined the Guild Hardiman was given a wage of between nine and eleven shillings a week, see MGH, 2 July 1891.

74 For a fuller account of this phase of Guild metalwork, see Chapter 12.

75 'Letters', First Annual Report of the School of Handicraft, June 1889; see also Fifth Annual Report of the Universities' Settlement in East London, 1889, p. 22, GLRO.

76 'Letters', First Annual Report of the School of Handicraft, June 1889.

77 Laurie, op. cit, p. 75.

78 MSH, 9 Sept 1892.

79 J, end of 1888.

80 Beatrice Webb, *My Apprenticeship* (1926), p. 209; see also Barnett, op. cit, vol. 1, pp. 317–18.

81 J, 29 Jan 1889.

82 Laurie, op. cit, p. 73.

83 J, 25 March 1889.

84 For Llewellyn Smith, see Roger Davidson, 'Sir Hubert Llewellyn Smith and Labour Policy 1886–1916' (Ph.D. thesis, Cambridge University, 1971); for Rogers and Fairfax-Cholmeley, Laurie, op. cit., p. 73 and 81. Hugh Fairfax-Cholmeley later became Master of the Guild of St George, see Edith Hope Scott, *Ruskin's Guild of St. George* (1931), p. 127.

85 'Letters', May 1889.

86 MSH, 8 April 1889.

87 J, 10–23 April 1888.

88 See 'Sketch Book 1880–1889', KCC, almost all of which is devoted to a diary of this Kent trip, with illustrations in pen, pencil and water-colour; also Ashbee to Janet Forbes, 15 Sept 1897, FA.

89 MSH, 8 Oct 1889.

90 'Letters', 17 June 1890.

91 Charles Kegan Paul to Arthur Rogers, 1 Aug 1890, Thorold Rogers Papers, Box 2, folio 416, Bodleian Library, Oxford.

92 The relevant minutes are MGH, 14 and 18 Aug, 12 and 22 Sept and 16 Oct 1890; MSH, 14 and 28 Aug, 24 Sept and 30 Oct 1890; also 'Letters', circulars of Nov 1890 and 3 Nov 1890.

93 MSH, 30 Oct 1890.

94 'Letters', circular of Nov 1890.

95 Davidson, op. cit, p. 29.

96 Prospectus dated 17 Feb 1891 in the possession of Arthur Llewellyn Smith.

97 V. Adoratsky (ed.), *Karl Marx: Selected Works* (1942), vol. 1, p. 236.

98 Stopford Brooke's diary for 9 Nov 1888; I am grateful to Mary Lago for telling me of this passage.

99 Ashbee seems to have been particularly fond of Hubert Baines, who was perhaps never a Guildsman or an apprentice, but was a pupil in the School; and of Walter Taylor, who was an apprentice in 1889 and 1890; see Ashbee to Janet Forbes, 15–16 Oct 1897 and 11 Jan 1898, FA.

100 *Birmingham Post* 27 Sept 1890; Montague Fordham, *The Birmingham Kyrle Society and the Birmingham Guild of Handicraft* (Birmingham, n.d. [1890]), p. 6; Alan Crawford (ed.), *By Hammer and Hand: The Arts and Crafts Movement in Birmingham* (Birmingham, 1984), pp. 30–2.

101 The exact publication date of *Transactions* is uncertain. The title-page has the date 1890, but an advertisement facing the half-title is dated January 1891. Despite its title, no further volumes were issued so far as I know.

102 *Endeavour*, p. 36.

103 Booth, op. cit, Third Series, vol. 1, p. 11.

104 File for the Guild of Handicraft Ltd., PRO. BT31. 8064/58132, indenture dated 26 July 1898.

105 J, March 1900; Miller, p. 50. For the emblematic role of the pink, see pp. 224–5.

CHAPTER THREE
THE NINETIES
1891–1897

1 J, 3 April 1891.
2 Ashbee to F. A. Forbes, 22 Sept 1891, FA.
3 Ibid.; MGH, 6 Feb 1891; *Endeavour*, p. 15.
4 MGH, 2 and 23 July, 19 Oct 1891, 19 Feb, 3 March and 14 April 1892.
5 MGH, 4 Feb and 13 July 1892, and analysis of profit-sharing at 1 Sept 1897; drawings for Bryngwyn in GWRB. The client at Bryngwyn was James Rankin MP; he added a wing to the existing house of 1868 and asked Ashbee to furnish the interior.
6 MGH, 23 June, 26 and 29 Aug, and 3 Sept 1892.
7 Ibid., 8 Sept 1892.
8 See the record of profits at MGH, 1 Sept 1897. 1895 saw neither profit nor loss.
9 *A*, 1891, vol. 46, p. 82; *Times*, 30 June 1891.
10 MSH, 21 May 1891.
11 Blanchet, op. cit, pp. 188–91.
12 MSH, 31 July 1891; *CMAF*, 1892, vol. 13, pp. 51–2.
13 *CMAF*, loc. cit.
14 School of Handicraft, Fourth Annual Report, V&A Library.
15 'Statement relating to the School of Handicraft', Jan 1891, in School of Handicraft, Annual Reports 1888–1895, V&A Library; C. R. Ashbee, *A Nine Years' Experiment in Technical Education* ... (1895), p. 9.
16 H. Llewellyn Smith, *Report to the Special Committee on Technical Education* (1892), p. 19.
17 Ashbee, *A Nine Years' Experiment* ..., p. 11.
18 School of Handicraft, Third Annual Report, V&A Library; Ashbee, *A Nine Years' Experiment* ..., pp. 3–4, 11.
19 MSH, 25 Oct 1893.
20 School of Handicraft, Sixth Annual Report, V&A Library.
21 MSH, 30 June 1894.
22 Minutes of the LCC Technical Education Board, 19 Nov 1894, item 6, GLRO; MSH, 30 Jan and 5 Nov 1895.
23 Ashbee, *A Nine Years' Experiment* ..., p. 12; *Endeavour*, p. 10; Llewellyn Smith, op. cit, p. 11. The business connection was given as the reason for the LCC's lack of co-operation by W. Fred in *K und K*, 1900, vol. 3, p. 170.
24 *The Technical Movement in its future relation to the skilled artisan, the elementary teacher and all such as are directly interested in handicraft*, undated leaflet in School of Handicraft, Annual Reports 1888–1895, V&A Library; Minutes of the Joint Board of the London Society for the Extension of University Teaching, 9 Feb 1892, University of London Library.
25 N. A. Jepson, *The Beginnings of English University Adult Education—Policy and Problems* (1973), Chapters 1–10.
26 J, July/Aug 1884, 1 Nov 1885, 4 Jan 1886.
27 *Chapters*, p. 95.
28 Ibid., pp. 93, 114.
29 Minutes of the Joint Board, 9 Feb and 26 March 1892, University of London Library.
30 Syllabus of a course of six lectures on 'Design in its application to Furniture', in the archives of the Department of External Studies, Oxford University (DES). References below to syllabuses, examiner's reports and lecturer's reports are to this archive. The reference to Pugin appears to be an adaptation of the second rule in *The True Principles of Pointed or Christian Architecture* (1841), that 'all ornament should consist of enrichment of the essential construction of the building' (p. 1).
31 Syllabus.
32 Ibid. See also the report of this lecture in *CMAF* 1891–2, vol. 12, pp. 291–2 and 319.
33 Ibid.
34 Examiner's Report.
35 Lecturer's Report.
36 1892–3, vol. 3, pp. 10–11. A revised version of this article appeared as Chapter 9 of *Chapters*.
37 He was T. C. Sutton, J, March 1907.
38 Lecturers' and Examiners' Reports, Autumn 1892, p. 130.
39 Syllabus, p. 12.
40 Ibid.; Examination paper, DES.

41 Lecturers' and Examiners' Reports, Autumn 1892, p. 124.
42 Ibid., Spring 1893, p. 25.
43 Ibid., Autumn 1893, p. 423.
44 Ibid., p. 395.
45 Marriott to Ashbee, 11 July 1898, Letter Book, DES.
46 Correspondence between Ashbee and Marriott, c. June–July 1898 and 23 Nov 1898, Letter Book, DES; Minutes of the University Extension Delegacy, 2 Dec 1898, DES.
47 Jepson, op. cit., pp. 169–76.
48 A marginal exception is that University Extension organizations taught a good many applied science classes in the early 1890s under the Technical Instruction Act, see Jepson, op. cit., pp. 225ff.
49 *The English Catalogue of Books 1890–1897* (1898), p. 46.
50 *Chapters*, p. 18.
51 Richter, op. cit., Chapter 11.
52 The obvious and fundamental limitation of Ashbee's ideas, that they did not extend to industries unconnected with the decorative arts, was acknowledged here but only in passing, p. 10.
53 *Chapters*, p. 47.
54 Ibid., p. 19.
55 Ibid., p. 23.
56 These personae seem to be based on real people, but it is not easy to identify them, apart from Barnett. Thomas Trudge may have been based on Tom Jelliffe, an elderly Guild cabinet-maker of great skill, or on Jelliffe and C. V. Adams together, see Miller, p. 14; and Pushington may have been partly based on Sir George Young of Formosa Place, Cookham, Berkshire, a Charity Commissioner who had a good deal to do with higher education, see *Dictionary of National Biography 1922–1930* (1937) and *Who Was Who, 1929–1940* (1967), J, c. 5 Nov 1900 and 7 June 1901, and *Chapters*, p. 93.
57 *Chapters*, pp. 160–1.
58 Edward Carpenter, *The Intermediate Sex* (fourth edition 1916), pp. 116 and 146–7.
59 Jeffrey Weeks, *Coming Out* (1977), pp. 118–25 and J, 1 Nov 1899.
60 Weeks, op. cit, pp. 118 and 133.
61 Timothy d'Arch Smith, *Love in Earnest* (1970), pp. xix, 59–65.
62 So Ashbee told Alec Miller in a letter of 5 March 1905, FA.
63 Ibid. Ashbee wrote a manuscript called 'Confessio Amantis' which would probably have told us more about the homosexual side of his life. It certainly referred to Hugh Holmes Gore whom Ashbee met at Millthorpe in October 1888 and who seems to have been homosexual; he visited 'The Ding's Club' in Bristol which Gore ran; the Guild of Handicraft published *The Ding's Song Book* for Gore in about 1894; and when Gore was involved in some kind of scandal in 1899 Ashbee wrote him a letter of sympathy and support, see J, 17 Jan 1899; and a letter from Alec Miller to Felicity Ashbee of 27 April 1958 concerning the 'Confessio', which was destroyed by Ashbee's literary executors.
64 Roland W. Paul, *Vanishing London* (1894), p. 21 and plate 40; Ernest Godman, *The Old Palace of Bromley-by-Bow* (1902); C. R. Ashbee (ed.), *The Survey of London: Volume 1: The Parish of Bromley-by-Bow* (1900), pp. xxxiii, 38–9; letter from T. F. Moberley to Ashbee, 17 June 1894, LSC; *B*, 1894, vol. 66, p. 239; Society for the Protection of Ancient Buildings, Report 1894, pp. 20–3.
65 In the introduction to Godman, op. cit., p. 9.
66 E.G., *Chapters*, pp. 18–19, all published material of the Watch Committee and, most picturesquely, in his song 'The Old Palace of Bow' in *The Essex House Song Book* (1903–5), X-30.
67 Jane Fawcett (ed.), *The Future of the Past: attitudes to conservation 1174–1974* (1976), pp. 17–24.
68 G. Baldwin Brown, *The Care of Monuments* (1905), Part 2.
69 Circular dated March 1894, tipped into the Minute Book of the Watch Committee, LSC.
70 *B*, 1894, vol. 66, pp. 239–40.
71 Correspondence, 17 June, June and 18 June 1894, LSC.
72 Minute Book of the Watch Committee, 25 June 1894, LSC.
73 Correspondence, 21 July 1894, LSC.
74 Correspondence, 25 Aug 1894. For the allocation of districts, see Minute Book, 2 July 1894, LSC.

75 *AJ*, 1894, p. 156; Minute Book, 10 Sept 1894, LSC.

76 Correspondence, 3 Oct 1894, 20 March 1895; Minute Book, 17 April 1895, LSC. There are a number of completed survey sheets surviving in LSC, filled in by Ashbee and Godman.

77 Trinity Hospital was bombed in 1941, and has since been restored and modernized.

78 J, 30 June 1901. The letters to the press stimulated by Ashbee are mostly reprinted in Ashbee, *The Trinity Hospital in Mile End* (1896), pp. 25–33. For the campaign, see Minute Book, 19 Nov 1895, LSC, and *Times*, 28 Nov 1895.

79 In the Trinity Hospital case *Times*, 28 Nov 1895 reported that Murray did not wish to hear evidence on grounds of aesthetics or public interest, but *Daily Chronicle* of the same date said that he felt architectural and historical matters might have a bearing. For Emmanuel Hospital, see National Trust, Report, March–July 1896, pp. 5, 20–3.

80 It was published in 1896 as the first Monograph of the Committee.

81 Ashbee, *The Trinity Hospital in Mile End*, p. 16.

82 Ibid., prefatory note.

83 Correspondence, 7 May 1896, LSC.

84 LCC, Minutes of Proceedings, 21 Jan 1896, 23 Feb and 27 July 1897. The turning point in the Council's attitude to the recording of historic buildings seems to have been the conference with interested societies organized by the General Purposes Committee on 4 Dec 1896, see *B*, 1897, vol. 72, p. 202.

85 A statement from the Committee in 1900 spoke of some 2,000 drawings, photographs and sketches 'arranged in great albums'. (*Builder's Journal and Architectural Record*, 1900, vol. 11, p. 464.) I have not located anything like this number of drawings etc., nor any albums. Topographical drawings by Varley and Godman, with some of the Committee's early photographs and measured drawings passed to the National Monuments Record, presumably in 1965 when the Committee was wound up. Some early measured drawings seem to have passed to the London Society, and there are early photographs of Chelsea in GLRO.

86 J, 22 Oct 1899.

87 Minute Book, 19 April 1900, and Fourth Report of the Committee in Minute Book, 21 June 1900, LSC. For Gomme, see *Times*, 25 Feb 1916, and his *Lectures on the Principles of Local Government* (1897). His son Austin was a pupil in Ashbee's architectural office from *c.* 1896.

88 Ashbee (ed.), *The Survey of London: Volume 1* (1900). p. xxviii.

89 Ibid., p. xxxvi.

90 Society for the Protection of Ancient Buildings, Report 1899, pp. 41–2, and 1898, pp. 23–5.

91 Minute Book, 21 June 1900, LSC. The earliest use of the long title I have found is on the menu for a supper on 19 May 1897 in Minute Book, 13 April 1897, LSC. It would be interesting to know whether the use of the word 'Survey' reflected the influence of Patrick Geddes whose work in Edinburgh Ashbee was certainly aware of.

92 Minute Book, 13 December 1906, LSC; see also W. H. Godfrey's useful account 'The London Survey Committee, 1894–1952', *London Topographical Record*, 1958, vol. 21, pp. 79–92.

93 F. H. W. Sheppard, 'Sources and Methods used for the Survey of London' in H. J. Dyos (ed.), *The Study of Urban History* (1968), pp. 131–3.

94 J, 20 March 1896.

95 Walt Whitman, *The Complete Poems* (Harmondsworth 1975), pp. 96–7.

96 Oxford University Extension, Fifth Summer Meeting ... Timetable of Lectures and Programme ... 1892, DES; for Rolfe see Peter Stansky, 'C. R. Ashbee visits Stanford University', *The Imprint of the Stanford Libraries Associates* 1977, vol. 3, pp. 16–23; and further information kindly supplied by Professor Stansky.

97 Cutting from the *Reading Herald* 24 March 1896, in J, Ashbee's syllabus, of which there is a copy in the Library of Congress, Washington, and J, 13 April 1896.

98 J, 23–4 March 1896.

99 J, 28 March 1896.

100 J, 25 March 1896.

101 J, *c.* 8 April 1896.

102 J, 10 April 1896.

103 E. T. Cook and Alexander Wedderburn (eds.), *The Works of John Ruskin* (1903–12), vol. 35, p. 521; J, 21 April 1896.

104 J, *c.* 21 April 1896.

105 J, 23 April 1896,

106 Ibid.

107 J, 27 April 1896.

108 J, 30 April 1896.

109 J, *c.* 1 May 1896.

110 J, 11 May 1896.

111 J, 2 May 1896.

112 Architectural drawings and papers relating to 115–16 Cheyne Walk in CPL, particularly a 'Plan on Indenture of Conveyance dated 4 May 1896', various drawings for Guild of Handicraft workshops on the site, and a draft letter to G. L. Gomme, 1 April 1901.

113 Quoted in Mrs E. T. Cook, *Highways and Byways in London* (1903), p. 225.

114 Charles Booth, *Life and Labour of the People in London* (1902–3), Third Series, vol. 3, p. 111.

115 Cook, op. cit, p. 223.

116 William Rothenstein, *Men and Memories . . . 1872–1900* (1931), p. 167.

117 Ibid.

118 New English Art Club. *Catalogue of the first Winter Exhibition of Modern Pictures . . . 1891*, nos. 117, 118.

119 *Who's Who in Architecture*, 1914, p. 16; Ashbee's application papers for Fellowship of the RIBA, RIBA Library; Register of Fees Paid, 9 March, 27 May and 30 Nov 1893, Slade School of Art.

120 Letter from Abbey to E. A. Walton, 1 Dec 1896, FA; information from T. H. Hancock, Chelsea Arts Club.

121 J, 26 Feb 1915.

122 Notes by Sir Nikolaus Pevsner on a meeting with Janet Ashbee and Felicity Ashbee, 25 Sept 1958, among Sir Nikolaus's papers.

123 The eyeglass did not survive long enough to be remembered by his children. It was referred to in J, 1 Nov 1899 and may have been a temporary remedy for the strain caused by working on his typeface, Endeavour. Ashbee's Hungarian friend, Zsombor de Szász, also thought he looked like Whistler, see *Magyar Iparmüvészet* (Budapest), 1910, vol. 13, p. 62.

124 'Grannie', p. 61.

125 Phoebe Haydon, 'The Memoirs of a Faithful Secretary' (Typescript, n.d.), p. 1, FA; for a fuller account of the interior of the Magpie and Stump, see pp. 297–30.

126 Agnes exhibited with La Libre Esthétique in Brussels in 1901, see Octave Maus, *Trente Années de lutte pour l'art* (Brussels, 1926), p. 255.

127 For Brett, 'Memoirs', vol. 7, p. 289; for Elsa, 'Rachel', p. 43. The account of Janet Forbes's early life which follows is mainly based on 'Rachel', her autobiographical novel.

128 'A Modern Morality Play' (Typescript [1895]), KCC.

129 Felicity Ashbee, 'Nevill Forbes, 1883–1929: Some Family Letters from Russia', *Oxford Slavonic Papers*, 1976, vol. 9, pp. 79–90.

130 Janet Forbes's journal, 28 Feb 1896, FA.

131 Ibid., 15 Oct 1896.

132 'Rachel', p. 44.

133 Letter of 28 April 1897, FA.

134 Letter of 2 September 1897, FA.

CHAPTER FOUR
SUCCESS
1897–1902

1 'Rachel', pp. 49–50.

2 Letter of 4 Sept 1897, FA.

3 Letters from Ashbee to Mrs H. S. Ashbee, *c.* 2 Sept and 9 Sept 1897, FA.

4 Letter of 15 Sept 1897, FA.

5 Letter of 11 Jan 1898, FA.

6 Letter to Janet of 1 Oct 1897, FA; MGH, 24 Sept, 2 and 17 Oct 1897; information from Anthony S. Heal.

7 Janet to Ashbee, 3–5 Oct 1897, and Ashbee's reply, 7 Oct 1897, both FA.

8 Simeon Samuels, 'My appreciation of C. R. Ashbee' (Typescript, *c.* 1950), p. 2, FA.

9 J, *c.* 15 July 1901.

10 Letters of 29 Oct and 8 Nov 1897, FA.

11 Ashbee to Janet, 25 Nov 1897, FA.

12 30 Nov 1897, FA; invitation for the performance at the Magpie and Stump, 6 July 1897, JJ Coll.

13 Janet to Ashbee, 25 (28?) Dec 1897, FA.

14 Ashbee to Janet, 31 Dec 1897, FA.

15 Ibid.; for the clocks, see original designs in GWRB and executed work in *DK*, 1899, vol. 4, pp. 14–15.

16 Letter of 11 Jan 1898, FA.

17 Walter Crane to Ashbee, 19 Feb 1898, FA; correspondence 20 March 1898, LSC; Ashbee to Janet, 2 and 18 March 1898, FA.

18 Wolverhampton Art and Industrial Exhibition, *Catalogue of the Exhibits in the Fine Art Section* (Wolverhampton, 1902); Ray Watkinson, *William Morris as Designer* (1967), p. 52. See also the fuller account of Hodson's collections and his part in the setting up of the Essex House Press in pp. 375–6.

19 Ashbee seems to have met Hodson in the early 1890s, see J, 14 Dec 1902.

20 Letter of March 1898, FA.

21 Miller, p. 148; Henry Osborn to the author, 4 March 1982.

22 Letters to Janet, 4 May and May 1898, FA.

23 Letter of 30 Jan 1898, FA.

24 MGH, 29 Jan 1898.

25 *Endeavour*, p. 15.

26 MGH, 6 Feb 1891, 28 Nov 1896, 30 April 1897; letter from Ashbee to Janet, 29 Oct 1897, FA; PRO. BT31. 8064/58132; Marriott is included in a list of Ashbee's pupils and apprentices loose at the end of MGH, volume 2, V&A Library.

27 'Memorandum and Articles of Association of The Guild of Handicraft (Limited)' items 3(c) and 66(a), PRO. BT31. 8064/58132. The 2½% deduction was already in force, see MGH, 4 Aug 1897.

28 Summary of capital and shares, 22 Aug 1898, PRO. BT31. 8064/58132.

29 See Chapter 15.

30 *Endeavour*, p. 25; J, Jan 1900.

31 'Rachel', pp. 53–6; Ashbee to Mrs H. S. Ashbee, 9 Sept 1898, FA.

32 Ashbee to Mrs H. S. Ashbee, 9 Sept 1898, FA, and another letter to Mrs H. S. Ashbee, 21 Sept 1898, FA; also 'Rachel', p. 58.

33 J, 1 Oct 1898.

34 J, 16 Oct 1898.

35 Ashbee to Janet, 11 Jan 1898, FA.

36 'Rachel', pp. 57–8.

37 Mary Newbery Sturrock in a letter to Fiona MacCarthy, 15 July 1981; for Sun Court, J, 22 Oct 1901.

38 'Rachel', pp. 57–8.

39 J, 8 Dec 1901; for Read see *Craftsmanship*, p. 228; for Jelliffe see Miller, p. 14; for Curtis, Henry Osborn to the author, 4 March 1982.

40 J, March 1900.

41 J, Aug 1901.

42 J, 30 Jan 1903.

43 Ibid.

44 J, 20 Feb 1902.

45 J, 9 Dec 1901.

46 Ibid., and information from William Cameron.

47 J, 14 Nov 1901.

48 Ibid.

49 J, 13 Aug 1899 and 16–25 Aug 1901.

50 J, Nov 1901.

51 Miller, p. 5; and for Ashbee sketching interviewees, Phoebe Haydon, 'First Impressions' (Typescript, n.d.), FA.

52 There was such, of course, see A. L. Lloyd, *Folk Song in England* (1967), Chapter 5. But Lloyd's 'industrial songs' were almost all from mining and textile areas in the North of England.

53 'Rachel', pp. 59–61; J, 30 Jan 1903. For slices of mutton, Simeon Samuels, 'My appreciation of C. R. Ashbee' (Typescript, *c.* 1950), p. 2, FA.

54 Introduction, pp. x–xi.

55 Report to the vicar and churchwardens, 31 Jan 1899, Horndon-on-the-Hill parish chest.

56 It was Walter Crane who first thought of the masque, and he had been involved in similar productions, notably 'The Masque of Painters', a series of *tableaux vivants* put on in 1885 by the Royal Society of Painters in Watercolour; see Julian Treuherz, 'A Victorian tableau vivant', *Connoisseur*, 1979, vol. 200, pp. 28–33.

57 C. R. Ashbee, Walter Crane, Selwyn Image, C. H. Townsend, Christopher Whall and Henry Wilson, *Beauty's Awakening: A Masque of Winter and of Spring* (1899), p. 28.

58 Selwyn Image's diary, 2, 4, 5, 9, 16 March 1899, Bodleian Library, Oxford, MS. Eng. misc. d.349; undated letter from Whall to Ashbee, J, *c.* June 1899.

59 J, 9 May 1899.

60 J, July 1899 and 10 January 1901.

61 C. R. Ashbee, *From Whitechapel to Camelot* (1892) is dedicated to the five boys of the first river expedition.

62 J, 13 Aug 1899.

63 S, 1899–1900, vol. 18, p. 119.

64 S, loc. cit, pp. 118–26; *Artist*, 1899, vol. 26, p. 179.

65 It was performed once again, at Charterhouse. For Poel, see Fiona MacCarthy, *The Simple Life: C. R. Ashbee in the Cotswolds* (1981), p. 139.

66 J, Dec 1899.

67 Programme, JJ Coll.

68 J, 7–11 Jan 1900.

69 J, 11 Dec 1899 and Dec 1899/Jan 1900. For arguments against the view that the Fabians did not care about the arts, see Ian Britain, *Fabianism and Culture* (Cambridge, 1982).

70 J, 26 Jan 1900, 14 Feb 1902, June 1900, May 1901.

71 For the Spottiswoode family, see Walter Crane, *An Artist's Reminiscences* (1907), pp. 189–91.

72 This was probably the Healthy and Artistic Dress Union; Janet and Gwendolen were on the committee in 1906.

73 J, 22 Feb 1903; obituary of Gerald Bishop, FA.

74 'Rachel', p. 64.

75 Advertisement for the opening of the shop, May 1899, JJ Coll.; Guild of Handicraft Limited, Annual Report for 1899, V&A Library.

76 Letter of 22 March 1900, FA.

77 J, Easter 1900.

78 Henry Spencer Ashbee's will; probate was granted on 21 Sept 1900.

79 Alec Miller to Felicity Ashbee, 14 Dec 1951, FA.

80 J, 25 Dec 1901.

81 J, 3–12 Aug 1900.

82 J, 29 Aug 1900.

83 J, Aug 1900.

84 *American Sheaves*, preface.

85 National Trust, Report for 1899–1900, pp. 23–30.

86 J, 23 Oct 1900.

87 *American Sheaves*, p. 13.

88 Ibid., pp. 10–11.

89 J, 26 Oct 1900.

90 J, 3 Nov 1900.

91 Ibid.

92 Ibid.

93 *Report*, pp. 16–17.

94 'Rachel', pp. 65–6.

95 *Report*, p. 11.

96 J, *c.* 8 Dec 1900.

97 *Chicago Tribune*, 6 Dec 1900.

98 Ibid.

99 See p. 407.

100 *American Sheaves*, pp. 90–2; *Chicago Tribune*, 9 Dec 1900.

101 See the lecture 'The National Trust to the Great Vainglorious City of Chicago', *American Sheaves*, pp. 90–108.

102 Ashbee to Wright, 6 Aug 1934, archives of the Frank Lloyd Wright Foundation, Taliesin West, Arizona.

103 J. *c.* 8 Dec 1900.

104 *Chicago Tribune*, 6 Dec 1900.

105 J, *c.* 8 Dec 1900.

438

106 Ibid.
107 See pp. 11–12, 17–19, 54, 160, 417–20.
108 J, c. 8 Dec 1900; for a sympathetic account of Wright's point of view see Ashbee's article on 'American Architecture' in *Munsey's Magazine* (New York), 1901, vol. 26, pp. 8–9.
109 J, mid-Dec 1900.
110 J, 28 Dec 1900.
111 Ibid.
112 For a fuller account of Janet at East Aurora, see Robert W. Winter, 'American Sheaves from "C.R.A." and Janet Ashbee', *Journal of the Society of Architectural Historians* (Philadelphia), 1971, vol. 30, pp. 317–22.
113 J, mid-Jan 1901; this visit is recalled in *Craftsmanship*, p. 34.
114 *Report*, pp. 4–8, 18–19; Ashbee to Wright, 2 April 1901, archives of the Frank Lloyd Wright Foundation, Taliesin West, Arizona; J, 23 Aug 1901.
115 *Report*, p. 7.
116 J, 3 Feb 1901.
117 Fredson Bowers (ed.), *The Dramatic Works in the Beaumont and Fletcher Canon: Volume 1* (Cambridge, 1966), p. 30.
118 Robert E. Spiller and Alfred R. Ferguson (eds.), *The Collected Works of Ralph Waldo Emerson: Volume I: Nature, Addresses and Lectures* (Cambridge, Mass., 1971), p. 21. The range of ideas implied in the late Victorian cult of the countryside are well described in Avner Offer, *Property and Politics 1870–1914: Land ownership, law, ideology and urban development in England* (Cambridge, 1981), Chapters 20 and 21, and in Jan Marsh, *Back to the Land: The Pastoral Impulse in England, from 1880–1914* (1982).
119 *The Scout: A Journal for Socialist Workers*, 30 March 1895, quoted in David Prynne, 'The Clarion Clubs, Rambling and the Holiday Associations in Britain since the 1890s', *Journal of Contemporary History*, 1976, vol. 11, p. 68.
120 *Endeavour*, pp. 40–1.
121 Jesse Collings, *The Colonisation of Rural Britain* (1914); L. Jebb, *The Small Holdings of England: A Survey of various existing systems* (1907).
122 Richard Soloway, 'Counting the Degenerates: The Statistics of Race Deterioration in Edwardian England', *Journal of Contemporary History*, 1982, vol. 17, pp. 137–64.
123 J, 25 Dec 1901; *AJ*, 1903, pp. 147–8; *Craftsmanship*, p. 11.
124 Indenture of 26 July 1898, PRO. BT31. 8064/58132.
125 Drawings for 115–16 Cheyne Walk and a draft letter to G. L. Gomme, 1 April 1901, CPL; J, 2 Nov 1901. Little Davis Place is now called Apollo Place.
126 'Memoirs', vol. 2, p. 7; for other London locations looked at see *Craftsmanship*, p. 42; MGH, 6 Dec 1901 says twenty-four possible schemes were looked into.
127 Ashbee to Wright, 2 April 1901, archives of the Frank Lloyd Wright Foundation, Taliesin West, Arizona.
128 J, late July 1901.
129 Ibid.
130 Philip Norman, *London Vanished and Vanishing* (1905), p. 144; *Times*, 30 July 1901.
131 J, 16–25 Aug 1901.
132 J, 3 June 1902.
133 Ashbee went back to Campden in September and wrote to Janet that it was 'divine', J, 5 Sept 1901.
134 Prospectus of 18 Oct 1901, JJ Coll.; drawings for 75 Cheyne Walk, RIBA Drawings Collection; *Times*, 18 Oct and 1 Nov 1901.
135 J, 24 Nov 1901.
136 Guild of Handicraft Limited, Annual Report for 1901, V&A Library; MGH, 6 Dec 1901 suggests that, according to Lord Gainsborough's agent, twenty-five houses would become vacant during the coming year.
137 J, 14 Nov 1901.
138 See 'Arrangements proposed by the Board for the removal of the Guild Workshops into the country and an account of the negociations that have led up to this', typescript at MGH, 6 Dec 1901; J, 8 Dec 1901.
139 J, 25 Dec 1901.
140 J, 24 Dec 1901.
141 Ibid.
142 J, Jan 1902.
143 J, 6 March 1902; for Whistler in 74 Cheyne Walk, see Felicity Ashbee, 'Dandy in decline: Whistler's last home', *Country Life*, 1984, vol. 176, pp. 1560–1.

CHAPTER FIVE
THE COTSWOLDS
1902–1908

1 For example, Charles Rowley, *A Workshop Paradise and other Papers* (1905), pp. 1–6.
2 Christopher Whitfield, *A History of Chipping Campden* (Windsor, 1958), *passim*.
3 Philip Mairet, *Autobiographical and other papers* (Manchester, 1981), p. 31.
4 J, 3 June 1902.
5 Campden School of Arts and Crafts, Report for 1904–5, p. 33, V&A Library.
6 Alan Crawford, 'New Life for an Artist's Village: Broadway, Worcestershire: I' and 'The Turning Point: Broadway, Worcestershire: II', *Country Life*, 1980, vol. 167, pp. 252–4 and 308–10.
7 *Country Life*, 1902, vol. 12, pp. 524–5; J, 15 Feb 1902.
8 J, c. 6 April 1905; for Ashbee dictating, information from Sir Basil Blackwell, 10 Aug 1970.
9 Whitfield, op. cit., pp. 59–60; *Cottages*, pp. 66–70.
10 Janet Ashbee, 'The Dress and the House, No. 2.', *Dress Review*, 1903, vol. 1, p. 43. Woolstaplers' Hall is now a museum of nostalgic bric-à-brac, and it is impossible to appreciate the character of the house among the relics of the Golden Age of the Cinema, the early vacuum cleaners, and the remains of Lieutenant Lemprière's air balloon.
11 J, 3 June 1902.
12 The Guild of Handicraft Ltd., Annual Report for 1902, V&A Library; for working hours, MGH, 30 April 1902 and Miller, pp. 12–13.
13 Will Hart, 'The Guild of Handicraft and Mr. C. R. Ashbee, F.R.I.B.A.' (Typescript, 1959), p. 2, FA.
14 Frederic Allen Whiting, 'A Successful English Experiment', *Handicraft* (Boston, Mass.), 1903, vol. 2, pp. 151–2.
15 J, June 1902; The Guild of Handicraft Ltd., Annual Report for 1902, V&A Library; MGH, 6 Dec 1901.
16 Recollections of their second son, Henry Osborn, in a letter to Fiona MacCarthy of 1 May 1981.
17 Whiting, op. cit., p. 154; MGH, 6 Dec 1901, 26 March 1902. It should be said that Ashbee *did* think about Guild wives and daughters during the move to Campden: the Guild bindery was set up partly to provide them with work, see MGH, 6 Dec 1901.
18 J, Jan 1902.
19 J, April 1902, Jan 1906.
20 J, 12 June 1902.
21 Guild of Handicraft Ltd. Annual Report for 1902, V&A Library.
22 J, June 1902, 11 Aug 1902 and 4 May 1903.
23 Miller, p. 71.
24 J, Oct 1903.
25 J, June 1902.
26 Birmingham Municipal School of Art, Student Registers for 1898–1901, in the archives of the Art and Design Centre, City of Birmingham Polytechnic; S, 1901–2, vol. 24, pp. 202–4; 1902–3, vol. 27, pp. 212–4; J, June 1902.
27 J, June 1902, 11 Aug 1902.
28 Henry Osborn to Fiona MacCarthy, 1 May 1981; Whiting, op. cit., p. 150.
29 Miller, p. 97.
30 J, 8 April 1903; draft letter from Phoebe Haydon to John Rothenstein, 1934, FA; *Craftsmanship*, p. 200.
31 J, June 1902, 8 April 1903; Whitfield, op. cit., p. 241.
32 J, Feb 1905.
33 C. R. Ashbee, *A Description of the Work of the Guild of Handicraft* (1902).
34 Ibid., pp. 12–13.
35 J, 14 Nov 1902.

36 Ibid.

37 J, 3, 4, 8, 14 and *c.* 15 Dec 1902, 9 and 14 Jan 1903; copies of Ashbee's letters are also in J.

38 J, 14 Jan 1903.

39 Quoted in Constance Babington Smith, *John Masefield: A Life* (Oxford, 1978), pp. 77–8.

40 J, Christmas 1902.

41 Henry Osborn to Fiona MacCarthy, 1 Sept 1981.

42 J, 28 Feb 1903.

43 Ibid.

44 J, 2 March 1903.

45 J, 3 March 1903.

46 J, 28 Feb 1903.

47 J, 29 May 1902.

48 *Evesham Journal*, 6 June 1903, p. 6.

49 J, 18 Oct 1904.

50 *Dictionary of National Biography 1951–1960* (1971); Susan Beattie, *A Revolution in London Housing: LCC Housing Architects and their Work 1893–1914* (1980), p. 21; J, Easter 1900.

51 See pp. 259–60.

52 Walter Nimocks, *Milner's young men: the 'kindergarten' in Edwardian Imperial affairs* (1970), passim.

53 Ashbee to Janet, 15 Oct 1897 and 11 Jan 1898, FA; J, *c.* 15 July 1903.

54 C. R. Ashbee, *Socialism and Politics: A Study in the Readjustment of the Values of Life* (1906), pp. 42–50.

55 J, *c.* 7 June 1903.

56 J, *c.* 22 June 1903.

57 J, 29 June 1903.

58 J, *c.* July 1903.

59 Herbert Baker, *Architecture and Personalities* (1944), p. 47.

60 Ibid., p. 50.

61 J, 7 July 1903.

62 Correspondence between Ashbee and Francis Masey, 21 Aug and 2 Sept 1903, Jagger Library, University of Cape Town. Correspondence at the Jagger Library shows that some work was done for Curtis, but The White House at Pretoria which Baker designed for him was not begun tutil 1905, and I have seen no evidence that it contained furniture designed by Ashbee or made by the Guild.

63 Typescript at J, July 1903.

64 J, 22 July 1903.

65 J, 23 July 1903.

66 E. R. and J. Pennell, *The Life of James McNeill Whistler* (1908), vol. 2, pp. 277, 279. Whistler's irate notes to the foreman on Ashbee's building works are in Glasgow University Library, dated 20 June and 6 Oct 1902.

67 J, Aug 1903.

68 J, Sept and 22 Oct 1903.

69 J, Sept 1903 and 14 Nov 1907; see also pp. 270–1 and Appendix I, no. 30.

70 Diary of Beatrice Webb, 4 Aug 1903, British Library of Political and Economic Science.

71 J, Sept 1902.

72 Circulars of 8 April and 21 Nov 1903, JJ Coll.

73 Janet thought of the *Song Book* as a rival to *English County Songs*, see J, 26 Oct 1901; and Ashbee referred to it as 'a collection of English folk song' in 1910 in his application for the Slade Professorship at Oxford, p. 4, Bodleian Library, Oxford, MS. Top. Oxon. *c.* 178.

74 S. Baring Gould, *English Minstrelsie: A National Monument of English Song* [1895], vol. 1, p. xxiii; and Mary Neal, *The Esperance Morris Book* (1910), p. 2; both quoted in Vic Gammon, 'Folk Song Collecting in Sussex and Surrey 1843–1914', *History Workshop Journal*, 1980, vol. 10, pp. 61–89; see also Dave Harker, 'May Cecil Sharp Be Praised?', *History Workshop Journal*, 1982, vol. 14, pp. 44–62.

75 Ashbee to Francis Masey, 26 Feb 1904, Jagger Library, University of Cape Town.

76 Draft lecture scheme of 1910 and manuscript copies of Hedges's songs, 1910, both FA.

77 Gammon, op. cit, p. 73.

78 For example, the Song Book version of *Sumer is icumen in* has the archaic spelling found in the 1893 edition; but the tune for *The Leather Bottel* is the one said in 1855–9 to be more traditional. I am grateful to Felicity Ashbee for pointing out these comparisons.

79 Proposal for *The Essex House Song Book*, June 1901, JJ Coll.

80 Preface, p. iii.

81 *The Campden Maypole Song* by Laurence Housman, section V, p. 36.

82 X: 30 and VIII: 10. When *The Master Craftsman's Song* was reprinted in C. R. Ashbee, *Echoes from the City of the Sun* (1905), it was inscribed 'Written for S.C.'.

83 Circular, Midsummer 1901, JJ Coll.

84 J, 15 Jan 1903.

85 J, 9 March 1903; *Craftsmanship*, p. 22. Isabelle Anscombe and Charlotte Gere, *Arts and Crafts in Britain and America* (1978), p. 38 imply that Liberty's investment was not as Janet put it. See also pp. 340–1, pp. 366–7.

86 Guild of Handicraft Ltd., Annual Report for 1903, V&A Library.

87 Gerald Bishop, *A May-Day Interlude* (Chipping Campden, 1904), p. 7.

88 Ibid., p. 17.

89 *Evesham Journal*, 28 May 1904, p. 5.

90 J, Aug 1904.

91 J, 23 June 1904.

92 MGH, 25 July 1905.

93 J, Aug 1904.

94 Miller, p. 115.

95 J, Aug 1904.

96 Letter of 17 Aug 1904, FA.

97 MSH, 13 Jan 1903; Ashbee stated here that the scheme began in Oct 1891, but the context suggests that this is an error for 1901, and MGH, 6 Dec 1901 confirms this.

98 MSH, 18 Dec 1902, in error for 1901, and 13 Jan 1903; Campden School of Arts and Crafts, Report for 1903–4, pp. 3–4, V&A Library.

99 Lord Redesdale, *Second Address at the Campden School of Arts and Crafts* (1905), p. 7; BN, 1905, vol. 89, p. 494; conversion plans for Elm Tree House, 20 April 1904, CT; Campden School of Arts and Crafts, Report for 1904–5, p. 8, V&A Library.

100 Campden School of Arts and Crafts, Report for 1905–6, pp. 22–3, V&A Library.

101 J, 12 June 1902.

102 Campden School of Arts and Crafts, Report for 1904–5, pp. 4–6, 11, 12–16; *Evesham Advertiser*, 11 March 1905.

103 J, mid-Sept 1904.

104 J, *c.* Sept 1904.

105 Lord Redesdale, *An Address at the opening of the Campden School of Arts and Crafts* (1904).

106 J, late Nov 1904.

107 Prospectus, JJ Coll.

108 J, 20 Dec 1904.

109 Guild of Handicraft Ltd., Annual Report for 1904, V&A Library.

110 MGH, 25 Feb 1905.

111 Ibid., and a letter from Henry Osborn to Fiona MacCarthy, 1 Sept 1981.

112 Fiona MacCarthy, *The Simple Life: C. R. Ashbee in the Cotswolds* (1981), pp. 123–4.

113 Programme note, JJ Coll.

114 J, Jan 1905.

115 J, Nov 1904; drawings for a studio-house, 1902, etc., CT.

116 Whitfield, op. cit., p. 245; 'Memoirs', vol. 7, pp. 341–3; letter from Phoebe Haydon to Janet Ashbee, '6 December', FA.

117 J, 29 Nov 1904; Joseph Nuttgens to Fiona MacCarthy, 5 Oct 1978; drawings for Woodroffe's cottage and studio, CT.

118 Minutes of the Board to Promote the Extension of University Teaching, London University, 23 June 1904, London University Library.

119 Report by Ashbee dated 2 Feb 1905, London University Library.

120 Two campaign leaflets, J, March 1905; *Evesham Journal*, 25 March and 8 April 1905.

121 Alec Miller to Felicity Ashbee, 14 Dec 1951, FA; where, however, Alec Miller appears to date this holiday *c.* 1907.

122 J, 20 June 1905; Ashbee to Alec Miller 21 June 1905, FA.
123 J, 26 June 1905. Zsombor de Szász apparently came from Transylvania and was probably new to Budapest in 1905; he was a Member of Parliament from 1905 to 1910; a specialist on minorities in Hungary, he wrote *The Minorities in Rumanian Transylvania* (1927). Elsa de Szász published a novel in London in 1912, *The Temple on the Hill: A Tale of Transylvania*.
124 Ashbee to Alec Miller, July 1905, FA; see also J, 26 June 1905.
125 J, Aug/Sept 1899 and *c.* 14 Jan 1900. Mandello was a professor at the Academy of Law in Bratislava from 1900 to 1910; he also represented the Hungarian Economic Association, of which he was later secretary, in the progressive Sociological Society. For Ashbee's designs for him, see silver in *MES*, plates 37, 50, 57, 58, plus photographs of a sports cup and a casket in Ashbee's own copy of *MES*, V&A Library; furniture and jewellery in Ashbee Collection, vol. 2, pp. 307–13, 319; and W. Shaw Sparrow (ed.), *Flats Urban Houses and Cottage Homes* (n.d.) facing p. 9 for what may be the interior in Budapest. *MES* plate 34 shows silver for de Szász. Later, in 1910, Mandello seems to have sent Mihály Biró, who became an important revolutionary poster artist, to study under Ashbee in Campden, see J, 12 Oct 1910; and it seems to have been through Mandello that the Hungarian Ministry of Education asked Ashbee to write 'A Survey of English-Speaking Universities' from an architectural point of view in 1912, of which there is a typescript in KCC.
126 J, *c.* 14 Jan and 22 Jan 1900; see also Viktória Kondor and Zsuzsa Zoldhely-Deák, 'P. A. Kropotkin and Count Ervin Batthyány', *Studia Slavica Academiae Scientiarum Hungaricae* (Budapest), 1978, vol. 14, pp. 12–35. At one time Batthyány thought of joining the Guild.
127 Dering Yard Visitors' Book, 7 June 1904, V&A Library; J, 26 June 1905.
128 Ashbee in a letter to *Times*, 24 Aug 1905.
129 Ervin Pamlényi (ed.), *A History of Hungary* (1975), pp. 380–96.
130 Ashbee to Alec Miller, July 1905, FA.
131 Ibid.; illustration of the scheme from an unidentified periodical, Ashbee Collection, vol. 1, p. 357.
132 J, 26 June 1905.
133 Private diary, FA.
134 Ibid.
135 J, 28 June 1905.
136 J, July 1905.
137 'Rachel', pp. 68–77.
138 J, 18 Aug 1905; *Times*, 24 Aug 1905.
139 Guild of Handicraft Ltd., Annual Report for 1905, V&A Library; MGH, 25 July 1905.
140 Deighton Bell Ltd., Booksellers, Cambridge. Catalogue 141, item 397.
141 Campden School of Arts and Crafts, Report for 1905–6, V&A Library.
142 J, 13 Jan 1906.
143 Ibid.
144 Ibid. and J, Jan and Feb 1906.
145 J, 13 Jan 1906.
146 Guild of Handicraft Ltd., Annual Report for 1905, V&A Library.
147 J, 5 March 1906.
148 J, 11 Dec 1899.
149 J, 5 March 1906.
150 MGH, 8 March 1906.
151 Guild of Handicraft Ltd., Annual Report for 1906, V&A Library; MGH, 16 and 27 March 1906; J, 17 June 1906; Catalogue I.
152 J, 22 April 1906.
153 J, 29 May 1906.
154 J, Oct 1903 and 17 June 1906.
155 J, 31 Aug 1906; for the detailed history of the presses, see Chapter 14, note 96.
156 *Kunst und Handwerk* (Munich), 1907–8, vol. 58, pp. 114–20. Berlepsch-Valendas signed the Guild Visitors' Book in Campden on 2 Aug 1906; this book is still in use in the workshop of Henry, David and Rex Hart in the Mill, Chipping Campden.

157 J, 15 Aug 1906.
158 J, 9 March and 20 April 1903; see also pp. 264–7.
159 Philip Mairet, *Autobiography and other papers* (Manchester, 1981), pp. 40–1; Roger Lipsey, *Coomaraswamy: 3: His Life and Work* (Princeton, N.J., 1977), pp. 7–33.
160 The photographs were used, for instance, in Catalogue J.
161 Advertising leaflet, V&A Library.
162 *AR*, Oct 1906–Nov 1907.
163 See particularly Catalogue K.
164 J, 15 Dec 1906.
165 Richard Jenkyns, *The Victorians and Ancient Greece* (Oxford, 1980), p. 291; Timothy d'Arch Smith, *Love in Earnest* (1970), pp. 62–3.
166 J, 1 Jan 1907.
167 J, 8 Jan and Jan 1907.
168 Ashbee to Alec Miller, 6 Feb 1907, FA.
169 Ibid.
170 Ibid.
171 J, 9 Feb 1907.
172 Guild of Handicraft Ltd., Annual Report for 1906, V&A Library; see also Special Resolution of the Guild of Handicraft Ltd., 18 May 1907, PRO. BT31. 8064/58132.
173 *Craftsmanship*, pp. 236–8.
174 Ibid., pp. 250 and 239–50.
175 J, 9 June 1907.
176 Ibid.
177 *Craftsmanship*, pp. 23 and 27.
178 MGH, 26 Oct 1907.
179 J, 20 Dec 1907; *Connoisseur* 1906, vol. 15, pp. 261–2 for Hodson's sales.
180 J, *c.* 1 Jan 1908.
181 J, 29 Nov 1907.
182 See, for instance, a pamphlet issued by the Guild, J, May 1914, and Miller, p. 129.
183 *Craftsmanship*, pp. 27 and 77–8.
184 Ibid., pp. 22, 40, 236; and Guild of Handicraft Ltd., Annual Reports for 1904 and succeeding years, V&A Library.
185 *Craftsmanship*, pp. 30–8.
186 Ibid., p. 24.
187 Ibid., p. 236.
188 A. R. Prest and A. A. Adams, *Consumers' Expenditure in the United Kingdom 1900–1919* (Cambridge, 1954), p. 117 for Furniture and Soft Furnishings; and Pottery, Glassware, Holloware and Hardware (which latter do, however, dip slightly between 1905 and 1906); p. 133 for Books and Periodicals; and p. 160 for 'Other Goods' including jewellery.
189 *Craftsmanship*, p. 40.
190 For Elmdon and Company, see *AJ*, 1905, p. 188; for the Coldrum Pottery, the Fine Art Society, *The Arts and Crafts Movement* (Catalogue of an exhibition, 1973), nos. C13 and C14; for the Crafts, see Glasgow Museums and Art Galleries, *The Glasgow Style 1890–1920* (1984), p. 14.
191 Helen Fitzrandolph and M. D. Hay, *The Rural Industries of England* (1926–7), passim.
192 R. E. D. Sketchley, 'Haslemere Arts and Crafts', *AJ*, 1906, pp. 337–42.
193 Mary Comino, *Gimson and the Barnsleys* (1980), pp. 97, 101–2, 158, 170–1.
194 Information from Douglas Webster and letters of 7 Feb and 31 March 1908 in his possession.
195 Anscombe and Gere, op. cit., plate 296 illustrates three cigarette boxes with Varley's enamels said to be from Liberty's, though the top box was made by the Guild in 1903.
196 J, April 1913 and late Aug 1917.
197 J, 17 March 1909.
198 Circular dated June 1908, CPL.
199 J, 25 Jan 1908.
200 Ibid.
201 For Coomaraswamy generally, see Lipsey, op. cit; for Ethel who, as Ethel Mairet, made a different and distinguished life for herself as a weaver, see Margot Coatts, *A Weaver's Life: Ethel Mairet 1872–1952* (1983).
202 e.g., *Craftsmanship*, p. 115.
203 J, April 1908; *Craftsmanship*, p. 46.

204 Mary Fels, *Joseph Fels* (1920).
205 J, April 1908 and March 1914.
206 MGH, 25 July, 18 Aug, 26 Sept, 3 and 13 Oct 1908; J. P. Nelson, *Broad Campden* (Privately printed, 1971), p. 57.
207 *AR*, 1908, vol. 24, p. 107.
208 J, 2 March 1908.
209 J, 4 May 1908.
210 J, 16 July and 14 Aug 1908; 'Rachel', pp. 86–95.
211 Janet wrote to Ashbee on 15 Dec 1908: 'It seems to me all the while that Gerald is dead.' (Journals)

CHAPTER SIX
WHERE THE GREAT CITY STANDS
1908–1918

1 J, *c.* 7 Nov 1908; Brandywine River Museum, Chadds Ford, Pennsylvania, *A Poor Sort of Heaven, A Good Sort of Earth: The Rose Valley Experiment* (Catalogue of an exhibition, 1983).
2 J, late Nov 1908.
3 *Times Educational Supplement*, 3 Oct 1911.
4 J, Dec 1908.
5 J, 21, 25 Dec and Dec 1908.
6 J, Dec 1908.
7 J, Jan 1909.
8 J, 20 Jan 1909.
9 J, late Jan 1909; *Daily Palo Alto*, 20 Jan 1909. For a fuller account of this episode see Peter Stansky, 'C. R. Ashbee visits Stanford University', *Imprint of the Stanford Libraries Associates*, 1977, vol. 3, pp. 16–23.
10 J, Jan 1909.
11 Ibid.
12 Ibid.
13 Ibid.
14 Ibid. For a fuller account of Ashbee and Greene, see Robert W. Winter, 'American Sheaves from "C.R.A." and Janet Ashbee', *Journal of the Society of Architectural Historians* (Philadelphia), 1971, vol. 30, pp. 321–2.
15 J, 17 Feb and *c.* 28 Feb 1909.
16 J, 11 Dec 1908, *c.* 28 Feb, 5 and 15 March 1909.
17 J, 5 March 1909.
18 MGH, 7 Dec 1909, 10 Jan, 17 Sept, 31 Oct and 7 Nov 1910.
19 Ashbee's application for the Slade Professorship, Bodleian Library, Oxford, MS. Top. Oxon. c.178.
20 J, 3 Dec 1910.
21 J, April 1910; letter to Alec Miller, 7 May 1910, FA; Diary of Selwyn Image, 6 May 1910, Bodleian Library, Oxford, MS. Eng. misc. d.349.
22 J, Feb 1914.
23 J, 22 April 1913 and Feb 1914. Ashbee's designs for the gallery are so far untraced.
24 J, 31 March 1910.
25 J, 13 April 1910 (draft letter to Wright) and 8 July 1910.
26 Wright signed the Visitors' Book still in use in the Mill in Chipping Campden on 17 Sept 1910; see also J, 26 Sept 1910 and a letter from Ashbee to Wright of 2 April 1901 in the archives of the Frank Lloyd Wright Foundation, Taliesin West, Arizona.
27 The monograph was published in Berlin in 1911 as *Sonderheft der Architektur des XX Jahrhunderts: 8: Frank Lloyd Wright*, though it is usually known by its cover-title of *Frank Lloyd Wright: Ausgeführte Bauten*. A new edition was published as Edgar Kaufmann Jr. (ed.), *Frank Lloyd Wright: The Early Work* (New York, 1968), with the difference that the bulk of Ashbee's introduction was printed in 1968 from his original English text. See also Alan Crawford, 'Ten Letters from Frank Lloyd Wright to Charles Robert Ashbee', *Architectural History*, 1970, vol. 13, pp. 64–73.
28 J, 26 Sept 1910; Robert C. Twombly, *Frank Lloyd Wright: His Life and His Architecture* (New York, 1979), pp. 123–5.
29 Kaufmann, op. cit, p. 4.
30 Ibid., p. 8.
31 e.g., H. Allen Brooks, 'Chicago Architecture: Its Debt to the Arts and Crafts', *Journal of the Society of Architectural Historians* (Philadelphia), 1971, vol. 30, p. 315.

32 Kaufmann, op. cit, p. xiv.
33 Reyner Banham, *Theory and Design in the First Machine Age* (1960), p. 147.
34 *AR*, 1910, vol. 27, p. 51.
35 ———, 'The Ruislip Manor Competition', *AR*, 1911, vol. 29, pp. 171–80.
36 May Morris, *William Morris Artist Writer Socialist* (Oxford, 1936), vol. 2, p. 474. For Ashbee and the Italian Renaissance, cf. pp. 347–9.
37 J, 25 Dec 1910.
38 S. D. Adshead, 'An Introduction to Civic Design', *Town Planning Review* (Liverpool), 1910, vol. 1, p. 13.
39 J, 20 Nov 1907.
40 Helen Meller, 'Cities and evolution: Patrick Geddes as an international prophet of town planning before 1914' in Anthony Sutcliffe (ed.), *The Rise of Modern Urban Planning 1800–1914* (1980), pp. 199–223.
41 J, 28 Jan 1913.
42 Patrick Geddes, *Cities in Evolution* (1968), pp. 60–83; the first edition of *Cities in Evolution* was only published in 1915, but the germ of the Palaeotechnic/Neotechnic idea was present in his *City Development: A Study of Parks, Gardens and Culture-Institutes: A Report to the Dunfermline Trust* (London, Edinburgh and Birmingham, 1904), pp. 174–5.
43 J, 14 Sept 1910.
44 J, 5 Feb 1909; *SWS*, introduction.
45 e.g., J, 25 Feb 1912.
46 *SWS*, p. 2.
47 Ibid., p. 4.
48 Ibid., p. 3.
49 Ibid., p. 13.
50 Paddy Kitchen, *A Most Unsettling Person: An Introduction to the Ideas and Life of Patrick Geddes* (1975), p. 224.
51 *WGC*, p. 85; see also pp. 251–2.
52 J, 26 May 1912.
53 *WGC*, pp. 85–6 for the design, and Minutes of the Professional Defence Committee, 2 Feb 1914 in Special Committee Minutes, vol. 6, pp. 446–7, archives of the RIBA.
54 J, 22 July 1912.
55 J, 20 Dec 1912.
56 J, May 1913.
57 J, 13 May 1913.
58 J, 20 April 1909.
59 *Evesham Journal*, 23 April 1910, 20 April and 29 June 1912.
60 J, 5 Jan 1912.
61 J, Jan 1914.
62 J, 30 March 1914.
63 Hermann Levy, *Large and Small Holdings: A Study of English Agricultural Economics* (Cambridge, 1911), pp. 124–47.
64 J, May 1913; MGH, 2 Feb 1912.
65 MGH, 24 May 1912 and 2 June 1914; J, 28 Jan and May 1913.
66 J, 5 Aug 1914.
67 J, 13 Sept 1914 (draft letter to Hodson).
68 J, 3 Dec 1914 and 1 Jan 1915.
69 J, 23 July 1915.
70 E. M. Forster, *Goldsworthy Lowes Dickinson* (1934), pp. 156 and 163–4; Dennis Proctor (ed.), *The Autobiography of G. Lowes Dickinson* (1973), p. 180.
71 Keith G. Robbins, 'Lord Bryce and the First World War', *Historical Journal*, 1967, vol. 10, pp. 265–6; Henry R. Winkler, *The League of Nations Movement in Great Britain in 1914–19* (New Brunswick, N.J., 1952), pp. 16–17.
72 J, 12 Feb 1915.
73 J, 6 Feb 1915.
74 J, 17 June 1915; C. R. Ashbee, *The American League to Enforce Peace: An English Interpretation* (1917), pp. 21–2, 25–6.
75 J, 18 June 1915.
76 J, 15 July 1915.
77 J, 11 Nov 1915.
78 J, 24 May, early June, 6 June and 8 Nov 1915.
79 J, 10 March 1916.
80 J, 12 June 1915.
81 J, 5 Dec 1915, late March 1916 and cutting from *St Louis Post Dispatch* for 2 March 1916; see also C. R. Ashbee, 'Kansas City

Missouri: The Influence of a Park System', *Town Planning Review* (Liverpool), 1915–16, vol. 6, pp. 233–7.

82 J, 11 April 1916.
83 J, 25 Feb 1916.
84 J, 14 May 1916.
85 J, May 1916, mid-Nov 1917 and 29 Aug 1918.
86 J, 21 Oct 1915.
87 J, 19 Feb 1916.
88 J, 20 March 1916.
89 J, 28 Jan 1916.
90 J, late Dec 1915, Dec 1916 and Jan 1919.
91 J, 11 Jan 1916.
92 J, Jan 1913, 11 Sept 1915.
93 J, 14 Oct 1916.
94 So family tradition goes; the nearest thing to such an advertisement is *Times Educational Supplement*, 16 Nov 1916, an advertisement for English teachers in secondary schools in Egypt.
95 J, 25 March 1917.
96 Ibid.
97 J, April and 5 May 1917.
98 J, 25 March 1917.
99 J, 22 March 1917.
100 J, 11 May and 25 March and April 1917.
101 J, 3 June 1917.
102 Ibid.
103 *WGC*, p. 3.
104 *American Sheaves*, p. 93.
105 *Craftsmanship*, pp. 44–5.
106 *WGC*, pp. 63, 70–2, 100–6; William H. Wilson, 'The ideology, aesthetics and politics of the City Beautiful Movement', in Sutcliffe, op. cit., pp. 165–98.
107 *WGC*, p. 113.
108 Ibid., pp. 113–26.
109 It perhaps owed something to Patrick Geddes's sketch of an Art Institute in *City Development* (1904), pp. 174–5, a passage which ends with a portrait of the Art Director as 'some many-sided and deeply socialised artist', which might almost be Ashbee himself.
110 It was very favourably reviewed in *Town Planning Institute: Papers and Discussions*, 1917–18, vol. 4, p. 30.
111 The wartime writings of the Arts and Crafts architect and designer Henry Wilson show the same sense of the city, idealism, inclusiveness and debt to Geddes as do Ashbee's; see the typescript volumes of Wilson's writings in the V&A Library.
112 From 'Song of the Broad Axe', Walt Whitman, *The Complete Poems* (Harmondsworth, 1975), pp. 219–20.
113 J, 27 Dec 1917.
114 J, 23 April 1918.
115 J, 2 May and 23 April 1918.
116 J, May 1918.
117 J, 11 Feb 1918; see also Ashbee to Alec Miller, 26 Jan 1918, FA.
118 J, 10 April 1918.
119 J, 11 and 26 July and 2 Aug 1918.
120 J, 16 Sept 1918.
121 There is a fully illustrated carbon copy in Box I, FA Jerusalem.
122 J, 14 Sept 1918.
123 J, 21 Oct 1918.
124 MGH, 25 Jan 1919; J, Jan and 2 Feb 1919.

CHAPTER SEVEN
JERUSALEM
1919–1922

1 Ashbee had these words from the 48th Psalm printed on the covers of his reports on behalf of the Pro-Jerusalem Society, whose titles are abbreviated here as *Jerusalem 1918–1920* and *Jerusalem 1920–1922*. These two volumes are one of the principal sources for Ashbee's work in Jerusalem; the other is the collection of Ashbee's drawings and plans in the possession of Felicity Ashbee, and here referred to as FA Jerusalem.
2 W. H. Bartlett, *Walks about the City and Environs of Jerusalem*

(1843) quoted in Martin Gilbert, *Jerusalem: Illustrated History Atlas* (1977), p. 39.
3 Gilbert, op. cit., pp. 55, 59.
4 Howard M. Sachar, *The Emergence of the Middle East 1914–1924* (1969), Chapter 7.
5 Bernard Wasserstein, *The British in Palestine: The Mandatory Government and the Arab-Jewish Conflict 1917–1929* (1978), p. 42.
6 *Palestine Notebook*, p. 4.
7 Ibid., pp. ix, 68–9, 107–8, 245–7.
8 J, 10 Feb 1920 and 24 July 1918.
9 J, Jan and 13 Feb 1919.
10 'Reconstruction in Jerusalem', *Times*, 5 Feb 1919; a cutting in J attributes the article to Ashbee.
11 *Palestine Notebook*, p. 240; see also pp. 3, 9, 18; *Times* loc. cit; and *Jerusalem 1918–1920*, p. 41.
12 Felicity Ashbee, 'The Golden String' (Typescript, 1981), Chapter 19, p. 11.
13 E. Keith Roach, Typescript recollections of Ashbee, FA.
14 Wasserstein, op. cit, pp. 2–41.
15 Ibid., pp. 49–50; Ronald Storrs, *Orientations* (1937), *passim*.
16 *Jerusalem 1918–1920*, p. v.
17 J, Jan and 5 July 1919.
18 Storrs, op. cit., p. 24.
19 J, 29 Aug 1918; Sir John Richmond, 'Prophet of Doom: E. T. Richmond, F.R.I.B.A., Palestine 1920–1924', *Islamic Quarterly*, 1975, vol. 19, pp. 187–94.
20 J, 9 March 1924.
21 *Palestine Notebook*, pp. vii–viii.
22 *Jerusalem 1918–1920*, pp. v–vi.
23 Storrs, op. cit, p. 364.
24 Roach, op. cit.
25 Ibid.
26 'Report by Mr. C. R. Ashbee on the Arts and Crafts of Jerusalem and District' (Typescript, 1918), p. 69, Box I, FA Jerusalem.
27 *Jerusalem 1918–1920*, pp. 1, 14; cutting from *St Louis Post Dispatch*, 3 Aug 1919 in J.
28 *Jerusalem 1918–1920*, pp. 6–8.
29 Ibid., p. 34.
30 J, 14 May 1920; *Jerusalem 1918–1920*, pp. 30–1.
31 Ernest Richmond, *The Dome of the Rock in Jerusalem: A Description of Its Structure and Decoration* (Oxford, 1924), pp. 39, 75, 104–6.
32 *Jerusalem 1918–1920*, pp. 8–10, 31–2; 'Memoirs', vol. 3, pp. 131–2; letter from William De Morgan to Ashbee, 28 Nov 1909, CT; Richmond, op. cit., pp. 73–4; Storrs, op. cit., p. 367; and Clive Aslet, *The Last Country Houses* (1982), plate XV.
33 *Times*, 5 Feb 1919.
34 Richmond, op. cit., p. 3; *Jerusalem 1918–1920*, pp. 32–3.
35 *Jerusalem 1918–1920*, pp. 2–4.
36 Ibid., p. 21; see also Box I, Folder 2, FA Jerusalem.
37 Ibid., p. 1.
38 Ibid., p. 21.
39 Ibid., pp. 1–2, 19–21; see also Box I, Folders 3 and 5, and Box II, Folder 1, FA Jerusalem.
40 See for example Box II, Folder 5 (David Street Market) and Folder 6 (Karaim Synagogue), FA Jerusalem.
41 *Jerusalem 1918–1920*, pp. 19–24.
42 The plans are reproduced in *Jerusalem 1918–1920*, figs. 21 and 22 and in David H. K. Amiran and others (eds.), *Atlas of Jerusalem* (Berlin and New York, 1973), Maps 9:1 and 9:2. The variant inscriptions in 9:2 are taken from an original map in Jerusalem assumed to have been drawn by Geddes.
43 *Jerusalem 1918–1920*, pp. 12–13.
44 Ibid., p. 24.
45 Ibid., p. 12.
46 J, 10 Feb 1920. The rebuilding of Nebi Samuel refers to a village outside Jerusalem all but destroyed during the war; Ashbee and Richmond were involved in its reconstruction. The important buildings referred to may have included his design for the YMCA in Jerusalem; the large hotel he designed for Thomas Cook and Son seems to belong to a later date. See Appendix 1, nos. 69–72.
47 J, late March 1920.

48 J, 16 and 17 March 1920.

49 Sachar, op. cit, pp. 391–3; Wasserstein, op. cit, pp. 64–71.

50 J, 6 April 1920.

51 J, 14 May 1920.

52 J, July 1920.

53 J, 4 Dec 1920, April and *c*. April 1921.

54 Sir John Richmond, op. cit., pp. 188–9, 193–4.

55 Fragmentary and undated letter from Samuel to Ashbee, J, late June 1920; see also *Palestine Notebook*, p. xii and *Jerusalem 1920–1922*, pp. 5–13, 20.

56 *Jerusalem 1920–1922*, pp. 26–8.

57 Ibid., pp. 1–2.

58 *Jerusalem 1918–1920*, fig. 21.

59 Ibid., pp. 11–14; *Jerusalem 1920–1922*, pp. 15–19 and figs. 34–5; Henry Kendall, *Jerusalem: The City Plan: Preservation and Development during the British Mandate 1918–1948* (1948), pp. 4–10. Shahar Shapiro, 'Planning Jerusalem: The First Generation, 1917–1968' in Amiran and others. *Urban Geography of Jerusalem* (Berlin and New York, 1973), pp. 140–4 suggests that Ashbee drew up a town plan in 1922 in collaboration with Patrick Geddes. This may be so, but no evidence is produced to support the idea, and I do not know of any. There is a draft zoning plan dated Jan 1921 among Ashbee's papers, Box IV, Folder 1, FA Jerusalem. It is annotated 'In this plan the MacLean and the Geddes plans have been co-ordinated'. This remark can be sufficiently explained by the fact that Ashbee's town plan drew on McLean's plan of 1918 and Geddes's of 1919.

60 *Jerusalem 1920–1922*, p. 18; Kendall, op. cit, p. 10.

61 J, 16 Oct 1919.

62 J, 2 May 1921.

63 Ibid.

64 J, 29 May 1921.

65 Ibid.

66 J, 14 June 1921.

67 J, 2 May 1921.

68 J, 18 May 1921.

69 'Sixth Exhibition. Deposits on Sale', archives of the A&CES, V&A Library.

70 *Jerusalem 1920–1922*, pp. 60–3, and Box IV, Folder 5, FA Jerusalem.

71 Ibid., pp. 62–3; J, 4 and 8 Sept 1921.

72 J, Nov 1921.

73 Sir John Richmond, op. cit., pp. 190–1.

74 *Times*, 5 Feb 1919; 'Report by Mr. C. R. Ashbee on the Arts and Crafts of Jerusalem and District' (Typescript, 1918), pp. 49–51, Box I, FA Jerusalem. The latter source is a particularly interesting and full discussion of Bezalel, drawing parallels with the Guild of Handicraft.

75 *Jerusalem 1918–1920*, p. 33; *Palestine Notebook*, p. 246.

76 *Palestine Notebook*, p. 188.

77 J, 25 Jan 1921.

78 J, *c*. July 1921; for Storrs's account of this decision, which he regretted, see *Orientations*, pp. 351–2.

79 J, May 1922.

80 J, 9 March 1922.

81 *Jerusalem 1920–1922*, pp. 1–2; J, Nov 1921.

82 J, 11 July 1922.

83 J, Oct 1922.

84 *Palestine Notebook*, p. ix.

85 Ibid., pp. 227–8; J, 16 Dec 1922; *English Catalogue of Books 1923*.

86 J, 24 Jan 1924.

87 Storrs, op. cit, pp. 514–15.

88 Arthur Kutcher, *The New Jerusalem: Planning and Politics* (1973), *passim*; Penny Maguire, 'A Great and Golden City', *AR*, 1979, vol. 165, pp. 343–50; Ulrik Plesner, 'Holy City Girdled in Green', Ibid., pp. 351–4.

CHAPTER EIGHT
IN A KENTISH GARDEN
1923–1942

1 10 and 14 Jan 1923, FA.

2 J, 28 Jan 1923.

3 J, March 1923; letter from Ashbee to H. W. Rolfe, 21 Dec 1931, in the possession of Beatrice Huntsman-Trout.

4 'The Magpie and Stump House, 37 Cheyne Walk, Chelsea', catalogue of a sale, 18 Oct 1921, V&A Library.

5 J, 5 Aug 1923.

6 Ibid., see also loose notes, correspondence etc. in C. R. Ashbee, 'Trivialities of Tom' (Typescript, 1940–1), V&A Library; papers in C. R. Ashbee Supplementary Gift, Box II, KCC; and Miller, p. 23.

7 In 1926 there was talk of his being offered the job of professor of English literature at Cairo University, but nothing came of this; J, 27 Aug 1926.

8 The transformation was very like that of Kerfield House, Ollerton, Cheshire, by Percy Worthington, which was published by Lawrence Weaver in *Small Country Houses of To-Day: Volume Two* (1922). Had Ashbee seen it?

9 C. R. Ashbee, *Caricature* (1928), p. 148.

10 Sevenoaks and District Housing and Town Planning Association. Notice of a public meeting 12 Nov 1923, and Statement of Objects and Constitution, Kent County Library, Sevenoaks Division; *Times*, 9 Oct 1926.

11 *Times*, loc. cit.

12 10 Jan 1924, in the possession of Nina Griggs; see also *Listener*, 1929, vol. 1, pp. 233–4 and 361.

13 Information from Meg Nason and Felicity Ashbee.

14 J, 21 July 1929.

15 J, 19 March 1940. '*Grannie*' seems to have been complete in manuscript form by 1926; in 1939 Ashbee had 100 copies printed and sent them out as Christmas presents to his friends.

16 C. R. Ashbee (ed.), *Peckover: The Abbotscourt Papers 1904–1931* (1932), p. 210.

17 *Chipping Campden Exhibition of Arts and Crafts . . . 1924*.

18 J, 20 Feb 1930.

19 Ibid.

20 Programme for St Mark's in-the-Bouwerie, 31 Oct to 8 Nov 1931, in J.

21 *Yale Alumni Weekly*, 25 Dec 1931, cutting in J.

22 Letter from Gordon Place of 16 Nov 1931, tipped into Ashbee's own copy of *Conradin*, FA.

23 Letter of 21 Dec 1931, in the possession of Beatrice Huntsman-Trout.

24 J, 5 Aug 1932.

25 J, 27 Nov 1937.

26 Ashbee to Alec Miller, 12 Aug 1939, FA. It appears that only four volumes of the Memoirs actually reached the Library of Congress; but these have been supplemented by microfilm copies of two volumes from KCC; Ashbee's own copies are in the Library of the V&A.

27 J, 4 July 1934.

28 J, 13 Feb 1935.

29 1936, vol. 14, pp. 536–62; a translation appeared in *Manchester Review* 1956, vol. 7, pp. 437–58.

30 *Manchester Review* loc. cit, p. 451.

31 Ibid., pp. 457–8.

32 Letter of 15 Feb 1935 among Sir Nikolaus Pevsner's papers. It is not easy to see where Ashbee stood in relation to the Modern Movement in the 1930s. He was a founder member of the MARS (Modern Architectural Research) group, and the only figure from the old world of the Arts and Crafts among them. (See MARS, *New Architecture* (Catalogue of an exhibition, 1938), p. 23.) But on the other hand he was slightly dismissive in the *Studio* in 1933, describing functionalism as 'a new and rather terrifying [word] added in the present century to the already overburdened glossary of architecture. It means very little . . .' (*S*, 1933, vol. 105, p. 239.)

33 Information from Felicity Ashbee.

34 J, 5 April 1938; see also 15 Feb 1935 and 15 April 1938.

35 Janet Ashbee to her nephew Guy Langham, letter dated '21 February' among the papers of the late Capt. Langham.

36 J, April 1940; Janet Ashbee to the Rolfe family, 21 June 1942, Rolfe papers, University of California, Los Angeles.

37 15 May 1940, in the possession of Beatrice Huntsman-Trout.

38 Janet Ashbee to the Rolfe family, 21 June 1942, Rolfe papers, University of California, Los Angeles.

39 Ashbee to Alec Miller, 21 Aug 1940, FA.
40 Ashbee to Alec Miller, 1 March 1941, FA.
41 The date of the bombing is recorded on the site.
42 Janet Ashbee to the Rolfe family, 21 June 1942, Rolfe papers, University of California, Los Angeles.
43 Ashbee to Alec Miller, 20 April 1942, FA.
44 Ashbee to Alec Miller, 3 May 1942, FA.
45 Janet Ashbee to the Rolfe family, 21 June 1942, Rolfe papers, University of California, Los Angeles.
46 *Lancaster Guardian and Observer*, 19 May 1961.

CHAPTER NINE
THE ELEMENTS OF DESIGN

1 Peter Savage, *Lorimer and the Edinburgh Craft Designers* (Edinburgh, 1980), p. 68.
2 Raphael Samuel, 'The Workshop of the World: Steam Power and Hand Technology in mid-Victorian Britain', *History Workshop Journal*, 1977, vol. 3, pp. 6–72.
3 Ashbee to Alec Miller, 17 Aug 1904, FA.
4 Ibid.
5 pp. 4–5; see also Ashbee in *Munsey's Magazine* (New York), 1901, vol. 26, p. 8: 'there is in the language of architecutre, the spoken word of stone, also a philosophic idea . . .'.
6 J, 8 Dec 1902 and Ashbee to Alec Miller, 17 Aug 1904, FA.
7 Edgar Kaufman Jr. (ed.), *Frank Lloyd Wright: The Early Work* (New York, 1968), p. 7.
8 Ibid.
9 *Chapters*, p. 156; see also J, 15 Jan 1903 and 30 March 1914.
10 *Chapters*, p. 120.
11 *Craftsmanship*, p. 150.
12 J, Jan 1900. See also Ashbee to Hodson, J, *c.* 15 Dec 1902; and Ashbee to Alec Miller, 17 Feb 1911, FA, where he mentions Ted Horwood, Will Hart, Jack Baily and Charley Downer as examples of the worthwhile but untalented human stuff of the Guild.
13 *Chapters*, p. 24; see also J, 14 Nov 1902, and *Cottages*, p. 104 where Ashbee gives the authority of neo-platonism for this idea.
14 J, 6 Dec 1900.
15 J, 14 Sept 1885.
16 *WGC*, p. 5.
17 J, *c.* 7 Nov 1908.
18 See Edward Teitelman and Richard W. Longstreth, *Architecture in Philadelphia: A Guide* (1974), p. 85.
19 *American Sheaves*, p. 70.
20 *Cottages*, p. 41; see also *Chapters*, pp. 81 and 90.
21 *MES*, p. 6; see also *Chapters*, p. 45.
22 'Architecture as the Language of the English People, Part II', p. 8, DES.
23 Ibid., Part I, p. 13, DES.
24 When lecturing to University Extension summer schools in 1892, 1894 and 1895, Ashbee prepared large printed *Tables* of the Arts and Crafts of the Renaissance, seventeenth and eighteenth centuries, in which the material was laid out in columns, architectural history and the history of the crafts running in parallel with social, cultural and political history. See Appendix 4, nos. 10, 17 and 20.
25 Green, op cit, p. vi; and Ashbee's syllabus, 'The History of English Handicraft', p. 5, DES.
26 *MES*, p. 8.
27 As they were, Ashbee thought, in Frank Lloyd Wright's 'American System Ready-Cut' scheme of 1915; see *WGC*, pp. 20–1; see also C. R. Ashbee, *The Private Press* (1909), pp. 46–7.
28 The Mother Art: 'The History of English Handicraft', p. 3 and 'Architecture as the Language of the English People, Part I', p. 9, both DES; the union of the fine and decorative arts: *Chapters*, pp. 16 and 21–2; materials and construction: 'Design in its Application to Furniture', p. 5, DES and *Chapters*, p. 41; mere ornament: *AJ*, 1898, p. 232.
29 Minutes of the Art Workers' Guild, January 1891. The election date of 5 Nov 1897 given in H. J. L. J. Massé, *The Art-Workers' Guild 1884–1934* (Oxford, 1935), p. 144 is presumably an error.

30 'Rachel', p. 44; for 15 Lincoln's Inn Fields see the circular of Sept 1890 in 'Letters'; for rooms at the Magpie and Stump, B, 1904, vol. 86, p. 315.
31 In the Foreword to *Cottages*, Ashbee acknowledged Ernest Godman and Gabriel Stevenson as the authors of much of the work on several houses.
32 J, 14 Nov 1901 and Phoebe Haydon, 'Memoirs of a faithful secretary' (Typescript, n.d.), FA. The earliest dated evidence connecting Godman with Ashbee is a small perspective sketch of Essex House signed by Godman and dated 9 July 1892, now in the measured drawings collection of the National Monuments Record, no. 1949/125.
33 For Gomme, see the list of articled pupils and apprentices in MGH for 1900–1904; for Stevenson, who worked in later life for Selfridge's and as chief architect to the Boots Pure Drug Company and the Midland Bank, see *Evesham Journal*, 22 Nov 1930, *Who's Who in Architecture 1914*, and J, 8 Jan 1931; for Chettle, see J, Aug 1904; he was the son of Ashbee's childhood tutor and later had a distinguished career as an inspector of Ancient Monuments; he was instrumental, with Sir John Summerson, in the establishment of the National Buildings (now Monuments) Record, see *AR*, 1960, vol. 128, p. 322. For Mairet, see Philip Mairet, *Autobiographical and other papers* (Manchester, 1981), pp. 19–21. Other figures in the office of whom little is known were Arthur Nutter, *c.* 1895, Ernest Marriott in the 1890s, Bill Crockart a draughtsman of *c.*1906, and W. G. Cox, a pupil of *c.* 1913.
34 Philip Mairet first realized how unsophisticated their draughtsmanship was when Louis de Soissons came to stay in Campden to finish off some competition drawings in the Beaux-Arts manner. (Interview, 11 October 1971.)
35 Charles Hutton, 'Dr. Charles Holden, D.Lit., Litt.D., F.R.I.B.A., M.T.P.I., Architect', *Artifex*, 1969, vol. 3, p. 37; 'Memoirs', vol. 1, p. 111; *Dictionary of National Biography 1951–1960* (1971), pp. 493–4.
36 V&A Library has the 'Guild Workshop Record Book' which contains *c.* 90 drawings; they extend over most of the 1890s but the majority belong to 1890–2. V&A Prints and Drawings has a bound volume of 146 sheets of drawings covering the period of *c.* 1903–7 but confined to enamelwork and jewellery. CPL has a bound volume of *c.* 120 drawings covering all kinds of work between Feb 1900 and Nov 1901. There are also a few individual surviving drawings.
37 It is a question of extrapolation: there are a number of designs which can be firmly attributed, on the basis of signed drawings or attributions in periodicals etc.; of these the great majority belong to Ashbee, and one assumes that the same applies to those not at present attributable. But the attributable designs account for only about a quarter of known Guild products. It is worth noting that Alec Miller wrote that Ashbee designed 'almost all' the work made at the Guild; Miller, p. 18.
38 Baillie Scott: furniture and fittings in the Grand Ducal Palace at Darmstadt in 1897; Charles Spooner: a 'new screen' mentioned in J, 5 Sept 1901; Charles Holden: furniture in the chapel, King Edward VII Sanatorium, Midhurst, Sussex. A list of other architect-clients is given in catalogue G.
39 *AJ*, 1898, p. 232.
40 *S*, 1899, vol. 18, p. 118; *K und K*, 1900, vol. 3, pp. 173–4; *Artist*, 1902, vol. 33, pp. 17–18; *Craftsman* (Eastwood, N.Y.), 1908, vol. 5, p. 174. Hermann Muthesius, on the other hand, said he thought that the craftsmen of the Guild were, on the whole, artistically dependent on Ashbee, *DK*, 1898, vol. 2, p. 47.
41 Interview, July 1969.
42 See Chapter 12.
43 *S*, loc. cit; J, 25 Dec 1901.
44 J, 28 Nov 1886.
45 MSH, 13 Jan 1903.
46 Ibid.
47 *Craftsmanship*, p. 19; Miller, p. 98; H. Waentig, *Wirtschaft und Kunst* (Jena, 1909), p. 133.
48 *S*, 1897–8, vol. 12, p. 30, where it is said that some Guild wares were displayed in the Guild meeting room at Essex House 'mostly for a short period only, pending, in fact, their delivery to purchasers'. See also *DK*, 1898, vol. 2, p. 41.

49 Memorandum of Sale and Receipt of Deposit for 1893 and 1896, Deposits on Sales for 1899, A&CES archives, V&A Library.

50 See the list of catalogues in the note on Abbreviations and Conventions, above.

51 Various records of sales at A&CES, 1893, 1896, 1899 and 1903 in A&CES archives, V&A Library; and Dering Yard Visitors' Book, V&A Library.

52 J, Sept 1903. For work at the Duchess of Leeds's villa at Bordighera see drawings for furniture at CPL, dated Nov 1900, and silver and tableware in V&A Metalwork.

53 For Horsfall see p. 33 and Deposit on Sales for 1899, A&CES archives, V&A Library; for Rowley, Memorandum of Sale and Receipt of Deposit for 1896 and Deposit on Sales for 1899, in the same archive; for Mandello, see Chapter 5 above, note 125.

54 See p. 306. C. R. Ashbee, 'An Experiment in Cast-Iron Work' S, 1898, vol. 14, pp. 254–6, and information from Godfrey Rubens quoting a letter from J. W. Yuille of the Falkirk Iron Company to the British Institute of Industrial Art, 25 July 1928; also B, 1898, vol. 74, p. 562.

55 SWS, p. 100. The clocks may have been designed for Wylie and Lochhead of Glasgow; S, 1901, vol. 23, p. 170 illustrates a clock designed by Ashbee and exhibited by Wylie and Lochhead at the Glasgow Exhibition; this clock is now in the collection of Cheltenham Art Gallery and Museums. CMAF, 1900, vol. 20, p. 191 illustrates the 'Unconventional Fireplace Suite' made by the Dudley firm of Adshead and Smellie; it consists of a series of metal plaques as on the enamelled fireplace at 37 Cheyne Walk, with Ashbee motifs so crowded together on them that it is hard to believe he designed it; but he did. For Broadwoods, see pp. 287–92.

56 Carl Bode and Malcolm Cowley (eds.), The Portable Emerson (Harmondsworth, 1981), p. 20.

57 For neo-Platonism and Swedenborg, see J, 22 and 23 April 1888, Jan 1889; for Burne-Jones and Watts, J, c. 12 July 1904; for Puvis, J, Jan 1889, WGC, p. 52 and Miller, p. 60.

58 Roger Fry to Lowes Dickinson, 24 Feb 1889, Fry Papers, KCC.

59 See p. 314.

60 J, 28 Nov 1886: 'Went in the morning as "per usual" on Saturday to South Kensington and worked among the embroideries.' For the fireplace, see pp. 297–9, 302.

61 J, Jan/Feb 1888.

62 Ibid.

63 Geoffrey Keynes (ed.), The Complete Writings of William Blake (1957), pp. 525 and 509.

64 Ibid., pp. 630–1.

65 Transactions, p. 31.

66 Deborah Dorfman, Blake in the Nineteenth Century (1969); Robert Schmutzler, 'Blake and Art Nouveau', AR, 1955, vol. 107, pp. 90–7.

67 The drawings from the title-page etc. of Jerusalem in J are preceded by a copy of Blake's design for 'A Divine Image', a poem rejected by Blake from The Songs of Innocence and Experience and only printed a few times after his death; the British Museum acquired a copy in 1864.

68 Alongside the drawings from Jerusalem in J are the words 'Golgonooza: inspired art by which salvation must come (Swinb)'.

69 The Ideals of the Craftsman (n.d. [1889]), p. 5, pamphlet in 'Letters'.

70 John H. Harvey, 'Gilliflower and Carnation', Garden History, 1978, vol. 6, pp. 46–57; J. L. Nevinson, 'English Domestic Embroidery Patterns of the Sixteenth and Seventeenth Centuries', Walpole Society, 1939–40, vol. 28, pp. 1–13; Aileen Ribeiro, '"A Paradice of Flowers": Flowers in English Dress in the late sixteenth and early seventeenth centuries', Connoisseur, 1979, vol. 201, pp. 110–17.

71 The circular is in 'Letters'. There is an undated design for a certificate for the Guild and School in GWRB with what appears to be a pink for an emblem and the address 34 Commercial Street, which would argue against the connection between pinks and Essex House suggested here; but it is probably not earlier than the summer of 1890 as it was designed by J. Eadie Reid who joined the Guild in July 1890.

72 The earliest references to Essex House are MSH and MGH for 14 Aug 1890.

73 The drawing of Essex House on p. 28 has pinks to one side.

74 For pinks in the garden at Essex House, see the Essex House Alphabet, J, March 1900.

75 This was presumably the plaster medallion designed by Ashbee and executed by Bill Hardiman which was exhibited at A&CES:1889:196, and in Glasgow early in 1890, see Corporation Galleries, Glasgow. Arts and Crafts Exhibition. 1890, no. 196.

76 The roundel is on, e.g., Ashbee's pamphlet The Ideals of the Craftsman in 'Letters'; the second image is in Transactions, p. 25.

77 See also the cover design for Chapters, discussed on pp. 374–5.

78 E. T. Cook and Alexander Wedderburn (eds.), The Works of John Ruskin (1903–12), vol. 15, p. 485; Thomas Carlyle, Collected Works (1870), vol. 13, p. 47.

79 In his application for the Slade Professorship at Oxford Ashbee wrote 'the "theory and practice" of Architecture have their roots deep down in modern Industry, in social life and in economic conditions . . .', Bodleian Library, Oxford, MS. Top. Oxon. c. 178.

80 Two of the medallions are indistinct, even in early photographs; they were perhaps gilded but not painted, waiting to celebrate some future development of the Guild.

81 There is a drawing of John Williams on the beach at Seasalter with such a sun shining in his face, done by Bill Hardiman; Ashbee has written 'the sun is drawn according to the correct tradition of the Guild of Handicraft'. See 'Sketch Book 1880–1889', KCC.

82 Edward N. Hooker (ed.), The Critical Works of John Dennis (Baltimore, 1939), vol. 1, p. 339.

83 J, 11 Jan 1888.

84 Ibid.

85 J, 23 April 1896.

86 The design was illustrated in S, 1895, vol. 5, p. 128, but it appears to date from 1889 or earlier, being exhibited at A&CES:1889:76.

87 The half-title, title-page and verso of the title-page of the large paper edition of Chapters feature naked youths upholding, standing on or chasing spheres, but they are not winged.

88 MES, p. 10.

89 Ashbee Collection, vol. 2, p. 98 and possibley AJ, 1896, p. 348; the coal scuttle illustrated in the drawing-room at 37 Cheyne Walk in S, 1895, vol. 5, p. 68 may be identical.

90 Ashbee to Elizabeth MacColl, 5 Dec 1892, Glasgow University Library. The binding is now in the Bodleian Library. See also AJ, 1896, p. 149.

91 E. T. Cook and Alexander Wedderburn (eds.), The Works of John Ruskin (1903–12), vol. 9, p. 72.

92 The Sirens Three was first published in the English Illustrated Magazine 1884–5, pp. [486] ff.

93 The winged youth is a case in point and it may be no accident that Ashbee's frontispiece to the Essex House Press edition of Prometheus Unbound is in the style of Ricketts.

94 W. B. Yeats, Mythologies (1959), p. 268.

CHAPTER TEN
ARCHITECTURE

1 E. P. Warren, 'The Life and Work of George Frederick Bodley', RIBA Journal, 1909–10, vol. 17, p. 334.

2 For Hoar Cross and Clumber, Ashbee's application for the Slade Professorship at Oxford, Bodleian Library, Oxford, MS. Top. Oxon. c. 178; for Hewell Grange, J, 22 April 1913.

3 A, 1893, vol. 49, p. 83.

4 Elevation of the west front, RIBA Drawings Collection; Ashbee Collection, vol. 2, p. 194; photographs of the house before Ashbee's alterations, at The Wodehouse.

5 American Sheaves, p. 35.

6 Designs for public buildings: Appendix 1, nos. 1, 56 and 68, for instance.

7 Hugh Seebohm's house, Poynder's End, Hitchin, was designed by Geoffry Lucas; Rob Martin Holland employed Ernest Newton and Herbert Baker at Overbury; E. Peter Jones asked Ashbee to design workers' houses for him at Ellesmere Port, but

had his own house, Greenbank, Eaton Road, Chester, altered and added to by Charles Reilly; Wilfred Buckley, who sold Essex House Press books in America, employed Reginald Blomfield to build his Hampshire mansion, Moundsmere, near Preston Candover.

8 *Chapters*, chapters 11, 12 and 13; Lethaby employed workmen directly on his church at Brockhampton in Herefordshire in 1901, and Prior at St Mary's Church, Burton Bradstock, Dorset, in the mid-1890s.

9 *Chapters*, pp. 134–5.

10 Ibid., p. 142.

11 Ibid., p. 143.

12 DSR, 4 Dec 1896 for 72–3 Cheyne Walk; 24 Dec 1897 for 74 Cheyne Walk; 11 March 1898 for 118–19 Cheyne Walk; 25 April 1898 for 37 Cheyne Walk; 7 June 1898 for 3 and 4 Little Davis Place; and 24 Sept 1898 for 38 and 39 Cheyne Walk.

13 *Endeavour*, p. 30; see also *Craftsmanship*, pp. 142, 145 and 147.

14 See below, pp. 240–1.

15 *Endeavour*, p. 31.

16 *Chapters*, p. 121.

17 Alan Crawford, 'Changes on Cheyne Walk', *AR*, 1983, vol. 174, p. 78/9, fig. 2.

18 Donald J. Olsen, *The Growth of Victorian London* (1976), pp. 147–54.

19 Mark Girouard, *Sweetness and Light* (1977), pp. 177–85.

20 *S*, 1895, vol. 5, pp. 66–74. Building work must have begun in 1893 as there is an entry for 28 July 1893 in DSR. Ashbee put the date 1894 on the rainwater head; and used the address from at least 10 May 1894, see a letter of that date to Oscar Browning, Hastings Public Library.

21 Ibid., p. 71; for the interior see below, Chapter 11, pp. 22–9.

22 *B*, 1897, vol. 72, p. 9.

23 The blank aedicules on the Electricity Transformer Station, Upper Street, Islington, by the General Section of the LCC Architect's Department, 1905–6, are among several tributes to Dance's Newgate Prison, demolished in 1902.

24 Philip Webb had designed an office building in brick with a tall stone bay in 1868 at 19 Lincoln's Inn Fields, a few doors from Ashbee's office where the Magpie and Stump was designed; but Webb's design was much more disciplined than Ashbee's.

25 *British Architect*, 1895, vol. 44, pp. 5–6; *Cottages*, pp. 57–61.

26 On 7 Sept 1898, six days after he had acquired a lease of 74 Cheyne Walk, F. A. Forbes mortgaged it to Henry Owen, the Ashbee family lawyer, and Willie Gibbins, a Birmingham friend of Ashbee's; on the same day, Mrs H. S. Ashbee mortgaged 37 Cheyne Walk to Forbes, Owen and Gibbins. This mortgage was discharged in 1899. The dates and circumstances suggest that these mortgages were designed to raise funds to pay for the freehold and building of 39 Cheyne Walk. See MDR for these dates.

27 Drawings in the RIBA Drawings Collection and at CPL.

28 Some sense of his tactics can be gained from a typescript sheet relating to 4 Danvers Street in Chelsea Miscellany, Book 13(1) at CPL: Ashbee designed a studio in the garden, got the agreement of the District Surveyor, and then offered a 40-year lease for sale; the price was £750, reduced to £650 if he were employed to build the studio.

29 Little Davis Place is now Apollo Place.

30 See Chapter 3 above, note 112. The 'Plan on Indenture of Conveyance dated the 4th May 1896' refers only to 3 and 4 Little Davis Place; 115–16 may not have been bought at this date, but it seems to have been by 1 April 1901, when Ashbee wrote to Gomme. For work on 3 and 4 Little Davis Place in 1898, see DSR, 7 June 1898. In 1914 the whole property, including 27 Riley Street, was described as Ashbee's freehold in the prospectus and correspondence from estate agents at CPL, C.M. 1704. The possibility that Janet's father helped to buy 27 Riley Street is suggested by the fact that she was entitled to most of the rental income from the property, see J, 3 March 1927.

31 The final design, 'World's End House', was offered for sale with the freehold at £11,000. See drawings in the RIBA Drawings Collection and CPL, and prospectus and correspondence at CPL, C.M. 1704.

32 For Sloane Stanley, see his obituary in *West London Press*, 1 Dec 1944; for the probable date of agreement, see plans of the properties 72–7 Cheyne Walk and 4 Danvers Street at CPL, including one made by Ernest Godman and dated 27 Aug 1896.

33 See the 'Ground Plan of London', GLRO.

34 7 Oct and 1 Nov 1897, FA.

35 How large his property was: Ashbee made designs at one time or another for every plot between Old Church Street and Danvers Street; but Godman's plans of Aug 1896 seem to refer only to 72–7 Cheyne Walk and 4 Danvers Street. Numbers 70–1 were in any case not part of the Sloane Stanley estate, and Ashbee acquired the freehold, perhaps in 1897; see entry for 14 Oct 1897 in MDR, and Ashbee's annotations to a prospectus for 64–9 Cheyne Walk etc., offered for sale on 13 July 1899 by Farebrother, Ellis, Egerton, Breach and Co. at CPL.

36 The windows had octagonal glazing bars like the one Philip Webb had designed at 35 Glebe Place, just behind Cheyne Walk, almost thirty years before. Curiously, Guthrie bought 35 Glebe Place in 1897. For Walton at the Magpie and Stump, Janet Forbes's journal, 18 Dec 1896, FA; there are drawings for the Guthrie house at the RIBA Drawings Collection and at CPL. It is not clear where on Cheyne Walk the house was to go and none of the drawings is dated; there is, however, a letter from Guthrie to Ashbee of 4 Nov 1896 discussing 'plans' Ashbee had sent, FA.

37 James L. Caw, *Sir James Guthrie, P.R.S.A., LL.D.: A Biography* (1932), pp. 70–2.

38 DSR, 4 Dec 1896; drawings for interior details of June, July and Aug 1897, CPL; letter of 19 Sept 1897 from Walton to Ashbee, FA.

39 By Godwin at 36 Tite Street in 1878 and by Maclaren at 10 and 12 Palace Court, Bayswater in 1889–90.

40 Drawings in the RIBA Drawings Collection; for Rollins see Susan Beattie, *The New Sculpture* (1983), p. 249.

41 Mark Girouard, 'The Victorian Artist at Home: I: The Holland Park Houses' and '... II: Chelsea's Bohemian Studio Houses', *Country Life*, 1972, vol. 152, pp. 1278–81 and 1370–4; plans for 35 Tite Street and 44 Tite Street, V&A Prints and Drawings.

42 e.g., Gerald Horsley writing in W. Shaw Sparrow (ed.), *Flats Urban Houses and Cottage Homes* (n.d.), p. 111.

43 Girouard, *Sweetness and Light* (1977), p. 180.

44 Though Voysey would have liked to use roughcast on 14 and 16 Hans Road, Kensington, of 1891–2 and on some proposed terraced houses in Chelsea of 1891.

45 A letter from Edwin Abbey to E. A. Walton of 1 Dec 1896, FA, suggests that Ashbee had begun work on the scheme by then, though Abbey did not see plans. The earliest dated drawing is of Jan 1897, RIBA Drawings Collection. The properties were auctioned on behalf of the LCC on 30 March 1897, and Ashbee's offer is documented in LCC, Corporate Property, Charities and Endowment Committee, Presented Papers, 1 March, 5 April and 17 May 1897, and LCC, Minutes of Proceedings, 1 June 1897, GLRO.

46 LCC, Corporate Property, Charities and Endowment Committee, Presented Papers, 28 March 1898. There are drawings for the original scheme in RIBA Drawings Collection and CPL, giving the clients' names. In 'Memoirs', vol. 1, p. 111 Ashbee wrote, 'There were studios for John, Sargent and Abbey and other artists.' But the drawings make no mention of J. S. Sargent, or of Augustus John if he is meant. For Walton's part, see the letter from Abbey referred to in n. 45 above.

47 Drawings for the second scheme in RIBA Drawings Collection and CPL, one at CPL having the LCC, Architect's Department stamp of 19 Feb 1898. LCC, Corporate Property, Charities and Endowment Committee, Presented Papers, 20 Dec 1897 and 28 March 1898.

48 Letter to Janet Forbes, March 1898, FA; LCC, Corporate Property, Charities and Endowment Committee, Presented Papers, 28 March 1898 and LCC. Minutes of Proceedings, 5 April 1898. The negotiations were complicated at all stages by Ashbee's insistence that his plans should be approved before he signed a lease, the reverse of the LCC's normal procedure. After the collapse of negotiations, the site was leased to Patrick Geddes's Town and Gown Association Ltd. of Edinburgh, who pro-

posed to build 'ideal residential flats' to designs by W. R. Lethaby and Frank Troup; the scheme was not executed but Geddes's connection with the site was long and influential; see LCC, Minutes of Proceedings, 1 Nov 1898 and 23 Jan 1900, and p. 158.

49 Godwin's Tower House still stands; for Voysey see *British Architect* 1889, vol. 31, p. 70 and 1891, vol. 36, p. 210, the latter being the house built as 14 South Parade, Bedford Park, London.

50 For Fleming, Ashbee and Lionel Curtis, see above Chapter 5, pp. 16–17. There are references to Fleming in J from 1900 onwards, but I am not sure when Ashbee first met him. See also Susan Beattie, *A Revolution in London Housing: LCC Housing Architects and their Work 1893–1914* (1980), p. 21 and Chapter 2 *passim*.

51 According to Ashbee in 'Memoirs', vol. 1, p. 111.

52 Holden may not have been involved in the early stages of Danvers Tower which seem to date from 1896, whereas his arrival in Ashbee's office appears to date from 1897, see *Dictionary of National Biography 1951–1960* (1971), p. 493.

53 DSR, 24 Dec 1897; Ashbee to Janet, 7 Oct 1897, FA.

54 Plans in the RIBA Drawings Collection and at CPL.

55 The interior of 74 Cheyne Walk is illustrated in BN, 1902, vol. 82, p. 846.

56 Ashbee to Janet, 4 May 1898, FA.

57 Webb in a letter to Sidney Barnsley quoted in W. R. Lethaby, *Philip Webb and his work* (1979), p. 259.

58 Ashbee designed a cottage for Mrs Hunt at Findon in Sussex, see Appendix 1, no. 81.

59 Drawings for 75 Cheyne Walk in the RIBA Drawings Collection and at CPL: some legal plans dated 1900 and 1901, architectural drawings dated 1902; building work had begun by 4 April 1902, DSR. For 38 and 39 Cheyne Walk, drawings in both the above collections dated 1898 and 1899; building work had begun by 24 Sept 1898, DSR.

60 For 39 as a speculation by Ashbee see *Neubauten in London* (Berlin, 1900), plate 8, where the sale notice on the house directs enquirers to apply at 37 Cheyne Walk; and note 26 above. As an example of Miss Christian's requirements, the ground floor windows on Number 38 were made particularly long, allowing large canvases to be taken out of her studio.

61 *Survey of London: Parish of Chelsea (Part I)* (n.d. [1909]), plate 88, and the inscription on a drawing of Shrewsbury House, filed with Ashbee's drawings for Shrewsbury Court, RIBA Drawings Collection; for Bracknell bricks, see *Builders' Journal and Architectural Record*, 1901–2, vol. 15, pp. 82–3.

62 Dennis Farr, *English Art 1870–1944* (1978), p. 144; Alastair Service, *Edwardian Architecture and Its Origins* (1975), p. 355.

63 B, 1900, vol. 78, p. 584.

64 See pp. 58–9.

65 Reginald Blomfield, *History of Renaissance Architecture in England 1500–1800* (1897), John Belcher and Mervyn Macartney, *Later Renaissance Architecture in England* (1901), and the series published as 'The Practical Exemplar' in *AR* under Macartney's editorship, were among the most influential publications.

66 WGC, pp. 26–8. Of Blomfield Ashbee wrote: 'he does not think much about the meaning of the Arts and builds in "Neo-Georgian", a style more than all others suitable for mechanical reduplication. But no one I suppose ever charged Reg. Blomfield with idealism...' J, 14 Jan 1915.

67 Drawings in the RIBA Drawings Collection and at CPL.

68 See above Chapter 6, pp. 160–1.

69 Site plan by Harry B. Measures among Ashbee's drawings at CPL; 'Ground Plan of London', GLRO.

70 Drawings in the RIBA Drawings Collection and at CPL; for the cost of the scheme, see RIBA, *Catalogue of the Drawings Collection of the RIBA: A* (Farnborough, 1969), p. 34.

71 WGC, pp. 84–5. Among American university buildings the Michigan Union at Ann Arbor could serve as a parallel; Ashbee illustrated it in his 'A Survey of English-Speaking Universities' (Typescript, 1912), KCC.

72 For an Outlook Tower in Chelsea, see *Re-erection of Crosby Hall on More's Garden, Chelsea* (n.d. [1908]), p. 7, pamphlet, GLRO; for 70 and 71 Cheyne Walk, see note 35 above.

73 Early drawings at CPL, e.g., July and 24 Aug 1912; refer to Miss Ladenburg; later drawings refer to Mrs Trier; Daisy Ladenburg married Paul Schlesinger-Trier in the autumn of 1912.

74 DSR, 27 Sept 1912.

75 The principal drawings for the executed scheme are undated, but there are drawings for details of the final scheme in the RIBA Drawings Collection and at CPL dated Sept 1912.

76 Drawings for the penultimate and executed schemes at CPL.

77 BN, 1904, vol. 86, p. 617, *British Architect*, 1904, vol. 61, p. 327 and B, 1904, vol. 86, p. 602, all re: 75 Cheyne Walk; BN, 1913, vol. 104, p. 638 re: 71 Cheyne Walk; Hermann Muthesius, *The English House* (trans. Janet Seligman) (1979), p. 46; and, more recently, Gavin Stamp in *Architectural Design Profiles: 13: London 1900* (1978), p. 315.

78 *Twentieth Century Houses* (1934), p. 74.

79 *Cottages*, p. 6.

80 K und K, 1901, vol. 4, p. 462.

81 The series 'Coaching Days and Coaching Ways' in *English Illustrated Magazine* for 1887–8, illustrated by Hugh Thomson and Herbert Railton, provides many good examples of this kind of standardized picturesque image.

82 Paintings by Whistler's unhappy acolyte Walter Greaves and photographs by James Hedderley could also have served as sources.

83 *American Sheaves*, pp. 52 and 67.

84 Ibid., p. 70.

85 Ibid.

86 Ibid. p. 52.

87 Margaret Richardson, *Architects of the Arts and Crafts Movement* (1983), pp. 28 and 51.

88 John Cornforth, 'Birthplace of Urban Conservation: The Royal Mile, Edinburgh: 1', *Country Life*, 1981, vol. 170, pp. 572–4.

89 His tenants included not only Whistler but Epstein, at 72 Cheyne Walk who, being short of money for the rent on one occasion, paid it in kind with a naked male torso, member erect, dumped in the garden of the Magpie and Stump to the scandal of Ashbee's mother. (Interview with Philip Mairet, 11 Oct 1971.)

90 *Illustrated Carpenter and Builder*, 23 May 1941.

91 *Cottages*, p. 9.

92 Circular advertising the opening of the Guild of Handicraft shop at 16A Brook Street, May 1899, JJ Coll.

93 It is not clear exactly when Ashbee bought the houses. They first came to notice in 1895 when they were to be sold for building purposes and Mrs Haweis tried to save them. (Philip Norman, *London Vanished and Vanishing* [1905], pp. 265–7.) Ashbee surveyed the buildings in Oct and Nov 1897 (drawings in the RIBA Drawings Collection) and on 11 Jan 1898 could write to Janet, 'The Turner house is settled and I am starting to rebuild it.' (FA) He transferred the property to Max Balfour on 16 May 1898 (MDR), but there are detail drawings at CPL as late as Oct 1898.

94 Reports of 7 July 1898 and 31 Jan 1899, Horndon-on-the-Hill parish chest. I am grateful to Shirley Bury for bringing these reports to my notice.

95 The Minories, Colchester, *The Eccentric A. H. Mackmurdo 1851–1942* (Catalogue of an exhibition 1979), n.p.

96 *Cottages*, pp. 7–11; drawings at CT.

97 *Cottages*, pp. 10–13; drawings at CT.

98 *Cottages*, pp. 50–1 and frontispiece; drawings at CT.

99 *Cottages*, p. 44.

100 SPAB, *Notes on the repair of ancient buildings* (1903), p. 17.

101 The Annual Reports of the Society for the years round 1900 contain few references to small domestic buildings, and its first statement on cottages seems to be A. H. Powell's *Report on the treatment of old cottages* (1919).

102 Lawrence Weaver, *Small Country Houses of To-Day* (n.d.), pp. 1–7.

103 Photographs in the Ashbee Collection, vol. 1, pp. 194–5; drawings at CT; Miller, p. 123.

104 J, 16 Jan, 9 March, 20 April and April 1903, and 24 Nov 1905. In 1919 J. J. Glynn, representing the Earl of Gainsborough

Estates, noted that Ashbee owned a ground lease on the Norman Chapel expiring in the year 2002; see his letter of 12 April 1919 in the records of Bruton Knowles, estate agents, at Gloucestershire Record Office, D2299–1891. I am grateful to Craig Fees for telling me of this correspondence.

105 Drawings at CT.

106 The 'nave' was occupied by the Essex House Press soon after the Coomaraswamys moved in and may never have been used as a music room.

107 *B*, 1907, vol. 93, p. 223.

108 E. T. Cook and Alexander Wedderburn (eds.), *The Works of John Ruskin* (1903–1912), vol. 8, p. 234.

109 See pp. 199–200.

110 Alan Crawford, 'A Tour of Broadway and Chipping Campden' (Victorian Society tour notes, 1978).

111 e.g., Arthur Martin, *The Small House* (1906); G. Ll. Morris and Esther Wood, *The Country Cottage* (1906); J. H. Elder-Duncan, *Country Cottages and Week-End Homes* (n.d. [1906]); Lawrence Weaver, *The 'Country Life' Book of Cottages* (1913).

112 *Cottages*, pp. 23–5; drawings submitted to the District Surveyor, Bromley Rural District Council; now in the possession of the London Borough of Bromley.

113 Fred Griggs felt it ought to have been pretty; in his drawing for *Cottages* he filled the shallow tympanum over the front door with ornament in the Adam manner.

114 *Cottages*, p. 23.

115 Elder-Duncan, op. cit, p. 27.

116 The only exception would be the houses at Gidea Park, Appendix 1, no. 55, the most suburban of his designs.

117 *Cottages*, pp. 19–23; drawings submitted to the District Surveyor, Eton Rural District Council, dated 2 and 3 April 1903, now in the possession of South Bucks District Council.

118 Alec Clifton-Taylor, *The Pattern of English Building* (1972), pp. 360–5.

119 *AR*, 1914, vol. 36, p. 50.

120 *Cottages*, p. 37.

121 James D. Kornwolf, *M. H. Baillie Scott and the Arts and Crafts Movement* (1972), pp. 300–2. There are photographs of Five Bells in the Ashbee Collection, vol. 1, pp. 129, 131, and drawings submitted to the District Surveyor, Eton Rural District Council, approved 10 Oct 1905, now in the possession of South Bucks District Council. The building appears to have been demolished.

122 E. M. Forster, *A Room with a View* (Harmondsworth, 1978), p. 195.

123 J, 26 June 1905.

124 J, 9 Feb 1907 and Jan 1907.

125 Above these two single-storey bays on the north front Ashbee built wooden pergolas like those on the house called Welgelegen at Cape Town which Baker restored for Cecil Rhodes; see Herbert Baker, *Architecture and Personalities* (1944), p. 24. On this front also there is a circular window recalling that on a church at Savoca in Sicily; there are drawings by Ashbee of the church in a sketchbook in V&A: Prints and Drawings, and photographs in J, Jan 1907.

126 Box 5, Folder 2, FA Jerusalem.

CHAPTER ELEVEN
FURNITURE AND
INTERIOR DECORATION

1 Elizabeth Aslin, *Nineteenth Century English Furniture* (1962), p. 71. One account which does not ignore Ashbee's furniture is B. G. Burrough, 'Three Disciples of William Morris: 2. Charles Robert Ashbee', *Connoisseur*, 1969, vol. 172, pp. 85–90 and 262–6.

2 MGH, 27 May and 21 Nov 1889 for the elections of Phillips and Curtis; advertisement sheet of Sept 1889 in 'Letters' for the first mention of Atkinson.
The whereabouts of the following early pieces of Guild furniture is known: a frame for a reproduction of *The Triumph of the Innocents* by Holman Hunt, made for the Manchester Art Museum, Ancoats, 1888–9, now in Manchester City Art Gal-

lery; an oak cupboard, painted with verses from William Blake's *Auguries of Innocence*, an oak trestle table, and a hall bench attributable to Ashbee on stylistic grounds, all of 1889, at Abbotsholme School, Rocester, Uttoxeter, Staffordshire; a similar trestle table formerly in the possession of the descendants of Gerald Bishop and now in the V&A; a desk to a design of 1890 though possibly made up later, in the possession of Haslam and Whiteway Ltd. of London; an octagonal oak table stained green to a design of 1890 and almost certainly made up later, in the possession of Felicity Ashbee, see *Connoisseur*, 1969, vol. 172, p. 90; a walnut cabinet, now slightly altered, to a design of 1890–1, see *Connoisseur*, 1971, vol. 176, pp. 106–7. A cabinet in oak, now at Standen, East Grinstead, West Sussex, though not precisely dated, is a variant of a design exhibited at A&CES:1890:374.

3 Design for chairs dated 1890 in GWRB.

4 GWRB, 28 Aug 1890.

5 A group of undated photographs in the Essex House Photograph Book, V&A Library, shows 25 designs for rush-seated chairs, some of which are identical to those produced by Morris and Company. The standard character of these chairs raises the question whether they were designed by Ashbee, or made by the Guild, at all.

6 Ball and claw feet: GWRB, 1 Jan 1890 and *Connoisseur*, 1969, vol. 172, p. 90. On the stained oak cabinet at Standen Ashbee used a cornice with a groove cut into the underside of the corona, a treatment which is commoner in architectural woodwork of c. 1680–1720 than in furniture.

7 Aslin, op. cit, plate 105. The all-over painted decoration and the fact that the carcase is not of a frame and panel construction make this cabinet atypical among early Guild furniture.

8 Designs attributable to this period include a writing desk made for Henry Owen in 1892 and now in the Scolton Manor Museum, Haverfordwest, Dyfed; furniture for the Magpie and Stump, discussed later in this chapter; a cabinet in light wood in the possession of Haslam and Whiteway Ltd. of London, decorated with a frieze of pinks in copper and enamel, which is the reason for attributing it to the Guild of Handicraft and to this period; two upholstered chairs and a desk illustrated in *CMAF* 1895, vol. 16, pp. 61–2; and the five items exhibited at A&CES:1896, see note 12 below.

9 Fine Art Society, *Morris and Company* (Catalogue of an exhibition 1979), nos. 18 and 19, for instance.

10 Mary Comino, *Gimson and the Barnsleys* (1980), Chapter 4. The contribution of the fifth architect-member of Kenton and Company, Sidney Barnsley, remains unclear.

11 A&CES:1893:45, 85, 96, 134. The Wood Handicrafts Society was only mentioned in connection with Voysey's work, but Spooner's pieces were partly carried out by a craftsman consistently associated with the Society; and in 1896 its address was Eyot Cottage, Chiswick Mall, Hammersmith, where Spooner lived. For illustrations, see *BN*, 1893, vol. 65, pp. 508–9.

12 Joseph Barlow, H. T. Dennis, Tom Jelliffe, Jim Pyment, Dick Read and G. Yonwin, all cabinet-makers, were elected on 13 July 1894 (MGH). Guild exhibits at the A&CES:1896 included the oak music cabinet discussed below; an oak chest stained green, illustrated in *Artist*, 1896, vol. 18, pp. 22 and 28, and now in a private collection; a lectern in oak and copper illustrated in *British Architect*, 1896, vol. 46, facing p. 292; and an oak sideboard inlaid with pewter and a writing cabinet decorated with gesso which, though not catalogued, can be seen in the background of a photograph of the exhibition in Ashbee Collection, vol. 2, p. 57; the sideboard is illustrated in *Artist*, 1897, vol. 19, p. 170, the writing cabinet in *S*, 1897–8, vol. 12, p. 33.

13 *S*, 1897, vol. 9, p. 127; *Artist*, 1896, vol. 18, p. 22. See also *DK*, 1898, vol. 2, p. 43.

14 M. H. Baillie Scott, 'Some furniture for the new palace, Darmstadt' and 'Decoration and furniture for the new palace, Darmstadt', *S*, 1898, vol. 14, pp. 91–7 and 1899, vol. 16, pp. 107–15. Photographs of some of the work executed for Darmstadt are in Ashbee Collection, vol. 2, pp. 70–93. For Ashbee's leather-backed chair, see *CMAF*, 1890, vol. 11, p. 119.

15 As an example of Scott's influence on Ashbee, compare a writ-

ing cabinet designed by Ashbee and exhibited in 1899 (*S*, 1899, vol. 18, p. 120) with a needlework cabinet designed by Scott for Darmstadt (*S*, 1899, vol. 16, p. 108). There is a variant of Ashbee's design in the *Badisches Landesmuseum* at Karlsruhe, West Germany, and another in a private collection in England. The question of how far Scott influenced Ashbee turns to some extent on an undated design for a toilet cabinet now in the library of the Art Workers' Guild, and illustrated in *DK*, 1898, vol. 2, p. 47. It has a boxy form, dark exterior and light interior, and heavy strap hinges with pierced ornament at the end, all 'Baillie Scott' elements in Ashbee's mature style. If the design was made before the Darmstadt commission, the case for Scott's influence would be weaker.

16 For the sideboard at 39 Cheyne Walk, see Ashbee Collection, vol. 1, pp. 40–5.

17 The two most striking examples of Guild metalwork on furniture were a music cabinet exhibited in Turin in 1902 and illustrated in *Deutsche Kunst und Dekoration* (Darmstadt) 1902–3, vol. 11, p. 231, and a tall cupboard illustrated on p. 18 of catalogue D.

18 *Furniture History*, 1977, vol. 13, pp. 52–3 and plate 31.

19 The earliest example of inlay is on a design for a sideboard for 2 Eaton Place of *c*. 1890 in GWRB; then comes the oak sideboard referred to in note 12 above; and then the two writing cabinets exhibited in 1899 and at the A&CES, see note 21 below.

20 *WGC*, p. 18.

21 See, for example, the needlework cabinet at *S*, 1899, vol. 16, p. 108. Ashbee's mahogany cabinet was exhibited at the A&CES: 1899:235, and no. 167 in the same exhibition was a writing cabinet designed by Ashbee in limewashed oak with similar inlays.

22 A&CES:1899:235; for Jelliffe's skill, Miller, p. 14.

23 There were such chairs, though without the curve in the central splat, among the dining-room furniture made for E. Peter Jones in 1900, and they may be among the earliest.

24 Arts Council of Great Britain, *Burne-Jones* (Catalogue of an exhibition, 1975), no. 208.

25 *Artist*, 1894, vol. 15, pp. 387–9; Michael Wilson, 'The Case of the Victorian Piano', *V&A Museum Yearbook*, 1972, vol. 3, pp. 133–53; David Wainwright, *Broadwood By Appointment: A History* (1982), pp. 209–14.

26 A&CES:1903:494.

27 *Artist*, 1901, vol. 9, pp. 174–5.

28 The Zumpe instrument was illustrated in an article by John F. Runciman, 'The Pianoforte: Past, Present and Future' in *AJ*, 1894, pp. 142–6, a volume to which Ashbee himself contributed several articles.

29 *The English House* (trans. Janet Seligman) (1979), p. 218.

30 C. R. Ashbee, *Echoes from the City of the Sun* (1905), p. 30, where the poem is reprinted.

31 The musical women sit in front of trellis work, an echo perhaps of the scene painted on a Dolmetsch harpsichord by Helen Coombe, shortly before she married Roger Fry, in 1896. The instrument was exhibited at A&CES:1896:178.

32 The piano now stands in the dining-room at Toynbee Hall, scene of Ashbee's first decorative endeavours.

33 Letter to the author from S. E. Broadwood, 10 Sept 1980; the piano cost 180 guineas.

34 *Artist*, 1901, vol. 32, p. 186 attributes this piano to Ashbee; *S*, 1901–2, vol. 24, pp. 135–6 attributes it to T. M. Shallcross. The *Studio* is the more circumstantial of the two; but the involvement of Varley and the choice of materials (oak stained green, Hungarian ash stained blue, and panels of white holly) point to Ashbee having played a part. A third 'square' piano belonged to Ananda Coomaraswamy at the Norman Chapel, and the Guild blacksmiths can be seen making the wrought iron hinges for its lid in plate 63; but it is not clear whether Ashbee or Broadwoods had anything to do with the design of the case as such. I know of only one other 'square' grand piano by an Arts and Crafts designer, that by Voysey illustrated in *Artifex*, 1970, vol. 4, p. 60. This design is undated, but John Brandon-Jones tells me that it may belong to the period 1906–9.

35 A&CES:1896:513; *Artist*, 1896, vol. 18, 'Arts and Crafts Special Number', p. 38.

36 *S*, 1897, vol. 10, p. 154; *Artist*, 1901, vol. 32, p. 188.

37 The four uprights were: one dated 1900 with painted decoration for E. Peter Jones, now in a private collection in Cambridge: see Catalogue G, p. 17; one in oak of 1903 with inlays and enamel plaques, now at Standen, East Grinstead, West Sussex; one in Spanish mahogany, undated, decorated with inlays of clover, now in the collection of Jimmy Page: see J. H. Elder-Duncan, *The House Beautiful and Useful* (n.d. [1907]), p. 153; and a fourth, in Spanish mahogany with elaborate strap hinges, whereabouts unknown, illustrated in Simon Nowell Smith (ed.), *Edwardian England* (1964), plate xlviib, and there dated 1904.

38 It is difficult to date this cabinet precisely. It made its first appearance in an exhibition of the Guild's work at the Woodbury Gallery in London in the autumn of 1902, see *K und K*, 1902, vol. 5, p. 597. A date of 1901–2 seems probable.

39 *Chapters*, p. 78.

40 *K und K*, 1902, vol. 5, p. 596. Earlier intricacy can be found on toilet cabinets and writing cabinets of *c*. 1898, see for example Cheltenham, C7, and the veneers on a desk in ebony for the Duchess of Leeds, *c*. 1900, see Ashbee Collection, vol. 3.

41 See Chapter 15 below, pp. 411–12.

42 For the Wodehouse screen, now destroyed, see GWRB, p. 40 and Ashbee Collection, vol. 2, p. 189; for Seal, which survives, see J, 8 Nov 1897 and *Builders' Journal and Architectural Record*, 1900, vol. 11, p. 228. Ashbee designed two more screens at Seal after he had retired to Godden Green, in the south aisle and the chancel arch.

43 The nearest Ashbee came to a Bodleyesque treatment was the reredos he designed for the church of St James in Walthamstow, London, now destroyed, see Ashbee Collection, vol. 1, pp. 324–5 and *Christian Art* (Boston, Mass), 1908, vol. 4, p. 112.

44 For the lectern, *S*, 1899, vol. 18, p. 118 and V&A Museum, *Victorian Church Art* (Catalogue of an exhibition 1971), O:16. For Shottermill, drawings at CPL and Ashbee Collection, vol. 1, p. 289. Ashbee designed a pulpit for Shottermill, *c*. 1901. All his work in the church survives, though the chancel has been rearranged.

45 For Bramwell, see A&CES:1903:213 A, B.

46 The church of St Mary the Virgin, Urswick, Lancashire contains an interesting late collection of church furniture by Ashbee and the Guild, of *c*. 1907.

47 Correspondence relating to work at Calne in J and FA covers the period August 1907 to April 1909. The organ was presented to the church by Henry George Harris on 19 Feb 1908 and Ashbee's case may have been designed after that. Besides the work described here Ashbee designed the parclose screen to the Epiphany chapel.

48 Ashbee to Alec Miller, 5 Aug 1907, FA. For the reredos, see *Craftsmanship*, pp. 141 and 143.

49 Edward G. Caple, 'Calne and its Organs', *Organ*, 1940–1, vol. 20, pp. 18–24; the echo organ was removed *c*. 1960.

50 Miller, p. 121.

51 See pp. 141, 143 and pp. 274–6. He had almost certainly seen the mosaics on the west wall of the Palatina in Palermo.

52 In a design for the case which hangs in the church, there are unexecuted designs for the easternmost chancel bay with pilasters of a broadly seventeenth-century type.

53 The principal sources of information for the interior of the Magpie and Stump are (1) ———, 'The new "Magpie and Stump". A successful experiment in domestic architecture', *S*, 1895, vol. 5, pp. 66–74; (2) 'The Magpie and Stump House, 37 Cheyne Walk, Chelsea' (Catalogue of a sale, 18 October 1921), of which there is a copy in the V&A Library; (3) 'Rachel'; (4) 'Notes on a visit to 37 Cheyne Walk. Jan.11.1964' by Dulcie Langham, Ashbee's niece, FA; (5) a tape-recording of childhood memories of the house by Dulcie Langham, FA; (6) Original photographs of the house in the Ashbee Collection; (7) Record photographs taken for the Greater London Council shortly before demolition, GLRO. The fittings now in the possession of the V&A include the copper and enamel chimney-piece from the hall, some leatherwork, newel posts and wrought iron balusters from the staircase, and light fittings.

54 Ashbee had used repoussé copper tiles from the early days of

the Guild; see the design for 'Furniture for Mrs Reynolds' in GWRB. There is a photograph of panels of copper tiles with many of the motifs used on the Magpie and Stump fire-place, and some others, in Essex House Photograph Book, p. 19, V&A Library.

55 *Chapters*, p. 90.

56 *A*, 1891, vol. 46, p. 82.

57 A&CES:1888:15, 62–7, 404–5.

58 F. Kruekl, 'Leather Embossing as an Artistic Handicraft', *S*, 1894, vol. 3, pp. 51–4. For Hulbe see Thieme-Becker, *Allgemeines Lexikon der Bildender Künstler* (Leipzig, 1925), vol. 18, and C. R. Ashbee (ed.), *The Manual of the Guild and School of Handicraft* (1892), p. 89. The earliest Guild leatherwork seems to have been on the chair for the President of the Craftsman Club which was exhibited at A&CES:1890:190, see *CMAF*, 1890, vol. 11, p. 119. This seems to have been the chair which Baillie Scott so much admired. In the winter of 1891 Ashbee exhibited a 'Set of experiments in Design in its application to Leather' at the New English Art Club, catalogue no. 117. And in 1892 he designed a frieze of twenty leather panels decorated with the Craft of the Guild, the pink, and stylized pomegranates, for a sitting-room at Bryngwyn, Wormelow Tump, Herefordshire; this frieze has recently been removed and about half of the panels have been acquired by Cheltenham Art Gallery and Museums.

59 Oddly enough, Ashbee did not follow up this work. I know of no leather wall coverings by him after this until *c.* 1905 when he supplied leather panels decorated with peacocks for the spandrels in the entrance hall at the Royal Victoria Infirmary, Newcastle-upon-Tyne. See Ashbee Collection, vol. 3. The panels were removed in the 1950s.

60 1895, vol. 5, p. 73.

61 The attribution is stylistic; the paper was close to Watts' 'Kinnersley'.

62 e.g., Conder's decorations for Edmund Davis, *AR*, 1904, vol. 16, pp. 253–5.

63 The fittings at 37 Cheyne Walk are best illustrated in Ashbee's article 'Suggestions for electric light fittings', *AJ*, 1895, pp. 91–3. For light fittings of a later date, see *DK*, 1897–8, vol. 1, p. 9 and *British Architect*, 1905, vol. 64, p. 478.

64 *AJ*, 1895, p. 92.

65 Ibid. Ashbee's designs for electric table lamps were often versions, with softened curves, of the remarkable brass lamps made by the Birmingham Guild of Handicraft in the mid-1890s and probably designed by A. S. Dixon. Dixon gave one of these as a wedding present to Ashbee, and it is now in the V&A; see Alan Crawford (ed.), *By Hammer and Hand: The Arts and Crafts Movement in Birmingham* (Birmingham, 1984), figs. 77 and 80. For Ashbee's designs, see e.g., *British Architect*, 1903, vol. 60, p. 442.

66 *AJ*, 1895, p. 93.

67 *S*, 1895, vol. 5, p. 72.

68 Such a table, made in 1889, survives at Abbotsholme School, and another belongs to the V&A.

69 The attribution to Agnes Ashbee is in *S*, 1895, vol. 5, p. 73; the Ashbee Collection, vol. 2, p. 38 shows the frieze without boys or deer; the frieze as a whole was attributed to Walter Taylor in the sale catalogue of 18 October 1921 which seems to reflect information provided by Ashbee.

70 The evidence for this inscription is in items (4) and (5), note 53 above. I have not been able to discover where the phrase comes from, or whether it is part of a longer quotation.

71 *B*, 1946, vol. 170, p. 30. The house still stands, but the interior had been dismantled even before Ansell wrote.

72 15 Stratton Street was built and furnished for H. A. Johnstone. At 1A Palace Gate, Kensington, Cooper employed many of the same artist-craftsmen and in the same way, for his brother W. A. Johnstone, in 1896–8, and the interior survives. See *Survey of London: Vol. 38: The Museums Area of South Kensington and Westminster* (1978), pp. 39–41.

73 Ashbee's 'interiors only' were the flat for Gyula Mandello in Budapest of 1899–1900, which may be that illustrated in W. Shaw Sparrow (ed.), *Flats Urban Houses and Cottage Homes* (n.d.), facing p. 9; interiors for the Duchess of Leeds at

Bordighera on the Italian Riviera of *c.* 1900, see drawings at CPL; and three rooms at The House by the Hill, Tettenhall, Wolverhampton for E. Peter Jones, also of *c.* 1900 which were, by virtue of walls hung with printed fabrics and decorated with modelled plasterwork, the most elaborate of his interiors apart from the Magpie and Stump, see catalogue G, pp. 16–19. Only the plasterwork now survives.

74 J, 4 July 1934.

75 For Balfour's frieze, see *BN*, 1902, vol. 82, p. 845. Modelled plasterwork was used at Tettenhall, see note 73 above, and at 39 Cheyne Walk.

76 There are designs for built-in settles alongside upright fire-places among the drawings in CPL; his only notably broad hearths were in old houses he restored, such as the Norman Chapel, and in the de Szász house in Budapest.

77 At Uplands, Ledbury, for Lionel Curtis in 1905, he had episodes from *The Jackdaw of Rheims* carved above the fire-place; at Byways, Yarnton, of 1907, he used the George and Dragon roundel.

78 C. R. Ashbee, 'An Experiment in Cast-Iron Work', *S*, 1898, vol. 14, pp. 254–6; for the date of these designs see *S*, 1897–8, vol. 12, p. 30. Ashbee also seems to have designed railings for Falkirk, see *DK*, 1898, vol. 2, p. 268.

79 Sylvia Backemeyer and Theresa Gronberg, *W. R. Lethaby 1857–1931: Architecture, Design and Education* (1984), p. 87; W. R. Lethaby, 'Cast Iron and Its Treatment for Artistic Purposes', *A*, 1890, vol. 43, pp. 103–6; *House*, 1898, vol. 3, p. 177.

80 *S*, 1898, vol. 14, p. 255.

81 Ibid.

82 Adolf Loos, *Spoken into the Void: Collected Essays 1897–1900* (trans. Jane O. Newman and John H. Smith) (1982), pp. 125–7.

83 Clive Aslet, *The Last Country Houses* (1982), pp. 250–5.

84 Photographs in an album at Madresfield Court show the library before Ashbee worked on it. The chimney-piece and the ceiling have been altered since these photographs were taken, as well as the doors and the ends of the free-standing bookcases; but I do not know whether Ashbee had any hand in these alterations.

85 The dating of this work is based on entries in J of March 1902 and 17 Dec 1902 by Ashbee, and the fact that some of the door panels are illustrated in catalogue D which was issued in 1903. There is a fourth door between the library and the chapel which was almost certainly designed by Ashbee, for it includes the Guild pink; I do not know when this was designed or executed.

86 J, 3 March 1905.

CHAPTER TWELVE
METAL WORK

1 A&CES:1888:454.

2 Cutting of 21 Oct 1888, apparently from *Sunday Times*, in 'Letters'.

3 Pearson was in the habit of marking his wares with his name or initials, the year of production, and often some kind of stock or design number. Some pieces marked in this way and dating from his time of employment with the Guild have come on to the art market recently; and on the majority no reference is made to the Guild. It may be, though, that some of them were made outside the Guild, for MGH, 16 October 1890 records that 'Mr. Pearson had been outside the Guild supplying Messrs. Morris and others with goods and also employing two men to help him in metalwork outside.'

4 The Keswick School of Industrial Art, started by Canon Rawnsley in 1884, and the Lyzwick Hall Art School class run by J. W. Oddie, also in Keswick in the Lake District, both specialized in repoussé work, see *BN*, 1886, vol. 50, p. 1029; *AJ*, 1886, p. 184; A&CES:1888; and *BN*, 1889, vol. 57, pp. 72 and 91.

5 *A*, 1889, vol. 41, p. 309 shows typical repoussé plaques in the studio of Alma-Tadema. See also Madeline A. Wallace-Dunlop, 'Some Oriental Brasswork', *MA*, 1885, vol. 8, pp. 56–60 and 109–12; and Rose G. Kingsley, 'Some Flemish Brass', *AJ*, 1887, pp. 330–2.

6 *S*, 1897–8, vol. 12, p. 32.

7 Information from Jon Catleugh.

8 There were a number of such brass dishes in the collections of the British Museum before 1888; but few, it seems, in the South Kensington Museum.

9 Shirley Bury, 'An arts and crafts experiment: the silverwork of C. R. Ashbee', *V&A Museum Bulletin*, 1967, vol. 3, p. 18; *AJ*, 1886, p. 184; *BN*, 1886, vol. 50, p. 779. The *Star*, reviewing the 1889 Arts and Crafts Exhibition, remarked on the resemblance between the Guild's repoussé work and Leland's designs, see the cutting of 5 Oct 1889 in 'Letters'. For Leland, student of gipsy life and legend, inexhaustible publicist for the useful arts, and (for which he was best known) pseudonymous author of *Hans Breitmann's Ballads* (1869), see Elizabeth Robins Pennell, *Charles Godfrey Leland: A Biography* (1906).

10 The earliest dated design for metalwork by Ashbee seems to be the drawings for 'Mr. Baillie's sconces' of 14 June 1889 in GWRB.

11 'Letters', broadsheet of Sept 1889; Underhill is listed as an 'Affiliated Craftsman'.

12 *B*, 1890, vol. 58, p. 397; cf. a design for a coal box, 1 Jan 1890 in GWRB.

13 See note 3 above.

14 An almost identical box was illustrated at *B*, 1901, vol. 81, p. 513 and attributed to 'J. Witham', a name which, since it is not otherwise connected with the Guild, may be an error for Williams. The ornament of the box may have been based on a silver cup of 1664 in the South Kensington Museum, which was illustrated in an article by W. A. S. Benson on 'The Embossing of Metals' in *English Illustrated Magazine*, 1889–90, p. 46.

15 See p. 46.

16 *Craftsmanship*, p. 96.

17 *S*, 1896, vol. 8, pp. 43–5; Newlyn Art Gallery, *Artists of the Newlyn School 1880–1900* (Catalogue of an exhibition 1979), p. 51.

18 *S*, 1896, vol. 8, pp. 95–6, 98–9 and 1897, vol. 11, p. 111; *Artist*, 1898, vol. 28, p. 146; *AJ*, 1898, p. 219; *S*, 1907, vol. 40, p. 67.

19 H. J. L. J. Massé, *The Art-Workers' Guild 1884–1934* (Oxford, 1935), p. 148; for Williams lecturing to leading members of the Arts and Crafts Movement, see *Arts and Crafts*, 1905, vol. 2, pp. 113–17.

20 It was also, like the furniture of the early 1890s, poorly documented. Few pieces made between 1890 and 1896 can be precisely dated and they cannot be arranged in a clear sequence.

21 MGH, 28 Feb and 10 June 1890; *Craftsmanship*, p. 214; J, 30 Jan 1903.

22 'Letters', Second Annual Report of the School of Handicraft, June 1890; *BN*, 1892, vol. 62, p. 661. There are original and rather finished designs for metalwork by Hardiman, Walter Taylor and Arthur Cameron in GWRB which may have been prepared for these exhibitions.

23 For Cameron, MGH, 20 Nov 1891 and J, 9 Dec 1901. I do not know exactly when Baily joined; he is listed among Guild craftsmen in A&CES:1896 but not in A&CES:1893.

24 *Craftsmanship*, p. 214. Ashbee is referring to the 'Bust of a Woman' in the V&A, attributed to Donatello, and sometimes known at that date as 'St Cecilia'.

25 Ashbee and modelling: he did the gesso work on the signboard of the Guild of Handicraft exhibited at A&CES:1889:195.

26 *MES*, p. 5; The Armourers' and Brasiers' Company, *Exhibition of Art Brass Work and Arms &c.* May 1890, nos. 170b and 170c.

27 Apart from allusions in the notes of *MES*, the substantial references to lost-wax casting as used by Ashbee are *S*, 1897–8, vol. 12, p. 34, where it is said that Guild jewellery 'is partly cast and partly hammered in gold and silver. If cast the process is that known as waste wax ...'; *S*, 1900, vol. 16, p. 165: 'the subsidiary parts of cups are made by sand-casting from patterns originally modelled in wax'; and *AJ*, 1894 in which Ashbee refers to two little figures which he had modelled for a ring: 'They have been cast in bronze, and when worked up will be re-cast in silver ...' (p. 184). For methods other than lost wax see, e.g., A&CES:1890:83.

28 *The New Sculpture* (1983), p. 185; and pp. 184–94 for a full discussion of lost-wax casting and the cult of the statuette.

29 Quoted in Beattie, loc. cit.

30 If he was the same person as the A. L. Collie whom Ashbee proposed for the committee, see MSH, 3 June 1889, and 'Letters', June 1889 and Sept 1890. For Stirling Lee see advertisement for a course of Easter Lectures, 1890, in 'Letters'; his talk was reprinted as 'The Language of Sculpture' in *Transactions*, pp. 85–98.

31 The balance of Guild output was reflected at an Arts and Crafts exhibition in Manchester City Art Gallery in 1895 when the Guild exhibited about thirty items of base metalwork, fourteen items of jewellery in silver and semi-precious stones, five pieces of silverwork and one of electroplate.

32 See *AJ*, 1894, p. 183. It was exhibited in the exhibition of Victorian and Edwardian Decorative Arts at the V&A in 1952, catalogue no. P5, but I do not know of its present whereabouts.

33 New English Art Club, *Catalogue of the Ninth Exhibition of Modern Pictures* (1892), no. 121. Surviving Guild silver, firmly datable to 1895 or earlier consists, so far as I know, only of the Dixon spoon mentioned above; the silver and onyx salt cellar discussed below; and a cup with a red enamel cover illustrated at *MES*, plate 7 and referred to below, note 36.

Other pieces which, though less clearly documented, probably belong to this period are the silver mustard-pot referred to on page 11; a handsome silver bowl on five cast legs in the V&A dated *c.* 1893–6 on stylistic grounds; and a silver spoon belonging to the descendants of Gerald Bishop, which family tradition attributes to the Guild: it has one mark which is similar to the CA monogram on Ashbee's 1892 silver medallion portrait of Cecil Langham (see pp. 351–2 below), and another which may be the workman's mark registered by Samuel Smith of 6 Grand Hotel Buildings, Trafalgar Square, between 23 February 1893 and June 1896.

34 Catalogue A; this catalogue is undated but in a letter of 12 Sept 1895 to Ashbee the lithographer T. R. Way gave an estimate for the printing of a catalogue of this description, see correspondence in LSC. The date of 1895 is consistent with the work illustrated. See also *British Architect*, 1893, vol. 40, p. 310; GWRB, design for two cups, Aug 1892. The fullest illustration of these cups is in an article by Ashbee on 'Challenge Cups, Shields and Trophies', *AJ*, 1898, pp. 230–2.

35 Anna Somers Cocks, *The Victoria and Albert Museum: The Making of the Collection* (1980), p. 18.

36 *MES*, plate 7; the cup and cover is still in the possession of the Ashbee family, but the enamel has perished. In catalogue A it is illustrated as a sugar bowl.

37 *AJ*, 1898, p. 231; the Ashbee Swimming Cup was last awarded in 1948, according to Mr J. Wilson of the Association, and is now untraced.

38 *AJ*, loc. cit.

39 The soup tureen is now in the collections of the V&A; for the cup see *MES*, plate 6 where it is described as a goblet and *AJ*, 1898, p. 338 where it is described as a salt-cellar; for the sixteenth-century spoon, *AJ*, 1894, p. 183; and for other spoons, catalogue A. Ashbee Collection, vol. 2, p. 101 seems to show Mrs H. S. Ashbee's collection of silver and jewellery designed by her son.

40 See p. 228.

41 This is not a complete list of all silver and enamels exhibited.

42 A&CES:1893:77A.

43 A&CES:1893:110.

44 John Culme, *Nineteenth-Century Silver* (1977), p. 223; *AJ*, 1896, p. 348.

45 *AJ*, 1896, pp. 347–8; *Artist*, 1891, vol. 12, p. 237.

46 Cameron's name does not appear in the lists for Fisher's class, which are in the archives of the City and Guilds of London Institute, City of London Guildhall Library. I am grateful to C. R. H. Cooper of the Guildhall Library for this information, and to Peter Stevens of the City and Guilds of London Institute. Ashbee made plans for Alexander Fisher to teach a class in enamelling at the School of Handicraft in 1894–5, but they were frustrated by lack of funds; see C. R. Ashbee, *A Nine Years' Experiment in Technical Education* (1895), p. 10. He also knew Constance Blount, a supporter of home industries who set up an enamelling workshop *c.* 1891; when Ashbee was translating Cellini's *Trattati dell'oreficeria e della scultura* she gave him advice

on points of enamelling, see *Treatises*, p. xiv and *Artist*, 1891, vol. 12, p. 237.

47 For the trades generally, see Clive Gilbert, 'The Evolution of an Urban Craft: The Gold, Silver and Allied Trades of the West Midlands' (M.Soc.Sc. thesis, University of Birmingham, 1972); for style, catalogues issued by James Deakin and Sons Ltd., 1899, Mappin and Webb, *c*. 1900, John Round and Sons, 1898, and Streeter and Company, 1900, all V&A Library; for the influence of art training, see the series on 'Original Designs for Art Manufacture' in *AJ*, 1880.

48 *Chapters*, p. 45; *MES*, p. 9; *Treatises*, p. x; *Craftsmanship*, p. 98.

49 *MA*, 1896–7, vol. 20, p. 67; see also *S*, 1897, vol. 9, pp. 126–31.

50 A&CES: 1896:176, 180.

51 Quoted in Peter Savage, *Lorimer and the Edinburgh Craft Designers* (Edinburgh, 1980), p. 67.

52 For the trade craftsmen, see *MES*, p. 5; for lists, *Craftsmanship*, pp. 256–8 and PRO. BT31. 8064/58132.

53 For the rough measure of datable pieces known to me as being in public and private collections, or as having passed through the London sale rooms, gives the following figures: 1899:11; 1900:40; 1901:38; 1902:23; 1903:39; 1904:31; 1905:20; 1906:16; 1907:8; 1908:1.

54 It is sometimes said that the CRA mark indicates a design specifically by Ashbee. I know of no evidence to support this view. In *MES*, p. 5, Ashbee rather suggested that the first mark, CRA, was in use from the start of the Guild, but Shirley Bury has shown that this was not the case; see Bury, op. cit, pp. 20, 22, 25.

After it was decided that the Guild of Handicraft Ltd. should go into liquidation, a new mark, 'G of H', in a rectangle chamfered at the corners was registered in the name of 'The Guild of Handicraft', the workmen being listed as George Henry Hart, John Kirsten Baily, George Edward Horwood, and William Mark. This was on 22 July 1908, but the entry in the Mark Book is annotated 'This firm dissolved 28.11.12'. (Mark Book 14, p. 245, Goldsmiths' Hall, London.) On 28 Nov 1912, Baily registered his own mark, JKB, trading as 'The Handicrafts' from 7 Church Street, Stratford-on-Avon; and on 5 Dec 1912, George Hart, trading as 'The Guild of Handicraft', re-registered the mark 'G of H' as at 22 July 1908. (Mark Book 17, pp. 167 and 170, Goldsmiths' Hall, London.) This mark has been used by the Campden workshop of George Hart, his son and grandsons, ever since.

55 C. R. Ashbee, 'On Table Service', *AJ*, 1898, p. 336.

56 Ibid., pp. 336–7.

57 Ibid., p. 337.

58 J, 3 Feb 1896.

59 Though there was a fashion in the late nineteenth century for oxidized silver, which has a matt grey finish close to the Arts and Crafts taste; see Patricia Wardle, *Victorian Silver and Silver-Plate* (1963), p. 103.

60 *A*, 1892, vol. 48, pp. 277 and 318; *S*, 1900, vol. 19, p. 165.

61 Cheltenham Art Gallery and Museums have a two-handled cup hallmarked 1903 but exactly reproducing a design of the early 1890s; its handles are cast. See plate 159.

62 *Artist*, 1896, vol. 18, p. 27; *S*, 1897, vol. 9, p. 130.

63 The twisted wires forming a grip are found on what may be the earliest of Ashbee's decanter designs, illustrated at *AJ*, 1898, p. 337; there are loop handles made of wires soldered together, though without the graceful curve, on a copper bowl in the Österreichisches Museum für angewandte Kunst in Vienna, which is of 1898 or earlier.

64 1897, vol. 9, p. 126.

65 At *AJ*, 1898, p. 338 Ashbee referred to sixteenth-century Italian cups and tankards in the Uffizi as examples of how stones too large for jewellery could be used with honour; it is a puzzling reference; he was perhaps referring to the very large stones used as ornamental vessels in the Museo degli Argenti in the Pitti Palace.

66 *S*, 1903, vol. 28, p. 184.

67 Varley had perhaps joined the Guild by the summer of 1899, see J, 13 Aug 1899, Mark by the end of 1900, see MGH, 3 July 1901. The earliest datable example of their brand of painted enamels is the plaque on a presentation trowel at the Belgrave

Hospital for Children, Clapham Road, London SW9, of 1900.

68 J, 29 Oct 1904. Varley's seemingly endless variations on this theme can be seen in an album of designs for enamel work and jewellery, *c*.1903–7, now in V&A Prints and Drawings.

69 J, 11 May 1914. The V&A owns a rectangular enamel plaque painted with a design of a cock by Mark in 1906; it is based on a water-colour drawing by Joseph Crawhall published in *S*, 1904, vol. 32, facing p. 219; see Cheltenham, D56.

70 Other techniques: for champlevé work, *MES*, plate 64; for cloisonné, a fruit stand of 1904 in the possession of St Cross College, Oxford, and a candlestick of 1905 in the Art Gallery and Museum, Brighton; for *plique-à-jour*, *MES*, plate 70.

71 For the continuing use of bosses etc. see *MES*, plate 62, a cup and cover made for presentation to the Leathersellers' Company in 1899; plate 72, a challenge cup first illustrated in 1900; and plate 74, a challenge cup designed by W. A. White and exhibited at the Arts and Crafts Exhibition in 1903.

72 This point is most eloquently made by Shirley Bury, op. cit, pp. 24–5. Table baskets: a design almost identical to that illustrated here was exhibited at the Arts and Crafts Exhibition in 1896, see *B*, 1896, vol. 71, p. 304. Beakers: two, for example, were in the same exhibition, see *S*, 1897, vol. 9, p. 128 and *MES*, plates 8 and 75. Teapots: see *DK*, 1898, vol. 2, p. 53, and *MES*, plate 24. *MES*, plate 37A is a handsome sugar caster made for Gyula Mandello presumably *c*. 1900, closely modelled on English examples of *c*. 1700 and freshly detailed in the manner of 1900.

73 *MES*, p. 18. Ashbee gave the bottles and other relics to Chelsea Public Library in 1924.

74 It is not clear whether this idea came from Ashbee or from the glassworks. Harry Powell, who ran the firm, was a member of the Art Workers' Guild; he was interested, in a typically Arts and Crafts way, in the adaptation of old forms and techniques to new uses, see his article on 'Table Glass' in *AR*, 1899, vol. 6, pp. 51–5; and he had been sketching old glass in museums since about 1889. He may have suggested the idea to Ashbee. But at the same time he seems to have learned from Ashbee, and in the early 1900s Powells produced decanters which owed a good deal to Ashbee's design, especially in their silver mounts; see particularly a decanter based on a seventeenth-century 'sack bottle' which Powell had sketched in the Guildhall Museum in 1903 (Powell's archive, Museum of London, photograph album 80. 547/3239/1); and *AJ*, 1905, p. 65; and a decanter of 1903 in Birmingham Museum and Art Gallery.

75 *AJ*, 1898, p. 337. In *MES* Ashbee described these bottles as Elizabethan; in the opinion of W. B. Honey they date from the late seventeenth century.

76 The earliest evidence of the design is at *AJ*, 1898, p. 337, an example which Ashbee described as 'recently designed'. For versions, besides this one and those illustrated here, see *MES*, plate 59; catalogue H, p. 41; and *Times*, 21 Jan 1981. *AJ*, 1904, p. 24 illustrates a decanter of a quite different design with mounts by the Guild; an almost identical decanter but with Powell mounts is at *AJ*, 1905, p. 65.

77 A&CES: 1903:490b.

78 An elaborate approximation to the design was exhibited at the Arts and Crafts Exhibition in 1899, see *S*, 1899, vol. 18, p. 122.

79 Catalogue F, pp. 20–1; catalogue J, p. 7. For vegetable or entrée dishes, see *MES*, plates 44, 45 and 53.

80 W. A. S. Benson, Alexander Fisher, Nelson Dawson and the Birmingham Guild of Handicraft all used electroplate.

81 V&A Metalwork have examples of a single-handled dish and the double-handled dish and cover, both of 1900; likewise the Österreichisches Museum für angewandte Kunst in Vienna has a single loop-handled dish, and the Hessisches Landesmuseum, Darmstadt has a double-handled dish and cover, both being of 1900; Sotheby's Belgravia, 8 December 1978, no. 139 is an example of a double-handled open dish of 1900.

82 Some variations: Sotheby's Belgravia, 8 Feb 1978, no. 114: openwork to the foot, two loop handles attached to the bowl rather than the foot, no stones; Sotheby's Belgravia, 12 July 1978, no. 202: two handles but no foot, and another example of this kind in the Nordenfjeldske Kunstindustrimuseum at

Trondheim; Sotheby's Belgravia, 8 Dec 1978, no. 139: a beaded rim to the bowl; Christie's, 15 July 1980, no. 85: a cover but no enamel.

83 Catalogue H, p. 31; catalogue J, p. 7; see also *MES*, plate 17.

84 *MES*, plates 5 and 71 illustrate the characteristically Scandinavian use of hanging discs; plate 84 is a chalice whose shape Ashbee described as Scandinavian.

85 A&CES:1903:490p and d; the two pieces are illustrated in *Der Moderne Stil* (Stuttgart) 1903, vol. 5, plate 49, nos. 3 and 6.

86 Catalogue J, p. 7.

87 For two pieces which approach the classic shape but have deeper dishes and thicker stems, see *AJ*, 1903, p. 151, and Sotheby's Belgravia, 10 Dec 1981, no. 86, a piece of 1903. The classic design can be seen in catalogue F, p. 18; catalogue H, p. 19, the original of which, dated 1904, is now in a private collection; Christie's, 3 March 1981, no. 179, an example of 1904; Essex House Photograph Book, p. 149, V&A Library; our illustration, an example of 1905, and *MES*, plates 78 and 99. Sotheby's 13 April 1984, no. 61 is a handsome variant with no enamels and set with stones, of 1904. *MES*, plate 77, and *Le Style Moderne: L'Art Appliqué* (Paris), 1904–5, plate 84 (another example of 1904, now in the possession of St Cross College, Oxford) stand somewhere between the fatter designs of 1903 and the classic shape.

88 Catalogue H, p. 19; *MES*, plates 12–14, 77–80, 99.

89 Catalogue of James Deakin and Sons Ltd., 1899, pp. 25–7, V&A Library.

90 *MES*, plate 99 stood one foot high; Christie's, 3 March 1981, no. 179, about fourteen inches. For the price, catalogue H, p. 19.

91 See note 87 above.

92 J, 25 Dec 1901; for Colverd, see J, *c.* 31 Jan 1903.

93 J, 20 Feb 1902, Jan, 1906. The spoon warmer was illustrated in *K und K*, 1902, vol. 5, p. 592, and attributed to Hardiman at *AJ*, 1903, p. 152. A striking design of this period, attributed to Hardiman and Ashbee jointly, is the cup and cover illustrated at *S*, 1903, vol. 28, p. 185 and *MES*, plate 66. Other designs by Hardiman: a beaker at *S*, 1900, vol. 19, p. 156; a necklace at *Artist*, 1902, vol. 33, p. 23; and a belt clasp at *S*, 1905, vol. 35, pp. 235–6.

94 George Hart joined about a year before the move to Campden, see his ms. reminiscences of Ashbee, FA; for Partridge, see p. 113; for Penny, see Birmingham Municipal School of Art, Student Registers for 1900–1901, in the archives of the Art and Design Centre, City of Birmingham Polytechnic, J, *c.* 7 March 1903 and *MES*, p. 6; for Keeley, J, 14 Dec 1914.

95 For falling off of work, see note 53 above. The design of the kettle is a little earlier than 1906; a version was illustrated in catalogue H, of 1905–6.

96 Catalogue H. Catalogue G, covering furniture and architectural metalwork, is eighty-four pages long, with the same format and typography, and must have been issued between April 1905 and May 1906; catalogue H does not have so precise a *terminus ante quem*, but seems to have been a companion volume.

97 Catalogue H, pp. 15, 34, 40, 43–4, 46–7. There were trinket boxes and whimsical ornaments *c.* 1900; but there were more *c.* 1905.

98 *Craftsmanship*, p. 22.

99 V&A, *Liberty's 1875–1975* (Catalogue of an exhibition 1975) particularly pp. 13–16; Shirley Bury, 'New Light on the Liberty Metalwork Venture', *Bulletin of the Decorative Arts Society 1890–1940*, no. 1, pp. 14–27.

100 *MA*, 1901–2, vol. 26, p. 271. There are some debts to Ashbee's work of *c.* 1896–1900 in early Liberty's designs for silver, scarcely strong enough to be called plagiarisms, see Liberty and Co. Ltd., 'Record Books: I: Silver Sketches 1900–1912', p. 221, no. 517; p. 260, no. 5687; p. 304, no. 280; p. 305, nos. 2077 and 2078; p. 419, no. 5859. (Photocopy, V&A Library.)

101 *Craftsmanship*, pp. 96–7.

102 Liberty and Co., *Cymric Silver* [1899/1900], introduction, V&A Library.

103 MGH, 29 March 1906. White's designs include a bronze and enamel plaque, *AJ*, 1898, p. 232; a cup and cover, *S*, 1902–3, vol. 27, p. 210; another cup and cover, *S*, 1903, vol. 28, p. 186 and *MES*, plate 74; a silver and enamel necklace, *AJ*, 1903,

p. 149; a two-handled dish and cover, *Der Moderne Stil* (Stuttgart), 1903, vol. 5, plate 49, no. 6; a gold pendant and a gold and enamel necklace, *AJ*, 1905, p. 12; a cup and cover, *S*, 1905, vol. 35, p. 236; and a centre-piece, *Deutsche Kunst und Dekoration* (Darmstadt), 1906–7, vol. 19, p. [218].

104 Catalogue I, pp. 7 and 11.

105 One of the most striking pieces in an eighteenth-century manner, a dessert dish and stand sold at Sotheby's Belgravia on 1 March 1973, no. 34, is as early as 1903; see also Essex House Photograph Book, pp. 45–6, V&A Library. Other pieces in this group are not easy to date, and include *MES*, plate 28; the series of 'Adapted Designs' which survive as dyeline prints in Ashbee Collection, vol. 3; and several pieces recorded in photographs in GWRB, pp. 87–8, and other photographs in the possession of Douglas Webster whose father was manager of the Guild from 1906–7: a coffee pot closely modelled on early eighteenth-century chocolate pots, and three sugar casters equally closely modelled on late seventeenth- and early eighteenth-century examples, two of which are in *MES*, plate 36. *MES*, plate 28 is of this character, though not datable, and Ashbee's own copy of *MES* in the V&A Library contains further designs of this kind, signed but not dated.

106 They fall into three groups:

(1) Those which can be fairly precisely dated: a fruit stand hallmarked 1906 and now in a private collection, a variant of *MES*, plate 14; a fruit stand and a tureen made for Count Lionel de Hirschel de Minerbi, *MES* plates 99 and 100, dated 1906 on the evidence of a variant design for 99, dated 3 April 1906, in Ashbee's copy of *MES*, V&A Library; a cup and cover, *MES*, plate 69, illustrated in *Magyar Iparművészet* (Budapest), 1907, vol. 10, p. 314; a ciborium hallmarked 1909, made for St Aidan's Church, Small Heath, Birmingham, see Gillian Naylor, *The Arts and Crafts Movement* (1971), plate 80; a bowl and cover, hallmarked 1912, in the possession of the Ashbee family, see Cheltenham D52.

(2) Designs which can only be dated '1909 or earlier': *MES*, plates 1, 10, 11, 45, 61, 64, 83 and 84; an unhallmarked cup and cover given by Ashbee to Janet at Christmas 1909 and in the possession of the Ashbee family.

(3) A salt-cellar which can only be dated '1914 or earlier', see Musée des Arts Décoratifs, *Arts décoratifs de Grande Bretagne et de l'Irlande* (Paris, 1914), no. 762.

107 For Miller's modelling, see *MES*, plates 45, 64 and presumably 69; for Ashbee, see the similarity in scale and treatment between the naked youth of *MES*, plate 14 and the naked winged youth of plate 76, attributed to him.

108 *MES*, p. 34; for the date of this work, see note 106 above.

109 C. R. Ashbee, *Modern English Silverwork* (1909). A fuller account of this book can be found in the introductions to the reprint published in 1974 by B. Weinreb Ltd. of London. At least two of the designs in *MES*, plates 70 and 74, appear to be by W. A. White and not by Ashbee; see note 103 above.

As for the statistics of Ashbee's output in silver, a conservative estimate of his total output is 600 designs; there is documentary evidence for about 450, but it is likely that more were executed than are documented for, taking only the pieces whose whereabouts are known, about half are not represented in the documents. The principal sources of documentary evidence are *MES*, contemporary periodicals, Guild catalogues and the Ashbee Collection.

110 *MES*, plate 86, and Hugh Honour, *Goldsmiths and Silversmiths* (1971), pp. 290–1. The gilding and enamelling of the cross are no longer in their original condition.

111 *MES*, p. 3.

112 The Birmingham Guild began to produce silverware in quantity in about 1898, see Alan Crawford (ed.), *By Hammer and Hand: The Arts and Crafts Movement in Birmingham* (Birmingham, 1984), p. 100.

113 *British Architect* thought that the Guild's wares were 'far above the senseless vagaries of *l'art nouveau* and the like'. (1904, vol. 62, p. 438.)

114 J, 9 Dec 1901.

115 *MES*, p. 7.

CHAPTER THIRTEEN
JEWELLERY

1 Quoted in Margaret Flower, *Victorian Jewellery* (1967), p. 11.
2 In *The Stones of Venice* Ruskin had said that people who wore cut jewels for the sake of their money-value were slave-drivers; E. T. Cook and Alexander Wedderburn (eds.), *The Works of John Ruskin* (1903–1912), vol. 10, p. 198.
3 *AJ*, 1894, p. 155.
4 *Treatises*, p. xii.
5 *AJ*, 1894, p. 153.
6 *AJ*, 1893, p. 247. Ashbee's ideas about jewellery and the Cinquecento are chiefly contained in two articles in *AJ*: 'How to wear jewellery. As illustrrated by the "Trattato della oreficeria" of Cellini', 1893, pp. 247–9, and 'Cinque-cento Jewelry. As illustrated by the "Trattati" of Benvenuto Cellini', 1894, pp. 152–5. See also the introduction to *Treatises*; and the syllabus of a lecture 'On Jewelry' in the series 'Design in its application to Metal Work', DES.
7 *AJ*, 1893, p. 248. In the syllabus mentioned above and at *AJ*, 1893, p. 247 Ashbee mentioned Crivelli, Verrochio, Zucchero, Piero della Francesca, Holbein and Dürer as artists in whose portraits the achievements of Renaissance jewellery could be studied.
8 Typescript reminiscences entitled 'First Impressions', FA.
9 *AJ*, 1893, p. 247.
10 *AJ*, 1893, p. 248, and p. 247 for the suggestion that he knew the collections in Paris and Vienna.
11 *AJ*, 1893, p. 248; lecture syllabus 'On Jewelry', see note 6 above.
12 John Culme, '"Benvenuto Cellini" and the nineteenth-century Collector and Goldsmith', *Art at Auction*, 1973–4, pp. 293–6.
13 *Treatises*, p. xiii.
14 *AJ*, 1894, p. 155; a translation to be published by the Guild was advertised as 'in preparation' at the back of C. R. Ashbee, *The Trinity Hospital in Mile End* (1896).
15 'Memoirs', vol. 7, p. 263.
16 Henry Wilson, *Silverwork and Jewelry* (1903), p. 265.
17 *Craftsmanship*, p. 98.
18 A critic in *MA*, 1896, vol. 19, p. 240 wrote of 'beetles, miniature frogs, chickens, cocks' heads, spiders, mimic banjoes etc . . .'.
19 *Treatises*, p. x.
20 This clasp was in the possession of the Ashbee family until recently, when it was stolen; another version of the left-hand disc, fitted as a brooch, is still in the possession of the family, see Cheltenham E1.
21 *AJ*, 1894, p. 183. The medallion is in the possession of the Ashbee family.
22 Paris, 1883. Ashbee reproduced several *enseignes* from this book in *Treatises*.
23 ———, 'Italian Medals', *AJ*, 1882, pp. 77–80. Ashbee illustrated two medals in his articles on jewellery as examples of breadth of decorative treatment, see *AJ*, 1893, p. 248 and 1894, p. 155.
24 Mark Jones, *The Art of the Medal* (1979), pp. 114–9.
25 A. Graves, *The Royal Academy of Arts . . .* (1905–6), 1889: no. 2106; *MA*, 1896, vol. 19, p. 236.
26 See Elfrida Manning, *Marble and Bronze: The Art and Life of Hamo Thornycroft* (1982), p. 198.
27 J, 25 Nov 1886 shows that Ashbee knew and admired Thornycroft.
28 *A*, 1891, vol. 46, p. 82.
29 *CMAF*, 1892, vol. 13, p. 51.
30 ———, *Illustrated catalogue of Gems, Cameos & Amber Collected by A. Booth, Gloucester* ([Gloucester?] n.d. [1886?]), p. 3.
31 See *AJ*, 1894, p. 184 and PRO. BT31. 8064/58132, Schedule of Liabilities as at 1 Jan 1898 where 'Booth' is listed among the creditors of the Guild. I am grateful to the Divisional Librarian, Gloucester Library, for information about Booth.
32 *AJ*, 1893, p. 359.
33 A&CES:1893:70A.
34 On Schonwerk: the preparation and setting of stones was something quite outside the Guild's expertise; and the execution of two rings in which stone-setting is all-important, was attributed

to Schonwerk in Manchester City Art Gallery, *Catalogue of the Manchester Arts and Crafts Exhibition* (1895), nos. 443 and 446. The evidence is no more substantial than this, and his name appears to be missing from the internal records of the Guild.
35 A buckle with rather similar cast ornament of fish was until recently in the possession of the Ashbee family, see Cheltenham E4 and Sotheby's, 29 Nov 1984, Decorative Arts, Part 1, no. 181.
36 The design of Jane Whitehead's brooch seems to belong to 1893 or 1894. It may be the silver and moonstone brooch bought by her husband, Ralph Radcliffe Whitehead, at the Arts and Crafts Exhibition in 1893, see Memorandum of Sale and Receipt of Deposit, 1893, A&CES archives, V&A Library; a version of the same design, with carbuncles, now in a private collection in Australia, was illustrated in *AJ*, 1894, p. 182.
37 See for instance *Journal of Indian Art*, 1892, vol. 5, plates 36–9, and Jamila Brij Bhushnan, *Indian Jewellery Ornaments and decorative designs* (Bombay, 1964), pp. 60–1. The silver and enamel brooch set with a Brazilian topaz illustrated in catalogue H, p. 60 and in *Craftsmanship*, p. 205 is very Indian in feeling. Ethel Coomaraswamy sent Ashbee a dozen or so photographs of Indian jewellery on 7 June 1903, see her Ceylon Journal, Book 1, in the possession of S. Durai Raja Singam.
38 *AJ*, 1893, p. 359.
39 *S*, 1897, vol. 9, p. 128.
40 For Janet's pendant, see Margaret Flower, *Victorian Jewellery* (1967), p. 228; it is still in the possession of the Ashbee family.
41 *S*, 1897, vol. 9, p. 131 illustrates an enamel brooch very like that proposed for Lady Pollock; and V&A Metalwork has a variant design of *c*. 1897, illustrated in *DK*, 1898, vol. 2, p. 57; see Shirley Bury, *Jewellery Gallery Summary Catalogue* (1982), Case 22, Board A, No. 3.
42 *AJ*, 1894, pp. 182–3.
43 Ibid., pp. 183–4.
44 *AJ*, 1893, p. 248.
45 Following a lecture on 'The discrimination and artistic use of precious stones' in 1881, A. H. Church referred to 'a lecture given by Mr. Ruskin some years ago at Oxford in which he objected to any facetted stones at all'; see *Journal of the Society of Arts*, 1881, vol. 29, p. 448. Ruskin's objections to the cutting of stones are many and specific, but I have not been able to trace any objection to faceting as distinct from cutting *en cabochon* in the Cook and Wedderburn edition.
46 There is a peacock jewel in the collection of Cheltenham Art Gallery and Museums which is attributed to Ashbee on good stylistic grounds, but which seems to have faceted garnets in the tail; in *AJ*, 1894, p. 182 Ashbee wrote that garnets should always be cut *en cabochon*.
47 See Memorandum of Sale and Receipt of Deposit for 4 Oct and 30 Nov 1893, A&CES archives, V&A Library; for average prices see Manchester City Art Gallery, op. cit.
48 In Charles Holme (ed.), *Modern Design in Jewellery and Fans* (1902), pp. 1–3.
49 Ibid., p. 3.
50 Ibid., p. 4. For similar opinions of Ashbee as a pioneer of Arts and Crafts jewellery see *S*, 1897, vol. 9, p. 129 and *K und K*, 1900, vol. 3, p. 175.
51 Guild records identify the new jewellers as Charlie Daniels, Adolf Gebhardt, Ted Horwood, Joseph McQueen, Alexander Riddell, Herbert Rome, William Scurr, Edwin Viner and, as an apprentice, Cyril Kelsey. In addition J, 15 Nov 1899 refers to 'Brook' as a jeweller and A&CES:1899:Case DD refers to 'W. Jones'.
52 J, 15 Nov 1899.
53 The dating of this piece is speculative. It must have been completed before the beginning of 1902 when it was illustrated in Charles Holme (ed.), *Modern Design in Jewellery and Fans* (1902), the '*Studio* Special Number' for Christmas 1901. But it may have been made early in 1900. On 15 Nov 1899 Cyril Kelsey wrote to Janet, 'No. Brook has not started on your peacocks yet, no chance till after Christmas.' (Journals) On 22 March 1900 Ashbee wrote to Janet 'Your peacock is finished. He is at the present moment pinned on my coat and is preening his tail and looking at himself with his ruby eye . . .' (FA) He went

on to speak of Janet's father paying for the peacock. However, Janet owned another peacock jewel, also with a ruby in its eye— no. 2 in note 51 below—and that may have been the one referred to in March 1900.

54 There are two almost identical designs for this pendant dated 22 Jan 1901 in CPL.

55 The following peacock jewels are attibuted to Ashbee, some on stylistic grounds alone: (1) The brooch made for Janet and referred to in note 53 above; now on loan to V&A Metalwork, catalogue no. 21:F:1. (2) a brooch pendant also made for Janet, possibly early in 1900; now on loan to the Royal Pavilion, Art Gallery and Museums, Brighton; see Nikolaus Pevsner, *The Sources of Modern Architecture and Design* (1968), plate 126. (3) The pendant of January 1901 illustrated here and now in V&A Metalwork, catalogue no. 21:F:3. (4) A brooch now in a private collection in the United States; stylistic attribution, and date uncertain; see Delaware Art Museum. *The Pre-Raphaelite Era 1848–1914* (Catalogue of an exhibition 1976), no. 6:40. (5) A brooch or hair-piece now part of the Hull Grundy Gift in Cheltenham Art Gallery and Museums; stylistic attribution, and date uncertain. (6) A brooch now in the collection of John Jesse; stylistic attribution, and date uncertain; see the Fine Art Society, *Jewellery and Jewellery Design 1830–1930 and John Paul Cooper 1869–1933* (Catalogue of an exhibition 1975–6), no. 110. (7) A pendant with rubies, emeralds, pearls and enamels, now in a private collection; stylistic attribution, and date uncertain. (8) A brooch advertised in catalogue H, p. 64. (9) A brooch advertised in catalogue K, p. 2. (10) A brooch now in a private collection with the mark G of H Ltd. and 1907. (Nos. 1–10 have tails in the 'proud' position.) (11) A pendant in the form of a peacock pecking a turquoise matrix, illustrated here and dated *c.* 1901; now in V&A Metalwork, catalogue no. 21:F:4. (12) A brooch in white enamel, pearls and turquoises illustrated in Charles Holme (ed.), *Modern Design in Jewellery and Fans* (1902), plate 20A. There are also designs for a pendant in the form of a proud peacock dated May 1905 in V&A Prints and Drawings, E.125:1968; and several other examples of jewellery with peacock designs in enamels, e.g. Holme (ed.), op. cit, plate 20B.

56 Another strikingly colourless design is the necklace of gold and silver, moonstones and black and white enamel illustrated in Margaret Flower, *Victorian Jewellery* (1967), plate 105A, in which, however, Hugh Seebohm is said to have had a hand. The enamels on this necklace are signed by William Mark which suggests a date of 1900 or later.

57 A&CES: 1903:163b; it was probably illustrated at *S*, 1902–3, vol. 27, p. 209.

58 V&A Metalwork, catalogue nos. 21:F:5, and 22:A:2. 21:F:5 is discussed by Shirley Bury in V&A Museum, *Princely Magnificence: Court Jewels of the Renaissance, 1500–1650* (Catalogue of an exhibition 1980–1), no. H15.

59 *S*, 1902–3, vol. 27, p. 208. There is a design for this pendant at CPL dated Sept 1901. For other ship pendants, see *AJ*, 1903, p. 151, and *House Beautiful* (Chicago), 1910, vol. 27, p. 4 which may be identical with A&CES:1903:163f. Both this and the squirrel pendant were made by Edwin Viner whom Janet Ashbee counted among the new faces of the Guild in June 1901, see J, 24 June 1901.

60 The necklace and pendant are now in the John Holden Gallery, Manchester Polytechnic.

61 *B*, 1901, vol. 18, p. 513. With the spiralling wires compare the lines which wreathe round 'the tulip of the new civilisation' in *Chapters*, p. 48; the cocoon surrounding a female figure perhaps suggestive of time and evolution on a Christmas card by Ashbee at *British Architect*, 1896, vol. 45, p. 24; and the bands from which the Spirit of Modern Hungary escapes in Ashbee's sculptural group of Szombor de Szász, *S*, 1906, vol. 37, p. 129. For other human figure pendants see a design for 'The Red Lady with the Pearls' at CPL of September 1901, and a pendant with a female figure in a cocoon-like setting at catalogue H, p. 61.

62 Catalogue H, p. 67. When this piece appeared in a sale room recently, it was catalogued alongside trade jewellery of a typically lifelike kind, see Christie's and Edmiston's, Glasgow, 13 March 1984. It is now in a private collection.

63 *Treatises*, plate facing p. 24.

64 The pendants came from the treasury of the Cathedral of the Virgin of the Pillar at Saragossa in 1870; Ashbee used one of these, a pendant of the Pelican in her Piety (catalogue no. 26: 12), as an illustration in *AJ*, 1893, pp. 247–8.

65 See Chapter 9 above, pp. 229–30.

66 It is noticeable how often gold is used at this period, or gold together with silver, but I hesitate to say that the use of gold is more common in the 1900s, for lack of sufficient information about its use in the 1890s.

67 So Felicity Ashbee tells me.

68 This pendant was originally designed as the finial of a hair-comb and has since been reset as a brooch; it was first exhibited at the Woodbury Gallery in the autumn of 1902, and at the Arts and Crafts Exhibition in the following year it seems to have been priced at £33; properly speaking, it belongs with the costly figurative pieces of the previous section; see *S*, 1902–3, vol. 27, p. 209 and A&CES:1903:163a.

69 For other examples of *plique-à-jour* enamel, see the squirrel pendant at *S*, 1902–3, vol. 27, p. 209 and A&CES:1903:163b; a lantern pendant at *S*, 1906, vol. 37, p. 138 and catalogue H, p. 63; a small peacock pendant at *S*, 1906, vol. 37, p. 139 and catalogue H, p. 64; a pendant at catalogue H, p. 63; and a brooch at Ibid., p. 66.

70 Examples can be seen in catalogue H, pp. 62, 64–5 and *Der Moderne Stil* (Stuttgart) 1904, vol. 6, plate 45.

71 This is also seen in the long chains for hanging muffs etc., from which Ashbee designed with a mixture of rigid and flexible links, see *B*, 1901, vol. 18, p. 513; *K und K*, 1902, vol. 5, p. 594; catalogue H, pp. 68–9. These chains resemble the '*sautoirs*' which came into fashion *c.* 1890.

72 See for instance a necklace and pendant in gold and peridots in V&A Metalwork, catalogue no. 21:F:2; *Artist*, 1902, vol. 33, p. 22; *Der Moderne Stil* (Stuttgart), 1903, vol. 5, plate 41; *AJ*, 1903, p. 151; catalogue H, pp. 55–7, 60–2.

73 Design at CPL of Nov 1901; see also *AJ*, 1903, p. 151 and a photograph in the Ashbee Collection, vol. 3, for variations on this theme.

74 In an article dealing with 'peasant' jewellery in *AJ*, 1893, Aymer Vallance wrote 'Pendant drops ... are extensively used in ancient and traditional jewellery of many countries, and might, with advantage, be adopted by ourselves.' (p. 358) In the same article he illustrated four pieces of Guild jewellery as exemplary modern work on traditional lines.

75 For brooches and pendants see catalogue H, pp. 62–3, 66–7; and compare the tree pendant with similar designs in 'Liberty and Co. (Jewellery Sketches)' (Photocopy 1975), V&A Library.

76 An early version was in pink enamel and reddish stones, the insect a dragonfly of gathered wires; it was designed for Mrs Rudyard Kipling in about May 1900, see the design at CPL; and *Artist*, 1902, vol. 33, p. 24; *Deutsche Kunst und Dekoration* (Darmstadt), 1902–3, vol. 11, p. 223; catalogue H, p. 73; and *AJ*, 1903, p. 88 (possibly the Kipling design).

77 *J*, 9 March 1903; and Chapter 5 above, p. 124.

78 There are two books of crudely copied jewellery designs from the Liberty's archive, of which there are photocopies in the V&A Library; both of them show a broad similarity between much Liberty's jewellery and that of the Arts and Crafts in general: (1) 'A Book of Tracings for Liberty Jewellery, *c.* 1898– 1906' (Photocopy 1963); and (2) 'Liberty and Co. (Jewellery Sketches)' (Photocopy 1975). The second of these also shows a probable debt to Ashbee in a number of brooches and pendants designed in the form of a central stone with leaves spiralling around it, Ashbee's favourite type of the 1890s; see p. 180, nos. 6269–6274 and 6281; p. 181, no. 6280; p. 300, nos. 8969–70; p. 309, nos. 9419 and 9453.

79 'A Book of Tracings for Liberty Jewellery, *c.* 1898–1906' (Photocopy 1963), pp. 1–50, V&A Library.

80 'Gold brooch set with river pearls', catalogue H, p. 67. This piece was sold at Sotheby's, 16 Feb 1984, no. 68 and is now in a private collection.

81 Catalogue K, p. 2.

CHAPTER FOURTEEN
THE ESSEX HOUSE PRESS

1 Los and Golgonooza: the original designs are at J, Jan/Feb 1888, and the earliest date for the letter-head that I have seen is in 'Letters' at 8 April 1889; see also pp. 222–3. The Craft of the Guild is on a pamphlet, *The Ideals of the Craftsman* (n.d. [1889]) in 'Letters'. For the Ash and Bee design, see the front of another pamphlet, *Decorative Art from a Workshop Point of View* (n.d. [*c.* 1889]) in 'Letters'. Compare H. W. Davies, *Devices of the Early Printers 1457–1560: Their History and Development* (1931), nos. 113, 122 and 176, which show a tree with roots against a criblé background.

2 See pp. 225–6.

3 See p. 43.

4 Ashbee sent complimentary copies to those who had supported the Guild with donations, and there are many letters of thanks in 'Letters', dated 12–20 Feb 1891.

5 *B*, 1891, vol. 60, p. 274.

6 Reid began working for the Guild in July 1890 and resigned in October 1891. The ornamental heading on p. 14, 'Guild and School of Handicraft', is signed by him, and that on p. 21, 'Apprentices and Franklins of the Guild', is signed 'R'. I would also attribute to him, on stylistic grounds, the illustrations on pp. 23–7 and the drawing of the workshop at 34 Commercial Street on p. 18.

7 Advertisement in *Transactions*, facing the half-title.

8 Vivian Ridler, 'Artistic Printing: A Search for Principles', *Alphabet and Image*, 1948, no. 6, pp. 4–17.

9 Charles S. Felver, *Joseph Crawhall: The Newcastle Wood Engraver (1821–1896)* (Newcastle, n.d. [1973]).

10 'Letters', 8 April 1889, H. H. Cunynghame to Ashbee, and cutting from *Manchester Examiner* for 21 Feb 1891.

11 An advertisement in 'Letters' at May–June 1890 for a series of lectures by Ashbee on 'Architecture as the Language of the English People' has the imprint 'P. & H. Typ., Lond.'. By comparison with the types and printing style of this item, much of the Guild ephemera may be tentatively attributed to Penny and Hull. Ashbee probably used them regularly until he acquired Morris's presses in 1898, for the printing styles of *From Whitechapel to Camelo* (1892), *A Few Chapters in Workshop Re-Construction and Citizenship* (1894) and *The Trinity Hospital in Mile End* (1896), all written by Ashbee and published by the Guild, are similar to that of *Transactions* in some respects. Penny and Hull are listed as creditors of the Guild in the Schedule of Liabilities as at 1 Jan 1898 in PRO. BT31. 8064/58132.

12 Cf. the early pages of *Century Guild Hobby Horse*, 1889, vol. 4. And on Crawhall, cf. Ashbee's treatments of the Guild pink with Crawhall's pomegranate motifs on pp. 129 and 133 of Andrew Tuer (ed.), *1,000 Quaint Cuts* (n.d. [1886]) and with the pink-like flower on p. 2 of 'The Taming of the Shrew' in Joseph Crawhall, *Olde Tayles Newly Related* (n.d. [1883]); also compare Crawhall's strange leaf-like motif on p. 34 of 'George Barnewel in *Olde Tayles Newly Related* with Ashbee's equally strange and frequently used rows of decorative 'leaves'.

13 *S*, 1893, vol. 1, p. 19. If, as is most probable, Ashbee was a student at the Westminster School of Art in 1891–2, he may have known Beardsley who was a student there in 1891.

14 *Chapters*, pp. 48 and 72. The tail-pieces in *Century Guild Hobby Horse* 1888, vol. 3 may have provided a suggestion for these designs. There are other new images in this book whose meaning I have not been able to make out: the naked youth with a violin on p. 60, derived from a common Renaissance motif, and the naked youths holding spheres or garlands, holding a pair of scales, and chasing spheres, on the title-page and prelims of the large paper edition.

15 The treatment of the binding may have been suggested by Ashbee's friend D. S. MacColl, whose *Greek Vase Paintings*, written with J. R. Harrison and published in 1894, was bound in the same way. The large paper copies of *Chapters* were bound in boards with a Guild pink on them and the cover design of the standard edition as the frontispiece, hand-coloured.

16 See p. 18.

17 Graphic design work by Ashbee after *Chapters* and before the establishment of the Essex House Press included an invitation card of 1894 with a romantic view of the Magpie and Stump, in *British Architect* 1896, vol. 45, p. 24; a book-plate for Janet Forbes of 1895 in, for instance, some of her books in the possession of the Ashbee family; two other examples of ephemera in *British Architect*, loc. cit.; and *The Trinity Hospital in Mile End* (1896).

18 Entries in the diaries of Sydney Cockerell for 10 Dec 1896, 18 Sept, 11 Oct and 20 Dec 1897, and a retrospect of 1897 written on the Memoranda pages of the 1897 diary but dated 5 Jan 1898; B.M. Add. MSS. 52633 and 52634.

19 J, 24 March 1913; see also note 96 below, for corroboration of Hodson's role.

20 See Wolverhampton Municipal Art Gallery, *Catalogue of the Arts and Crafts Exhibition Spring 1897*; and ms. notes for a paper on the Beautiful Book, apparently given by Hodson to a literary club in 1896, in the possession of Edward Newton. The Morris manuscripts that Hodson owned are listed in Cockerell's papers, B.M. Add. MSS. 52772, and most of them are now in the Huntington Library, San Marino, California. The designs for the *Aeneid* are in the Fitzwilliam Museum, Cambridge. Hodson's taste in books can be judged from the ms. notes on the Beautiful Book referred to above and from the Library Association, *Exhibition of English MSS in the Library of the University of Birmingham* (Birmingham, 1902) which he appears to have written.

21 Ashbee to Janet Forbes, 21 March and March 1898, FA. Note however that in *Endeavour*, p. 34 Ashbee said, 'I opened negotiations with the trustees of the Kelmscott Press...'

22 *A*, 1891, vol. 46, p. 82. In 1892 David Nutt published *Dante Map* by Mary Hensman; this consisted of a preface and gazetteer printed by letterpress, and a large folded sheet, about two feet high by three feet wide, on which were printed, apparently from woodblocks, two maps of Italy in the time of Dante surrounded by elaborate borders made up of Guild emblems, all from designs by John Williams and printed by the Guild of Handicraft. In 'Memoirs', vol. 3, p. 5, Ashbee wrote that F. W. Sargant practised wood-block cutting at the Guild in the 1890s; Sargant later ran the Basil Press.

23 *Catalogue Raisonné of Books Printed and Published at The Doves Press No. 1. The Terrace, Hammersmith* (1908), p. 4.

24 A&CES, *Catalogue of the First Exhibition* (1888), p. 94.

25 A notable exception is Susan Otis Thompson, *American Book Design and William Morris* (1977).

26 H. Halliday Sparling, *The Kelmscott Press and William Morris Master-Craftsman* (1924), p. 135.

27 A&CES:1888:462–3.

28 *Of the Decorative Illustration of Books Old and New* (1896), p. 186.

29 This classification of illustrators is borrowed from Rose Sketchley's *English Book Illustration of To-Day* (1903) which is still one of the best books on the subject despite its over-ambitious literary style and its startling omission of Beardsley.

30 Sparling, op. cit, pp. 144–7.

31 *Treatises*, colophon. For the question of which presses Ashbee acquired, see note 96 below.

32 Prospectus for *Treatises*, Dec 1898, JJ Coll. In addition to the Caslon founts regularly used, capitals in 10 or 12 point appear in F. W. Bourdillon, *Through the Gateway* (1900), capitals in 48 point on the title-pages of Ernest Godman, *Mediaeval Architecture in Essex* (1905) and Ibid., *Norman Architecture in Essex* (1905), and an odd size, rather bigger than 48 point, as the initials in *Treatises*.

33 C. R. Ashbee, *The Private Press* (Broad Campden, 1909), pp. 4–5. For bindings, see the note at the end of this chapter.

34 *Treatises*, colophon; Ashbee's correspondence with Florence Kingsford, B.M. Add.MSS. 52703, particularly 6 April 1901.

35 There is an extensive collection of such prospectuses in the John Johnson Collection of Printed Ephemera, Bodleian Library, Oxford, on which my research is based. There are other collections in New York Public Library and Princeton University Library, and in the possession of the Ashbee family. The dates on these prospectuses provide some indication of when a book was published; and when a month of publication is cited in this chapter it may be taken as based on a prospectus in JJ Coll.

However, the Ashbee-Kingsford correspondence in the British Library suggests that titles were not always available until a month or so after the issue of the prospectus.

36 J, Dec 1900. For Buckley, see Phililp Sheail. 'Hampshire man and the quest for clean milk', *Hampshire,* March 1981, pp. 60–2. J, April 1900 suggests that Ashbee had thought of giving the American agency for Essex House to John Lane.

37 Sparling, op. cit, pp. 168–9, 174.

38 Essex House Press books have two minor but distinct technical flaws: the printing on vellum is never as wholly good, see p. 384 below; and the printing in red is not consistent: sometimes the ink is bright, even and strong, sometimes it has black or silver specks in it; this fault is found in Kelmscott books as well.

39 There were four sets of decorative initials, in sizes ranging with three, four, six and ten lines of Caslon 14 point; they were first used in *Beauty's Awakening,* printed to accompany the Art Workers' Guild masque in June 1899; more of the four-line series appeared in Shakespeare. *The Poems,* published in April 1900, and the four sets were announced as complete in the prospectus for Baldassare Castiglione, *The Courtyer,* of Oct 1900, JJ Coll.

40 It appears with Endeavour in his *Report . . . to the National Trust* (1901), *American Sheaves and English Seed Corn* (1901), the preface to *The Essex House Song Book* (1903–5) and *The Private Press* (1909).

41 Apart from *The Courtyer,* she edited *Pilgrim's Progress, The Praise of Folie, The Psalter,* and *The Essex House Song Book.*

42 *Chapters,* p. 165.

43 *The Private Press,* p. 43.

44 Philip Athill is right to suggest that Ashbee would have been attracted by the extraordinary visual force of Strang's *Book of Giants* (1898), in which helpless, primitive and soft-hearted giants experience fatal encounters with some of the peculiarities of modern life. She Sheffield City Art Galleries, *William Strang RA 1859–1921* (Catalogue of an exhibition 1980–1), p. 82.

45 Prospectus for Woolman and Penn, Sept 1900, JJ Coll.

46 See p. 214.

47 *The Private Press,* pp. 41–2.

48 Prospectus, March 1900, JJ Coll.

49 Prospectus for Shakespeare. *The Poems,* April 1900 and *The Eve of Saint Agnes,* Sept 1900, JJ Coll. The fourteen poems in the series are listed in Appendix 3 as nos. 6, 9, 13, 14, 24, 29, 30, 31, 35, 42, 47, 50, 56 and 67. Shelley's *Hellas* and Cowper's *John Gilpin* were planned as part of the series, but not printed; Thomas Hood's *Miss Kilmansegg* was planned but printed on paper instead in 1904. Illustrations by William Rothenstein for Browning's *Flight of the Duchess,* by Selwyn Image for *Comus,* and by F. W. Sargant and J. D. Batten were proposed but not printed.

50 Edwin Greenlaw and others (eds.), *The Works of Edmund Spenser: The Minor Poems: Volume One* (Baltimore, 1943), p. 207.

51 The first book, *Adonais,* was in an edition of only 50 copies, but the editions rose quickly to 125 and then 150.

52 It has to be said that defects in printing on vellum are not peculiar to Essex House among private presses.

53 Ashbee to Florence Kingsford, 6 April 1901, B.M. Add.MSS. 52703.

54 She decorated nos. 24, 30, 31, 42 and 47; the Whitman went through her hands but was apparently coloured by her sister. Goldsmith's *Deserted Village* was decorated in part by her and in part by Annie Power.

55 *Hymn on the Death of Lincoln* is Ashbee's title for *When Lilacs Last in the Dooryard Bloom'd.*

56 I do not know of book illustrations by George Thomson earlier than his frontispiece to *Elegy written in a Country Churchyard* (1901) for the Essex House Press. He was a member of the New English Art Club, and his drawings were used to illustrate an article on the Magpie and Stump in *S,* 1895, vol. 5, pp. 66–74 and an article on Essex House in *S,* 1897–8, vol. 12, pp. 27–31. He translated the Essex House drawings, not very successfully, into decorative initials for Ashbee's *Endeavour* (1901). I do not know of much earlier work by Edith Harwood, but she had illustrated *Old English Singing Games* (1900) by Alice B. Gomme, Laurence Gomme's wife, which is perhaps where

Ashbee came across her. So far as illustration goes, Ashbee himself could also be considered a novice.

57 Ashbee provided frontispieces for *Adonais, Hymn on the Death of Lincoln* and *Deserted Village.*

58 In Appendix 3 they are 5, 8, 9, 17, 24, 31, 34, 41, 47 and 56. Much later in life, he provided rather weak illustrations for Ashbee's *Peckover: The Abbotscourt Papers* (1932).

59 For Savage's illustration work before 1899 see *Dial,* 1892, no. 2, frontispiece; 1893, no. 3, frontispiece and facing p. 38; 1896, no. 4, facing p. 32; *Pageant,* 1896, vol. 1, pp. 122 and 161; 1897, vol. 2, p. 29; and R. F. Sharp, *Wagner's Drama Der Ring Des Nibelungen* (1898). See also the entry in Brigid Peppin and Lucy Micklethwaite, *Dictionary of British Book Illustrators: The Twentieth Century* (1983), p. 269.

60 Savage appears between Pissarro and a Mr Riley in one of Ricketts's illustrations to *Daphnis and Chloe* (1893), see Joseph Darracott. *The World of Charles Ricketts* (1980), p. 37.

61 J, April 1900. I have not been able to identify this unfortunate address.

62 Ibid.

63 The photograph is dated by its position in J at June 1900; it may be earlier. *DK,* 1899, vol. 3, p. 239 describes the cutting of Endeavour as almost finished.

64 It may be that Ashbee's *Report . . . to the National Trust* was actually the first appearance of Endeavour; it is dated March 1901 in the colophon; the prospectus for *Endeavour* in JJ Coll. is dated April 1901. In addition to the main fount, capitals in 18 point and 24 point appeared in *The Psalter* published in Oct 1901. The punches were cut by Edward Prince who had worked for Morris and other private presses; I do not know which foundry supplied the type.

65 *A Bibliography of the Essex House Press* (Chiping Campden, 1904), p. 3.

66 Paul Needham (ed.), *William Morris and the Art of the Book* (1976), pp. 122–3.

67 William Blades had pointed out that Caxton's No. 1 type, which Ashbee perhaps took special note of, had only five letters in it that were not either combinations or variants; see D. B. Updike, *Printing Types: Their History, Forms and Use: A Study in Survivals* (1922), vol. 1, pp. 115–6.

68 Needham, op. cit, p. 72.

69 A number of the letters in the carved inscription on the reredos which Ashbee designed for St Stephen's, Shottermill, Surrey in 1900 are very similar to the upper case of Endeavour.

70 Echoes of Holbein: cherubs and children larking about and playing trumpets, figures climbing in and out of letters, the occasional note of ribaldry.

71 In a quite different context, Ashbee wrote of 'the bare soul of the man, naked as the Italian Quattrocentist might have drawn it in its progress to heaven or hell'. J, March 1902.

72 *The Private Press,* p. 40. Prospectus of Oct 1903, JJ Coll. As a more immediate celebration of the King's accession, Ashbee wrote *The Masque of the Edwards of England* and printed it at the Essex House Press in 1901 with lithographed illustrations by Edith Harwood.

73 Prospectus of 18 Oct 1901, JJ Coll. The private press movement had already produced one sumptuous edition of *The Book of Common Prayer* in *The Altar Book* printed by D. B. Updike at the Merrymount Press in Boston between 1893 and 1896. Ashbee could have seen this when it was exhibited at the Arts and Crafts Exhibition in London in 1896, or when he met Updike in Boston in November 1900.

74 There were fewer combined letters; the descenders, but not the curve in 'h', 'm' and 'n' were removed; the pennant-like 'f' remained.

75 The prospectus of 18 Oct 1901 refers to 'about One Hundred and Fifty Woodcuts' but this figure probably includes the decorative initials from *The Psalter* re-used here. The wood engraving for *The Prayer Book* was done by William Harcourt Hooper, who had worked for the Kelmscott Press, and Laurence Housman's sister Clemence. Hooper seems to have done most of the engraving for the Press, with lesser contributions from Clemence Housman, Bernard Sleigh and Reginald Savage.

76 Prospectus of Oct 1903, JJ Coll. This prospectus only mentions standard bindings in oak boards, but the copies in the Bodleian Library and the British Library are both bound in vellum.

77 Invitation to an exhibition at 67A New Bond Street on 20 November 1903, JJ Coll.

78 *The Private Press*, p. 38. I do not know whether any of the drawings survive. The woodblock of the frontispiece to *The Prayer Book*, a proof of the frontispiece, six sheets of trial pages and three sheets of proofs of illustrations are in V&A Prints and Drawings. See also note 96 below.

79 *A Defence of the Revival of Printing* (1899), p. 30.

80 Compare the circular domed structure on p. [103] recto of the *Hypnerotomachia*; and also the full page of close-set capitals on p. 6 of *The Prayer Book* with p. [129] recto of the *Hypnerotomachia*.

81 J, 3 Dec 1902.

82 *A Key to the Principal Decorations in the Prayer Book of King Edward VII* (1904), p. 10. This pamphlet and an article by Ashbee, 'The Coronation Prayer Book of King Edward VII', *AJ*, 1904, pp. 386–91, are the best sources for understanding Ashbee's choice of illustrations.

83 J, 24 Nov. 1901; see also *A Key*, p. 4 and *AJ*, 1904, p. 388.

84 Prospectus Dec 1901, JJ Coll.

85 J, 15 Feb 1886. *Transactions* is dedicated to Bradshaw. For the whole subject of Prayer Books, printing and liturgy, see Stanley Morison, *English Prayer Books* (Cambridge, 1949).

86 For the Revd. Percy Dearmer, who had a verger's wand by the Guild of Handicraft in his church of St Mary the Virgin, Primrose Hill, London, see V&A Museum, *Victorian Church Art* (Catalogue of an exhibition, 1971), no. O17 and Peter F. Anson, *Fashions in Church Furnishings 1840–1940* (1965), pp. 306–15.

87 In a letter to Janet of *c*. 1898 quoted in Miller, p. 35.

88 For Pierpont Morgan, see C. R. Ashbee, *Kingfisher out of Egypt* (1934), p. 28. For the *Bible*, prospectus Nov 1904, JJ Coll. Ashbee believed that this would not compete with the Bible printed by the Doves Press and published in 1903–5 because his was a two-volume book intended for use in churches; J, 17 June 1906.

89 J, 17 June 1906. The fact that *The Essex House Song Book*, which began publication in December 1903, did not sell well, and that a proposal of the same date to print the *Poems of Ben Jonson* met with a poor response, made the situation more serious. A copy of the Jonson proposal in JJ Coll has written on it: '*never published* because the English book lover will not read Ben Jonson. I love him. C.R.A.'

90 MGH, 25 July 1905. Prospectus of Nov 1904 for Cicero, *De Amicitia* in JJ Coll. The books published were nos. 48–76 in Appendix 3. Of these 57–60, 62, 66, 69 and 76 were probably not published at the expense of the Press.

91 J, 17 June, 1906.

92 J, 31 Aug 1906.

93 J, 25 Jan 1908 and 14 Sept 1910.

94 *Mediaeval Sinhalese Art* (Broad Campden, 1908), p. x.

95 Letter from Philip Mairet to the author, 24 Feb 1972.

96 The question of what happened to the equipment of the Essex House Press may be of interest, if only for its associations with Morris and Kelmscott. It falls under four heads:
    The presses. Ashbee probably acquired two Albion presses from the executors of William Morris, and possibly a small proofing press. An inventory was taken at the time of the transfer, but I have not seen a copy of it. (See a note in the miscellaneous collection of Sydney Cockerell's papers, B.M. Add.MSS. 52772.) According to Anthony Eyre (ed.), *William Morris's Printing Press* (1983), n.p., a third Albion was advertised for sale in May 1898 and therefore presumably did not go to Essex House. A photograph of the printing room in the workshops at Campden appears to show two full-sized Albions. (FA)
    It is interesting that Sydney Cockerell wrote that one of the Kelmscott presses had already passed into other hands by 4 Jan 1898, see Sparling, op. cit, p. 147. Since there were three Kelmscott Albions in all, this must have been one of the presses which came to Essex House, and the dates suggest that Hodson had already bought one press late in 1897.
    The subsequent career of the two Kelmscott Albions used

at Essex House is a little uncertain; but it appears that one was sold to A. H. Bullen of the Shakespeare Head Press in Stratford-on-Avon in about 1904; see Sir Basil Blackwell's memories in Eyre, op. cit; since then it has been in Sir Basil's care and has passed by way of Oxford Polytechnic, to the William Morris Society.
The other Albion must have been used by Coomaraswamy. Just how it passed from Ashbee's or Coomaraswamy's hands is not clear, though G. S. Tomkinson, *A Select Bibliography of the Principal Modern Presses Public and Private in Great Britain and Ireland* (1928), p. 67 states that the Essex House 'presses' were sold in 1910. It seems to have passed through the hands of Herbert Broome of the Old Bourne Press, James Guthrie of the Pear Tree Press, F. W. Goudy (who brought it to the United States in 1924), Spencer Kellogg of the Aries Press, and Melbert B. Cary of the Woolly Whale Press, before it came to its present owner, J. Ben Lieberman of the Herity Press, White Plains, N.Y., in 1961. This is the press which Cockerell says was sold before 4 Jan 1898; see Needham, op. cit, p. 139 and 'A Historian's Judgment', a keepsake printed at the Herity Press, 28 Jan 1984.
    The Caslon type. This was acquired by Coomaraswamy; a letter from Ethel Coomaraswamy to Ashbee, J, 14 Sept 1910, says 'Ananda is letting the Chiswick Press have his type . . .'
    The Endeavour and Prayer Book types. These were still in Ashbee's possession in February 1913 when, being short of money, he wrote to Janet that he had tried to sell the types, J, 26 Feb 1913. According to Tomkinson, 'the two founts were sold to an Indian gentleman but Mr Ashbee retained the matrices and blocks' (op. cit., p. 67). I do not know where the types, the matrices or the blocks now are. Ashbee gave the block for the frontispiece of *The Prayer Book* to the V&A in 1921 and perhaps disposed of the rest; Felicity Ashbee has no memory of any quantity of blocks or matrices among her father's possessions in the 1920s and 1930s.
    Original drawings and proofs. There are sixteen sheets of proofs and trial pulls for various Essex House Press titles in V&A Prints and Drawings, and some sets of proofs and trial pulls in the possession of the Ashbee family. A magnificent collection of original drawings, proofs and trial pulls, amounting in all to some 800 items, was auctioned by the American Art Association, Inc. in New York on 12 May 1924. I do not know who formed the collection, or who the buyers were, or the whereabouts of any of the items now. There is a copy of the sale catalogue in the Rare Book Room, New York Public Library.

97 See Appendix 3. The best collection of Essex House ephemera is probably that in JJ Coll.

98 J, 5 March 1916.

99 Stanley Morison, *Type Designs of the Past and Present* (1926), p. 56. D. B. Updike, *Printing Types . . .* (1922), vol. 2, p. 214.

100 *The Private Presses* (1969), p. 75.

101 *The Private Press*, p. 45.

102 *English Printed Books* (1946), p. 33.

103 The correspondence with Florence Kingsford, B.M. Add.MSS. 52703 shows how ready he was to accept her standards and preferences.

104 The single, two-colour wood engraving *Conscience* (1904) by Bernard Sleigh, another very fine engraver–illustrator, falls into the same category.

105 Prospectus, June 1901, JJ Coll.

106 Ashbee to Florence Kingsford, B.M. Add.MSS. 52703, 29 Oct and 29 Nov 1901.

107 Prospectus for *Pilgrim's Progress*, Sept 1899 and many following. Bindings for *Pilgrim's Progress* were advertised as designed by Ashbee or by Cockerell.

108 Prospectus of Oct 1902 for *The Flower and the Leaf*; *Craftsmanship*, p. 258.

109 For lavish bindings, see the Prospectus of Oct 1902 for *The Flower and the Leaf*, and *K und K*, 1902, vol. 5, p. 596; for others see *Le Style Moderne: L'Art Appliqué* (Paris), 1904–5, plate 4.

110 J, 6 July 1905.

CHAPTER FIFTEEN
REPUTATION AND INFLUENCE

1 Minute Books of the A&CES, 29 Jan and 27 Oct 1897, 2 Feb 1898, V&A Library.

2 For admiration mingled with criticism, see the letter from Cecil Brewer quoted above, Chapter 5, p. 144.

3 Letter to A. W. Simpson, 22 Aug 1909, in the possession of John Brandon-Jones.

4 Letter of Philip Norman to George Roebuck, 8 Oct 1908, William Morris Gallery, Walthamstow; and Sydney Cockerell in conversation with John Brandon-Jones, reported in a letter to the author, 4 Feb 1974. As an example of the presentation of Ashbee as the successor of Morris, common among German and American writers, see J. A. Lux, *Das Neue Kunstgewerbe in Deutschland* (Leipzig, 1908), p. 44.

5 So Norman Jewson told Jane Darke on 24 Aug 1967; I am grateful to Fiona MacCarthy for telling me this; see also W. R. Lethaby, A. H. Powell and F. L. Griggs, *Ernest Gimson, his life and work* (1924), p. 10.

6 J, 25 Feb 1912.

7 W. R. Lethaby, *Form in Civilization: Collected Papers on Art and Labour* (1922), p. 107.

8 The following is a list of the exhibitions at which Ashbee showed. Where the name of the exhibition or the exhibiting body is not known, only the place is given.
  1888: A&CES, London. *1889*: Arts and Crafts exhibition, Walker Art Gallery, Liverpool; A&CES, London. *1890*: Arts and Crafts exhibition, Corporation Art Galleries, Glasgow; Arts and Crafts exhibition, Mansfield; Arts and Crafts exhibition, Abbotskerswell; Armourers' and Brasiers' Company, London; A&CES, London. *1891*: Armourers' and Brasiers' Company, London; Falmouth; New English Art Club, London. *1892*: New School of Applied Art, Edinburgh; Armourers' and Brasiers' Company, London; New English Art Club, London; Royal Academy, London. *1893*: A&CES, London. *1894*: La Libre Esthétique, Brussels. *1895*: Arts and Crafts exhibition, City Art Gallery, Manchester; La Libre Esthétique, Brussels; L'Oeuvre Artistique, Liège; Royal Academy, London. *1896*: A&CES, London; East London Trades, Industries and Arts Exhibition. *1897*: Arts and Crafts exhibition, Municipal Art Gallery, Wolverhampton; Keller and Reiner, Berlin. *1898*: Arts and Crafts Society, Chicago; Glaspalast, Munich; Royal Academy, London; Art Metal Exhibition, Royal Aquarium, London; T Square Club, Philadelphia; Architectural Club, Chicago. *1899*: T Square Club, Philadelphia; A&CES, London. *1900*: Exposition Universelle, Paris; Secession, Vienna; Architectural Club, Chicago; Royal Academy, London; Arts and Crafts exhibition, Leeds; Stockholm; Howard Fine Art Gallery, London; Huddersfield; Keighley. *1902*: Art and Industrial Exhibition, Wolverhampton; Secession, Vienna; Esposizione Internazionale d'Arte Decorativa Moderna, Turin; Woodbury Gallery, London. *1903*: Cumberland and Westmorland Society of Arts and Crafts, Carlisle; A&CES, London. *1904*: Arts and Crafts exhibition, Leicester; Arts and Crafts exhibition, Port Sunlight; Hohenzollerns-Kunstgewerbehaus, Berlin; Louisiana Purchase International Exposition, St Louis; Royal Academy, London; Arts and Crafts exhibition, City Art Gallery, Leeds. *1905*: Clarion Guild, Manchester; Bristol and Clifton Arts and Crafts Society, Bristol; Royal Academy, London; Secession, Vienna. *1906*: Secession, Vienna; A&CES, London; Royal Academy, London; Architectural Congress, London; Esposizione Internazionale, Milan. *1906–7*: New Zealand International Exhibition. *1908*: Royal Academy, London. *1909*: Kunstschau, Vienna. *1910*: A&CES, London; Royal Academy, London. *1912*: A&CES, London. *1913*: Royal Academy, London. *1914*: Arts décoratifs de Grande Bretagne et de l'Irlande, Musée des Arts Décoratifs, Paris; Leipzig; Town Planning Exhibition, Dublin. *1916*: A&CES, London.
  In *Endeavour*, p. 12, Ashbee also refers to exhibitions in Dublin and Frankfurt, and at the Cape, which I have not been able to identify.

9 See Appendix 4, nos. 12, 14, 15, 18, 22 and 23.

10 S, 1897–8, vol. 12, pp. 27–36.

11 The *Studio* article was preceded by a rather similar one in *Artist* for April 1897 by Mabel Cox, 'The Guild and School of Handicraft' 1897, vol. 19, pp. 167–71; see also H. Dymoke Wilkinson, 'The Guild and School of Handicraft, Essex House', *Architectural Association Notes*, 1898, vol. 13, pp. 61–3.

12 I have come across some examples of Ashbee's stylistic influence in Britain, in several media, and there are no doubt many others. But he does not seem to have been imitated as obviously or as often as Beardsley for instance, or Voysey or Baillie Scott. The earliest and most obvious example is that the motif of a spreading tree used in *Transactions*, for instance on p. 23, was taken up and closely copied by Laurence Housman in his first success as an illustrator, George Meredith's *Jump to Glory Jane* (1892). There is no evidence that Housman knew Ashbee at this date.
  See also: a design by Aymer Vallance for playing cards possibly influenced by the Guild pink, see *Yellow Book* 1894, vol. 2, p. [361]; a binding for John Cowper Powys. *Poems* (1899) by G. W. (Gleeson White?), influenced by the same design, see G. Krishnamurti, *The Eighteen-Nineties: A Literary Exhibition* (1973), plate 3; an unexecuted design for a house at 68 Sloane Street, London by E. W. Filkins in which the street elevation seems to be based on 37 Cheyne Walk, see B, 1905, vol. 89, p. 421; a brooch by Bernard Cuzner and Alfred H. Jones very like an insect pendant exhibited by Ashbee in 1896, see the advertisement in *S*, for Oct 1901, p. xvii; and various silver bowls by the Birmingham silversmith A. E. Jones which echo Ashbee's loop-handled dishes, see Alan Crawford (ed.), *By Hammer and Hand: The Arts and Crafts Movement in Birmingham* (Birmingham, 1984), plate 91. In *European and American Jewellery 1830–1914* (1975) p. 220, Charlotte Gere refers to a book of designs for jewellery by Edgar Simpson in the Metropolitan Museum, New York, which plagiarize Ashbee; I have not seen them.

13 See Chapter 2 above, pp. 42–3.

14 For Lambeth see A&CES: 1899: 258, 429; for Gentlewomen, see S, 1899, vol. 16, p. 50; for Crediton, *Art Workers' Quarterly* 1903, vol. 2, p. 188.

15 Glasgow Museums and Art Galleries, *The Glasgow Style 1890–1920* (Glasgow, 1984), pp. 46–7; S, 1907, vol. 39, p. 72; and Peter Aitken, Cameron Cunningham and Bob McCutcheon, *The Homesteads: Stirling's Garden Suburb* (Stirling, 1984), p. 38 which shows that the principal figures in the Scottish Guild were not closely acquainted with Ashbee's. Other groups which may have had something in common with the Guild were the Guild of Art Craftsmen, see AJ, 1899, p. 351; and the Potteries' Cripples' Guild of Handicraft, see *Art Workers' Quarterly*, 1904, vol. 3, p. 137 and *Arts and Crafts*, 1905, vol. 2, p. 29.

16 *Clarion*, 30 March 1901, p. 98 and ff.

17 H. Allen Brooks, 'Steinway Hall, Architects and Dreams', *Journal of the Society of Architectural Historians* (Philadelphia), 1963, vol. 22, pp. 171–5.

18 Isabelle Anscombe and Charlotte Gere, *Arts and Crafts in Britain and America* (1978), p. 33; G.R.T., 'Workshop Reconstruction by C. R. Ashbee: A Review', *House Beautiful* (Chicago), 1896–7, vol. 1, no. 2, pp. 8–14.

19 *House Beautiful* (Chicago), 1898, vol. 3, p. 203; and information from Jerry Cinamon.

20 James D. Kornwolf, *M. H. Baillie Scott and the Arts and Crafts Movement* (1972), p. 366.

21 T Square Club, Philadelphia, *Catalogue of the Annual Architectural Exhibition 1899–1900*, nos. 10–18; *Inland Architect* (Chicago), 1900, vol. 35, p. 5.

22 H. Allen Brooks, *The Prairie School: Frank Lloyd Wright and his midwest contemporaries* (Toronto, 1972), p. 18.

23 See Chapter 4 above, pp. 96–7.

24 Christina Melk, 'Oscar Lovell Triggs and the Industrial Art League of Chicago: A Chapter in the History of the Arts and Crafts Movement' (MA Thesis, Tufts University, 1983). See also Sharon Darling, *Chicago Furniture: Art, Craft, Industry: 1833–83* (New York, 1984), pp. 229–30.

25 op. cit, (Chicago, 1902), pp. 142–57.

26 Ibid., p. 124.

27 *Artsman* (Philadelphia), 1903–4, vol. 1, p. 59.

28 *Craftsman* (Eastwood, N.Y.), 1902, vol. 3, at the end of the October number; *Handicraft* (Boston, Mass.), 1902, vol. 1, p. 168 and 1903, vol. 2, back cover of the October number; *Artsman* (Philadelphia), 1903–4, vol. 1, pp. 378 and 472.

29 *American Sheaves*, p. 88.

30 He has certainly seemed so to two scholars who have argued for the importance of Arts and Crafts influence on American architecture in the early twentieth century, James Kornwolf in his study of Baillie Scott, and H. Allen Brooks in his book on the Prairie School.

31 Frederic Allen Whiting, 'A Successful English Experiment' *Handicraft* (Boston, Mass.), 1903, vol. 2, pp. 139–58. Ashbee reprinted this article at the Essex House Press, see Appendix 3, no. 44.

32 1903, vol. 2, p. 198. Other references to Ashbee in American periodicals are *American Architect and Building News* (Boston, Mass.), 1896, vol. 52, pp. 45, 47; 1905, vol. 88, p. 208; *House and Garden* (Greenwich, Conn.), 1906, vol. 9, p. 209; and various articles written by Ashbee, see Appendix 4, nos. 31, 50, 55, 57–9, 76, 80.

33 For Voysey see, for example, *Craftsman* (Eastwood, N.Y.), 1912, vol. 22, p. 302.

34 For Stickley and Hubbard see Mary Ann Smith, *Gustav Stickley: The Craftsman* (Syracuse, N.Y., 1983) and Coy L. Ludwig, *The Arts and Crafts Movement in New York State 1890s–1920s* (Catalogue of an exhibition Oswego, N.Y., 1893–5). For comparable designs by Ashbee see *Le Style Moderne: L'Art Appliqué* (Paris), 1904–5, plates 8 and 55, and catalogue G, pp. 70–1, 75, 77. John Crosby Freeman, *The Forgotten Rebel: Stickley and His Craftsman Mission Furniture* (Watkins Glen, N.Y., 1966), pp. 44 and 53 says that Stickley met Ashbee and other Arts and Crafts figures in England in about 1898 and that he was particularly interested in the work of the Guild as an alternative to Art Nouveau; but no supporting evidence is given for either point.

35 For the Kalo Shop, Sharon Darling, *Chicago Metalsmiths: an illustrated history* (Chicago, 1977), pp. 45–55; for the Shreve, Crump and Low dish, information from Milo Naeve, Art Institute of Chicago.

36 See the excellent catalogue, *The Arts and Crafts Movement in America 1896–1916* (Princeton, N.J., 1972).

37 J, 8 July 1910.

38 See Robert-L. Delevoy, Giovanni Wieser and Maurice Culot. *Bruxelles 1900* (Brussels, 1972); and for socialism in the Belgian *avant-garde*, Isobel Spencer, *Walter Crane* (1975), pp. 182–3.

39 Madeleine Octave Maus, *Trente Années de lutte pour l'art* (Brussels, 1926), pp. 173 and 185; Pevsner, *Pioneers of Modern Design* (Harmondsworth, 1974), p. 110; Ashbee, *A Nine Years' Experiment in Technical Education . . .* (1895), p. 10.

40 Maus, loc. cit; Fernand Khnopff, 'Some English Art Works at the "Libre Esthétique" at Brussels', *S*, 1894, vol. 3, p. 32.

41 Ashbee, *A Nine Year's Experiment in Technical Education . . .* (1895), p. 10; Maus, op. cit., p. 179 refers to the Guild as exhibiting 'orfèvreries', but beyond this I do not know what was exhibited or which museum bought the Guild's work; it was not the Musées Royaux d'Art et d'Histoire in Brussels.

42 The only substantial reference to Ashbee that I have seen in French periodicals is in *Le Style Moderne: L'Art Appliqué* (Paris) for 1904–5. However, he seems to have had dealings with Samuel Bing of L'Art Nouveau in Paris: in the Schedule of Liabilities of the Guild as at 1 Jan 1898 'Bing' is mentioned among the creditors of the Guild, PRO. BT31. 8064/58132. And the Minutes of the A&CES for 2 Feb 1898 show that Ashbee brought a message from Bing advising the Society on exhibiting in Paris—presumably at the Exposition Universelle; V&A Library.

43 The Münchener Vereinigte Werkstätten für Kunst im Handwerk founded by Obrist, Pankok, Paul and Riemerschmid, and the Dresdener Werkstätte für Handwerkskunst.

44 *K und K*, 1900, vol. 3, p. 172.

45 Keller and Reiner: *DK*, 1897–8, vol. 1, p. 143; H. Muthesius, 'Die "Guild and School of Handicraft" in London', ibid., 1898, vol. 2, pp. 41–8; and other references: 1897–8, vol. 1, pp. 8–10,

19–20, 48, 68, 70–1; 1898, vol. 2, pp. 268–70; 1899, vol. 3, pp. 238–9, 247, 270; 1899, vol. 4, pp. 1, 11–15, 177–9. The volume numbers given here are taken from the bound volumes in the V&A Library and do not necessarily correspond to the numbering printed in the magazine itself.

46 op. cit, p. 48.

47 *Endeavour*, p. 20.

48 For the Viennese background, see Peter Vergo, *Art in Vienna 1898–1918* (1975).

49 *S*, 1899, vol. 16, p. 33. For Ashbee acquisitions, correspondence from the Österreichisches Museum of 25 June 1984.

50 Letter of 20 April 1900 in a private collection in Vienna. I am grateful to Hofrat Prof. Dr Wilhelm Mrazek for kindly transcribing this letter for me. A translation of virtually the whole letter will be found in Werner J. Schweiger, *Wiener Werkstaette: Design in Vienna 1903–1932* (1984), pp. 17–18.

51 Letter from Ashbee to von Myrbach of 19 July 1900 in the archives of the Secession, Vienna.

52 Letter from Ashbee to Franz Hancke, 15 Sept 1900 in the archives of the Secession, Vienna. Secession, *Katalog der VIII. Kunst-Ausstellung* (1900), nos. 50–5, 126–53, 387–8, 391–2, 402–15, 419; for the cabinet in a place of honour, Eduard F. Sekler, *Josef Hoffmann: Das architektonische werk* (Salzburg and Vienna, 1982), p. 265.

53 Ludwig Hevesi, *Acht Jahre Secession* (Vienna, 1906), p. 288; *DK*, 1901, vol. 7, pp. 178–84. Schweiger, op. cit, p. 18, has put forward the view that the Scottish contingent was not greeted with quite the acclaim that recent literature has suggested.

54 Ibid.

55 Ibid., pp. 289–90.

56 Ibid.

57 Quoted in Benedetto Gravagnuolo, *Adolf Loos: Theory and Works* (Milan, 1982), p. 61.

58 The Guild of Handicraft Ltd., Annual Report for 1900. V&A Library; letters from Ashbee of 8, 15 and 26 November, 5 and 22 December 1900 and 17 and 19 January 1901 in the archives of the Secession, Vienna, referring to sales; Eduard F. Sekler, 'Mackintosh and Vienna' in Pevsner and Richards (eds.), *The Anti-Rationalists* (1973), p. 139; the Österreichisches Museum acquired a mustard pot, a silver spoon, one of the new loop-handled dishes and a two-handled dish on a foot on 8 Nov 1900, a few days after the exhibition opened; the first three of these seem to correspond to catalogue nos. 127, 131, and 129; for the sale of the mahogany writing cabinet, information from Fischer Fine Art Ltd., of London.

For Örley, see a cupboard illustrated at *DK*, 1902, vol. 9, p. 71; for Moser, plate 203; for Hoffmann, Eduard F. Sekler, *Josef Hoffmann: Das architektonische werk* (Salzburg and Vienna, 1982), p. 40. Another influential Viennese architect who was impressed by Ashbee even before the Secession exhibition in 1900 was Rudolf Hammel; compare his cup for cigar ashes, *S*, 1899, vol. 16, p. 33 with the biscuit barrel which Ashbee exhibited in 1896, *Artist*, 1896, vol. 18, p. 27.

The articles in *K und K* were W. Fred, 'C. R. Ashbee. Ein Reformer Englischen Kunstgewerbes', 1900, vol. 3, pp. 167–76; B. Rendell, 'Charles Ashbee als Architekt und Baumeister', 1901, vol. 4, pp. 461–7; B. Kendell, 'Die Neueren arbeiten der Guild of Handicraft und das neue "Essex House" in Campden, Glous.', 1902, vol. 5, pp. 591–600.

59 Secession, *XV Ausstellung* (1902), no. 154; ———, *XXIV Ausstellung* (1905), nos. 55–8, 67–75; ———, *XXVII Ausstellung* (1906), nos. 73, 94–146, 151–7.

60 Vergo, op. cit, p. 202 and *S*, 1909, vol. 47, p. 240.

61 Horst-Herbert Kossatz, 'The Vienna Secession and its early relations with Great Britain', *Studio International*, 1971, vol. 181, p. 17. I know of no record of a meeting with Hoffmann in Ashbee's papers.

62 The idea that the Werkstätte were modelled on the Guild has been most clearly stated by Kossatz, op. cit., p. 17; see also Eduard F. Sekler, 'The Stoclet House by Josef Hoffmann' in Douglas Fraser, Howard Hibbard and Milton J. Lewine (eds.), *Essays in the history of architecture presented to Rudolf Wittkower* (1967), p. 240; Georg Eisler in *Apollo*, 1971, p. 47, and Wilhelm Mrazek in *Connoisseur*, 1971, vol. 176, p. 17.

63 Josef Hoffmann and Koloman Moser, *Katalog mit Arbeits-programm der Wiener Werkstätte* (Vienna, 1905) as translated in T. and C. Benton (eds.), *Form and Function* (1975), p. 36.

64 Österreichisches Museum für angewandte Kunst, *Die Wiener Werkstätte: Modernes Kunsthandwerk von 1903–1932* (Catalogue of an exhibition 1967), *passim*; for the 1904 cabinet, ibid. *Wiener Möbel des Jugendstils: Neuerwerbungen und Leihgaben* (Catalogue of an exhibition 1971), no. 6; see also Schweiger, op. cit, pp. 58, 213, 216, 218–19.

65 Vergo, op. cit., p. 134.

66 For the first see Ashbee's application for the Slade Professorship at Oxford, Bodleian Library MS. Top. Oxon. c. 178; for the second, Heinz Spielmann, *Museum für Kunst und Gewerbe, Hamburg: Die Jugendstil Sammlung: Band I: Künstler A–F* (Hamburg, 1979), p. 12.

67 Zsombor de Szász, 'C. R. Ashbee és a Guild of Handicraft', vol. 13, pp. 44–90. For British Arts and Crafts exhibits in Hungary see Isobel Spencer, *Walter Crane* (1975), pp. 186–7 and Orszagos Magyar Iparmüveszéti Museum. *Brit. Iparmüveszéti Kiallitas Katalogusa* (Catalogue of an exhibition, 1902).

68 Erika Gysling-Billeter, *Objekte des Jugendstils aus der Sammlung der Kunstgewerbemuseums im Museum Bellerive* (Zurich, 1975), p. 22 and correspondence with the Österreichisches Museum für angewandte Kunst, 25 June 1984, the cross being a variant of *MES*, plate 85; for Milan, 'A Survey of English-Speaking Universities' (Typescript 1912), KCC.

69 Spielmann, op. cit, pp. 16–17; for the *Deutsche Buchgewerbe Künstler*, J, 3 Sept 1914; B. Kendell in *K und K*, 1902, vol. 5, p. 595 said that the Essex House Press was the 'most stimulating' section of the Guild's work. For Ashbee's influence on jewellery in Germany and Austria see Ulrike von Hase, *Schmuck in Deutschland und Österreich 1895–1914* (Munich, 1977), pp. 22–3, which also documents (p. 134) a design by Moser of 1903–4, now in the Österreichisches Museum für angewandte Kunst, for a belt clasp which is very similar to a clasp designed by Ashbee, exhibited in Turin in 1902 and illustrated in *Deutsche Kunst und Dekoration*, 1902–3, vol. 11, p. 223; a clasp to this design is in the collections of Birmingham Museums and Art Gallery, Hull Grundy Gift. There is also a clasp in the Österreichisches Museum für angewandte Kunst which was made in the Kunstgewerbliche Fachschule at Gablonz in Bohemia, a straightforward copy of a clasp by Ashbee incorporating a medallion portrait of a girl and illustrated in *S*, 1897, vol. 9, p. 131; see von Hase, op. cit, p. 344. For Hirzel, see *DK*, 1898, vol. 2, pp. 28–33, 153.

70 For Berlepsch-Valendas, see Chapter 5 above, pp. 138–40. John Th. Uiterwijk of The Hague is said to have studied at the Guild, see *AJ*, 1902, p. 261; Karl Schmidt of the Dresdener Werkstätte visited Dering Yard on 11 May 1903, see Visitor's Book, V&A Library.

71 J, early Nov 1904.

72 Stefan Muthesius, *Das Englische Vorbild* (Munich, 1974), p. 183.

73 *Wirtschaft und Kunst* (Jena, 1909), pp. 135–6.

74 *SWS*, p. 4; see also *WGC*, p. 11 where Ashbee wrote that the 'most logical and consistent development' of the Arts and Crafts was in 'the co-ordinated workshops of Munich and Vienna'.

75 Ibid., pp. 32–3; 'Report of an address by C. R. Ashbee to members of the Walthamstow Public Libraries Committee concerning the proposed Morris Memorial Museum', *Walthamstow District Times*, 9 Oct 1908.

76 Edgar Kaufmann Jr (ed.), *Frank Lloyd Wright: The Early Work* (New York, 1968), p. 7.

77 Joan Campbell, *The German Werkbund: The Politics of Reform in the Applied Arts* (Princeton, N.J., 1978).

78 See the Prospectus and List of Original Members issued by the DIA in August 1915, V&A Library.

79 *Modern Architecture* (n.d. [1929]), p. 42. Henry-Russell Hitchcock's *Modern Architecture: Romanticism and Reintegration*, which

80 was published in the same year, does not mention Ashbee. A classic example of this ambiguity is P. Morton Shand's comment on Ashbee's Byways, Yarnton, Oxfordshire, in his pioneering series of articles, 'Scenario for a Human Drama' in *AR* in the early 1930s. Shand said 'The vernacular idiom is already wearing thin. Clearly the sort of house that is preparing to become quite another, where "scholarship" intervenes to prevent the design being carried to its logical conclusion.' (*AR*, 1934, vol. 76, p. 42). We have seen that Ashbee's reticent design was intended to 'fit in' with the building traditions of the area.

81 See p. 202.

82 p. 42.

83 p. 28.

84 Ibid.

85 See for instance Julius Posener (ed.), *Anfänge des Funktionalismus: Von Arts and Crafts zum Deutschen Werkbund* (Berlin, 1964), p. 95; Leonardo Benevolo, *History of Modern Architecture* (1966), vol. 1, p. 186; The Open University, *History of architecture and design 1890–1939: Art Nouveau* (1975), p. 14; Kenneth Frampton, *Modern Architecture: a critical history* (1980), p. 48; Lionel Lambourne, *Utopian Craftsmen: The Arts and Crafts Movement from the Cotswolds to Chicago* (1980), p. 143; Edward Lucie-Smith, *A History of Industrial Design* (1983), p. 79.

86 p. 172.

87 *WGC*, p. 19.

88 See p. 160.

89 *Chapters*, p. 23; see also C. R. Ashbee, *Socialism and Politics* (1906), p. 24.

90 *WGC*, p. 21.

91 'A Survey of English-Speaking Universities' (Typescript, 1912), pp. 7–8, KCC; J, Jan and 30 March 1914, early March 1918; *Palestine Notebook*, pp. 247 and 252. See also Ashbee's article on 'The province of the arts and handicrafts in a mechanical society', *Hibbert Journal*, 1915–16, vol. 14, pp. 95–104.

CHAPTER SIXTEEN
CONCLUSION

1 J, 13 Sept 1914.

2 *Endeavour*, p. 25.

3 Alec Miller wrote to Sir Nikolaus Pevsner: 'I *know* he never was a member of any Socialist group or organisation, and I doubt if he ever gave a vote for Labour in any party election.' Letter of 10 March 1957 among Sir Nikolaus's papers. See also Miller, pp. 26–7.

4 *Chapters*, p. 124.

5 *Endeavour*, p. 21.

6 May Morris (ed.), *The Collected Works of William Morris* (1910–1915), vol. 22, p. 9.

7 Shulamit Volkov, *The Rise of Popular Antimodernism in Germany: The Urban Master Artisans, 1873–1896* (Princeton, N.J., 1978).

8 For Ashbee on Guild socialism, see J, *c*. 30 Nov 1914 and early March 1918.

9 J, Oct 1887.

10 J, 8 Feb 1933.

11 J, 26 June 1939.

12 Phoebe Haydon to Alec Miller, 27 Jan 1952, FA.

13 J, Feb 1911.

14 Miller, p. 10.

15 He was apt to yoke his tastes and his social beliefs too closely together, as in the absurd proposition that 'Neo-Georgianism and genuine Democracy are, and always will be, incompatible'. (*WGC*, p. 28.)

16 *Transactions*, p. 25.

17 So William Gaunt explained in a letter to Fiona MacCarthy, 25 March 1977.

A NOTE ON SOURCES

The principal collections of unpublished material relating to Ashbee's life and work are sketched in here; the full range of sources is given only in the notes to the text.

BIOGRAPHICAL

The principal source of biographical information about C. R. Ashbee is the Ashbee Journals, a collection of manuscript journal entries, letters and other materials covering the years 1884 to 1941, and running to more than fifty volumes. The Journals belong to King's College, Cambridge, and can be consulted by appointment; enquirers should write to the Modern Archivist, King's College Library, Cambridge. The library also holds other miscellaneous Ashbee papers, and relevant material in other collections, such as the papers of Roger Fry.

In his retirement Ashbee produced a useful digest of the bulky Journals in the form of six typescript volumes, 'The Ashbee Memoirs'. Sets of the 'Memoirs', differing in their condition and pagination, can be seen in King's College Library, Cambridge, the London Library, and the Library of the Victoria and Albert Museum. The Library of Congress in Washington holds four of the typescript volumes and microfilm of the other two from copies in King's College Library.

There are letters and other papers in the possession of Felicity Ashbee.

THE GUILD OF HANDICRAFT

The Library of the Victoria and Albert Museum holds an album of letters and printed ephemera from the years 1887–91 (indexed as 'Letters from William Morris' and others); the Minute Books of the Guild of Handicraft 1888–1919; the Minute Book of the School of Handicraft, and of the Campden School of Arts and Crafts 1888–1907; and a photocopy of Alec Miller's typescript, 'C. R. Ashbee and the Guild of Handicraft' (c. 1941). The Board of Trade's file on the Guild as a limited company is in the Public Records Office, BT31. 8064/58132.

ARCHITECTURE

There are three principal collections of Ashbee's architectural drawings: in the Drawings Collection of the Royal Institute of British Architects (mainly for buildings on Cheyne Walk, London SW3); in Chelsea Public Library (also mainly for buildings on Cheyne Walk); and in the possession of the Campden Trust (for buildings in and around Chipping Campden). The Campden Trust drawings are in the care of Gordon Russell Limited, Broadway, Worcestershire. Few other papers from Ashbee's architectural office seem to have survived. The four albums of photographs in the Library of the Victoria and Albert Museum, known as the Ashbee Collection, contain many photographs of Ashbee's buildings.

DESIGN

There are original designs by Ashbee for furniture, metalwork, jewellery etcetera in the Library of the Victoria and Albert Museum (Guild Workshop Record Book), in the Prints and Drawings

Department of the Victoria and Albert Museum, and in Chelsea Public Library; but the majority of Ashbee's drawings seem to have been lost or destroyed. The various catalogues issued by the Guild of Handicraft, and the photographs of design work in the Ashbee Collection, all of which can be seen in the Library of the Victoria and Albert Museum, provide a useful visual survey of Ashbee's work as a designer. There is a good collection of prospectuses for the work of the Essex House Press, and other ephemera, in the John Johnson Collection of Printed Ephemera in the Bodleian Library, Oxford.

UNIVERSITY EXTENSION

There are letters, lecturer's reports and syllabuses relating to Ashbee's work in the archives of the Department of External Studies, Oxford University.

THE SURVEY OF LONDON

Minutes and correspondence from the early years of the Survey are in the Greater London Record Office; drawings and photographs are in the National Monuments Record and the Greater London Photograph Library.

JERUSALEM

There is a collection of papers, drawings and photographs relating to Ashbee's work in Jerusalem in the possession of Felicity Ashbee.

APPENDICES

APPENDIX ONE
A LIST OF C. R. ASHBEE'S
ARCHITECTURAL WORKS

This list includes all Ashbee's architectural works known to me, executed and unexecuted.

The entries are arranged as far as possible in order of the date of their design. When Ashbee designed for a particular site on more than one occasion, all the designs for that site are listed at the date of the earliest; except that, when one of the later designs was executed, the date of that design is preferred.

Works which I have not been able to date precisely will be found at the end of the list, numbers 75 to 91; the order in which they have been arranged reflects very conjectural dating.

The buildings are referred to by their original names where there was one, and any modern name is given later in brackets. In the case of executed designs the rest of the address, house-numbers, street- and road-names, and the names of counties, have been adapted to modern usage. Postal rather than administrative addresses have been used.

In the case of executed work, the dates should be taken to cover the period of design and execution.

The materials listed are those of the external walls; materials are not listed in the case of repair or restoration work.

'Drawings' refers to the whereabouts of original drawings, not of illustrations.

1   Oxford University Extension College
Model design for a centre for University Extension teaching
Date: *c.* 1892
Source: *A,* 1893, vol. 49, p. 83
Not built.

2   The Ancient Magpie and Stump,
37 Cheyne Walk, London SW3
New house, with offices and studio; garden studio adapted from an existing building
Date: 1893–4; alterations 1898
Client: Mrs H. S. Ashbee
Contractors: G. F. Wright, 25 Wood Street, Westminster; decorative work in the interior by the Guild of Handicraft, Roger Fry, Christopher Whall, J. Wenlock Rollins, Agnes Ashbee and Walter Taylor
Materials: brick and stone

Drawings: V&A Prints and Drawings
Sources: DSR 28 July 1893 and 25 April 1898
    Sources listed in Chapter 11, note 53, including Ashbee Collection, vol. 1, pp. 2–10; vol. 2, pp. 34, 36–50, 54
    Neubauten in London (Berlin 1900), plates 7 and 9
    B, 1904, vol. 86, p. 315.
Demolished 1968. Some fittings are now in the V&A.

3   Carlyle's House, 24 Cheyne Row,
London SW3
Repairs and restoration
Date: 1895
Client: Carlyle's House Purchase Fund Committee
Contractor: D. G. West, King's Road, London SW3
Drawings: RIBA Drawings Collection
Sources: Ashbee Collection, vol. 1, p. 11 *Cottages,*
    pp. 57–61

4   The Wodehouse, Wombourne, Wolverhampton, West Midlands
Addition of chapel and billiard room, alterations to gables and chimneys, and restoration of part of the interior
Date: 1895–7
Client: Thomas Bradney Shaw-Hellier
Materials: brick, stone, half-timber and roughcast
Drawings: RIBA Drawings Collection; The Wodehouse, Wombourne
Sources: Ashbee Collection, vol 1, pp. 12–19, vol. 2, pp. 185–99
  AR, 1898, vol 4, Royal Academy Supplement: Third Series
Further alterations to the house were made in 1912 by J. and H. E. Lavender of Wolverhampton. Both Ashbee's chapel and his billiard room have been altered internally.

5   House for James Guthrie, Cheyne Walk, London SW3
New studio-house
Date: probably 1896
Client: it is not clear whether the house was designed at Guthrie's suggestion, or on Ashbee's initiative.
Drawings: RIBA Drawings Collection; CPL
Sources: letter from Guthrie to Ashbee of 4 Nov 1896, FA
Not built.

6   72–3 Cheyne Walk, London SW3
Flat and separate sculptor's studio at 72; new studio-house at 73
Date: 1896–7
Clients: John Wenlock Rollins for 72; E. A. Walton for 73
Contractor: C. R. Ashbee
Materials: brick, stone and roughcast
Drawings: RIBA Drawings Collection; CPL
Sources: DSR 4 Dec 1896
  Ashbee Collection, vol. 1, pp. 21–5; vol. 2, pp. 61–9, vol. 3
  Neubauten in London (Berlin 1900), plates 10 and 12
Destroyed by bombs, 17 April 1941.

7   Danvers Tower, on the western corner of Cheyne Walk and Danvers Street, London SW3
Block of studio-flats
Date: 1896–8
Clients: Edwin Abbey, John Tweed and Ernest Oppler were thought of as potential clients at an early stage.
Drawings: RIBA Drawings Collection; CPL
Sources: London County Council: Corporate Property, Charities and Endowment Committee, Presented Papers 1 March, 5 April, 17 May and 20 Dec 1897, 17 Jan and 28 March 1898, and Minutes of Proceedings 20 July 1897, 5 April 1898.
  Rough estimate of costs, RIBA Library
  Letter from Ashbee to Janet Forbes, March 1898, FA
Not built.

8   118–19 Cheyne Walk, London SW3
Repairs and alterations; addition of studio in garden
Date: 1897–8
Clients: Maxwell Balfour and Lionel Curtis
Contractor: C. R. Ashbee
Materials: brick
Drawings: RIBA Drawings Collection; CPL
Sources: DSR 11 March 1898
  BN, 1901, vol. 81, p. 835
  Cottages, pp. 61–6
These houses were bombed during the Second World War; they have been rebuilt, and added to.

9   74 Cheyne Walk, London SW3
New studio-house
Date: 1897–8
Client: F. A. Forbes
Contractor: C. R. Ashbee
Materials: brick, stone and roughcast
Drawings: RIBA Drawings Collection; CPL
Sources: DSR 24 Dec 1897
  Letter from Ashbee to Janet Forbes, 7 Oct 1897, FA
  Ashbee Collection, vol. 1, pp. 50–63; vol. 2, pp. 151–63; vol. 3
  BN, 1902, vol. 82, p. 846
  Moderne Bauformen (Stuttgart), 1903, vol. 2, plate 75
Destroyed by bombs, 17 April 1941.

10   Hutton drinking fountain, Ashby, Wigginton and Comberford Roads, Tamworth, Staffordshire
Drinking fountain and horse trough
Date: 1898
Client: Mrs Hutton
Materials: blue Pennant sandstone, red Peterhead granite, wrought iron, gilt copper and hammered aluminium
Sources: Mitchell Scrapbooks, Tamworth Public Library
  Ashbee Collection, vol. 1, p. 313; vol. 2, p. 221
  House Beautiful (Chicago), 1910, vol. 27, p. 102
Demolished *c.* 1965.

11   38 and 39 Cheyne Walk, London SW3
38 a new studio-house with separate studio in the garden; 39 a new house
Date: 1898–9
Clients: Miss C. L. Christian at 38; probably C. R. Ashbee at 39
Contractor: C. R. Ashbee
Materials: Bath stone, Bracknell brick, roughcast
Drawings: RIBA Drawings Collection; CPL
Sources: DSR 24 Sept 1898
  Ashbee Collection, vol. 1, pp. 38–45; vol. 2, pp. 164–77, 371–8, 380–3
  Neubauten in London (Berlin 1900), plates 8 and 9
  Builders' Journal and Architectural Record, 1901–2, vol. 15, pp. 82–3
  B, 1901, vol. 80, p. 64
The interior of 39 has been very much altered.

468

12 4 Danvers Street, London SW3

Various schemes for alterations and additions to an existing house (1898–9); a new studio (1908); and a new house (1913)

Clients: 1898–9: Miss St John Partridge; 1908: Miss H. G. Liddle

Drawings: RIBA Drawings Collection; CPL

Sources: Ms specification for work in 1908, and undated bill of quantities, RIBA Library

Typescript in Chelsea Miscellany Book 13 (1), CPL

It is unlikely that any of these schemes was carried out. The house was bombed during the Second World War.

**13 Sts Peter and Paul,
Horndon-on-the-Hill, Essex**

Removal of plaster to reveal the roof timbers, and of encumbrances surrounding the timber structure of the tower

Date: 1898–1900

Client: The Reverend S. W. Fischel

Contractors: H. C. Mitchell of Tamworth, Staffordshire; the Guild of Handicraft

Sources: Reports of 7 July 1898 and 31 Jan 1899, Horndon-on-the-Hill parish chest

Ashbee Collection, vol. 1, pp. 315–20; vol. 2, pp. 242–55

Craftsmanship, pp. 137, 140, 142

14 St Mary, Stratford-le-Bow, London E3

Repair of walls, of roof to chancel, and of nave; addition of choir vestry, fitting of oak dado to walls and piers

Date: 1899

Client: Restoration Committee

Contractors: H. C. Mitchell of Tamworth, Staffordshire, for masons' work; Guild of Handicraft for carpentry and smiths' work

Sources: Ashbee Collection, vol. 1, p. 395; vol. 2, pp. 228–33

Osborn C. Hills, *Saint Mary, Stratford, Bow* (1900)

It is not clear just what part Ashbee played in this work. The detailed architectural work was in the care of Walter A. Hills and Osborn C. Hills, architects, and Ashbee was officially only a member of the Restoration Committee and of a supervising committee formed by the Society for the Protection of Ancient Buildings; however, he listed the repair of this church among his architectural works when applying for the Slade Professorship at Oxford.

**15 The Shoehorn, 15 Station Road,
Orpington, Kent**

New house

Date: 1900

Client: Henry Fountain

Contractor: B. J. White and Sons, 6 Camden Terrace, Chislehurst, Kent

Materials: brick

Cost: £1,260

Drawings: Drawings submitted to the District

Surveyor, now in the possession of the London Borough of Bromley

Sources: Ashbee Collection, vol. 1, pp. 75–8; vol. 2, pp. 331–9

Cottages, pp. 23–5

A single-storey extension has been added, and the chimney stack has been removed.

16 40–5 Cheyne Walk, London SW3

Six schemes for a group of studios and houses (undated—possibly the earliest scheme); for a block of flats (1900–01); for a block of larger flats with garages (July 1907); for a variant of the July 1907 scheme in two blocks (Nov 1907); for an adaptation of the Nov 1907 scheme to a 'University Hall Extension' (Nov 1907); and finally for a 'Fraternity House' for the University of London (1912)

Drawings: RIBA Drawings Collection; CPL

Sources: *WGC*, pp. 84–5 and plate 76

C. R. Ashbee, 'A Survey of English-Speaking Universities' (Typescript 1912), KCC

Undated estimate of costs, RIBA Library

W. Shaw Sparrow (ed.), *Flats Urban Houses and Cottage Homes* (n.d.) between pp. 16 and 17

Not built.

17 115–16 Cheyne Walk, London SW3

Scheme for workshops for the Guild of Handicraft (*c.* 1900?); undated designs for flats; undated design for a studio-house; final design for 'World's End House' a studio-house, dated 1914

Drawings: RIBA Drawings Collection; CPL

Sources: Prospectus at CPL

None of these schemes was built.

**18 Hallingbury Place,
Bishop's Stortford, Hertfordshire**

Addition of a billiard room, incorporating panelling and a mantelpiece from Coopersale in Essex

Date: 1901

Client: George Bramston Archer-Houblon

Contractor: Guild of Handicraft for carpenters' work, metalwork and decoration

Materials: brick

Source: Ashbee Collection, vol. 1, pp. 28–35; vol. 2, pp. 130–4, 136–9; vol. 3

Drawing of Coopersale inscribed by Ashbee at the National Monuments Record

'Memoirs', vol. 7, pp. 288–9

Builders' Journal and Architectural Record, 1901–2, vol. 15, p. 113

Part of Ashbee's work was obscured after a few years behind a ceiling designed by C. Harrison Townsend. All of Hallingbury Place was demolished in 1922.

19 75 Cheyne Walk, London SW3

New house

Date: 1901–2

Client: Mrs William Hunt

Contractor: General Builders Ltd., Notting Hill; carpenters' work by the Guild of Handicraft

Materials: brick, stone and roughcast
Drawings: RIBA Drawings Collection; CPL
Sources: DSR 4 April 1902
  Ashbee Collection, vol. 1, pp. 341–3, 345, vol. 3
  Moderne Bauformen (Stuttgart), 1903, vol. 2, plate 43
Destroyed by bombs, 17 April 1941.

20 Izod's Cottage, High Street, Chipping Campden, Gloucestershire (now Shreelaine)

New house
Date: 1902
Client: W. N. Izod
Contractor: C. R. Ashbee
Materials: stone and brick; some materials from a
  demolished house on the site were used.
Cost: £270
Drawings: CT
Sources: Ashbee Collection, vol. 1, pp. 90–3, vol. 3
  Cottages, pp. 7–11
  Craftsmanship, pp. 50–1, 54–5

21 1–4 Lion Cottages, Broad Campden, Gloucestershire (now Studio Cottage and Adelaide Cottage)

Repair and reconstruction of four cottages as two
dwellings
Date: 1902
Client: C. R. Ashbee
Cost: £158
Drawings: CT
Sources: *Cottages*, pp. 43–4
  Lawrence Weaver, *The 'Country Life' Book of Cotta-
  ges* (2nd ed. 1919), p. 207

22 The Mill, Chipping Campden, Gloucestershire

Addition of woodshed and engine house (1902); proposed pottery kilns (1909)
Client: The Guild of Handicraft
Drawings: CT
Sources: The Guild of Handicraft Ltd. Annual Report
  for 1902, V&A Library
The kilns, which were part of a scheme for carrying
on William De Morgan's work at Campden, were not
built.

23 Studio-house in Calf's Lane, Chipping Campden, Gloucestershire (now The Long House)

Adapted from an existing building
Date: 1902
Client: George Loosely
Drawings: CT
Sources: Ashbee Collection, vol. 1, pp. 97–9

24 Coombe End Farmhouse, Whitchurch, Reading, Berkshire

Addition of a wing at the north-east corner of the
house
Date: 1902

Client: Rickman J. Godlee
Materials: brick, flint and oak
Sources: Ashbee Collection, vol. 1, pp. 101–7, vol. 3
  Cottages, pp. 54–7

25 Labourers' cottages

Scheme for a block of five or six cottages
Date: 1902
Drawings: CT
The block was presumably intended for a site in or
near Chipping Campden; if so, it seems that it was
not built.

26 Cottage in Sheep Street, Chipping Campden, Gloucestershire (now High House)

New house
Date: 1902–3
Client: Lord Gainsborough
Contractor: C. R. Ashbee
Materials: Campden Hill stone
Cost: about £170
Drawings: CT
Sources: *Cottages*, pp. 10–12, 14

27 Porthgwidden, near Feock, Cornwall

Scheme for rebuilding; laying-out of a rose garden
Date: 1902–3
Client: William Hugh Spottiswoode
Sources: A&CES: 1903: 434
  Ashbee Collection, vol. 1, pp. 363, 365
  J, 14 Nov 1902 and 12 Jan 1913
It is not clear how extensive Ashbee's scheme was;
nor is it clear whether anything was built apart from
a verandah.

28 Houses at Catbrook, Chipping Campden, Gloucestershire (now Maryvale and Catbrook Furlong)

A pair of new semi-detached houses
Date: 1902–3
Client: J. Bell Gripper
Contractor: C. R. Ashbee
Materials: brick, stone and roughcast
Cost: £915
Drawings: CT
Sources: *Cottages*, pp. 14–17

29 Woolstaplers' Hall, High Street, Chipping Campden, Gloucestershire

Removal of internal partitions, and an outhouse
(1902–3); scheme for restoration of the west wing of
the building, additions to the east wing, and a new
entrance to the east wing (1907–9)
Client: C. R. Ashbee
Drawings: CT
Sources: *Cottages*, pp. 66–70
  British Architect, 1910, vol. 74, p. 309
  Ashbee Collection, vol. 1, pp. 231–42
Of the 1907–9 scheme, only the new entrance to the
east wing and some other minor changes were carried

out. For the present condition of the interior of Wool-staplers' Hall, see Chapter 5, note 10.

30 Little Coppice, Pinewood Road, Iver, Buckinghamshire

New house
Date: 1903; extension at the back, 1905
Client: Mr H. Wrightson
Contractor: W. Hartley of Wexham, Buckinghamshire
Materials: brick and roughcast
Cost: £875
Drawings: Drawings submitted to the District Surveyor, now in the possession of South Bucks District Council
Sources: Ashbee Collection, vol. 1, pp. 81–9; vol. 3
    Cottages, pp. 19–23

31 Dinah's Cottage, Park Road, Chipping Campden, Gloucestershire (now Brooklyn)

Reconstruction of two cottages as one dwelling
Date: 1903
Client: Rob Martin Holland
Drawings: CT
Sources: Ashbee Collection, vol. 1, pp. 113–17
    Cottages, pp.44–7

32 Market Hall, Chipping Campden, Gloucestershire

Repairs, particularly to the pier at the south-east corner
Date: 1903
Client: Lord Gainsborough
Sources: Ashbee Collection, vol. 1, pp. 109–11
    C. R. Ashbee, 'Chipping Campden and its Craftsmanship: I: The Village' *Christian Art* (Boston, Mass.), 1908, vol. 4, pp. 81–2
    Application papers for Fellowship of the RIBA, RIBA Library

33 Elm Tree House, High Street, Chipping Campden, Gloucestershire

Various unexecuted schemes for repairing Elm Tree House as a dwelling (1902–3); executed plans for the adaptation of Elm Tree House and the malthouse at the back as premises for the Campden School of Arts and Crafts (1904); moving a small slated cottage to stand next to the malthouse (1907–8)
Client: The Campden School of Arts and Crafts
Drawings: CT
Sources: Ashbee Collection, vol. 1, pp. 134–5, 149, 151, vol. 3
    Cottages, pp. 126–8
    WGC, pp. 86–7 and plates 78–85
The malthouse has been demolished.

34 Cottage in Westington, Chipping Campden, Gloucestershire (now Woodroffe House)

Repairs and alterations; addition of gabled wing to east front; conversion of stable in garden to studio
Date: 1904
Client: Paul Woodroffe
Contractor: Espley and Co. Ltd., 77 High Street, Evesham, Worcestershire
Material: stone
Drawings: CT
Sources: Ashbee Collection, vol. 1, pp. 216–19
    Cottages, pp. 50–1
Alterations have been made in the kitchen wing to the south.

35 St Stephen's, Springfield, Wolverhampton, West Midlands

Scheme for a new church, clergy house and parish hall
Date: 1904–5
Client: Laurence Hodson
Drawings: The Art Workers' Guild
Sources: J, 3 Dec 1902, 3 Feb 1903, Sept 1904, 12 April 1905, 9 March 1924
    BN, 1905, vol. 89, p. 471
Not built.

36 The Cedars, Westington, Chipping Campden, Gloucestershire (now Abbotsbury)

Demolition of one wing, addition of gable, bay window etc.
Date: 1904–5
Client: St John Hankin
Materials: stone and timber
Drawings: CT
Sources: Ashbee Collection, vol. 1, pp. 219–21, 223
    Cottages, pp. 52–4

37 House at Catbrook, Chipping Campden, Gloucestershire

New studio-house
Date: 1905
Client: G. F. Nicholls
Drawings: CT
Not built.

38 House at Catbrook, Chipping Campden, Gloucestershire

New house
Date: 1905
Clients: Canon and Mrs Glazebrook
Drawings: CT
Not built.

39 Cottages at Letchworth, Hertfordshire

A pair of semi-detached timber cottages, apparently built as part of the Cheap Cottages Exhibition at Letchworth
Date: 1905
Materials: timber
Cost: £300
Sources: *Cottages*, pp. 31–40
    BN, 1905, vol. 89, pp. 106 and 131

The reference in *BN* suggests that these cottages were built; but they no longer exist and there appears to be no evidence of their whereabouts.

40 House in Denham Road, Iver, Buckinghamshire (now High Larch)
New house
Date: 1905
Client: Alan Thompson
Contractor: W. Hartley, of Wexham, Buckinghamshire
Materials: brick and roughcast
Cost: £850
Drawings: Drawings submitted to the District Surveyor, now in the possession of South Bucks District Council
Sources: Ashbee Collection, vol. 1, p. 125
 Cottages, pp. 31–4
 S, 1906, vol. 36, pp. 50, 52
The house has been much added to.

41 Five Bells, Pinewood Road, Iver, Buckinghamshire
Pair of new semi-detached houses
Date: 1905
Client: Alan Thompson
Contractor: W. Hartley, of Wexham, Buckinghamshire
Materials: brick and roughcast
Drawings: Drawings submitted to the District Surveyor, now in the possession of South Bucks District Council
Sources: Ashbee Collection, vol. 1, pp. 129, 131
These houses appear to have been demolished.

42 Uplands Cottage, Wellington Heath, Ledbury, Herefordshire
Addition of a substantial wing to an existing house
Date: 1905
Client: Mrs Curtis
Materials: stone and roughcast
Sources: J July 1914
 Ashbee Collection, vol. 1, pp. 268–75
 Walter Shaw Sparrow (ed.), *Flats Urban Houses and Cottage Homes* (n.d.), facing p. 148
 Walter Shaw Sparrow, *Our Homes and How to Make the Best of Them* (1909), facing p. 48

43 Cottages at Catbrook, Chipping Campden, Gloucestershire (now Clapgat, Greenstead, The Haven and Paynsley)
A block of four new cottages
Date: 1903 (early schemes); 1905–6 (executed scheme)
Client: C. R. Ashbee
Contractor: C. R. Ashbee
Materials: brick, roughcast and stone
Cost: *c.* £900
Drawings: CT
Sources: Ashbee Collection, vol. 1, pp. 224–7
 Cottages, pp. 27–8

The thatch which crowned these cottages has recently been removed.

44 The Island House, High Street, Chipping Campden, Gloucestershire
Repairs and internal alterations
Date: 1905–6
Client: E. Peter Jones
Drawings: CT
Sources: Ashbee Collection, vol. 1, pp. 202–5
 Cottages, pp. 76–9
Alterations to Ashbee's work have been carried out recently.

45 The Norman Chapel, Broad Campden, Gloucestershire
Adaptation of a ruined Norman chapel and mediaeval priest's house to a dwelling; addition of a service wing; laying out of the garden
Date: 1905–7
Client: Ananda Coomaraswamy
Contractor: Guild of Handicraft for carpenters' work
Materials: stone, brick and roughcast
Drawings: CT
Sources: J, 24 Nov 1905
 Ashbee Collection, vol. 1, pp. 171–201
 B, 1907, vol. 93, pp. 223–4
 C. R. Ashbee, 'The "Norman Chapel" Buildings at Broad Campden, in Gloucestershire' *S*, 1907, vol. 41, pp. 289–96
 B, 1909, vol. 96, p. 441
Ashbee's service wing has been altered on the south side, and the building has been extended to the west.

46 House in Népstadion útca, Budapest, Hungary (Népstadion útca was formerly Stefania útca)
New house
Date: 1905–7
Client: Zsombor de Szász
Materials: brick and roughcast
Sources: J, 3 July 1905 and 28 Jan 1907
 Ashbee Collection, vol. 1, pp. 355, 357
 B, 1910, vol. 98, p. 326
 Builders' Journal and Architectural Engineer, 1906 vol. 24, pp. 56–7
 Magyar Iparmüvészet (Budapest), 1910, vol. 13, plates 66–8, 85
The house has been demolished.

47 The Poor House, Holcombe Rogus, Wellington, Somerset
Replacing timbers and repairs to screen and upper floor; new staircase
Date: 1906
Contractor: Guild of Handicraft
Sources: Ashbee Collection, vol. 1, pp. 206–15
 Cottages, pp. 71–2
 BN, 1906, vol. 91, p. 13
 Craftsmanship, p. 140

48 13, 15 and 17 Enfield Road,
1–55 (odd) Dudley Road, and
50, 52, and 54 Heathfield Road,
Ellesmere Port, Cheshire
New terraced and semi-detached houses
Date: 1906
Client: E. Peter Jones
Materials: brick and roughcast
Sources: Ashbee Collection, vol. 1, pp. 258–65
    Cottages, pp. 111–13
    B, 1910, vol. 98, p. 464
B, refers to fifty-six houses, but only thirty-four corresponding to Ashbee's designs can be identified today.

49 **Shops and cottages at Iver,
Buckinghamshire**
Scheme for a block of four cottages, village store and butcher's shop
Date: *c*. 1906
Client: Alan Thompson
Sources: *Cottages*, pp. 30–1
    S, 1906, vol. 36, pp. 49–50
It is not clear whether this scheme was built.

50 **St Nicholas, Saintbury, Gloucestershire**
Reroofing of chancel
Date: 1906–7
Contractor: Guild of Handicraft
Sources: J, 28 Jan 1907
    Ashbee Collection, vol. 4, pp. 46–51
    Craftsmanship, pp. 139, 142
A photograph of the church in the Ashbee Collection is annotated 'Tower restoration'; but it is not clear what work, if any, Ashbee may have done on the tower.

51 **Byways, Yarnton, Oxfordshire**
New house
Date: 1907
Client: H. A. Evans
Materials: brick, stone and roughcast
Sources: Ashbee Collection, vol. 4, pp. 81–7
    AR, 1914, vol. 36, p. 50 and plate IV

52 **Houses on the corner of Old Church Street
and Cheyne Walk, London SW3**
Schemes for a group, or groups, of houses and flats at 64–71 Cheyne Walk and the first properties on the west side of Old Church Street
Dates: 1907; *c*. 1912
Drawings: RIBA Drawings Collection; CPL
Not built.

53 **Villa San Giorgio, Taormina, Sicily**
New house
Date: 1907–9
Client: Thomas Bradney Shaw-Hellier
Contractor: decorative carving by Alec Miller and Will Hart
Materials: Basaltic and other stone, roughcast

Drawings: RIBA Drawings Collection; The Wodehouse, Wombourne, West Midlands
Sources: J, Jan 1907, 25 May 1908, 31 March 1909
    Ashbee Collection, vol. 4, pp. 2–38
    AR, 1911, vol. 29, pp. 84–7

54 **Farm buildings, whereabouts unknown**
Date: 1909
Client Miss Gardiner
Drawings: CT
It is not known whether this scheme was executed.

55 **23–37 (odd) Squirrels Heath Avenue,
Gidea Park, Romford, Essex**
A group of new detached and semi-detached houses
Date: 1910–11
Contractor: R. Emmott
Materials: brick
Source: Gidea Park Exhibition Committee, *The Book of the Exhibition of Houses and Cottages* (1911), pp. 141–2
These houses were designed in association with Gripper and Stevenson, architects. The scheme envisaged houses on both sides of Squirrels Heath Avenue, but they were built on one side only.

56 **Buildings for Morley College,
Webber Street and Waterloo Road,
London SE1**
New buildings, including lecture room gymnasium, classrooms, etc.
Date: 1911
Drawings: RIBA Drawings Collection
Sources: *WGC*, pp. 85–6 and plate 77
Not built.

57 **The Anchorage, St Mawes,
Truro, Cornwall**
Additions to a house (?)
Date: 1912–13
Client: Mrs Dudley Ryder
Materials: stone
Sources: J, 19 July and 23 Oct 1912, 11, 14 and 22 Jan 1913

58 **71 Cheyne Walk, London SW3**
Various schemes for adding to, adapting or replacing the existing buildings, between 1907 and 1910 (see Chapter 10 above, pp. 251–2); executed design for a studio-house (1912–13)
Client: Daisy D. Ladenburg
Contractors: G. Munday and Sons, 9 Botolph Lane, Eastcheap, London EC3; J. W. Pyment and Sons, and Thornton and Downer, both of Chipping Campden
Materials: red Old English and silver-grey facing brick
Drawings: RIBA Drawings Collection; CPL
Sources: DSR 27 Sept 1912
    Ashbee Collection, vol. 4, pp. 163–75
    AR 1922, vol. 51, p. 245
Destroyed by bombs 17 April 1941.

59 Kirklands, Hillyfields, Sidcot, Avon (now Penhaven)
New house
Date: 1913
Client: Mr S. Maltby
Materials: brick
Sources: J, April 1913

60 St Peter, Seal, Kent
Repairs to tower (1913); repairs to east window (1939)
Sources: Ashbee Collection, vol. 4, pp. 185, 198–201

61 Studios in Oakley Street and Glebe Place, London SW3
A group of thirteen studios
Date: 1913?
Drawings: CPL
Not built.

62 Barn, Broad Campden, Gloucestershire
Date: 1914
Drawings: CT
Probably not executed.

63 Cottages, Broad Campden, Gloucestershire
Various blocks of new cottages on the Guild of Handicraft estate at Broad Campden
Date: 1914–15
Drawings: CT
Sources: J, 12 Nov 1914
Not executed. The drawings may relate to attempts to provide housing for Belgian refugees.

64 27 Riley Street, London SW3
Adaptation of existing building as a studio-house
Date: 1915
Drawings: CPL
Not built.

65 Sûq el Qattanin, Jerusalem, Israel
Repairs
Date: 1919
Client: The Pro-Jerusalem Society
Sources: FA Jerusalem, Box 2, Folder 9
 Jerusalem 1918–1920, pp. 6–7

66 The Rampart Walk, Jerusalem, Israel
Repairs
Date: 1919–22
Client: The Pro-Jerusalem Society
Drawings: FA Jerusalem, Box 1, Folder 2
Sources: *Jerusalem 1918–1920*, pp. 2, 4, 21–2
 Jerusalem 1920–1922, pp. 12–13

67 The Citadel, Jerusalem, Israel
Repairs; laying out of the Citadel gardens
Date: 1919–22
Client: The Pro-Jerusalem Society
Drawings: FA Jerusalem, Box 1, Folders 3 and 5, Box 2, Folder 1
Sources: *Jerusalem 1918–1920*, pp. 1, 2, 19, 21
 Jerusalem 1920–1922, pp. 5–12

68 YMCA Building, Jaffa Road, Jerusalem, Israel
Date: 1920
Client: Dr Harte
Drawings: FA Jerusalem, Box 5, Folder 5
Not built.

69 Bible House, Jerusalem, Israel
Date: *c.* 1920
Client: The British and Foreign Bible Society
Drawings: FA Jerusalem, Box 6, Folder 1
Not built.

70 Post Office, Post Office Square, Jerusalem, Israel
Addition of gabled wing
Date: *c.* 1920
Drawings: FA Jerusalem, Box 5, Folder 6
Probably not built.

71 Hotel, Ard es Sillam, Jerusalem, Israel
Date: 1922
Client: Thomas Cook and Son
Drawings: FA Jerusalem, Box 5, Folder 2
Not built.

72 House at Godden Green, Sevenoaks, Kent (now Stormont Court)
Removal of attic storey and other alterations
Date: 1924–5
Client: C. R. Ashbee
Contractor: carving to porch by Alec Miller
Sources: Ashbee Collection, vol. 4, n.p.

73 Sts Peter and Paul, Shoreham, Kent
Repair of porch
Date: 1925
Source: Ashbee Collection, vol. 4, n.p.

74 The Hatch, Godden Green, Sevenoaks, Kent
Alterations
Date: 1932
Client: Lady Campbell
Sources: Ashbee Collection, vol. 4, n.p.

Works of uncertain date:

75 Houses in Christ Church Street, Queen's Road and Smith Street, London SW3 (Queen's Road is now Royal Hospital Road)
Scheme for fourteen houses in Christ Church Street, three or more in Queen's Road and twelve in Smith Street
Drawings: CPL
The drawing is not dated, but seems to be inscribed by Ernest Godman; this would give a date before 1906.
Not built.

76 Farm House, Broad Campden, Gloucestershire

Repairs, alterations and enlargement of an existing building

Drawings: CT

There are survey drawings of July 1902, and notes to the effect that the house was destroyed in 1904 and the stones numbered and stored by Ashbee. His proposals were not executed.

77 Roberts House, High Street, Chipping Campden, Gloucestershire

Repairs and alterations

Drawings: CT

Not executed.

78 Grammar School, High Street, Chipping Campden, Gloucestershire

Adaptation of seventeenth-century portion of the building to a dwelling

Drawings: CT

Not executed.

79 Cottage in Park Road, Chipping Campden, Gloucestershire

Repair and reconstruction

Clients: Mrs Gilchrist Thompson and Mrs H. W. Wrightson

Sources: Ashbee Collection, vol. 1, pp. 119, 121
    Cottages, pp. 48–50

The cottage was thatched when Ashbee worked on it, but is so no longer.

80 Cottage at Abbots Langley, Hertfordshire

New house

Client: Trinity College, Oxford

Materials: brick and roughcast

Cost: £230

Sources: Ashbee Collection, vol. 1, pp. 370–1
    Cottages, pp. 16–19

Exact whereabouts unknown.

81 House in The Square, Findon, West Sussex

New house, designed as a 'nursing cottage'

Client: Mrs William Hunt

Materials: brick, flint and roughcast

Cost: £400

Sources: Ashbee Collection, vol. 2, pp. 350, 352
    Cottages, pp. 23 and 26–7

82 4 Little Davis Place, London SW3 (Little Davis Place is now Apollo Place)

Alterations to an existing building (?)

Client: Mr Bird

Drawings: CPL

The drawings are not dated but are inscribed by George Chettle and must therefore date from 1904 or later. Probably not built.

83 Houses on the eastern corner of Cheyne Walk and Danvers Street, London SW3

A new house at 77 Cheyne Walk, and further building at 2, and possibly 4 Danvers Street

Drawings: CPL

The drawings are not dated but the plans are in George Chettle's hand and must therefore date from 1904 or later. Not built.

84 Houses on the western corner of Oakley Street and Cheyne Walk, London SW3

A group consisting of two houses at 35 and 36 Cheyne Walk, and further buildings in Oakley Street

Drawings: CPL

The drawings are not dated but are inscribed in George Chettle's hand and must therefore date from 1904 or later. Not built.

85 Gates at Poyston Hall, Haverfordwest, Dyfed

Two masonry piers and wrought iron gates with heraldic figures in lead

Client: Dr Henry Owen

Sources: Ashbee Collection, vol. 2, p. 345
    AR, Aug 1907, p. ix

The decorative leadwork has been removed.

86 Manor Gate Cottage, Holmsbury St Mary, Surrey

Repairs (?)

Client: Elsa Ashbee

Sources: J, March 1908 and 30 Oct 1919
    Ashbee Collection, vol. 4, pp. 124–7

Work on this building is attributed to Ashbee because photographs of it are in the Ashbee Collection, but it is not clear what the work was.

87 House at Wroxton, Oxfordshire (now the Wroxton Hotel)

Addition of one wing, and alterations

Material: stone

Sources: Ashbee Collection, vol. 4, pp. 39–41
    House Beautiful (Chicago), 1910, vol. 28, p. 53

88 House at Mackies Hill, Peaslake, Surrey

Repairs and alterations, addition of a studio

Client: Miss Liddle

Materials: brick, and salvaged timber for the studio

Cost: £460

Sources: Ashbee Collection, vol. 4, pp. 92–7
    Lawrence Weaver, *Small Country Houses: Their Repair and Enlargement* (1914), pp. 26–9

89 116 and 117 Cheyne Walk, London SW3

New house

Client: Mrs Hunt

Drawings: CPL

Not built.

90 68–9 Cheyne Walk, London SW3
Various designs for a house, flats and studio flats
Drawings: CPL
The drawings are not dated but show 71 Cheyne Walk (1912–13) as it was built. Not built.

91 Rosemary Hall, Greenwich, Connecticut, USA
Unidentified scheme for building
Source: J, 7 Aug 1924

APPENDIX TWO
PUBLIC COLLECTIONS
CONTAINING WORK
DESIGNED BY C. R. ASHBEE

It is impossible here to list Ashbee's work as a designer item by item; and the following list of public collections is by way of a substitute. It is probably incomplete, and I would be glad to hear of collections mistakenly omitted.

Libraries containing books designed by Ashbee and/or printed under his care are too numerous to list and their holdings duplicate each other; the largest accessible collections of these books in Britain will be found in the copyright libraries and in the United States there is a good collection in the New York Public Library.

AUSTRALIA
The Art Gallery of South Australia, Adelaide

AUSTRIA
Österreichisches Museum für angewandte Kunst

CANADA
Maltwood Memorial Museum of Historic Art, Victoria, British Columbia

CZECHOSLOVAKIA
Moravská Galerie, Brno

GREAT BRITAIN
The Victoria and Albert Museum in London has the finest collection of Ashbee's work. Its collection of metalwork, in particular, is large and contains some outstanding pieces. The jewellery collection is strong; and there are some interesting pieces of furniture; a number of decorative features were rescued from the Magpie and Stump, 37 Cheyne Walk, London SW3, before it was demolished in 1968.

Second only to the collection of the Victoria and Albert Museum is that of Cheltenham Art Gallery and Museum in Gloucestershire, which reflects the museum's interest in the Arts and Crafts Movement in the Cotswolds. The collection has been formed during the past few years, and includes two outstanding pieces of furniture; there is also a good selection of metalwork and jewellery, much of it given by the late Professor and Mrs Hull Grundy; and leatherwork of 1892.

Work by Ashbee can also be seen in the collections of Arlington Mill, Bibury, Gloucestershire; Birmingham Museums and Art Gallery; the Royal Pavilion, Art Gallery and Museums, Brighton; Bristol City Art Gallery; the Fitzwilliam Museum, Cambridge; Glasgow Museums and Art Galleries; the Worshipful Company of Goldsmiths, Goldsmiths' Hall, London; Leicestershire Museums, Leicester; Manchester City Art Gallery; Manchester Polytechnic, John Holden Gallery; Scolton Manor Museum, Haverfordwest, Dyfed; Sheffield City Museums, Weston Park, Sheffield; and at Standen, East Grinstead, West Sussex, a property of the National Trust.

NORWAY
Nordenfjeldske Kunstindustrimuseum, Trondheim

SWITZERLAND
Museum Bellerive, Kunstgewerbemuseum, Zurich

WEST GERMANY
Hessisches Landesmuseum, Darmstadt; Museum für Kunst und Gewerbe, Hamburg; Badisches Landes-museum, Karlsruhe; Wurttemburgisches Landesmuseum, Stuttgart

UNITED STATES
The Art Institute of Chicago, Chicago; Cleveland Museum of Art, Cleveland, Ohio; Delaware Art Museum, Wilmington, Delaware; the Museum of Modern Art, New York

APPENDIX THREE
A LIST OF BOOKS, PAMPHLETS
ETC. PRINTED AT
THE ESSEX HOUSE PRESS

Items are listed as far as possible in order of publication.

Recording the titles of Essex House Press books is not always a straightforward matter. Ashbee followed the irritating practice of Kelmscott and some other private presses in often dispensing with a title-page; and he gave idiosyncratic titles to some of his reprints of well-known books. In some cases, his titles have been altered to those in normal use.

The typefaces listed are those used for the setting of the body of the text; decorative typefaces are not listed.

A handmade paper with a special Essex House Press water-mark was used on most Essex House books, and its use can be assumed where no other paper is mentioned in this list. Where other papers were used they have been recorded, and described either as 'handmade' or 'ordinary'.

1 ————, 'Memorandum and Articles of Association of the Guild of Handicraft (Limited)' (1898). Caslon type. A few copies printed for the shareholders of the Company.

2 Benvenuto Cellini, *The Treatises on Goldsmithing and Sculpture* (1898). Translated by C. R. Ashbee. Caslon type. 600 copies at £1.15s.0d.

3 ————, *The Hymn of Bardaisan: The First Christian Poem* (1899). Translated by F. Crawford Burkitt. Caslon type. 300 copies at 7s.6d.

4 C. R. Ashbee, Walter Crane, Selwyn Image, C. H. Townsend, Christopher Whall and Henry Wilson, *Beauty's Awakening: A Masque of Winter and of Spring* (1899). The text of the Art Workers' Guild Masque, performed in June 1899. Caslon type. 25 copies on Essex House Press paper. A larger edition was printed by the *Studio*, presumably from plates, and issued as their Summer Number, with illustrations added.

5 John Bunyan, *The Pilgrim's Progress* (1899). Frontispiece by Reginald Savage. Caslon type. 750 copies at £1.10s.0d.

6 Percy Bysshe Shelley, *Adonais* (1900). Frontispiece by C. R. Ashbee. Caslon type. Printed on vellum. 50 copies at £1.10s.0d. The first of the 'Great Poems of the Language' series.

7 Osborn C. Hills, *Saint Mary Stratford Bow* (1900). Caslon type. Ordinary paper. 250 copies at 12s.6d.

8 William Shakespeare, *The Poems* (1900). Edited by F. S. Ellis. Frontispiece by Reginald Savage. Caslon type. 450 copies at £2.

9 John Keats, *The Eve of St Agnes* (1900). Frontispiece by Reginald Savage. Caslon type. Printed on vellum. 125 copies at £2.2s.0d. The second of the 'Great Poems of the Language' series.

10 Baldassare Castiglione, *The Courtyer* (1900). The 1561 translation by Sir Thomas Hoby, edited by Janet Ashbee. Caslon type. 200 copies at £3.3s.0d.

11 Francis William Bourdillon, *Through the Gateway* (1900). Caslon type. 50 copies. Privately printed for the author.

12 George Thompson, *Ruskin and Modern Business* (1900). Caslon type. Number of copies unknown. Privately printed.

13 Thomas Gray, *Elegy written in a Country Church-yard* (1901). Frontispiece by George Thomson. Decorative initials partly by Florence Kingsford. Caslon type. Printed on vellum. 125 copies at £2.2s.0d. The third of the 'Great Poems of the Language' series.

14 Walt Whitman, *Hymn on the Death of Lincoln* (1901). Frontispiece by C. R. Ashbee. Caslon type. Printed on vellum. 125 copies at £2.2s.0d. The fourth of the 'Great Poems of the Language' series.

15 C. R. Ashbee, *Report . . . to the National Trust* (1901). Endeavour type. Some copies on Essex House Press paper, some on ordinary paper. Number of copies unknown.

16 C. R. Ashbee, *An Endeavour towards the teaching of John Ruskin and William Morris* (1901). Frontispiece by George Thomson. Endeavour type. 350 copies at £1. A second impression was printed, apparently from plates, on ordinary paper, and sold at 1s.0d; the number of copies is unknown.

17 John Woolman, *A Journal of the Life and Travels of John Woolman in the Service of the Gospel* (1901). Frontispiece by Reginald Savage. Caslon type. 250 copies at £2.2s.0d.

18 Erasmus, *The Praise of Folie* (1901). The 1549 translation by Sir Thomas Chaloner, edited by Janet Ashbee. Illustrations by William Strang. Caslon type. 250 copies at £3.3s.0d.

19 ——, *A letter from Percy B. Shelley to T. Peacock July MDCCCXVL* (1901). Endeavour type. 50 copies, of which 5 were on vellum. Privately printed for Wilfred Buckley.

20 William Penn, *Some Fruits of Solitude* (1901). Frontispiece by T. Sturge Moore. Caslon type. 250 copies at £2.2s.0d.

21 C. R. Ashbee, *American Sheaves and English Seed Corn* (1901). Endeavour type. 300 copies at £1.10s.0d. A second impression on ordinary paper may have been issued.

22 ——, *The Psalter* (1901). Endeavour type. 250 copies on paper at £4.4s.0d; 10 copies on vellum at £16.16s.0d.

23 ——, *John Hunter leaves St George's Hospital* (1901). Caslon type. Handmade paper. Number of copies unknown. Privately printed.

24 Edmund Spenser, *Epithalamion* (1901). Frontispiece by Reginald Savage. Decorative initials by Florence Kingsford. 150 copies at £2.2s.0d. The fifth of the 'Great Poems of the Language' series.

25 William Strang, *The Doings of Death* (1901). A series of twelve woodcuts issued in portfolio or in book form. 140 copies at £6.6s.0d.

26 C. R. Ashbee, *The Masque of the Edwards of England* (1902). Illustrations by Edith Harwood. Endeavour type. Printed on grey paper except for 20 copies on vellum. The illustrations in the paper copies printed by chromolithography by Sprague and Company, and finished by hand; in the vellum copies the illustrations are coloured entirely by hand. 300 copies on paper at £3.3s.0d; 20 copies on vellum at £12.12s.0d.

27 Ernest Godman, *The Old Palace of Bromley-by-Bow* (1902). Caslon type. 300 copies on ordinary paper at £1.1s.0d.

28 ——, *Three Letters from R. L. Stevenson* (1902). Caslon type. 60 copies, of which 6 were on vellum. Privately printed.

29 Geoffrey Chaucer, *The Flower and the Leaf* (1902). Illustrations and decorative initials by Edith Harwood. Caslon type. Printed on vellum. 165 copies at £3.3s.0d. The sixth of the 'Great Poems of the Language' series.

30 Robert Burns, *Tam O'Shanter* (1902). Frontispiece by William Strang. Decorative initials by Florence Kingsford. Caslon type. Printed on vellum. 150 copies at £2.2s.0d. The seventh of the 'Great Poems of the Language' series.

31 John Milton, *Comus* (1902). Frontispiece by Reginald Savage. Decorative initials by Florence Kingsford. Caslon type. Printed on vellum. 150 copies at £3.3s.0d. The eighth of the 'Great Poems of the Language' series.

32 ——, *The Snow Lay on the Ground* (1902). Illustration by Paul Woodroffe. Endeavour and Prayer Book types. 400 copies of a Christmas carol printed for distribution to the subscribers of the Essex House Press; some for sale at 5s.0d.

33 Christopher Wren, *Life and Works of Sir Christopher Wren* (1903). Edited by E. J. Enthoven. Illustrations by E. H. New and others. Caslon type. 200 copies at £3.13s.6d.

34 Heinrich Heine, *Ausgewaehlte Lieder* (1903). Edited by Edmond Holmes. Frontispiece by Reginald Savage. Endeavour type. 250 copies on Essex House Press paper at £1.1s.0d., and 12 copies on vellum at £2.2s.0d.

35 William Wordsworth, *Ode on Intimations of Immortality* (1903). Frontispiece by Walter Crane. Decorative initials by Annie Power. Caslon type.

Printed on vellum. The ninth of the 'Great Poems of the Language' series.

36 ———, *The Prayer Book of King Edward VII* (1903). Illustrations by C. R. Ashbee. Prayer Book and Endeavour types. 400 copies on Essex House Press paper at £12.12s.0d. and 10 on vellum at £40.0s.0d.

37 C. R. Ashbee, *A Key to the principal decorations in The Prayer Book of King Edward VII* (1903). Endeavour type. 250 copies at 2s.6d.

38 ———, *Supplement to The Prayer Book of King Edward VII showing the American variants* (1903). Illustrations by C. R. Ashbee. Prayer Book and Endeavour types. 100 copies at 10s.6d.

39 Edwin Gunn, *The Great House, Leyton* (1903). Illustrations by Edwin Gunn and others. Caslon type. 350 copies on ordinary paper at £1.1s.0d.

40 Janet Ashbee (ed.), *The Essex House Song Book* (1903–5). Music drawn by Paul Woodroffe. Endeavour type. 200 copies on Essex House Press paper at £6.3s.0d. and 5 on vellum at £30.15s.0d.

41 Thomas Hood, *Miss Kilmansegg and her Precious Leg* (1904). Illustrations by Reginald Savage. Caslon type. 200 copies on Essex House Press paper at £1.5s.0d. and 4 on vellum at £3.3s.0d.

42 Samuel Taylor Coleridge, *The Ancient Mariner* (1904). Frontispiece by William Strang. Decorative initials by Florence Kingsford. Caslon type. Printed on vellum. 150 copies at £2.12s.6d. The tenth of the 'Great Poems of the Language' series.

43 Percy Bysshe Shelley, *Prometheus Unbound* (1904). Frontispiece by C. R. Ashbee. Prayer Book type. 200 copies on Essex House Press paper at £2.2s.0d. and 20 on vellum at £7.7s.0d.

44 F. Allen Whiting, *A successful English experiment* (1904). Illustrations by E. H. New and George Thomson. Caslon type. 50 copies on Essex House Press paper. A second impression, presumably from plates on ordinary paper, was issued at 1s.0d.

45 Gerald Bishop, *A May-Day Interlude* (1904). Illustration by E. H. New. Caslon type. 24 copies on Essex House Press paper; 500 copies on ordinary paper at 2s.6d.

46 C. R. Ashbee, *A Bibliography of the Essex House Press* (1904). Endeavour type. 50 copies on Essex House Press paper at 2s.6d. and 200 copies on ordinary paper at 1s.0d.

47 John Dryden, *Alexander's Feast* (1904). Frontispiece by Reginald Savage. Decorative initials by Florence Kingsford. Caslon type. Printed on vellum.

140 copies at £2.2s.0d. The eleventh in the 'Great Poems of the Language' series.

48 Cicero, *De Amicitia* (1904). With a translation by John Harrington, edited by E. D. Ross. Illustrations by C. R. Ashbee. Endeavour type. 150 copies on Essex House Press paper at £1.15s.0d. and 10 copies on vellum at £6.6s.0d.

49 Lord Redesdale, *An Address at the opening of the Campden School of Arts and Crafts* (1904). Caslon type. 50 copies at £1.1s.0d.

50 Oliver Goldsmith, *The Deserted Village* (1904). Frontispiece by C. R. Ashbee. Decorative initials by Florence Kingsford and Annie Power. Caslon type. Printed on vellum. 150 copies at £2.12s.6d. The twelfth in the 'Great Poems of the Language' series.

51 Thomas à Kempis, *The Imitation of Christ* (1904). Edited by Ernest Godman from translations of 1504 and 1580. Illustrations by C. R. Ashbee. Prayer Book and Endeavour types. 100 copies on Essex House Press paper at £5.5s.0d. and 10 copies on vellum at £15.15s.0d.

52 C. R. Ashbee (ed.), *The Last Records of a Cotswold Community* (1904). Illustrations by E. H. New. Endeavour type. 75 copies on Essex House Press paper at £1.1s.0d. and 150 copies on ordinary paper at 12s.6d.

53 ———, *Report on the Campden School of Arts and Crafts 1903–4* (1904). Caslon type. Printed on ordinary paper. Number of copies unknown.

54 Bernard Sleigh, *Conscience* (1904). A single woodcut. Number of copies unknown.

55 Ernest A. Mann, *Brooke House, Hackney* (1904). Caslon type. Printed on ordinary paper. Number of copies unknown.

56 Alfred Tennyson, *Maud* (1905). Frontispiece by Laurence Housman and Reginald Savage. Decorative initials by Annie Power. Caslon type. Printed on vellum. 125 copies at £3.3s.0d. The thirteenth in the 'Great Poems of the Language' series.

57 Lily Nightingale, *A Cycle of Sonnets* (1905). Caslon type. Printed on handmade paper. 250 copies, price unknown.

58 Ernest Godman, *Mediaeval Architecture in Essex* (1905). Illustrations by Ernest Godman and others. Caslon type. Printed on handmade paper. 250 copies, priced according to the binding.

59 Edward Fitzgerald, *The Rubaiyat of Omar Khayyam* (1905). Illustrations by C. R. Ashbee. Prayer Book and Endeavour types. 88 copies on Essex House

Press paper at £2.2s.0d. and 17 copies on vellum at £4.4s.0d. Printed for the Omar Khayyam Club.

60 Caroline Hazard, *The Illuminators* (1905). Prayer Book type. Number of copies unknown. Privately printed.

61 Lord Redesdale, *The Second Address . . . at the Campden School of Arts and Crafts* (1905). Illustration by E. H. New. Caslon type. 50 copies at £1.1s.0d.

62 Ernest Godman, *Norman Architecture in Essex* (1905). Illustrations by Ernest Godman and others. Caslon type. Printed on handmade paper. 300 copies at 12s.6d.

63 C. R. Ashbee, *Echoes from the City of the Sun* (1905). Decorations by C. R. Ashbee. Endeavour type. 250 copies on Essex House Press paper at 12s.6d. and one on vellum, not for sale.

64 Walter C. Pepys and Ernest Godman, *The Church of St Dunstan, Stepney* (1905). Illustrations by Ernest Godman and others. Caslon type. Printed on ordinary paper. 350 copies, price unknown.

65 ———, *Report on the Campden School of Arts and Crafts 1904–5* (1905). Illustration by E. H. New. Caslon type. Printed on ordinary paper. About 100 copies at 1s.0d.

66 F. A. Hyett, *An Octet of Sonnets* (1905). Caslon type. Privately printed for the author.

67 Robert Browning, *The Flight of the Duchess* (1906). Frontispiece by Paul Woodroffe. Decorative initials by Raymond Binns. Caslon type. Printed on vellum. 125 copies at £2.12s.6d. The fourteenth of the 'Great Poems of the Language' series.

68 John Fisher, *A Mornynge Rembrounce* (1906). Frontispiece by C. R. Ashbee. Prayer Book and Endeavour types. 125 copies on Essex House Press paper at £1.1s.0d. and 7 copies on vellum at £3.3s.0d.

69 Hugh E. Seebohm (trans.), *The Picture of Kebes the Theban* (1906). Caslon type. 50 copies on Essex House Press paper for Hugh Seebohm, and 250 copies on ordinary paper at 5s.6d.

70 Laurence Housman, *Mendicant Rhymes* (1906). Endeavour and Prayer Book types. Printed on handmade paper. 300 copies at 12s.6d.

71 C. R. Ashbee, *Socialism and Politics: A Study in the Re-adjustment of the Values of Life* (1906). Caslon type. Printed on handmade paper. 250 copies at 3s.6d.

72 C. R. Ashbee, *A Book of Cottages and Little Houses* (1906). Illustrations by F. L. Griggs and others. Caslon

type. 50 copies on Essex House Press paper at £1.5s.0d. and 200 copies on ordinary paper at 12s.6d.

73 Archibald Ramage, *An Essay on Dr Johnson* (1906). Frontispiece by Alec Miller. Caslon type. Printed on ordinary paper. 200 copies at 5s.0d.

74 C. R. Ashbee, *On the Need for the Establishment of Country Schools of Arts and Crafts* (1906). Caslon type. Printed on ordinary paper. 200 copies at 5s.0d.

75 ———, *Report on the Campden School of Arts and Crafts 1905–6* (1906). Illustration by E. H. New. Caslon type. Printed on ordinary paper. Number of copies unknown. Price 1s.0d.

76 Lord Redesdale, *A Tale of Old and New Japan* (1906). Caslon type. Printed on ordinary paper. Number of copies unknown. Privately printed for the author.

77 Ananda Coomaraswamy, *The Deeper Meaning of the Struggle* (1907). Caslon type. 75 copies on handmade paper at 1s.0d. and 1,000 copies on ordinary paper at 4d.

78 Ananda Coomaraswamy, *Nētra Maṅgalya* (1908). Caslon type. Printed on ordinary paper. 25 copies for private circulation.

79 Ananda Coomaraswamy, *The Aims of Indian Art* (1908). Caslon type. 225 copies on ordinary paper at 2s.6d.; 50 copies on handmade paper at 5s.0d.; and 2 copies on vellum, not for sale.

80 Ananda Coomaraswamy, *The Influence of Greek on Indian Art* (1908). Caslon type. 75 copies on ordinary paper for private circulation, followed by a second impression of 50 copies.

81 C. R. Ashbee, *Conradin: A Philosophical Ballad* (1908). Illustrations by Philippe Mairet. Prayer Book type. 250 copies on handmade paper at £1.1s.0d. and one copy on vellum.

82 Ananda Coomaraswamy, *The Two Painters* (1908). Caslon type. 30 copies on handmade paper and one on vellum. Not for sale.

83 Ananda Coomaraswamy, *Mediaeval Sinhalese Art* (1908). Caslon type. 400 copies on ordinary paper at £3.3s.0d. and 25 copies on handmade paper at £5.5s.0d.

84 Ananda Coomaraswamy (trans.), *Voluspa* (1909). Caslon type. 100 copies on handmade paper at 2s.6d. and one copy on vellum.

85 W. P. D. Stebbing, *The Church of Worth, in Sussex* (1909). Illustrations by C. Terry Pledge. Caslon type. 88 copies on ordinary paper at 3s.6d. and 25 copies on handmade paper at 5s.0d.

86 Vincent A. Smith (ed.), *The Edicts of Asoka* (1909). Caslon, Prayer Book and Endeavour types. Printed on handmade paper. 100 copies at £1.1s.0d.

87 C. R. Ashbee, *Modern English Silverwork* (1909). Lithograph illustrations by Philippe Mairet. Caslon type. 200 copies, of which some have the text printed on handmade paper, but most on ordinary paper. The ordinary paper copies cost £2.2s.0d. The lithographed plates were probably not printed at the Essex House Press.

88 C. R. Ashbee, *The Private Press: A Study in Idealism* (1909). Various illustrations. Endeavour type. 125 copies on handmade paper and two on vellum. Privately printed for the Club of Odd Volumes, Boston, Massachusetts.

89 C. R. Ashbee, *The Guild of Handicraft: Its Deed of Trust and Rules for the Guidance of its Guildsmen* (1910). Endeavour type. 100 copies on handmade paper at 5s.0d.

90 Ananda Coomaraswamy, *The Oriental View of Woman* (1910). Caslon type. 125 copies on ordinary paper. Price unknown.

91 Ananda Coomaraswamy, *Selected Examples of Indian Art* (1910). Caslon type. 400 copies on ordinary paper at £1.5s.0d. and 25 copies on handmade paper at £3.3s.0d.

92 Ananda Coomaraswamy, *Domestic Handicraft and Culture* (1910). Caslon type. Number of copies and price unknown.

93 Ananda Coomaraswamy, *Indian Drawings* (1910). Illustrations by Ananda Coomaraswamy. Caslon type. Printed on ordinary paper. 400 copies at £1.5s.0d.

94 William Rothenstein, *Two Drawings by Hok'sai* (1910). Caslon type. Printed on ordinary paper. 150 copies at 10s.6d.

APPENDIX FOUR
A LIST OF C. R. ASHBEE'S
PUBLISHED WRITINGS

1 'The Workman as an Artist', *BN*, 1884, vol. 47, pp. 200–1.

2 *The Ideals of the Craftsman* (n.d. [1889]). Pamphlet.

3 *Decorative Art from a Workshop Point of View* (n.d. [c. 1889]). Pamphlet. Also published in *Transactions of the National Association for the Advancement of Art and Its Application to Industry: Edinburgh Meeting 1889* (1890), pp. 451–60; and in a revised form as Chapter 4 of *Chapters*.

4 (ed.), *Transactions of the Guild & School of Handicraft. Vol. I.* (1890). A further large paper edition of 250 copies was issued.

5 *A Short History of the Guild and School of Handicraft* (1890). Pamphlet. An offprint from item 4.

6 *The Technical Movement in its future relation to the skilled artisan, the elementary teacher and all such as are directly interested in handicraft* (n.d. [1891]). Pamphlet.

7 *Some illustrations to a course of lectures on design in its application to furniture* (n.d. [1892]). Pamphlet.

8 (ed.), *The Manual of the Guild and School of Handicraft: being a Guide to County Councils and Technical Teachers* (1892).

9 *From Whitechapel to Camelot* (1892).

10 *A Table of the Arts and Crafts of the Renaissance* (Various editions, 1892–3). Pamphlet.

11 'University Extension and Working Men', *Oxford University Extension Gazette*, 1892–3, vol. 3, pp. 10–11.

12 'How to wear jewellery. As illustrated by the "Trattato della oreficeria" of Cellini', *AJ*, 1893, pp. 247–9.

13 *A Few Chapters in Workshop Re-Construction and Citizenship* (1894). A further large paper edition of 75 copies was issued.

14 'Cinque-Cento Jewelry. As illustrated by the "Trattati" of Benvenuto Cellini', *AJ*, 1894, pp. 152–5.

15 'A little talk on the setting of stones', *AJ*, 1894, pp. 182–4.

16 'A Proposal for the Preservation of the Few Remaining Ancient Buildings of Greater London and Essex', *AJ*, 1894, p. 156.

17 *A Table of the Arts and Crafts of the Seventeenth Century* (1894). Pamphlet.

18 'Suggestions for electric light fittings', *AJ*, 1895, pp. 91–3.

19 *A Nine Years' Experiment in Technical Education: Being the last Report of the School of Handicraft* (1895). Pamphlet.

20 *A Table of the Arts and Crafts of the Eighteenth Century* (1895). Pamphlet.

21 *The Trinity Hospital in Mile End: An Object Lesson in National History* (1896).

22 'Challenge cups, shields and trophies', *AJ*, 1898, pp. 230–2.

23 'On table service', *AJ*, 1898, pp. 336–8.

24 'An experiment in cast iron work', *S*, 1898, vol. 14, pp. 254–6.

25 (trans.), *The Treatises of Benvenuto Cellini on Goldsmithing and Sculpture* (1898).

26 With Walter Crane, Selwyn Image, C. H. Townsend, Christopher Whall and Henry Wilson. *Beauty's Awakening: A Masque of Winter and of Spring* (1899).

27 Foreword to Osborn C. Hills. *Saint Mary Stratford Bow* (1900).

28 (ed.), *The Survey of London: Volume 1: The Parish of Bromley-by-Bow* (1900).

29 *An Endeavour towards the teaching of John Ruskin and William Morris* (1901).

30 *A Report by Mr. C. R. Ashbee to the Council of the National Trust . . . on his visit to the United States . . .* (1901). Pamphlet.

31 'American Architecture', *Munsey's Magazine* (New York), 1901, vol. 26, pp. 1–9.

32 Foreword to Ernest Godman. *The Old Palace of Bromley-by-Bow* (1901).

33 *American Sheaves and English Seed Corn* (London and New York, 1901).

34 *A Description of the Work of the Guild of Handicraft* (1902). Pamphlet.

35 *The Masque of the Edwards of England* (London and New York, 1902).

36 Foreword to Edwin Gunn. *The Great House, Leyton* (1903).

37 'The Guild of Handicraft, Chipping Campden', *AJ*, 1903, pp. 147–52.

38 *A Key to the principal decorations in The Prayer Book of King Edward VII* (1903). Pamphlet.

39 'The Coronation Prayer Book of King Edward VII', *AJ*, 1904, pp. 386–91.

40 Foreword to Ernest A. Mann. *Brooke House, Hackney* (1904).

41 (ed.), *The Last Records of a Cotswold Community* (Chipping Campden, 1904).

42 *A Bibliography of the Essex House Press* (Chipping Campden, 1904).

43 *Echoes from the City of the Sun* (1905).

44 Foreword to Walter C. Pepys and Ernest Godman. *The Church of St. Dunstan, Stepney* (1905).

45 'On the Dromenagh Estate at Iver Heath', *S*, 1906, vol. 36, pp. 47–52.

46 *A Book of Cottages and Little Houses* (1906).

47 *On the Need for the Establishment of Country Schools of Arts and Crafts* (Chipping Campden, 1906). Chapter 8 of item 46 reprinted as a pamphlet.

48 *Socialism and Politics: A Study in the Readjustment of the Values of Life* (1906).

49 'The "Norman Chapel" Buildings at Broad Campden, in Gloucestershire', *S*, 1907, vol. 41, pp. 289–96.

50 'Chipping Campden and its Craftsmanship: I: The Village' and '. . . II: The Work of the Guild of Handicraft', *Christian Art* (Boston, Mass.), 1908, vol. 4, pp. 79–87 and 107–17.

51 *Conradin: A Philosophical Ballad* (Broad Campden, 1908).

52 *Craftsmanship in Competitive Industry* (London and Chipping Campden, 1908).

53 *Modern English Silverwork* (1909).

54 Foreword to Ananda K. Coomaraswamy. *The Indian Craftsman* (1909).

55 'Arts and Crafts in England: A Brief Sketch of the Development of the Movement: I' and '. . . II', *House Beautiful* (Chicago), 1909, vol. 26, pp. 14–16, 34–5, 46.

56 *The Private Press: A Study in Idealism* (Broad Campden, 1909).

57 'Man and the Machine: The Pre-Raphaelites and their influence upon life: I' and '. . . II', *House Beautiful* (Chicago), 1910, vol. 27, pp. 75–7, 101–4, 112.

58 'Man and the Machine: The soul of architecture: I' and '. . . II', *House Beautiful* (Chicago), 1910, vol. 28, pp. 23–5, 53–6.

59 'Man and the Machine: The return of the village: I' and '. . . II', *House Beautiful* (Chicago), 1910, vol. 28, pp. 88–90, 109–111.

60 *The Building of Thelema* (1910).

61 'Chipping Campden and Its Craftsmanship' in Percy H. Ditchfield (ed.), *Memorials of Old Gloucestershire* (1911), pp. 268–72.

62 'Frank Lloyd Wright: Eine Studie Seiner Würdigung' in *Sonderheft der Architektur des XX Jahrhunderts: 8: Frank Lloyd Wright* (Berlin 1911). This publication is usually known by its cover-title, *Frank Lloyd Wright: Ausgeführte Bauten*. Most of Ashbee's original English text is published in Edgar Kaufmann Jr (ed.), *Frank Lloyd Wright: The Early Work* (New York 1968).

63 *Should We Stop Teaching Art* (1911).

64 *Exhibition of University Planning and Building: being a Catalogue Raisonne together with an introductory study on the architectural significance of modern university development* (1912). Pamphlet.

65 *The Hamptonshire Experiment in Education* (1914).

66 'The province of the arts and handicrafts in a mechanical society', *Hibbert Journal*, 1915–16, vol. 14, pp. 95–104.

67 'Quality *versus* quantity as the standard of industry and life', *Hibbert Journal*, 1915–16, vol. 14, pp. 380–92.

68 'Kansas City, Missouri: the influence of a park system', *Town Planning Review* (Liverpool); 1915, vol. 6, pp. 233–7.

69 'The Arts and Crafts Exhibition: II: What the City should do for the Craftsman', *Sociological Review*, 1916–17, vol. 9, pp. 52–4.

70 *The American League to Enforce Peace: An English Interpretation* (1917).

71 'The Future of Craft Museums', *Museums Journal*, 1917, vol. 16, pp. 151–68.

72 *Where the Great City Stands: A Study in the New Civics* (1917).

73 *Lyrics of the Nile* (1919; second edition 1938).

74 'Reconstruction in Jerusalem', *The Times*, 5 Feb 1919.

75 (ed.), *Jerusalem 1918–1920: Being the Records of the Pro-Jerusalem Council during the Period of the British Military Administration* (1921).

76 'Pro-Jerusalem', *American Magazine of Art* (Washington), 1921, vol. 12, pp. 99–102.

77 *A Palestine Notebook 1918–1923* (London and Garden City, N.Y. 1923).

78 'Political Zionism without the Rose-Coloured Glasses', *English Review*, 1924, vol. 38, pp. 212–20.

79 'The Palestine Problem', *English Review*, 1924, vol. 38, pp. 804–7.

80 'Town Planning in Islam', *Asia* (Concord, New Hampshire), 1924, vol. 24, pp. 377–83, 406–7.

81 (ed.), *Jerusalem 1920–1922: Being the Records of the Pro-Jerusalem Council during the First Two Years of the Civil Administration* (1924).

82 *Caricature* (1928).

83 'The "Ugliness" Exhibition: Can We Save the Countryside?', *Listener*, 1929, vol. 1, pp. 233–4.

84 'Saving the Countryside: What the Listener Thinks', *Listener*, 1929, vol. 1, p. 361.

85 'Saving the Countryside', *Artwork*, 1929, vol. 5, pp. 278–84.

86 (ed.), *Peckover: The Abbotscourt Papers 1904–1931* (1932).

87 '40 years of British architecture', *S*, 1933, vol. 105, pp. 233–9.

88 'The Essex House Press: And the Purpose or Meaning of a Private Press', *Book Collector's Quarterly*, 1933, vol. 3, pp. 69–87.

89 'Recent American Town Planning Developments and their Bearing on the English Problem under the New Act', *Journal of the Town Planning Institute*, 1932–3, vol. 19, pp. 172–81.

90 *Kingfisher out of Egypt: A Dialogue in an English Garden* (1934).

91 'The Palestine Problem Reviewed after Ten Years', *English Review*, 1935, vol. 61, pp. 529–39.

92 Foreword to *Catalogue of An Exhibition of Cotswold Art and Craftsmanship . . . Campden, Glos.* (1935).

93 *The Kings of Min Zamān* (1938).

94 'Grannie': *A Victorian Cameo* (Privately printed 1939).

ACKNOWLEDGMENTS FOR ILLUSTRATIONS

In the case of copy-photographs of original drawings and of photographs, this list acknowledges the owner of the drawing or photograph, who is not necessarily the source of the copy-photograph.

Art Institute of Chicago 200. Art Workers' Guild 203. Felicity Ashbee frontispiece, 2, 4, 27, 30, 33, 36–7, 42, 57, 61, 66, 71, 76, 78–9, 81–3, 86–90, 135, 183, III–IV, XVIII. BBC Hulton Picture Library 1, 75. Bodleian Library, Oxford 3. British Architectural Library, RIBA, London 107, 109, 114. Brown Brothers 67. William Cameron 51–2. Campden Trust 43, 45, 55, 60, 63–4, 94, 102, 124–5, 136. Cheltenham Art Gallery and Museums 174. *Country Life* 153. Alan Crawford 16, 44, 70, 104, 111–3, 120–1, 123, 128, 134, 141, 145, 157–8, 160, 162, 165–6, 171, 175, 180, 196. David Cripps 101, 142, 167–9, 178, V, VII–VIII, X–XIV, XVI–XVII. Robert L. Edwards 181. First Garden City Heritage Museum 132. Ian Gee XIX. Greater London Council Photograph Library 149. Guildhall Library, City of London 8. Anthony F. Kersting 117. King's College Library, Cambridge 7, 9, 11, 19, 21, 29, 31, 34, 39–40, 46, 54, 56, 62, 68, 73–4, 77, 91, 95, 99, 191, I, II. Trustees of the National Library of Scotland 69. National Portrait Gallery 5, 38. Österreichisches Museum für angewandte Kunst, Vienna 202, IX. Oxford County Libraries 122. Protocol XX–XXI. Royal Borough of Kensington and Chelsea Libraries and Arts Services 115, 151. Royal Commission on Historical Monuments (England) 18, 22–3, 26. Guy Ryecart 127. Sheffield City Libraries, Carpenter Collection 6. Trustees of the Victoria and Albert Museum 10, 12, 17, 28, 35, 41, 58–9, 65, 93, 96–8, 110, 119, 126, 130–1, 137, 139, 143–4, 146–8, 152, 164, 173, 177, 179, 182, 184, XV. Elizabeth Watson 48. Sutton Webster 84–5, 116. John Whybrow Ltd 140, 154–5, 159, VI. Jane Wilgress 47, 156.

Copy photography by Birmingham City Libraries, Gordon Bishop Associates, Alan Crawford, GGS Photography, John Edward Leigh, Royal Borough of Kensington and Chelsea Libraries and Arts Services, Rodney Todd-White and Son, and John Whybrow Ltd.

INDEX

489

490